Cross Game

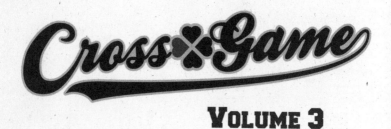

Volume 3

Mitsuru Adachi

Contents Volume 3

Cross✕Game

⑥

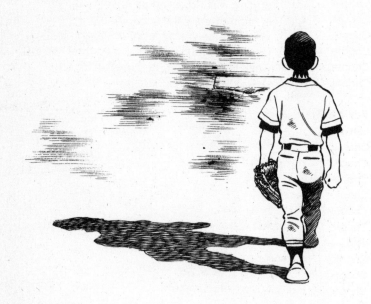

Story & Art by
Mitsuru Adachi

Story Wrap-Up

First-year high school student Ko Kitamura
is the only child of the family that runs
Kitamura Sporting Goods. Down the street
is a family of four sisters, whose second
daughter Wakaba tragically drowned when
she and Ko were in the fifth grade. Now in
high school, Ko joins the baseball team,
but coldhearted Coach Daimon banishes
Ko and his buddies from the varsity team
to a prefab portable shack. But when the
portable team goes up against varsity, the
game unexpectedly turns into a nailbiter
ending with Ko giving up a walk-off homer
in the bottom of the ninth. During summer
vacation the varsity team competes in the
preliminary tournament for Summer Koshien,
while the Portables get together for some
secret special training.

CHAPTER 41

THAT'S GREAT!

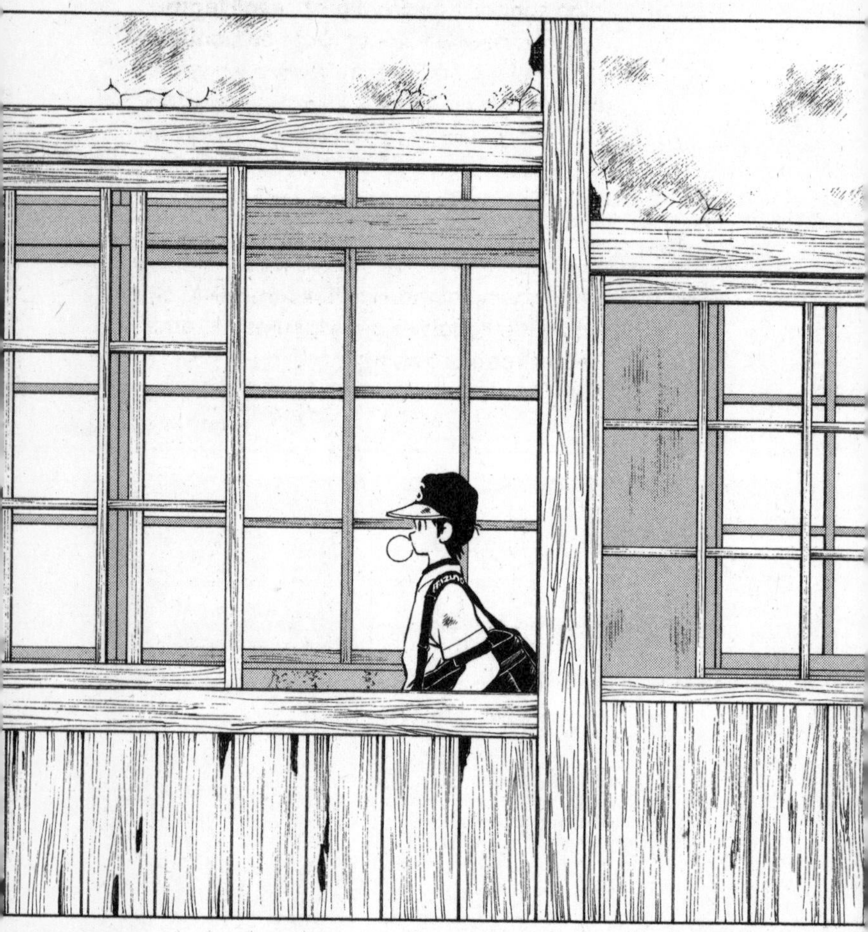

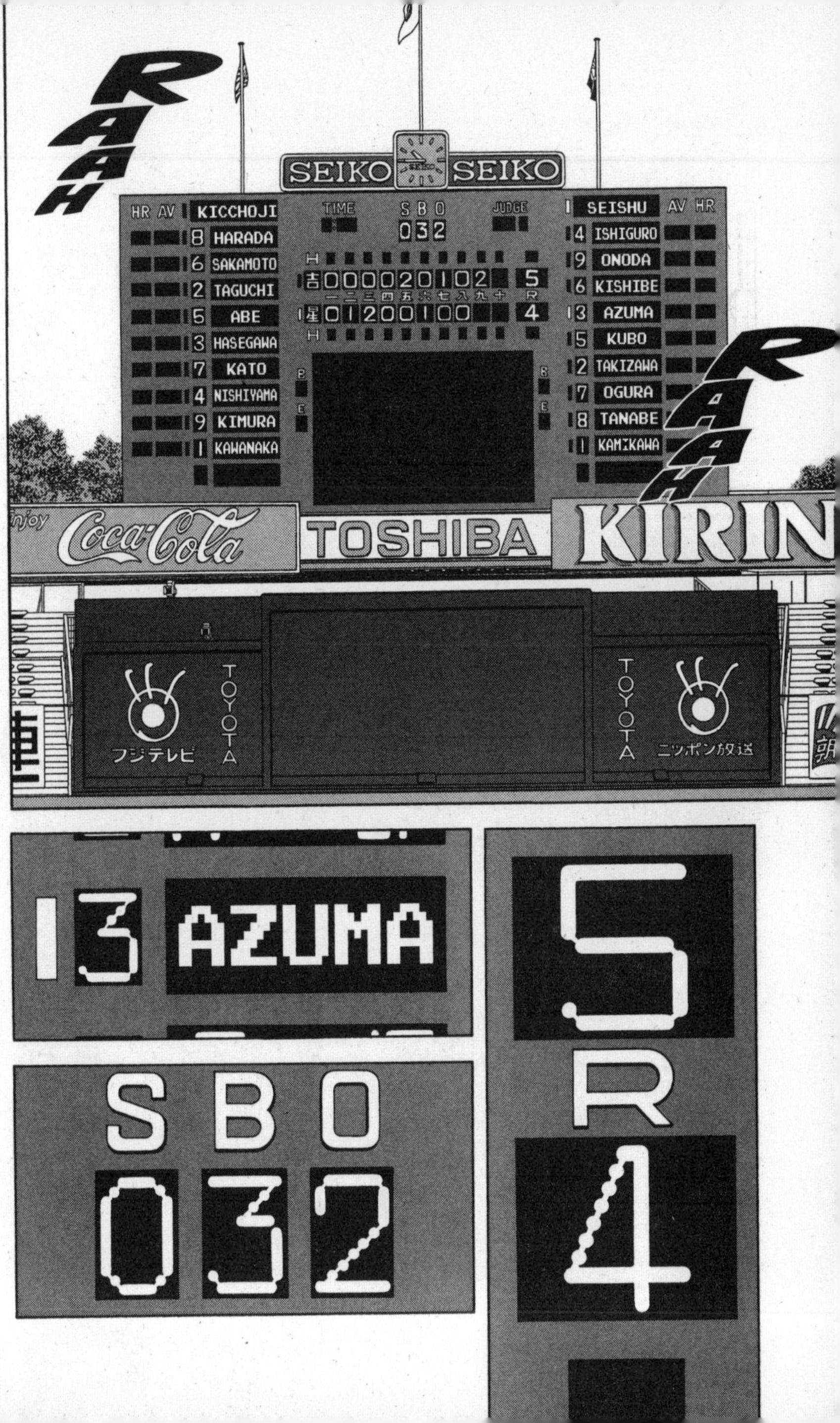
RAAAH
SEIKO SEIKO
HR AV KICCHOJI
8 HARADA
6 SAKAMOTO
2 TAGUCHI
5 ABE
3 HASEGAWA
7 KATO
4 NISHIYAMA
9 KIMURA
1 KAWANAKA
TIME
S B O
0 3 2
JUDGE
吉 0 0 0 0 2 0 1 0 2 5
一 二 三 四 五 六 七 八 九 十 R
星 0 1 2 0 0 1 0 0 4
SEISHU AV HR
4 ISHIGURO
9 ONODA
6 KISHIBE
13 AZUMA
5 KUBO
2 TAKIZAWA
7 OGURA
8 TANABE
1 KAMIKAWA
RAAAH
Enjoy Coca-Cola
TOSHIBA
KIRIN
フジテレビ
TOYOTA
TOYOTA
ニッポン放送
5
R
4
13 AZUMA
S B O
0 3 2

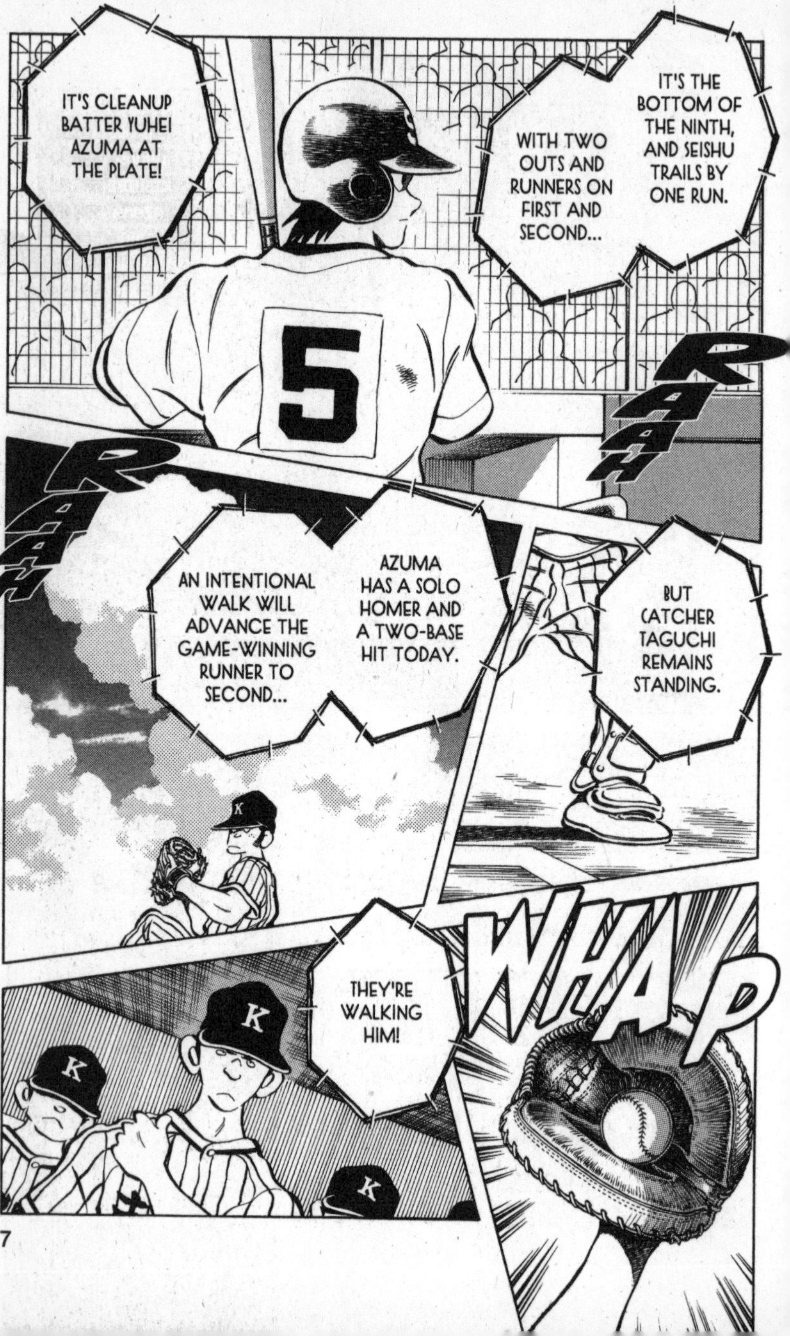
IT'S THE BOTTOM OF THE NINTH, AND SEISHU TRAILS BY ONE RUN.
WITH TWO OUTS AND RUNNERS ON FIRST AND SECOND...
IT'S CLEANUP BATTER YUHEI AZUMA AT THE PLATE!
RAAAH
RAAAH
BUT CATCHER TAGUCHI REMAINS STANDING.
AZUMA HAS A SOLO HOMER AND A TWO-BASE HIT TODAY.
AN INTENTIONAL WALK WILL ADVANCE THE GAME-WINNING RUNNER TO SECOND...
WHAP
THEY'RE WALKING HIM!

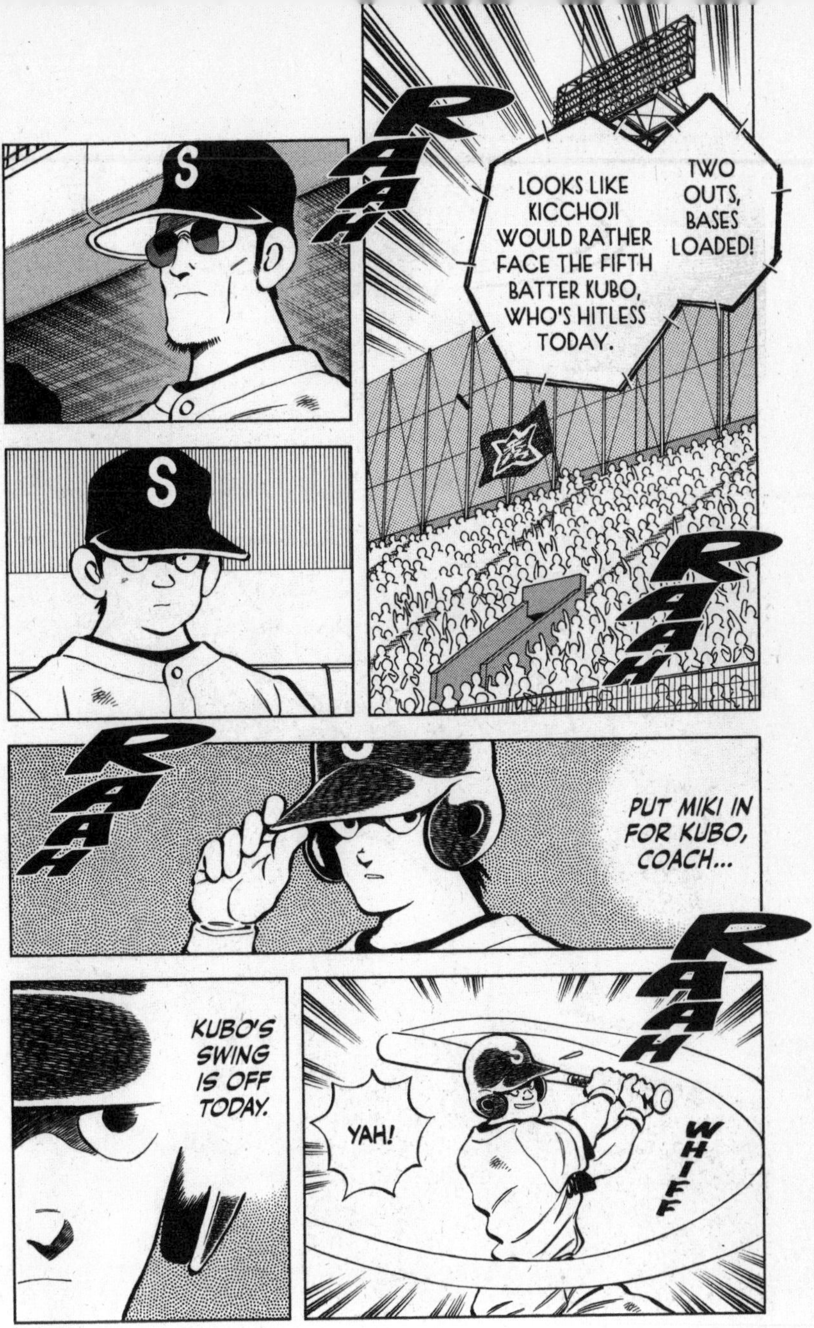
RAAAH
TWO OUTS, BASES LOADED!
LOOKS LIKE KICCHOJI WOULD RATHER FACE THE FIFTH BATTER KUBO, WHO'S HITLESS TODAY.
RAAAH
PUT MIKI IN FOR KUBO, COACH...
RAAAH
RAAAH
YAH!
WHIFF
KUBO'S SWING IS OFF TODAY.

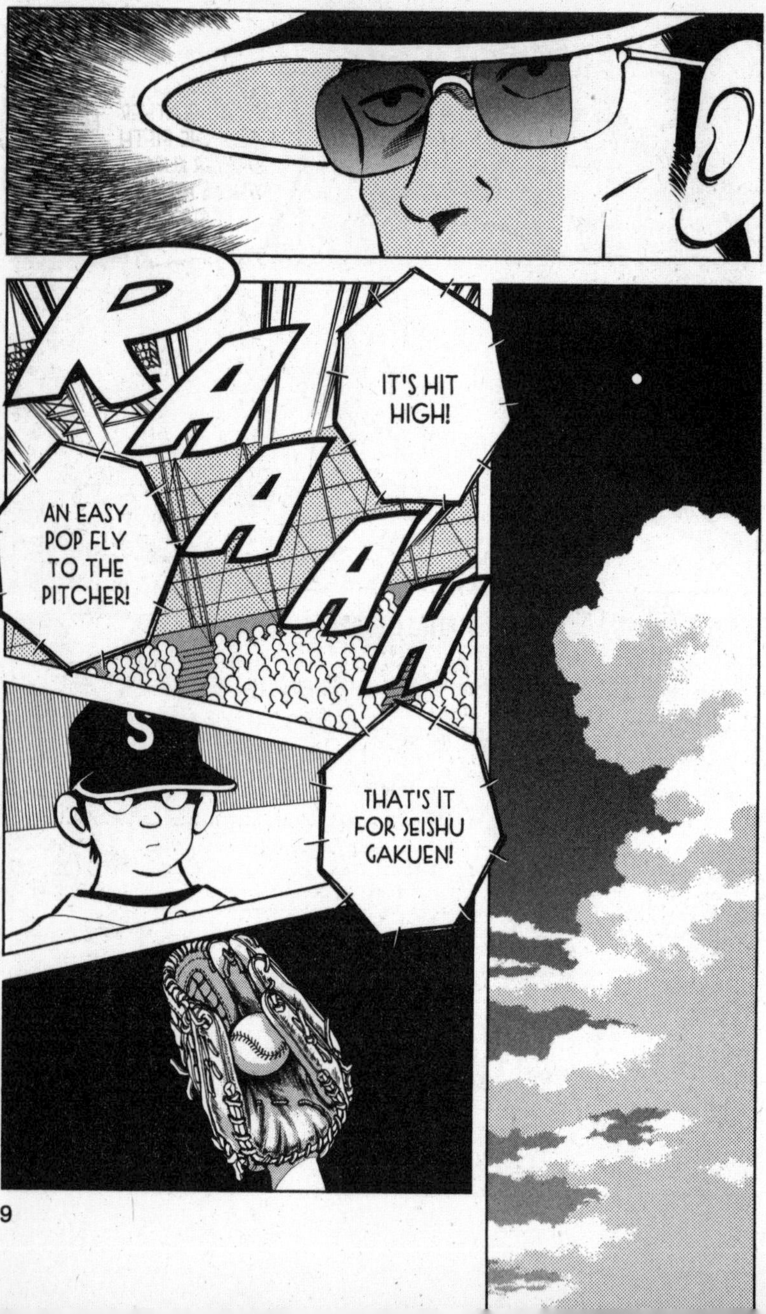
RAAAH
IT'S HIT HIGH!
AN EASY POP FLY TO THE PITCHER!
THAT'S IT FOR SEISHU GAKUEN!

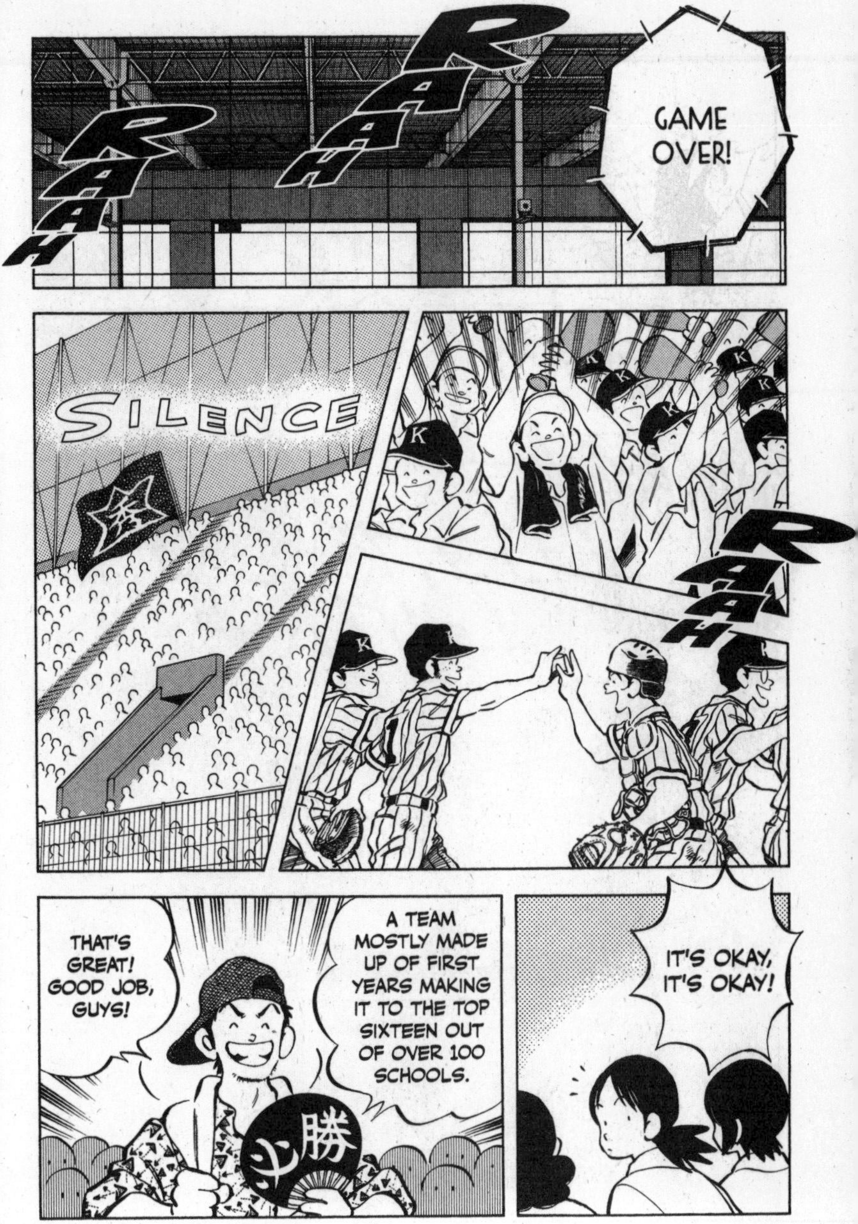
GAME OVER!
RAAAH
RAAH
RAAH
SILENCE
IT'S OKAY, IT'S OKAY!
A TEAM MOSTLY MADE UP OF FIRST YEARS MAKING IT TO THE TOP SIXTEEN OUT OF OVER 100 SCHOOLS.
THAT'S GREAT! GOOD JOB, GUYS!
勝

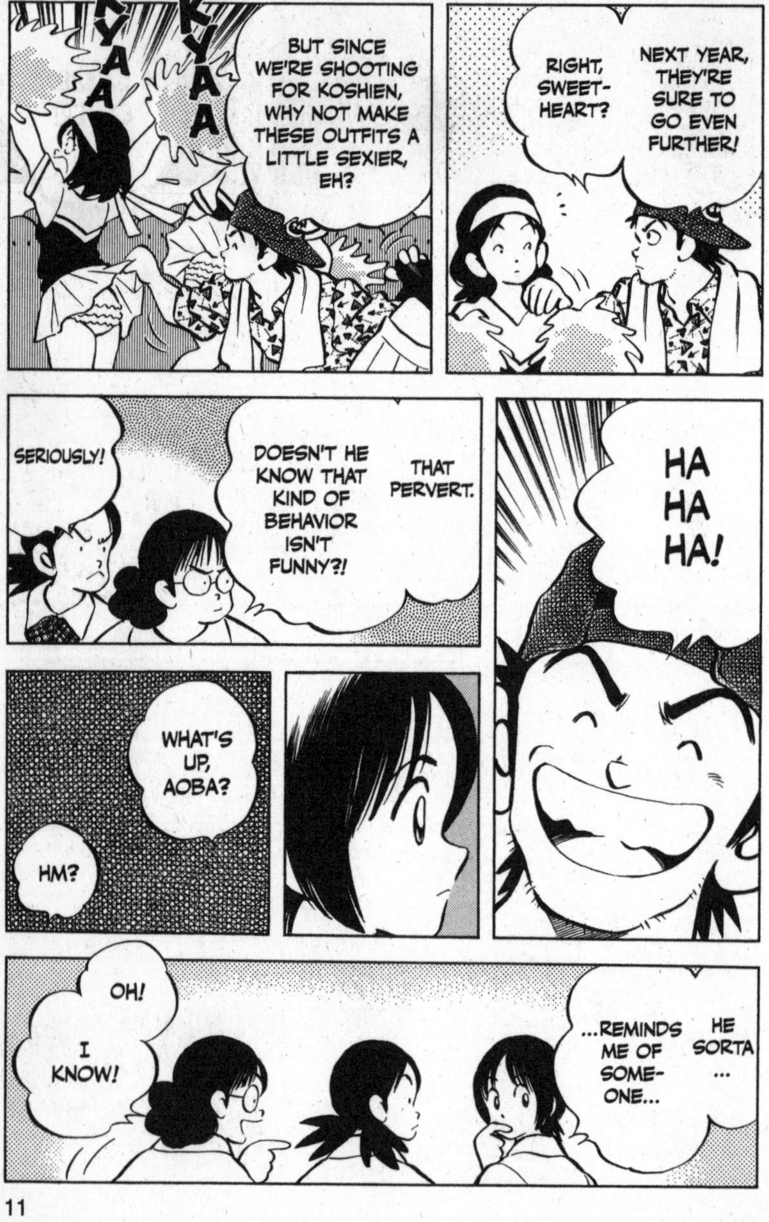
NEXT YEAR, THEY'RE SURE TO GO EVEN FURTHER!
RIGHT, SWEETHEART?
BUT SINCE WE'RE SHOOTING FOR KOSHIEN, WHY NOT MAKE THESE OUTFITS A LITTLE SEXIER, EH?
KYAA
KYAA
HA HA HA!
THAT PERVERT.
DOESN'T HE KNOW THAT KIND OF BEHAVIOR ISN'T FUNNY?!
SERIOUSLY!
WHAT'S UP, AOBA?
HM?
HE SORTA...
...REMINDS ME OF SOMEONE...
OH!
I KNOW!

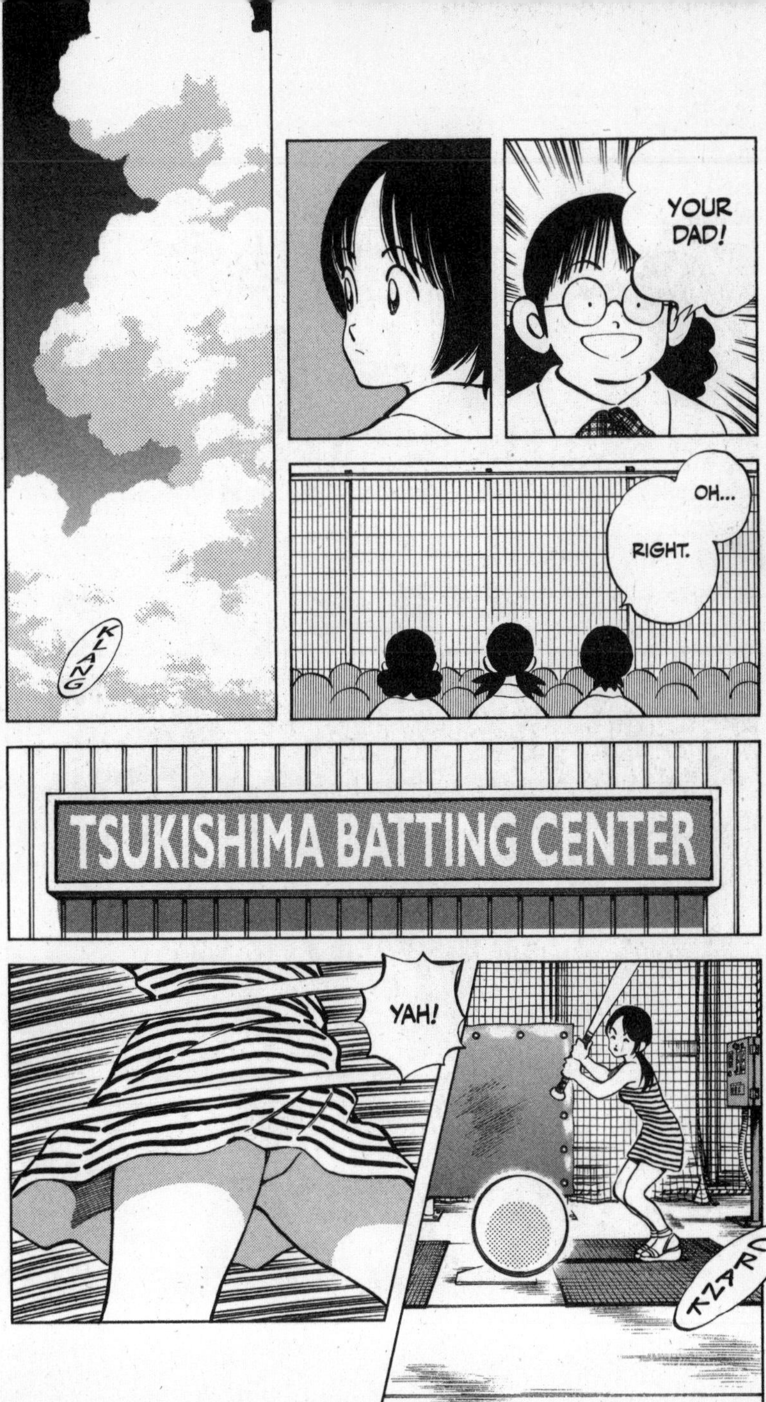
YOUR DAD!
OH... RIGHT.
KLANG
TSUKISHIMA BATTING CENTER
YAH!

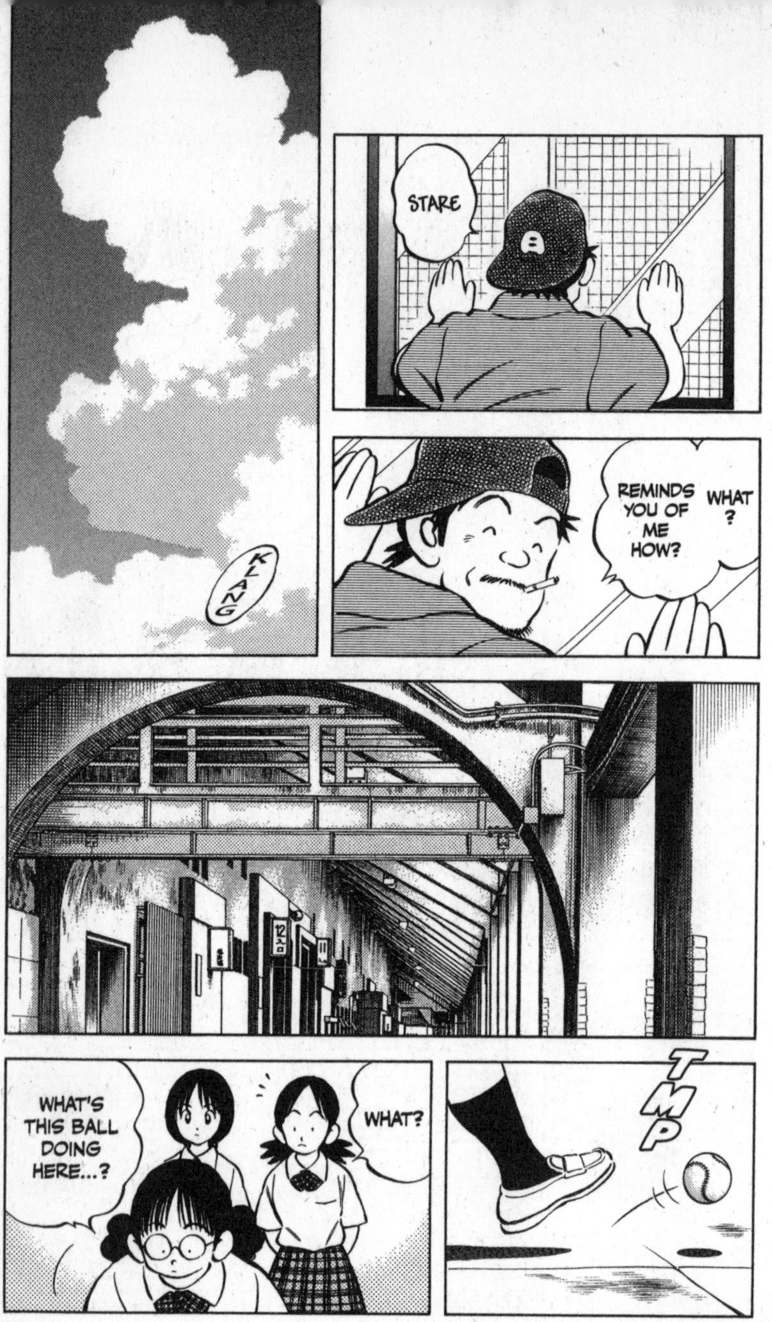
STARE
WHAT?
REMINDS YOU OF ME HOW?
KLANG
TMP
WHAT?
WHAT'S THIS BALL DOING HERE...?

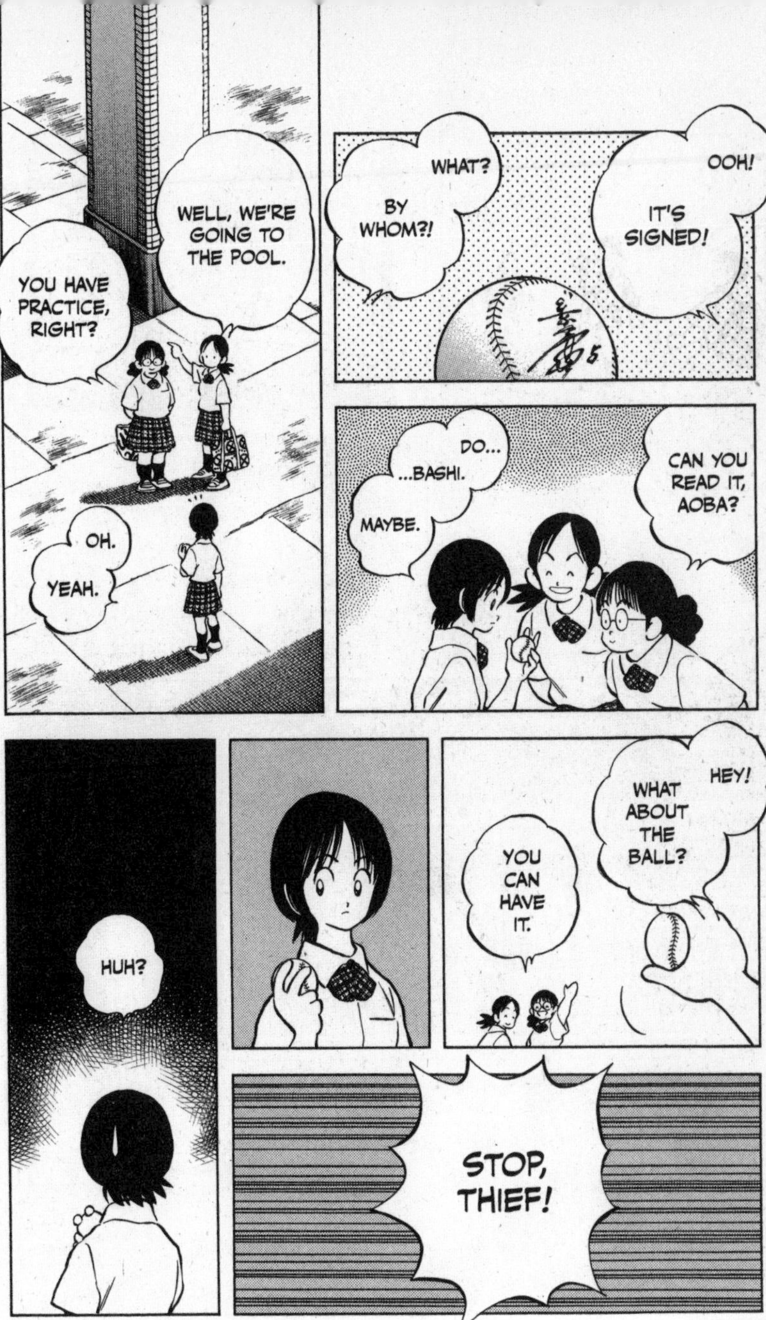
OOH! IT'S SIGNED!
WHAT? BY WHOM?!
CAN YOU READ IT, AOBA?
DO... ...BASHI.
MAYBE.
WELL, WE'RE GOING TO THE POOL.
YOU HAVE PRACTICE, RIGHT?
OH. YEAH.
HEY! WHAT ABOUT THE BALL?
YOU CAN HAVE IT.
STOP, THIEF!
HUH?

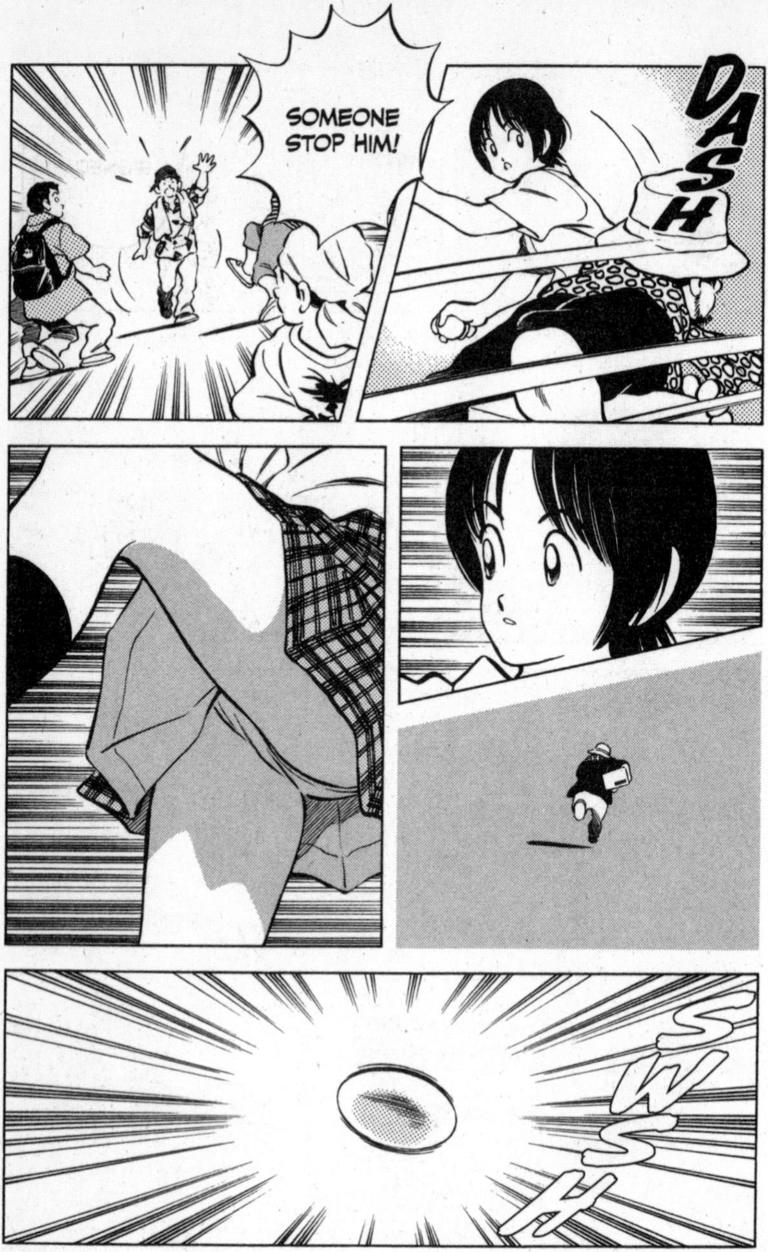
DASH
SOMEONE STOP HIM!
SWISH

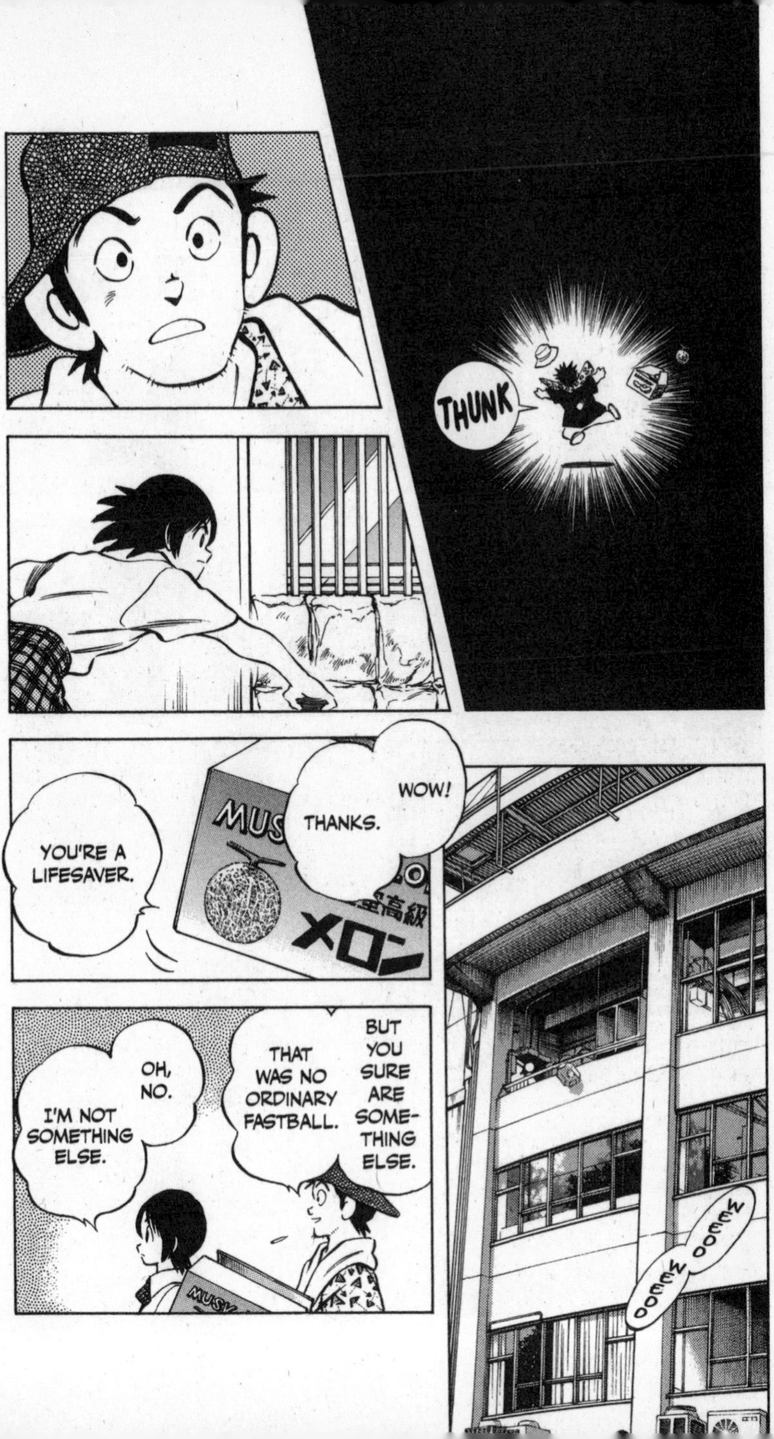

THUNK
WEEOO WEEOO
WOW!
THANKS.
YOU'RE A LIFESAVER.
メロン
THAT WAS NO ORDINARY FASTBALL.
BUT YOU SURE ARE SOMETHING ELSE.
OH, NO.
I'M NOT SOMETHING ELSE.

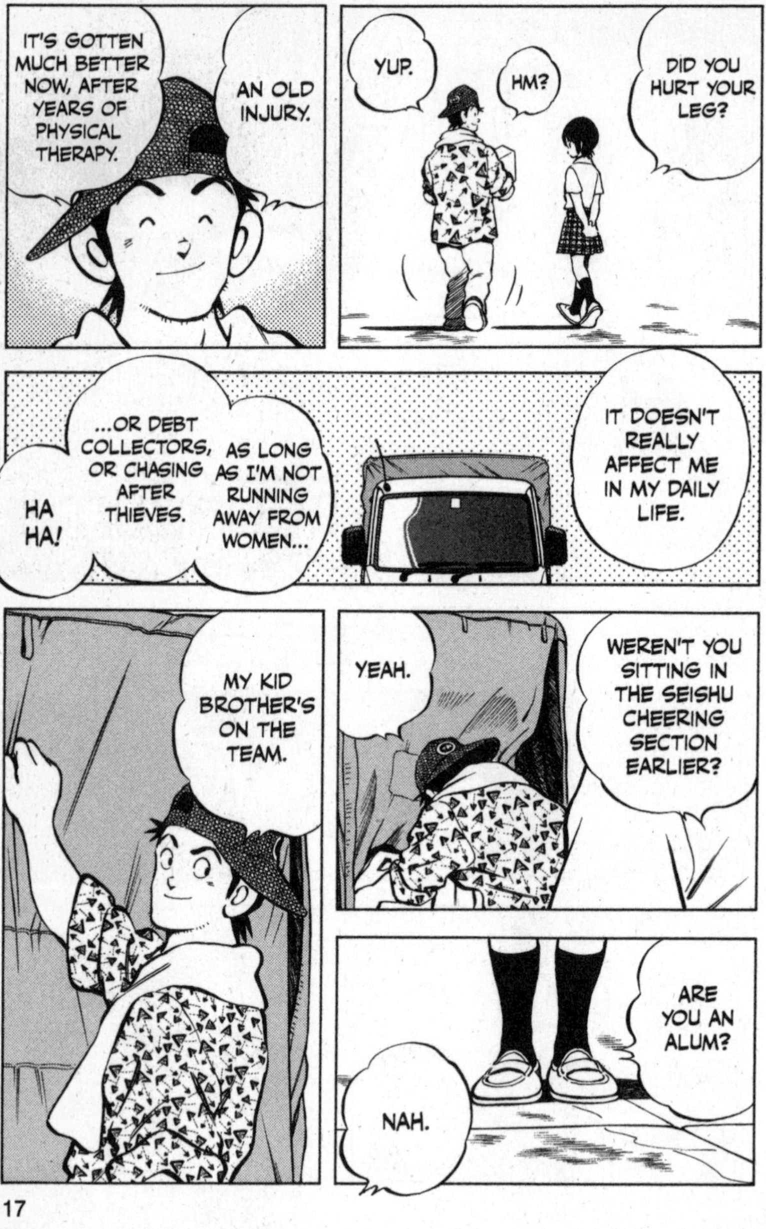
DID YOU HURT YOUR LEG?
HM?
YUP.
AN OLD INJURY.
IT'S GOTTEN MUCH BETTER NOW, AFTER YEARS OF PHYSICAL THERAPY.
IT DOESN'T REALLY AFFECT ME IN MY DAILY LIFE.
AS LONG AS I'M NOT RUNNING AWAY FROM WOMEN...
...OR DEBT COLLECTORS, OR CHASING AFTER THIEVES.
HA HA!
WEREN'T YOU SITTING IN THE SEISHU CHEERING SECTION EARLIER?
YEAH.
ARE YOU AN ALUM?
NAH.
MY KID BROTHER'S ON THE TEAM.

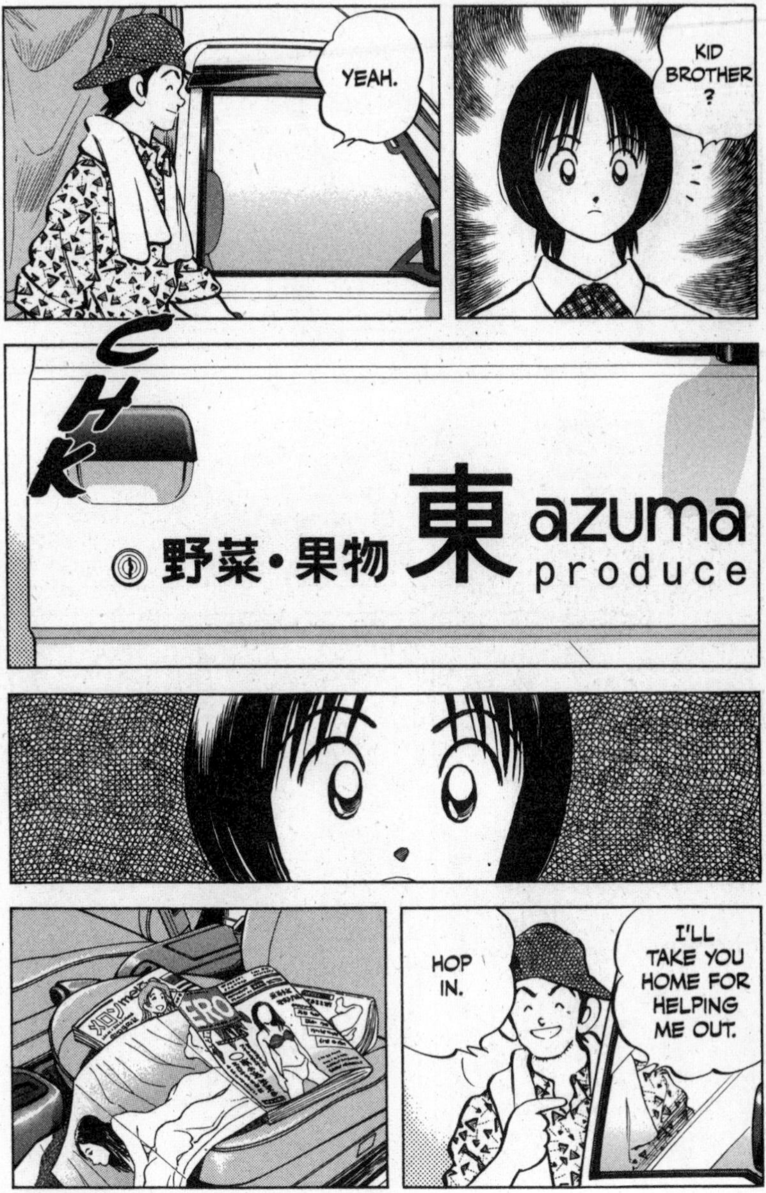
KID BROTHER ?
YEAH.
CHK
野菜・果物
東 azuma produce
I'LL TAKE YOU HOME FOR HELPING ME OUT.
HOP IN.
ERO

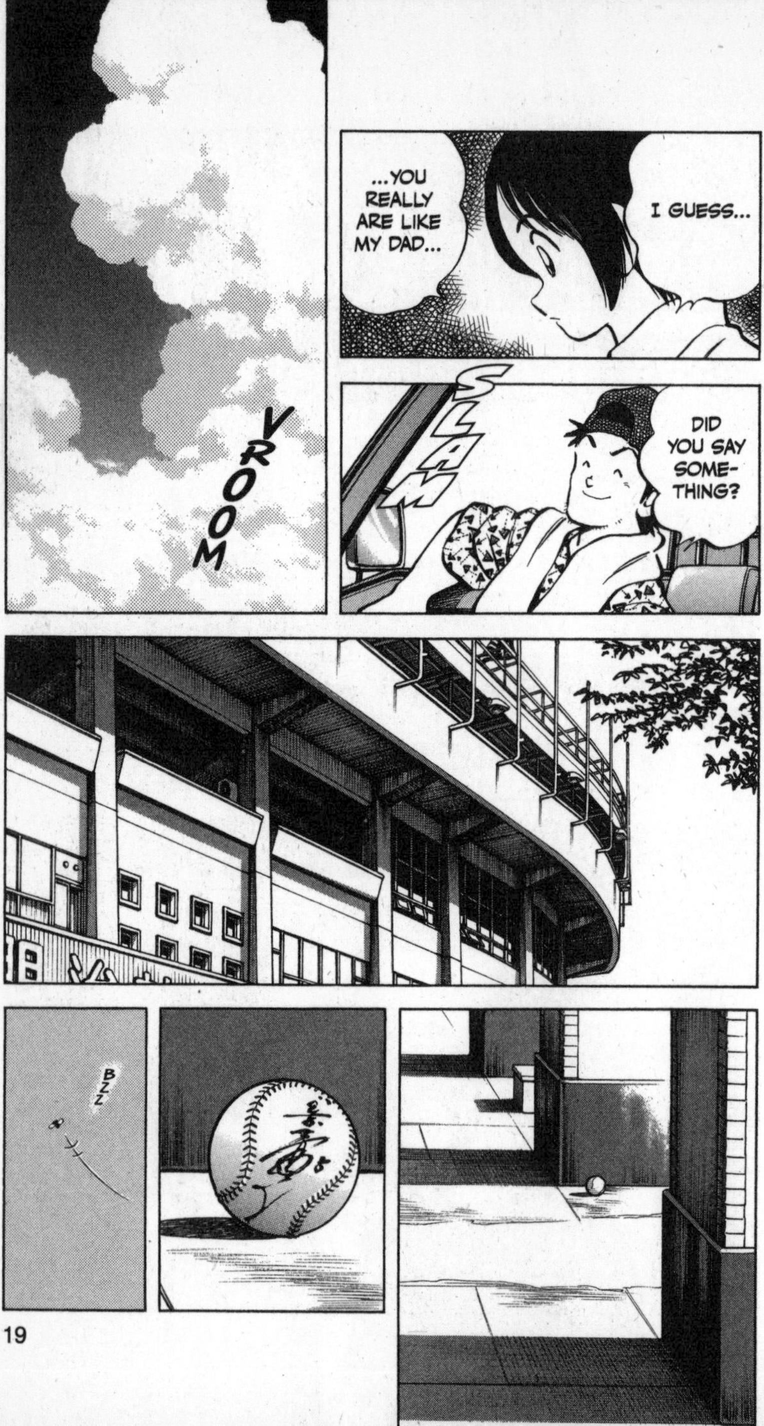
I GUESS...
...YOU REALLY ARE LIKE MY DAD...
SLAM
DID YOU SAY SOMETHING?
VROOM
BZZ

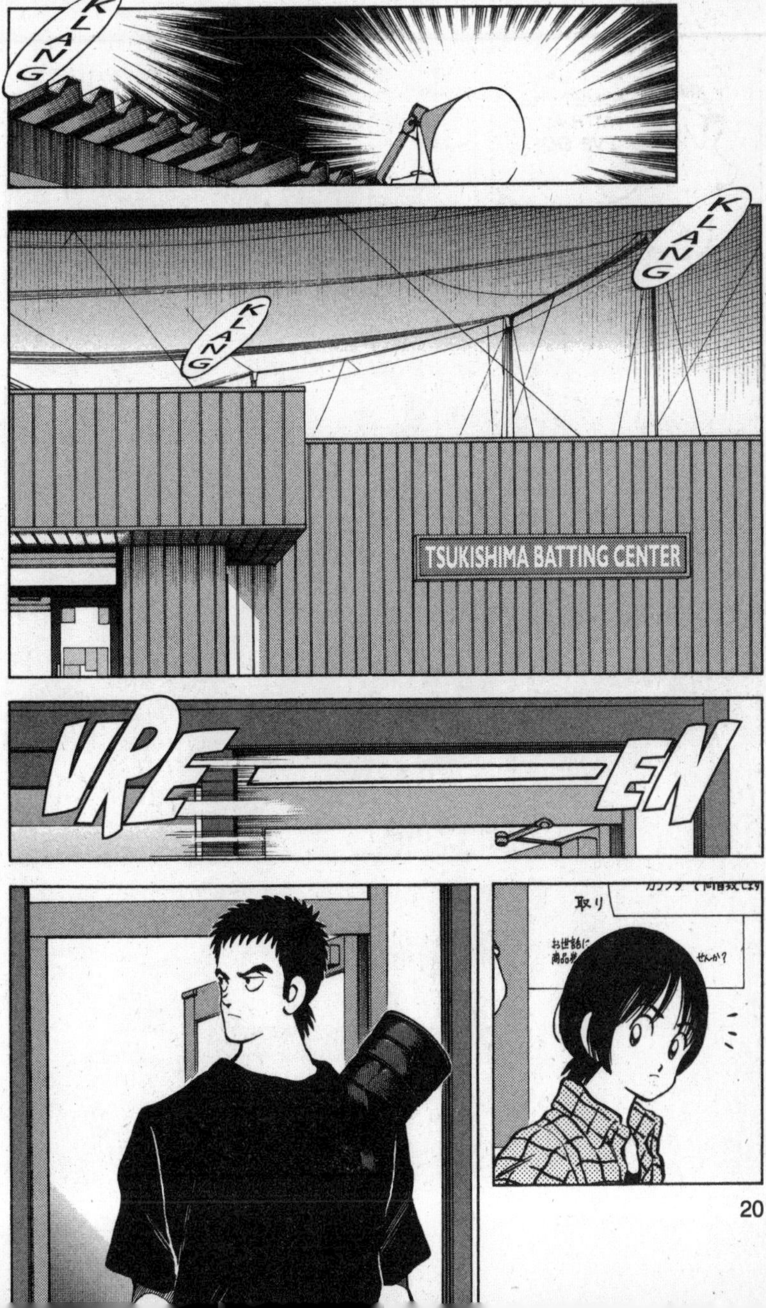
KLANG
KLANG
KLANG
TSUKISHIMA BATTING CENTER
VRE—EN

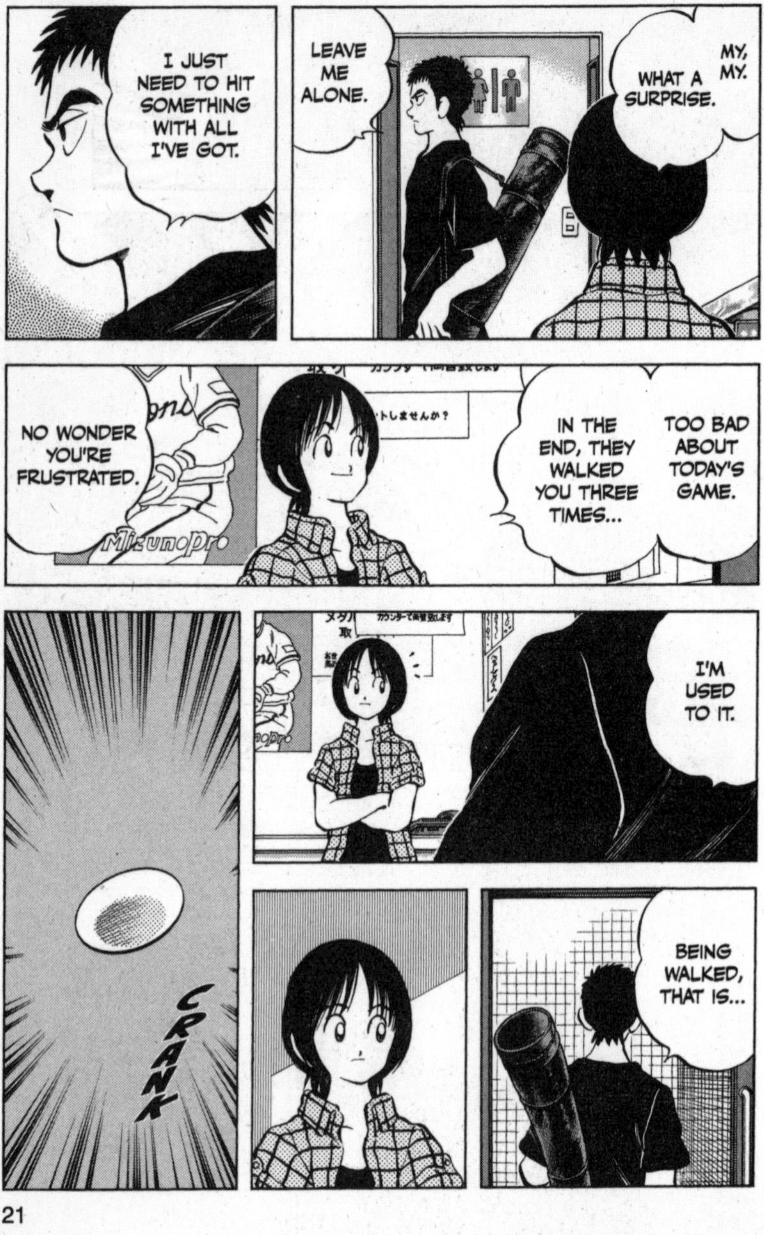
MY, MY.
WHAT A SURPRISE.
LEAVE ME ALONE.
I JUST NEED TO HIT SOMETHING WITH ALL I'VE GOT.
TOO BAD ABOUT TODAY'S GAME.
IN THE END, THEY WALKED YOU THREE TIMES...
NO WONDER YOU'RE FRUSTRATED.
Mizuno Pro
I'M USED TO IT.
BEING WALKED, THAT IS...
CRANK

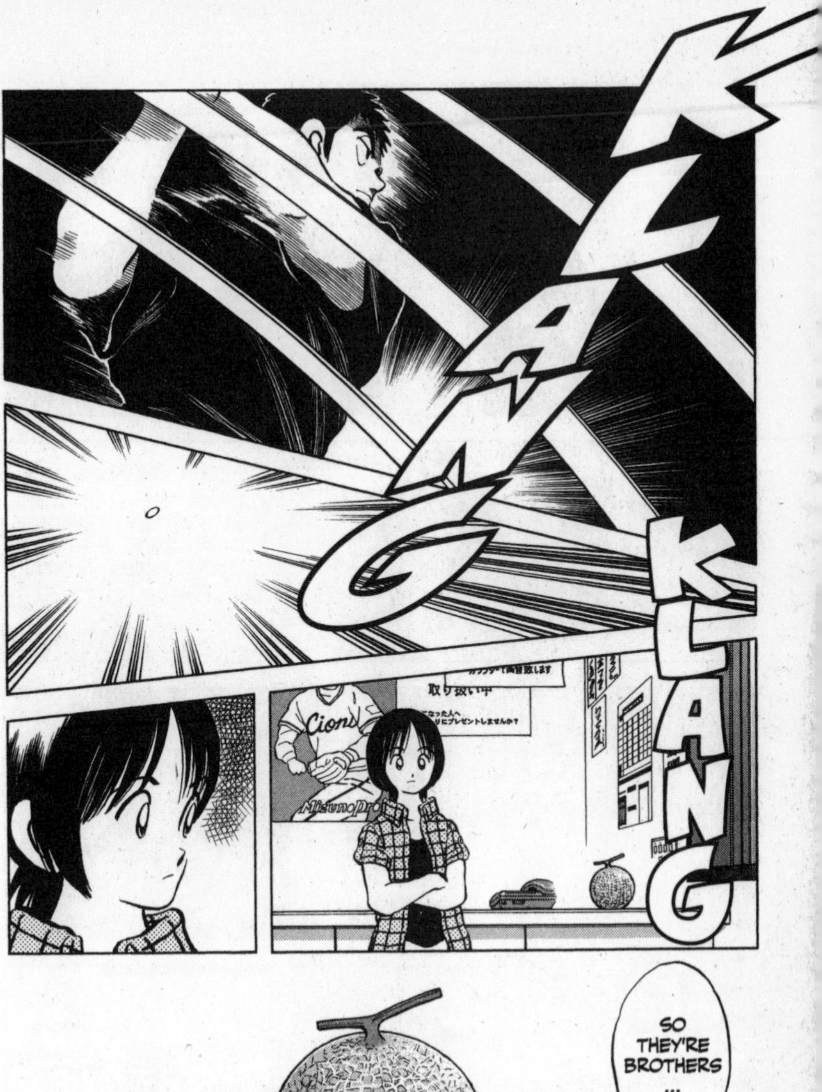
KLANG
KLANG
取り扱い中
Cions
SO THEY'RE BROTHERS ...

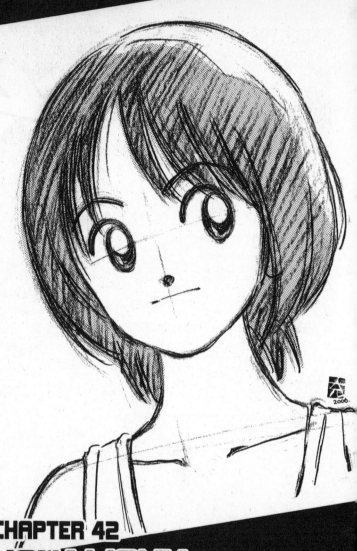

CHAPTER 42
HOW MANY POINTS?

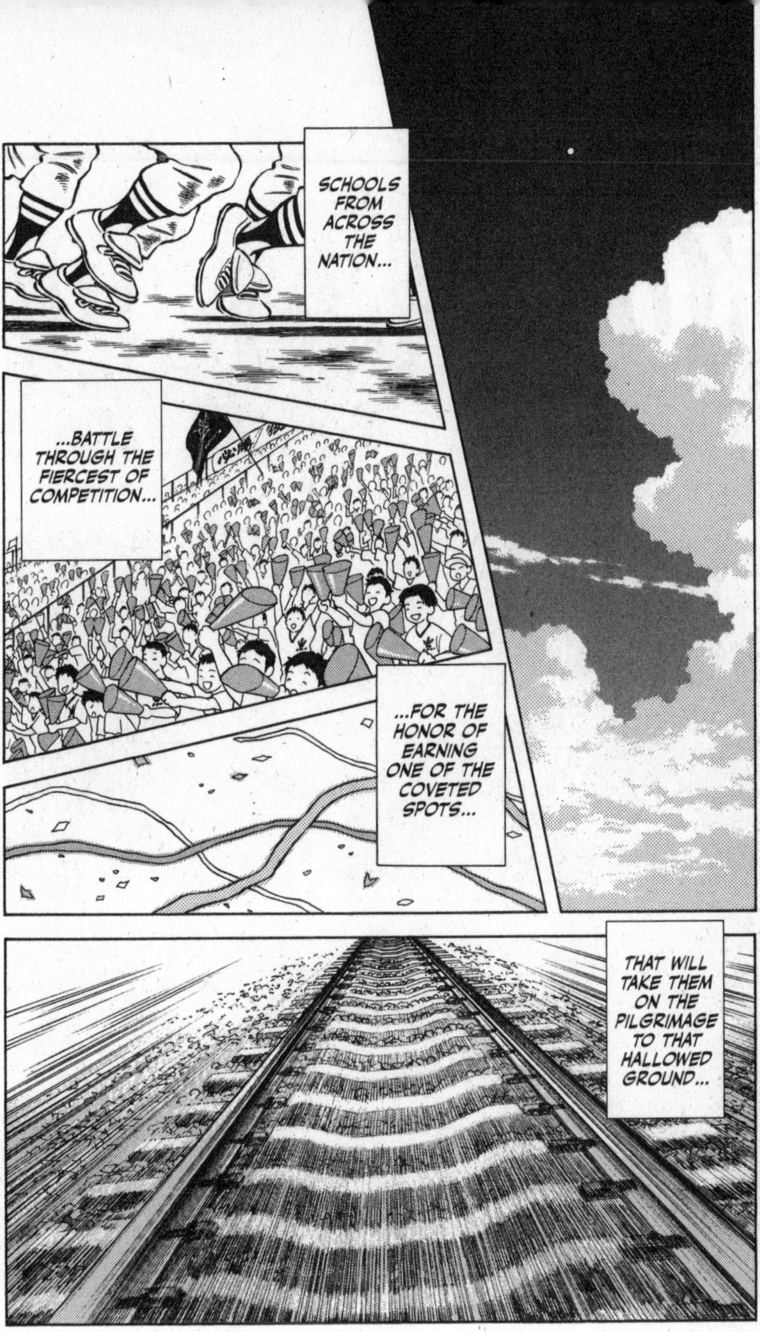
SCHOOLS FROM ACROSS THE NATION...
...BATTLE THROUGH THE FIERCEST OF COMPETITION...
...FOR THE HONOR OF EARNING ONE OF THE COVETED SPOTS...
THAT WILL TAKE THEM ON THE PILGRIMAGE TO THAT HALLOWED GROUND...

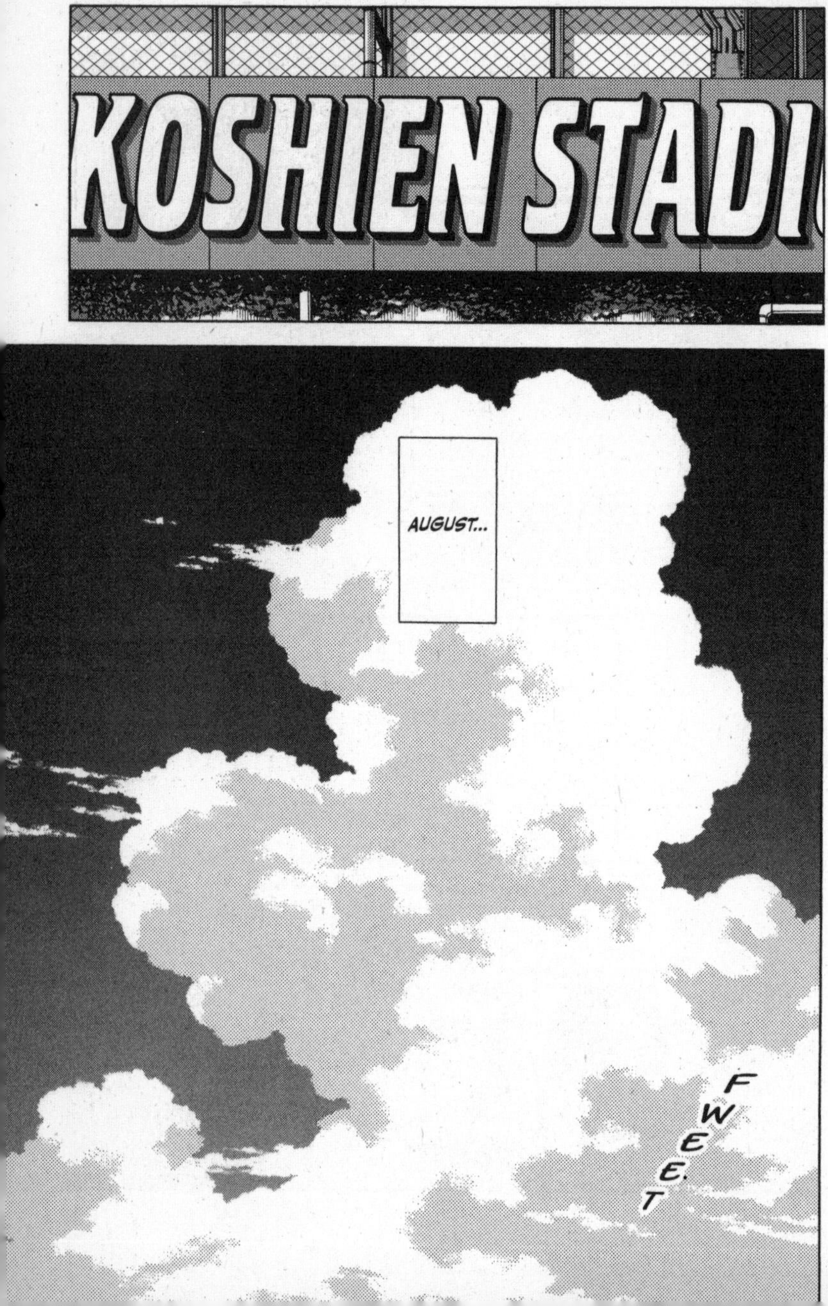
KOSHIEN STADI
AUGUST...
FWEEET

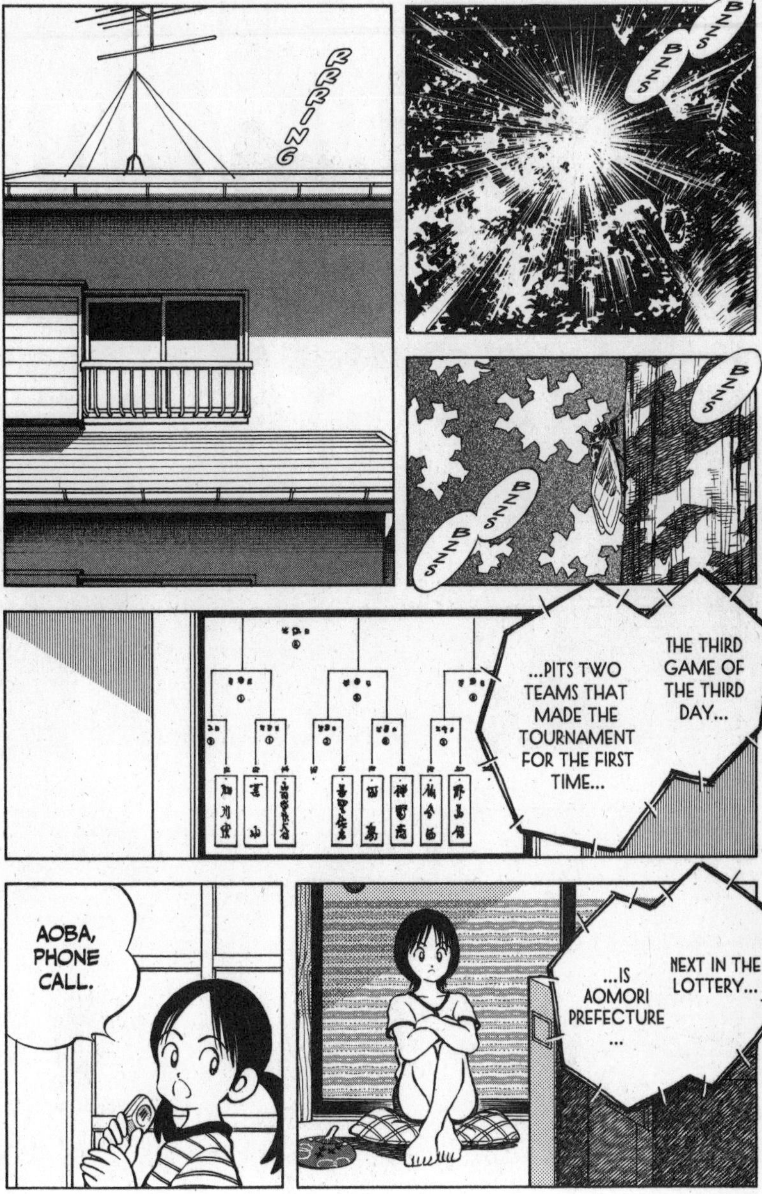
BZZS
BZZS
BZZS
BZZS
BZZS
RRRING
THE THIRD GAME OF THE THIRD DAY...
...PITS TWO TEAMS THAT MADE THE TOURNAMENT FOR THE FIRST TIME...
NEXT IN THE LOTTERY...
...IS AOMORI PREFECTURE ...
AOBA, PHONE CALL.

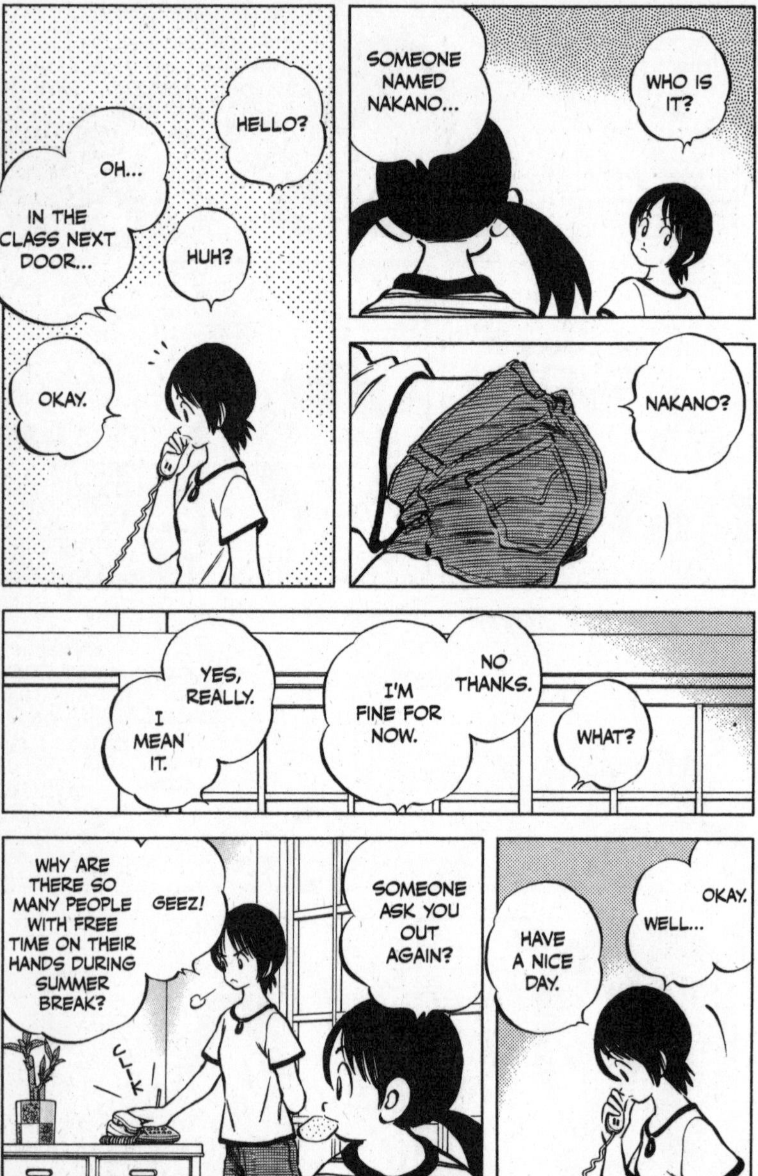
WHO IS IT?
SOMEONE NAMED NAKANO...
NAKANO?
HELLO?
OH...
IN THE CLASS NEXT DOOR...
HUH?
OKAY.
WHAT?
NO THANKS.
I'M FINE FOR NOW.
YES, REALLY.
I MEAN IT.
OKAY.
WELL...
HAVE A NICE DAY.
SOMEONE ASK YOU OUT AGAIN?
GEEZ!
WHY ARE THERE SO MANY PEOPLE WITH FREE TIME ON THEIR HANDS DURING SUMMER BREAK?
CLIK

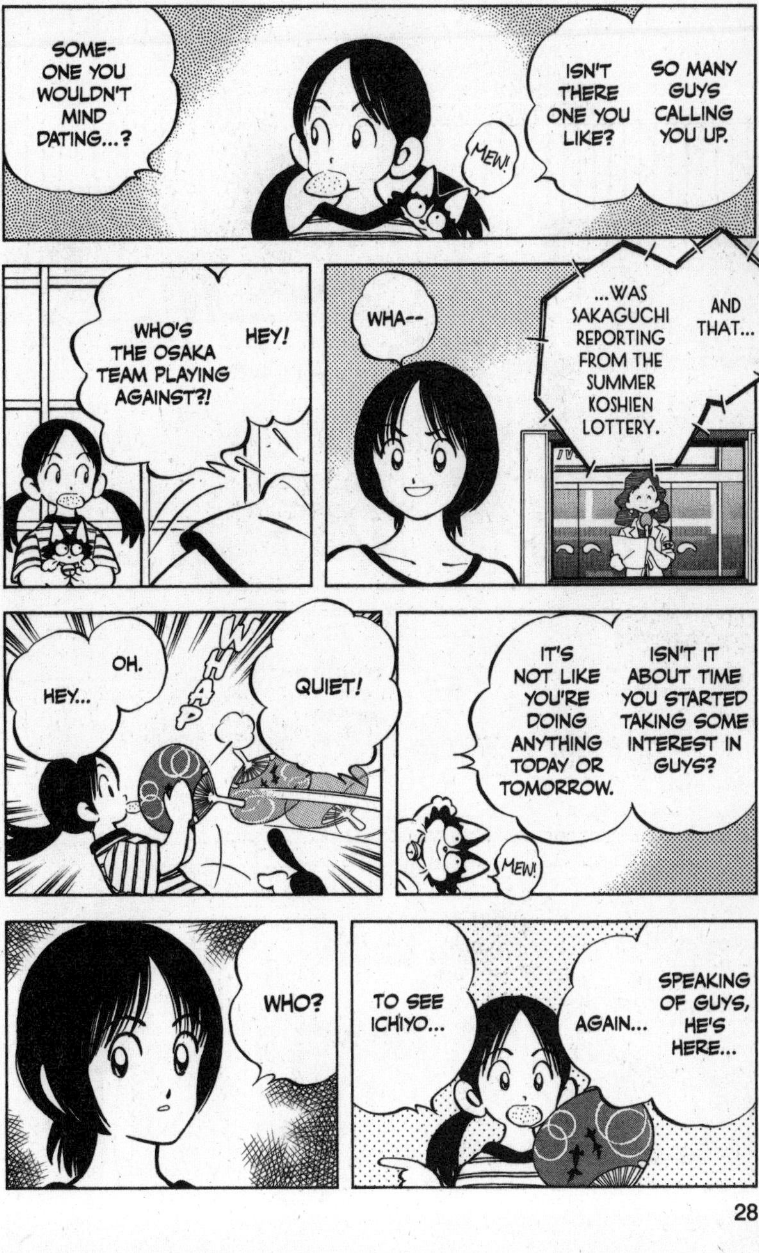
SO MANY GUYS CALLING YOU UP.
ISN'T THERE ONE YOU LIKE?
MEW!
SOME-ONE YOU WOULDN'T MIND DATING...?
AND THAT...
...WAS SAKAGUCHI REPORTING FROM THE SUMMER KOSHIEN LOTTERY.
WHA--
HEY!
WHO'S THE OSAKA TEAM PLAYING AGAINST?!
ISN'T IT ABOUT TIME YOU STARTED TAKING SOME INTEREST IN GUYS?
IT'S NOT LIKE YOU'RE DOING ANYTHING TODAY OR TOMORROW.
MEW!
QUIET!
WHAP
OH.
HEY...
SPEAKING OF GUYS, HE'S HERE...
AGAIN...
TO SEE ICHIYO...
WHO?

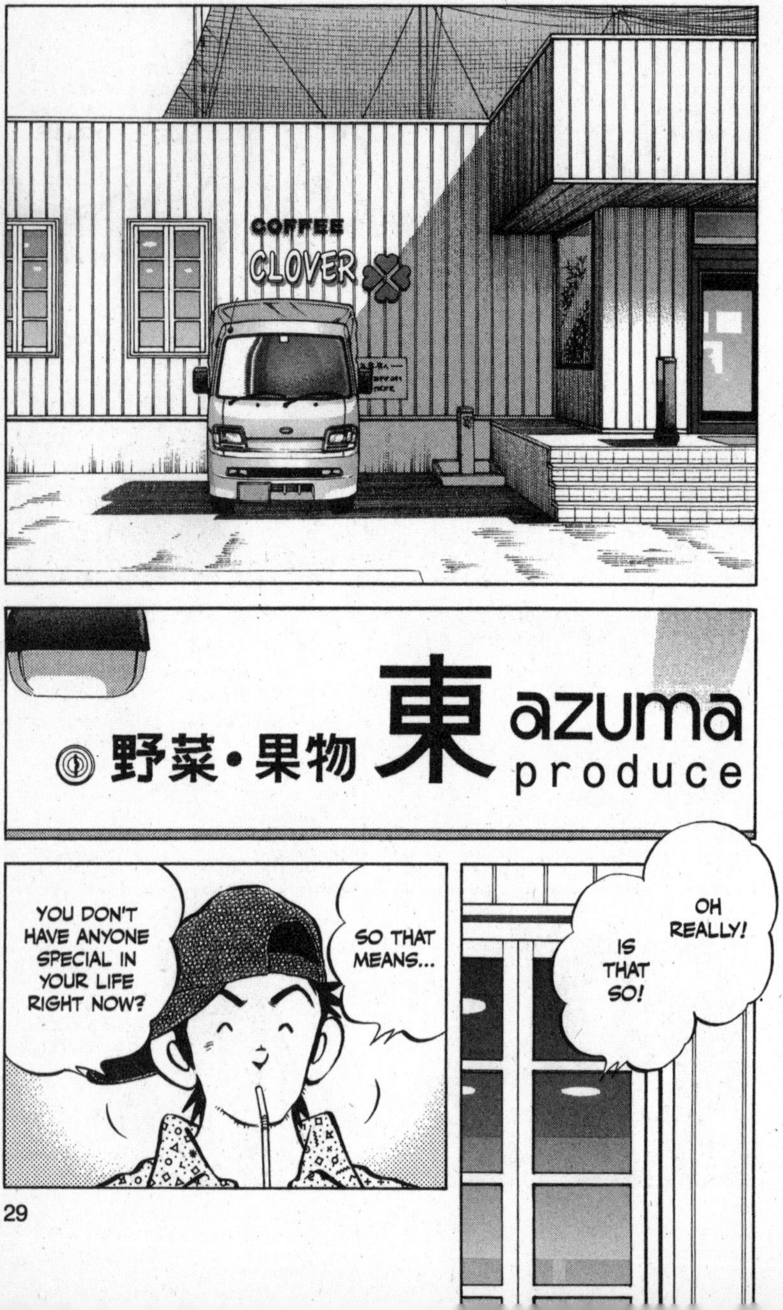
COFFEE
CLOVER
野菜・果物
東
azuma
produce
OH REALLY!
IS THAT SO!
SO THAT MEANS...
YOU DON'T HAVE ANYONE SPECIAL IN YOUR LIFE RIGHT NOW?

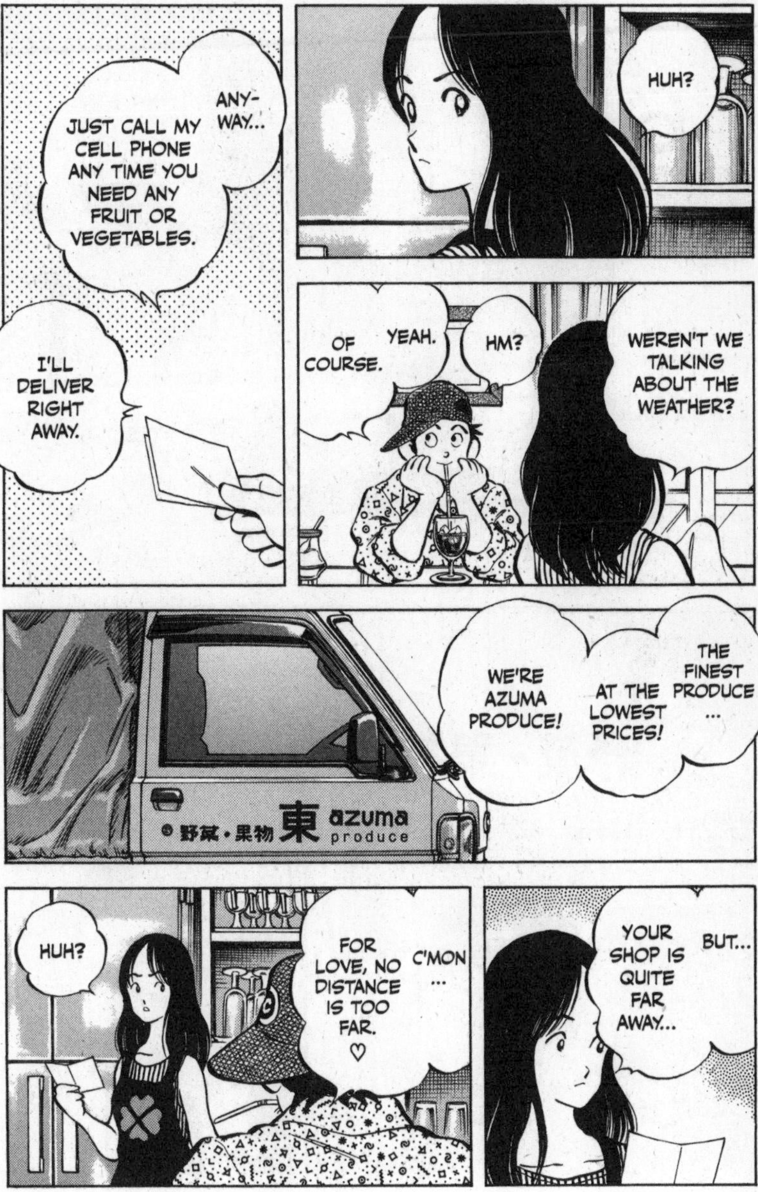
HUH?
WEREN'T WE TALKING ABOUT THE WEATHER?
HM?
YEAH.
OF COURSE.
ANY- WAY...
JUST CALL MY CELL PHONE ANY TIME YOU NEED ANY FRUIT OR VEGETABLES.
I'LL DELIVER RIGHT AWAY.
THE FINEST PRODUCE ...
AT THE LOWEST PRICES!
WE'RE AZUMA PRODUCE!
野菜・果物 東 azuma produce
BUT...
YOUR SHOP IS QUITE FAR AWAY...
C'MON ...
FOR LOVE, NO DISTANCE IS TOO FAR. ♡
HUH?

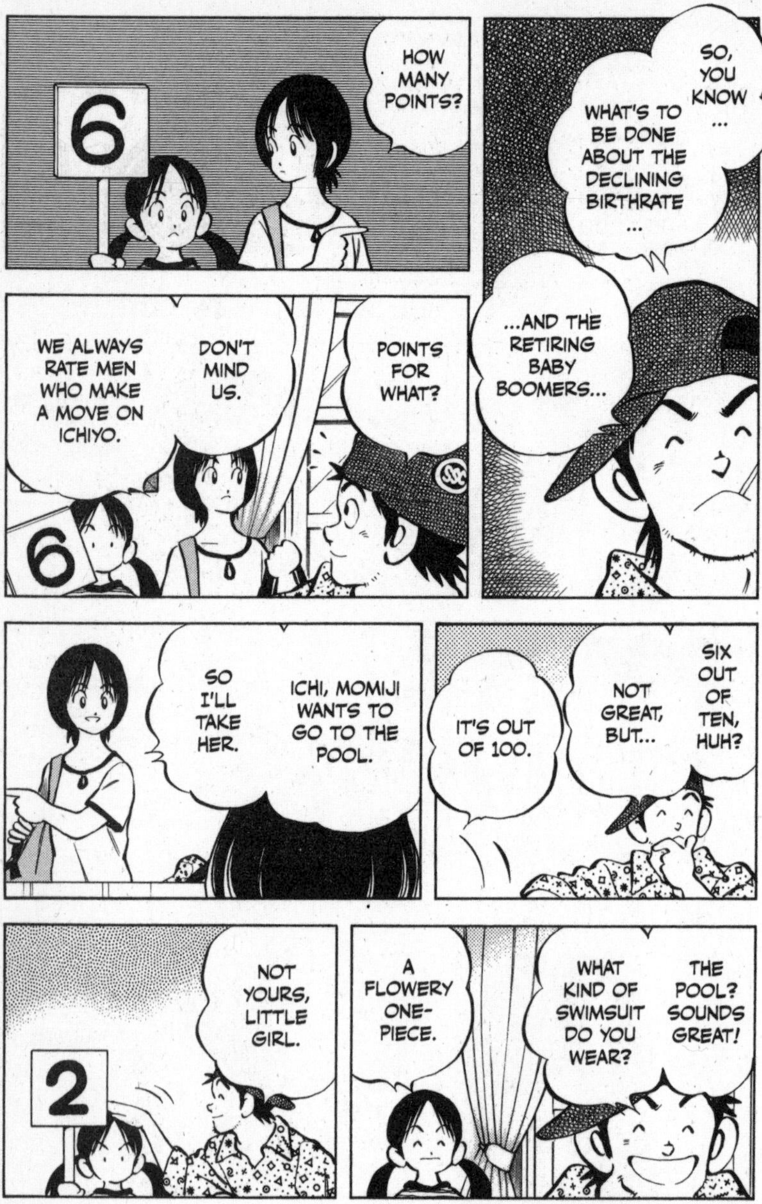
SO, YOU KNOW ...
WHAT'S TO BE DONE ABOUT THE DECLINING BIRTHRATE ...
...AND THE RETIRING BABY BOOMERS...
HOW MANY POINTS?
6
POINTS FOR WHAT?
DON'T MIND US.
WE ALWAYS RATE MEN WHO MAKE A MOVE ON ICHIYO.
6
SIX OUT OF TEN, HUH?
NOT GREAT, BUT...
IT'S OUT OF 100.
ICHI, MOMIJI WANTS TO GO TO THE POOL.
SO I'LL TAKE HER.
THE POOL? SOUNDS GREAT!
WHAT KIND OF SWIMSUIT DO YOU WEAR?
A FLOWERY ONE-PIECE.
NOT YOURS, LITTLE GIRL.
2

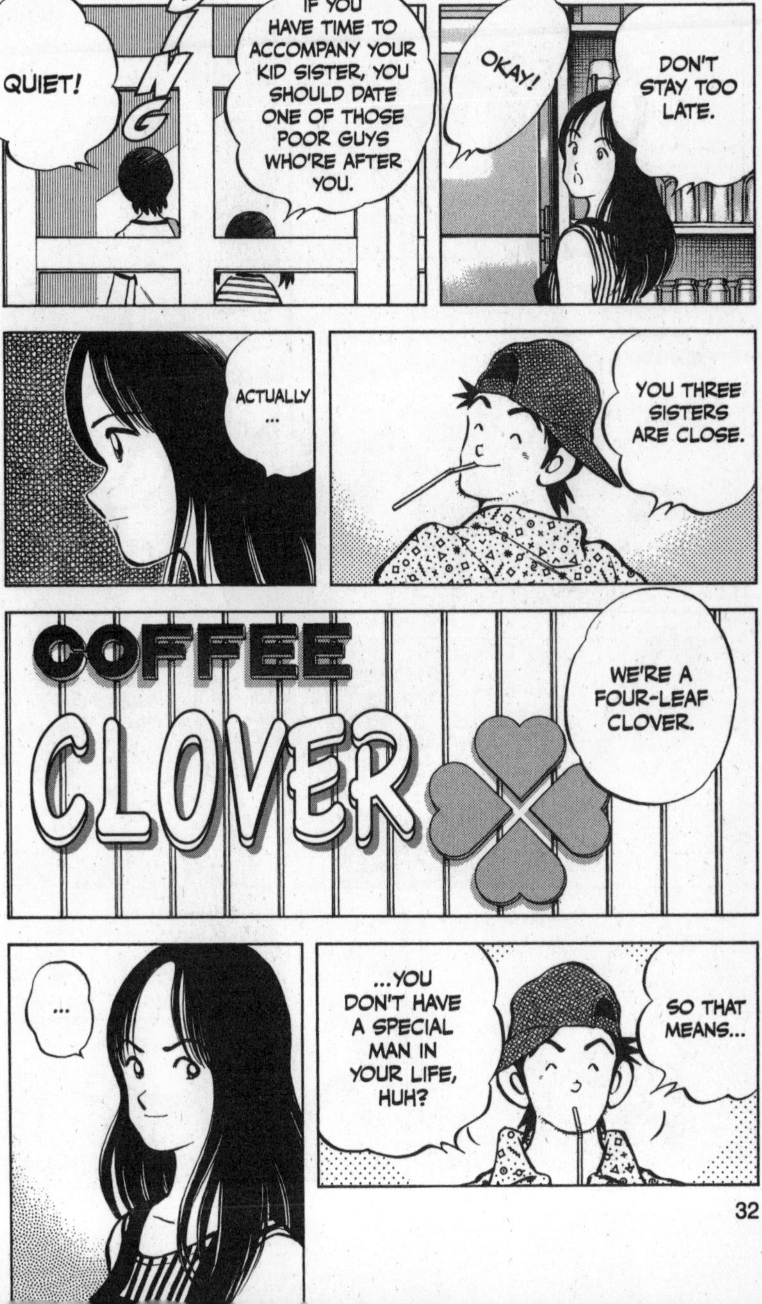
DON'T STAY TOO LATE.
OKAY!
IF YOU HAVE TIME TO ACCOMPANY YOUR KID SISTER, YOU SHOULD DATE ONE OF THOSE POOR GUYS WHO'RE AFTER YOU.
DING
QUIET!
YOU THREE SISTERS ARE CLOSE.
ACTUALLY ...
WE'RE A FOUR-LEAF CLOVER.
COFFEE
CLOVER
SO THAT MEANS...
...YOU DON'T HAVE A SPECIAL MAN IN YOUR LIFE, HUH?
...

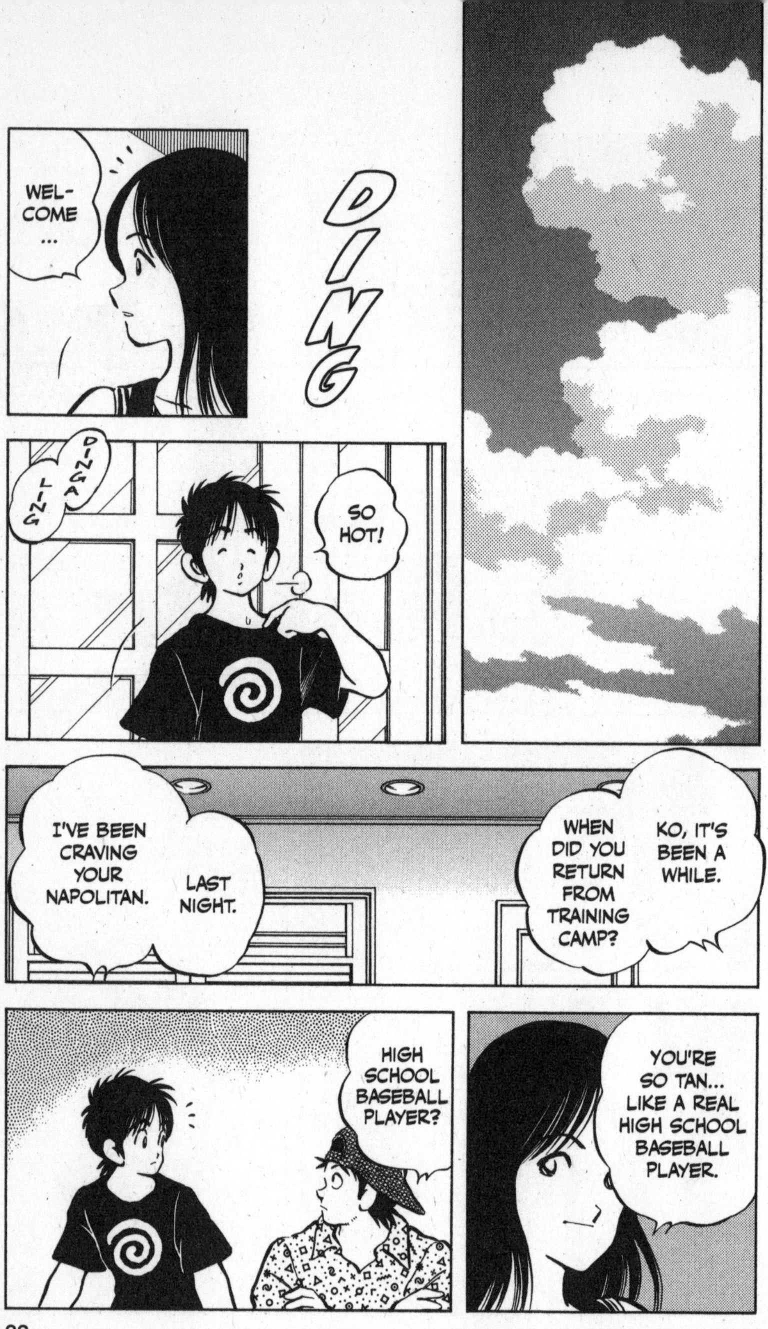
DING
WEL-COME ...
DINGA LING
SO HOT!
KO, IT'S BEEN A WHILE.
WHEN DID YOU RETURN FROM TRAINING CAMP?
LAST NIGHT.
I'VE BEEN CRAVING YOUR NAPOLITAN.
YOU'RE SO TAN... LIKE A REAL HIGH SCHOOL BASEBALL PLAYER.
HIGH SCHOOL BASEBALL PLAYER?

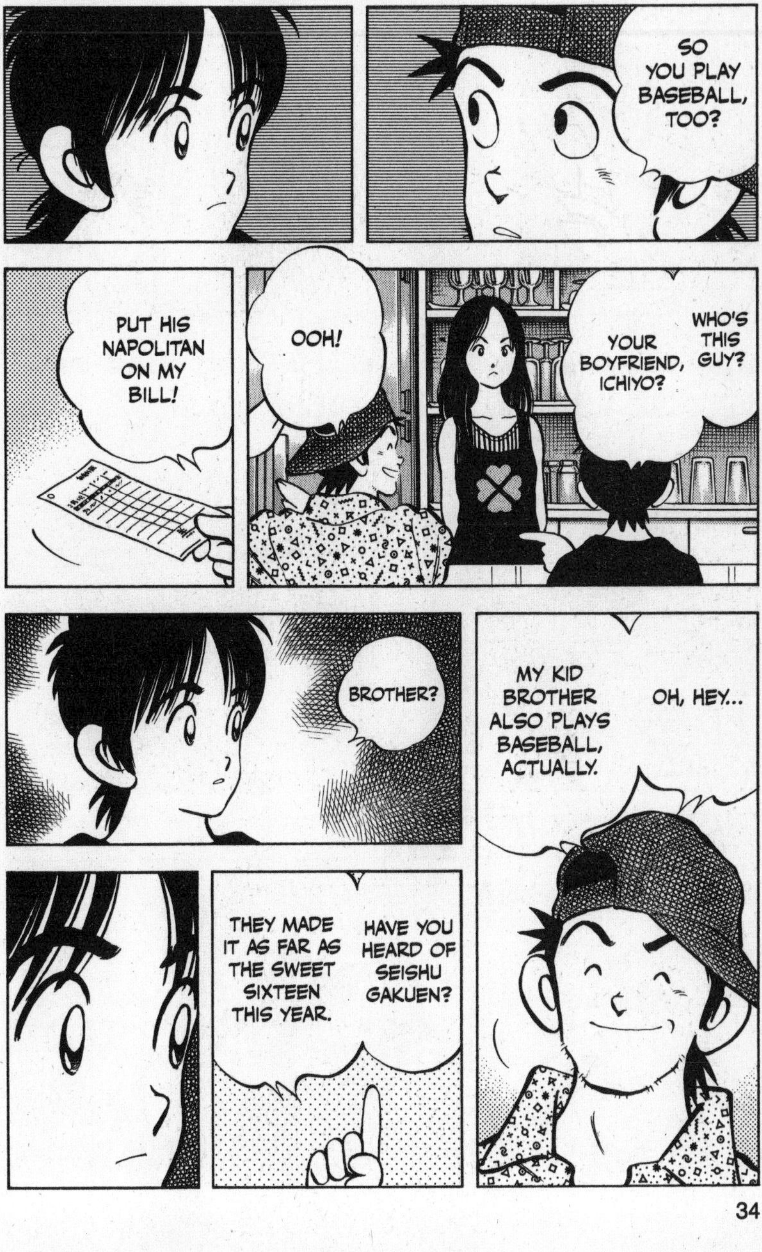
SO YOU PLAY BASEBALL, TOO?
WHO'S THIS GUY?
YOUR BOYFRIEND, ICHIYO?
OOH!
PUT HIS NAPOLITAN ON MY BILL!
OH, HEY...
MY KID BROTHER ALSO PLAYS BASEBALL, ACTUALLY.
BROTHER?
HAVE YOU HEARD OF SEISHU GAKUEN?
THEY MADE IT AS FAR AS THE SWEET SIXTEEN THIS YEAR.

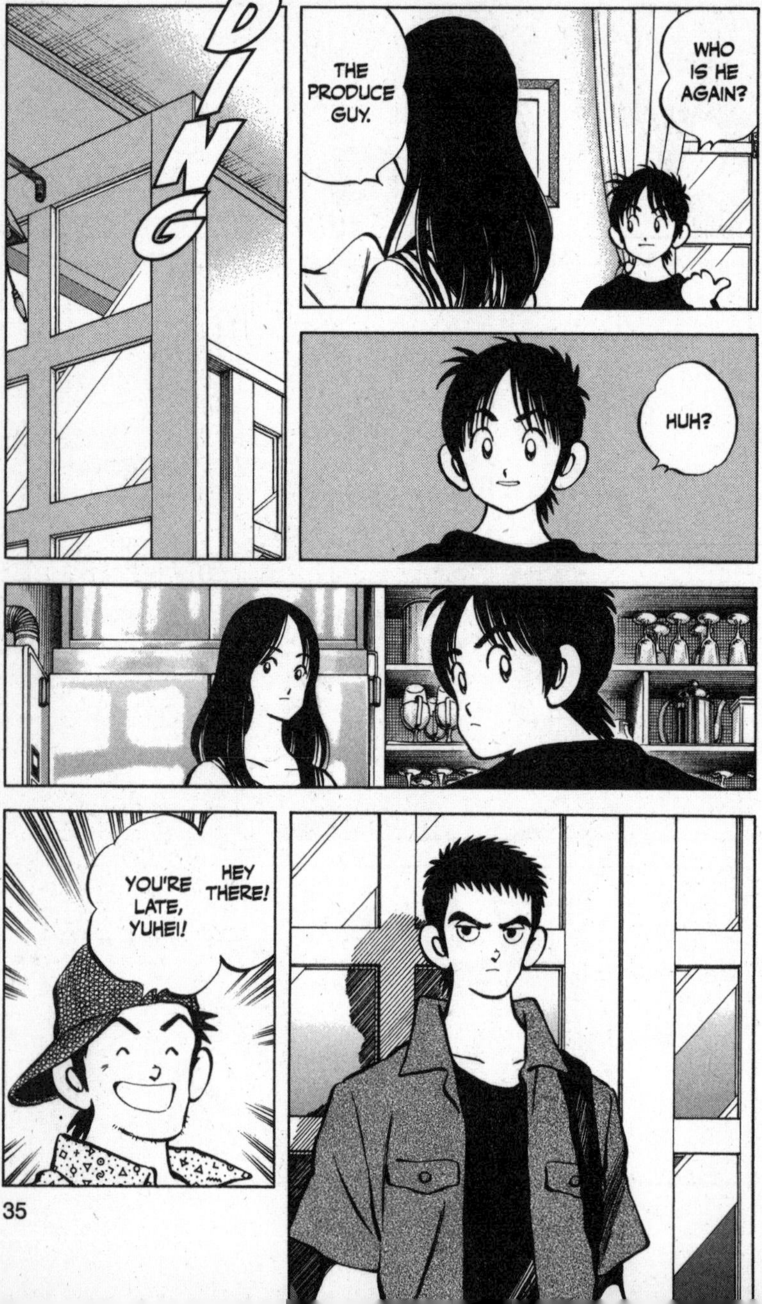
WHO IS HE AGAIN?
THE PRODUCE GUY.
HUH?
DING
HEY THERE!
YOU'RE LATE, YUHEI!

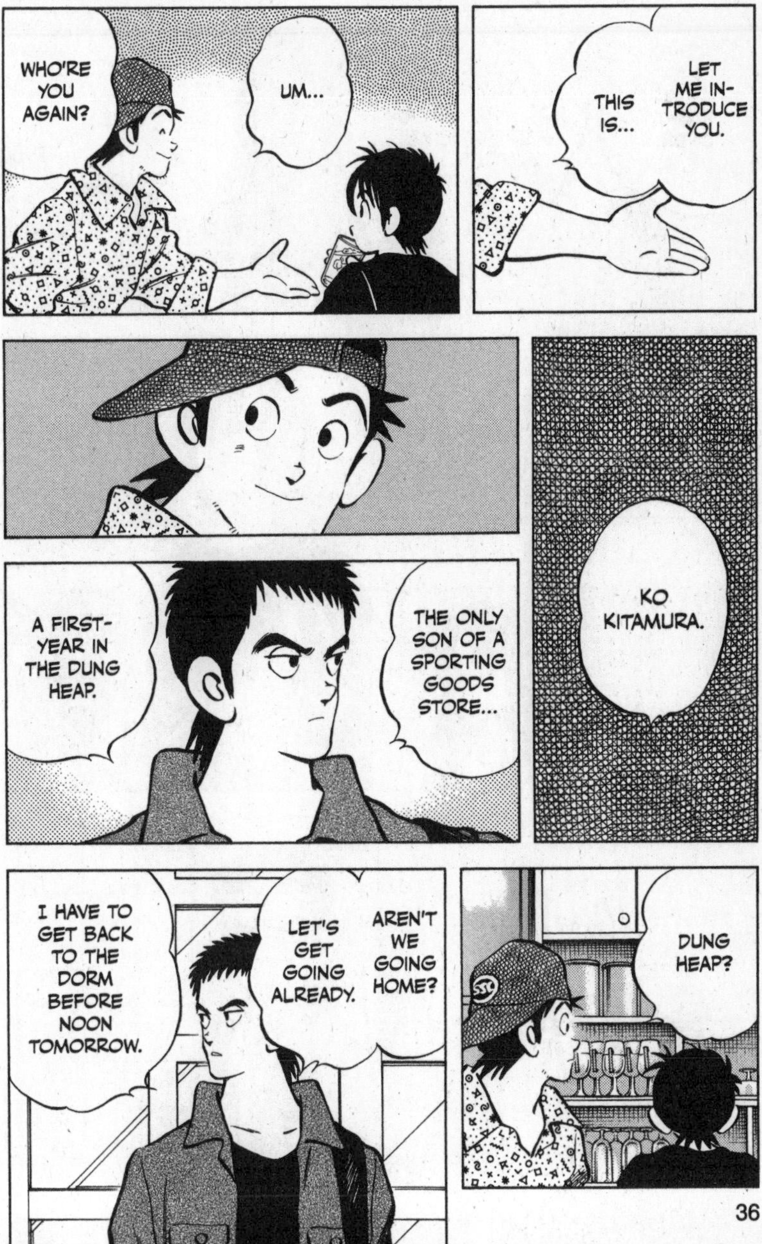
LET ME IN-TRODUCE YOU.
THIS IS...
UM...
WHO'RE YOU AGAIN?
KO KITAMURA.
THE ONLY SON OF A SPORTING GOODS STORE...
A FIRST-YEAR IN THE DUNG HEAP.
DUNG HEAP?
AREN'T WE GOING HOME?
LET'S GET GOING ALREADY.
I HAVE TO GET BACK TO THE DORM BEFORE NOON TOMORROW.

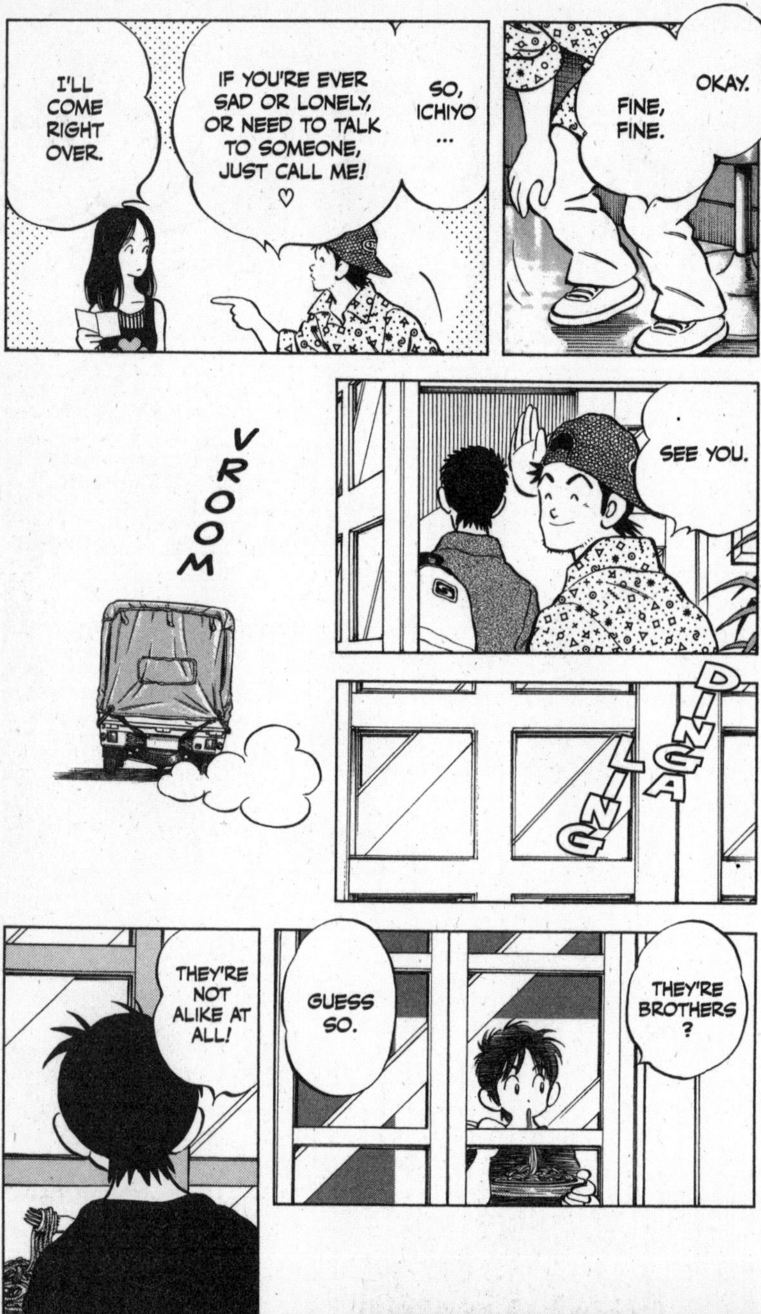
OKAY.
FINE, FINE.
SO, ICHIYO...
IF YOU'RE EVER SAD OR LONELY, OR NEED TO TALK TO SOMEONE, JUST CALL ME! ♡
I'LL COME RIGHT OVER.
SEE YOU.
DINGALING
VROOM
THEY'RE BROTHERS?
GUESS SO.
THEY'RE NOT ALIKE AT ALL!

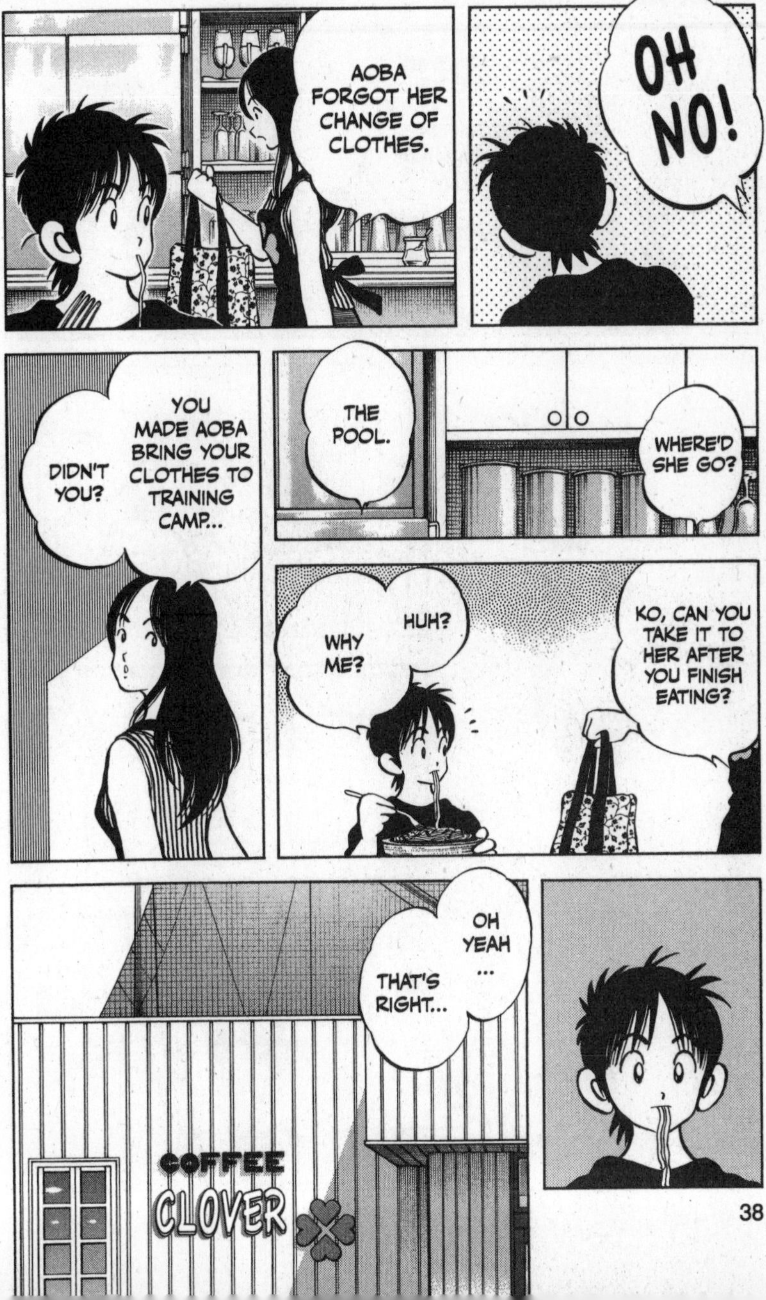
OH NO!
AOBA FORGOT HER CHANGE OF CLOTHES.
WHERE'D SHE GO?
THE POOL.
KO, CAN YOU TAKE IT TO HER AFTER YOU FINISH EATING?
HUH?
WHY ME?
YOU MADE AOBA BRING YOUR CLOTHES TO TRAINING CAMP...
DIDN'T YOU?
OH YEAH ...
THAT'S RIGHT...
COFFEE
CLOVER

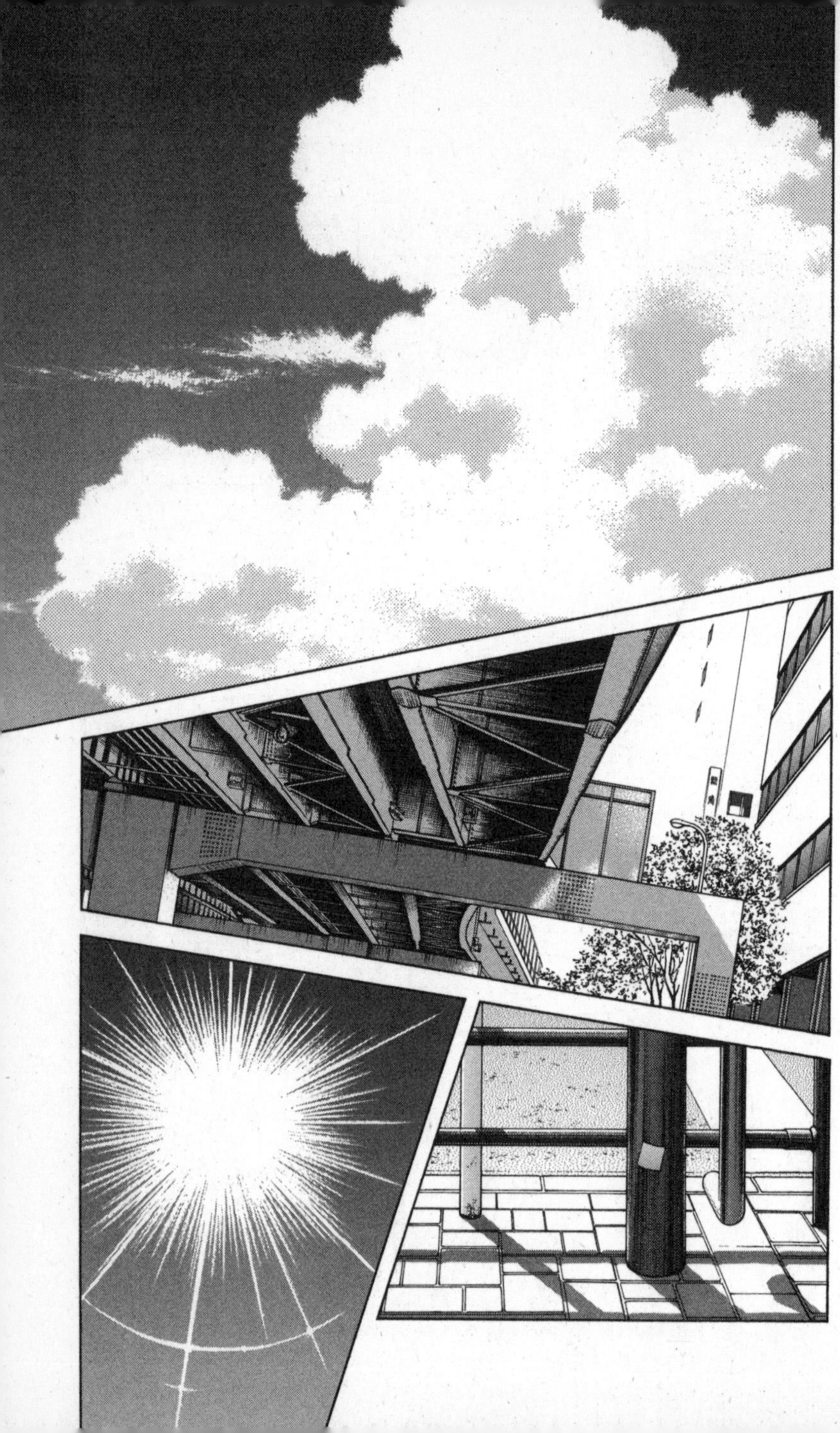

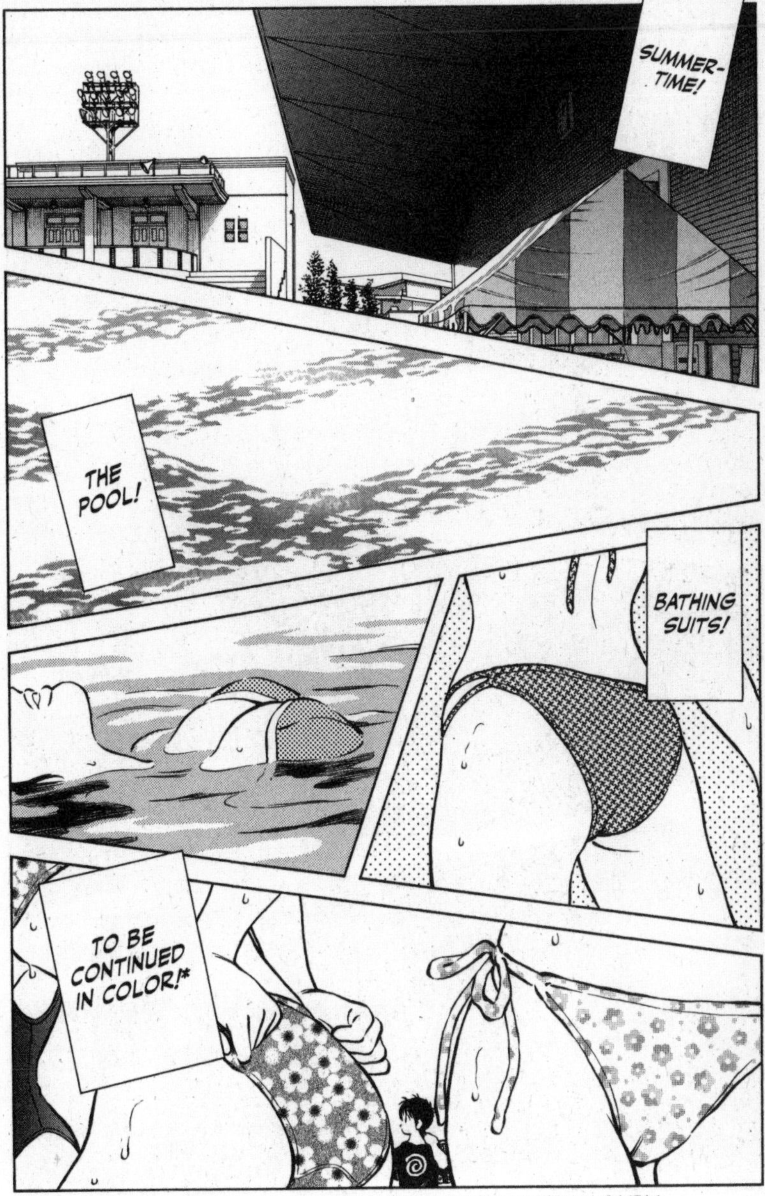
SUMMER-TIME!
THE POOL!
BATHING SUITS!
TO BE CONTINUED IN COLOR!*

*P.41-43 WERE PUBLISHED IN COLOR WHEN THEY RAN IN *WEEKLY SHONEN SUNDAY*.

CHAPTER 43 OBNOXIOUS FIRST-YEAR

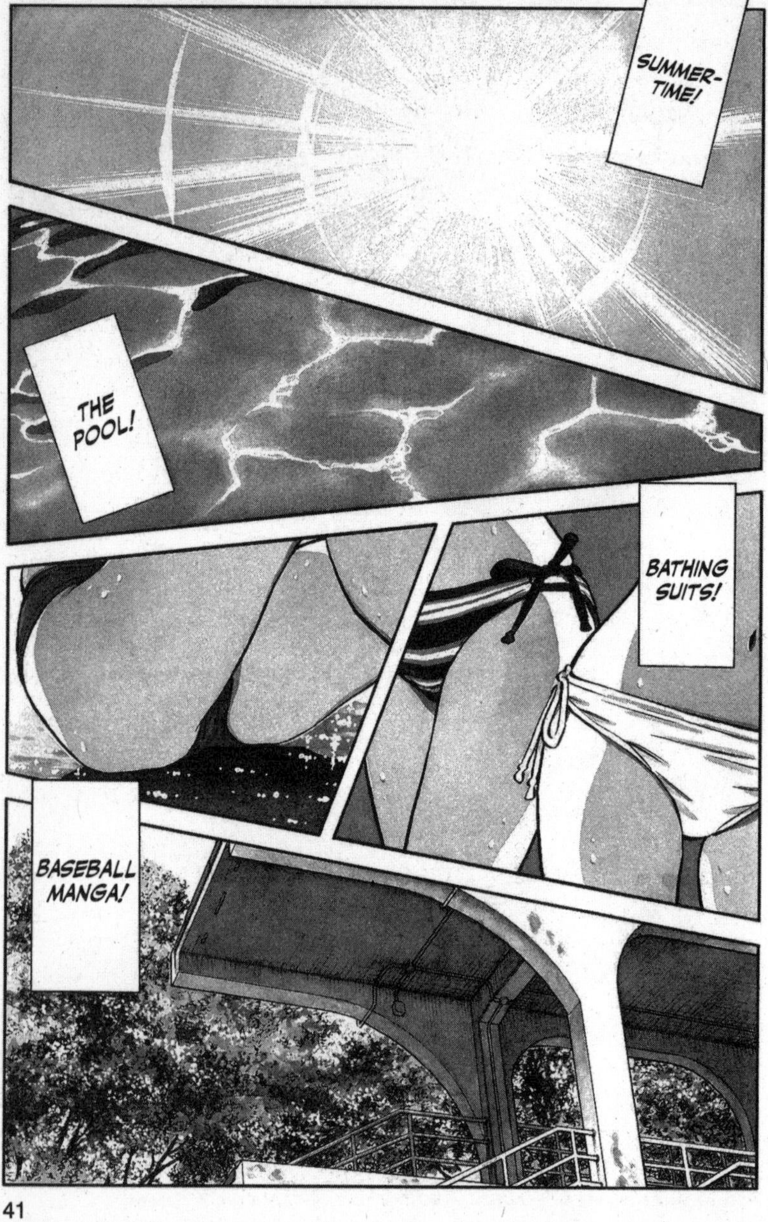
SUMMER-TIME!
THE POOL!
BATHING SUITS!
BASEBALL MANGA!

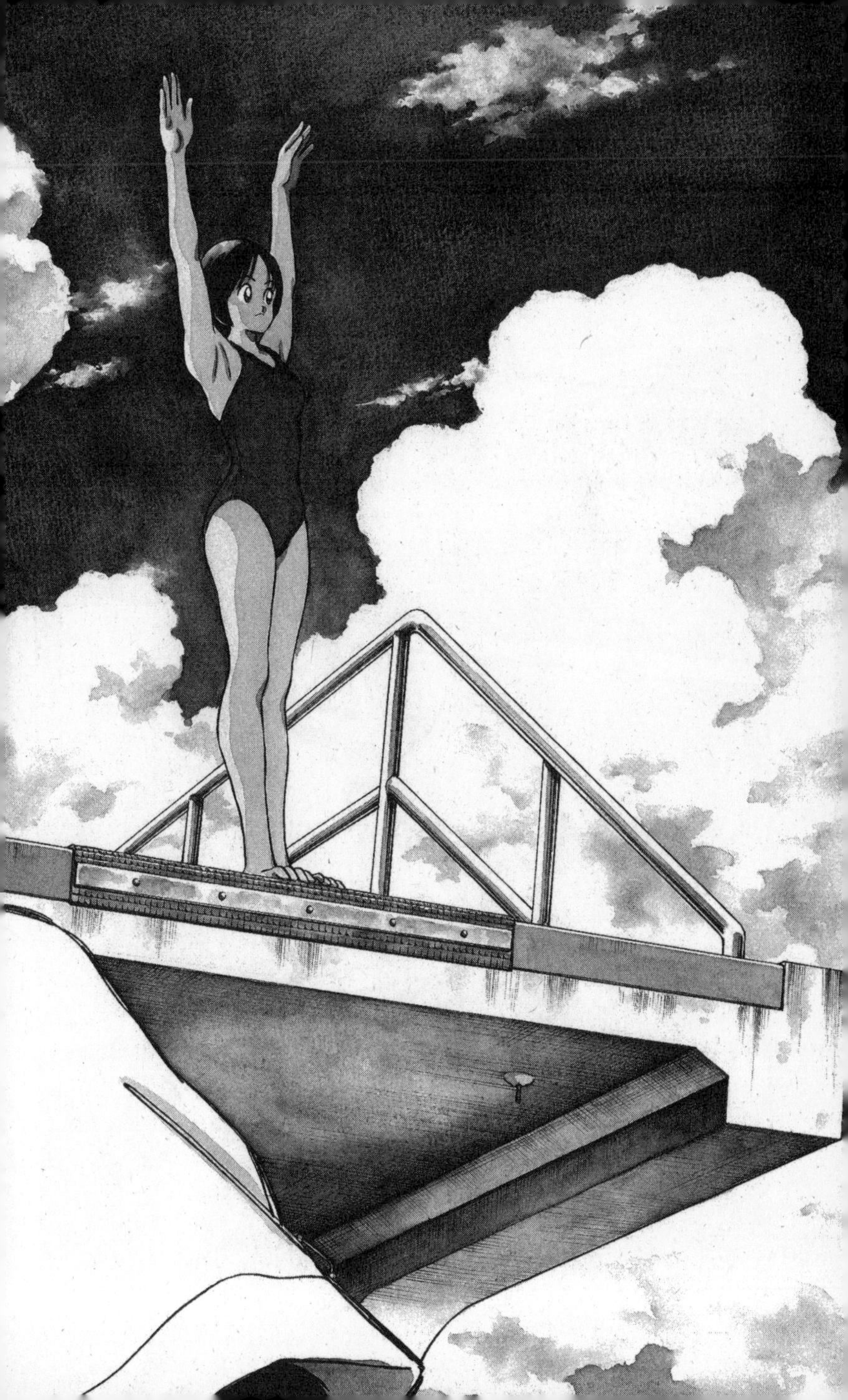

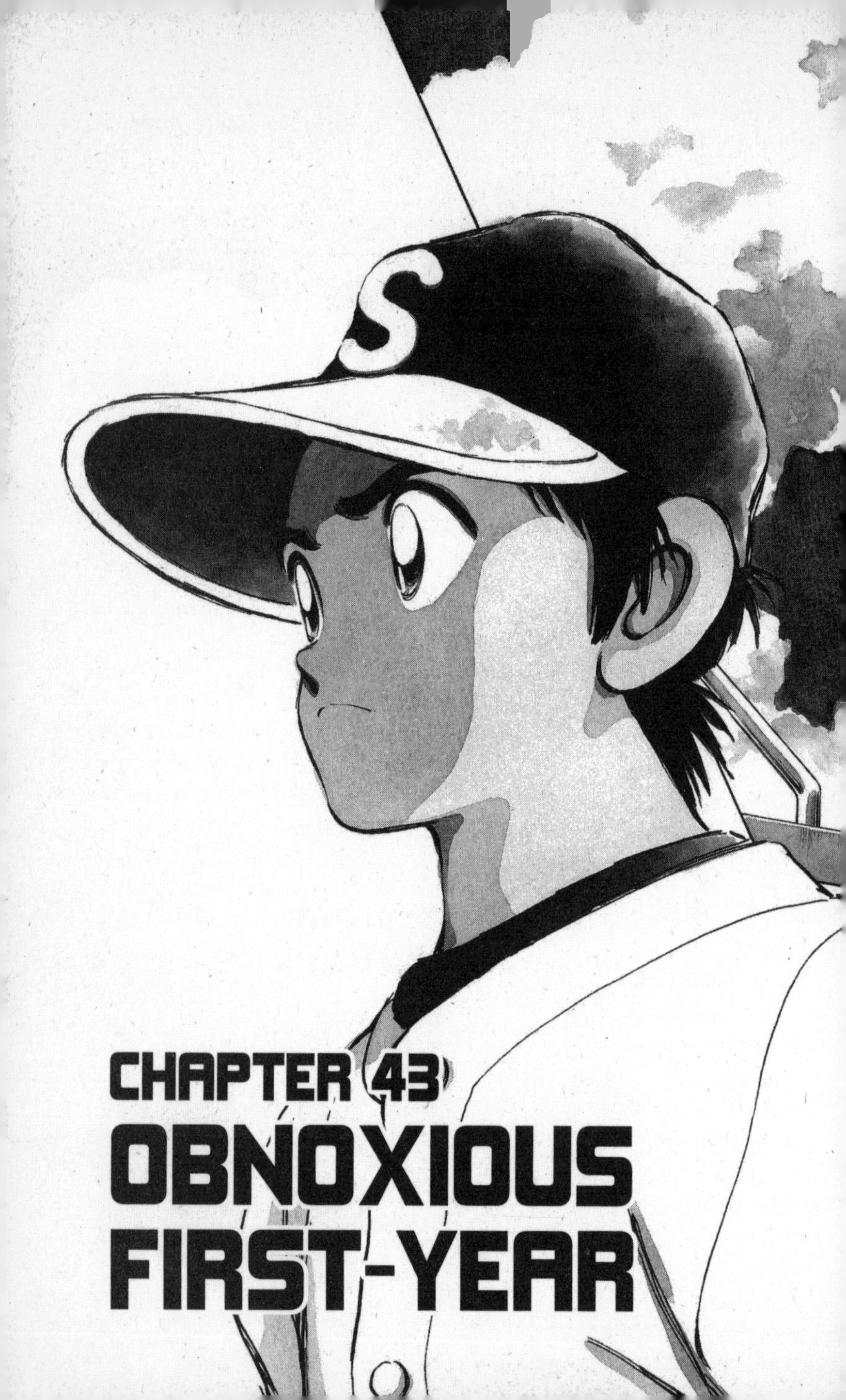
CHAPTER 43
OBNOXIOUS FIRST-YEAR

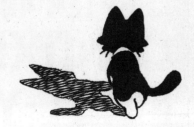

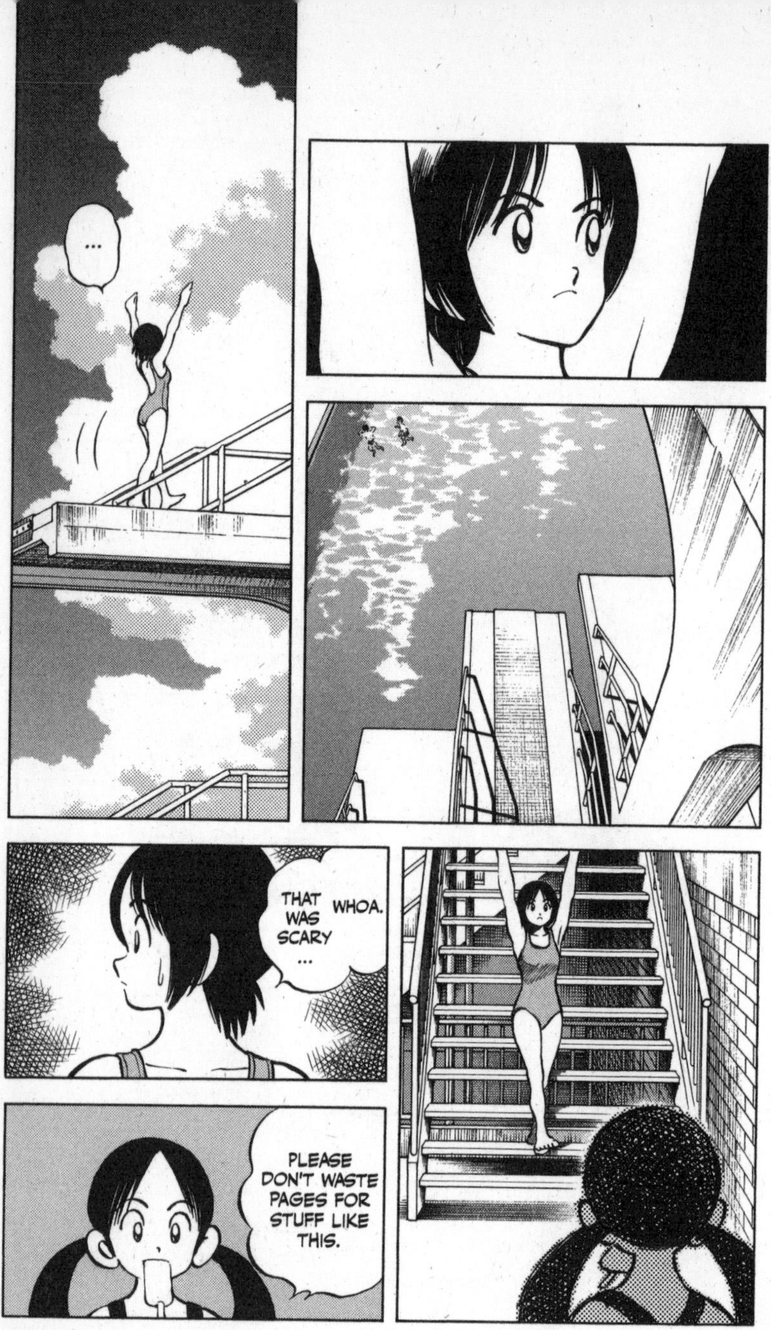
...
WHOA.
THAT WAS SCARY ...
PLEASE DON'T WASTE PAGES FOR STUFF LIKE THIS.

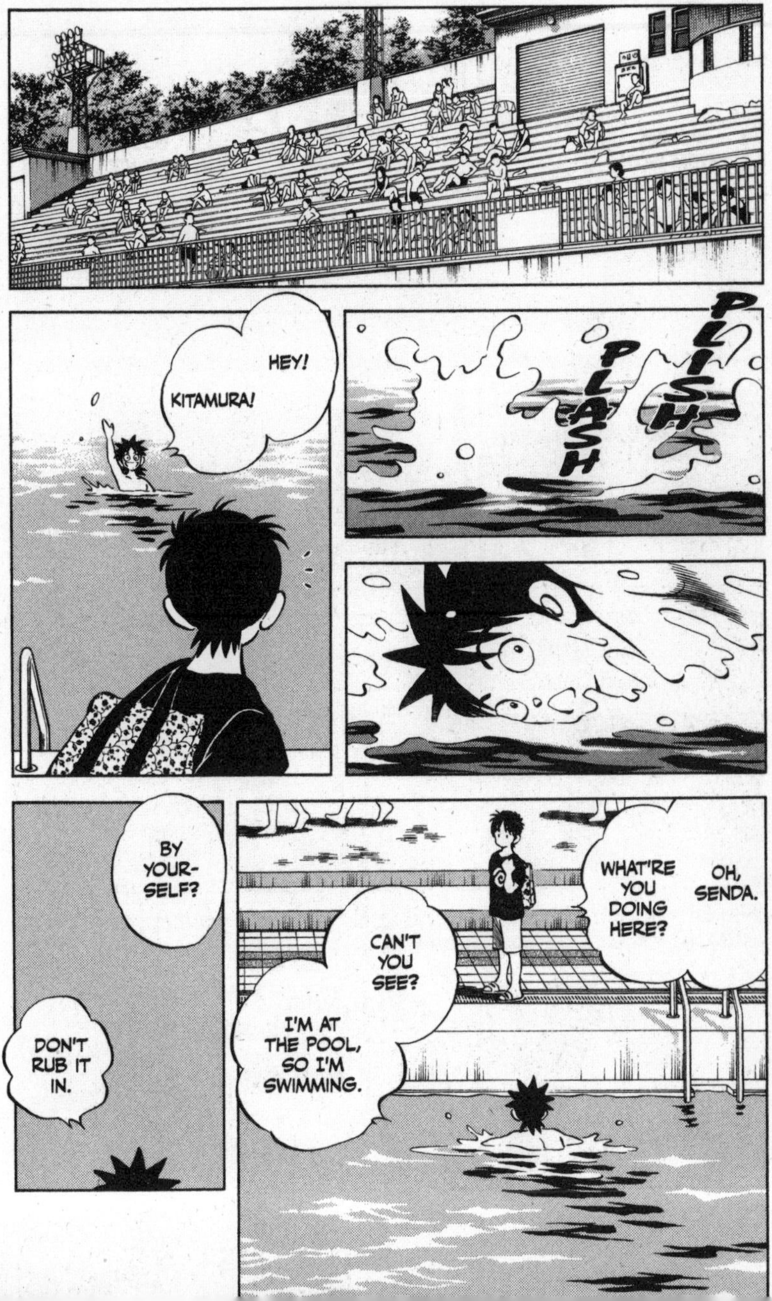
PLISH
PLASH
HEY!
KITAMURA!
OH, SENDA.
WHAT'RE YOU DOING HERE?
CAN'T YOU SEE?
I'M AT THE POOL, SO I'M SWIMMING.
BY YOURSELF?
DON'T RUB IT IN.

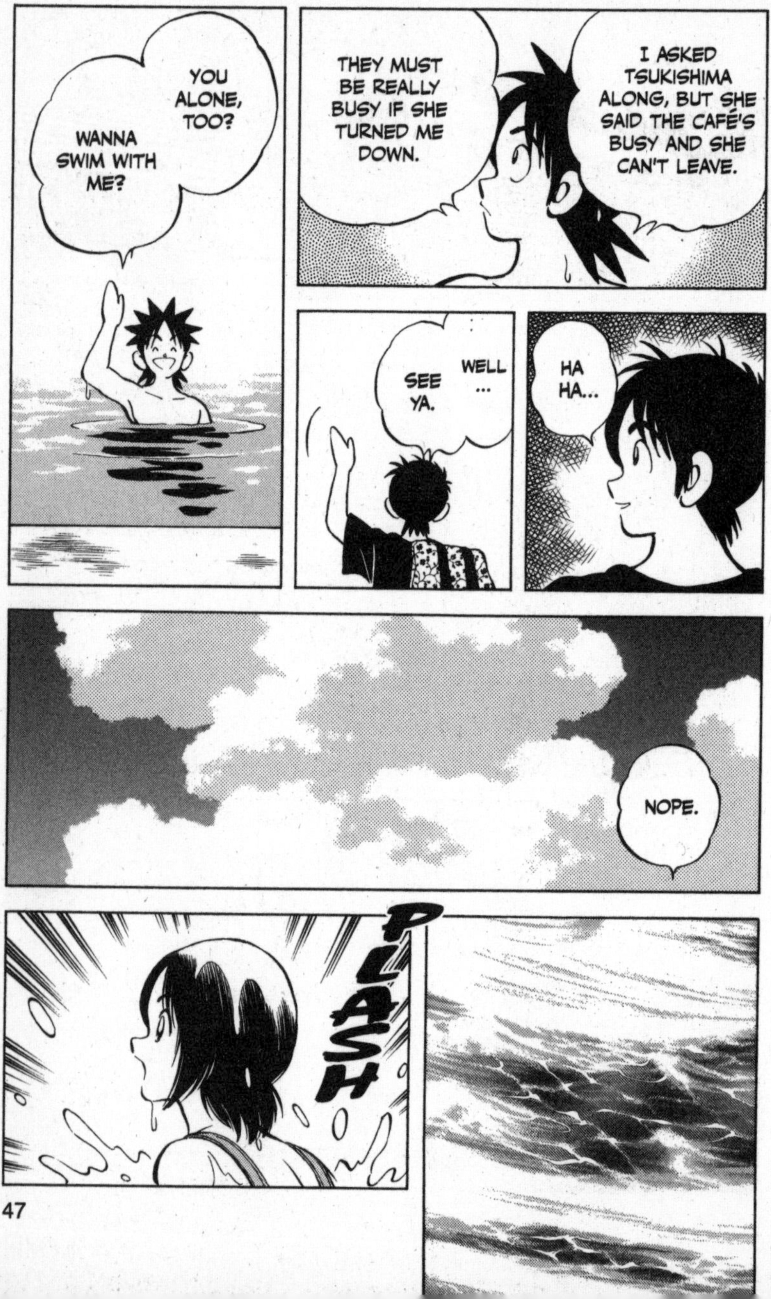
I ASKED TSUKISHIMA ALONG, BUT SHE SAID THE CAFÉ'S BUSY AND SHE CAN'T LEAVE.
THEY MUST BE REALLY BUSY IF SHE TURNED ME DOWN.
HA HA...
WELL ...
SEE YA.
YOU ALONE, TOO?
WANNA SWIM WITH ME?
NOPE.
PLASH

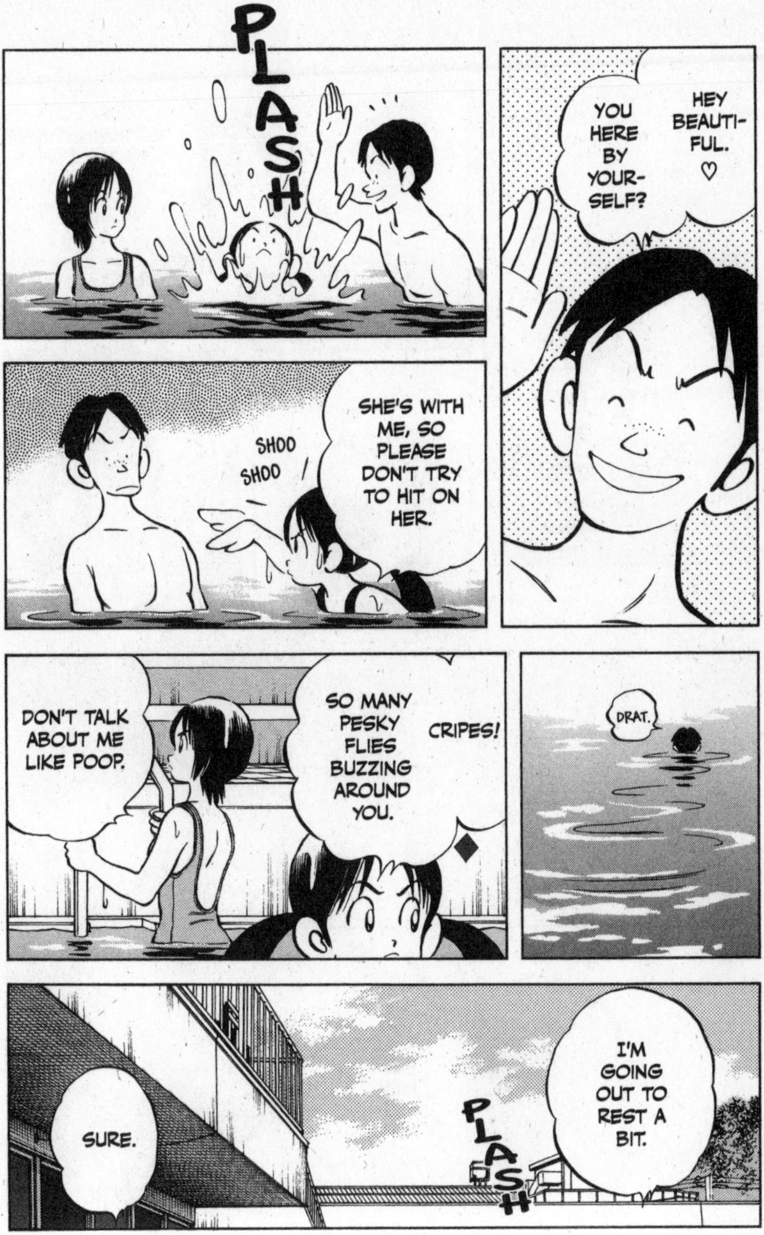
HEY BEAUTI-FUL. ♡
YOU HERE BY YOUR-SELF?
PLASH
SHE'S WITH ME, SO PLEASE DON'T TRY TO HIT ON HER.
SHOO SHOO
DRAT.
CRIPES!
SO MANY PESKY FLIES BUZZING AROUND YOU.
DON'T TALK ABOUT ME LIKE POOP.
I'M GOING OUT TO REST A BIT.
PLASH
SURE.

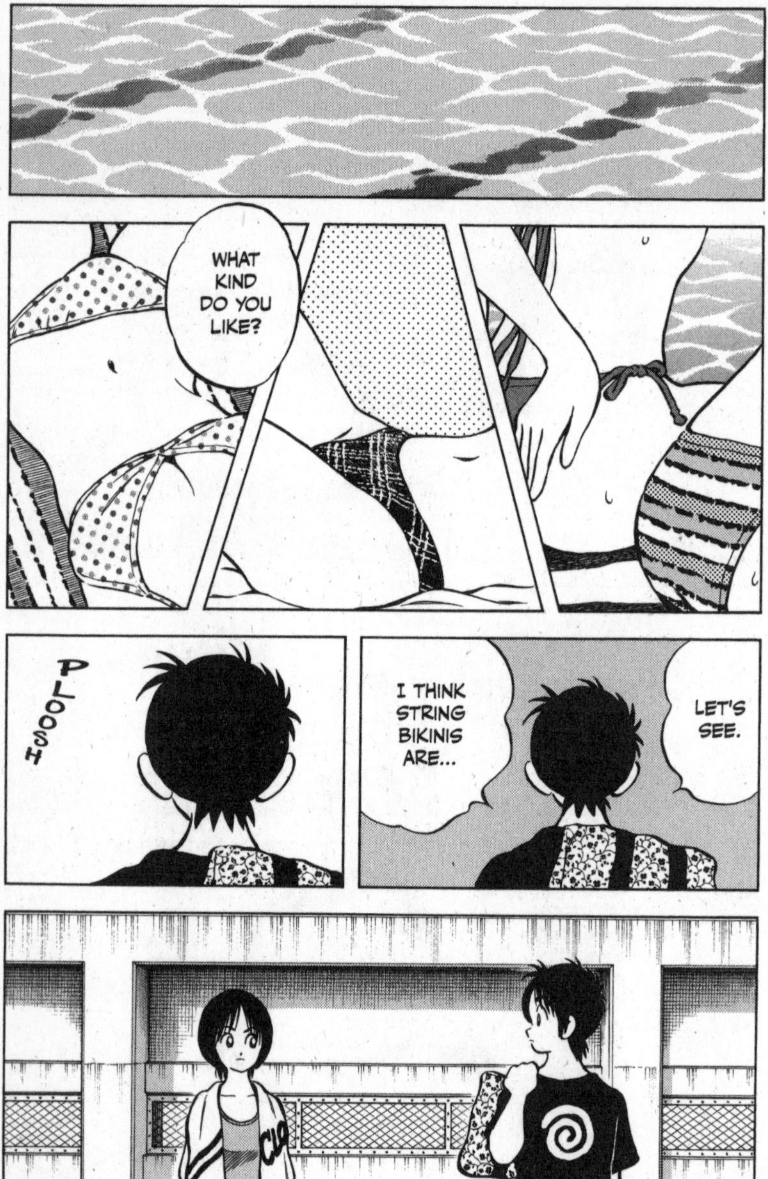
WHAT KIND DO YOU LIKE?
LET'S SEE.
I THINK STRING BIKINIS ARE...
PLOOSH

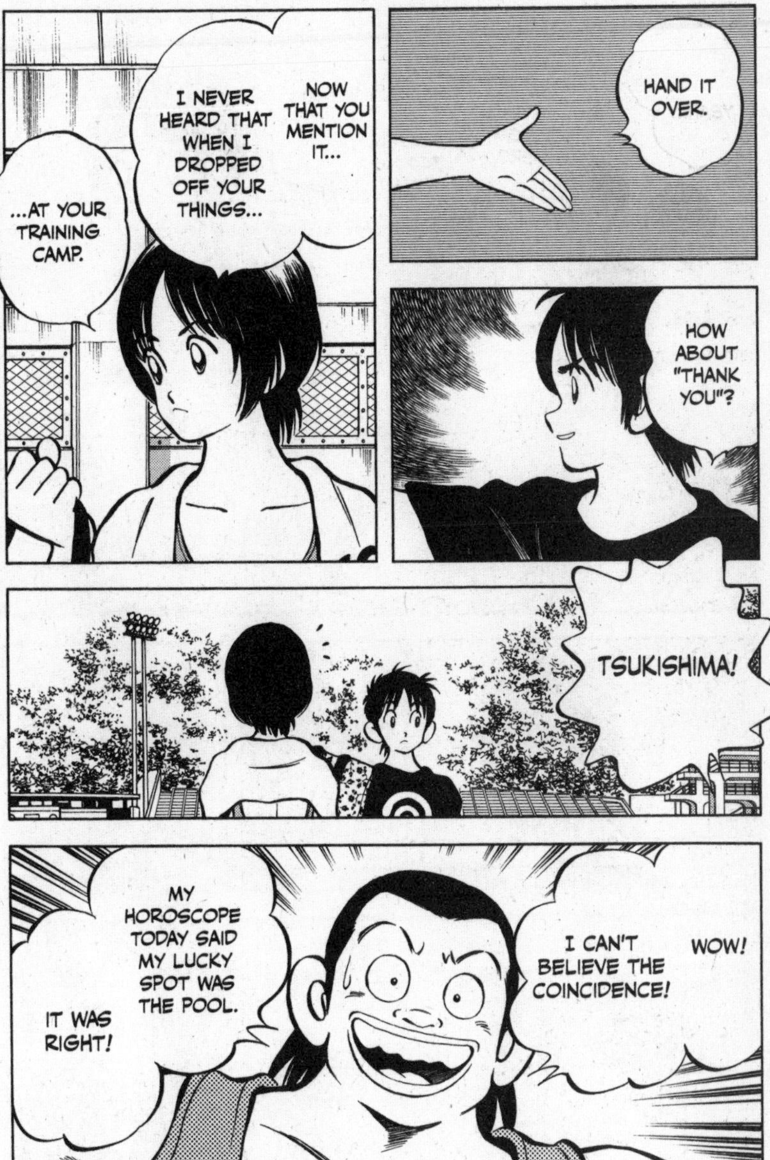
HAND IT OVER.
HOW ABOUT "THANK YOU"?
NOW THAT YOU MENTION IT...
I NEVER HEARD THAT WHEN I DROPPED OFF YOUR THINGS...
...AT YOUR TRAINING CAMP.
TSUKISHIMA!
WOW!
I CAN'T BELIEVE THE COINCIDENCE!
MY HOROSCOPE TODAY SAID MY LUCKY SPOT WAS THE POOL.
IT WAS RIGHT!

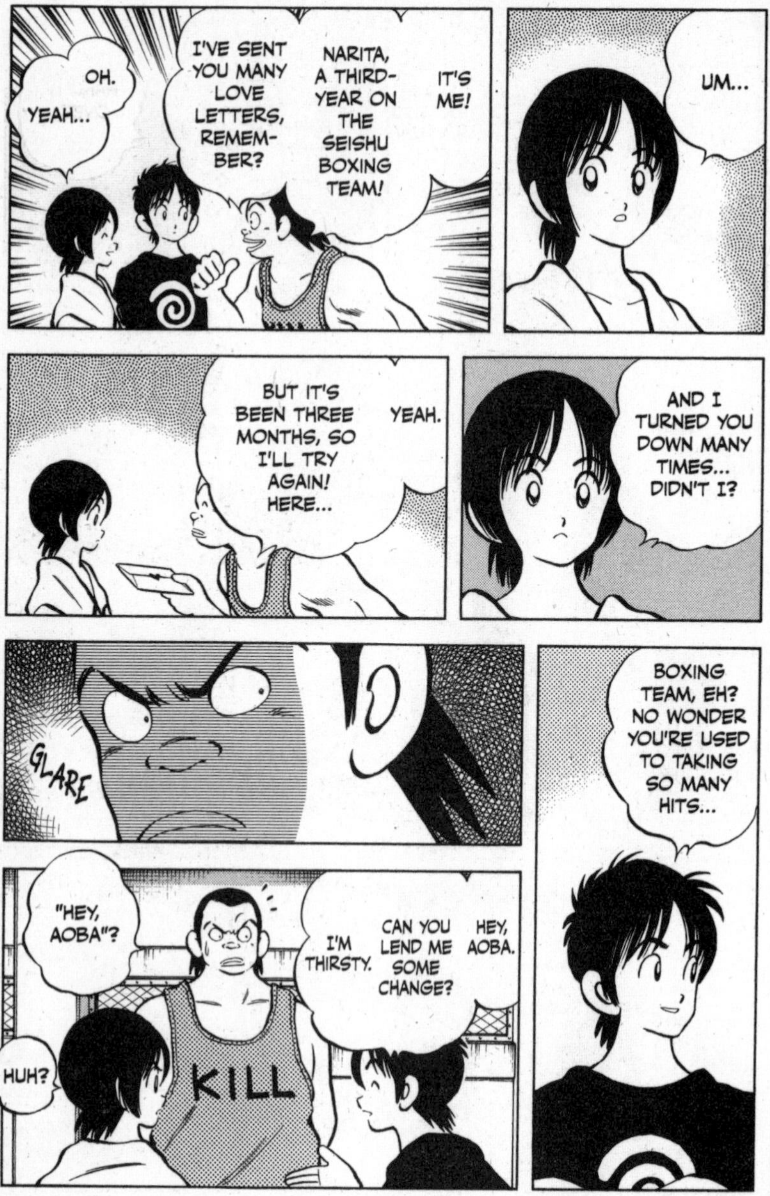
UM...
IT'S ME!
NARITA, A THIRD-YEAR ON THE SEISHU BOXING TEAM!
I'VE SENT YOU MANY LOVE LETTERS, REMEMBER?
OH. YEAH...
AND I TURNED YOU DOWN MANY TIMES... DIDN'T I?
YEAH.
BUT IT'S BEEN THREE MONTHS, SO I'LL TRY AGAIN! HERE...
BOXING TEAM, EH? NO WONDER YOU'RE USED TO TAKING SO MANY HITS...
GLARE
HEY, AOBA.
CAN YOU LEND ME SOME CHANGE?
I'M THIRSTY.
KILL
"HEY, AOBA"?
HUH?

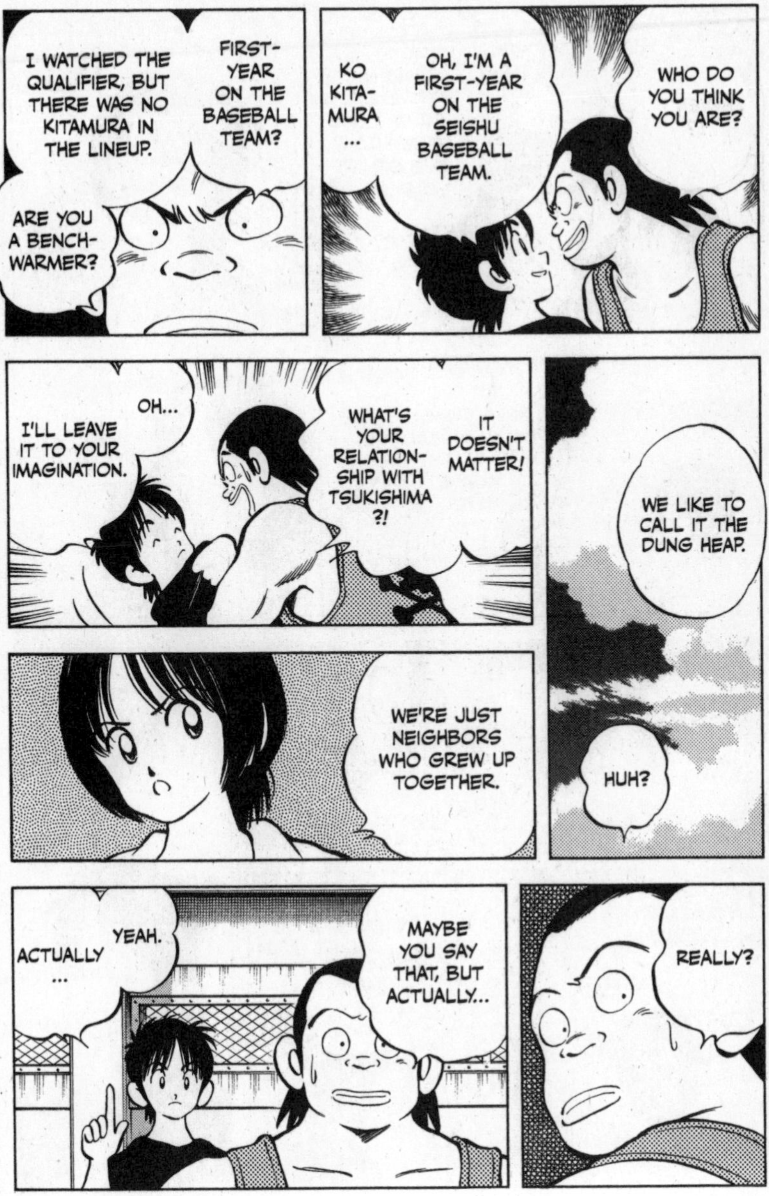
WHO DO YOU THINK YOU ARE?
OH, I'M A FIRST-YEAR ON THE SEISHU BASEBALL TEAM.
KO KITAMURA ...
FIRST-YEAR ON THE BASEBALL TEAM?
I WATCHED THE QUALIFIER, BUT THERE WAS NO KITAMURA IN THE LINEUP.
ARE YOU A BENCH-WARMER?
WE LIKE TO CALL IT THE DUNG HEAP.
HUH?
IT DOESN'T MATTER!
WHAT'S YOUR RELATIONSHIP WITH TSUKISHIMA ?!
OH...
I'LL LEAVE IT TO YOUR IMAGINATION.
WE'RE JUST NEIGHBORS WHO GREW UP TOGETHER.
REALLY?
MAYBE YOU SAY THAT, BUT ACTUALLY...
YEAH.
ACTUALLY ...

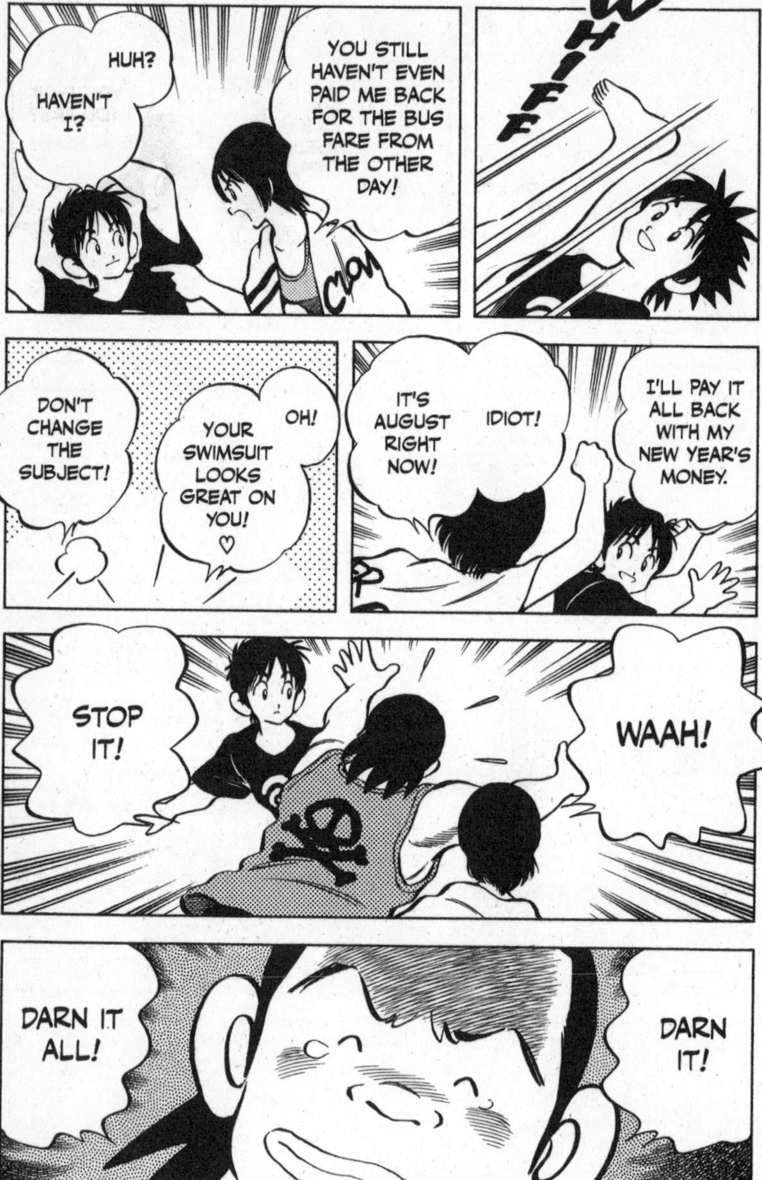
WHIFF
YOU STILL HAVEN'T EVEN PAID ME BACK FOR THE BUS FARE FROM THE OTHER DAY!
HUH?
HAVEN'T I?
I'LL PAY IT ALL BACK WITH MY NEW YEAR'S MONEY.
IDIOT!
IT'S AUGUST RIGHT NOW!
OH!
YOUR SWIMSUIT LOOKS GREAT ON YOU! ♡
DON'T CHANGE THE SUBJECT!
WAAH!
STOP IT!
DARN IT!
DARN IT ALL!

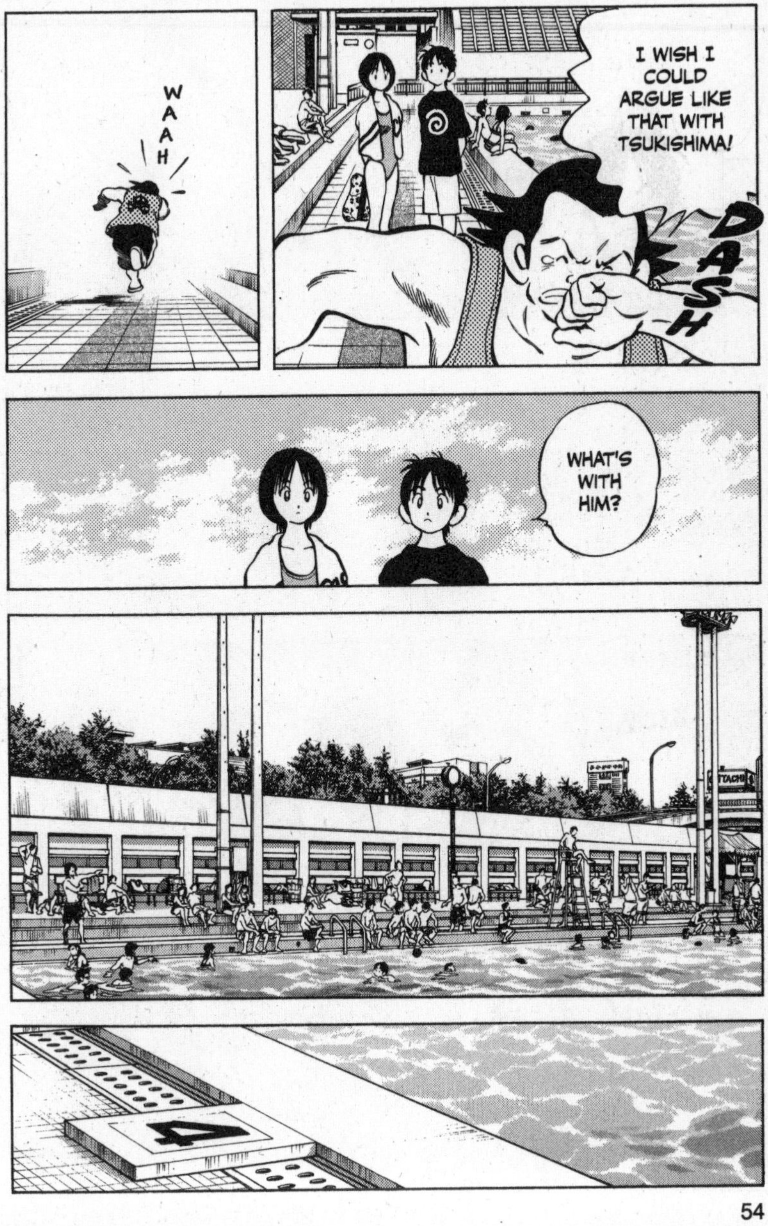
I WISH I COULD ARGUE LIKE THAT WITH TSUKISHIMA!
DASH
WAAH
WHAT'S WITH HIM?

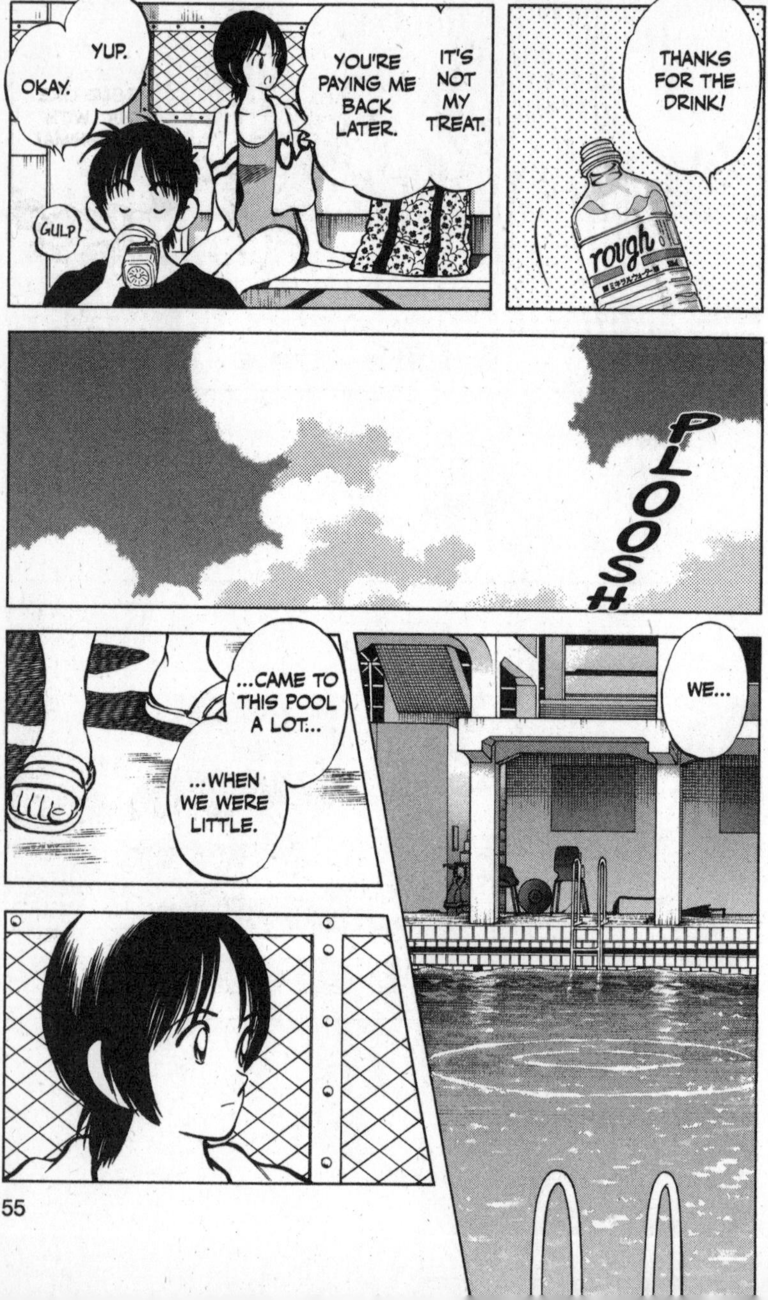
THANKS FOR THE DRINK!
rough
IT'S NOT MY TREAT.
YOU'RE PAYING ME BACK LATER.
YUP.
OKAY.
GULP
PLOOSH
WE...
...CAME TO THIS POOL A LOT...
...WHEN WE WERE LITTLE.

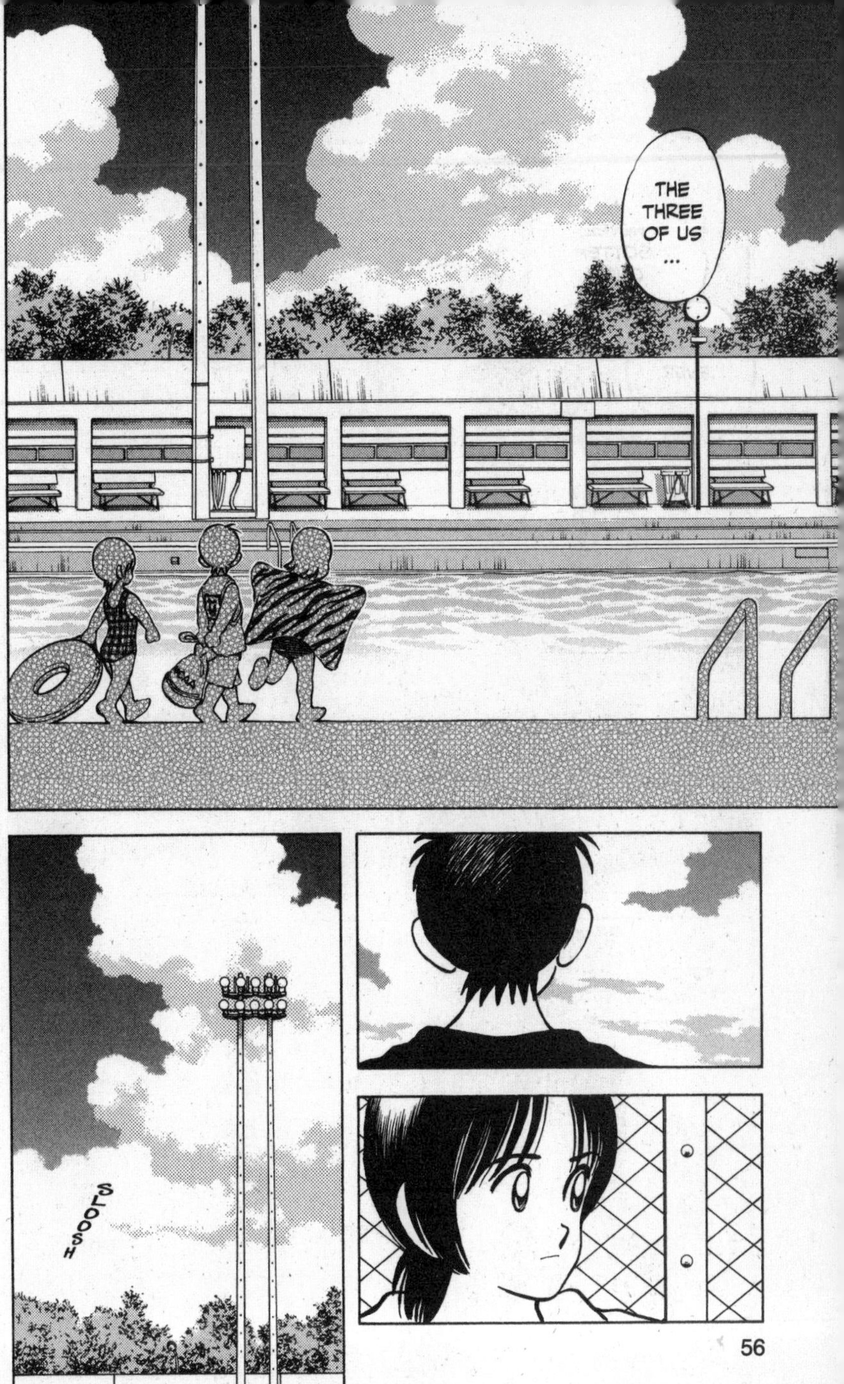
THE THREE OF US ...
SLOOSH

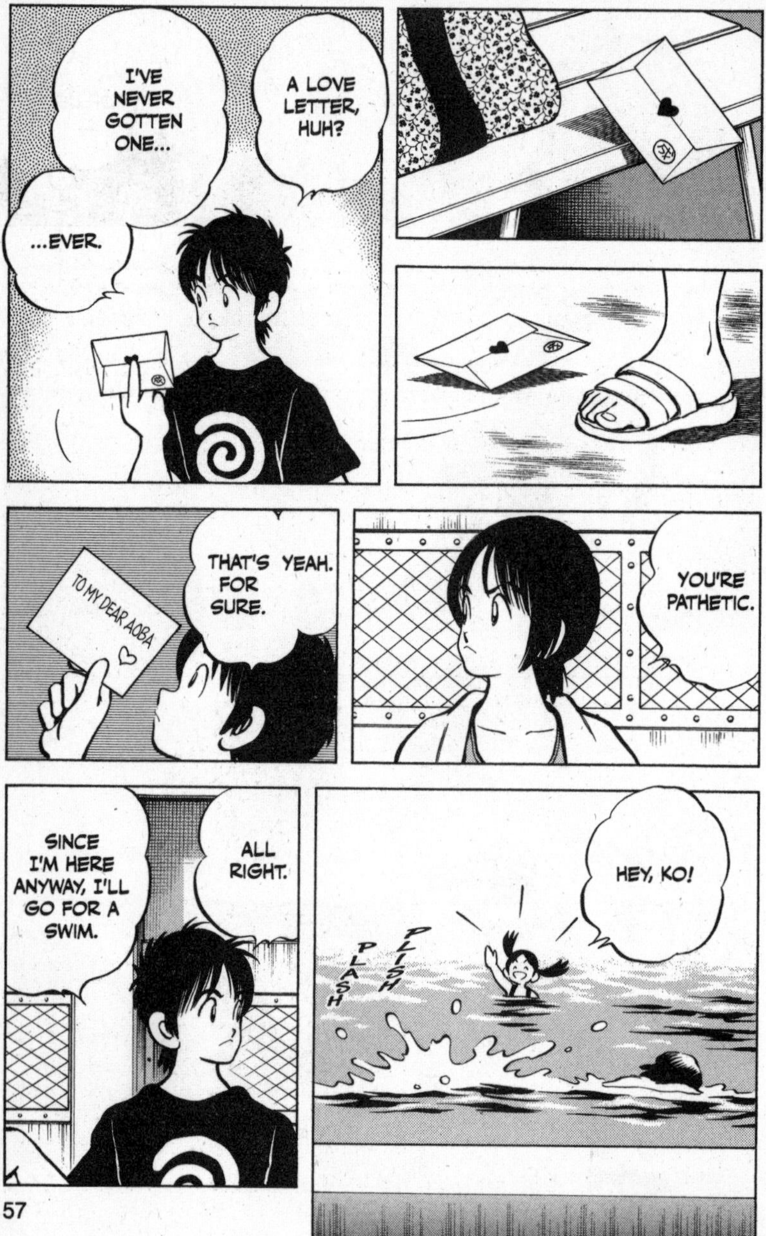
A LOVE LETTER, HUH?
I'VE NEVER GOTTEN ONE...
...EVER.
YOU'RE PATHETIC.
YEAH.
THAT'S FOR SURE.
TO MY DEAR AOBA
HEY, KO!
PLISH
PLASH
ALL RIGHT.
SINCE I'M HERE ANYWAY, I'LL GO FOR A SWIM.

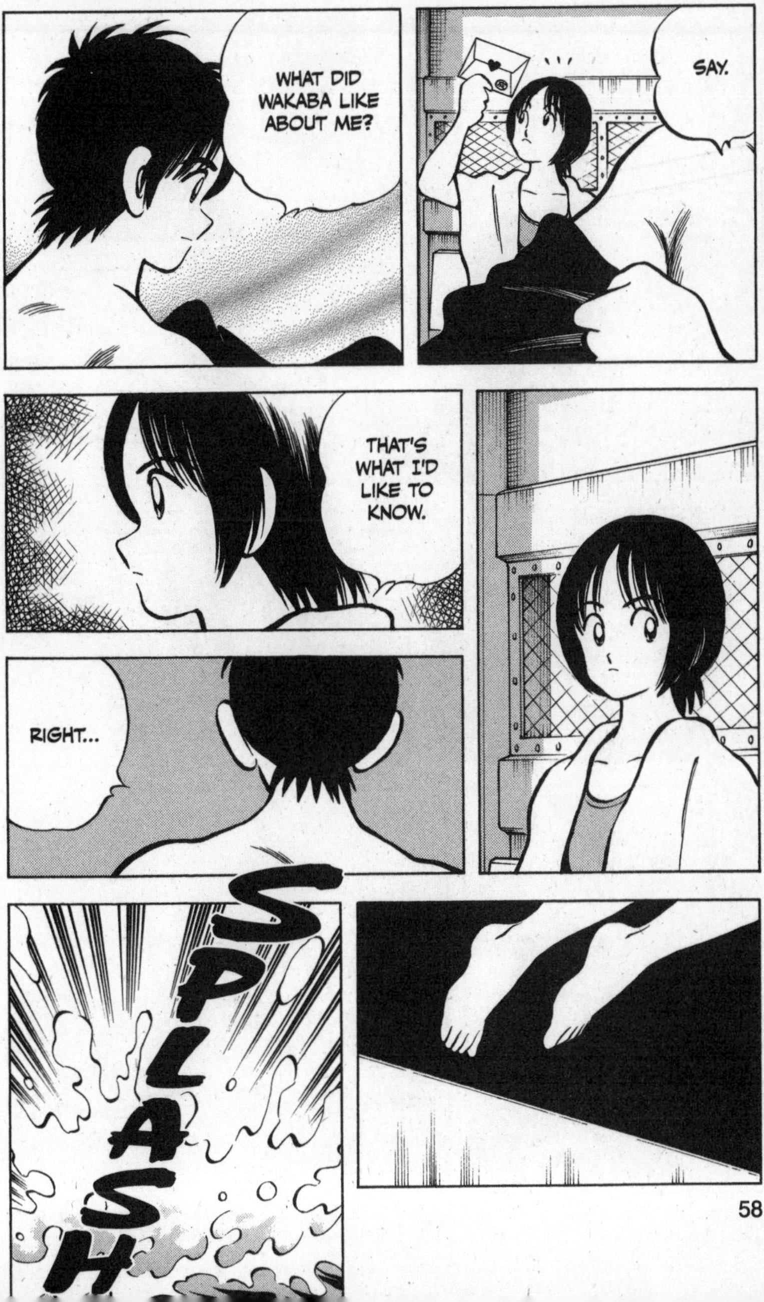
SAY.
WHAT DID WAKABA LIKE ABOUT ME?
THAT'S WHAT I'D LIKE TO KNOW.
RIGHT...
SPLASH

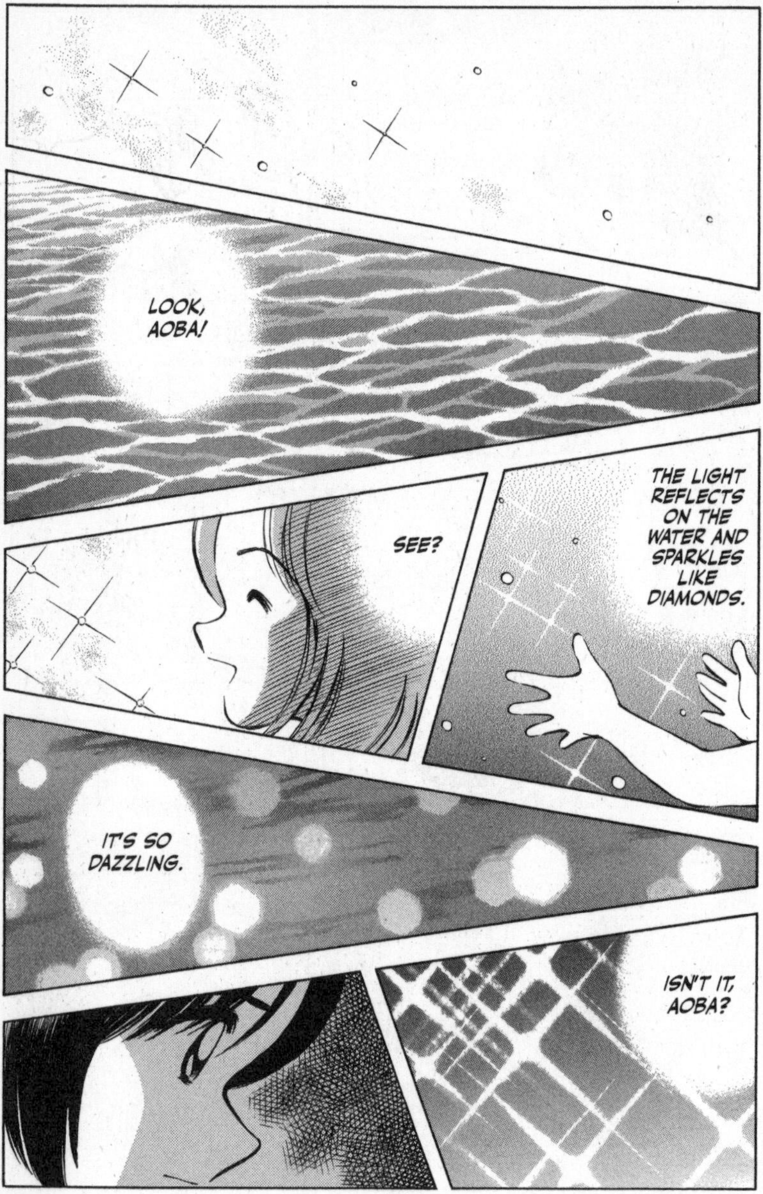
LOOK, AOBA!
THE LIGHT REFLECTS ON THE WATER AND SPARKLES LIKE DIAMONDS.
SEE?
IT'S SO DAZZLING.
ISN'T IT, AOBA?

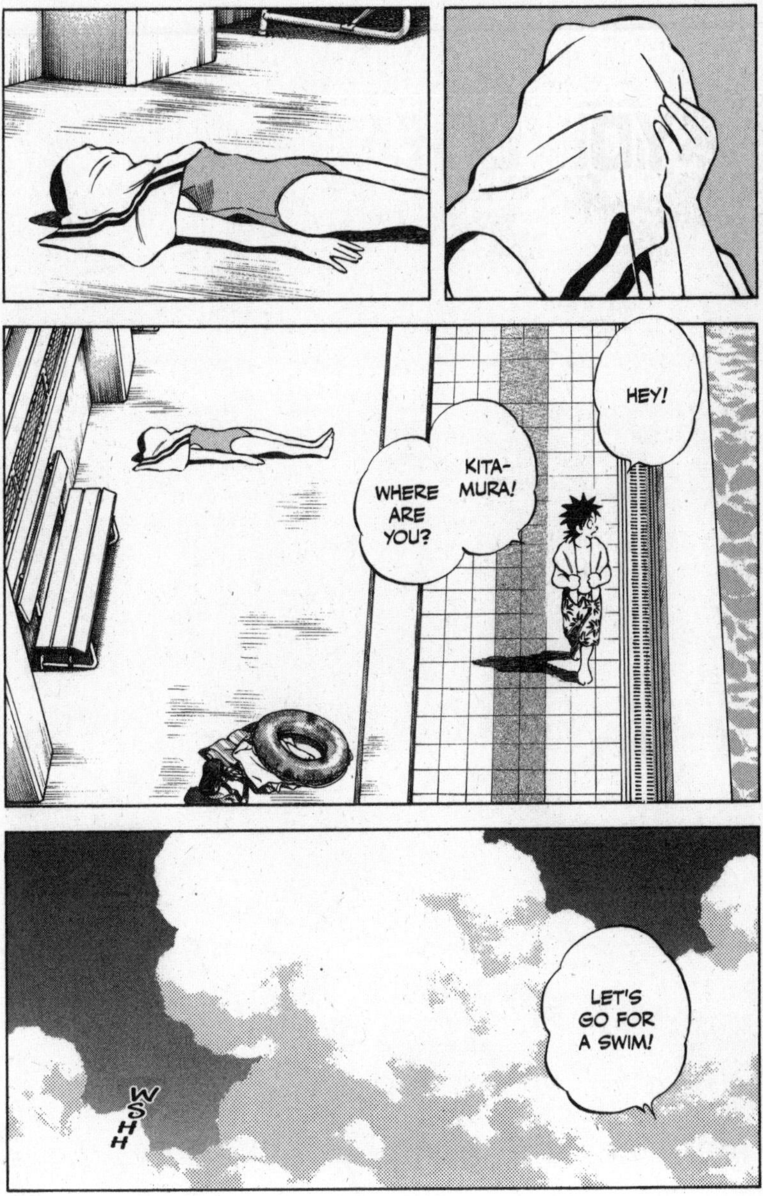
HEY!
KITA-MURA!
WHERE ARE YOU?
LET'S GO FOR A SWIM!
WSHH

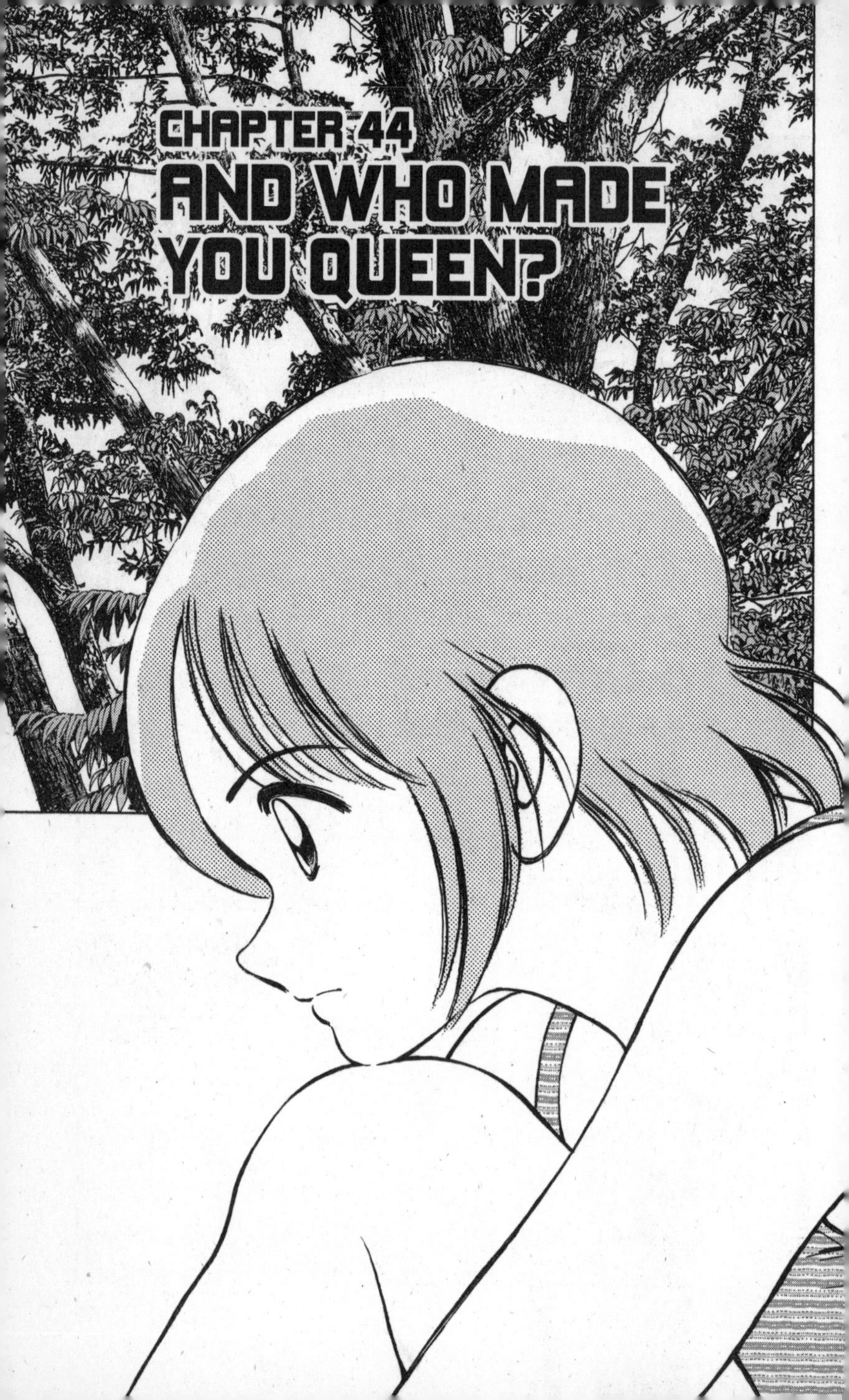
CHAPTER 44
AND WHO MADE YOU QUEEN?

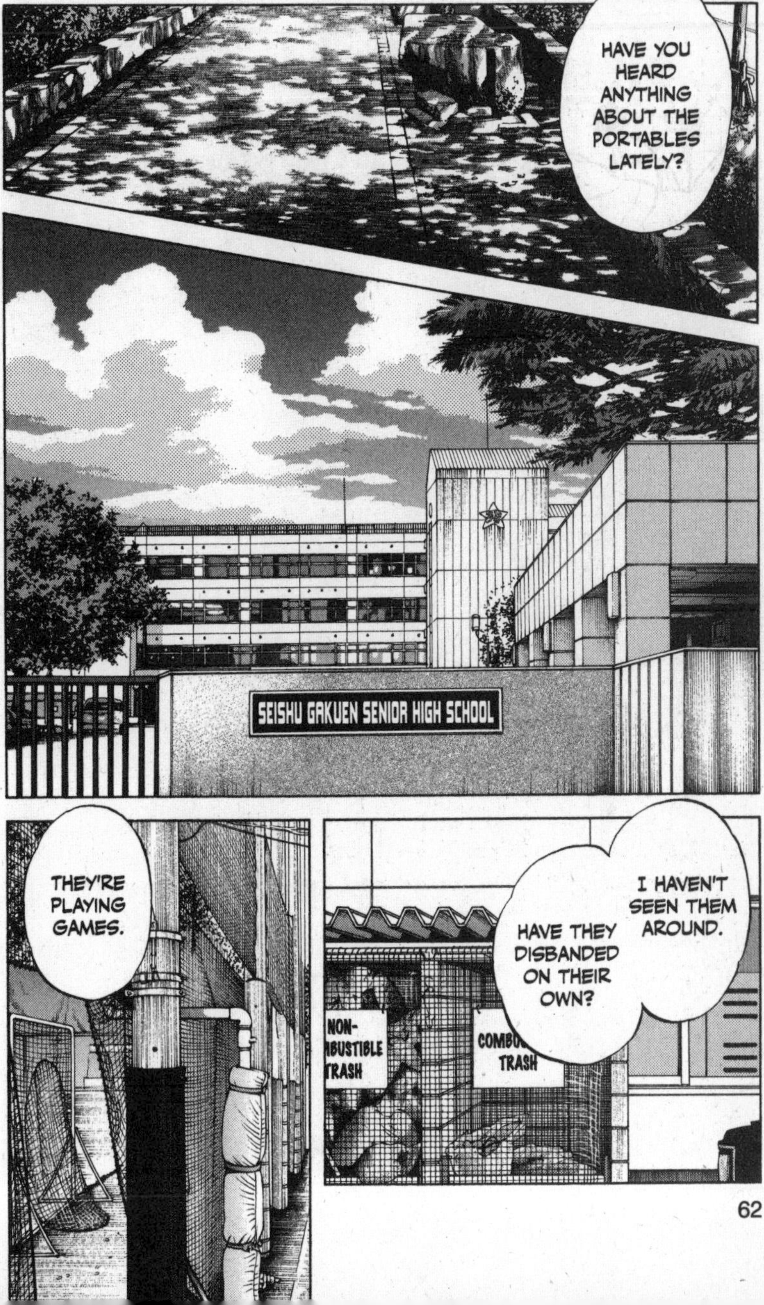
HAVE YOU HEARD ANYTHING ABOUT THE PORTABLES LATELY?
SEISHU GAKUEN SENIOR HIGH SCHOOL
I HAVEN'T SEEN THEM AROUND.
HAVE THEY DISBANDED ON THEIR OWN?
NON-
TRASH
TRASH
THEY'RE PLAYING GAMES.

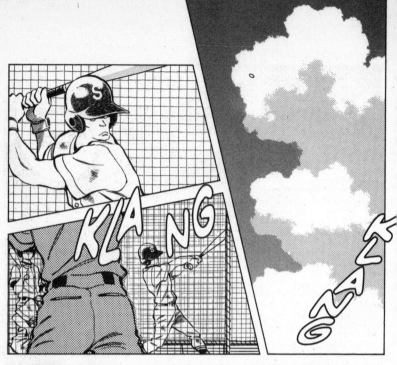

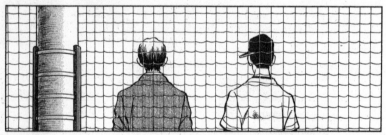

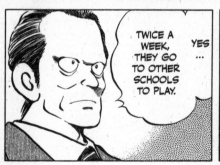

TWICE A WEEK, THEY GO TO OTHER SCHOOLS TO PLAY.

YES ...

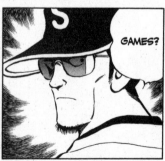

GAMES?

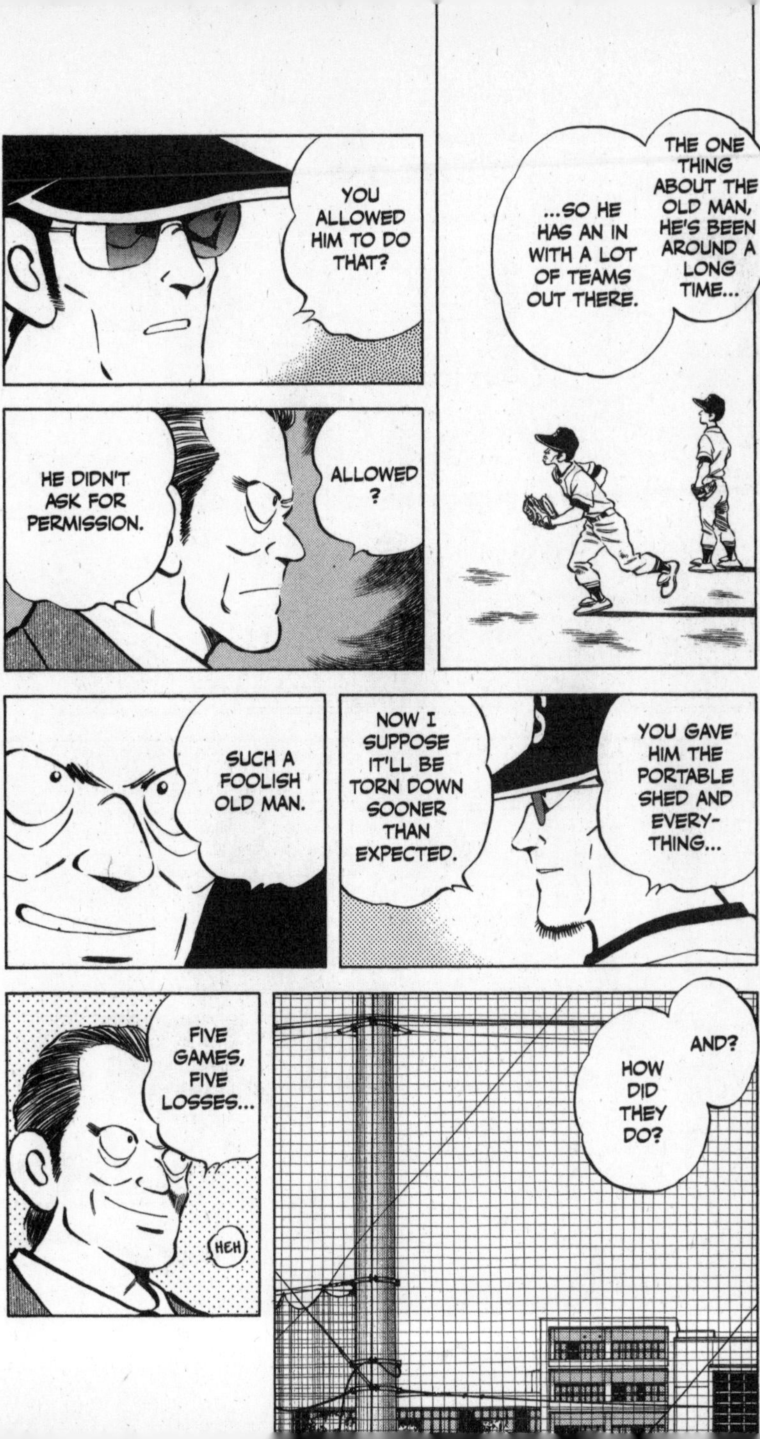
THE ONE THING ABOUT THE OLD MAN, HE'S BEEN AROUND A LONG TIME...
...SO HE HAS AN IN WITH A LOT OF TEAMS OUT THERE.
YOU ALLOWED HIM TO DO THAT?
ALLOWED?
HE DIDN'T ASK FOR PERMISSION.
YOU GAVE HIM THE PORTABLE SHED AND EVERYTHING...
NOW I SUPPOSE IT'LL BE TORN DOWN SOONER THAN EXPECTED.
SUCH A FOOLISH OLD MAN.
AND?
HOW DID THEY DO?
FIVE GAMES, FIVE LOSSES...
HEH

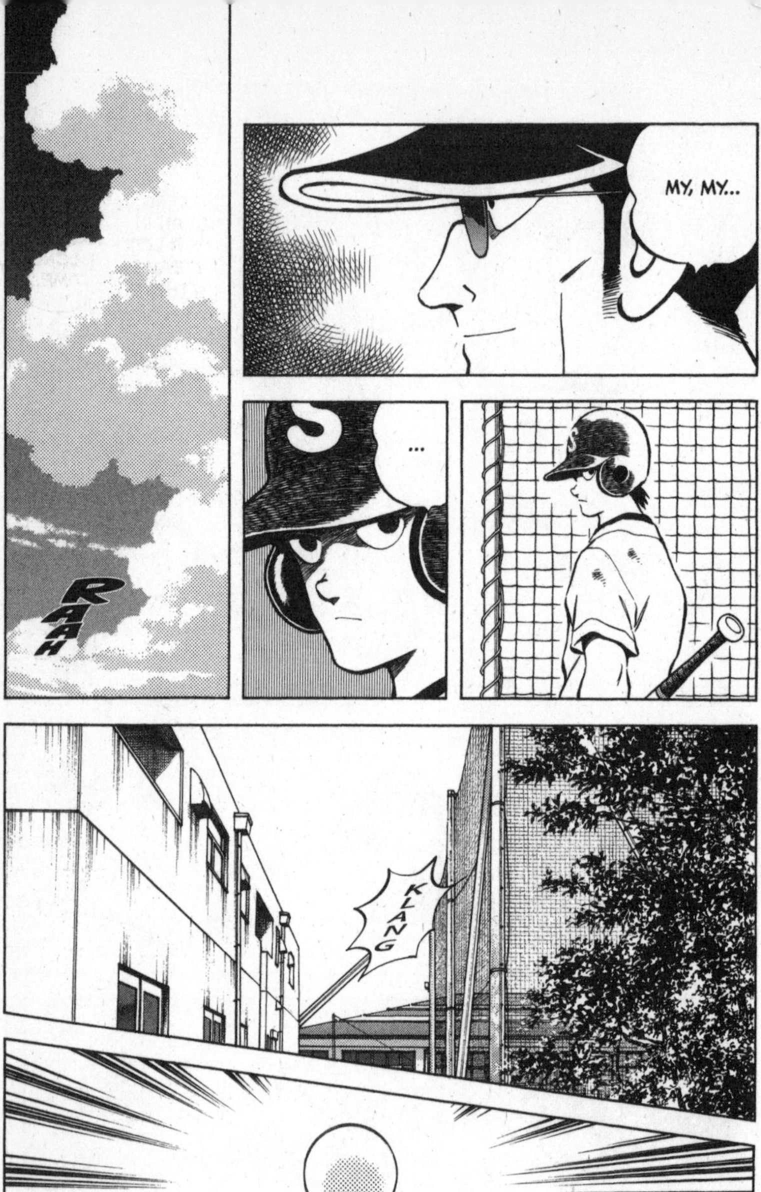
MY, MY...
...
RAAAH
KLANG

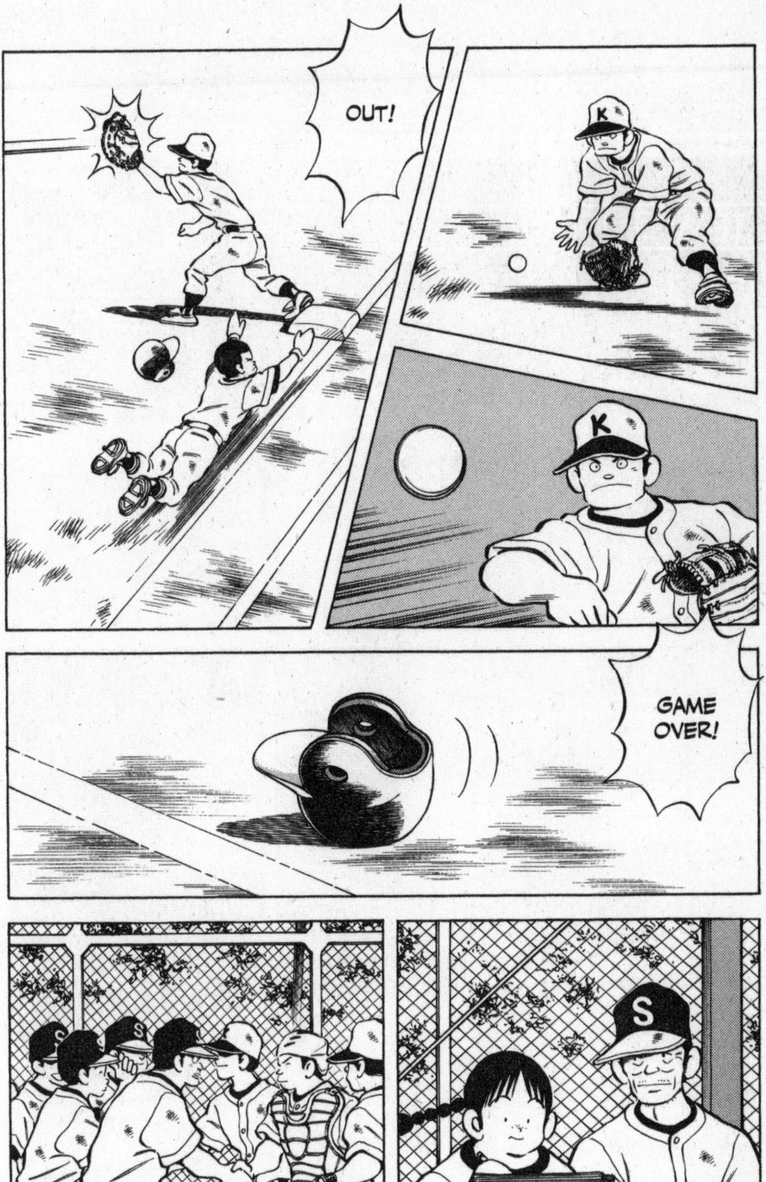
OUT!
GAME
OVER!

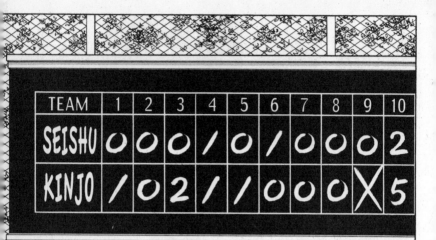

TEAM	1	2	3	4	5	6	7	8	9	10
SEISHU	0	0	0	1	0	1	0	0	0	2
KINJO	1	0	2	1	1	0	0	0	✕	5

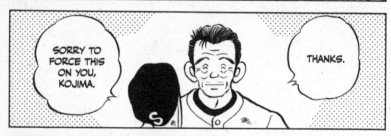

SORRY TO FORCE THIS ON YOU, KOJIMA.

THANKS.

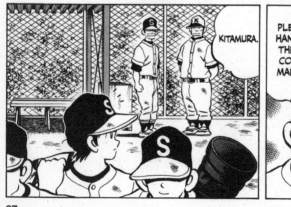

KITAMURA.

PLEASE HANG IN THERE, COACH MAENO.

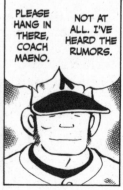

NOT AT ALL. I'VE HEARD THE RUMORS.

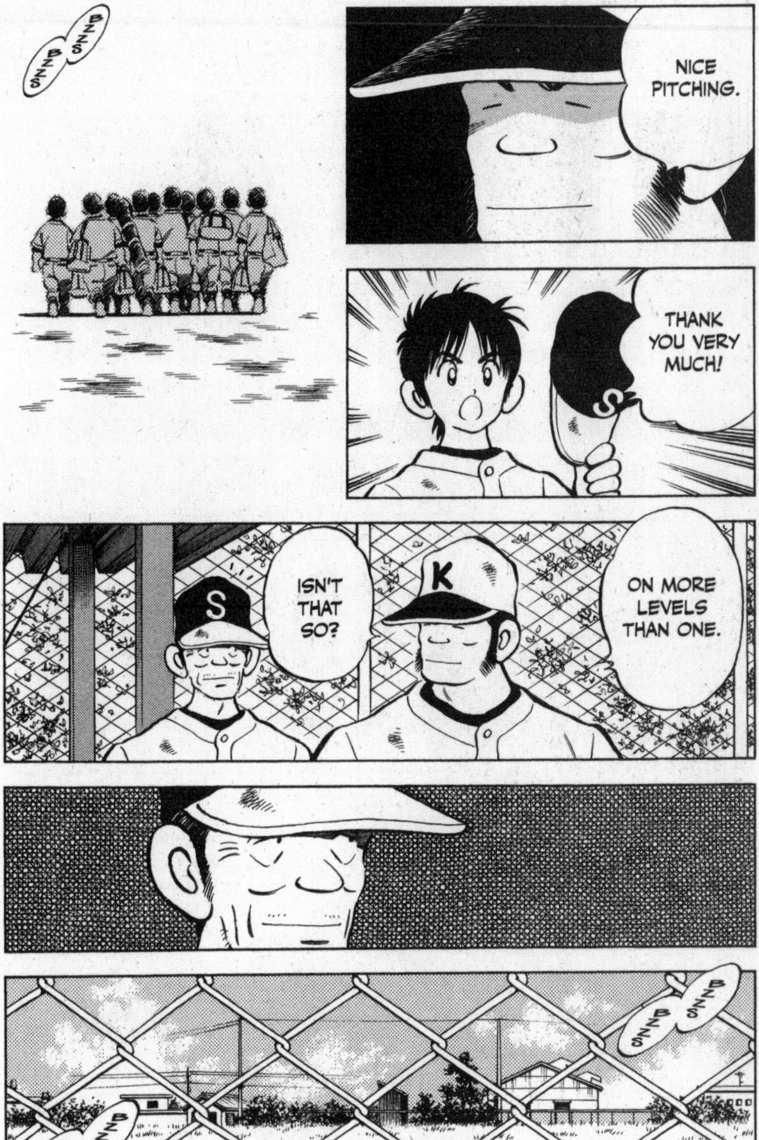
NICE PITCHING.
THANK YOU VERY MUCH!
BZZS BZZS
ON MORE LEVELS THAN ONE.
ISN'T THAT SO?
BZZS BZZS
BZZS BZZS

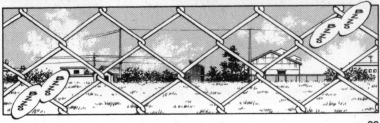

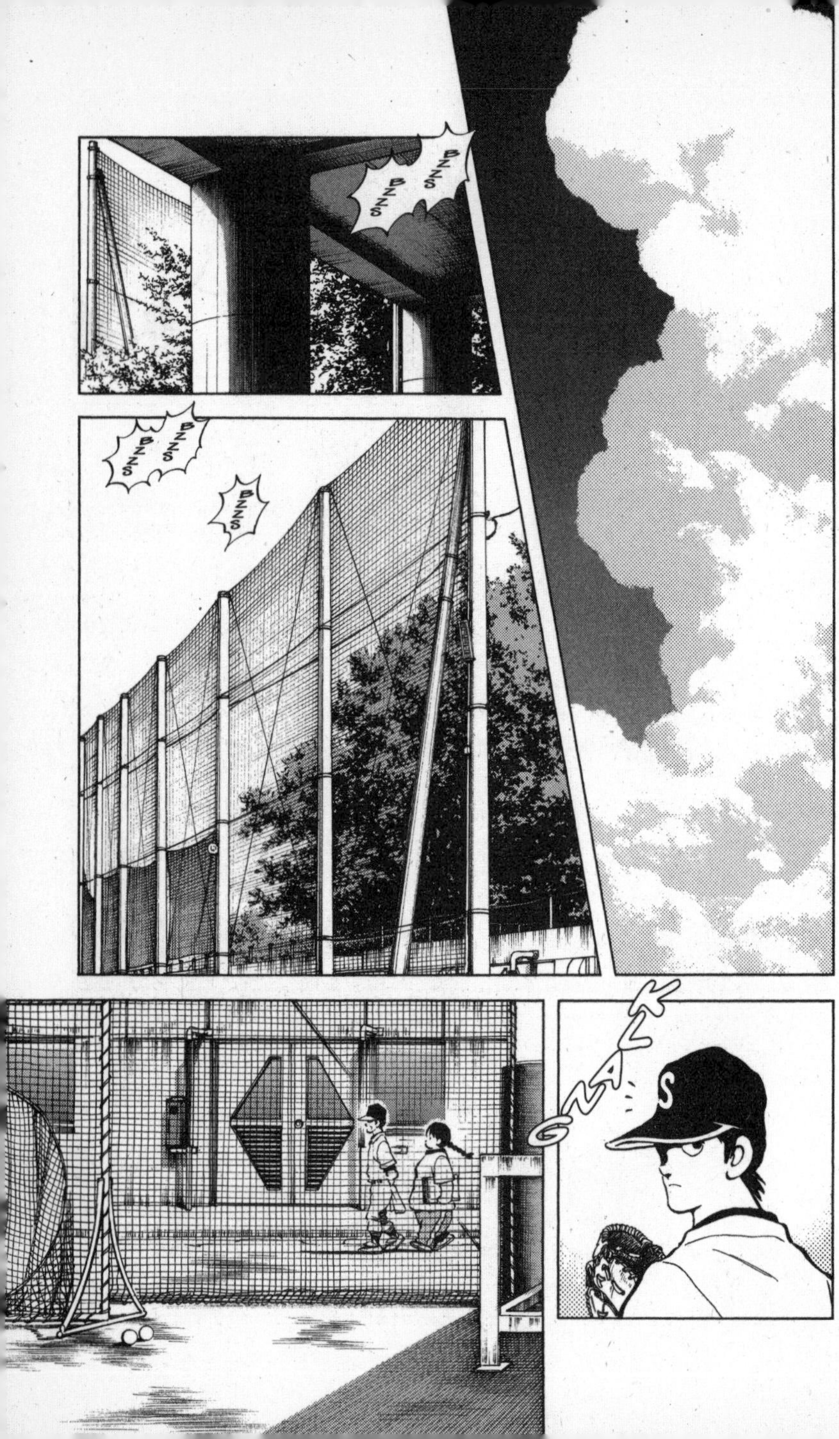
BZZS BZZS
BZZS BZZS
BZZS
GNAK

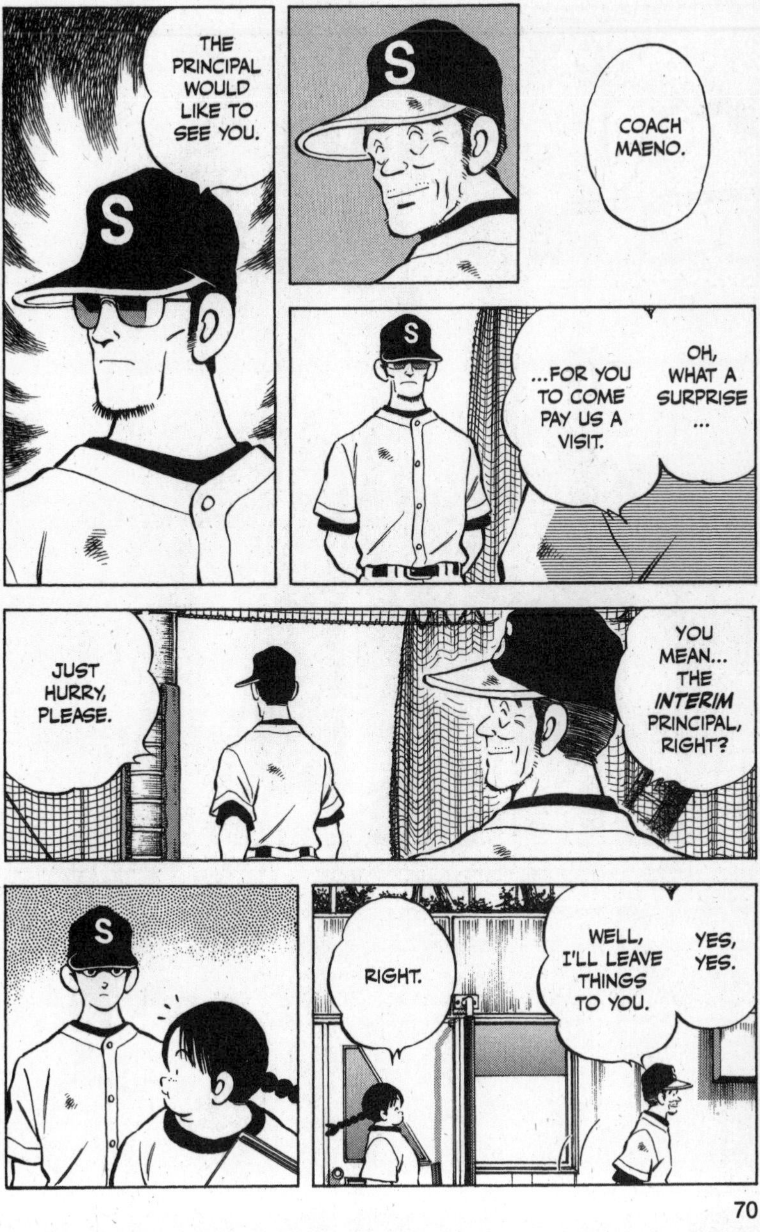
COACH MAENO.
OH, WHAT A SURPRISE...
...FOR YOU TO COME PAY US A VISIT.
THE PRINCIPAL WOULD LIKE TO SEE YOU.
YOU MEAN... THE *INTERIM* PRINCIPAL, RIGHT?
JUST HURRY, PLEASE.
YES, YES.
WELL, I'LL LEAVE THINGS TO YOU.
RIGHT.

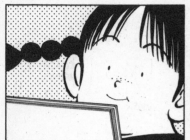

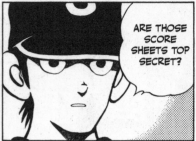

ARE THOSE SCORE SHEETS TOP SECRET?

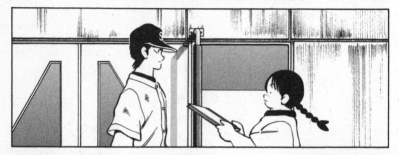

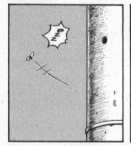

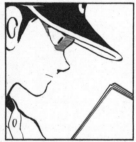

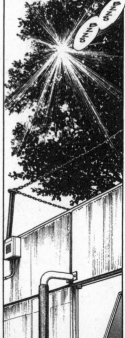

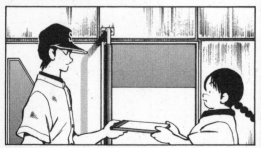

71

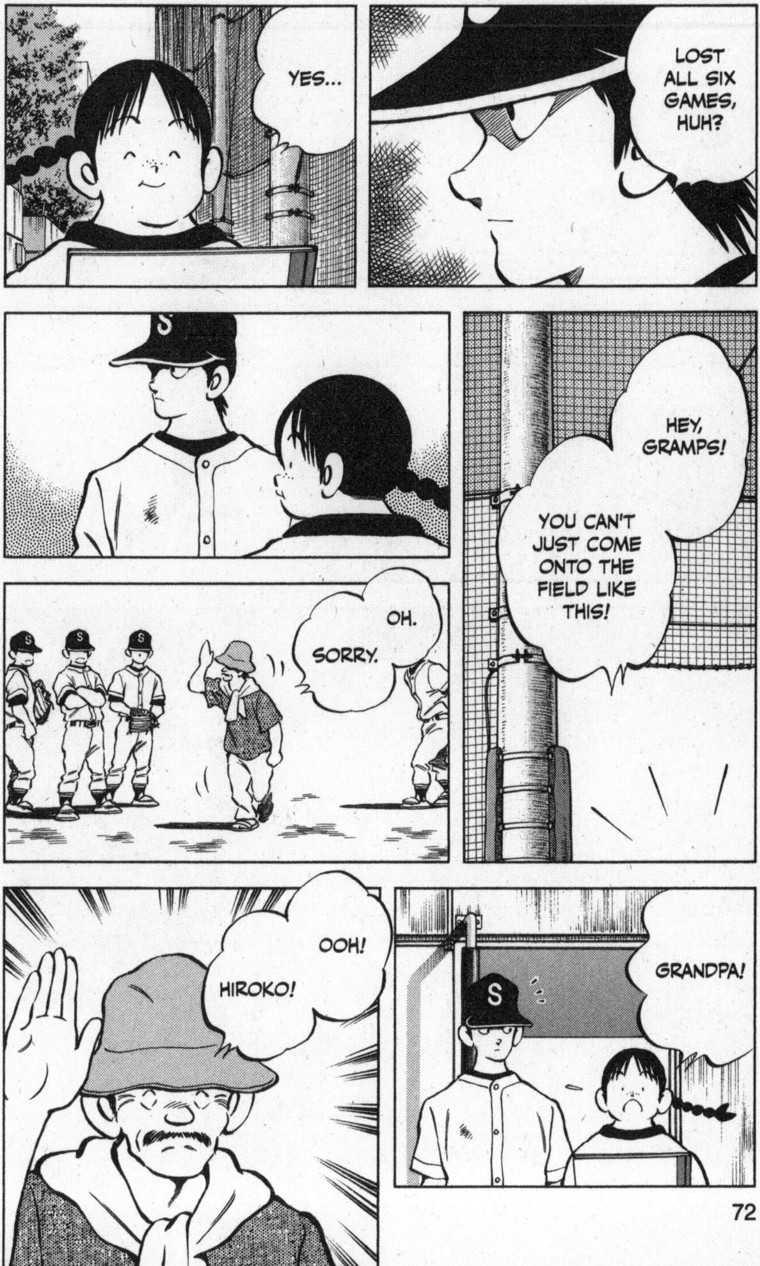
LOST ALL SIX GAMES, HUH?
YES...
HEY, GRAMPS!
YOU CAN'T JUST COME ONTO THE FIELD LIKE THIS!
OH.
SORRY.
GRANDPA!
OOH!
HIROKO!

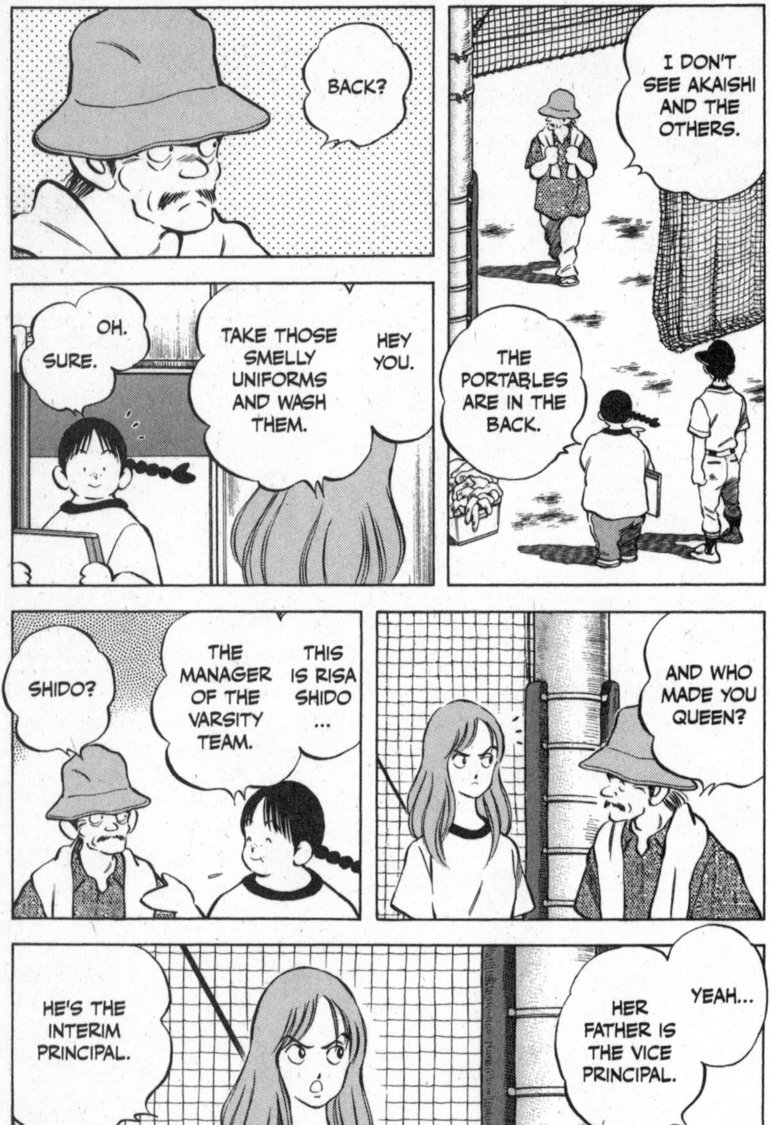
I DON'T SEE AKAISHI AND THE OTHERS.
THE PORTABLES ARE IN THE BACK.
BACK?
HEY YOU.
TAKE THOSE SMELLY UNIFORMS AND WASH THEM.
OH. SURE.
AND WHO MADE YOU QUEEN?
THIS IS RISA SHIDO ...
THE MANAGER OF THE VARSITY TEAM.
SHIDO?
YEAH...
HER FATHER IS THE VICE PRINCIPAL.
HE'S THE INTERIM PRINCIPAL.

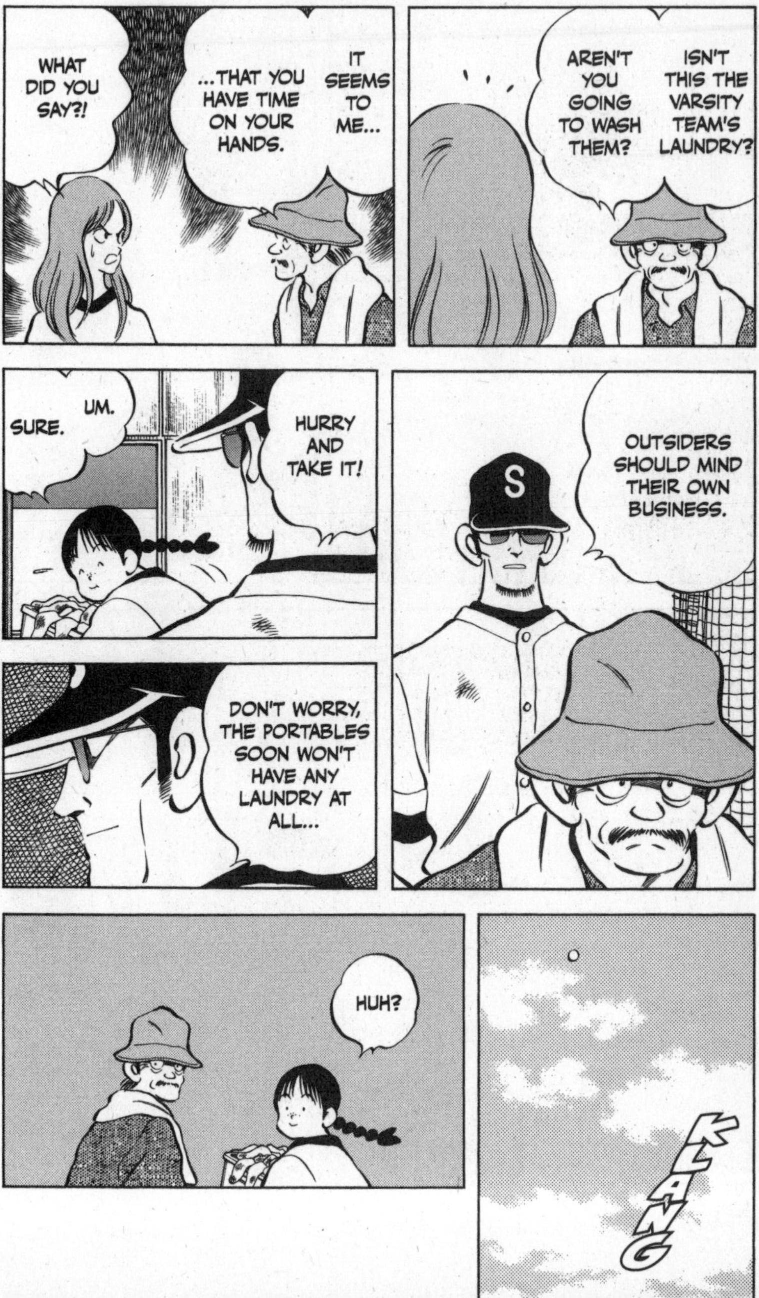
ISN'T THIS THE VARSITY TEAM'S LAUNDRY?
AREN'T YOU GOING TO WASH THEM?
IT SEEMS TO ME...
...THAT YOU HAVE TIME ON YOUR HANDS.
WHAT DID YOU SAY?!
OUTSIDERS SHOULD MIND THEIR OWN BUSINESS.
HURRY AND TAKE IT!
UM.
SURE.
DON'T WORRY, THE PORTABLES SOON WON'T HAVE ANY LAUNDRY AT ALL...
KLANG
HUH?

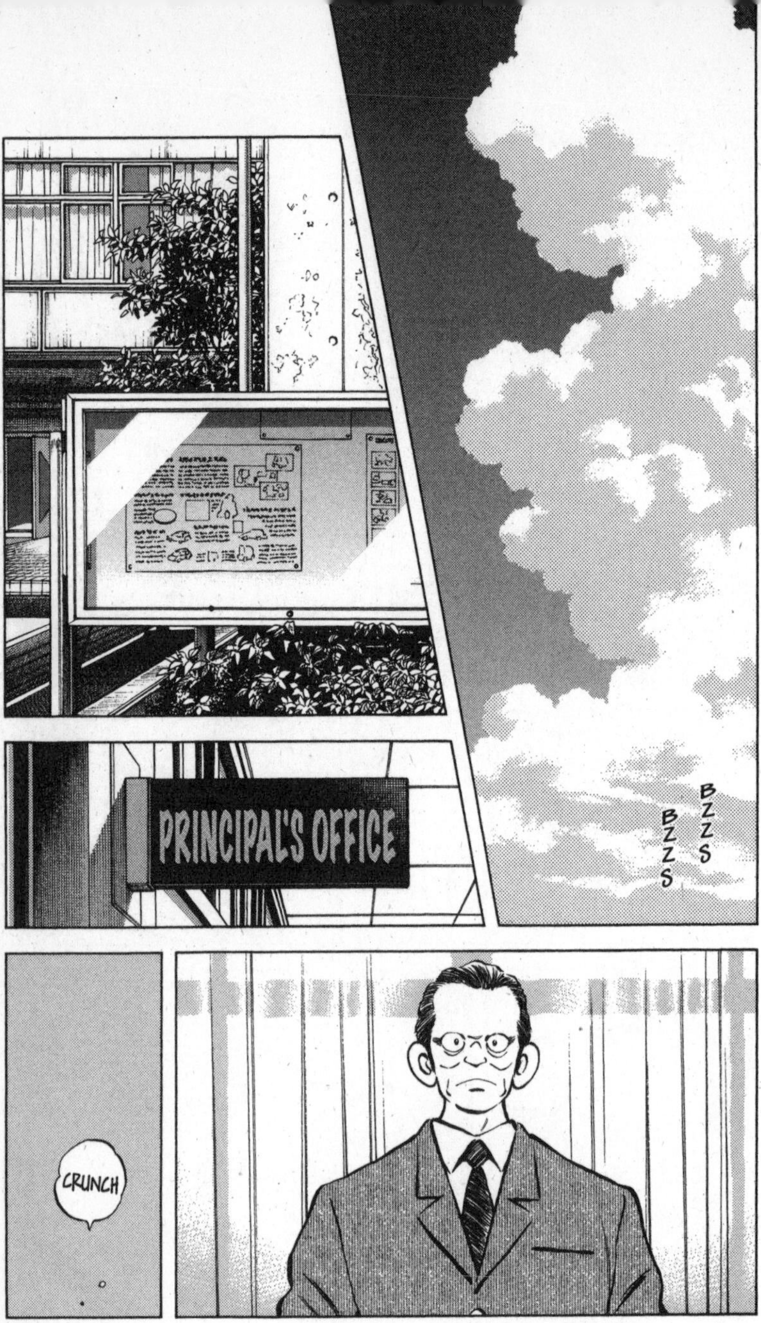
BZZS
BZZS
PRINCIPAL'S OFFICE
CRUNCH

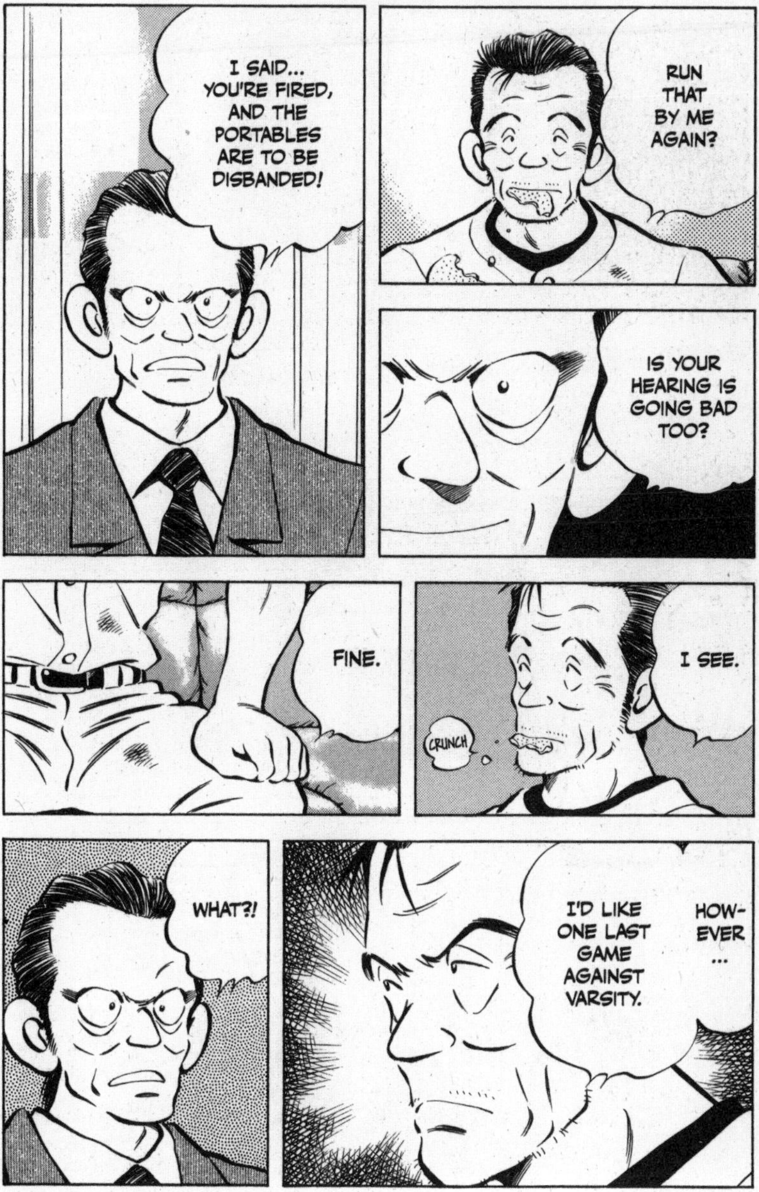
RUN THAT BY ME AGAIN?
IS YOUR HEARING IS GOING BAD TOO?
I SAID... YOU'RE FIRED, AND THE PORTABLES ARE TO BE DISBANDED!
I SEE.
CRUNCH
FINE.
HOW-EVER...
I'D LIKE ONE LAST GAME AGAINST VARSITY.
WHAT?!

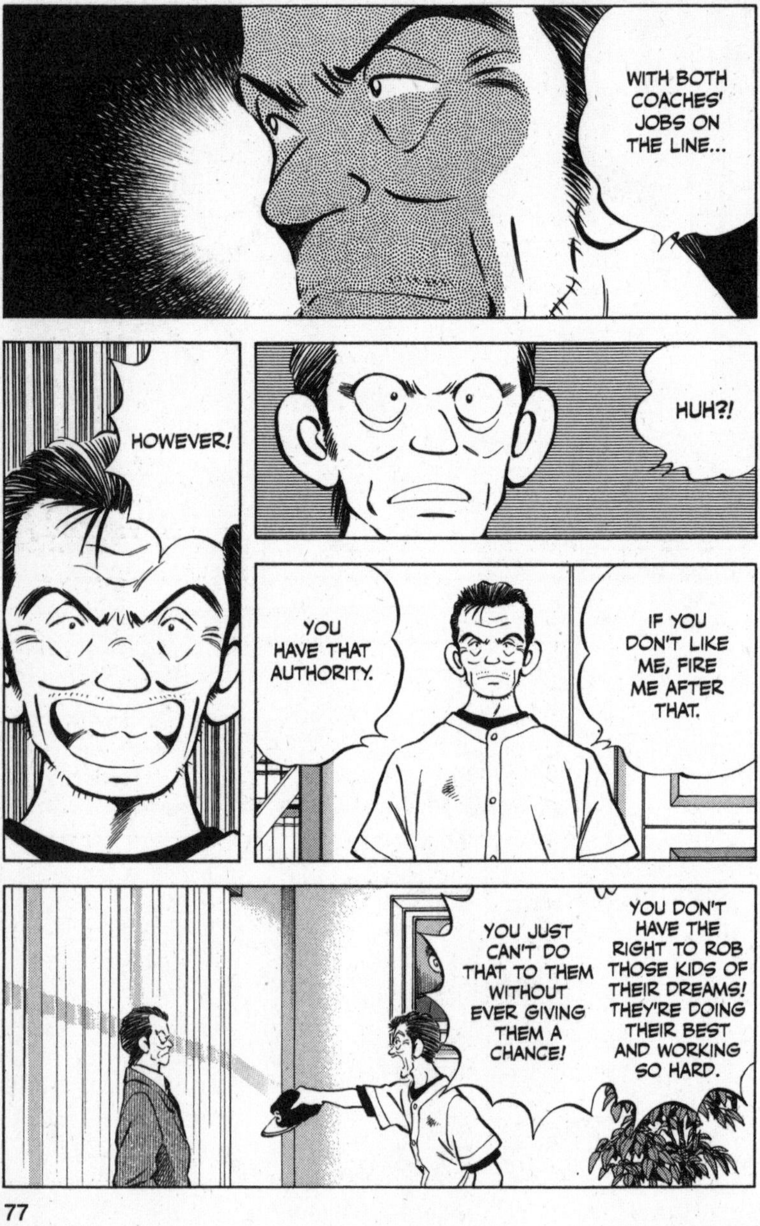
WITH BOTH COACHES' JOBS ON THE LINE...
HUH?!
IF YOU DON'T LIKE ME, FIRE ME AFTER THAT.
YOU HAVE THAT AUTHORITY.
HOWEVER!
YOU DON'T HAVE THE RIGHT TO ROB THOSE KIDS OF THEIR DREAMS! THEY'RE DOING THEIR BEST AND WORKING SO HARD.
YOU JUST CAN'T DO THAT TO THEM WITHOUT EVER GIVING THEM A CHANCE!

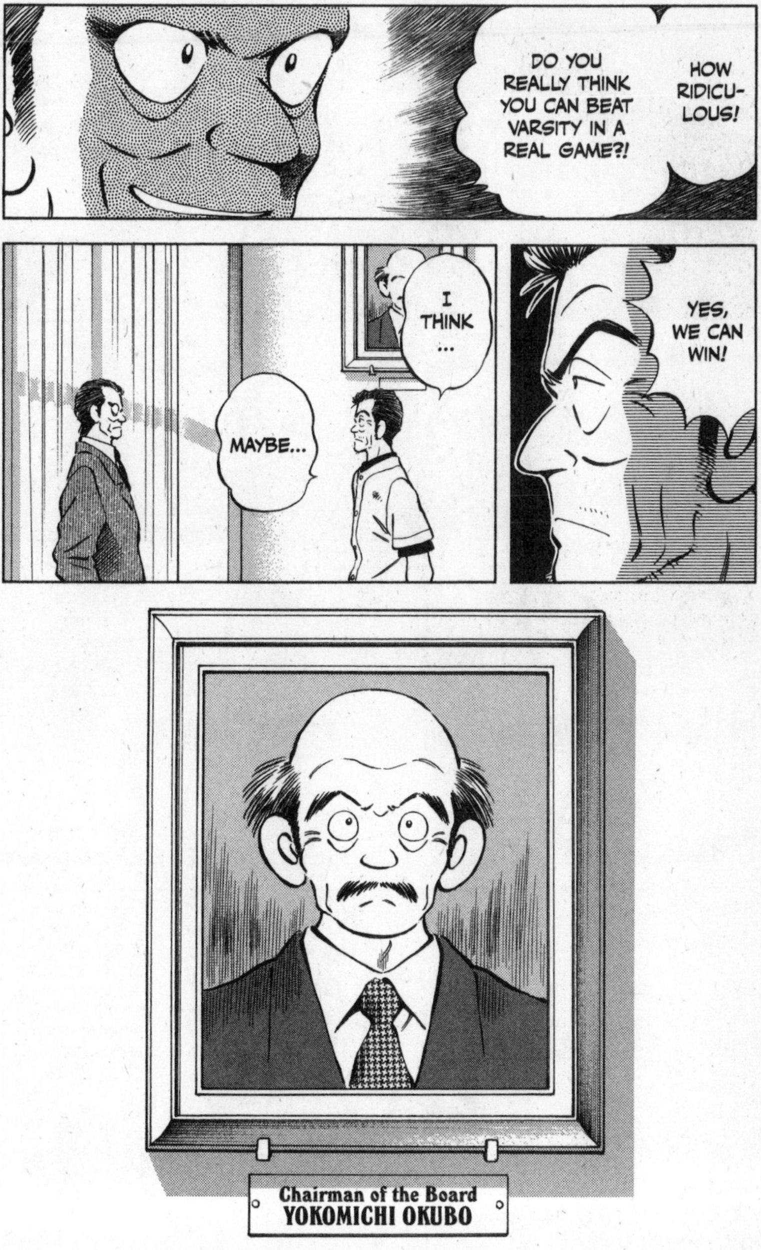
HOW RIDICU-LOUS!
DO YOU REALLY THINK YOU CAN BEAT VARSITY IN A REAL GAME?!
YES, WE CAN WIN!
I THINK...
MAYBE...
Chairman of the Board
YOKOMICHI OKUBO

CHAPTER 45
BROTHER

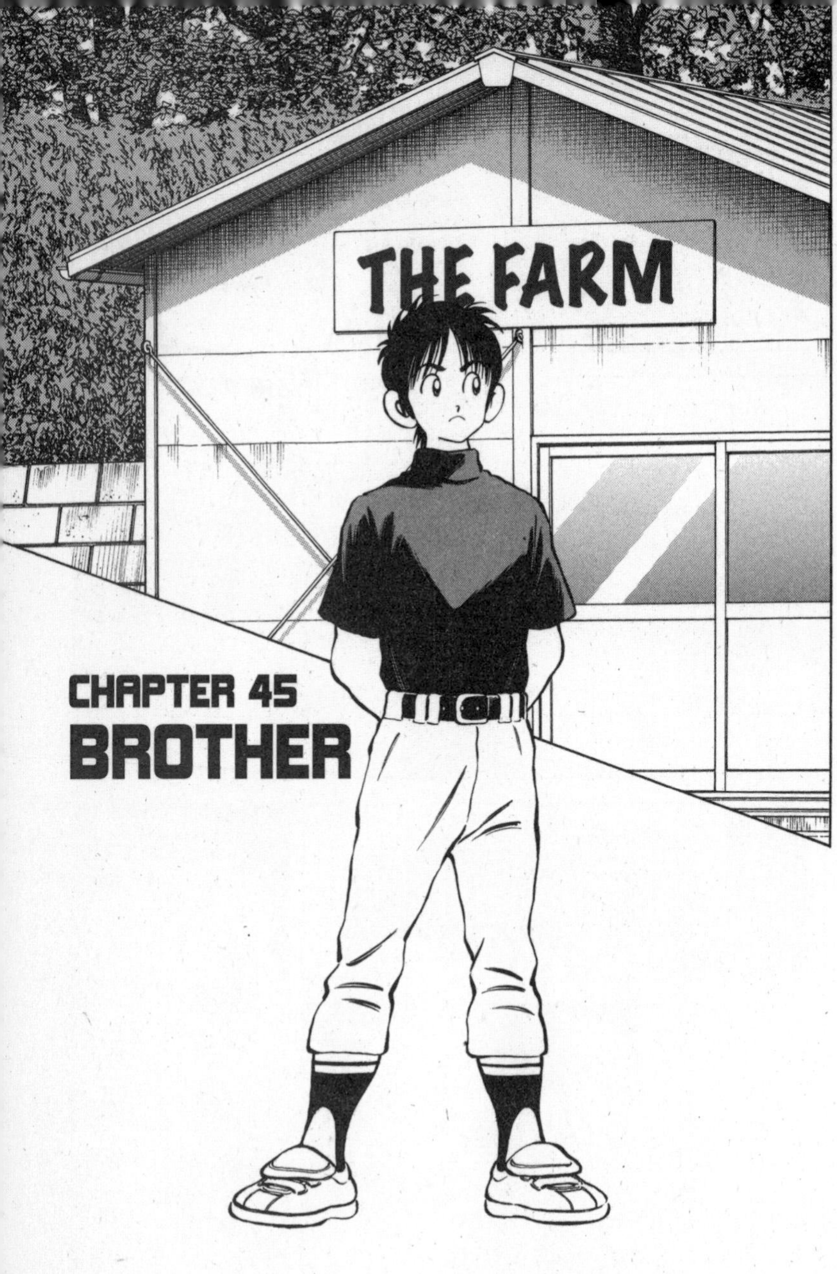
THE FARM

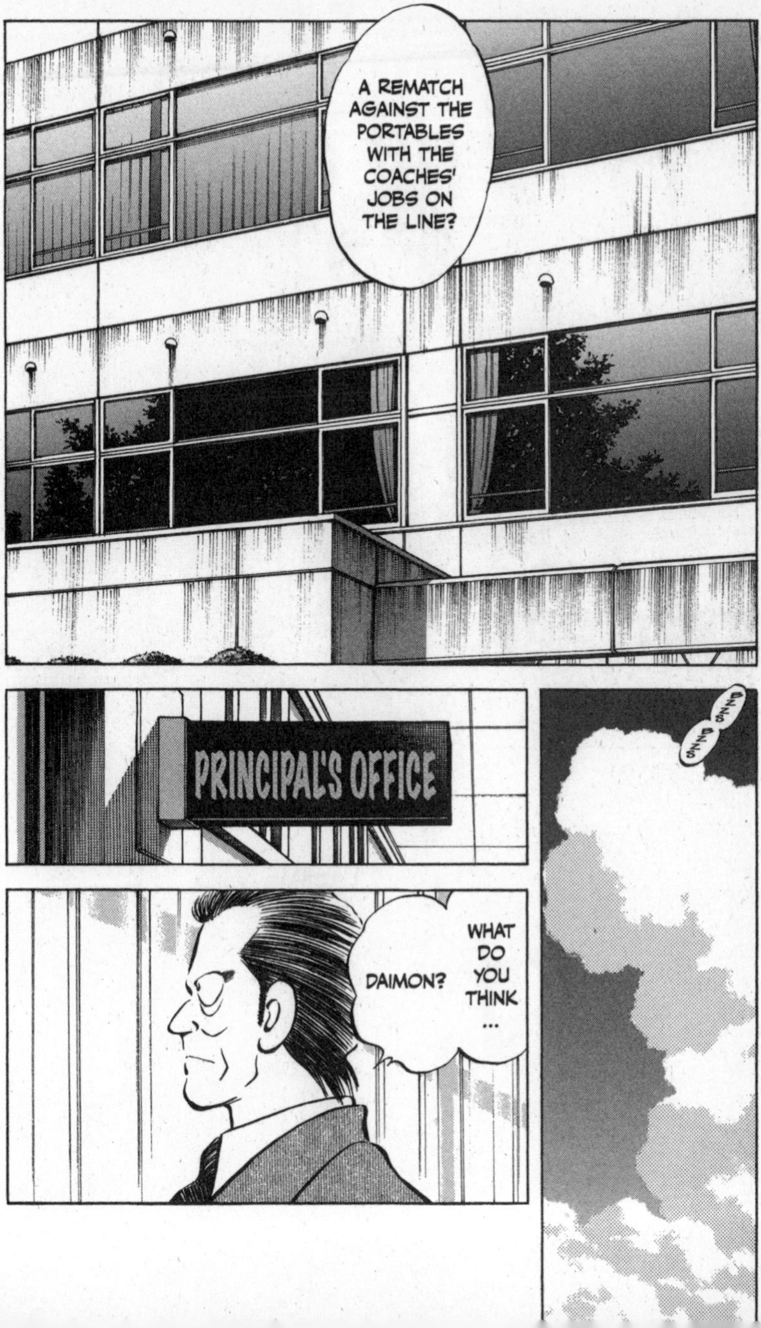
A REMATCH AGAINST THE PORTABLES WITH THE COACHES' JOBS ON THE LINE?
BZZS BZZS
PRINCIPAL'S OFFICE
WHAT DO YOU THINK ... DAIMON?

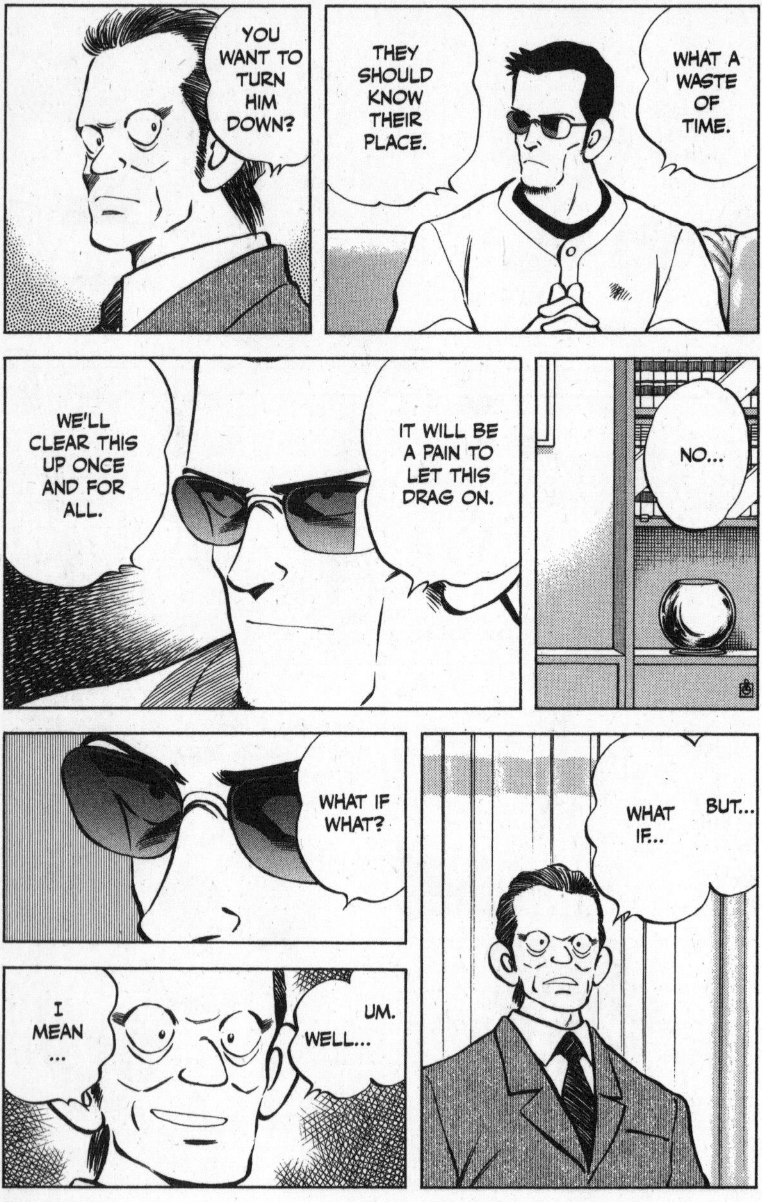
WHAT A WASTE OF TIME.
THEY SHOULD KNOW THEIR PLACE.
YOU WANT TO TURN HIM DOWN?
NO...
IT WILL BE A PAIN TO LET THIS DRAG ON.
WE'LL CLEAR THIS UP ONCE AND FOR ALL.
BUT...
WHAT IF...
WHAT IF WHAT?
UM. WELL...
I MEAN ...

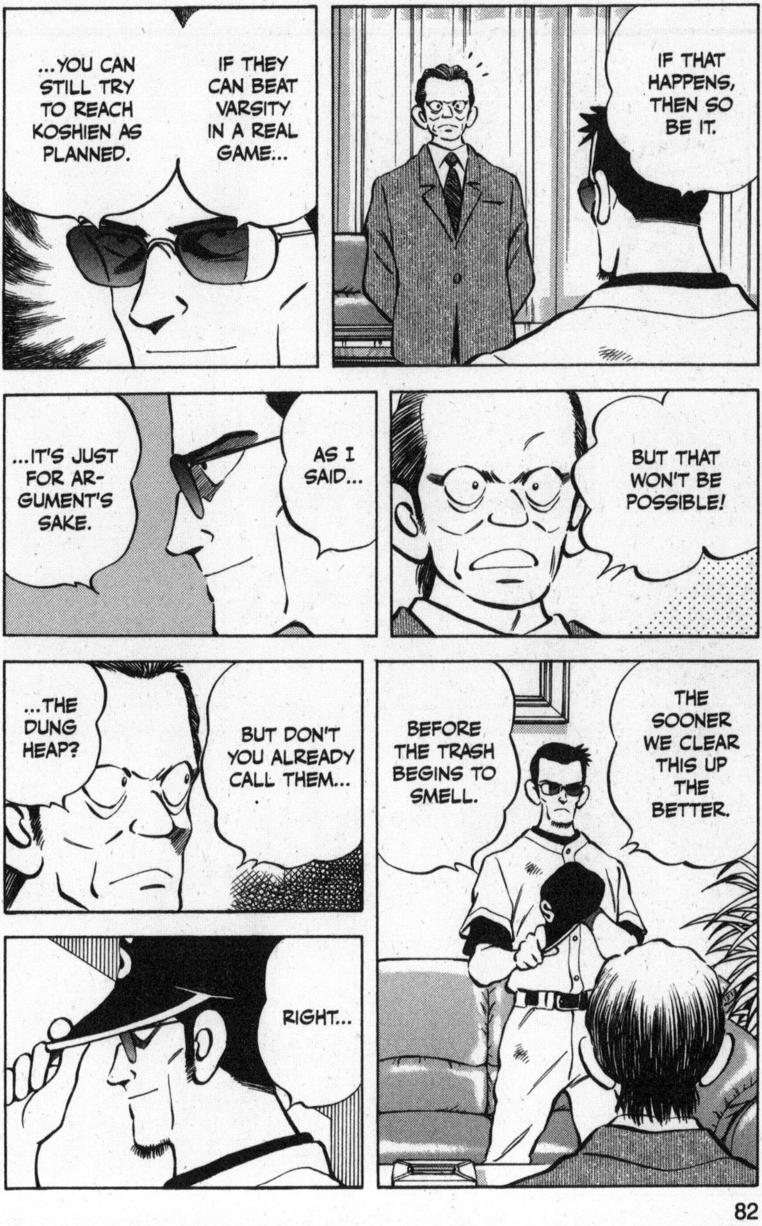
IF THAT HAPPENS, THEN SO BE IT.
IF THEY CAN BEAT VARSITY IN A REAL GAME...
...YOU CAN STILL TRY TO REACH KOSHIEN AS PLANNED.
BUT THAT WON'T BE POSSIBLE!
AS I SAID...
...IT'S JUST FOR AR-GUMENT'S SAKE.
THE SOONER WE CLEAR THIS UP THE BETTER.
BEFORE THE TRASH BEGINS TO SMELL.
BUT DON'T YOU ALREADY CALL THEM...
...THE DUNG HEAP?
RIGHT...

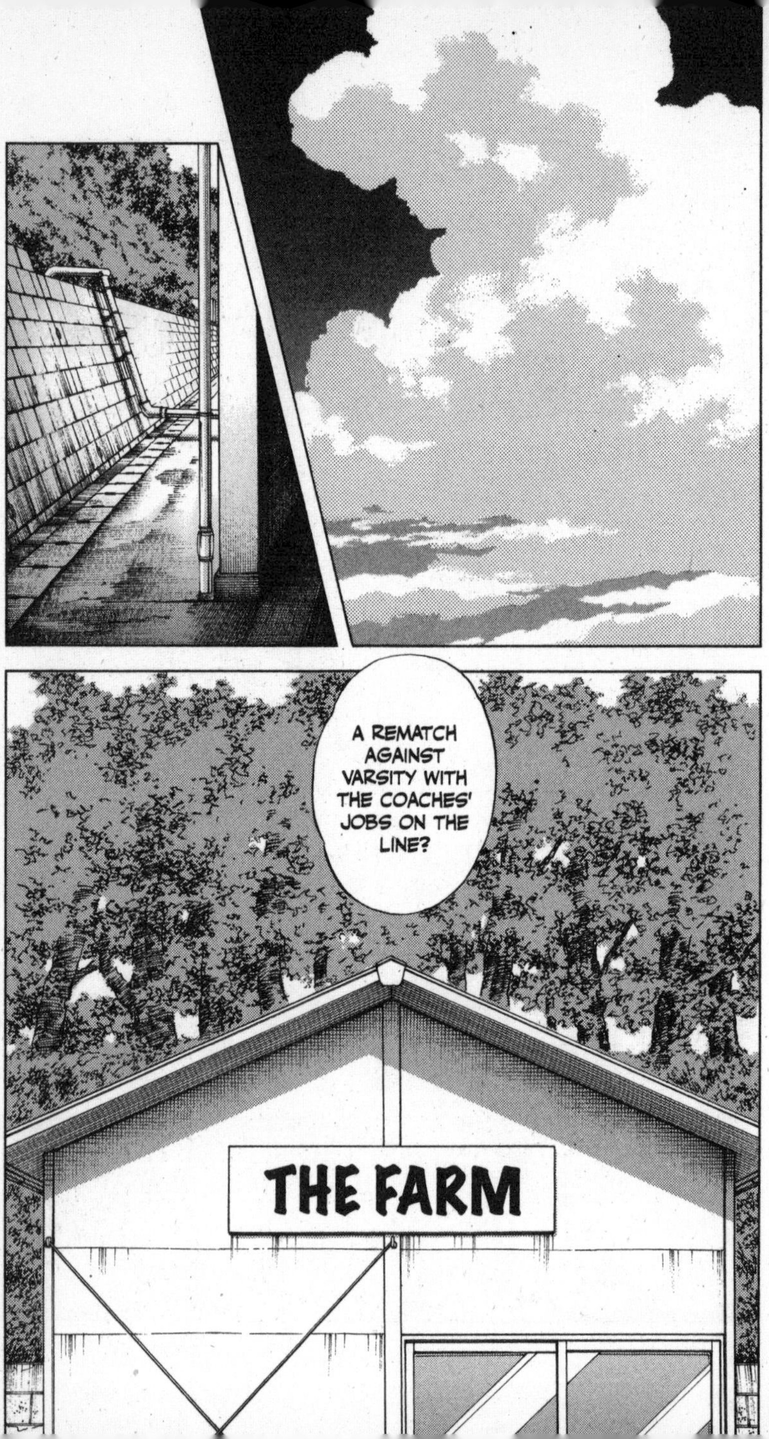
A REMATCH AGAINST VARSITY WITH THE COACHES' JOBS ON THE LINE?
THE FARM

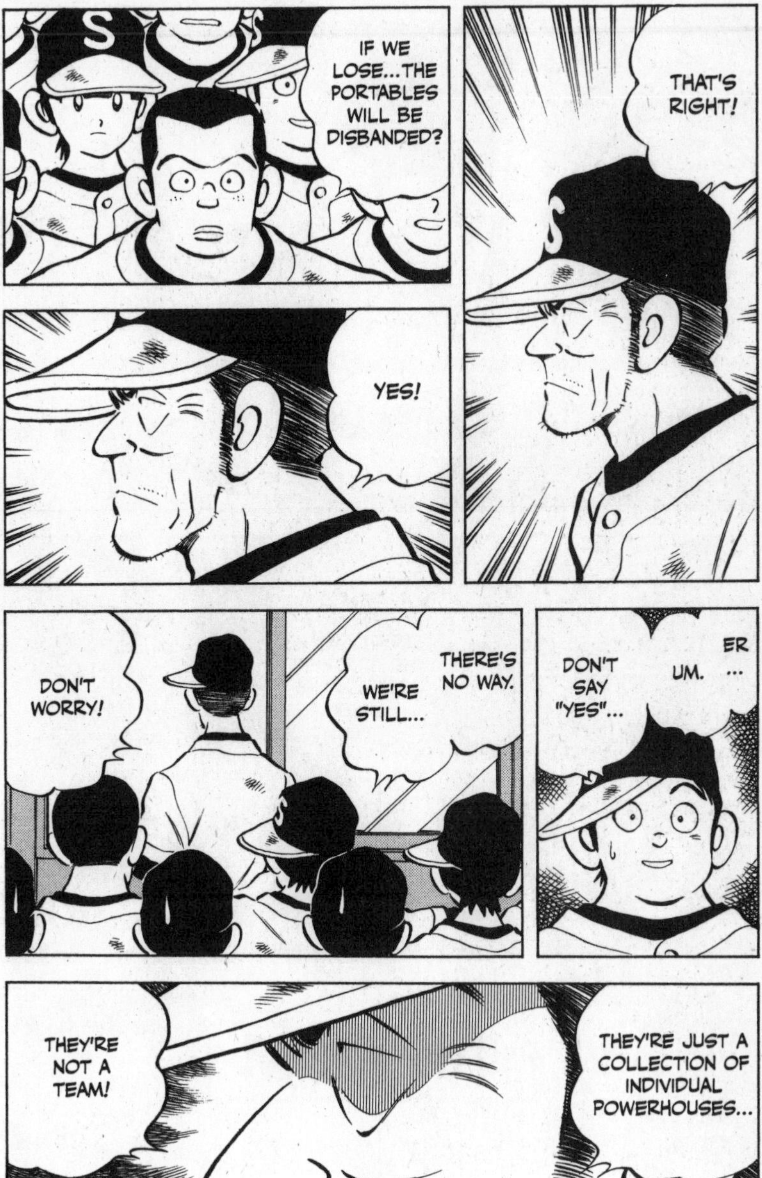
THAT'S RIGHT!
IF WE LOSE...THE PORTABLES WILL BE DISBANDED?
YES!
ER ...
UM.
DON'T SAY "YES"...
THERE'S NO WAY.
WE'RE STILL...
DON'T WORRY!
THEY'RE JUST A COLLECTION OF INDIVIDUAL POWERHOUSES...
THEY'RE NOT A TEAM!

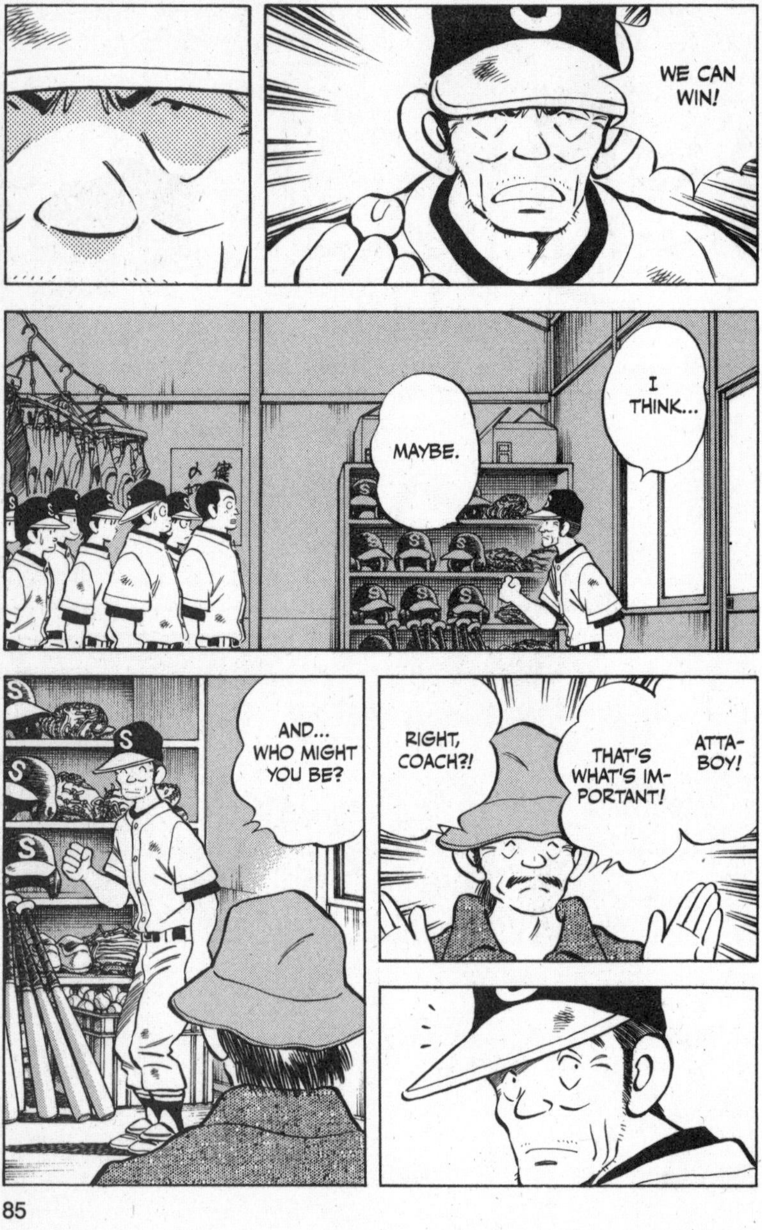
WE CAN WIN!
I THINK...
MAYBE.
ATTA-BOY!
THAT'S WHAT'S IMPORTANT!
RIGHT, COACH?!
AND... WHO MIGHT YOU BE?

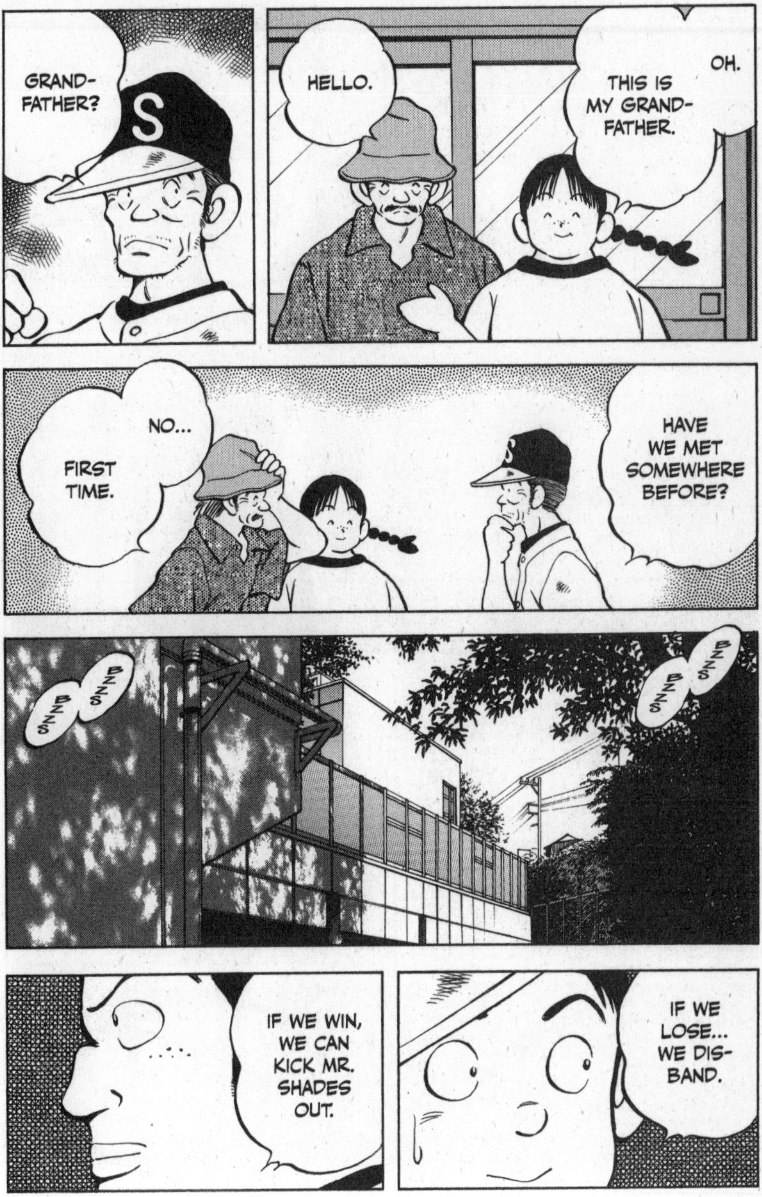
OH.
THIS IS MY GRAND-FATHER.
HELLO.
GRAND-FATHER?
HAVE WE MET SOMEWHERE BEFORE?
NO...
FIRST TIME.
BZZS BZZS
BZZS BZZS
IF WE LOSE... WE DIS-BAND.
IF WE WIN, WE CAN KICK MR. SHADES OUT.

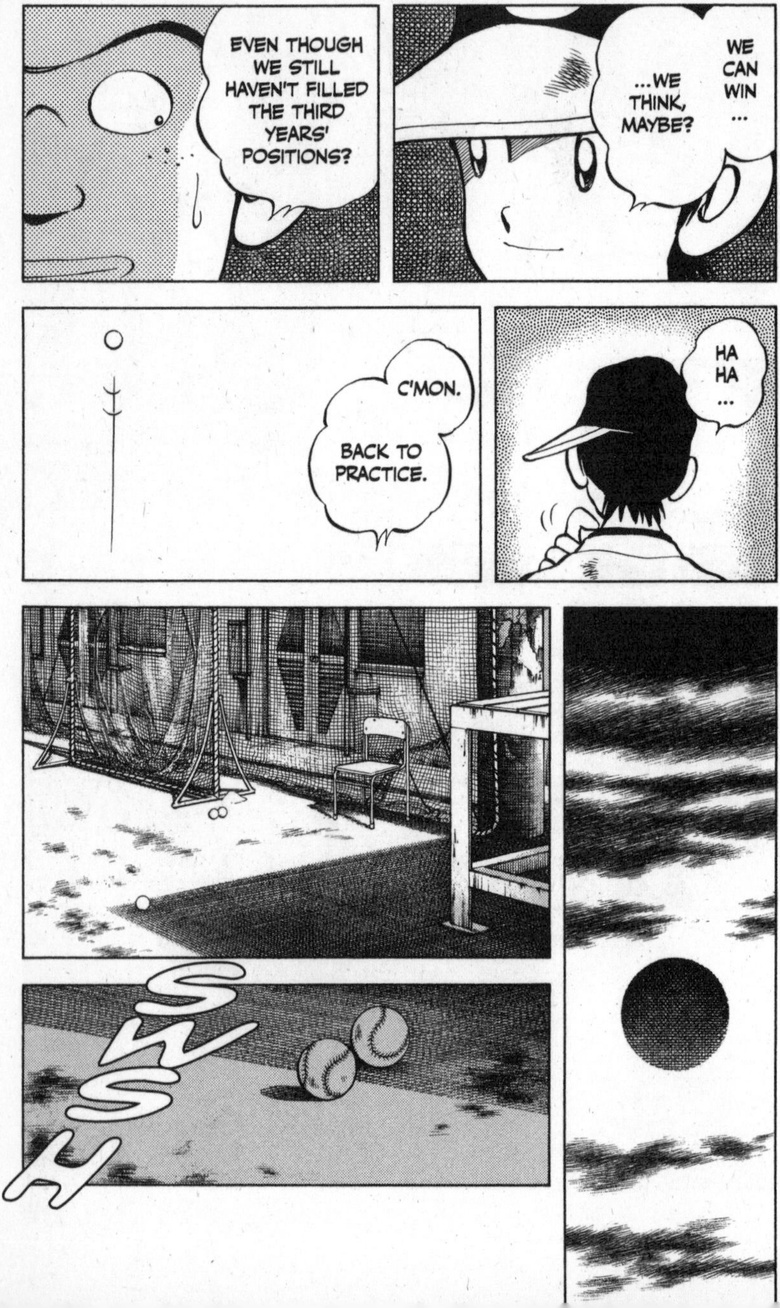
WE CAN WIN ...
...WE THINK, MAYBE?
EVEN THOUGH WE STILL HAVEN'T FILLED THE THIRD YEARS' POSITIONS?
HA HA ...
C'MON.
BACK TO PRACTICE.
SWSH

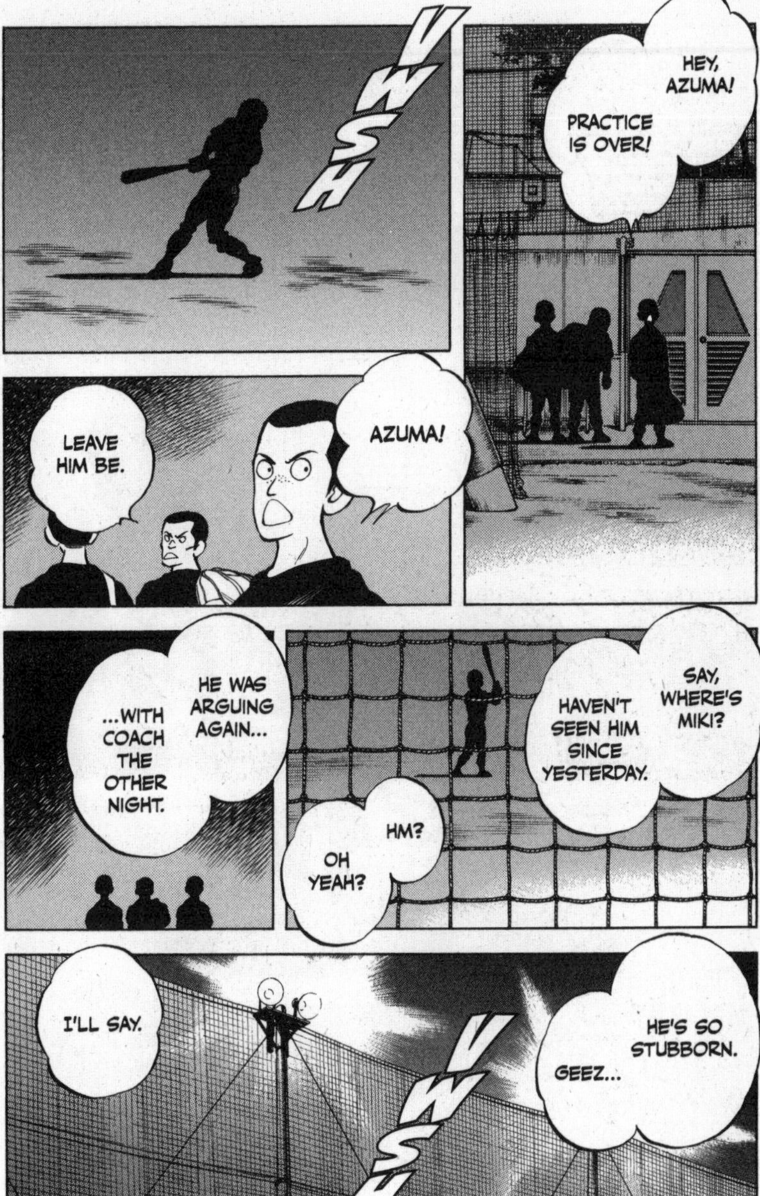
HEY, AZUMA!
PRACTICE IS OVER!
VWSH
AZUMA!
LEAVE HIM BE.
SAY, WHERE'S MIKI?
HAVEN'T SEEN HIM SINCE YESTERDAY.
HM?
OH YEAH?
HE WAS ARGUING AGAIN...
...WITH COACH THE OTHER NIGHT.
HE'S SO STUBBORN.
GEEZ...
VWSH
I'LL SAY.

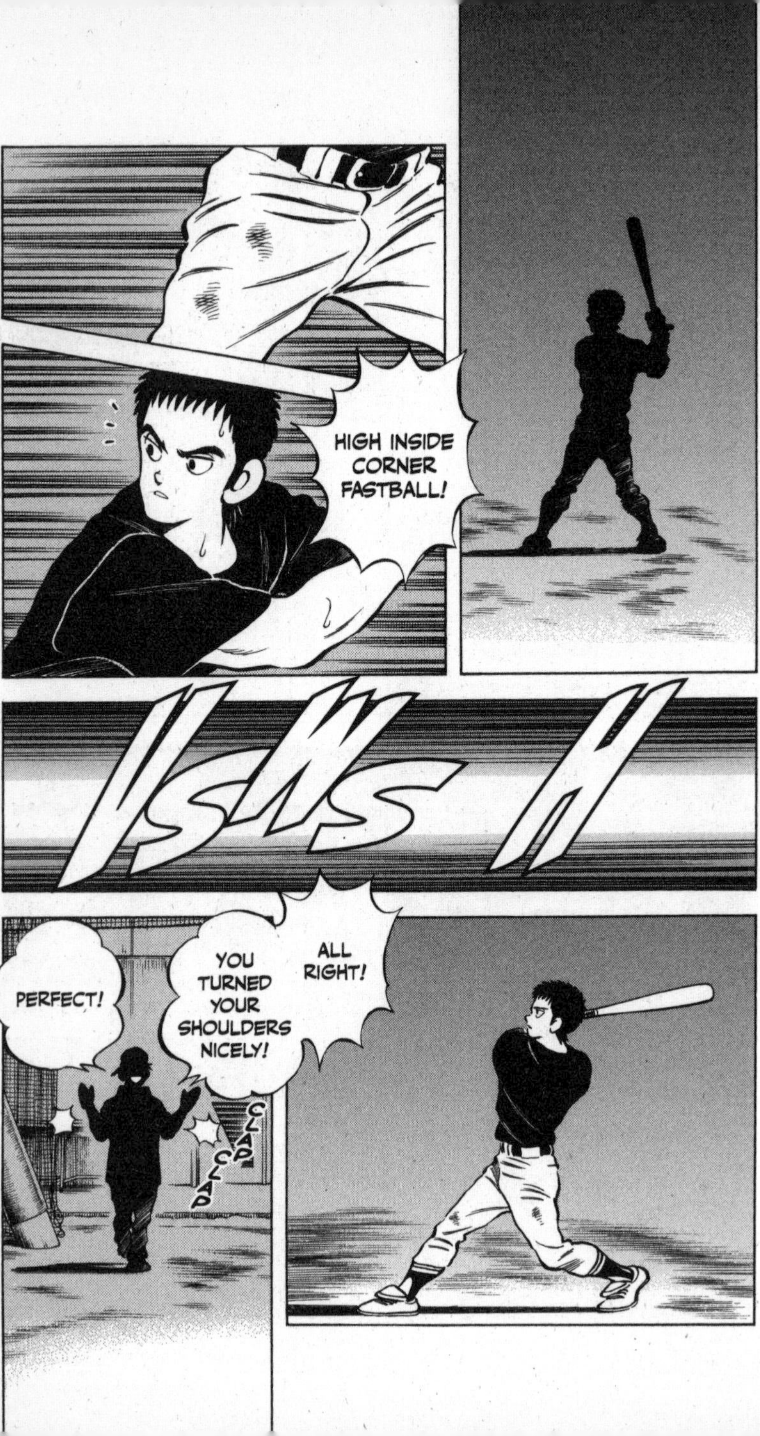
HIGH INSIDE CORNER FASTBALL!
VSHSH
ALL RIGHT!
YOU TURNED YOUR SHOULDERS NICELY!
PERFECT!
CLAP
CLAP

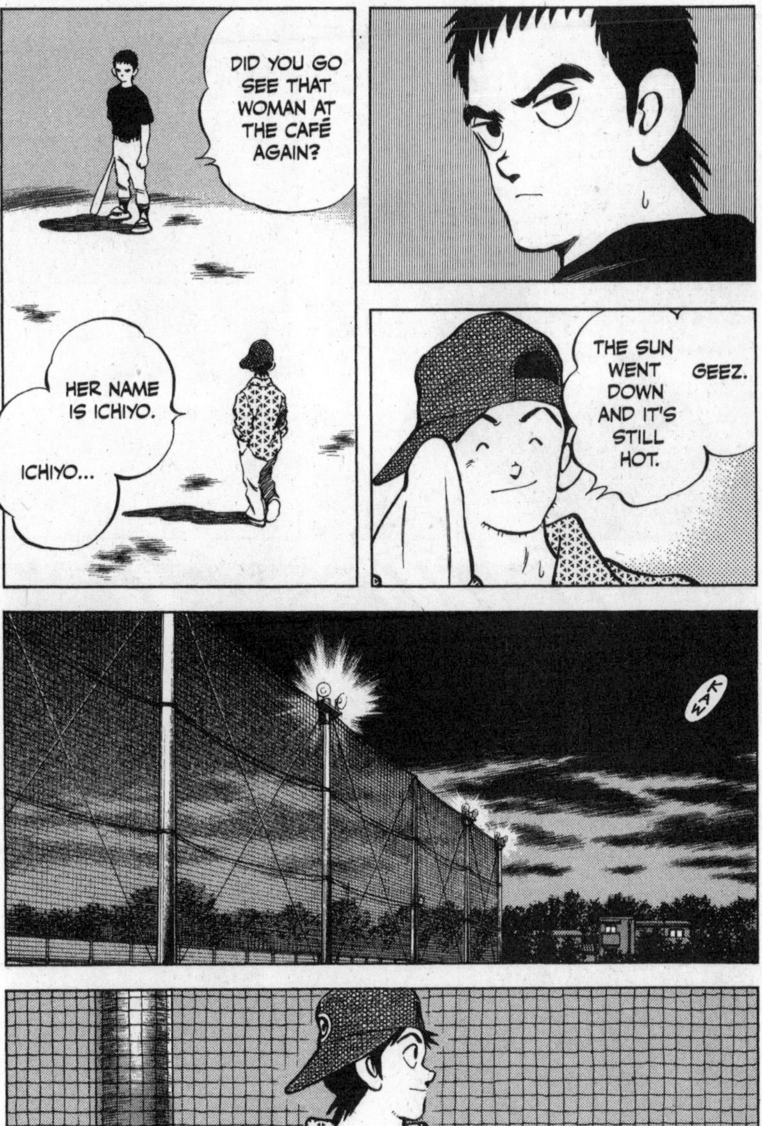
GEEZ.
THE SUN WENT DOWN AND IT'S STILL HOT.
DID YOU GO SEE THAT WOMAN AT THE CAFÉ AGAIN?
HER NAME IS ICHIYO.
ICHIYO...
KAW

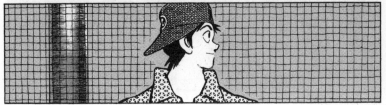

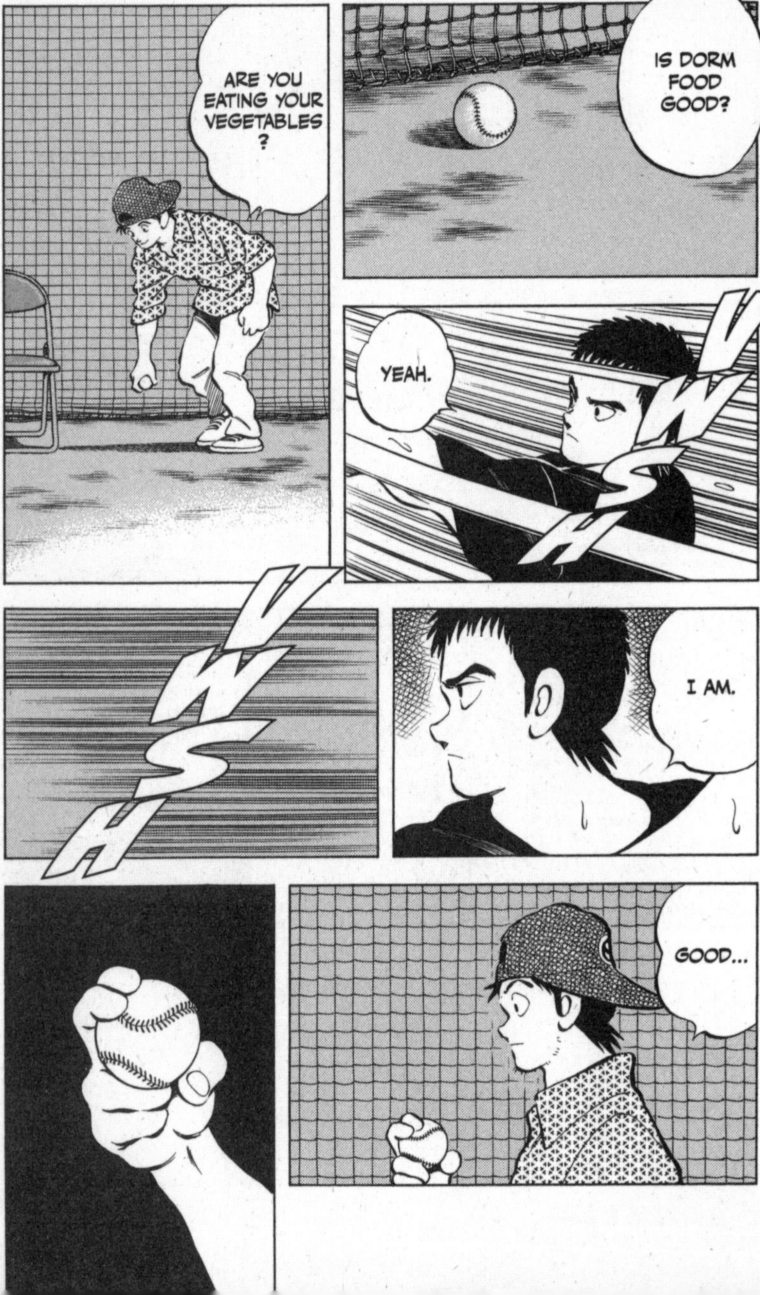
IS DORM FOOD GOOD?
YEAH.
VWSH
ARE YOU EATING YOUR VEGETABLES ?
I AM.
VWSH
GOOD...

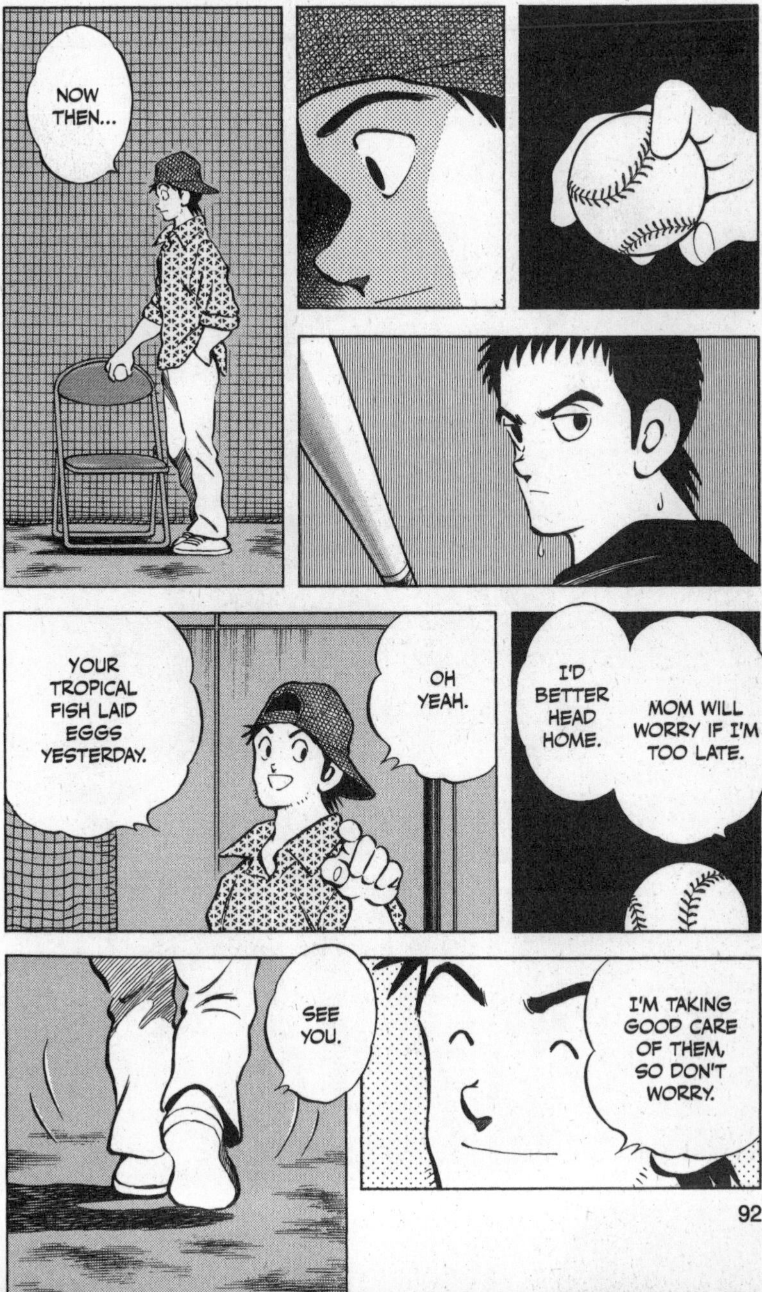
NOW THEN...
MOM WILL WORRY IF I'M TOO LATE.
I'D BETTER HEAD HOME.
OH YEAH.
YOUR TROPICAL FISH LAID EGGS YESTERDAY.
I'M TAKING GOOD CARE OF THEM, SO DON'T WORRY.
SEE YOU.

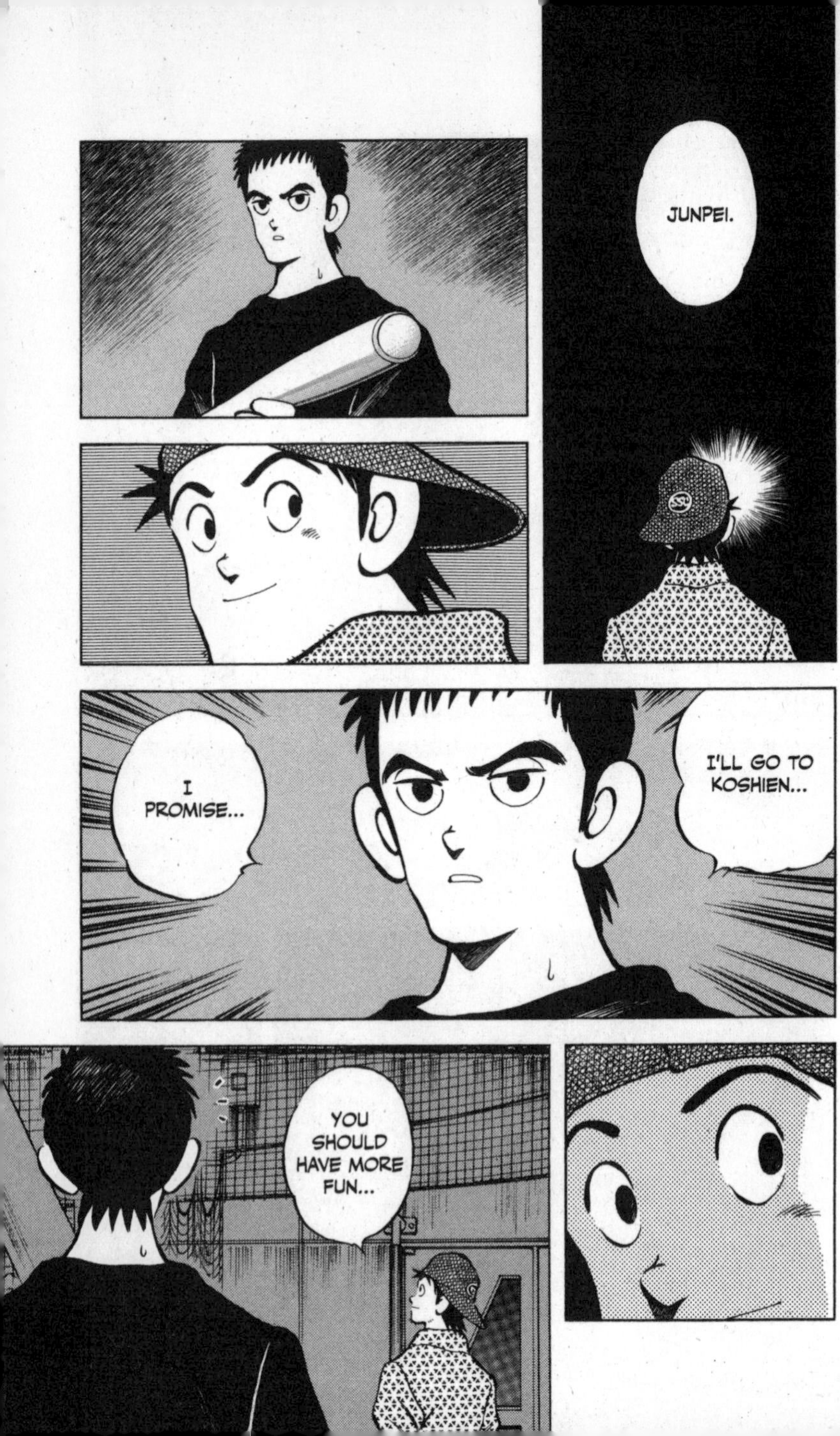
JUNPEI.
I'LL GO TO KOSHIEN...
I PROMISE...
YOU SHOULD HAVE MORE FUN...

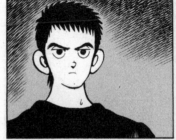

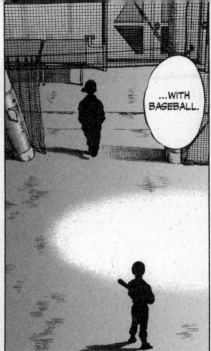

...WITH BASEBALL.

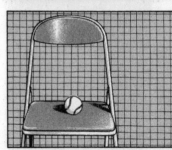

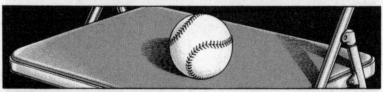

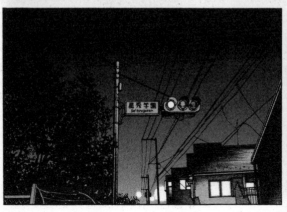

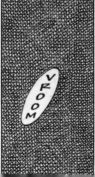

VROOM

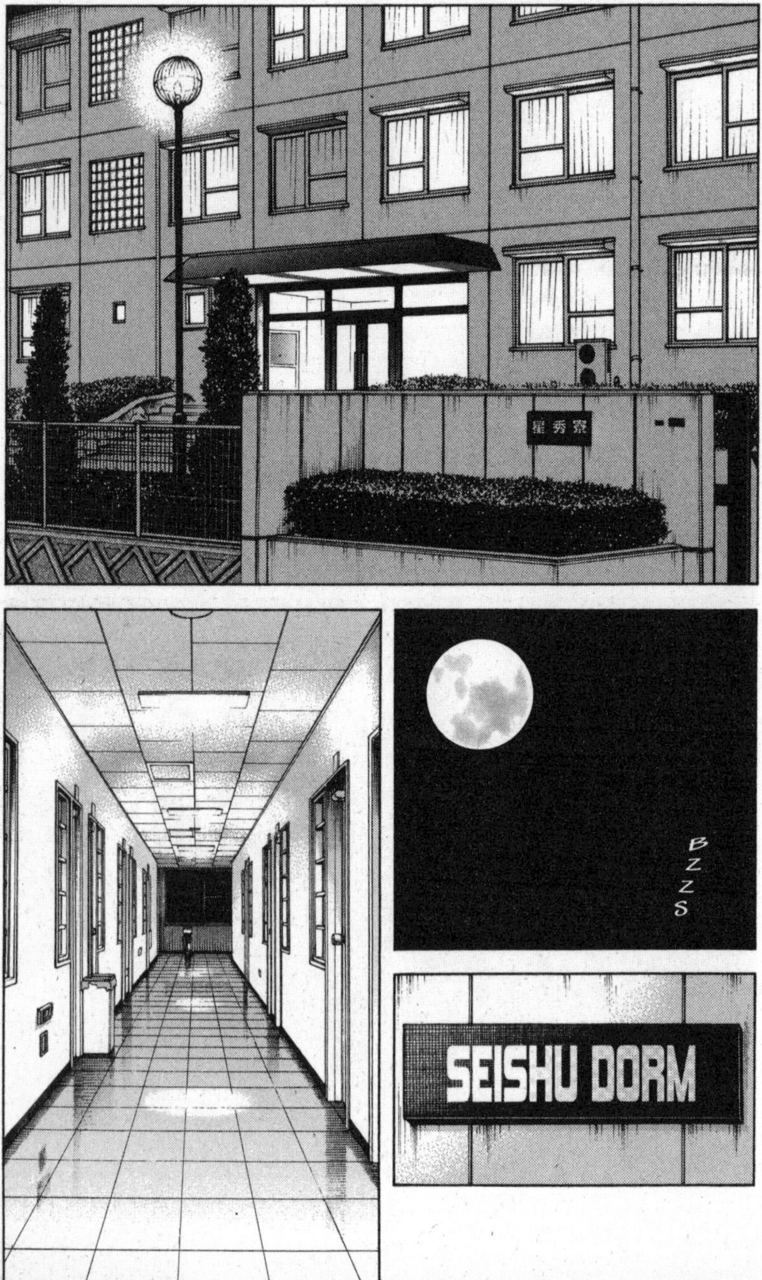
星秀寮
BZZS
SEISHU DORM

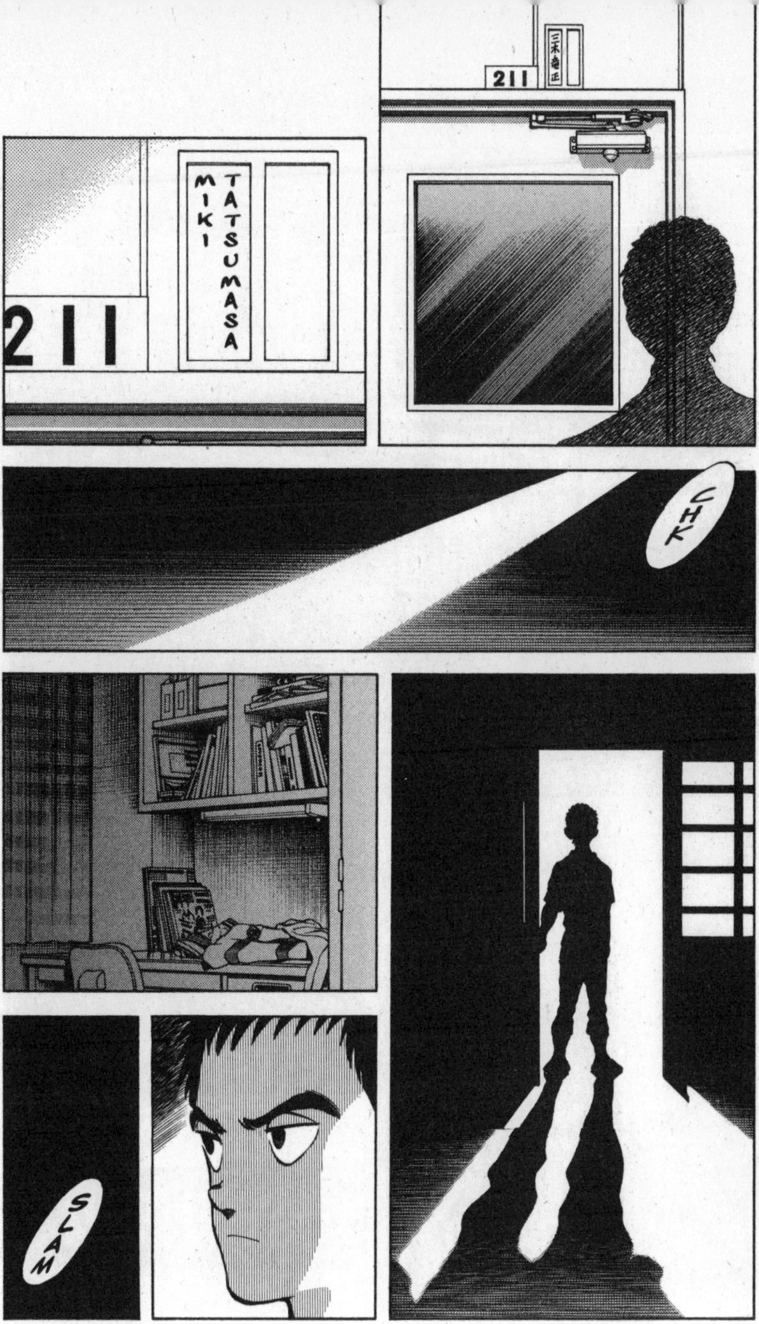
211
MIKI TATSUMASA
211
CHK
SLAM

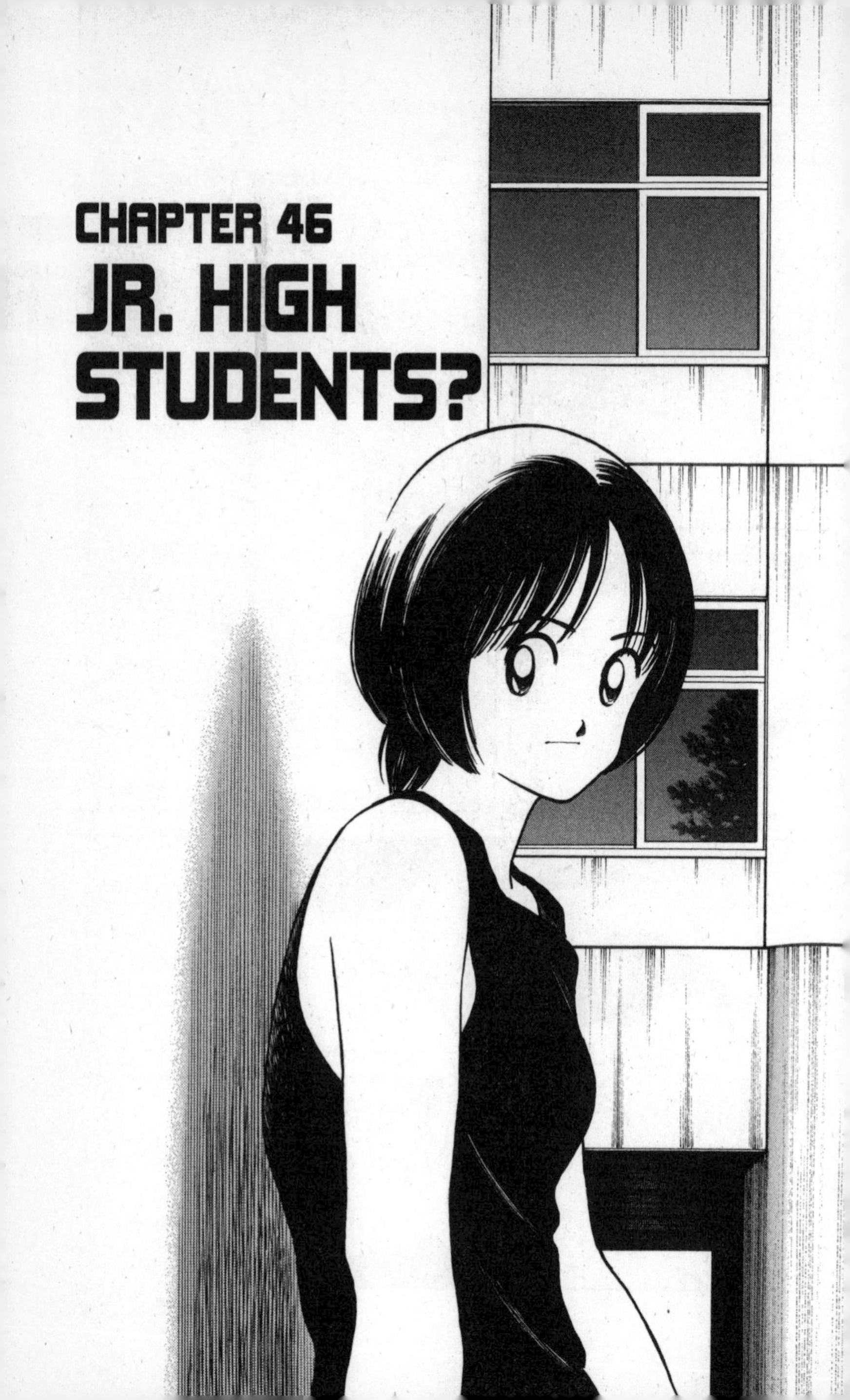
CHAPTER 46
JR. HIGH STUDENTS?

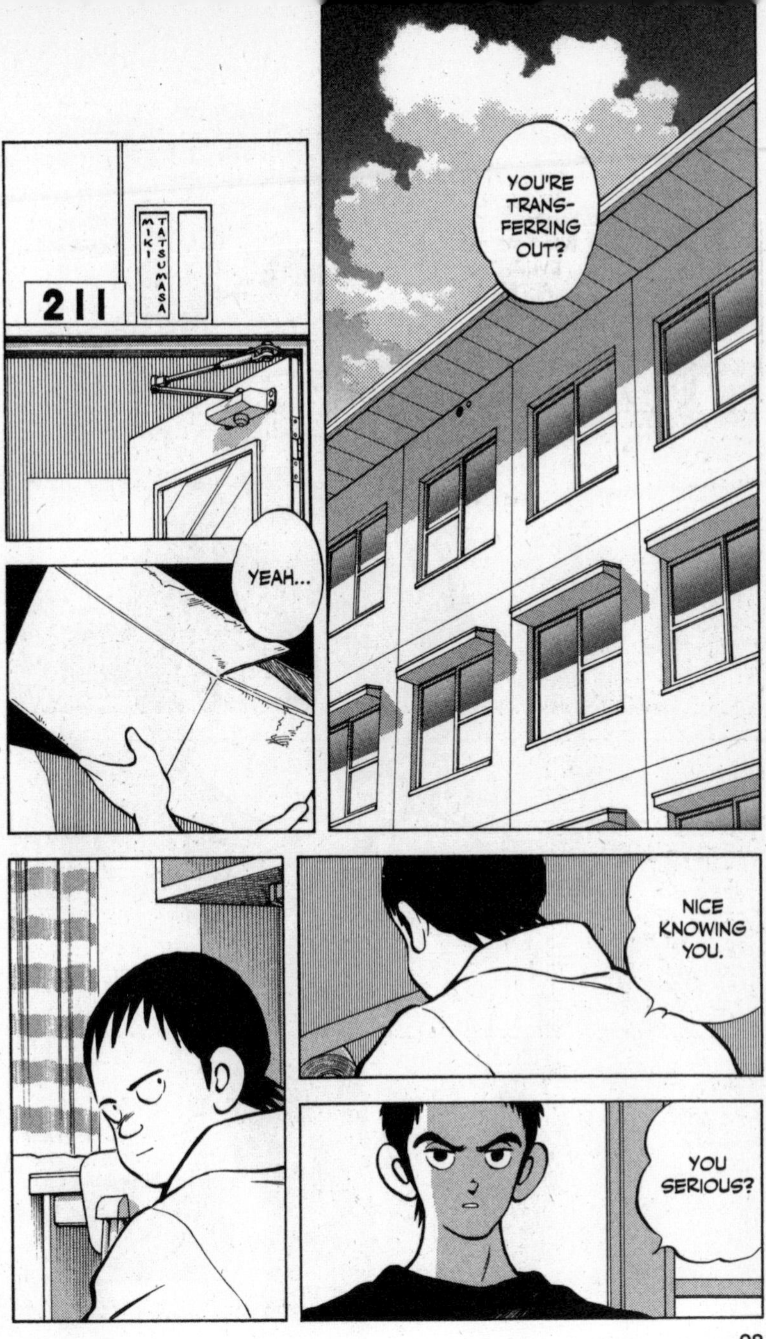
YOU'RE TRANS-FERRING OUT?
211
TATSUMASA
MIKI
YEAH...
NICE KNOWING YOU.
YOU SERIOUS?

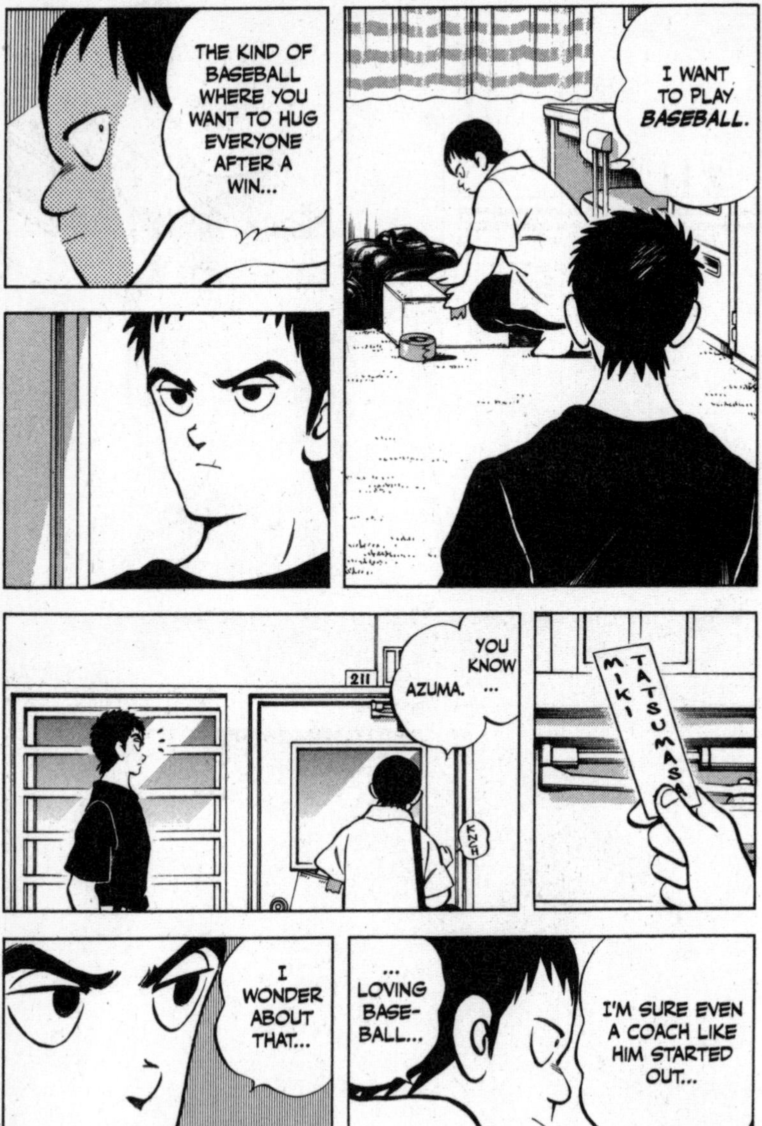
I WANT TO PLAY BASEBALL.
THE KIND OF BASEBALL WHERE YOU WANT TO HUG EVERYONE AFTER A WIN...
MIKI TATSUMASA
YOU KNOW ... AZUMA.
KNCH
I'M SURE EVEN A COACH LIKE HIM STARTED OUT...
... LOVING BASE-BALL...
I WONDER ABOUT THAT...

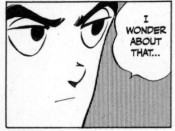

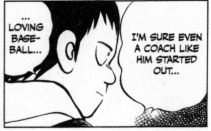

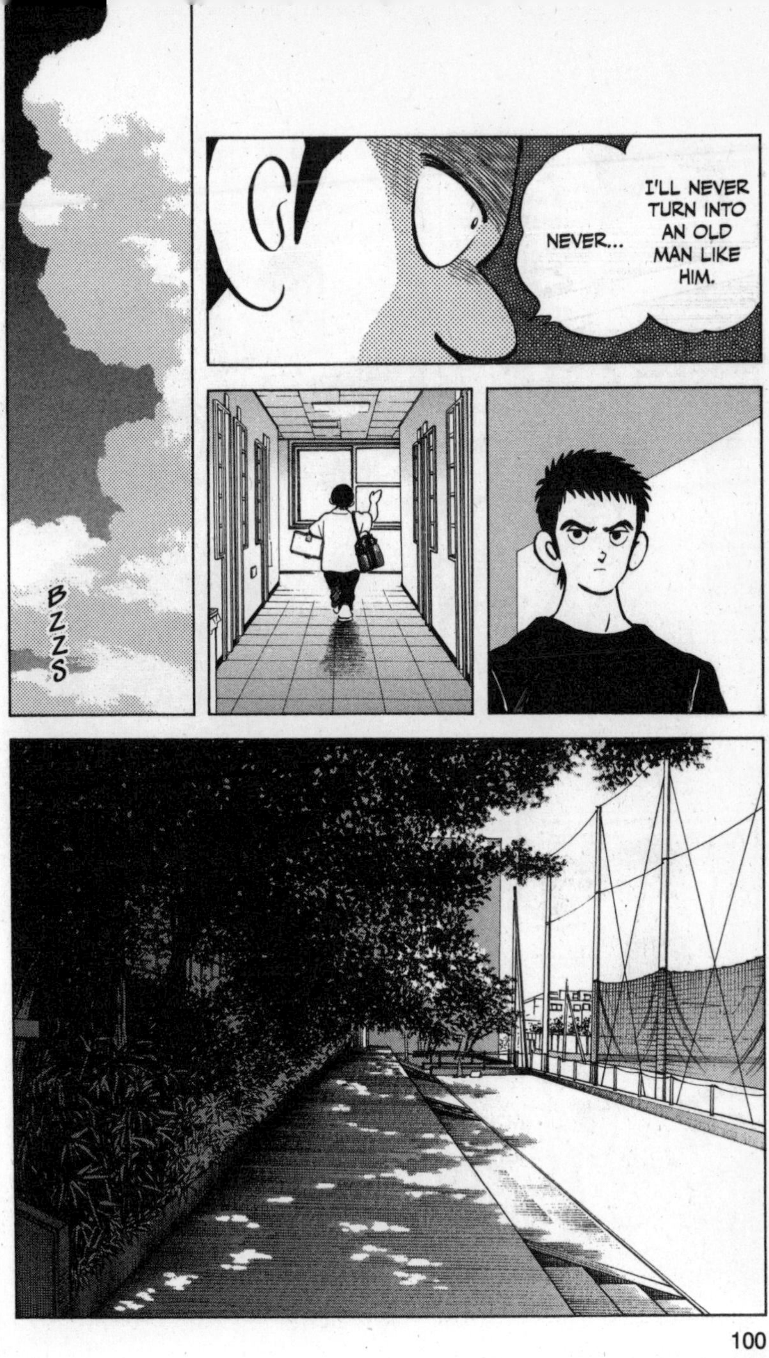
I'LL NEVER TURN INTO AN OLD MAN LIKE HIM.
NEVER...
BZZS

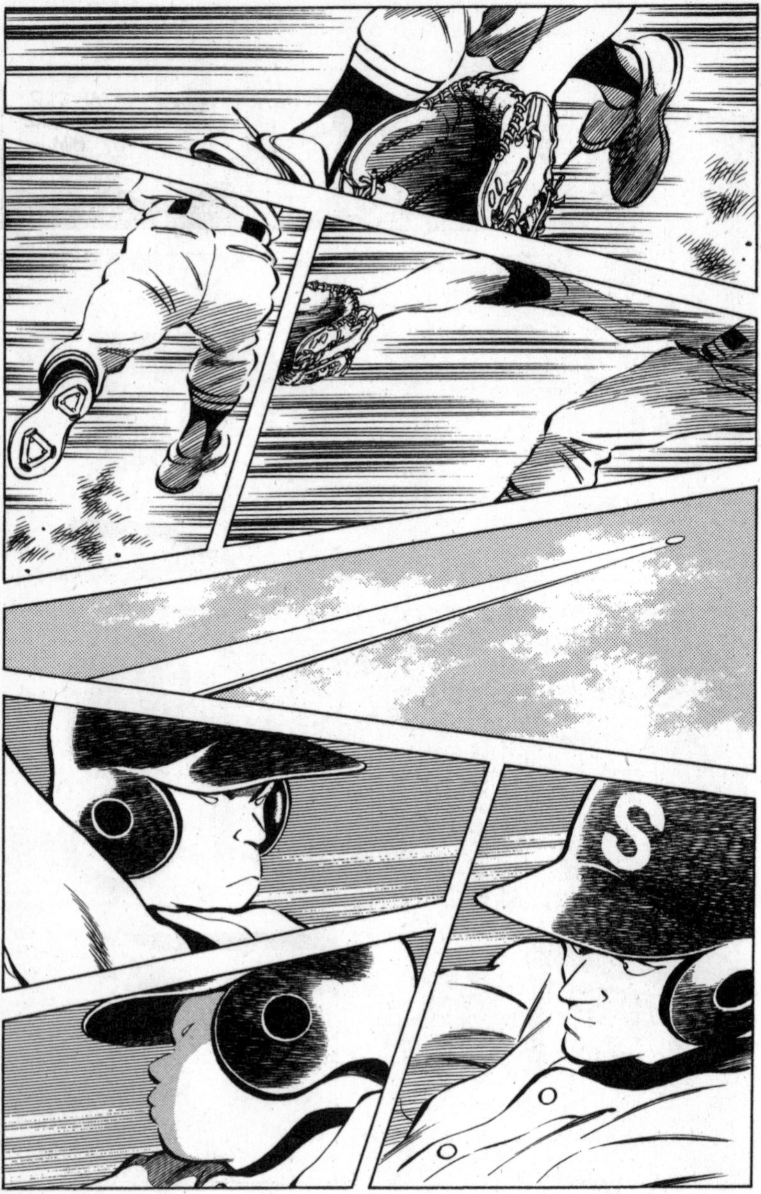

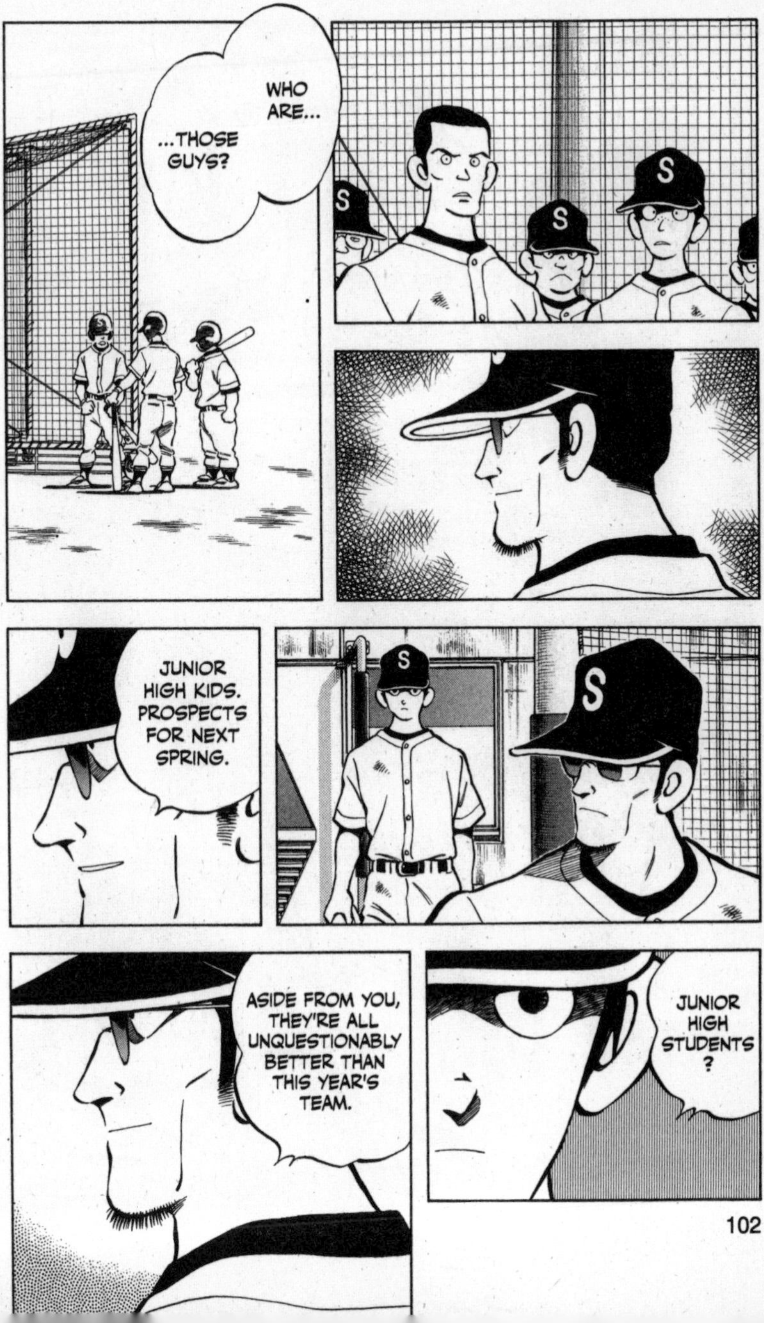
WHO ARE...
...THOSE GUYS?
JUNIOR HIGH KIDS. PROSPECTS FOR NEXT SPRING.
JUNIOR HIGH STUDENTS?
ASIDE FROM YOU, THEY'RE ALL UNQUESTIONABLY BETTER THAN THIS YEAR'S TEAM.

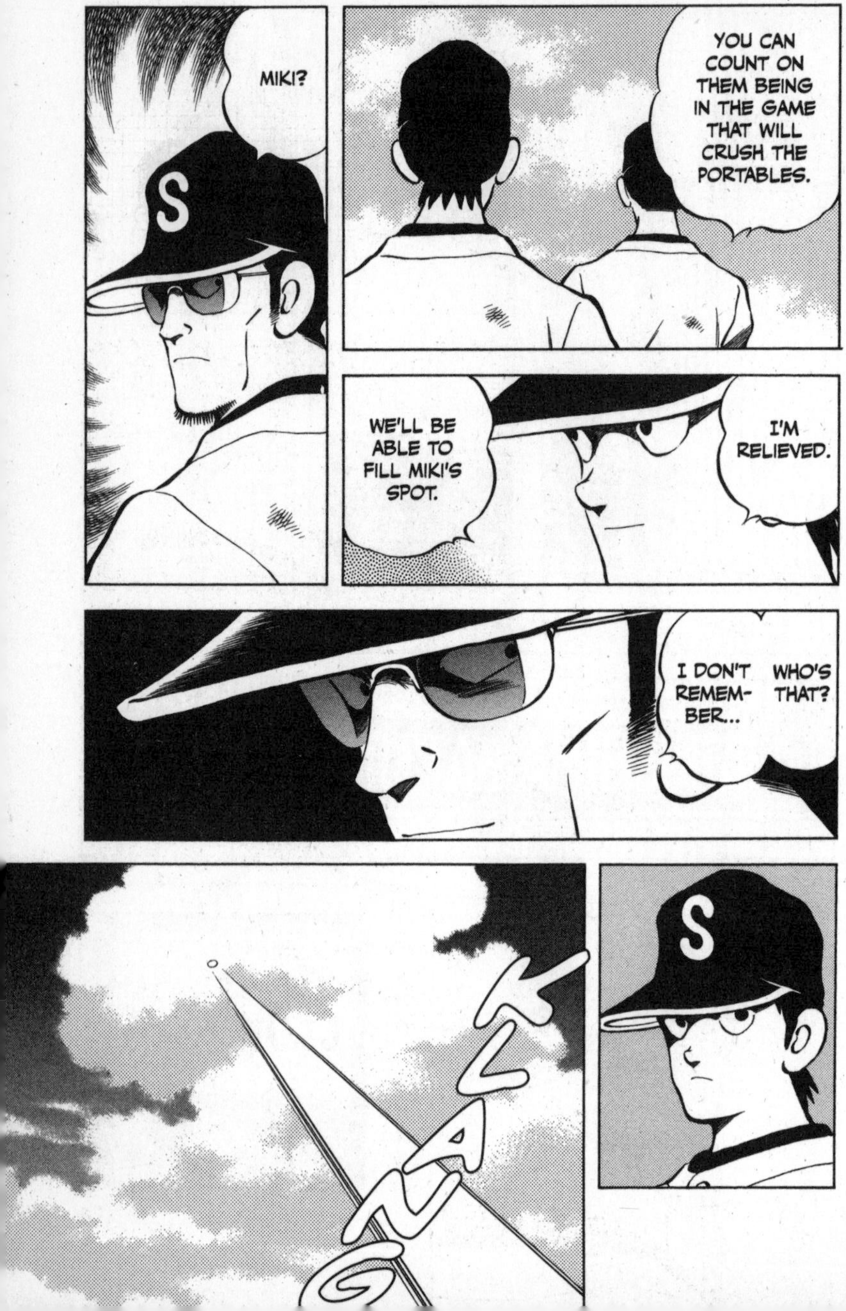
YOU CAN COUNT ON THEM BEING IN THE GAME THAT WILL CRUSH THE PORTABLES.
I'M RELIEVED.
WE'LL BE ABLE TO FILL MIKI'S SPOT.
MIKI?
WHO'S THAT?
I DON'T REMEMBER...
KLANG

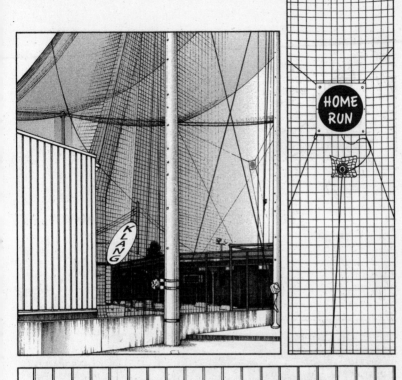

KLANG

HOME
RUN

TSUKISHIMA BATTING CENTER

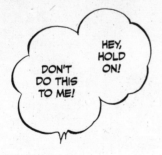

HEY,
HOLD
ON!

DON'T
DO THIS
TO ME!

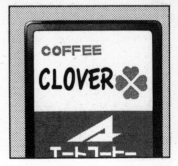

COFFEE

CLOVER

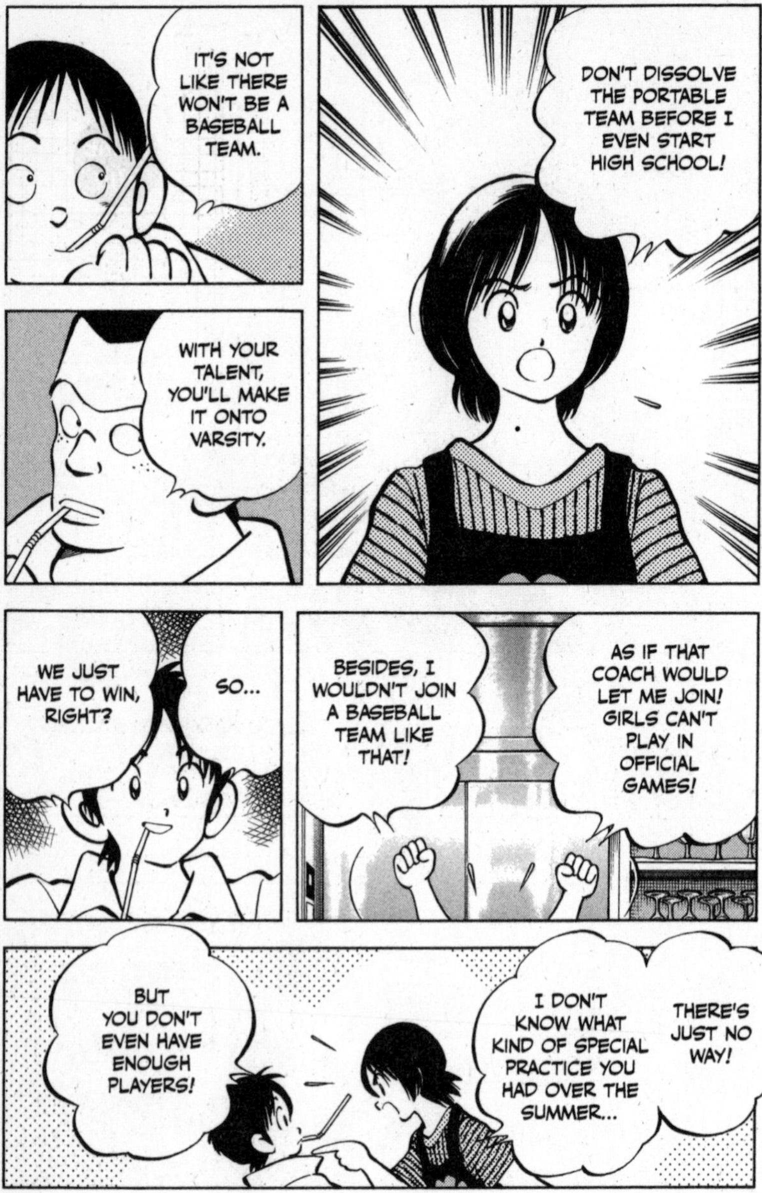
DON'T DISSOLVE THE PORTABLE TEAM BEFORE I EVEN START HIGH SCHOOL!
IT'S NOT LIKE THERE WON'T BE A BASEBALL TEAM.
WITH YOUR TALENT, YOU'LL MAKE IT ONTO VARSITY.
AS IF THAT COACH WOULD LET ME JOIN! GIRLS CAN'T PLAY IN OFFICIAL GAMES!
BESIDES, I WOULDN'T JOIN A BASEBALL TEAM LIKE THAT!
SO...
WE JUST HAVE TO WIN, RIGHT?
THERE'S JUST NO WAY!
I DON'T KNOW WHAT KIND OF SPECIAL PRACTICE YOU HAD OVER THE SUMMER...
BUT YOU DON'T EVEN HAVE ENOUGH PLAYERS!

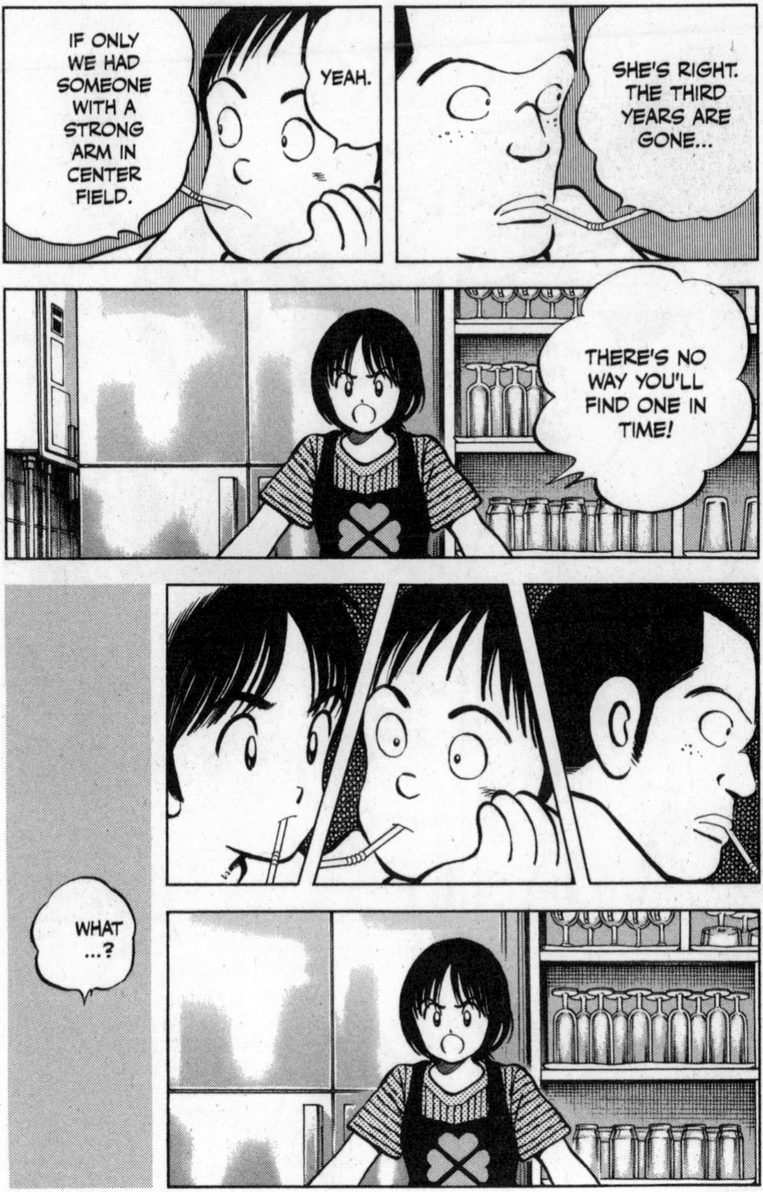
SHE'S RIGHT. THE THIRD YEARS ARE GONE...
IF ONLY WE HAD SOMEONE WITH A STRONG ARM IN CENTER FIELD.
YEAH.
THERE'S NO WAY YOU'LL FIND ONE IN TIME!
WHAT ...?

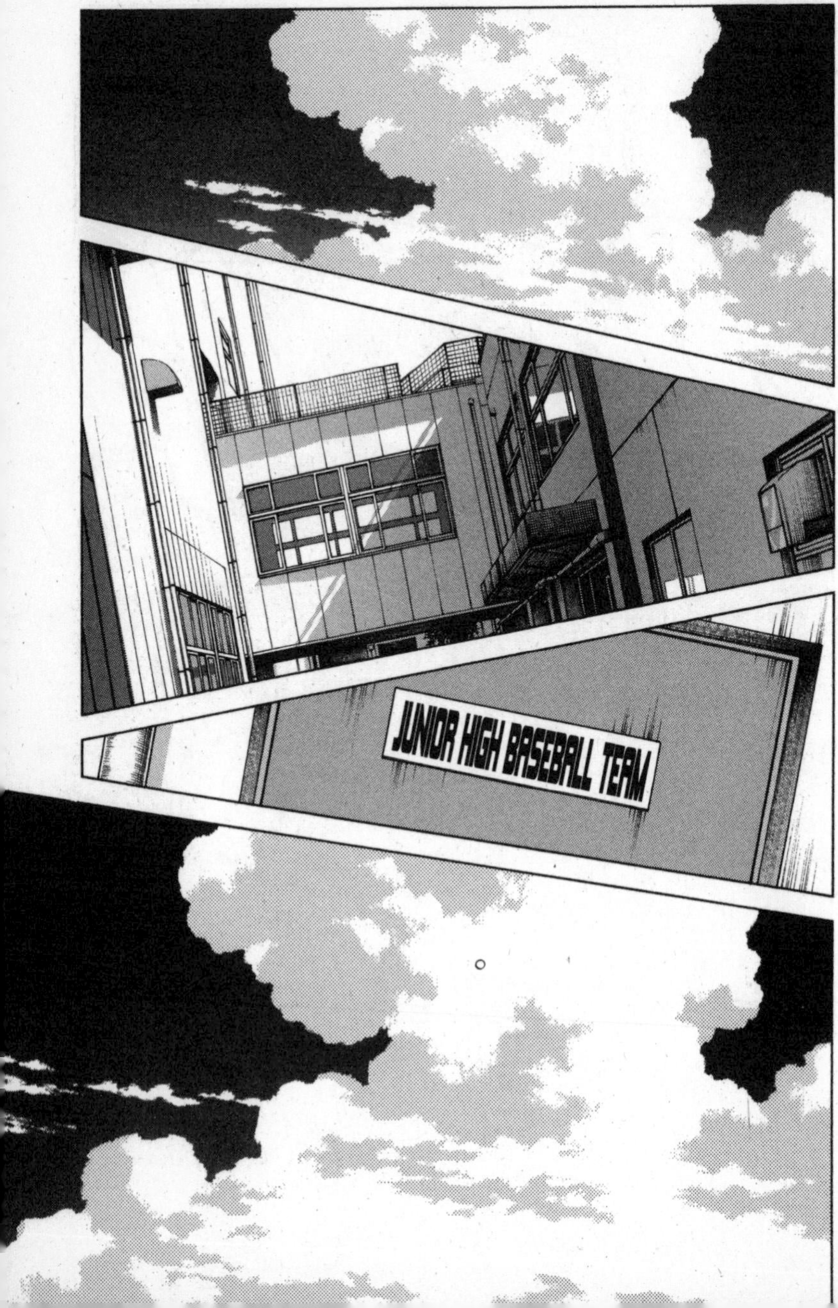
JUNIOR HIGH BASEBALL TEAM

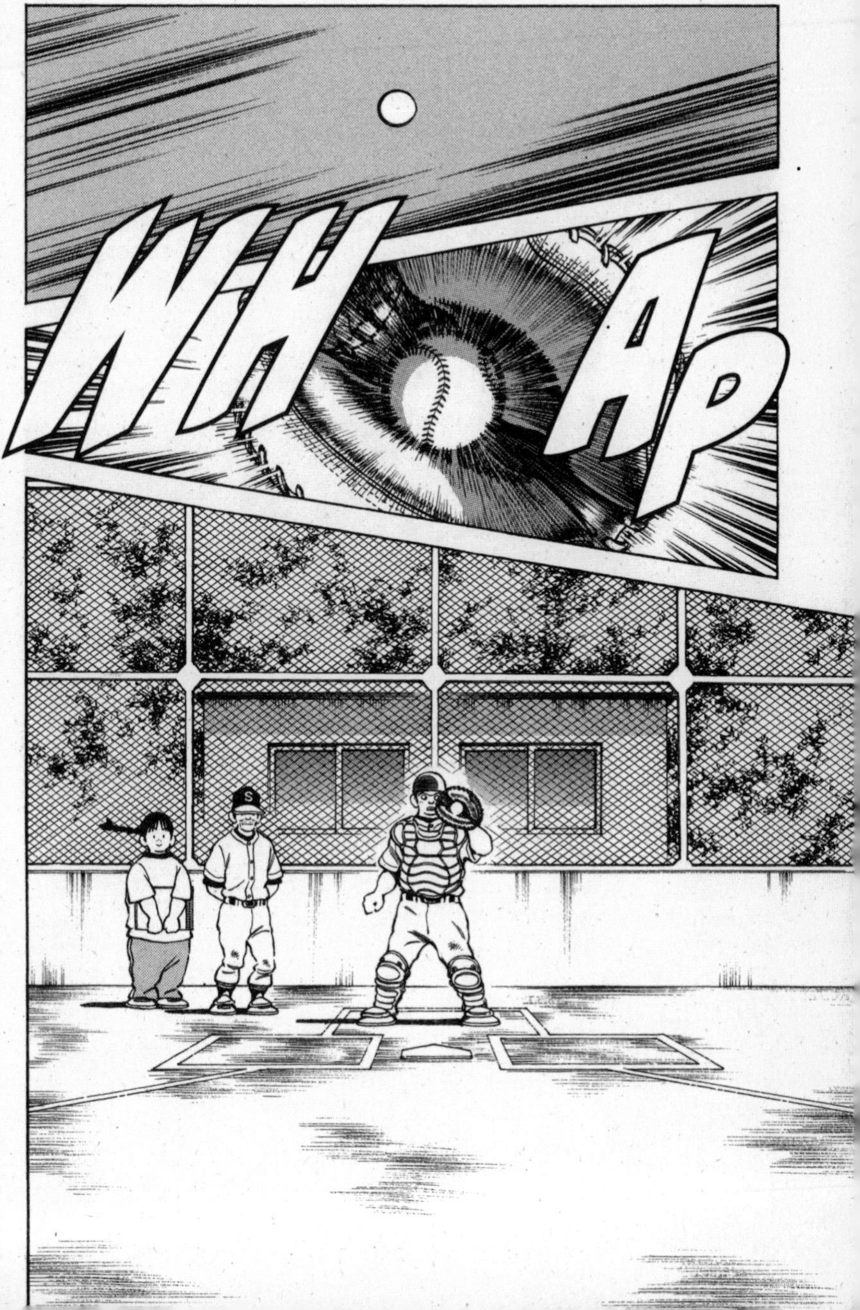
WHAP

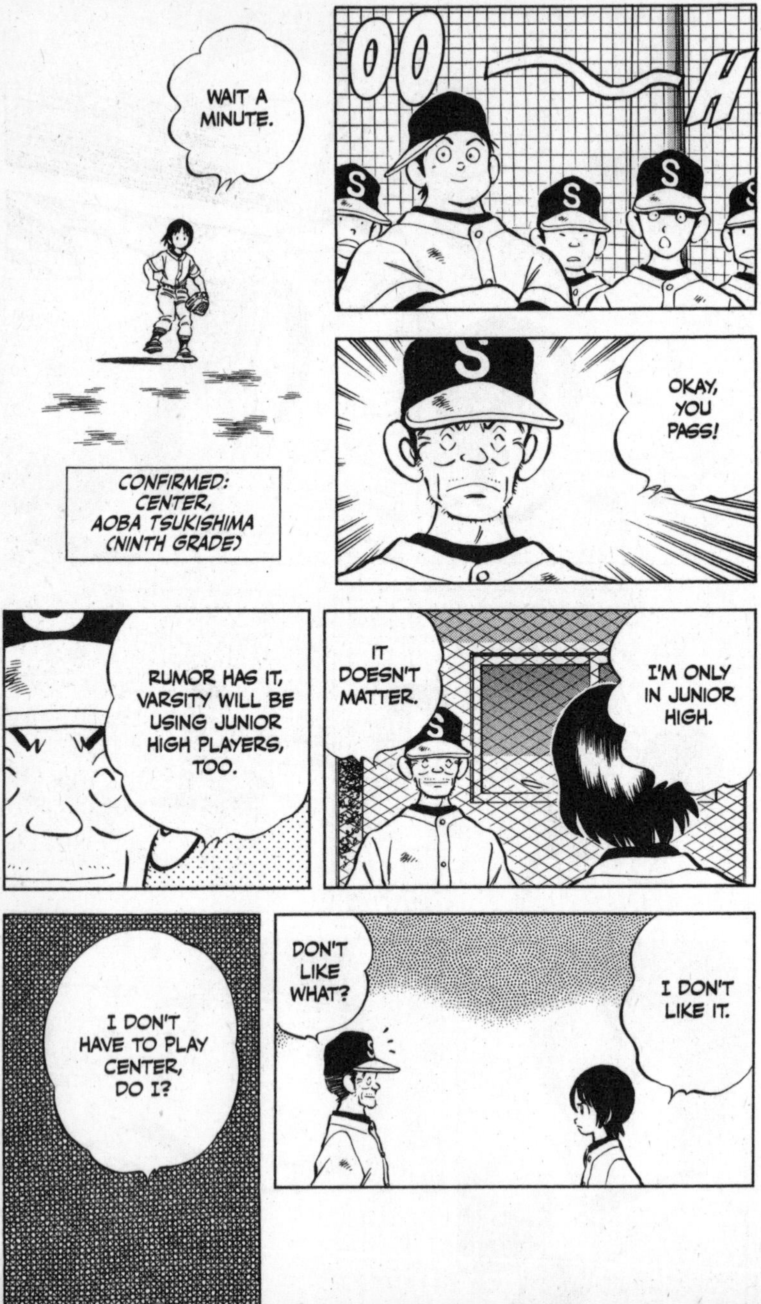
OOO~H
OKAY, YOU PASS!
WAIT A MINUTE.
CONFIRMED: CENTER, AOBA TSUKISHIMA (NINTH GRADE)
I'M ONLY IN JUNIOR HIGH.
IT DOESN'T MATTER.
RUMOR HAS IT, VARSITY WILL BE USING JUNIOR HIGH PLAYERS, TOO.
I DON'T LIKE IT.
DON'T LIKE WHAT?
I DON'T HAVE TO PLAY CENTER, DO I?

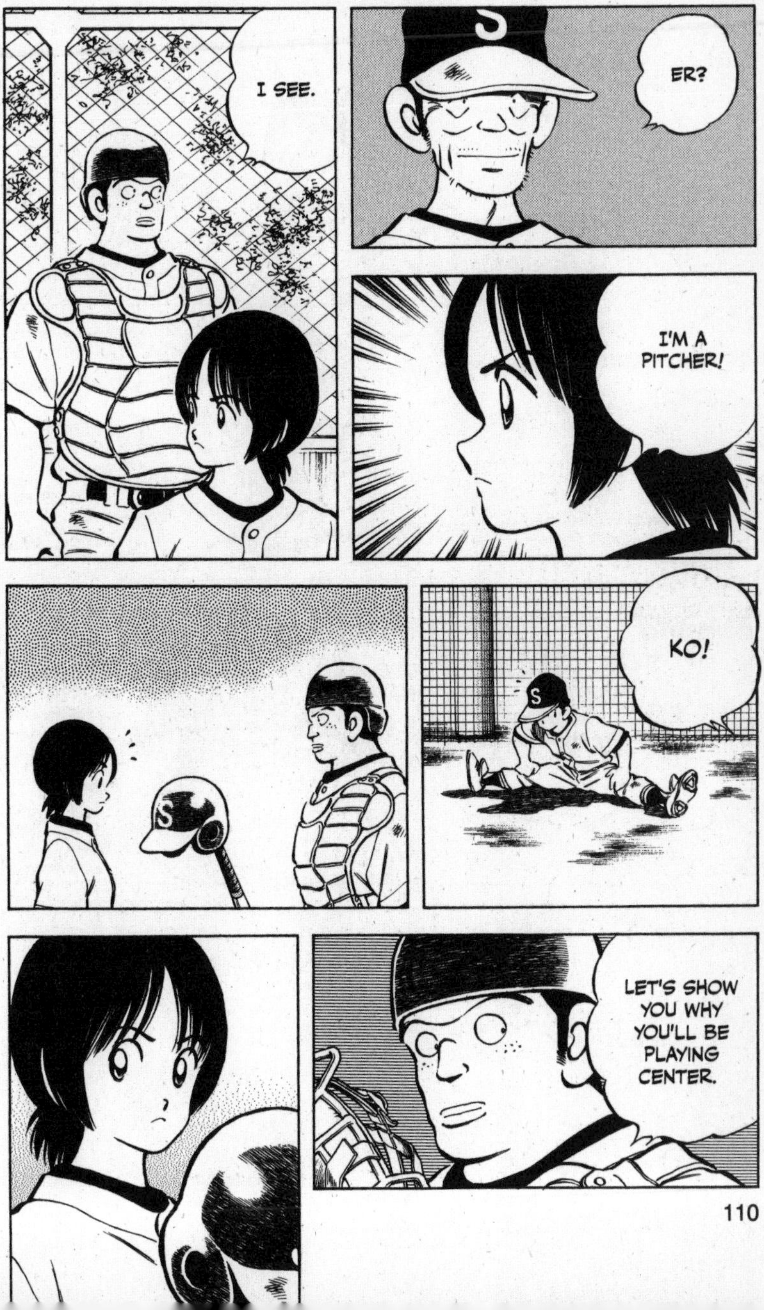
ER?
I'M A PITCHER!
I SEE.
KO!
LET'S SHOW YOU WHY YOU'LL BE PLAYING CENTER.

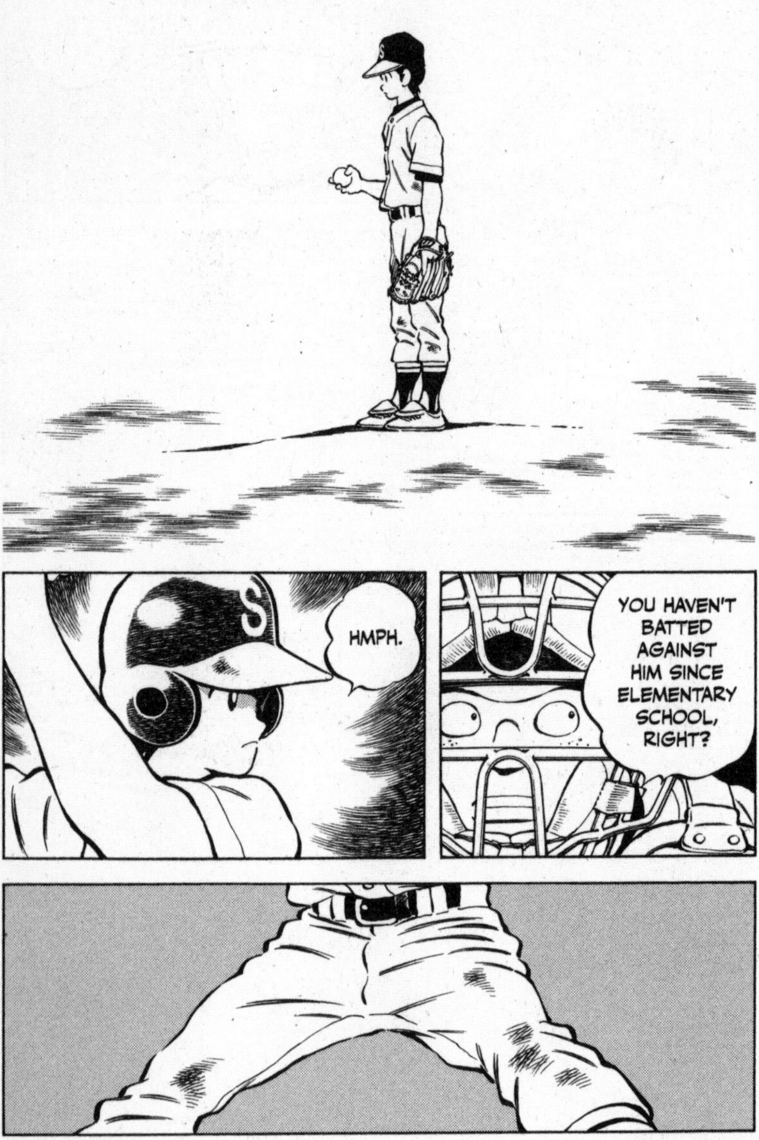
YOU HAVEN'T BATTED AGAINST HIM SINCE ELEMENTARY SCHOOL, RIGHT?
HMPH.

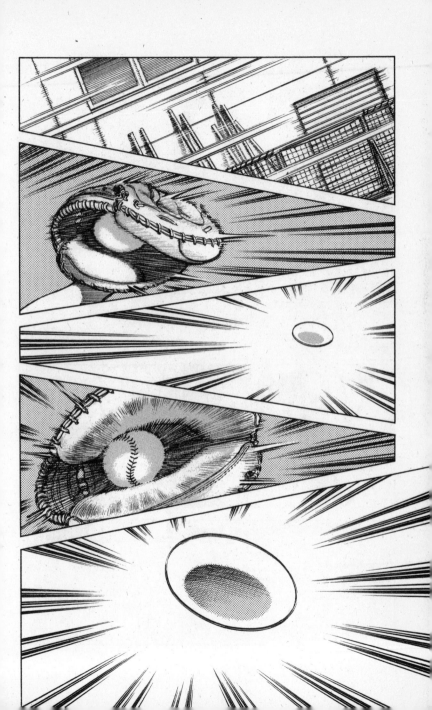

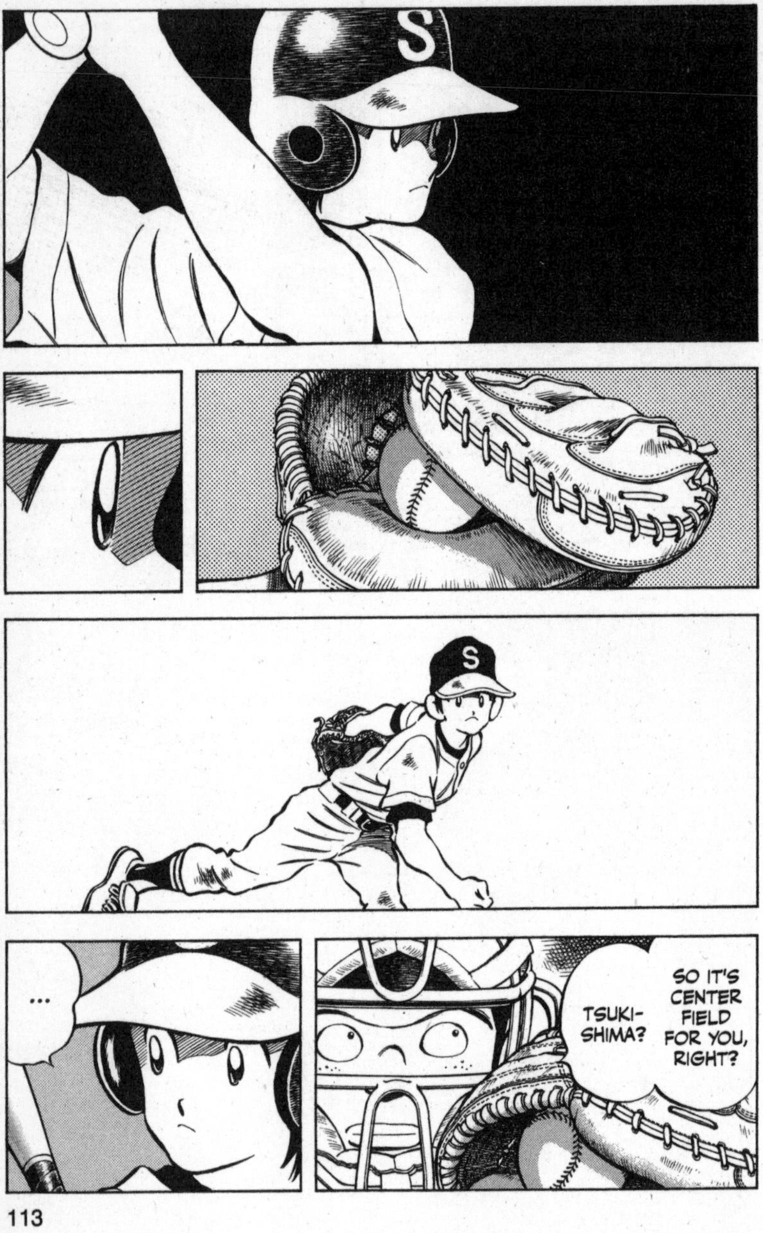
SO IT'S CENTER FIELD FOR YOU, RIGHT?
TSUKI-SHIMA?
...

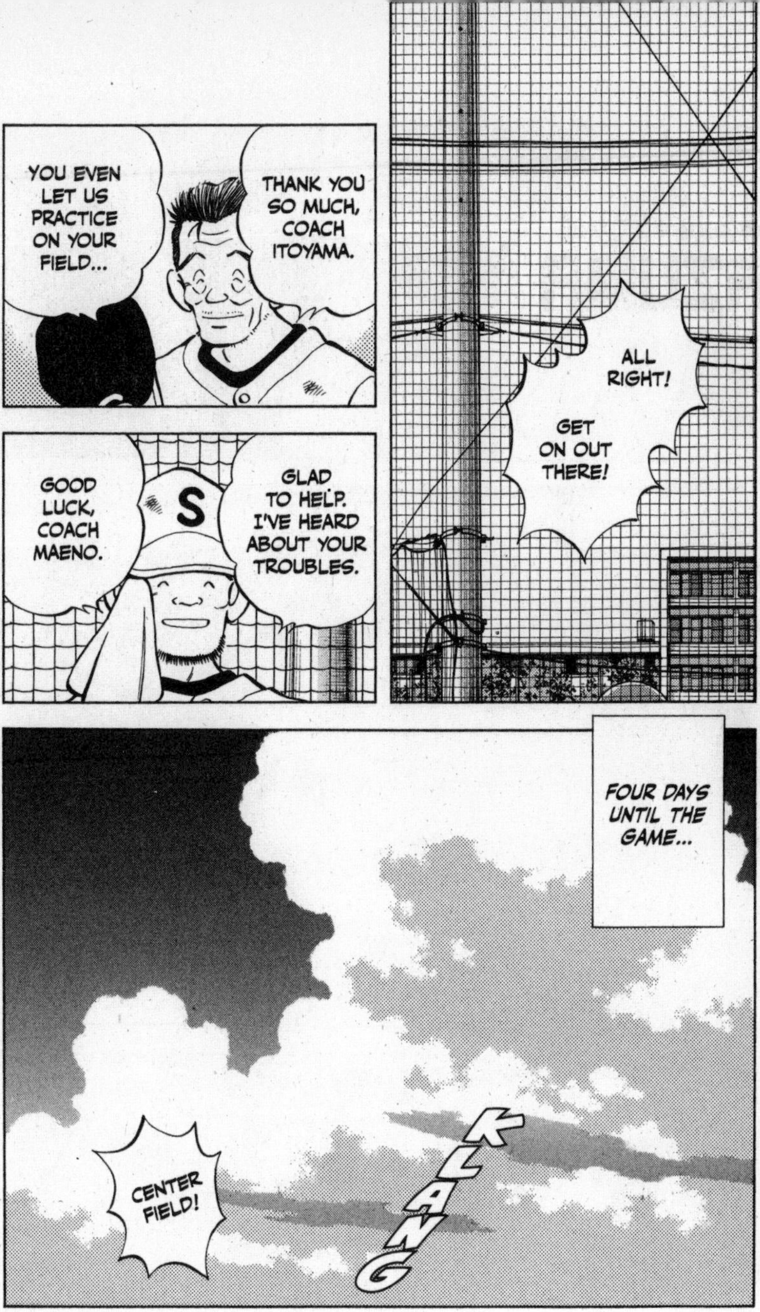
ALL RIGHT!
GET ON OUT THERE!
THANK YOU SO MUCH, COACH ITOYAMA.
YOU EVEN LET US PRACTICE ON YOUR FIELD...
GLAD TO HELP. I'VE HEARD ABOUT YOUR TROUBLES.
GOOD LUCK, COACH MAENO.
FOUR DAYS UNTIL THE GAME...
KLANG
CENTER FIELD!

CHAPTER 47
JUNPEI AZUMA

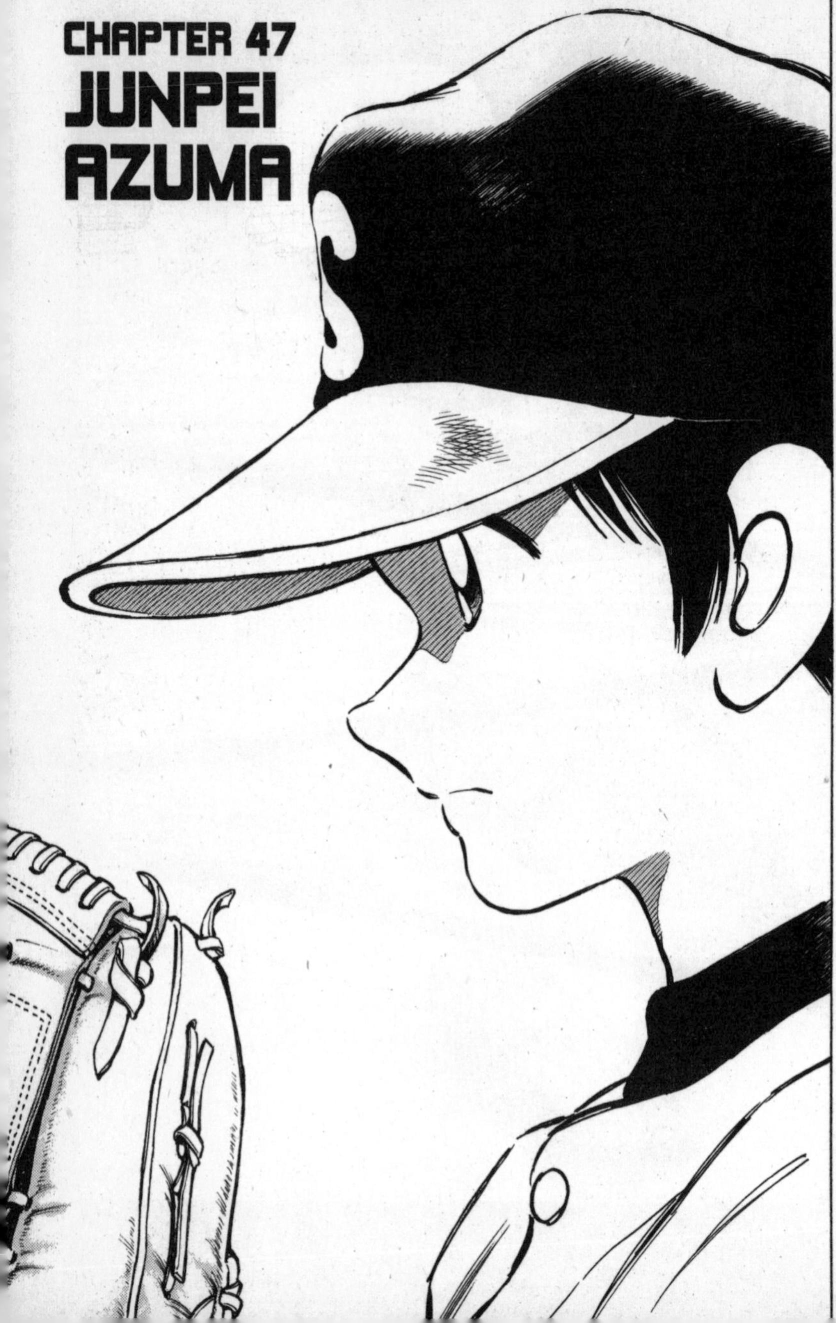

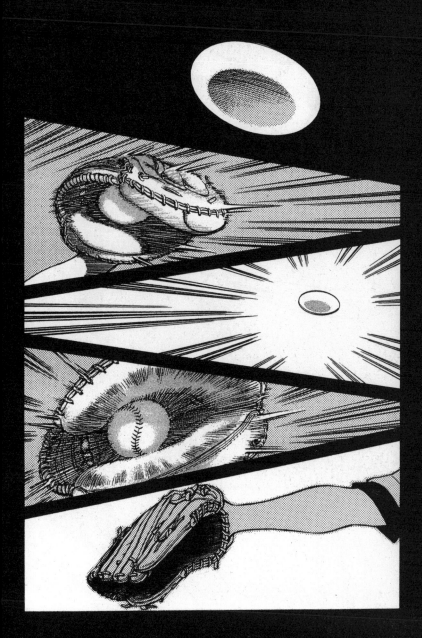

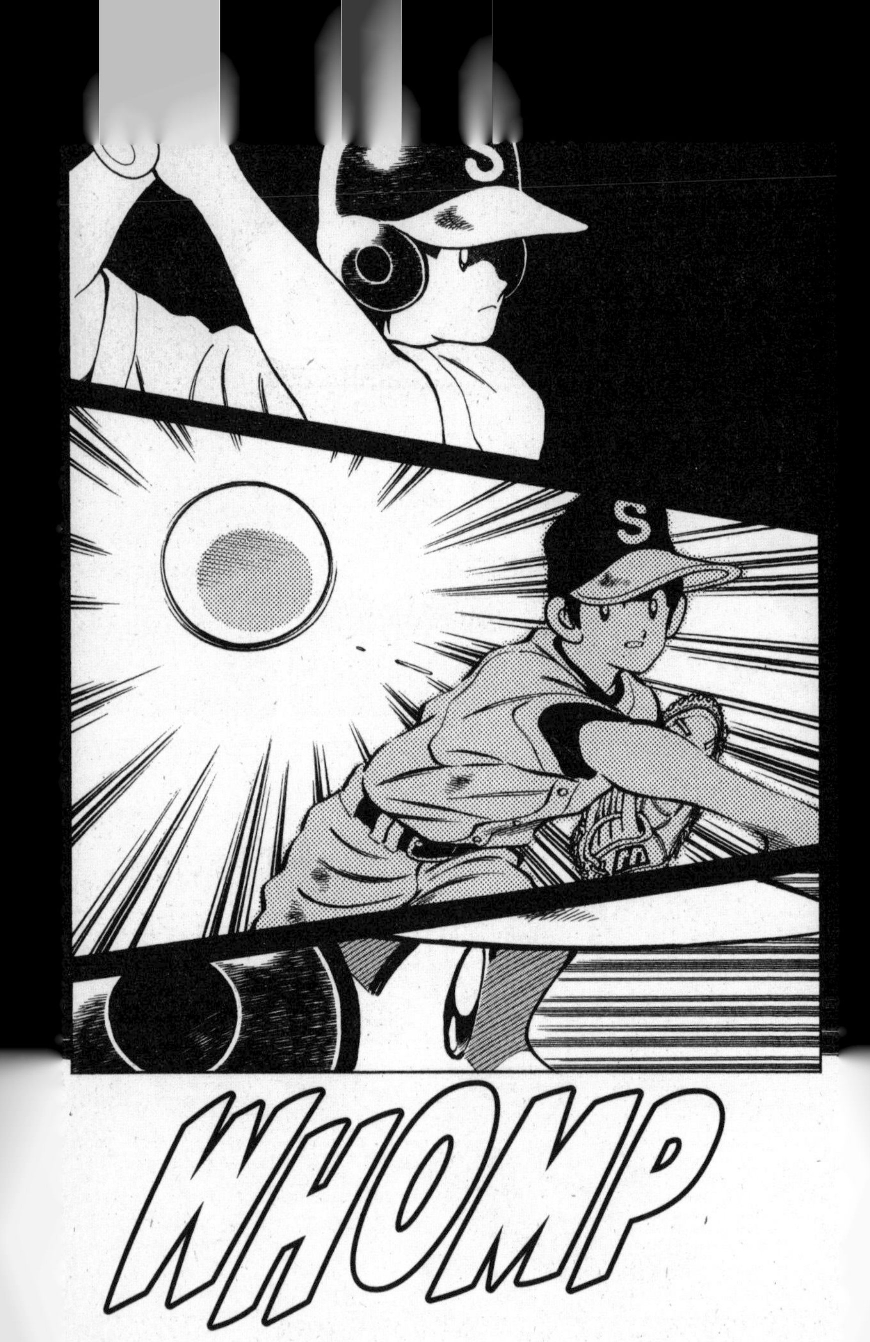
WHOMP

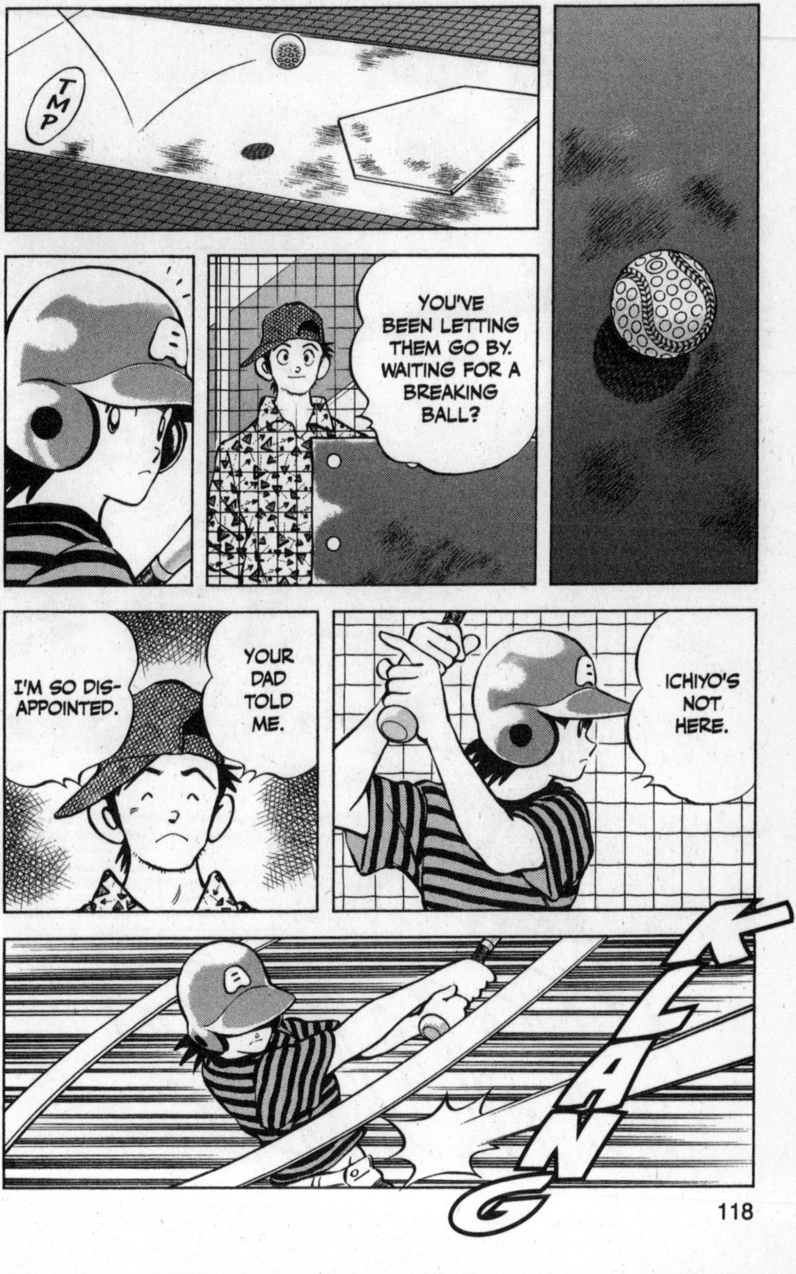
TMP
YOU'VE BEEN LETTING THEM GO BY. WAITING FOR A BREAKING BALL?
ICHIYO'S NOT HERE.
YOUR DAD TOLD ME.
I'M SO DIS-APPOINTED.
KLANG

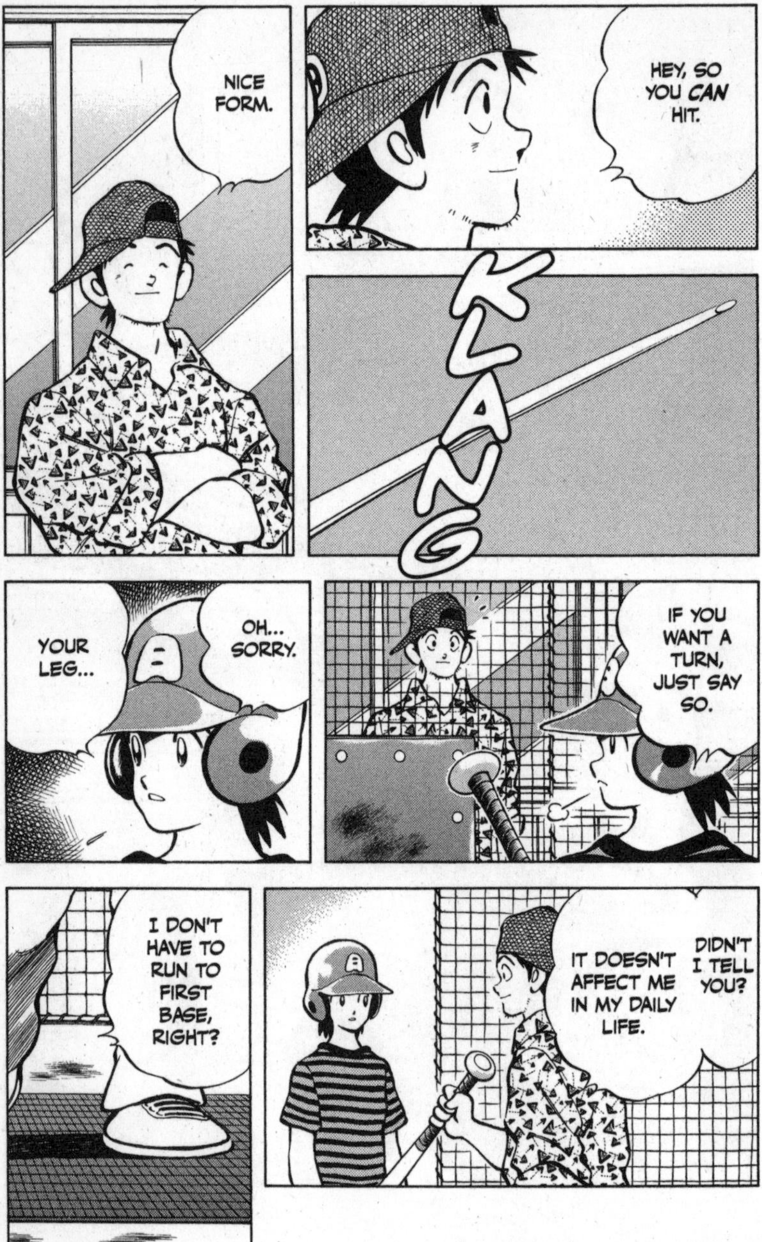
HEY, SO YOU CAN HIT.
KLANG
NICE FORM.
IF YOU WANT A TURN, JUST SAY SO.
OH... SORRY.
YOUR LEG...
DIDN'T I TELL YOU?
IT DOESN'T AFFECT ME IN MY DAILY LIFE.
I DON'T HAVE TO RUN TO FIRST BASE, RIGHT?

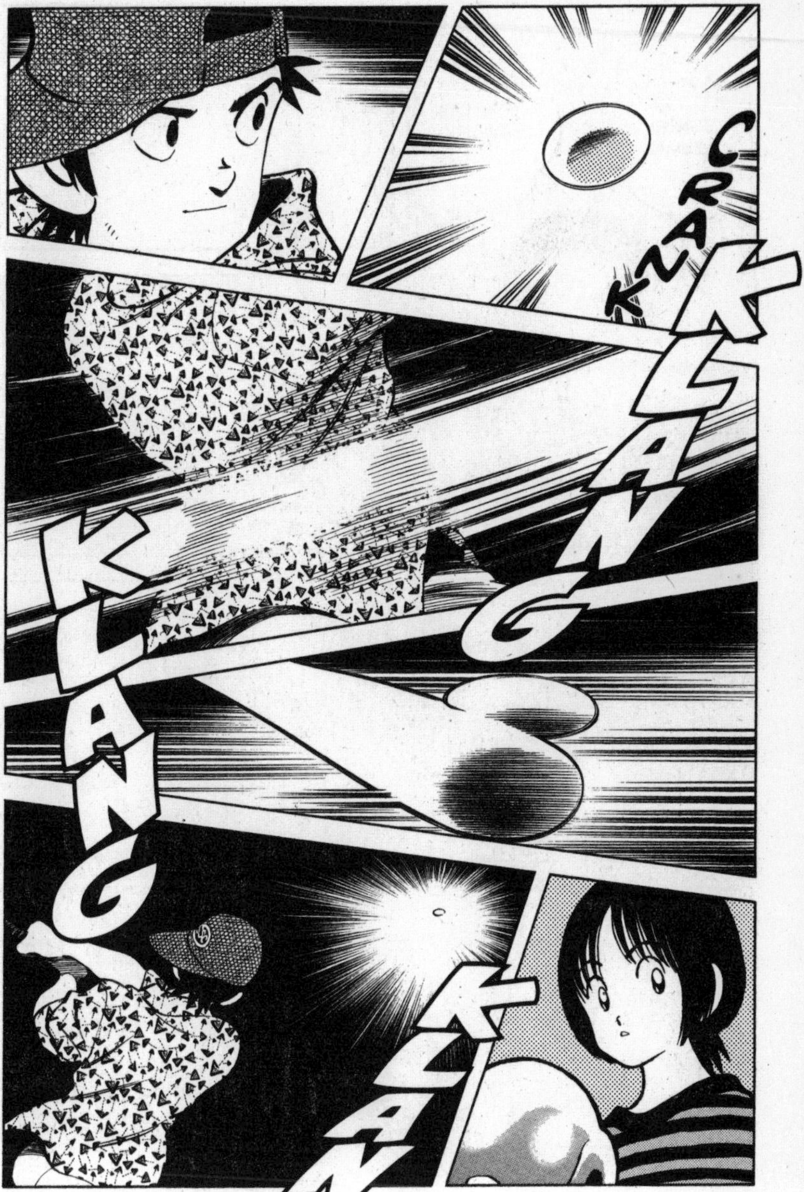
CRANK
KLANG
KLANG
KLANG

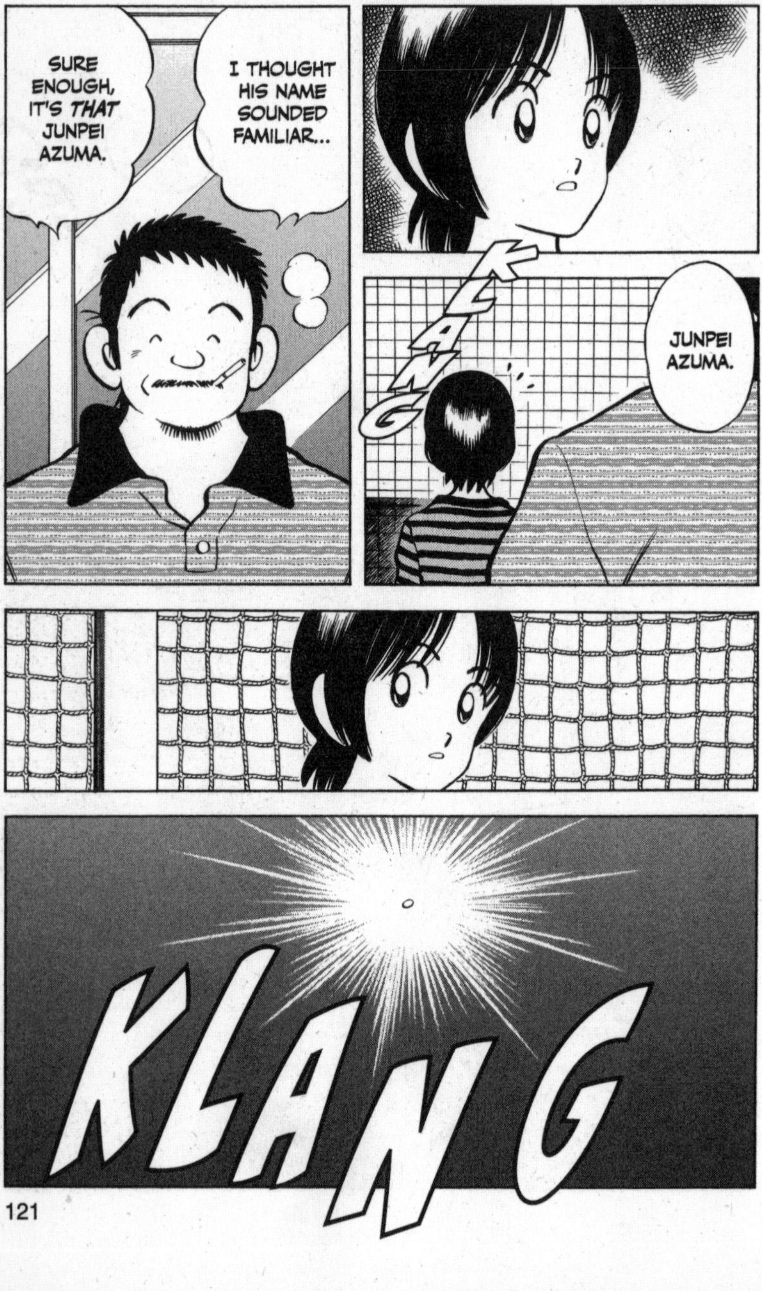
KLANG
JUNPEI AZUMA.
I THOUGHT HIS NAME SOUNDED FAMILIAR...
SURE ENOUGH, IT'S *THAT* JUNPEI AZUMA.
KLANG

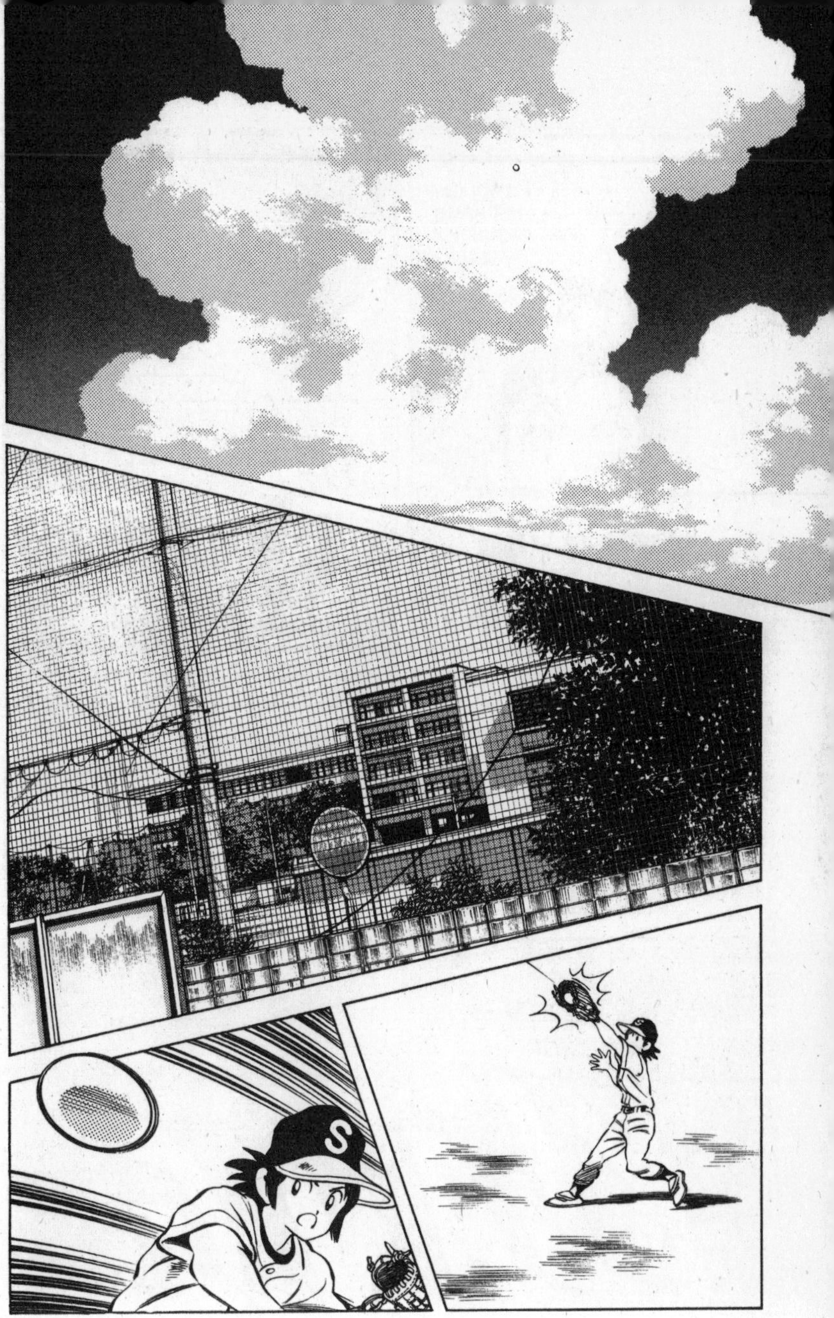

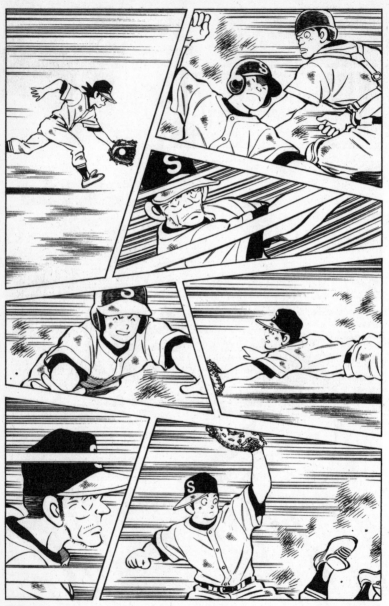

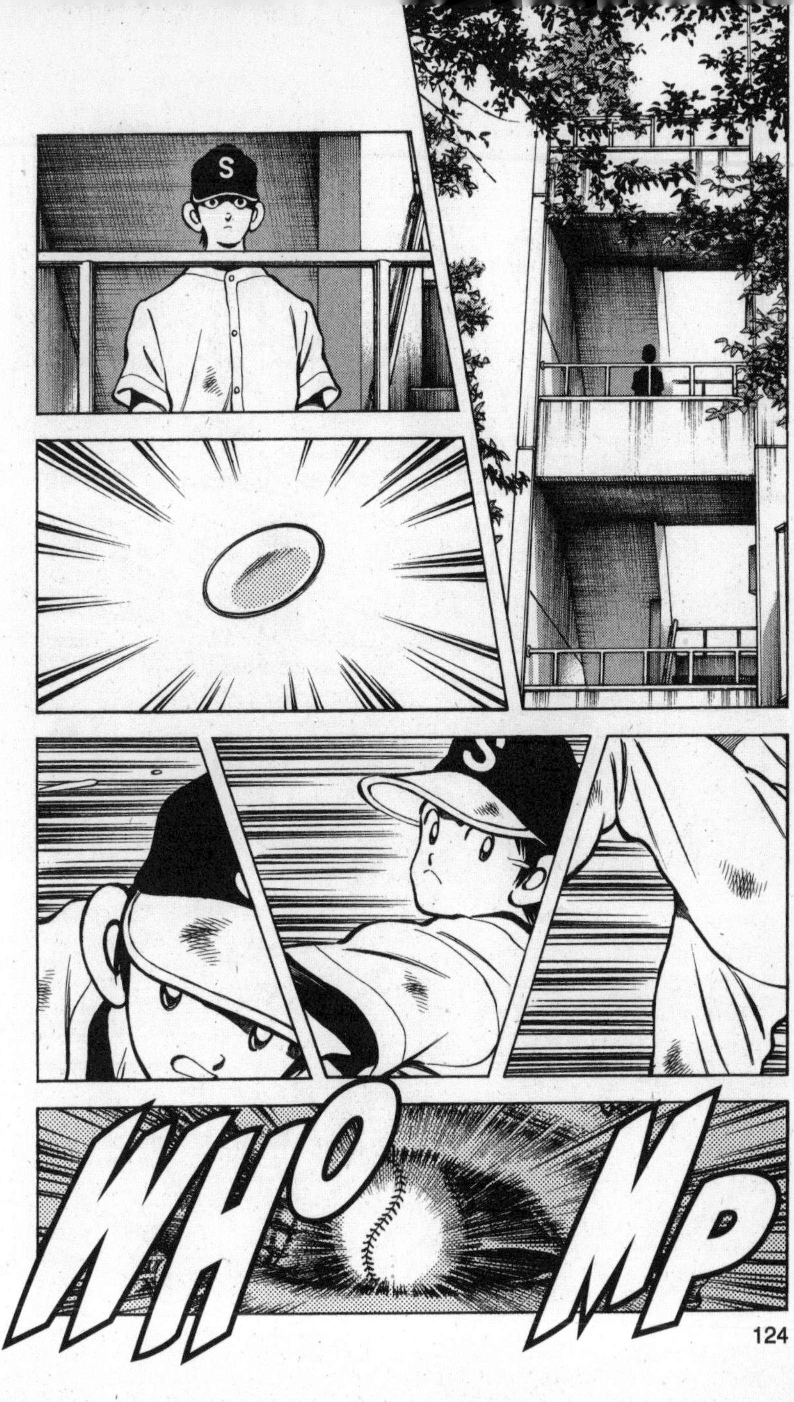
WHOOMP

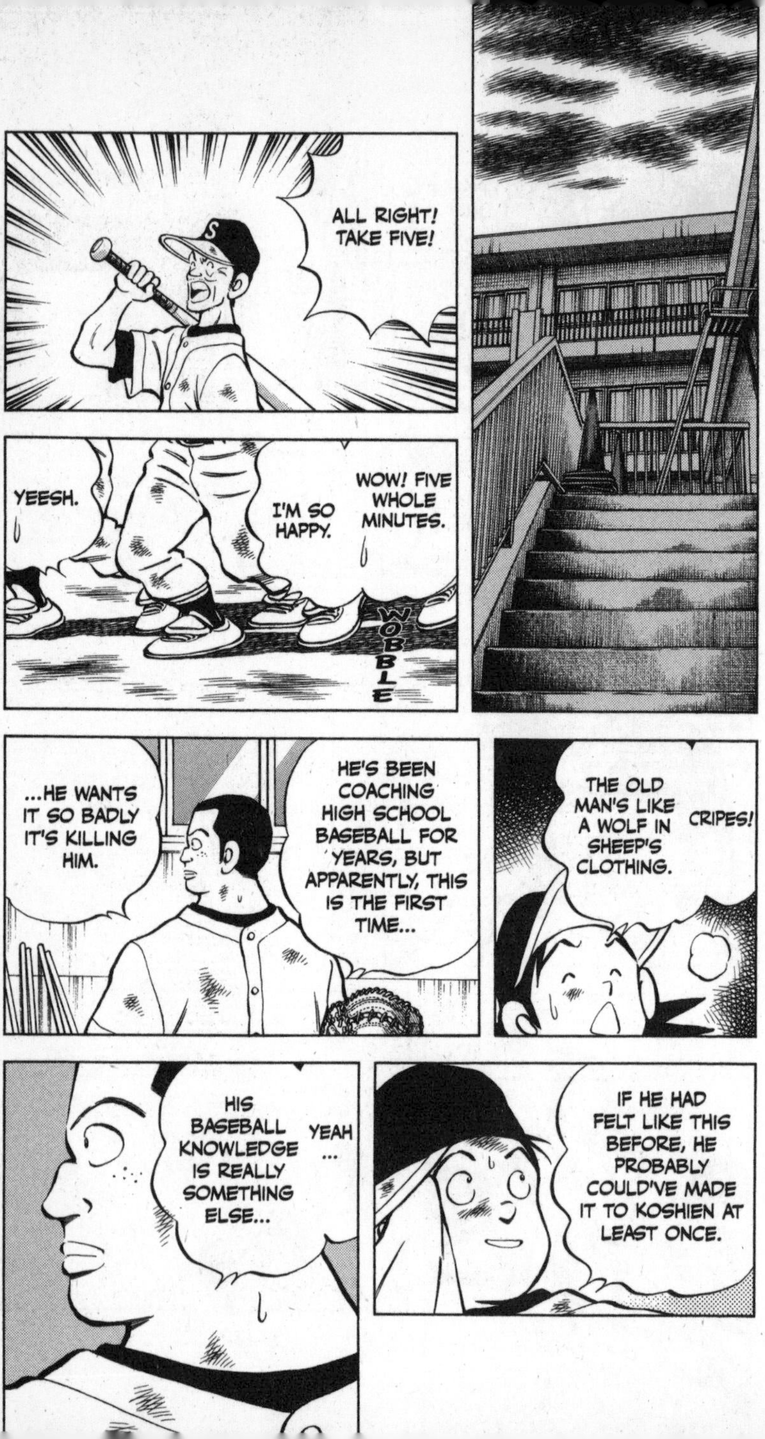
ALL RIGHT! TAKE FIVE!
WOW! FIVE WHOLE MINUTES.
I'M SO HAPPY.
YEESH.
WOBBLE
CRIPES!
THE OLD MAN'S LIKE A WOLF IN SHEEP'S CLOTHING.
HE'S BEEN COACHING HIGH SCHOOL BASEBALL FOR YEARS, BUT APPARENTLY, THIS IS THE FIRST TIME...
...HE WANTS IT SO BADLY IT'S KILLING HIM.
IF HE HAD FELT LIKE THIS BEFORE, HE PROBABLY COULD'VE MADE IT TO KOSHIEN AT LEAST ONCE.
YEAH...
HIS BASEBALL KNOWLEDGE IS REALLY SOMETHING ELSE...

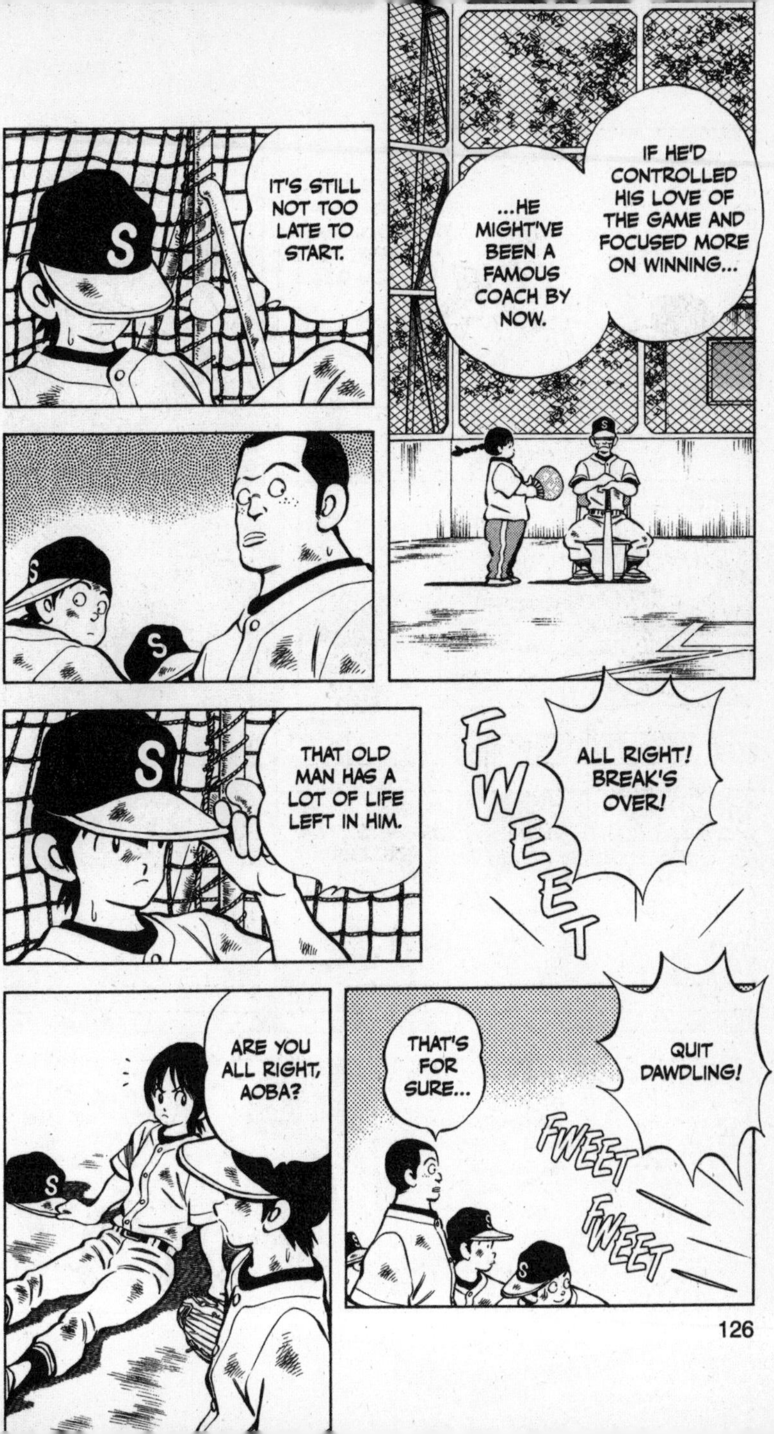
IF HE'D CONTROLLED HIS LOVE OF THE GAME AND FOCUSED MORE ON WINNING...
...HE MIGHT'VE BEEN A FAMOUS COACH BY NOW.
IT'S STILL NOT TOO LATE TO START.
ALL RIGHT! BREAK'S OVER!
FWEET
THAT OLD MAN HAS A LOT OF LIFE LEFT IN HIM.
QUIT DAWDLING!
THAT'S FOR SURE...
FWEET
FWEET
ARE YOU ALL RIGHT, AOBA?

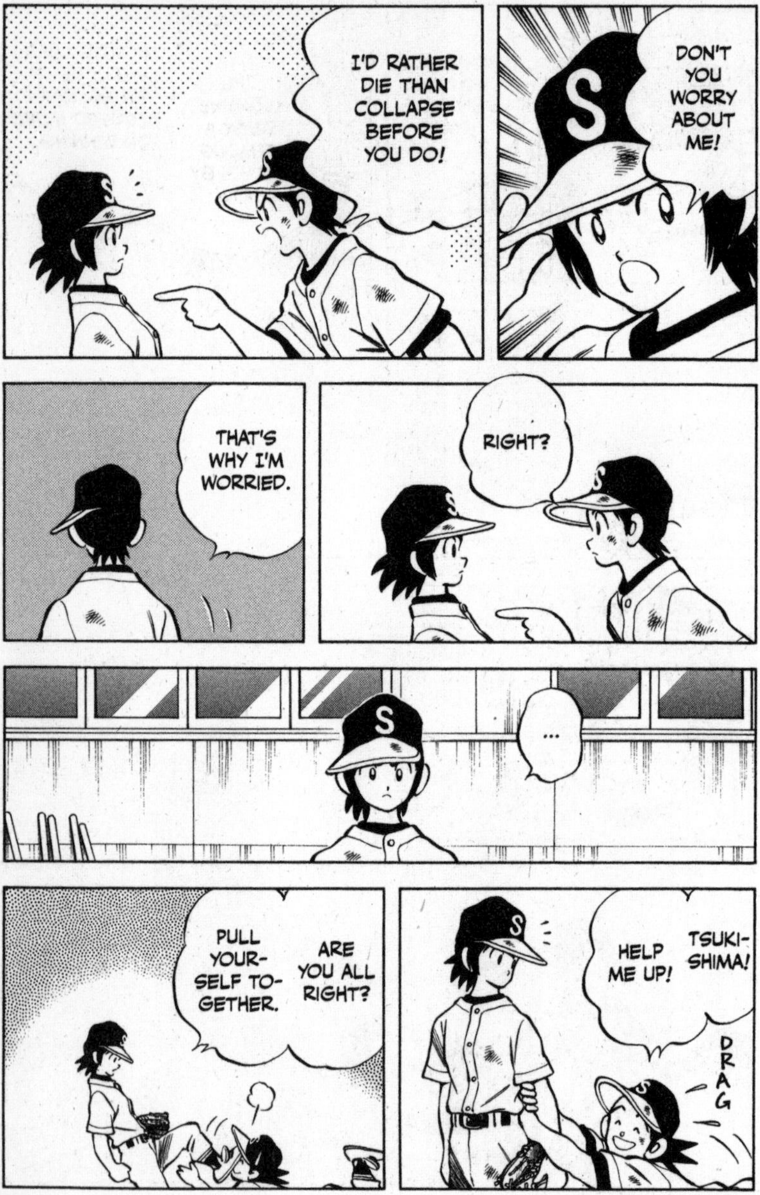
DON'T YOU WORRY ABOUT ME!
I'D RATHER DIE THAN COLLAPSE BEFORE YOU DO!
RIGHT?
THAT'S WHY I'M WORRIED.
...
TSUKI-SHIMA!
HELP ME UP!
DRAG
ARE YOU ALL RIGHT?
PULL YOUR-SELF TO-GETHER.

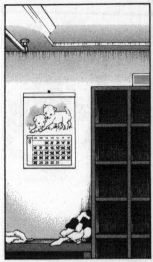

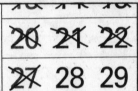

20 21 22

27 28 29

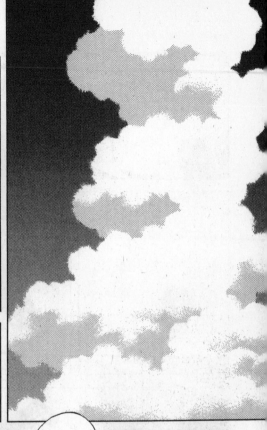

YOU WON'T PLAY IN TOMORROW'S GAME?!

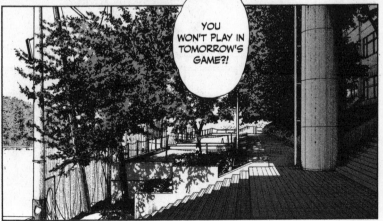

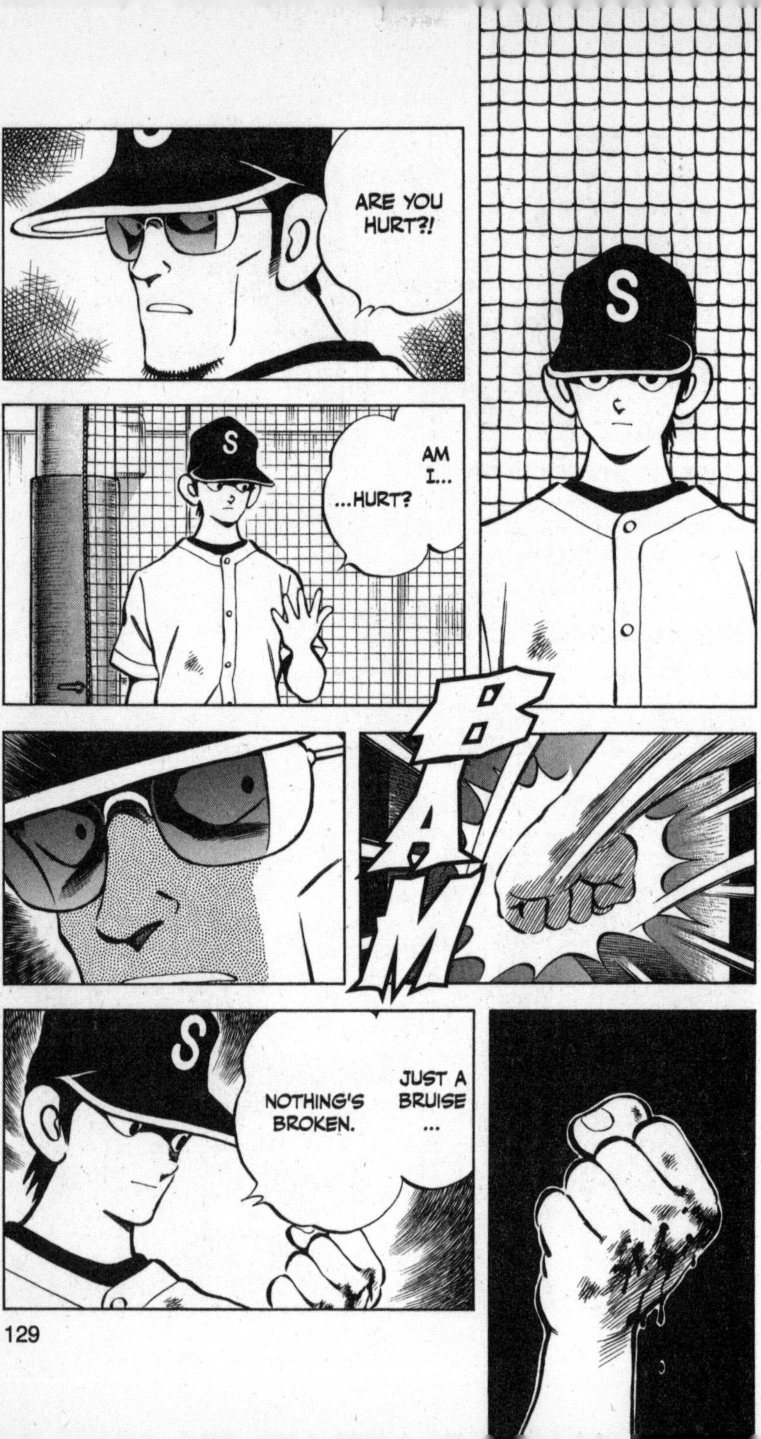
ARE YOU HURT?!
AM I... ...HURT?
BAM
JUST A BRUISE ...
NOTHING'S BROKEN.

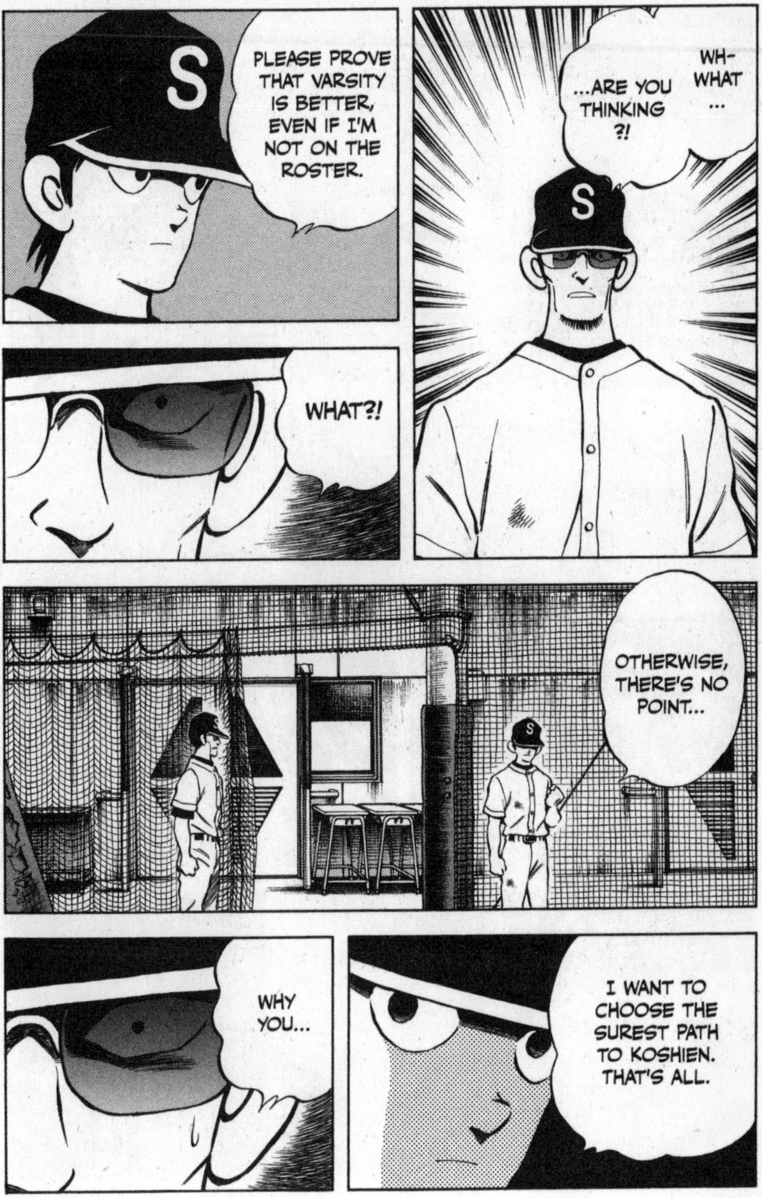
WH- WHAT ...
...ARE YOU THINKING ?!
PLEASE PROVE THAT VARSITY IS BETTER, EVEN IF I'M NOT ON THE ROSTER.
WHAT?!
OTHERWISE, THERE'S NO POINT...
I WANT TO CHOOSE THE SUREST PATH TO KOSHIEN. THAT'S ALL.
WHY YOU...

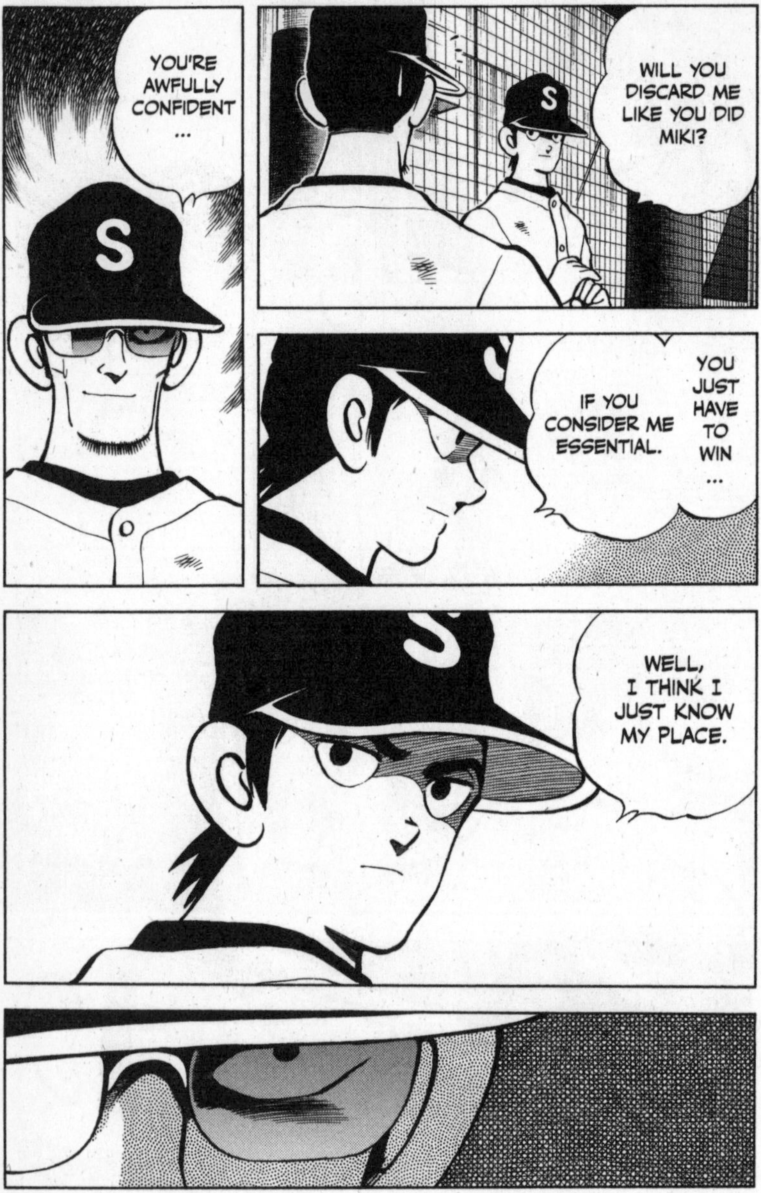
WILL YOU DISCARD ME LIKE YOU DID MIKI?
YOU JUST HAVE TO WIN ...
IF YOU CONSIDER ME ESSENTIAL.
YOU'RE AWFULLY CONFIDENT ...
WELL, I THINK I JUST KNOW MY PLACE.

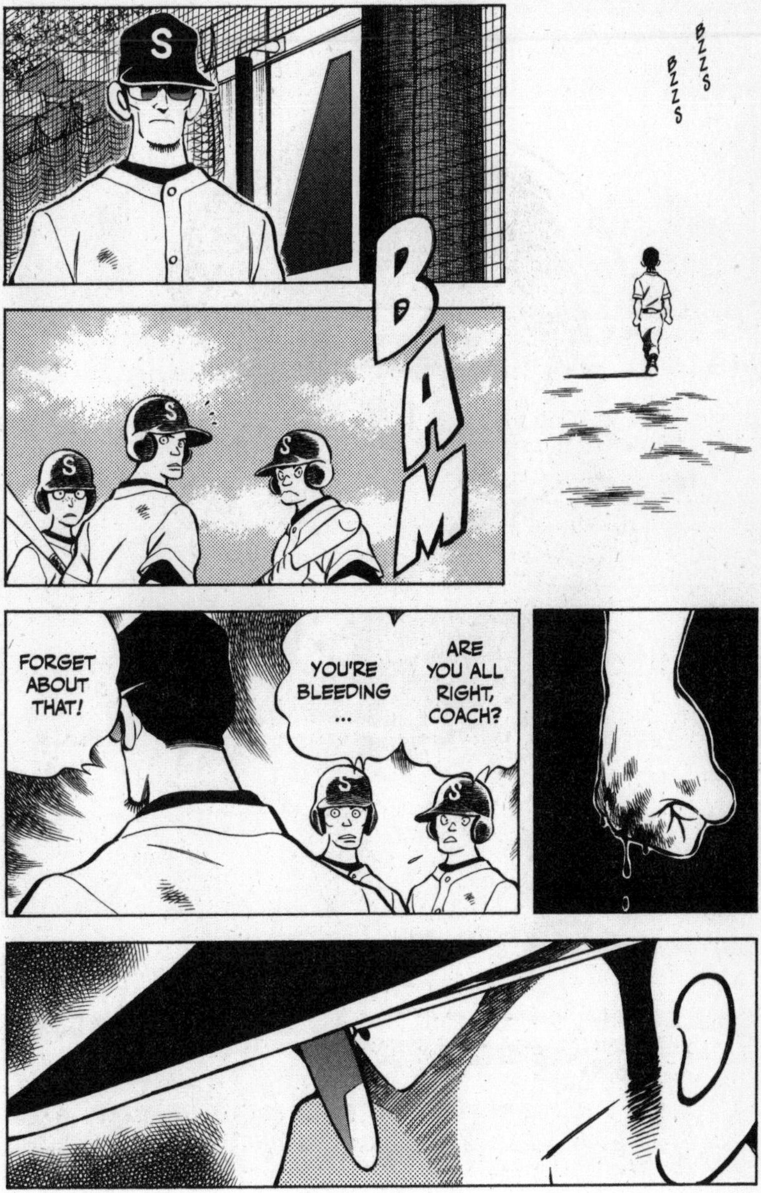
BZZS
BZZS
BAM
ARE YOU ALL RIGHT, COACH?
YOU'RE BLEEDING ...
FORGET ABOUT THAT!

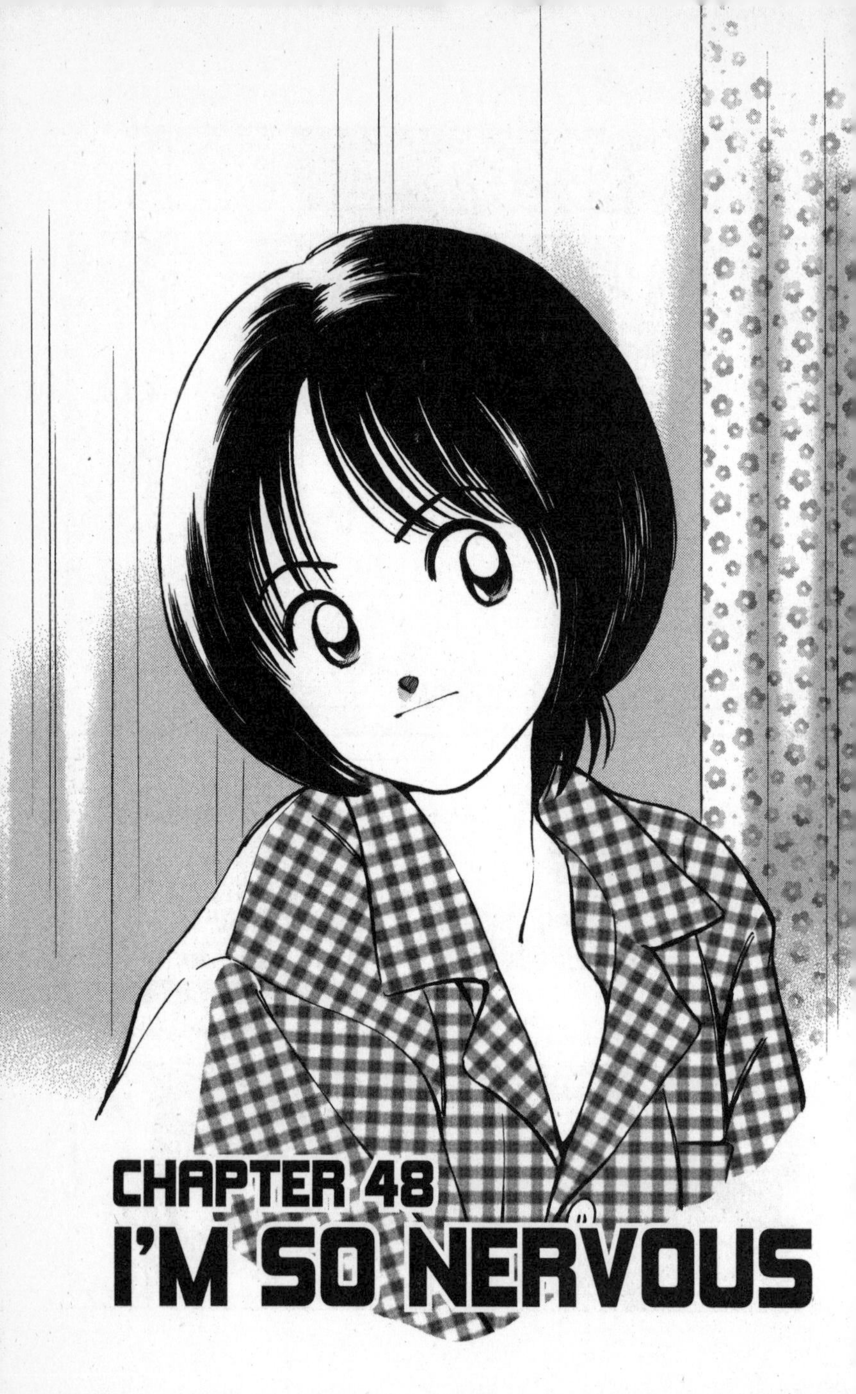

CHAPTER 48
I'M SO NERVOUS

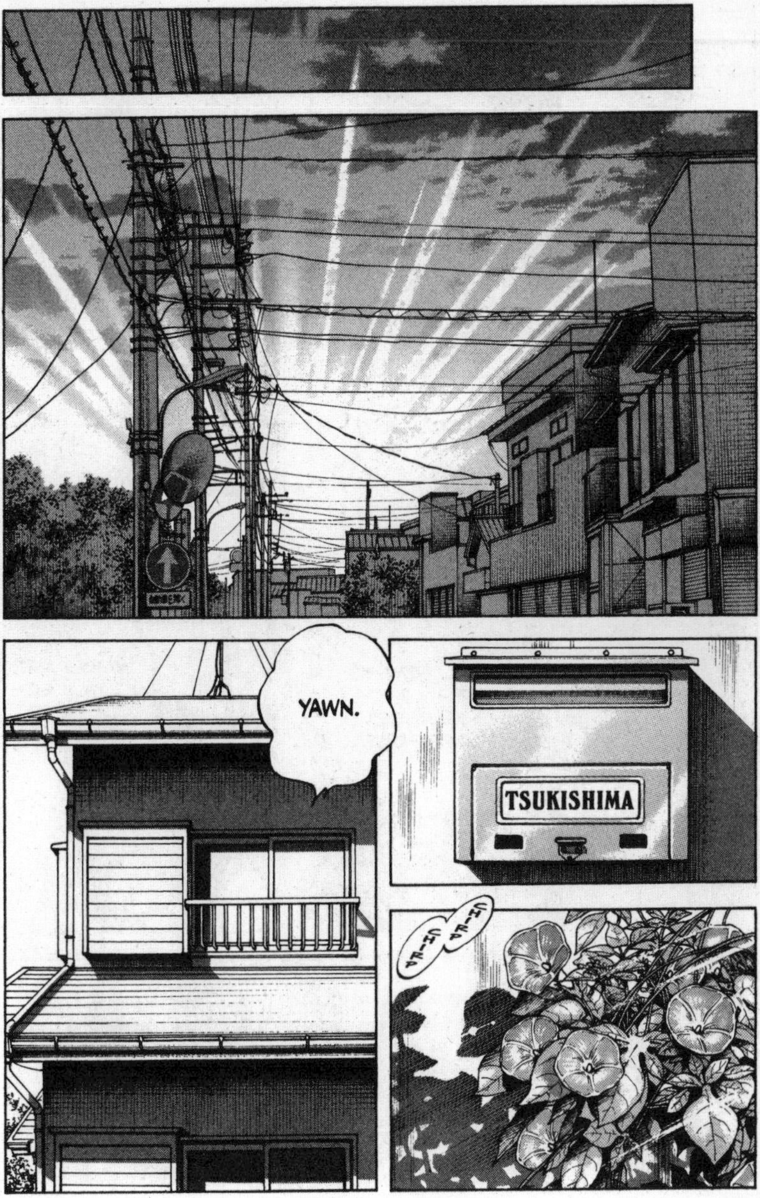
TSUKISHIMA
CHIRP
CHIRP
YAWN.

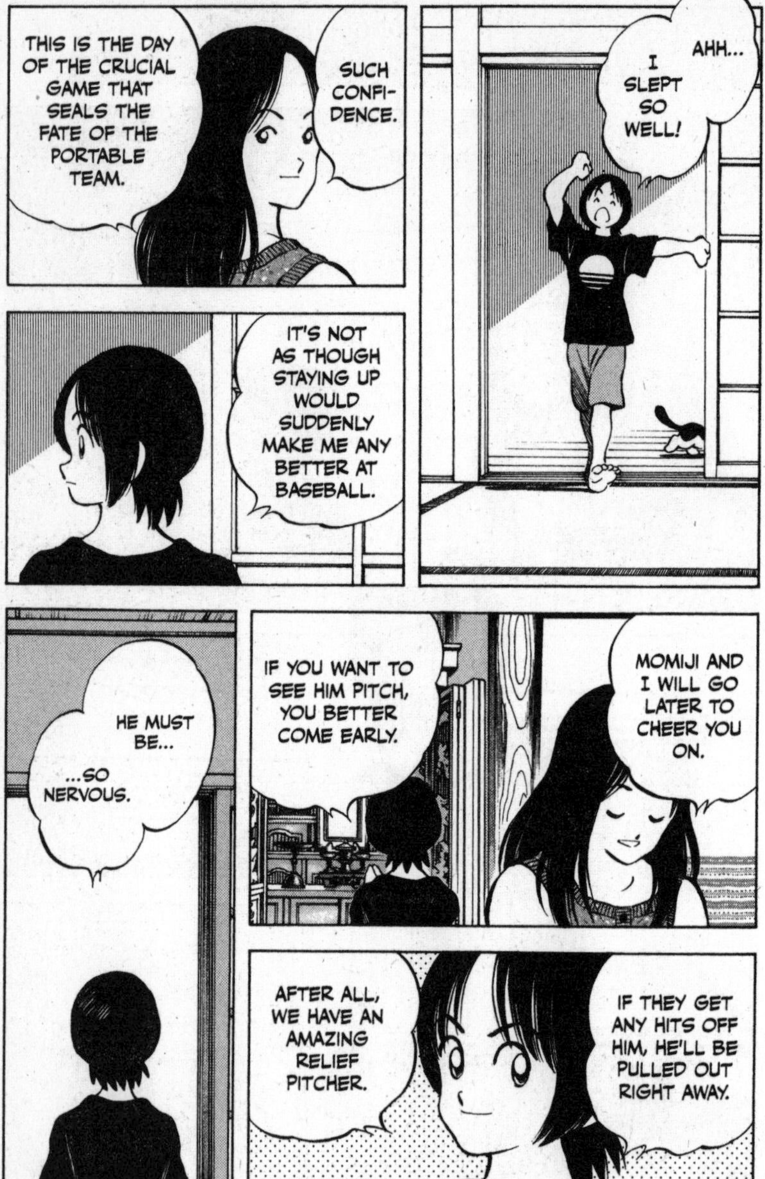
AHH... I SLEPT SO WELL!
SUCH CONFIDENCE.
THIS IS THE DAY OF THE CRUCIAL GAME THAT SEALS THE FATE OF THE PORTABLE TEAM.
IT'S NOT AS THOUGH STAYING UP WOULD SUDDENLY MAKE ME ANY BETTER AT BASEBALL.
MOMIJI AND I WILL GO LATER TO CHEER YOU ON.
IF YOU WANT TO SEE HIM PITCH, YOU BETTER COME EARLY.
IF THEY GET ANY HITS OFF HIM, HE'LL BE PULLED OUT RIGHT AWAY.
AFTER ALL, WE HAVE AN AMAZING RELIEF PITCHER.
HE MUST BE...
...SO NERVOUS.

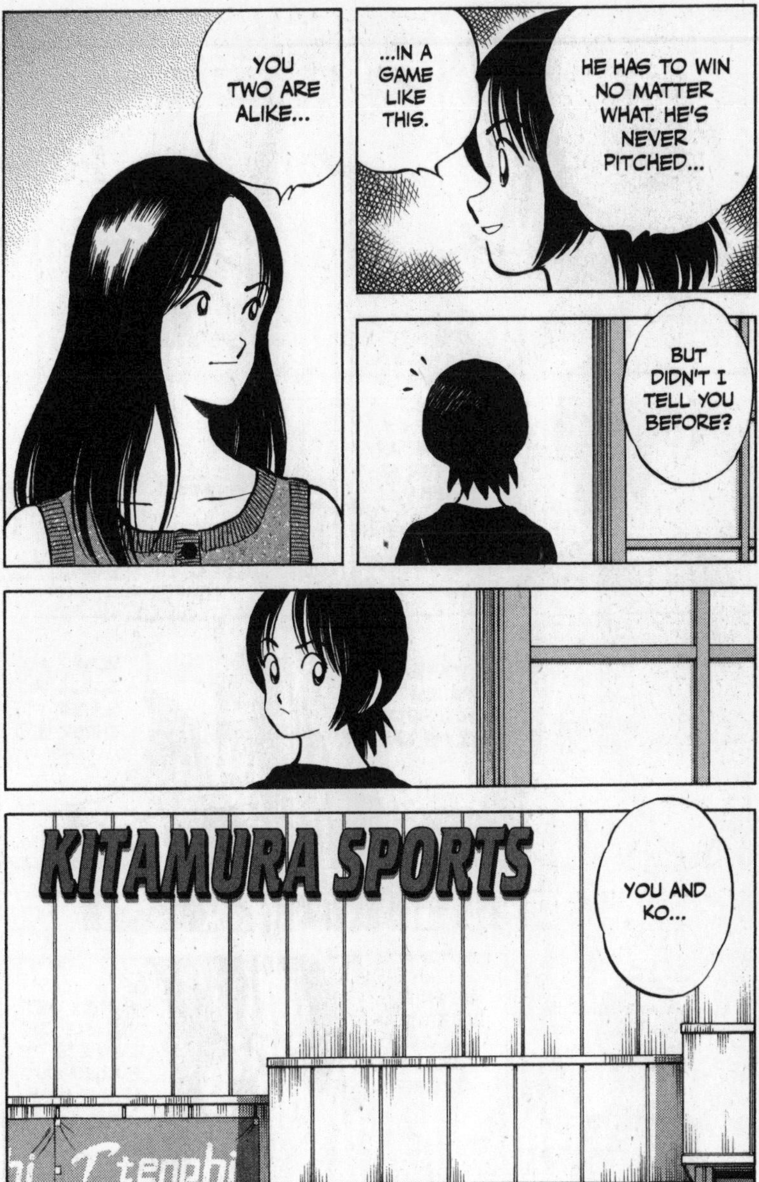
HE HAS TO WIN NO MATTER WHAT. HE'S NEVER PITCHED...
...IN A GAME LIKE THIS.
BUT DIDN'T I TELL YOU BEFORE?
YOU TWO ARE ALIKE...
YOU AND KO...
KITAMURA SPORTS
hi tenphi

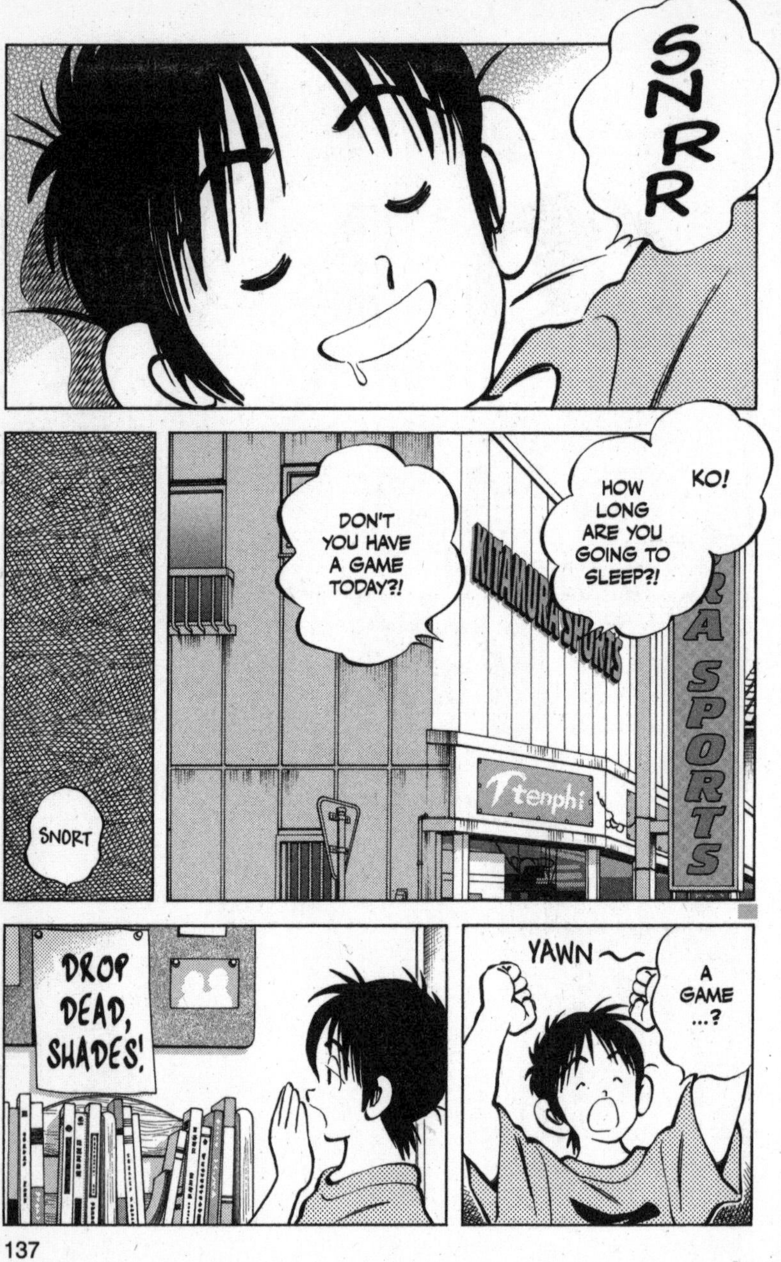
SNRR
KO!
HOW LONG ARE YOU GOING TO SLEEP?!
DON'T YOU HAVE A GAME TODAY?!
KITAMURA SPORTS
RA SPORTS
tenphi
SNORT
YAWN~
A GAME ...?
DROP DEAD, SHADES!

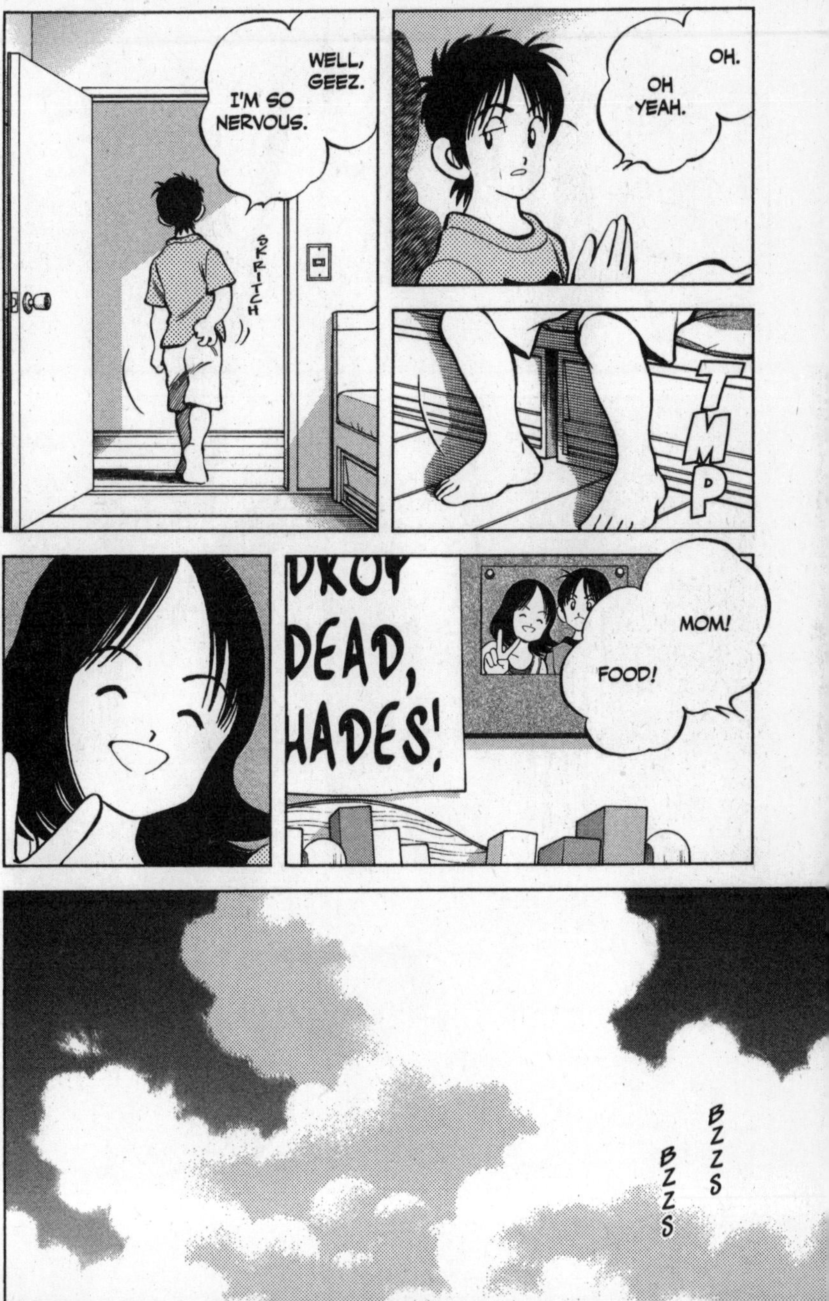
OH.
OH YEAH.
TMP
WELL, GEEZ.
I'M SO NERVOUS.
SKRITCH
MOM!
FOOD!
DEAD,
HADES!
BZZS
BZZS

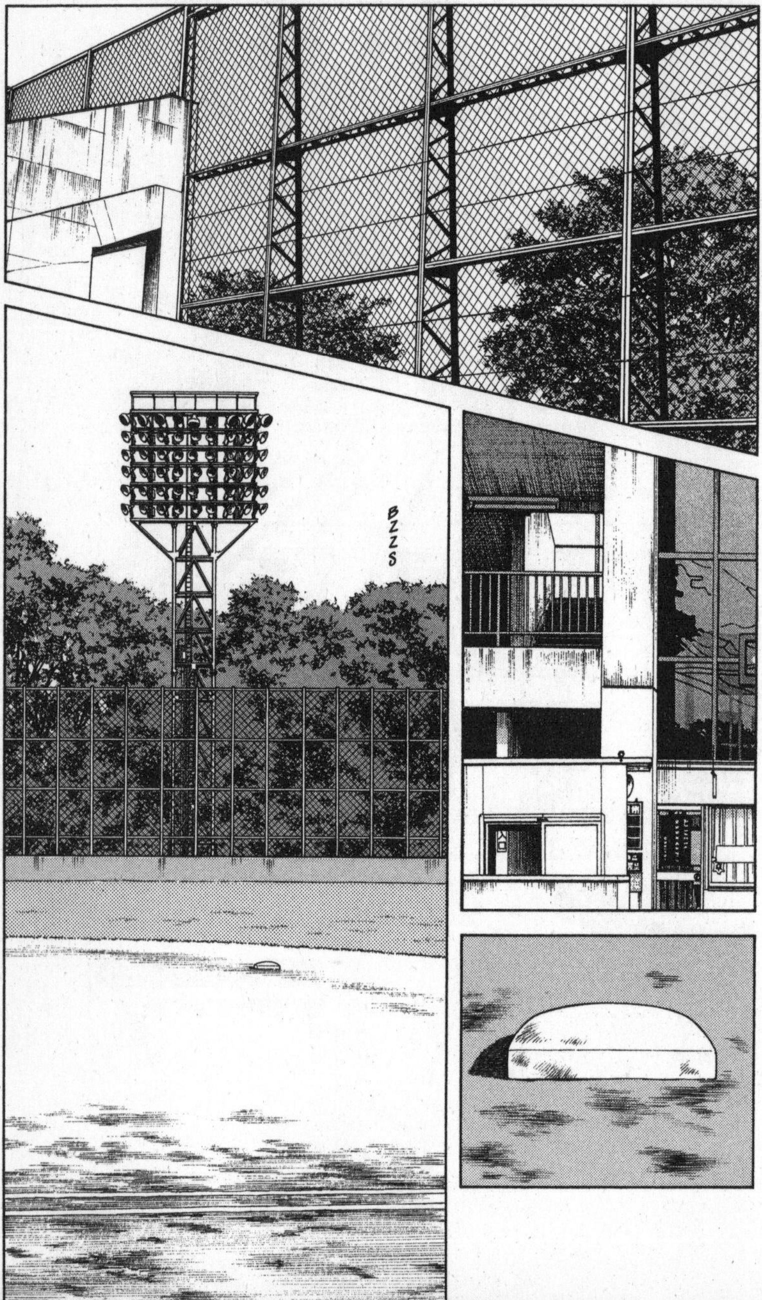
BZZS

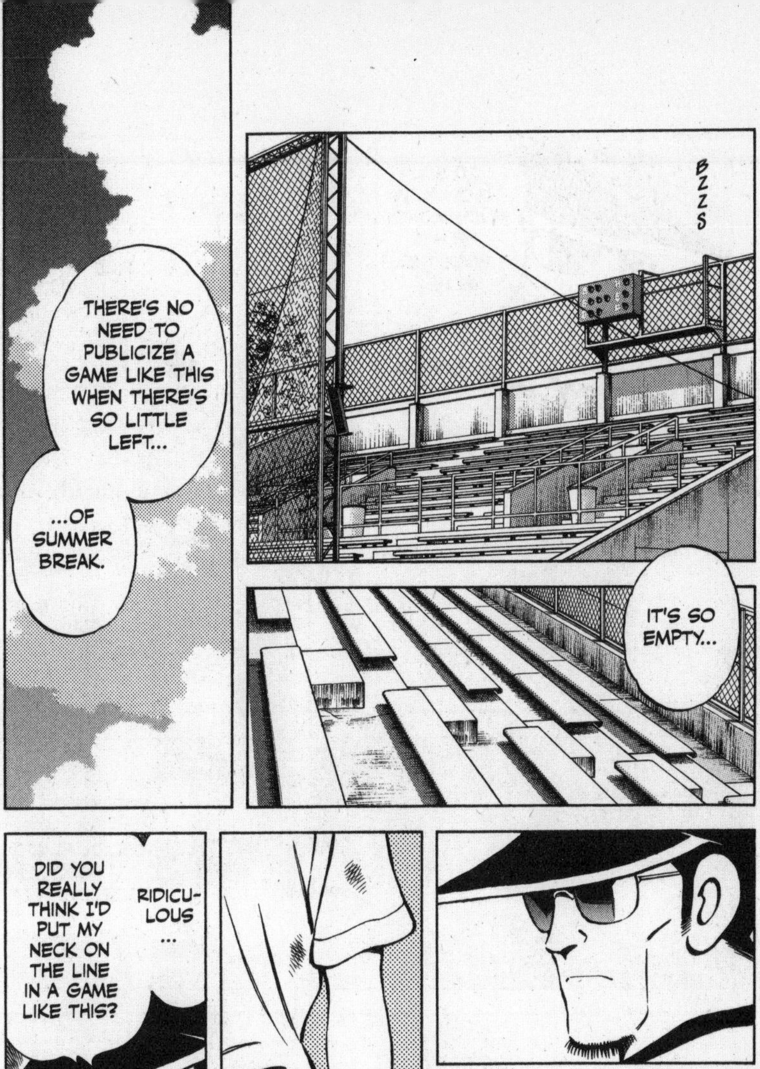
BZZS
IT'S SO EMPTY...
THERE'S NO NEED TO PUBLICIZE A GAME LIKE THIS WHEN THERE'S SO LITTLE LEFT...
...OF SUMMER BREAK.
RIDICU-LOUS...
DID YOU REALLY THINK I'D PUT MY NECK ON THE LINE IN A GAME LIKE THIS?

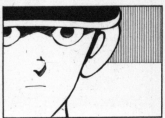

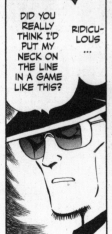

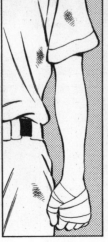

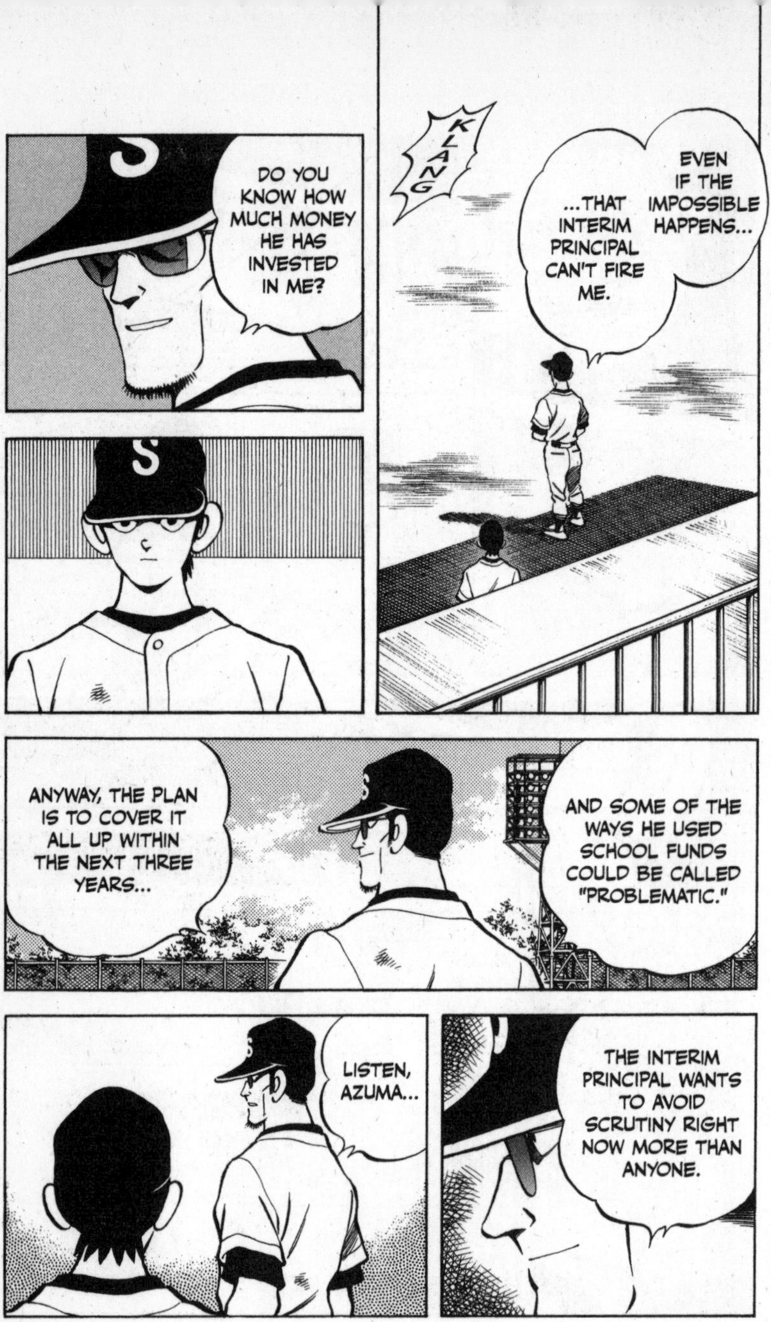
KLANG
EVEN IF THE IMPOSSIBLE HAPPENS...
...THAT INTERIM PRINCIPAL CAN'T FIRE ME.
DO YOU KNOW HOW MUCH MONEY HE HAS INVESTED IN ME?
AND SOME OF THE WAYS HE USED SCHOOL FUNDS COULD BE CALLED "PROBLEMATIC."
ANYWAY, THE PLAN IS TO COVER IT ALL UP WITHIN THE NEXT THREE YEARS...
THE INTERIM PRINCIPAL WANTS TO AVOID SCRUTINY RIGHT NOW MORE THAN ANYONE.
LISTEN, AZUMA...

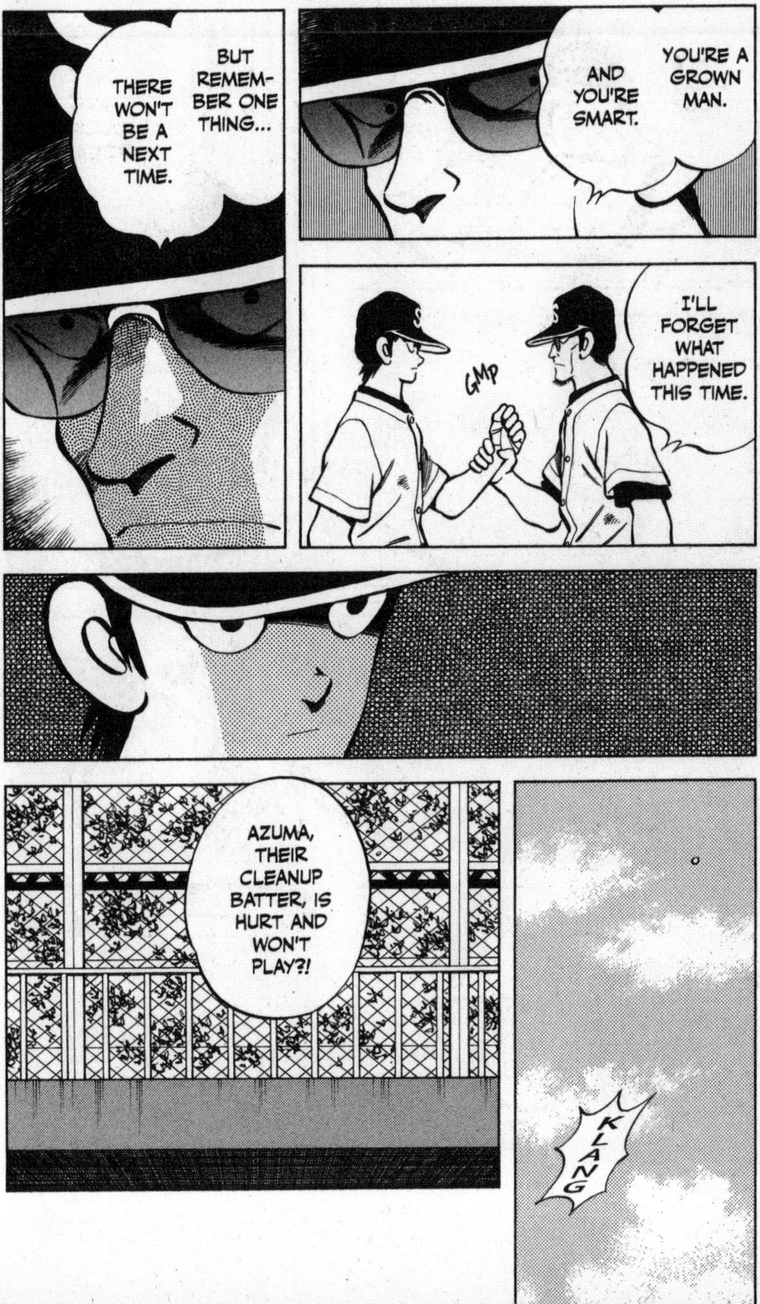

YOU'RE A GROWN MAN.
AND YOU'RE SMART.
I'LL FORGET WHAT HAPPENED THIS TIME.
GMP
BUT REMEMBER ONE THING...
THERE WON'T BE A NEXT TIME.
KLANG
AZUMA, THEIR CLEANUP BATTER, IS HURT AND WON'T PLAY?!

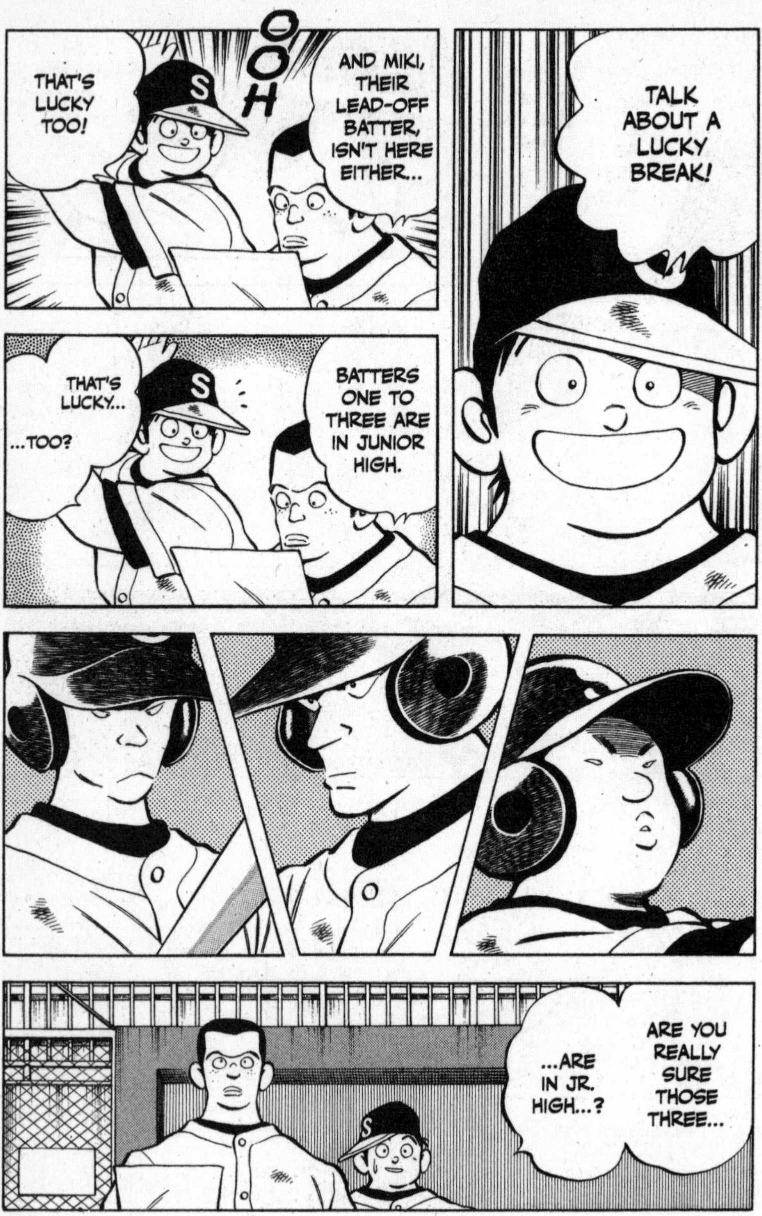
TALK ABOUT A LUCKY BREAK!
AND MIKI, THEIR LEAD-OFF BATTER, ISN'T HERE EITHER...
OOH
THAT'S LUCKY TOO!
BATTERS ONE TO THREE ARE IN JUNIOR HIGH.
THAT'S LUCKY...
...TOO?
ARE YOU REALLY SURE THOSE THREE...
...ARE IN JR. HIGH...?

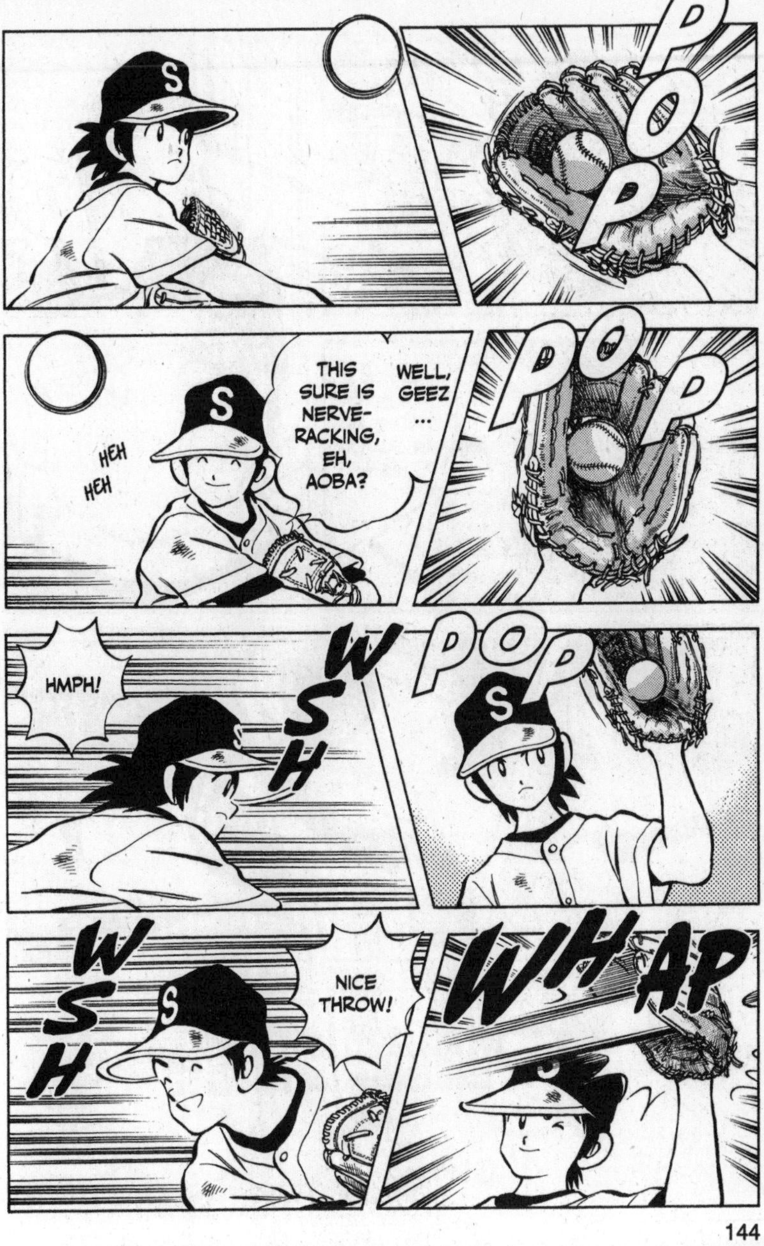
POP
POP
WELL, GEEZ ...
THIS SURE IS NERVE-RACKING, EH, AOBA?
HEH HEH
POP
WSH
HMPH!
WHAP
NICE THROW!
WSH

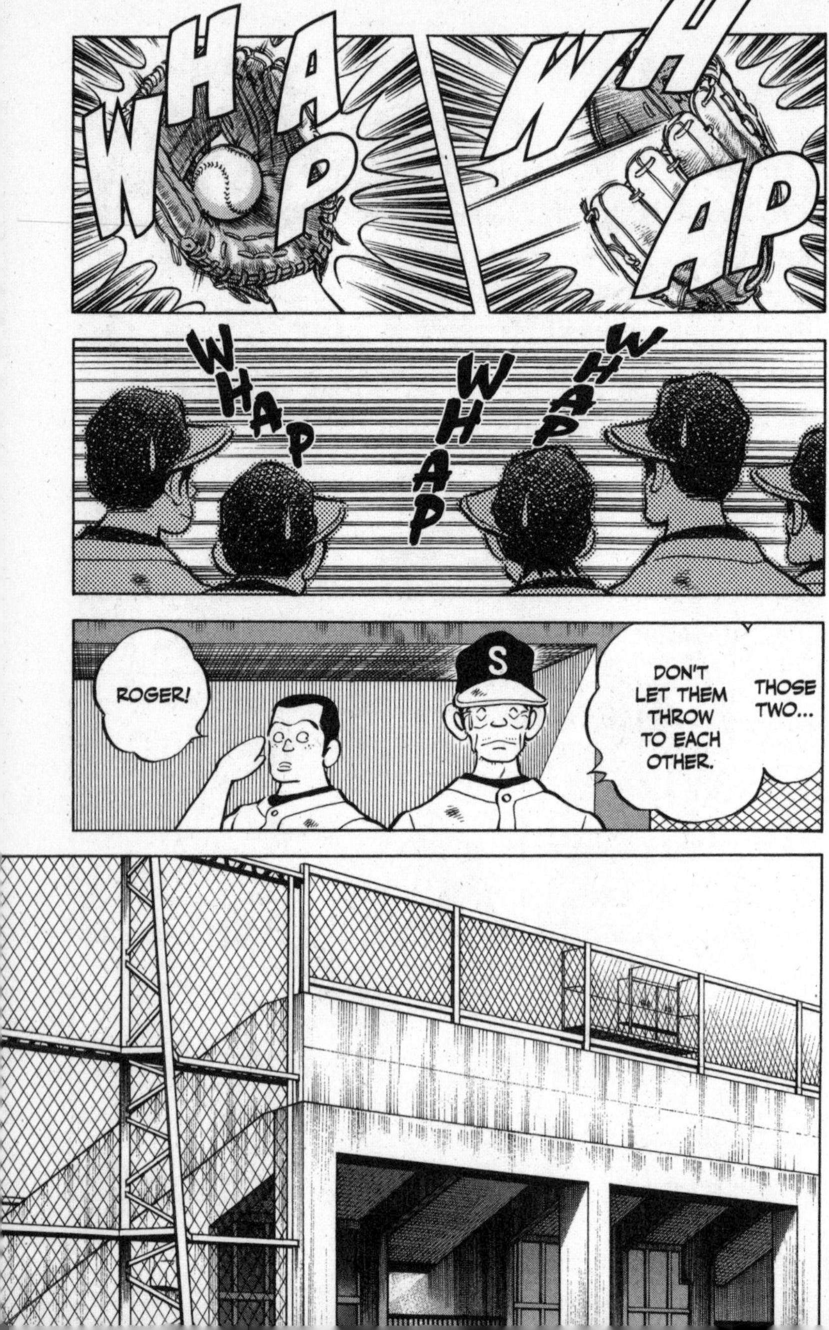
WHAP
WHAP
WHAP
WHAP
WHAP
THOSE TWO... DON'T LET THEM THROW TO EACH OTHER.
ROGER!

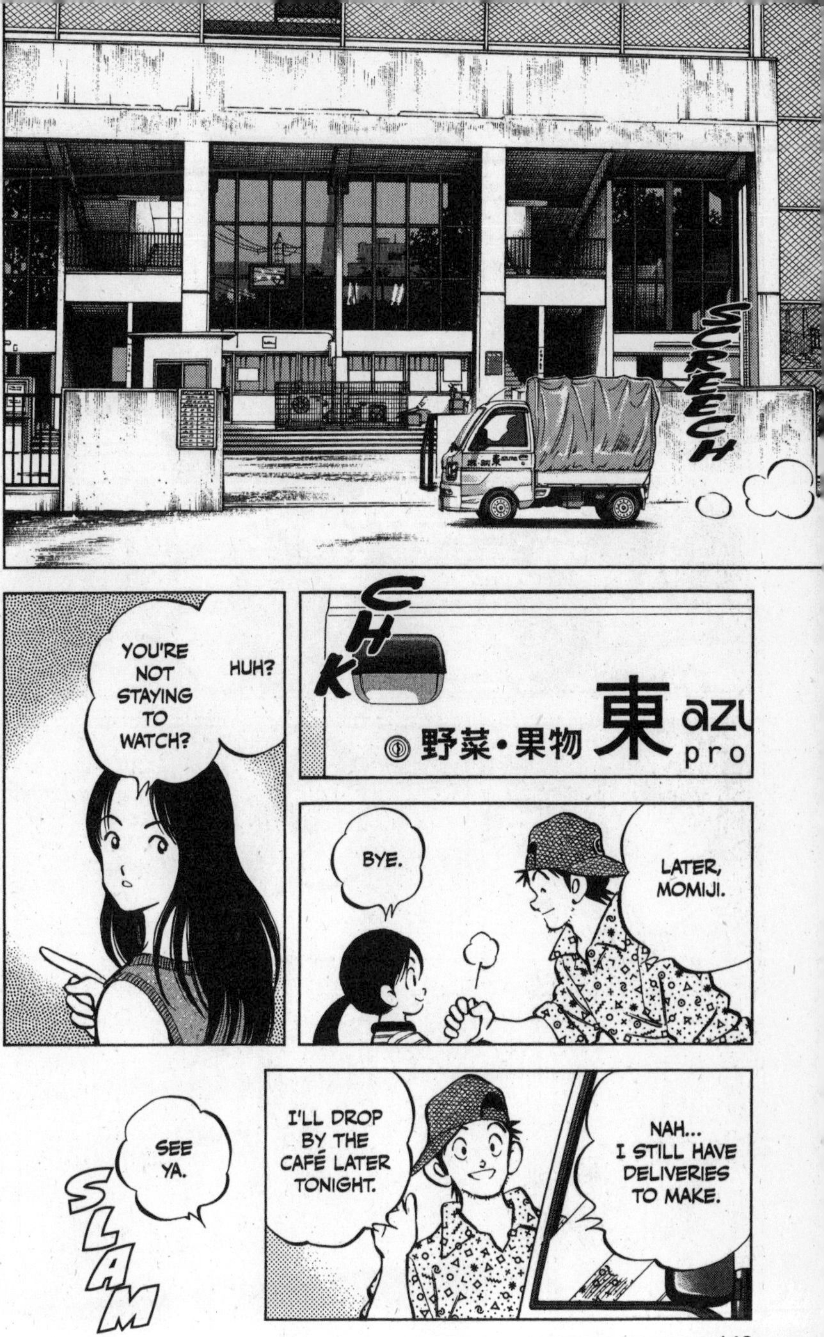
SCREECH
CHK
野菜・果物 東 azu
pro
LATER, MOMIJI.
BYE.
YOU'RE NOT STAYING TO WATCH?
HUH?
NAH... I STILL HAVE DELIVERIES TO MAKE.
I'LL DROP BY THE CAFÉ LATER TONIGHT.
SEE YA.
SLAM

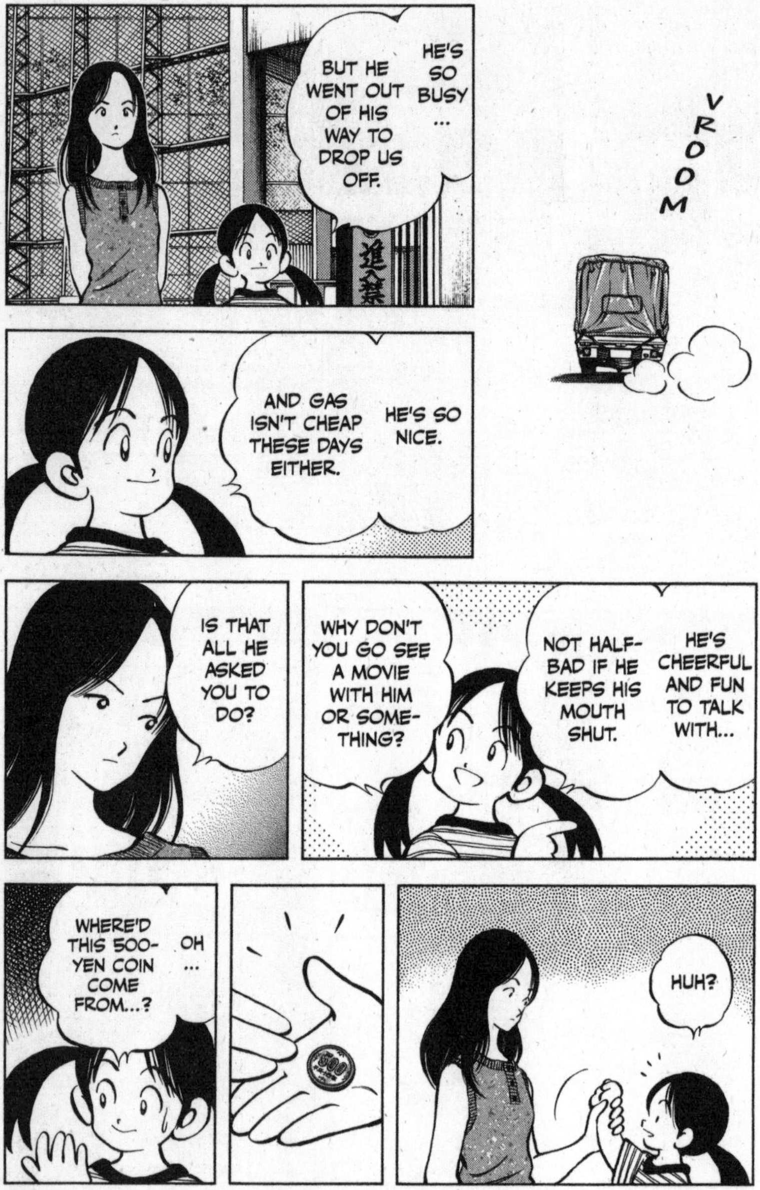
VROOM
HE'S SO BUSY...
BUT HE WENT OUT OF HIS WAY TO DROP US OFF.
HE'S SO NICE.
AND GAS ISN'T CHEAP THESE DAYS EITHER.
HE'S CHEERFUL AND FUN TO TALK WITH...
NOT HALF-BAD IF HE KEEPS HIS MOUTH SHUT.
WHY DON'T YOU GO SEE A MOVIE WITH HIM OR SOME-THING?
IS THAT ALL HE ASKED YOU TO DO?
HUH?
OH...
WHERE'D THIS 500-YEN COIN COME FROM...?

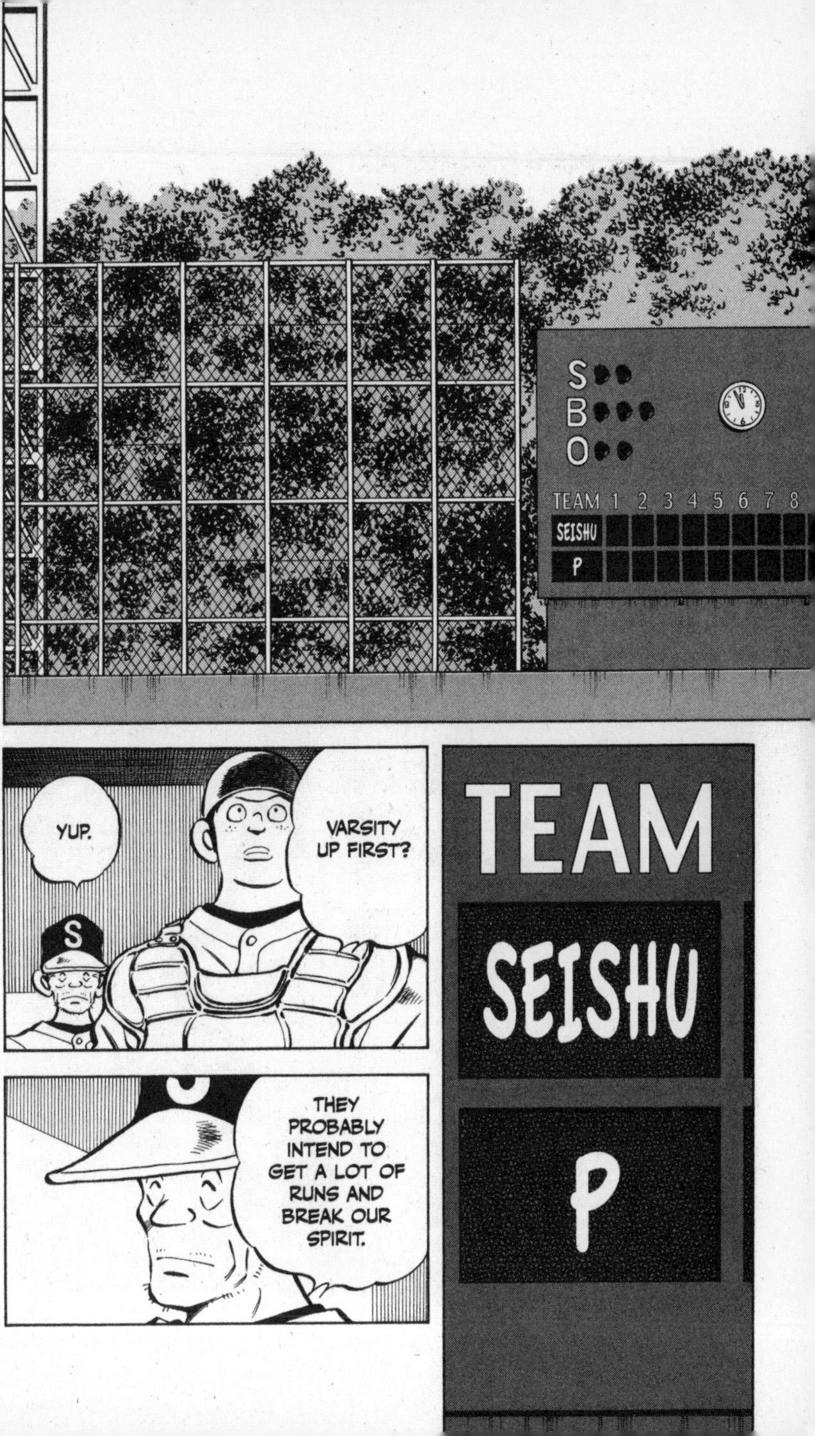
S
B
O
TEAM 1 2 3 4 5 6 7 8
SEISHU
P
TEAM
SEISHU
P
VARSITY UP FIRST?
YUP.
THEY PROBABLY INTEND TO GET A LOT OF RUNS AND BREAK OUR SPIRIT.

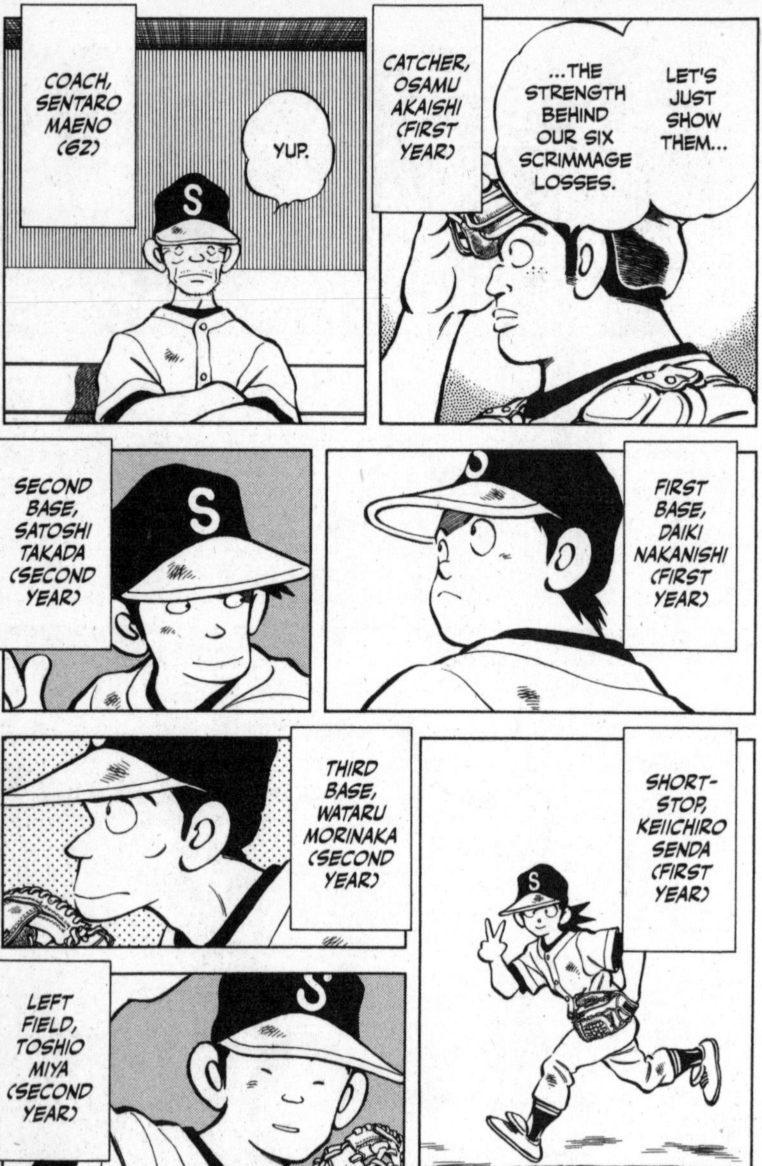
LET'S JUST SHOW THEM...
...THE STRENGTH BEHIND OUR SIX SCRIMMAGE LOSSES.
CATCHER, OSAMU AKAISHI (FIRST YEAR)
YUP.
COACH, SENTARO MAENO (62)
FIRST BASE, DAIKI NAKANISHI (FIRST YEAR)
SECOND BASE, SATOSHI TAKADA (SECOND YEAR)
SHORT-STOP, KEIICHIRO SENDA (FIRST YEAR)
THIRD BASE, WATARU MORINAKA (SECOND YEAR)
LEFT FIELD, TOSHIO MIYA (SECOND YEAR)

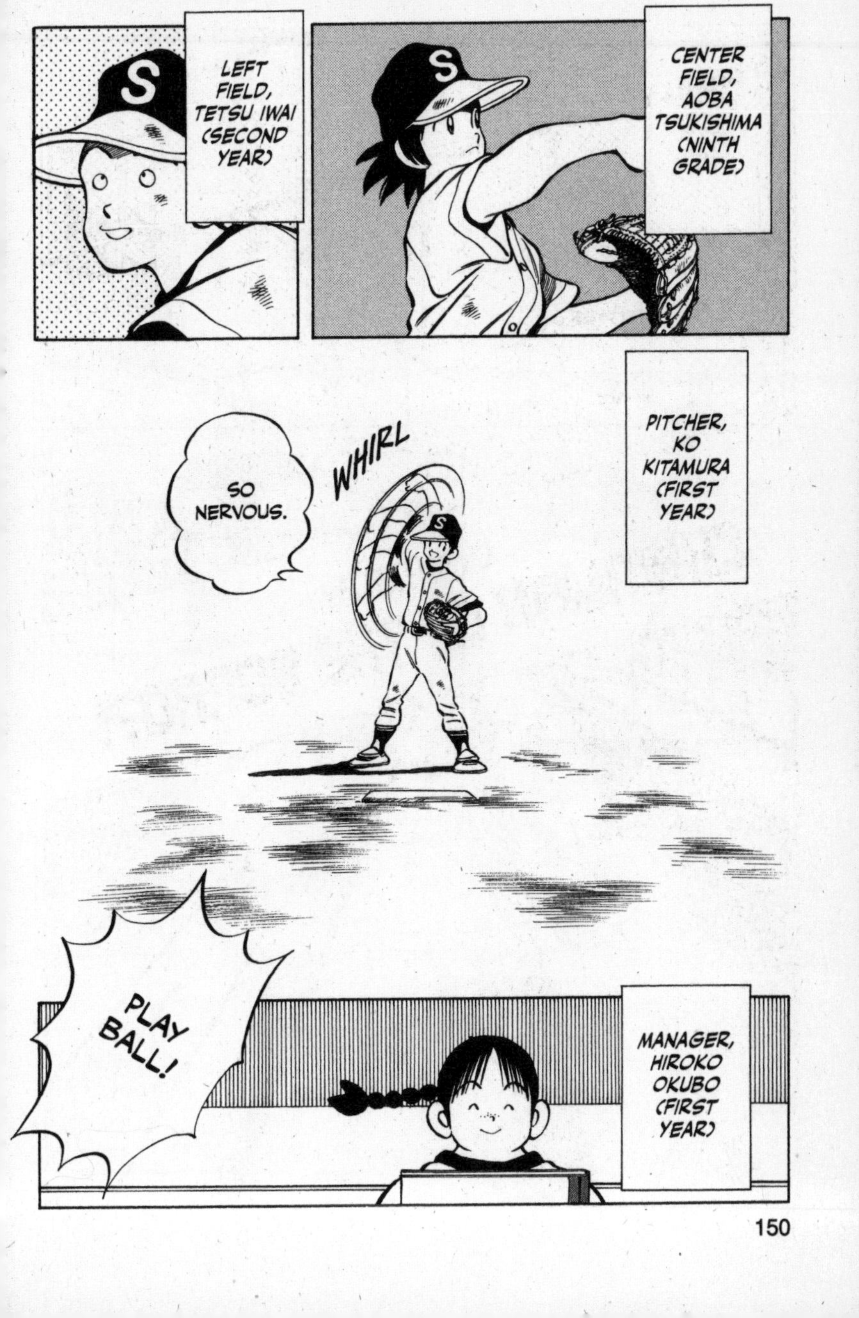
CENTER FIELD, AOBA TSUKISHIMA (NINTH GRADE)
LEFT FIELD, TETSU IWAI (SECOND YEAR)
PITCHER, KO KITAMURA (FIRST YEAR)
WHIRL
SO NERVOUS.
MANAGER, HIROKO OKUBO (FIRST YEAR)
PLAY BALL!

CHAPTER 49
CHAIRMAN OF THE BOARD?!

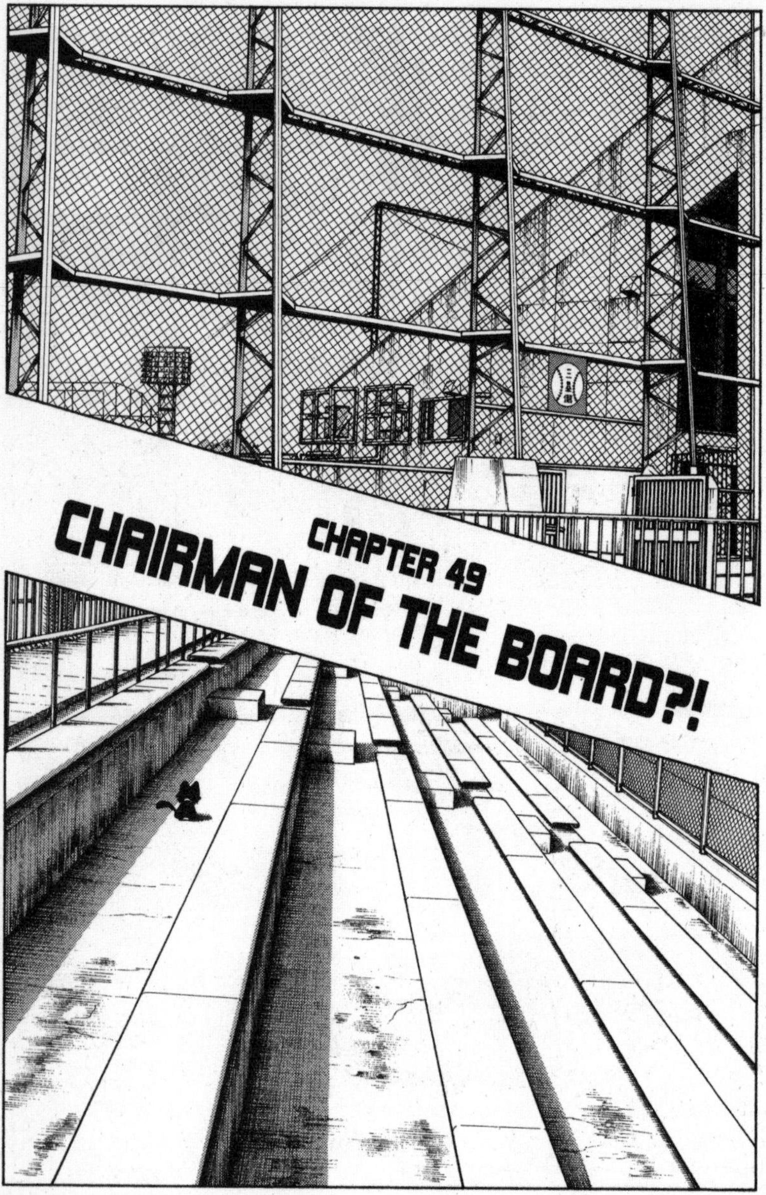

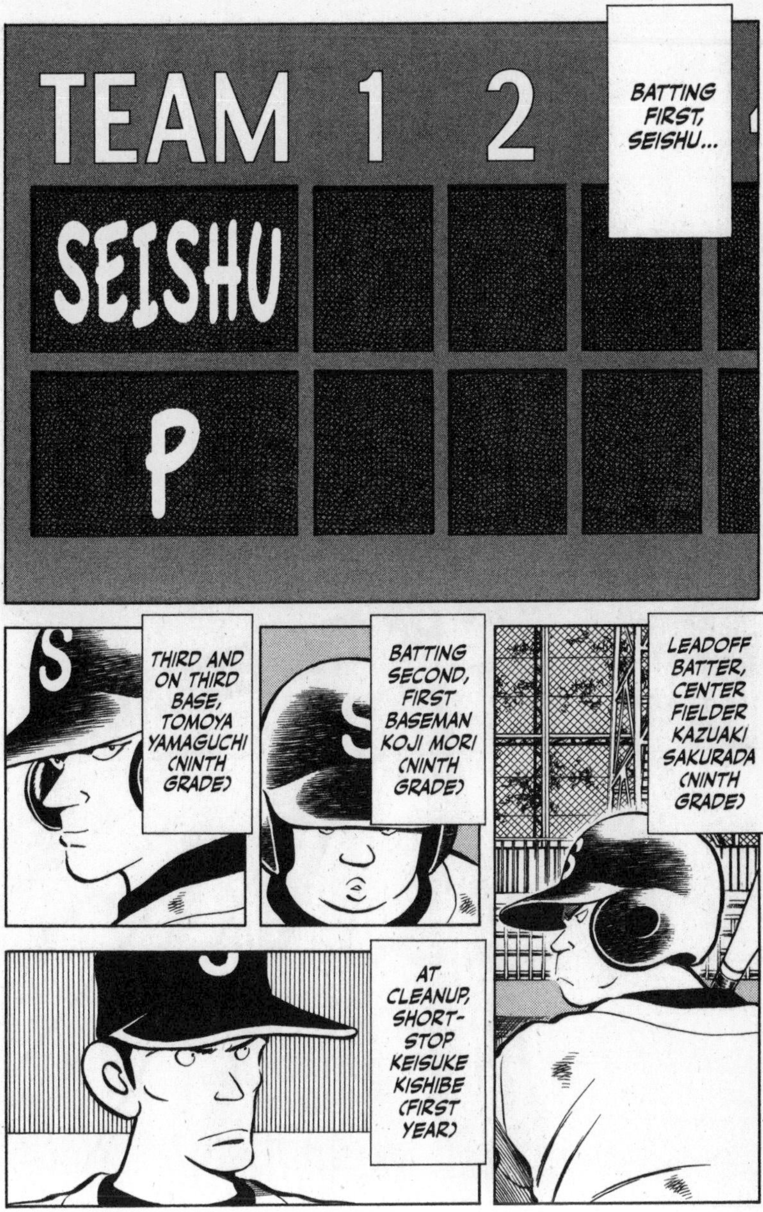
BATTING FIRST, SEISHU...
TEAM 1 2
SEISHU
P
LEADOFF BATTER, CENTER FIELDER KAZUAKI SAKURADA (NINTH GRADE)
BATTING SECOND, FIRST BASEMAN KOJI MORI (NINTH GRADE)
THIRD AND ON THIRD BASE, TOMOYA YAMAGUCHI (NINTH GRADE)
AT CLEANUP, SHORT-STOP KEISUKE KISHIBE (FIRST YEAR)

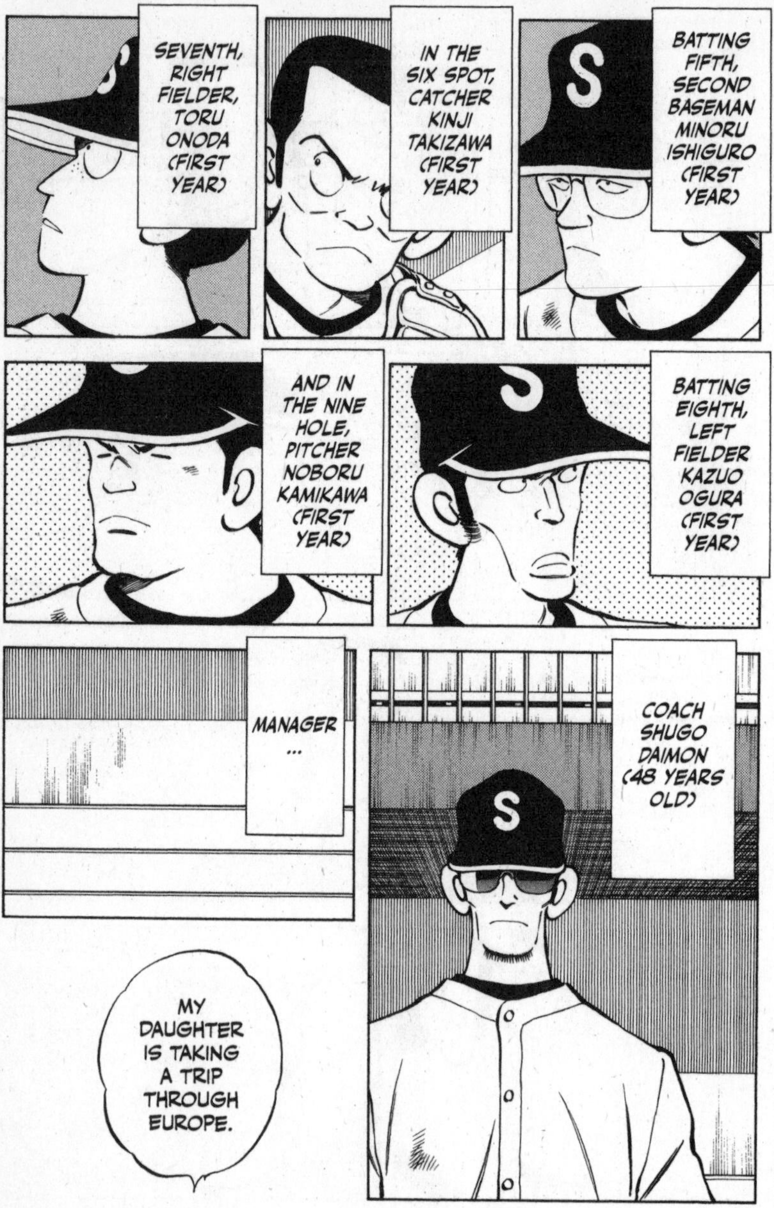
BATTING FIFTH, SECOND BASEMAN MINORU ISHIGURO (FIRST YEAR)
IN THE SIX SPOT, CATCHER KINJI TAKIZAWA (FIRST YEAR)
SEVENTH, RIGHT FIELDER, TORU ONODA (FIRST YEAR)
BATTING EIGHTH, LEFT FIELDER KAZUO OGURA (FIRST YEAR)
AND IN THE NINE HOLE, PITCHER NOBORU KAMIKAWA (FIRST YEAR)
COACH SHUGO DAIMON (48 YEARS OLD)
MANAGER ...
MY DAUGHTER IS TAKING A TRIP THROUGH EUROPE.

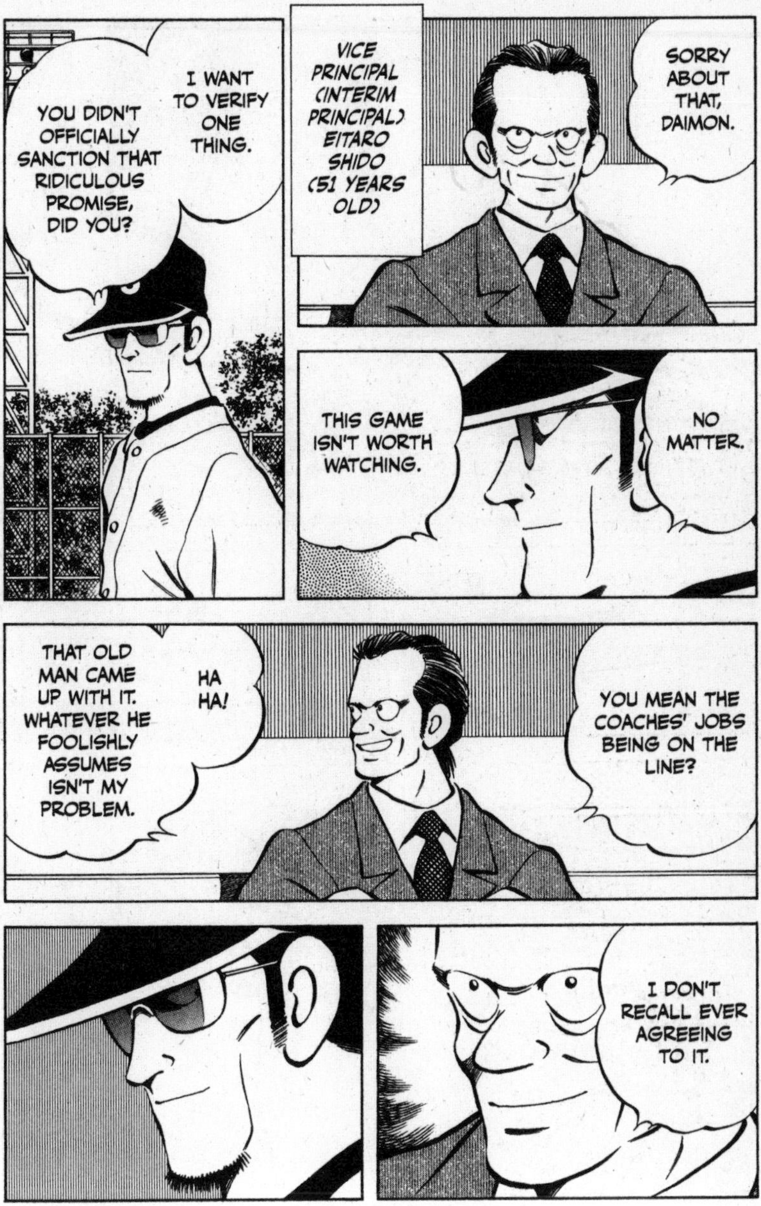
SORRY ABOUT THAT, DAIMON.
VICE PRINCIPAL (INTERIM PRINCIPAL) EITARO SHIDO (51 YEARS OLD)
NO MATTER.
THIS GAME ISN'T WORTH WATCHING.
I WANT TO VERIFY ONE THING.
YOU DIDN'T OFFICIALLY SANCTION THAT RIDICULOUS PROMISE, DID YOU?
YOU MEAN THE COACHES' JOBS BEING ON THE LINE?
HA HA!
THAT OLD MAN CAME UP WITH IT. WHATEVER HE FOOLISHLY ASSUMES ISN'T MY PROBLEM.
I DON'T RECALL EVER AGREEING TO IT.

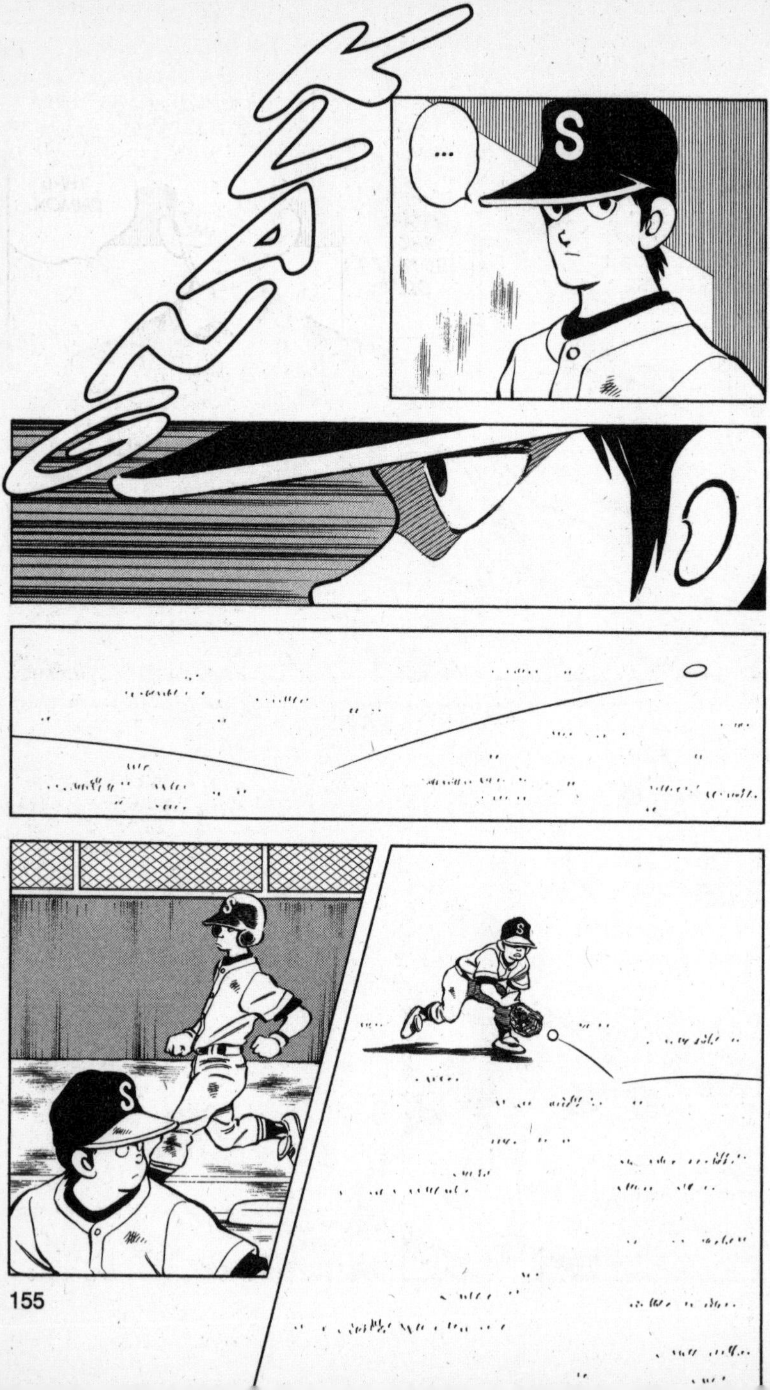
...
KLANG

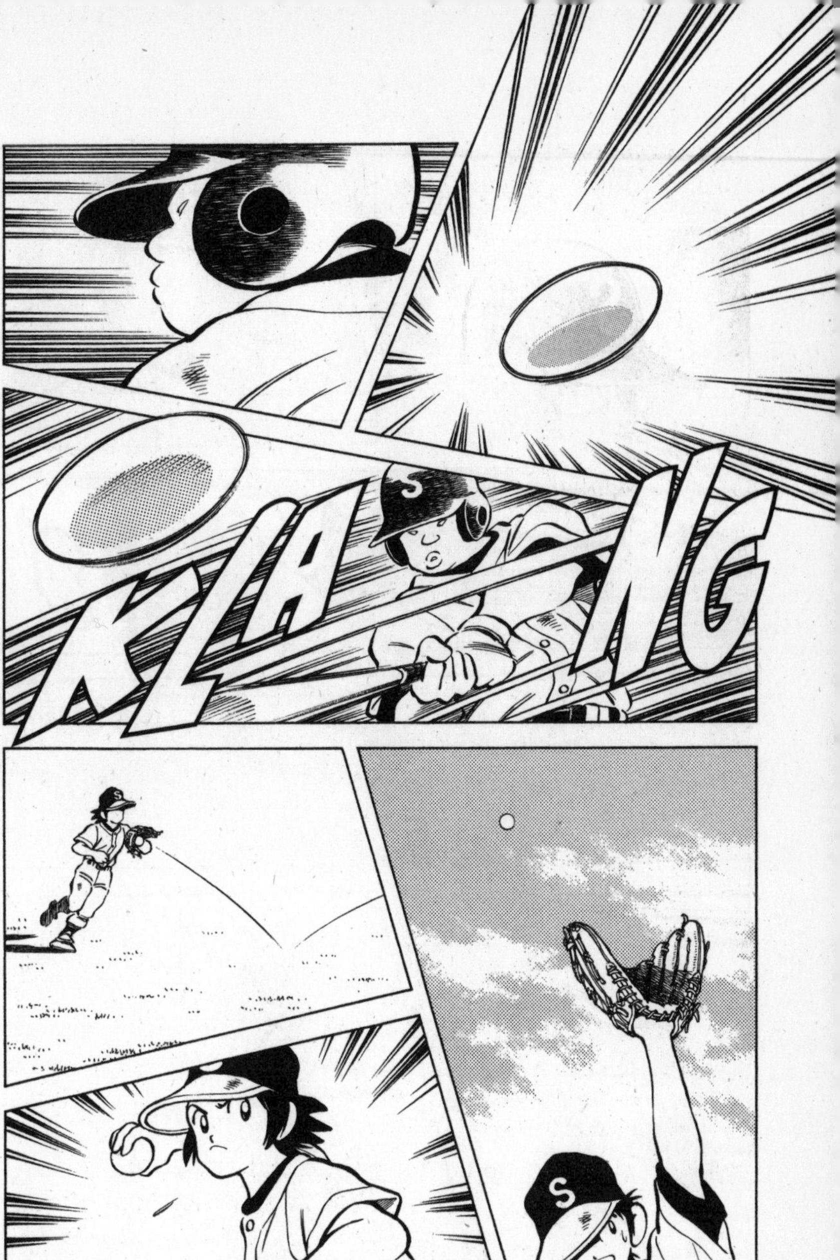
KLANG

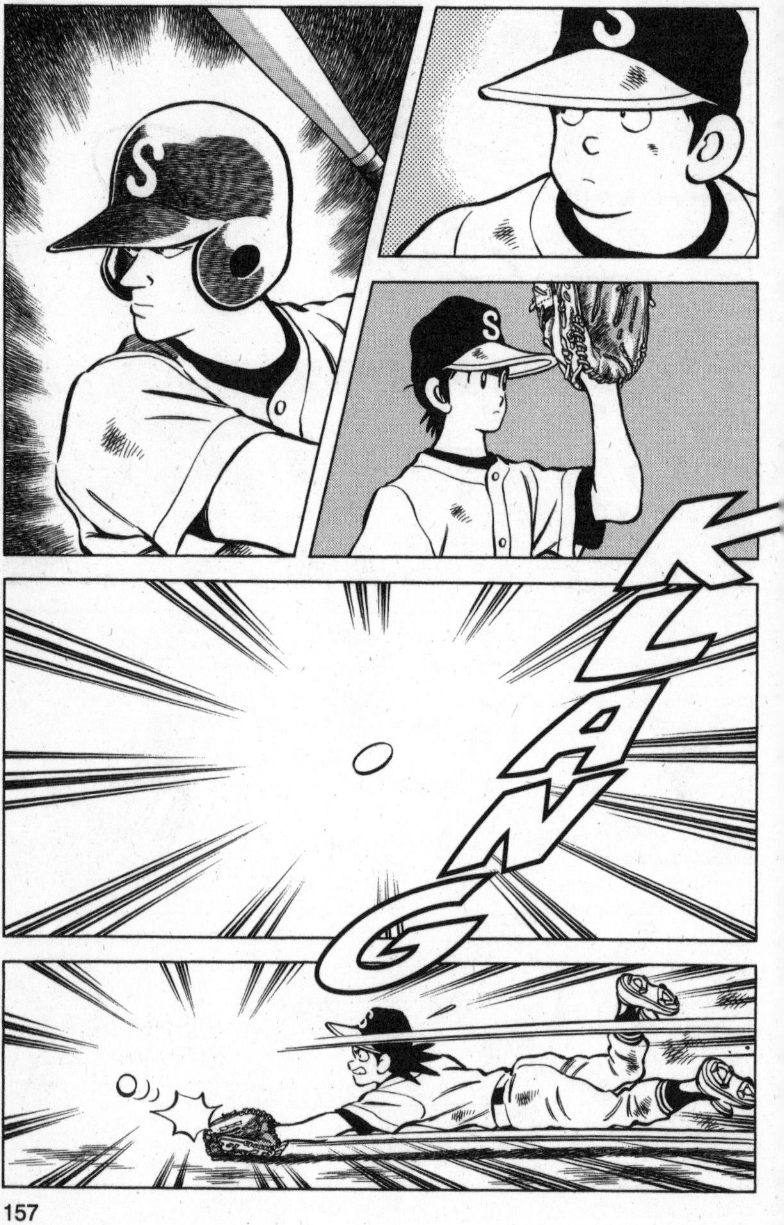
KLANG

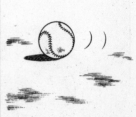

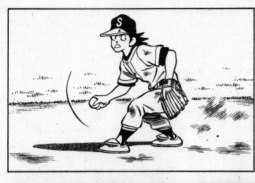

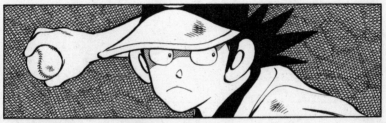

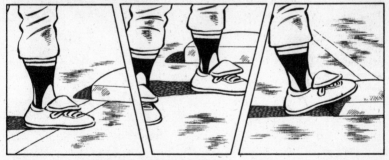

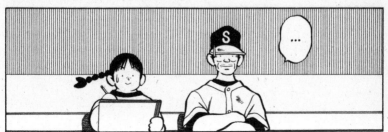

…

158

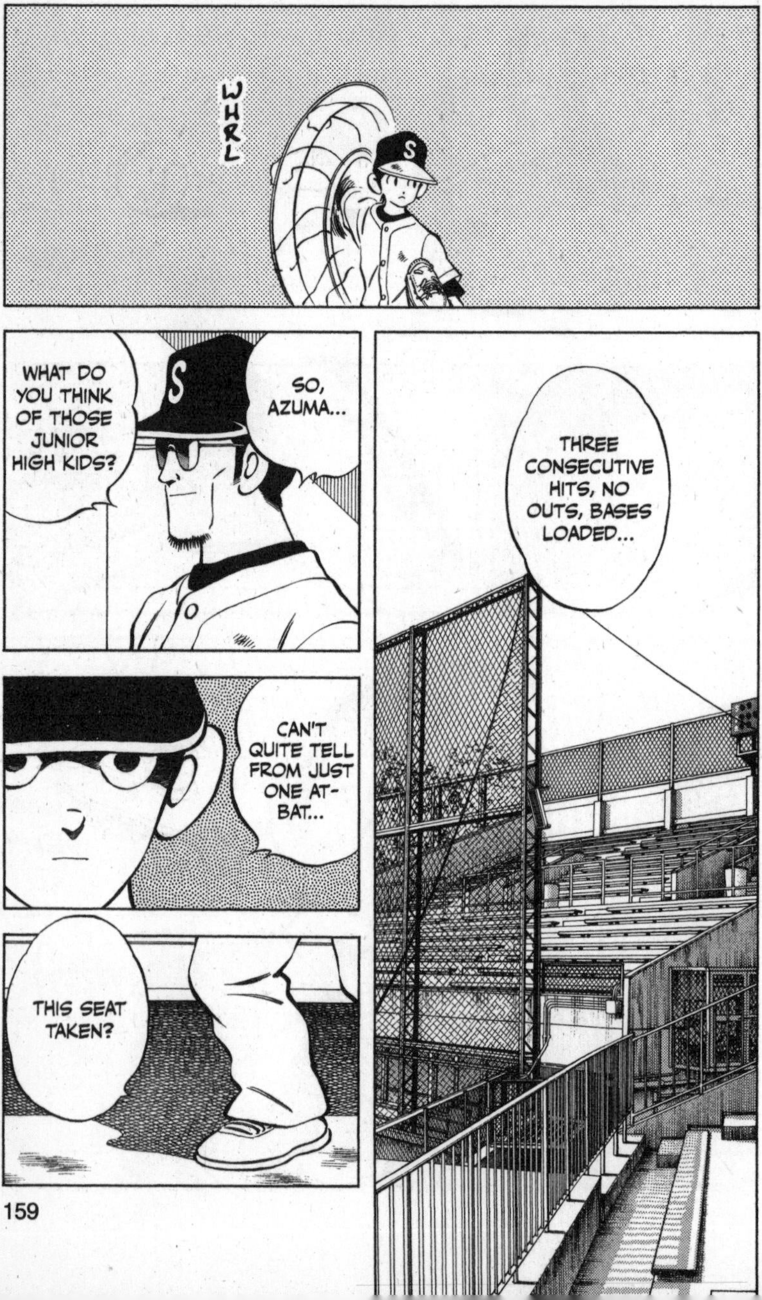
WHRL
THREE CONSECUTIVE HITS, NO OUTS, BASES LOADED...
SO, AZUMA...
WHAT DO YOU THINK OF THOSE JUNIOR HIGH KIDS?
CAN'T QUITE TELL FROM JUST ONE AT-BAT...
THIS SEAT TAKEN?

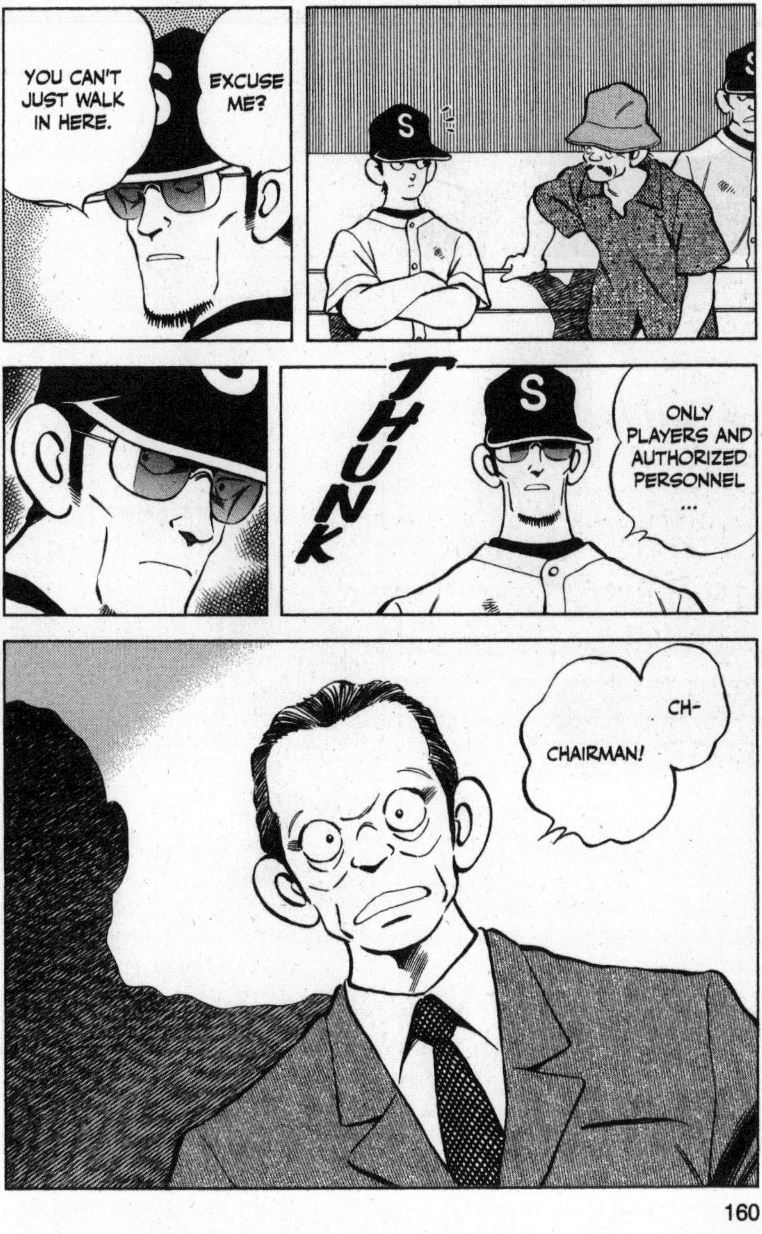
EXCUSE ME?
YOU CAN'T JUST WALK IN HERE.
ONLY PLAYERS AND AUTHORIZED PERSONNEL ...
THUNK
CH-
CHAIRMAN!

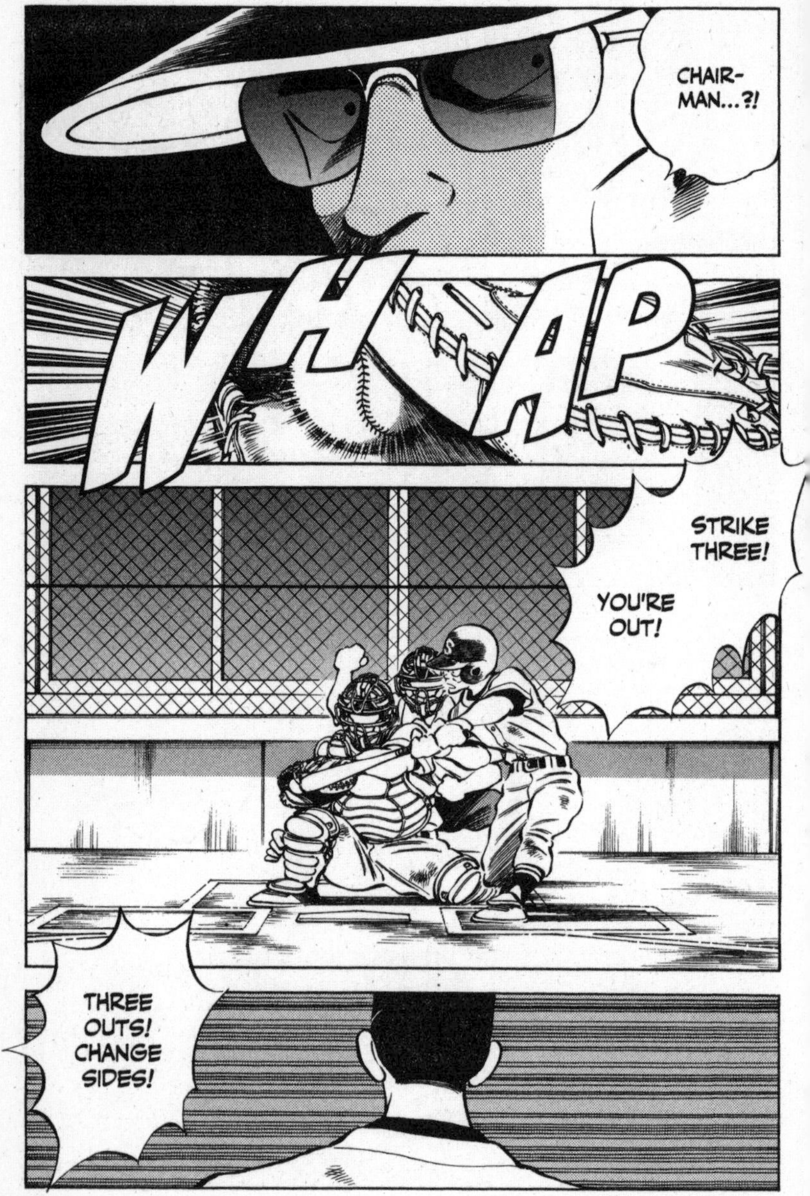
CHAIR-MAN...?!
WHAP
STRIKE THREE!
YOU'RE OUT!
THREE OUTS! CHANGE SIDES!

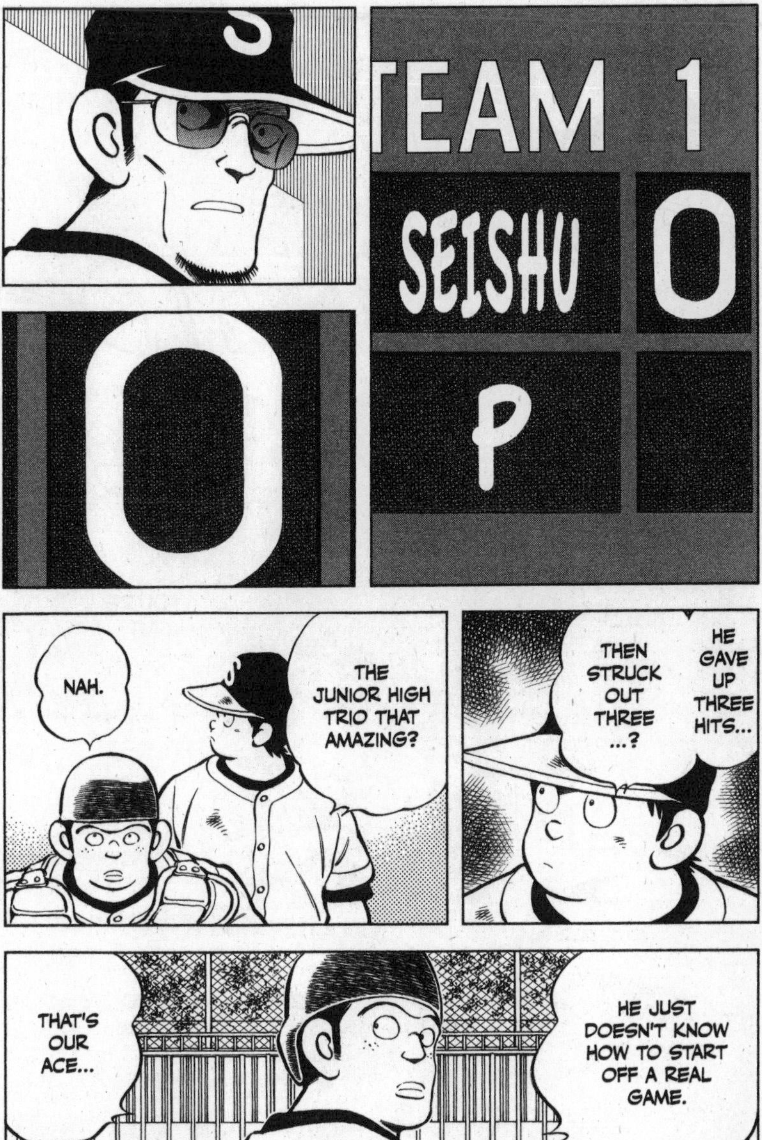
TEAM 1
SEISHU 0
P
0
HE GAVE UP THREE HITS...
THEN STRUCK OUT THREE ...?
THE JUNIOR HIGH TRIO THAT AMAZING?
NAH.
HE JUST DOESN'T KNOW HOW TO START OFF A REAL GAME.
THAT'S OUR ACE...

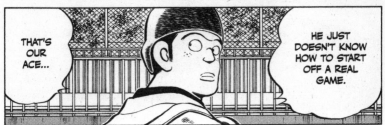

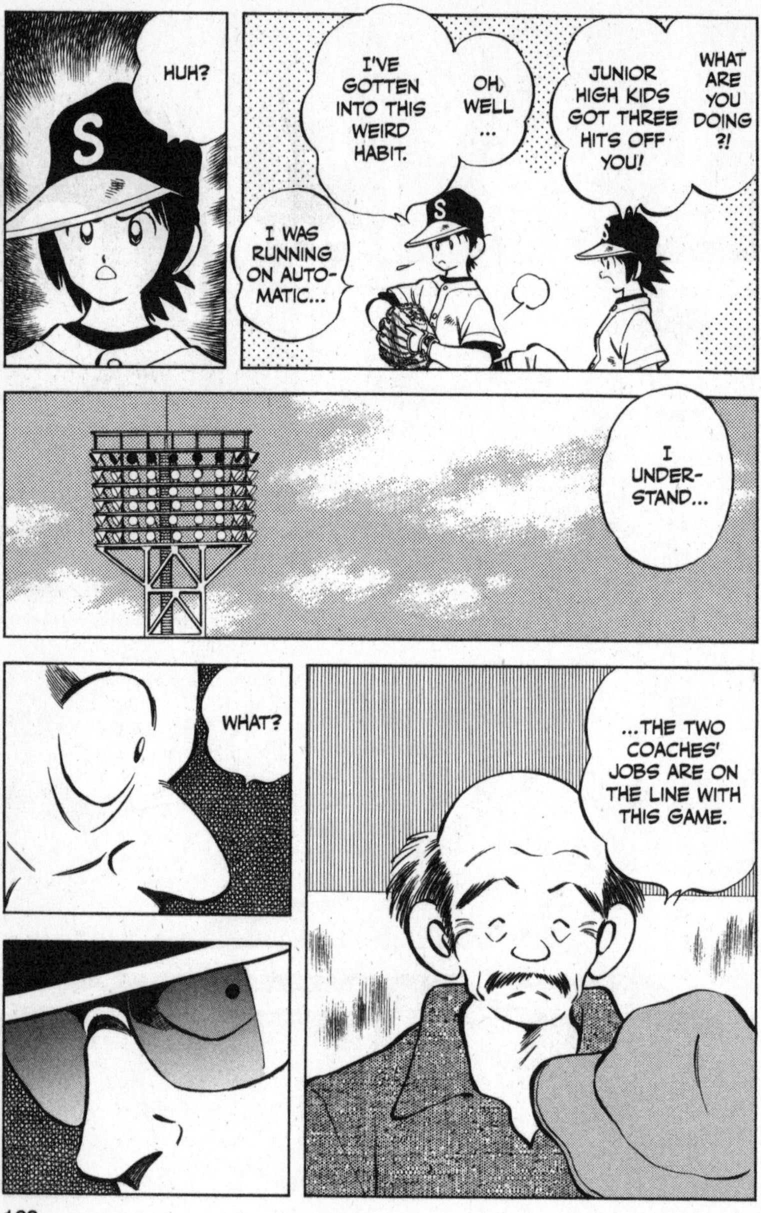
WHAT ARE YOU DOING?!
JUNIOR HIGH KIDS GOT THREE HITS OFF YOU!
OH, WELL...
I'VE GOTTEN INTO THIS WEIRD HABIT.
I WAS RUNNING ON AUTO-MATIC...
HUH?
I UNDER-STAND...
...THE TWO COACHES' JOBS ARE ON THE LINE WITH THIS GAME.
WHAT?

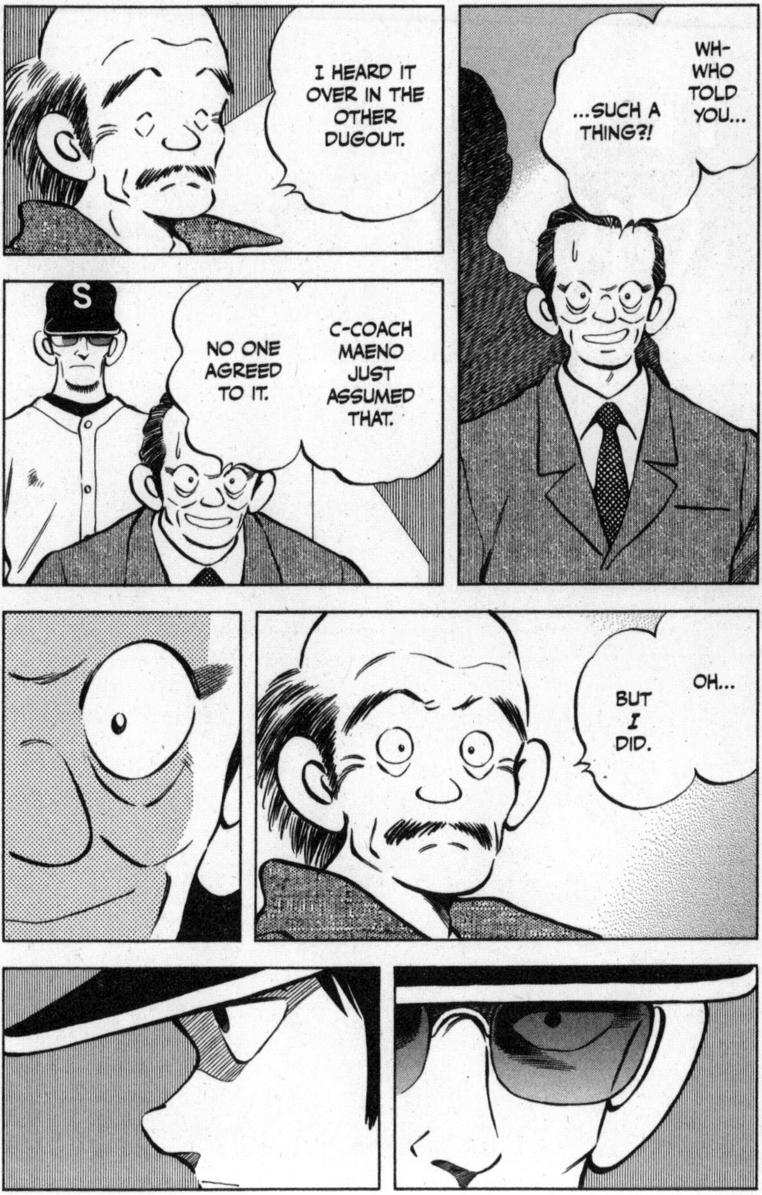
WH-WHO TOLD YOU...
...SUCH A THING?!
I HEARD IT OVER IN THE OTHER DUGOUT.
C-COACH MAENO JUST ASSUMED THAT.
NO ONE AGREED TO IT.
OH...
BUT *I* DID.

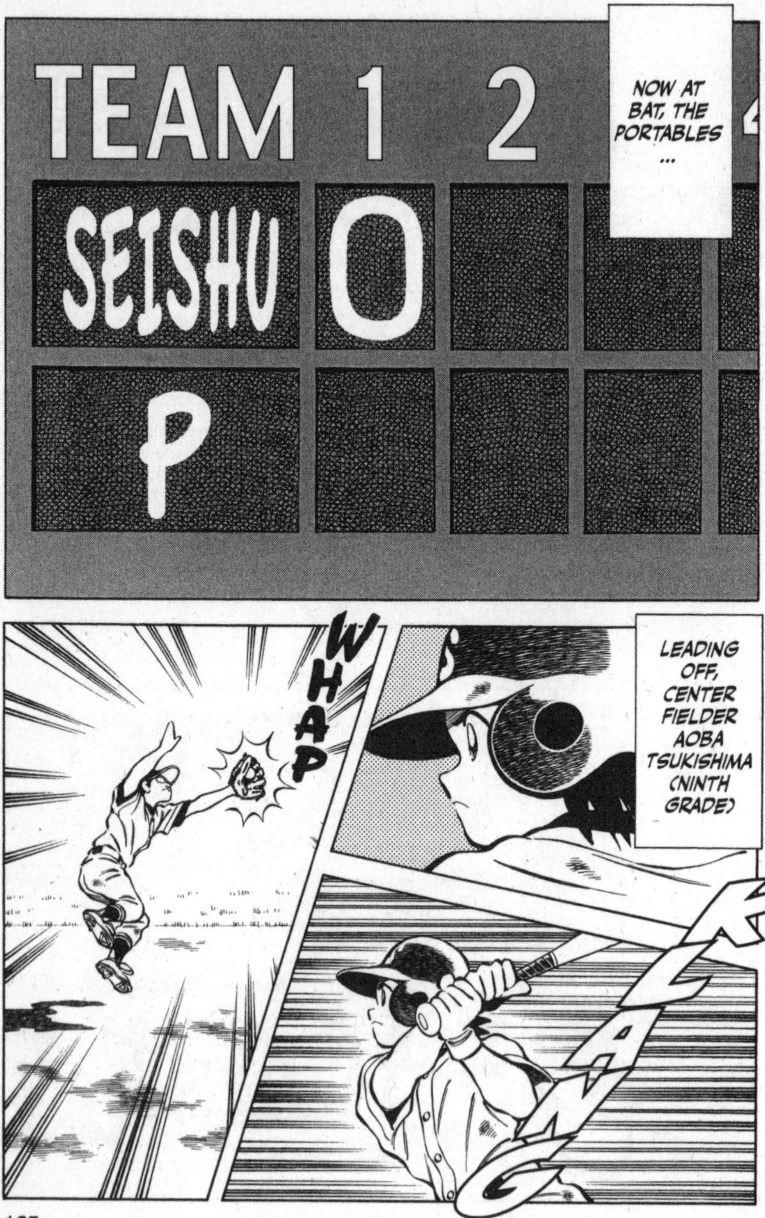
NOW AT BAT, THE PORTABLES ...
TEAM 1 2
SEISHU 0
P
LEADING OFF, CENTER FIELDER AOBA TSUKISHIMA (NINTH GRADE)
KLANG
WHAP

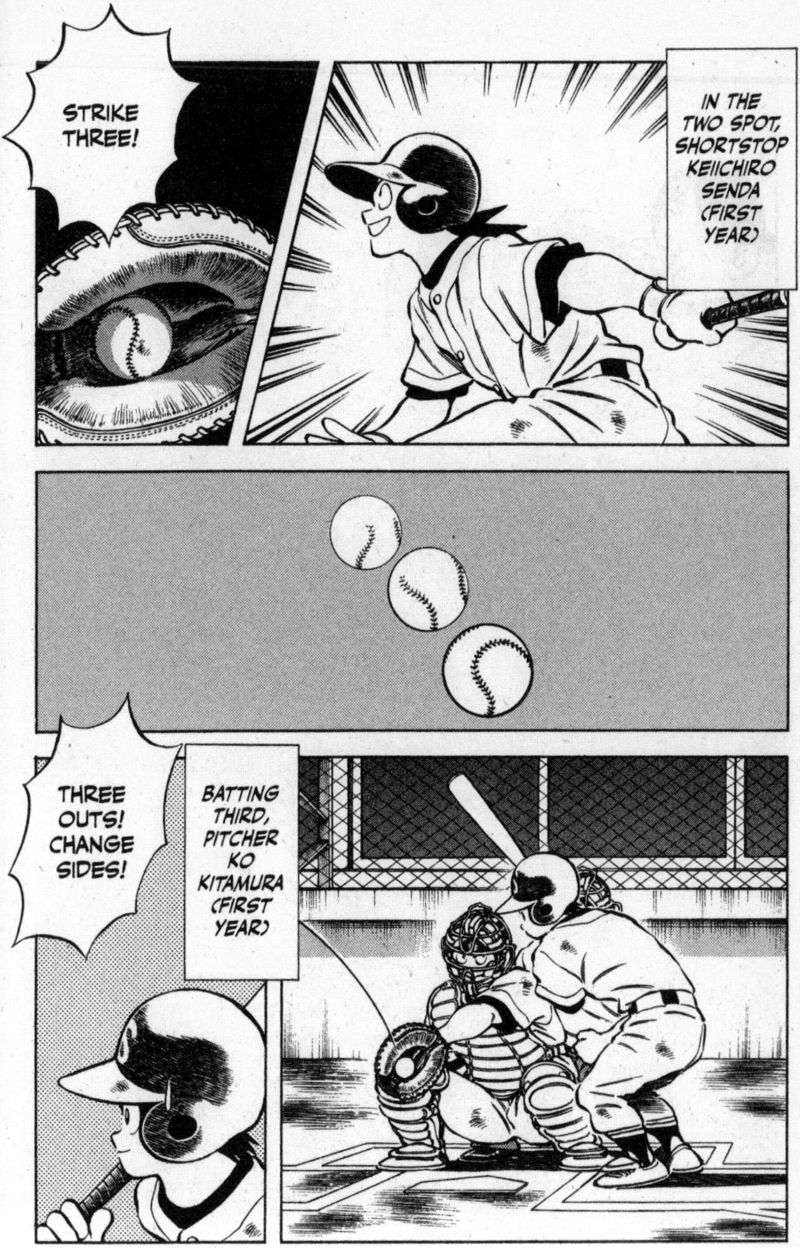
IN THE TWO SPOT, SHORTSTOP KEIICHIRO SENDA (FIRST YEAR)
STRIKE THREE!
THREE OUTS! CHANGE SIDES!
BATTING THIRD, PITCHER KO KITAMURA (FIRST YEAR)

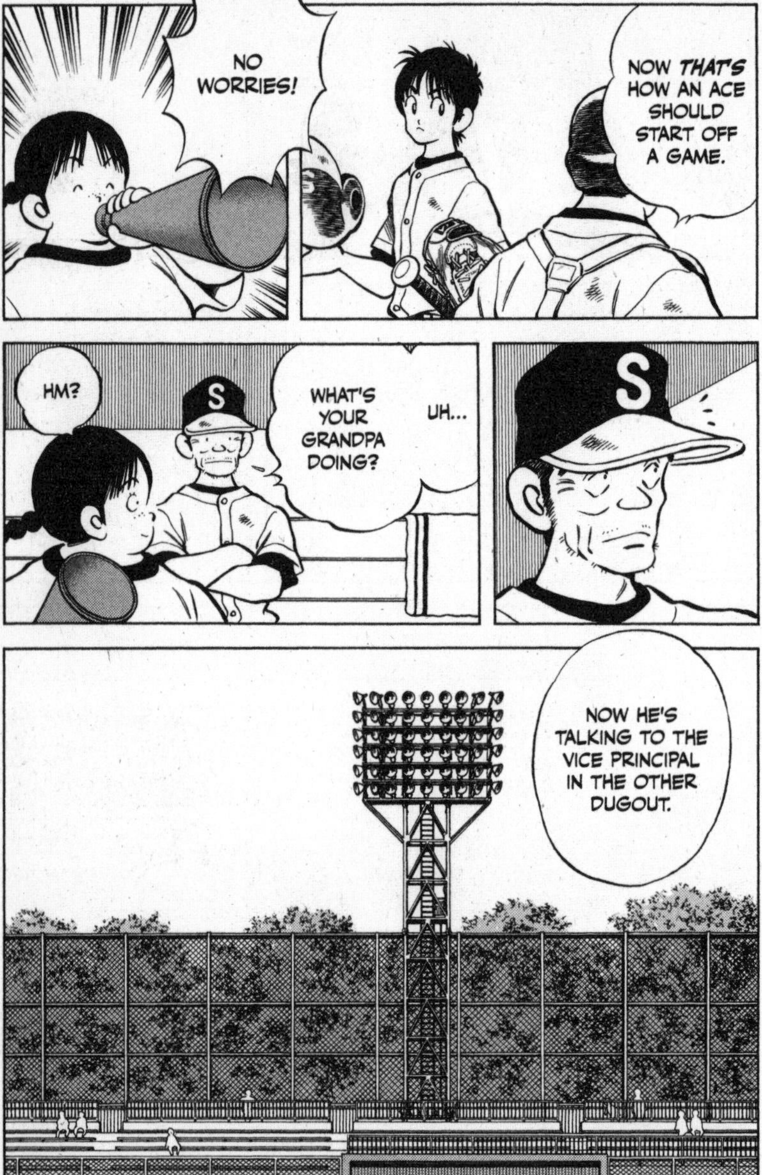
NOW THAT'S HOW AN ACE SHOULD START OFF A GAME.
NO WORRIES!
UH...
WHAT'S YOUR GRANDPA DOING?
HM?
NOW HE'S TALKING TO THE VICE PRINCIPAL IN THE OTHER DUGOUT.

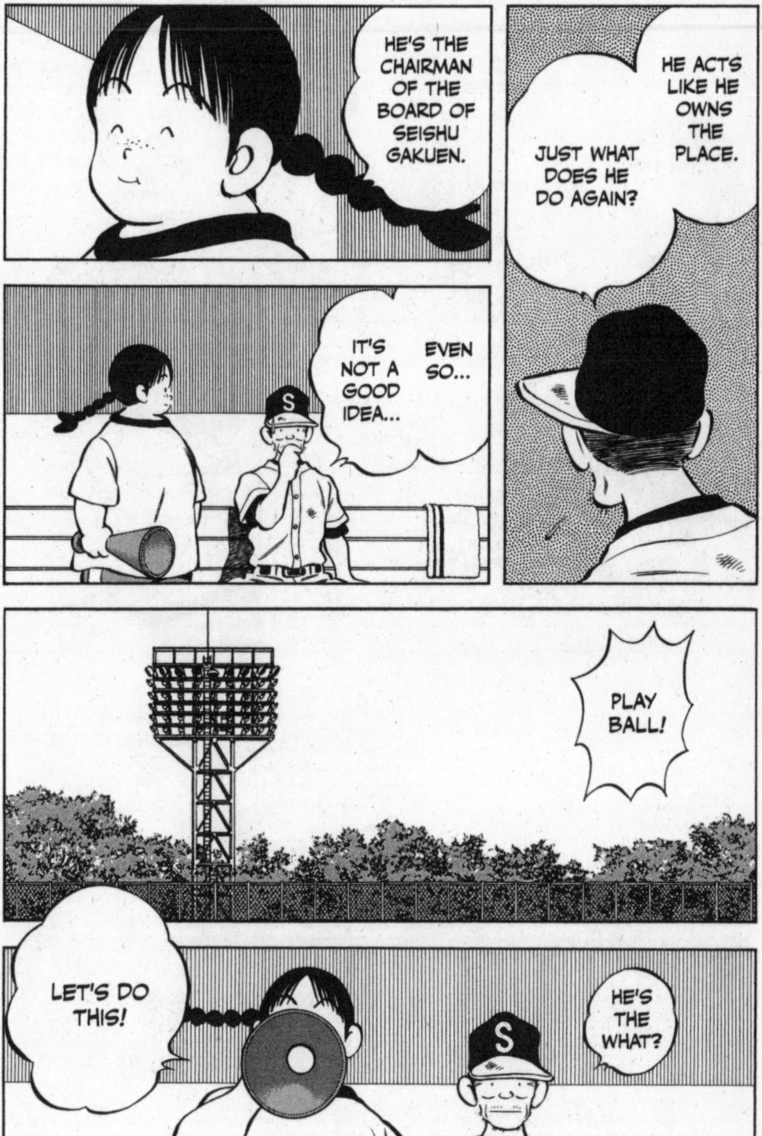
HE ACTS LIKE HE OWNS THE PLACE.
JUST WHAT DOES HE DO AGAIN?
HE'S THE CHAIRMAN OF THE BOARD OF SEISHU GAKUEN.
EVEN SO...
IT'S NOT A GOOD IDEA...
PLAY BALL!
HE'S THE WHAT?
LET'S DO THIS!

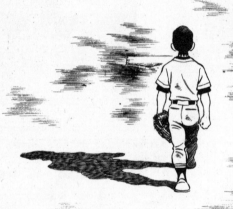

CHAPTER 50
HOW SHOULD I KNOW?

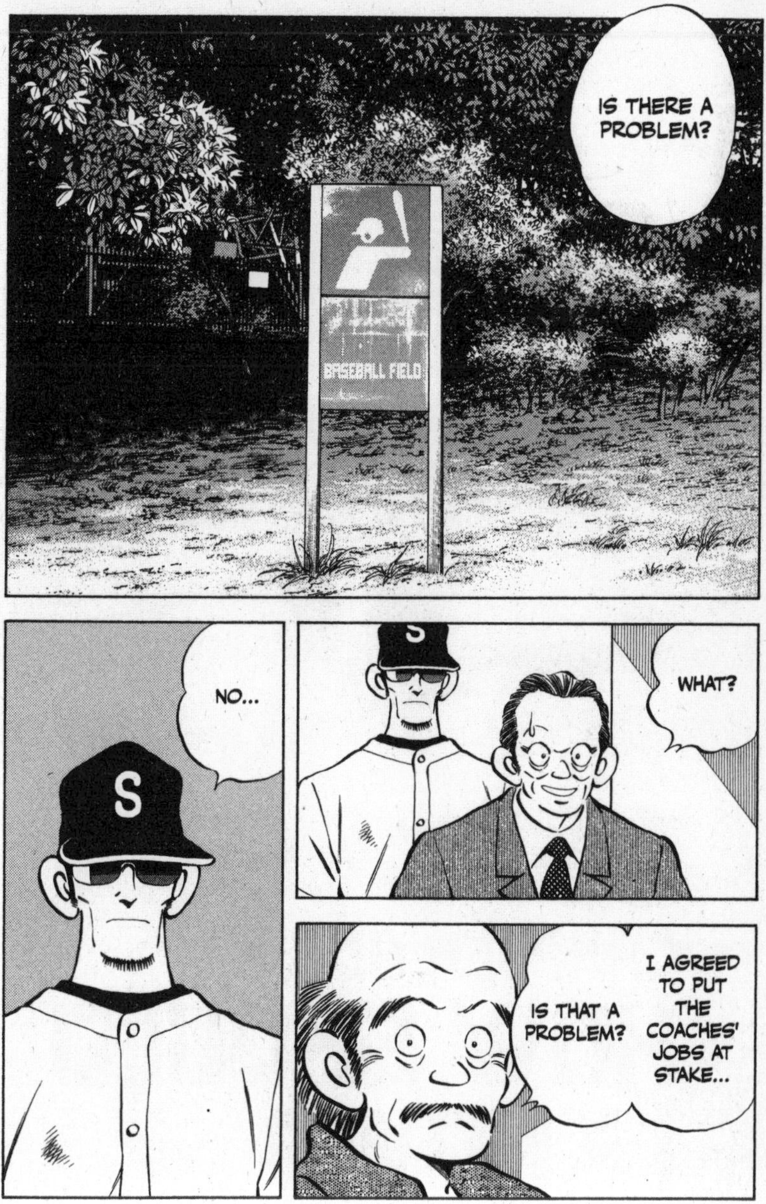
BASEBALL FIELD
IS THERE A PROBLEM?
WHAT?
I AGREED TO PUT THE COACHES' JOBS AT STAKE...
IS THAT A PROBLEM?
NO...

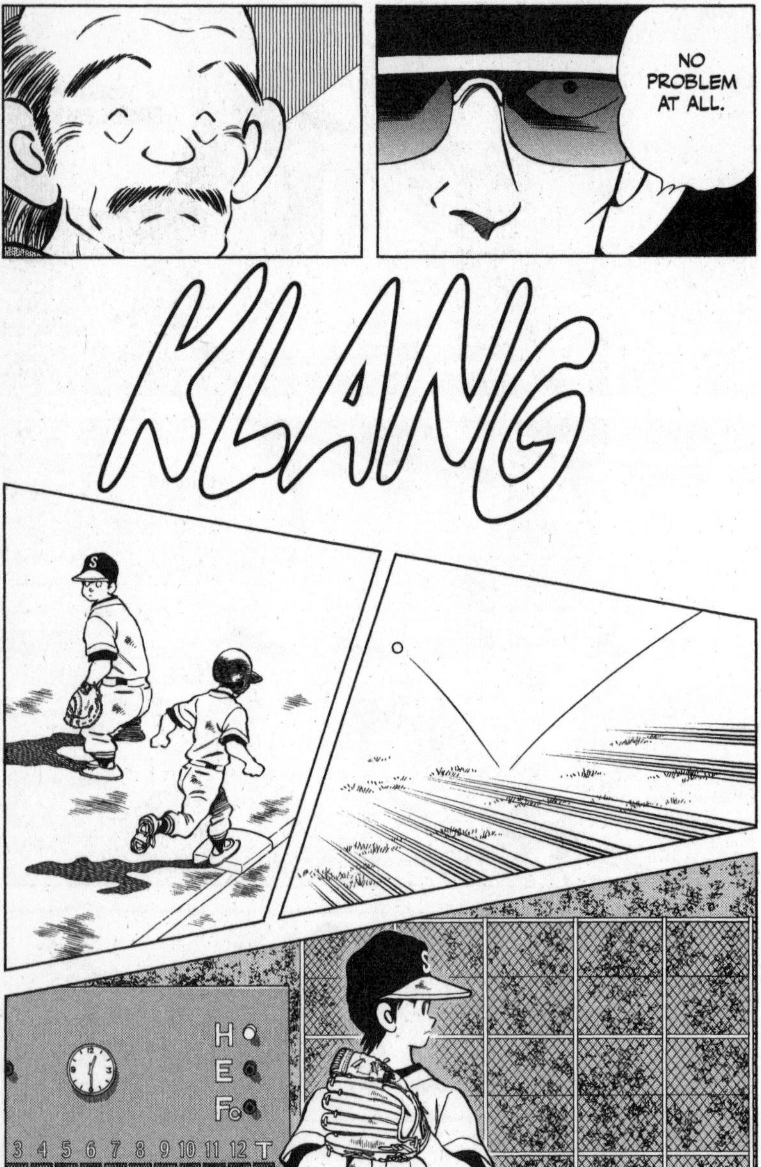
NO PROBLEM AT ALL.
KLANG
H
E
Fc
3 4 5 6 7 8 9 10 11 12 T

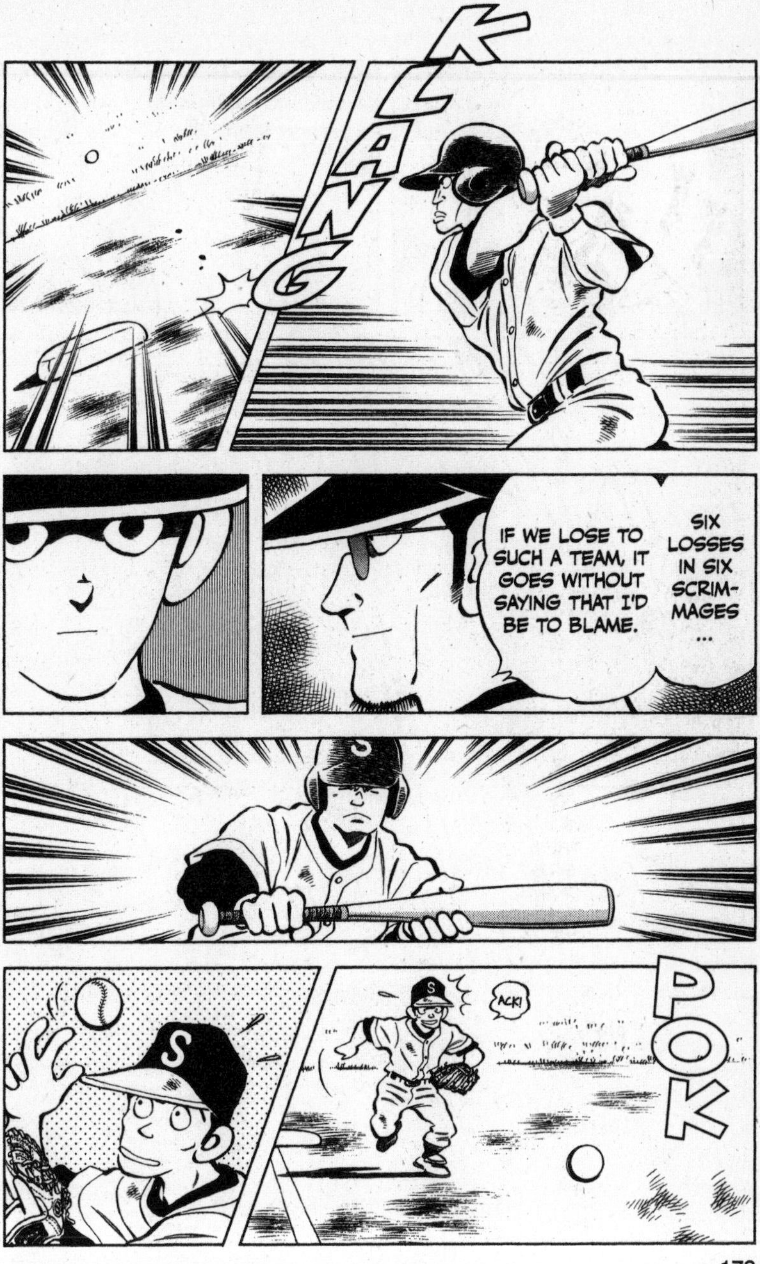
KLANG
SIX LOSSES IN SIX SCRIM-MAGES ...
IF WE LOSE TO SUCH A TEAM, IT GOES WITHOUT SAYING THAT I'D BE TO BLAME.
POK
ACK!

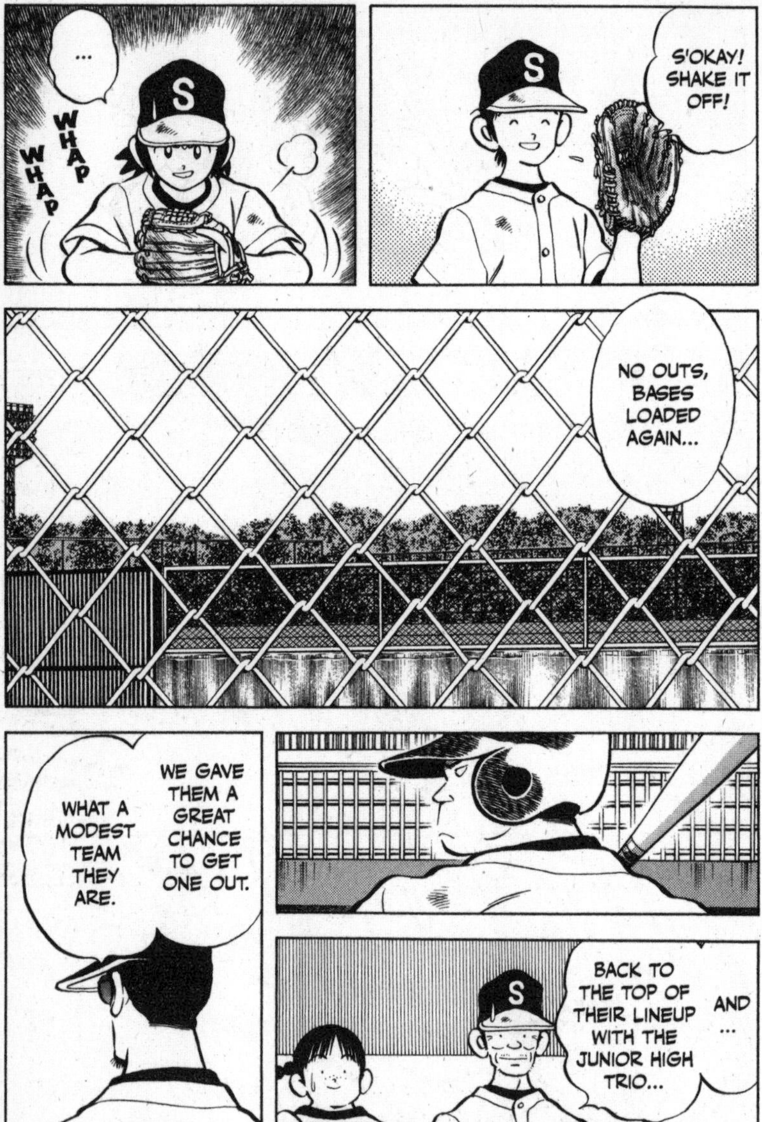

S'OKAY! SHAKE IT OFF!
...
WHAP WHAP WHAP
NO OUTS, BASES LOADED AGAIN...
BACK TO THE TOP OF THEIR LINEUP WITH THE JUNIOR HIGH TRIO...
AND ...
WE GAVE THEM A GREAT CHANCE TO GET ONE OUT.
WHAT A MODEST TEAM THEY ARE.

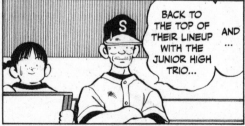

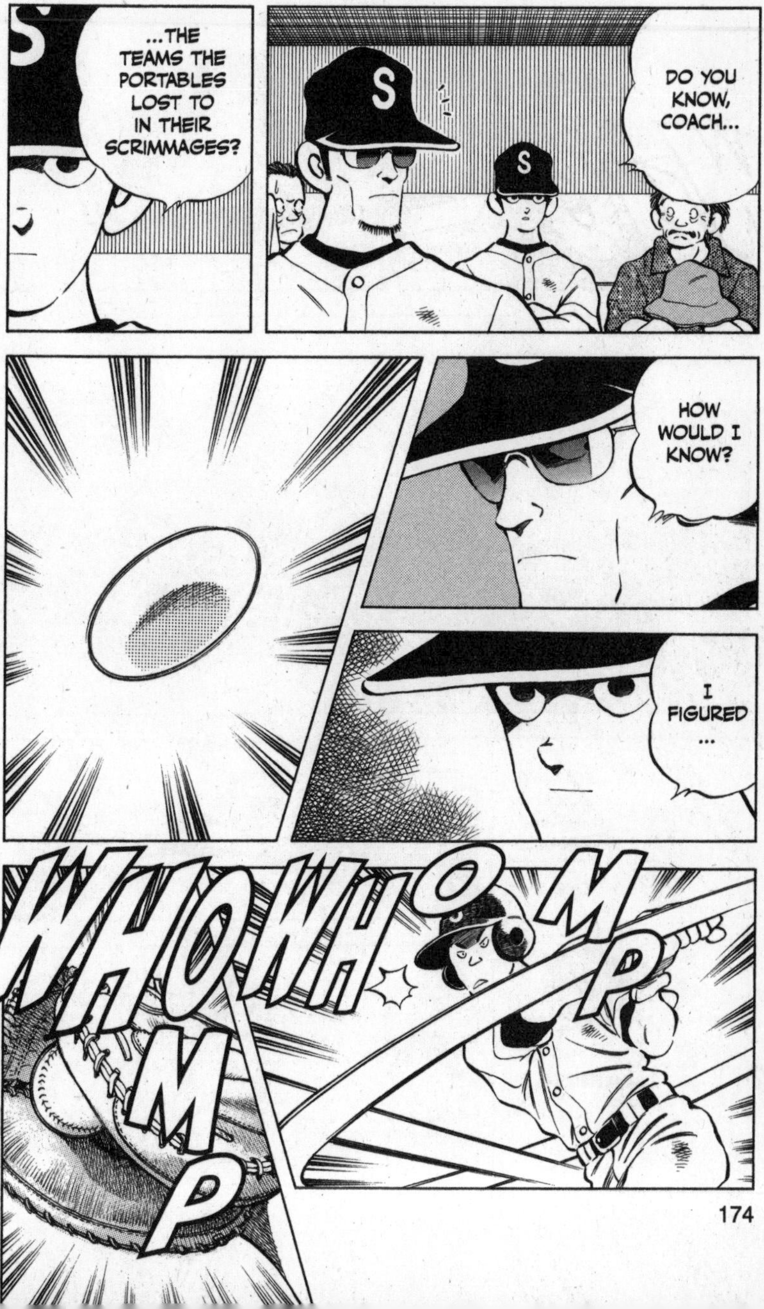
DO YOU KNOW, COACH...
...THE TEAMS THE PORTABLES LOST TO IN THEIR SCRIMMAGES?
HOW WOULD I KNOW?
I FIGURED ...
WHOMP
WHOMP

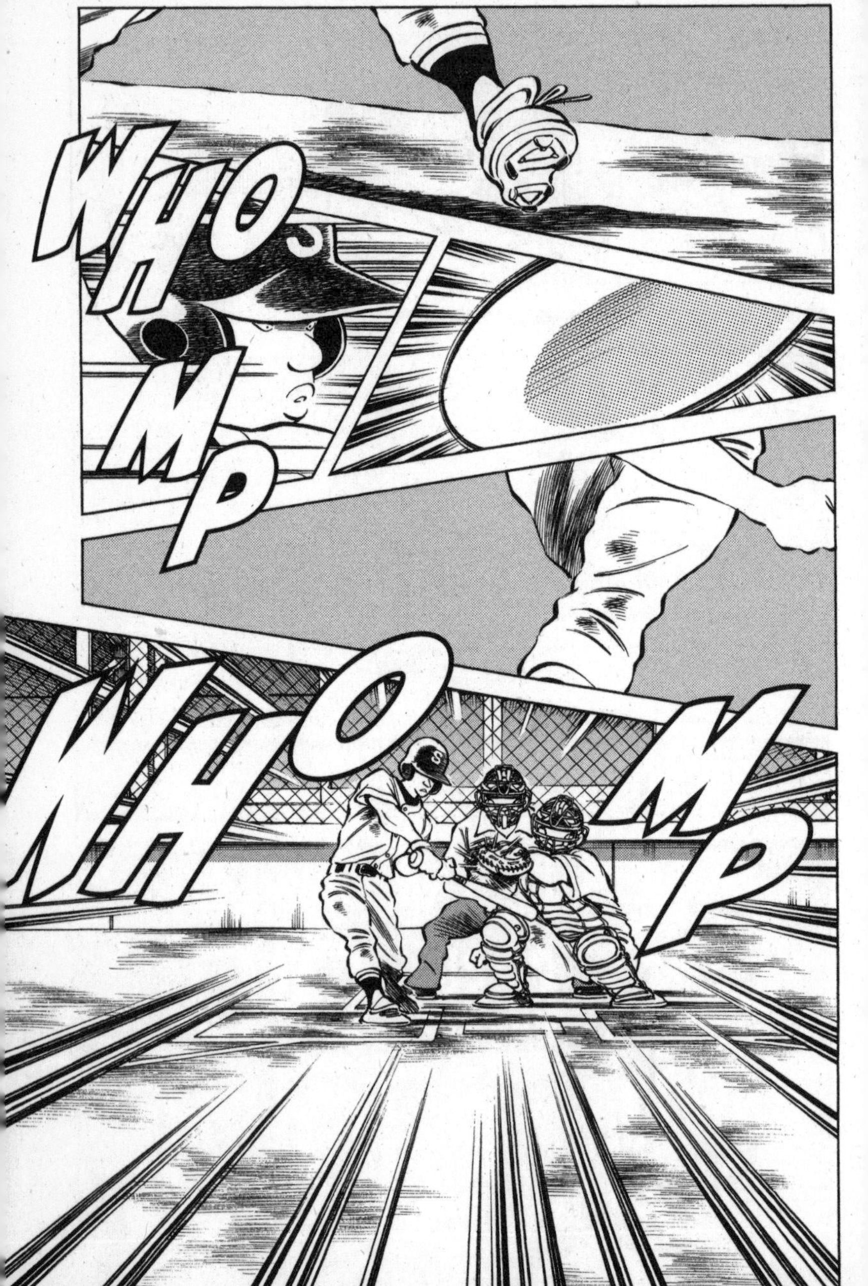
WHOMP
WHOMP

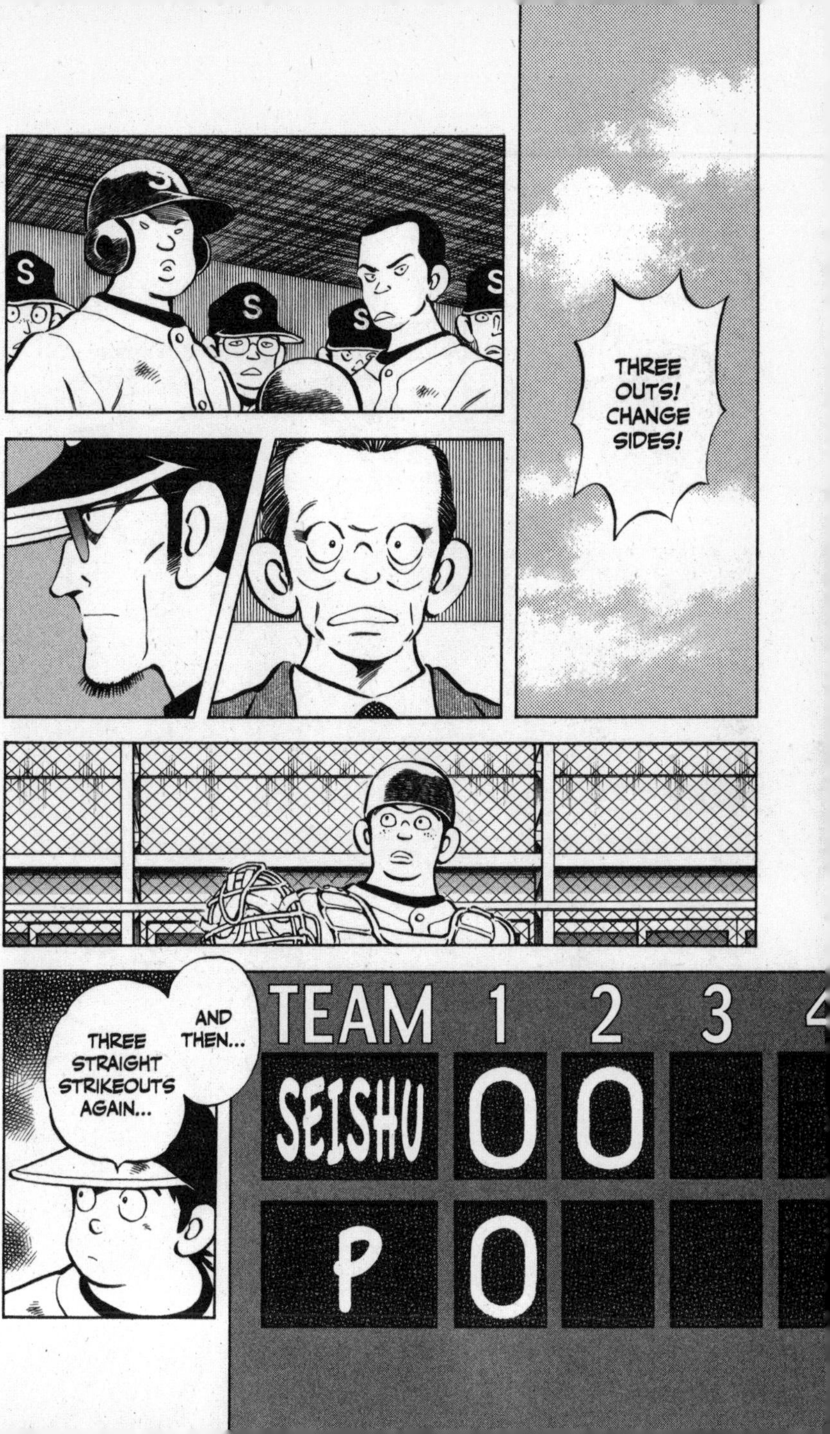
THREE OUTS! CHANGE SIDES!
TEAM 1 2 3 4
SEISHU 0 0
P 0
AND THEN...
THREE STRAIGHT STRIKEOUTS AGAIN...

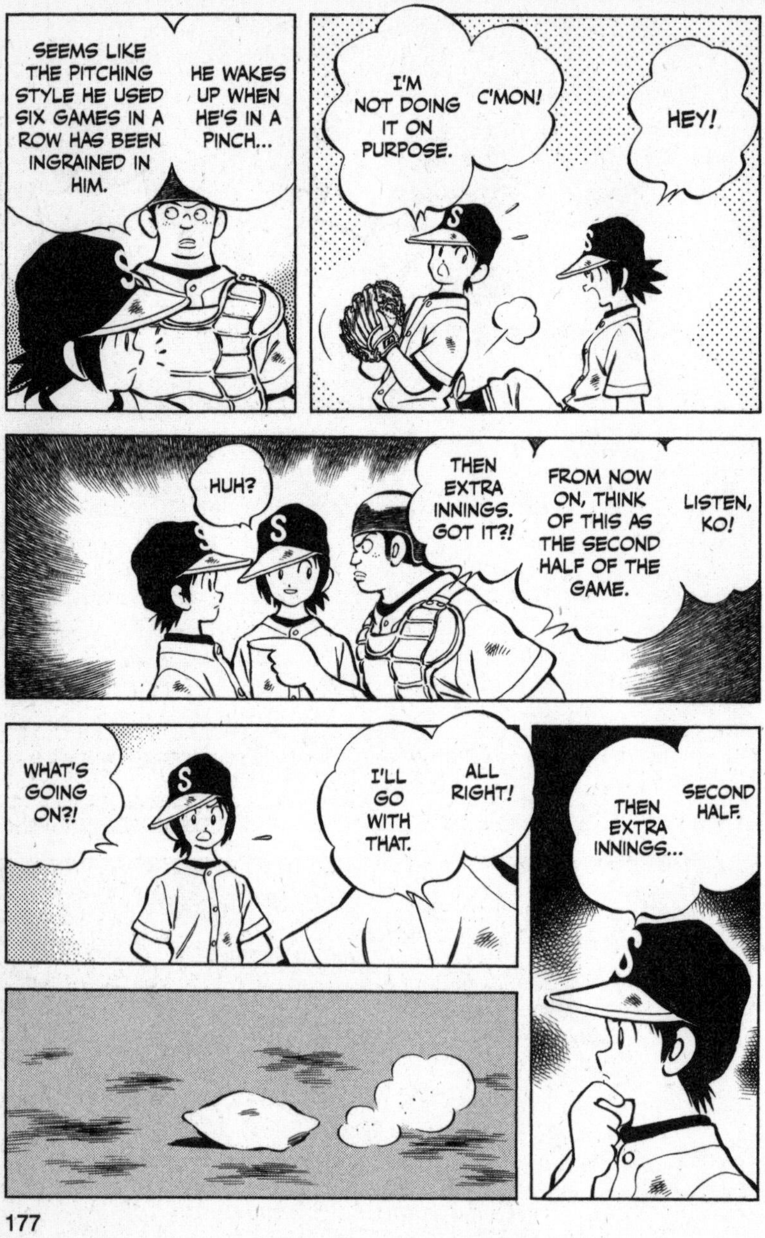
HEY!
C'MON!
I'M NOT DOING IT ON PURPOSE.
HE WAKES UP WHEN HE'S IN A PINCH...
SEEMS LIKE THE PITCHING STYLE HE USED SIX GAMES IN A ROW HAS BEEN INGRAINED IN HIM.
LISTEN, KO!
FROM NOW ON, THINK OF THIS AS THE SECOND HALF OF THE GAME.
THEN EXTRA INNINGS. GOT IT?!
HUH?
SECOND HALF.
THEN EXTRA INNINGS...
ALL RIGHT!
I'LL GO WITH THAT.
WHAT'S GOING ON?!

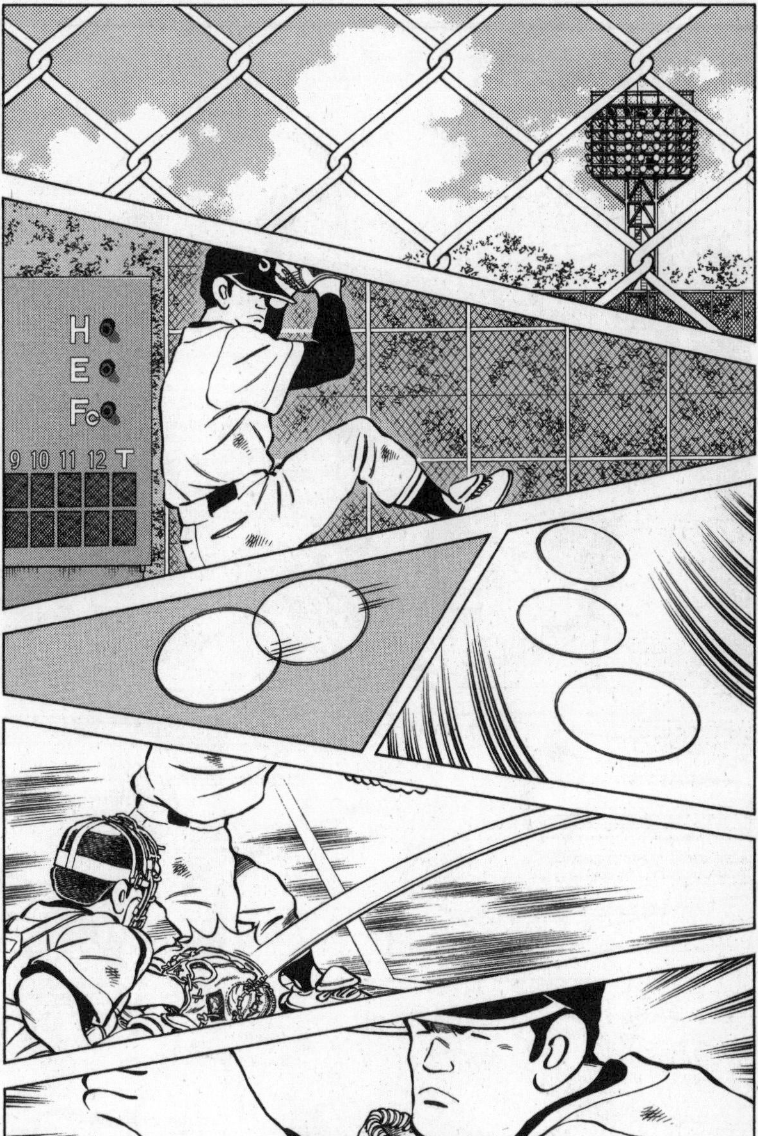
H
E
Fc
9 10 11 12 T

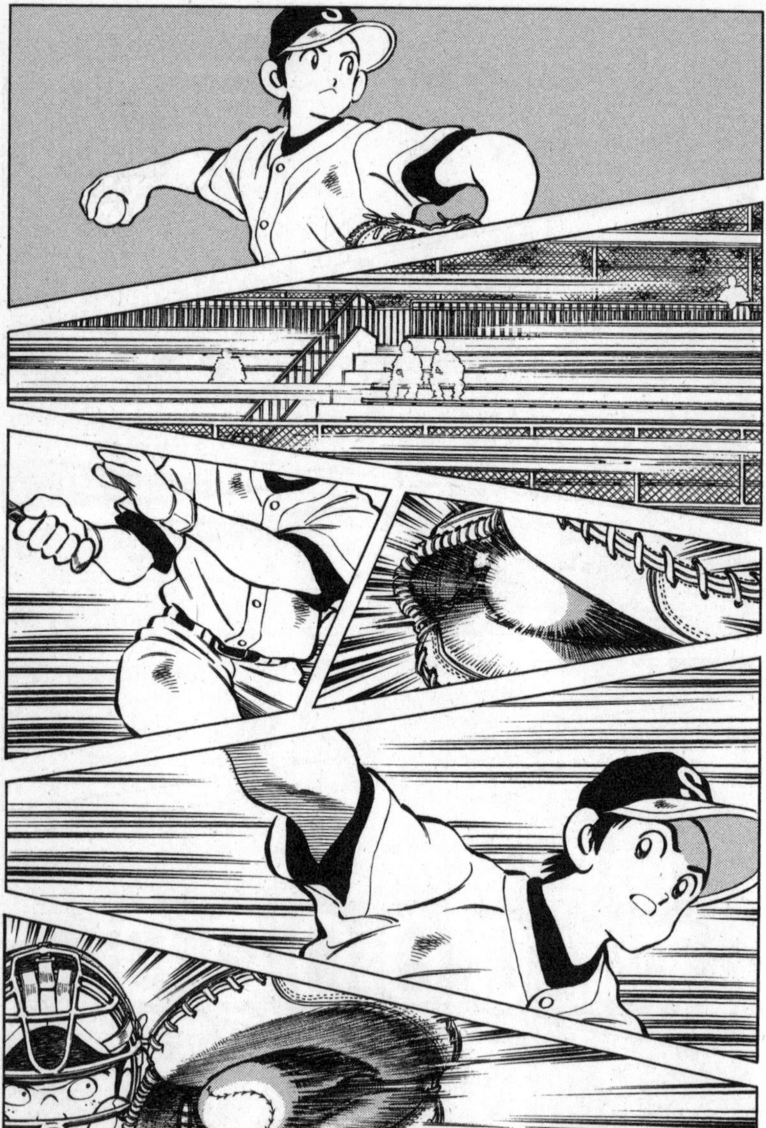

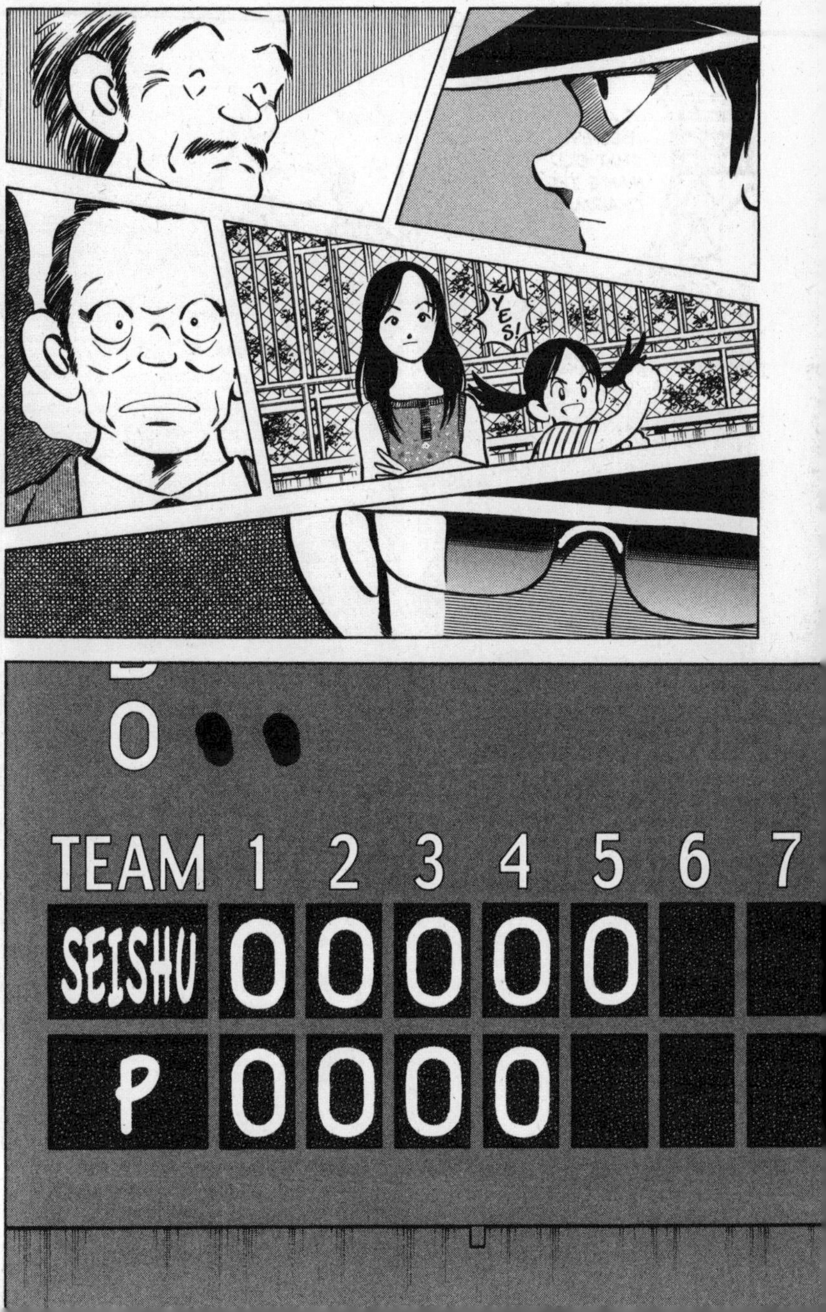
YES!
O
TEAM 1 2 3 4 5 6 7
SEISHU 0 0 0 0 0
P 0 0 0 0

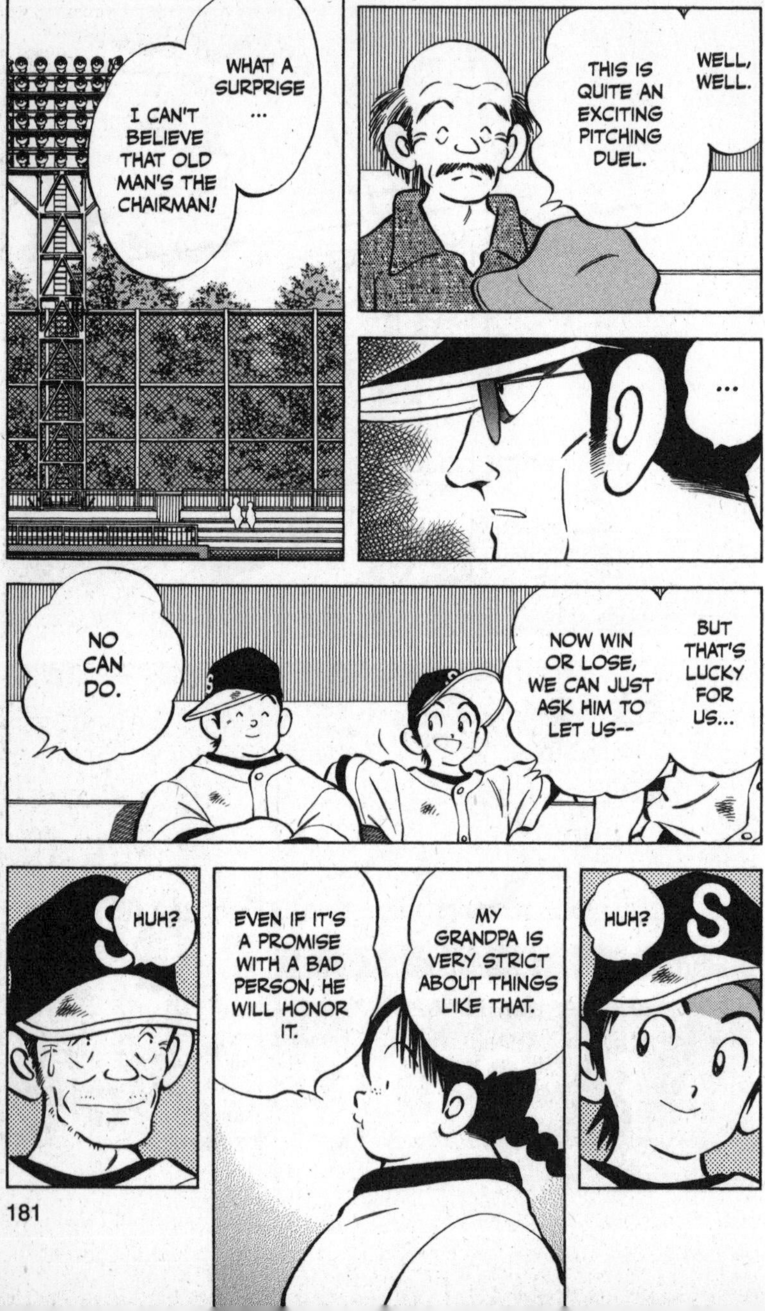
WELL, WELL.
THIS IS QUITE AN EXCITING PITCHING DUEL.
...
WHAT A SURPRISE ...
I CAN'T BELIEVE THAT OLD MAN'S THE CHAIRMAN!
BUT THAT'S LUCKY FOR US...
NOW WIN OR LOSE, WE CAN JUST ASK HIM TO LET US--
NO CAN DO.
HUH?
MY GRANDPA IS VERY STRICT ABOUT THINGS LIKE THAT.
EVEN IF IT'S A PROMISE WITH A BAD PERSON, HE WILL HONOR IT.
HUH?

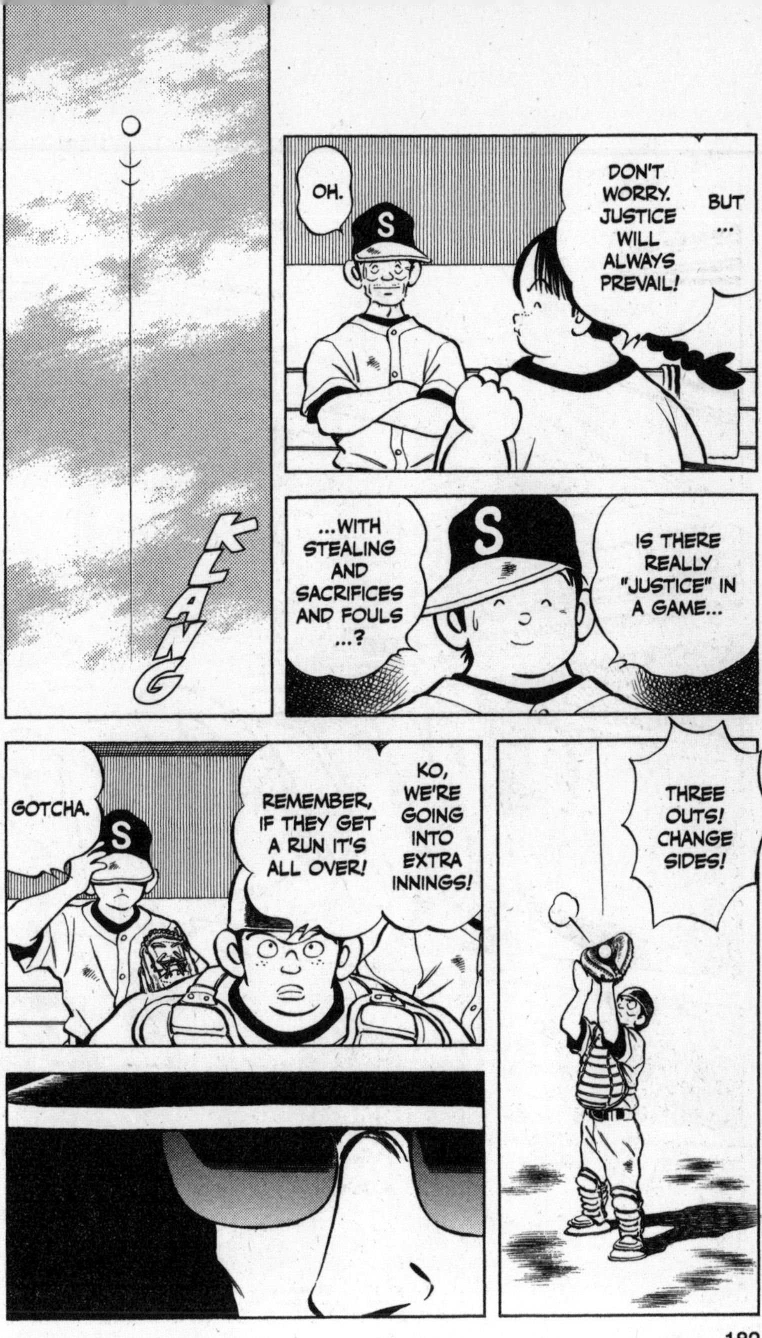
BUT ...
DON'T WORRY. JUSTICE WILL ALWAYS PREVAIL!
OH.
IS THERE REALLY "JUSTICE" IN A GAME...
...WITH STEALING AND SACRIFICES AND FOULS ...?
KLANG
THREE OUTS! CHANGE SIDES!
KO, WE'RE GOING INTO EXTRA INNINGS!
REMEMBER, IF THEY GET A RUN IT'S ALL OVER!
GOTCHA.

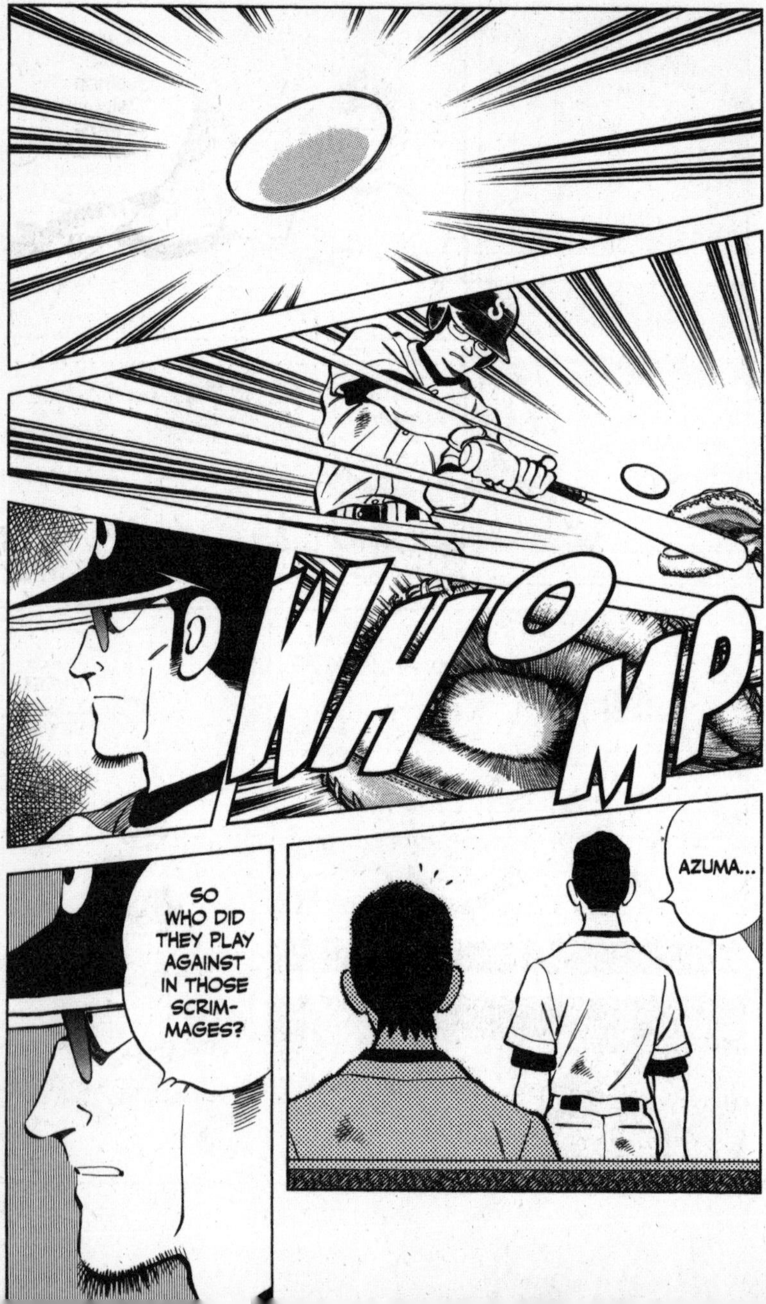
WHOMP
AZUMA...
SO WHO DID THEY PLAY AGAINST IN THOSE SCRIM-MAGES?

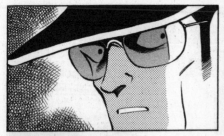

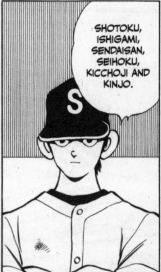

SHOTOKU, ISHIGAMI, SENDAISAN, SEIHOKU, KICCHOJI AND KINJO.

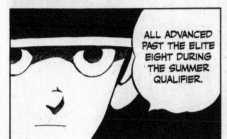

ALL ADVANCED PAST THE ELITE EIGHT DURING THE SUMMER QUALIFIER.

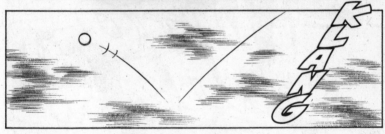

KLANG

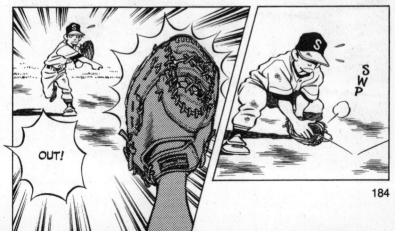

OUT!

SWP

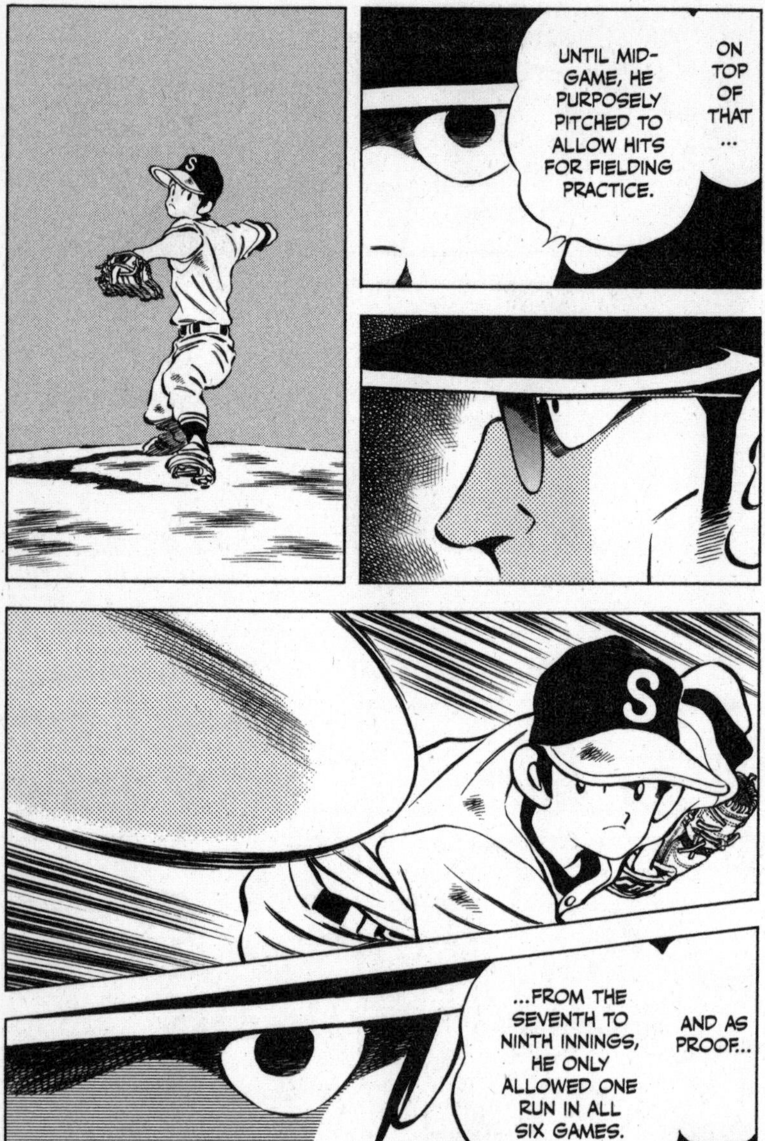

ON TOP OF THAT ...
UNTIL MID-GAME, HE PURPOSELY PITCHED TO ALLOW HITS FOR FIELDING PRACTICE.
AND AS PROOF...
...FROM THE SEVENTH TO NINTH INNINGS, HE ONLY ALLOWED ONE RUN IN ALL SIX GAMES.

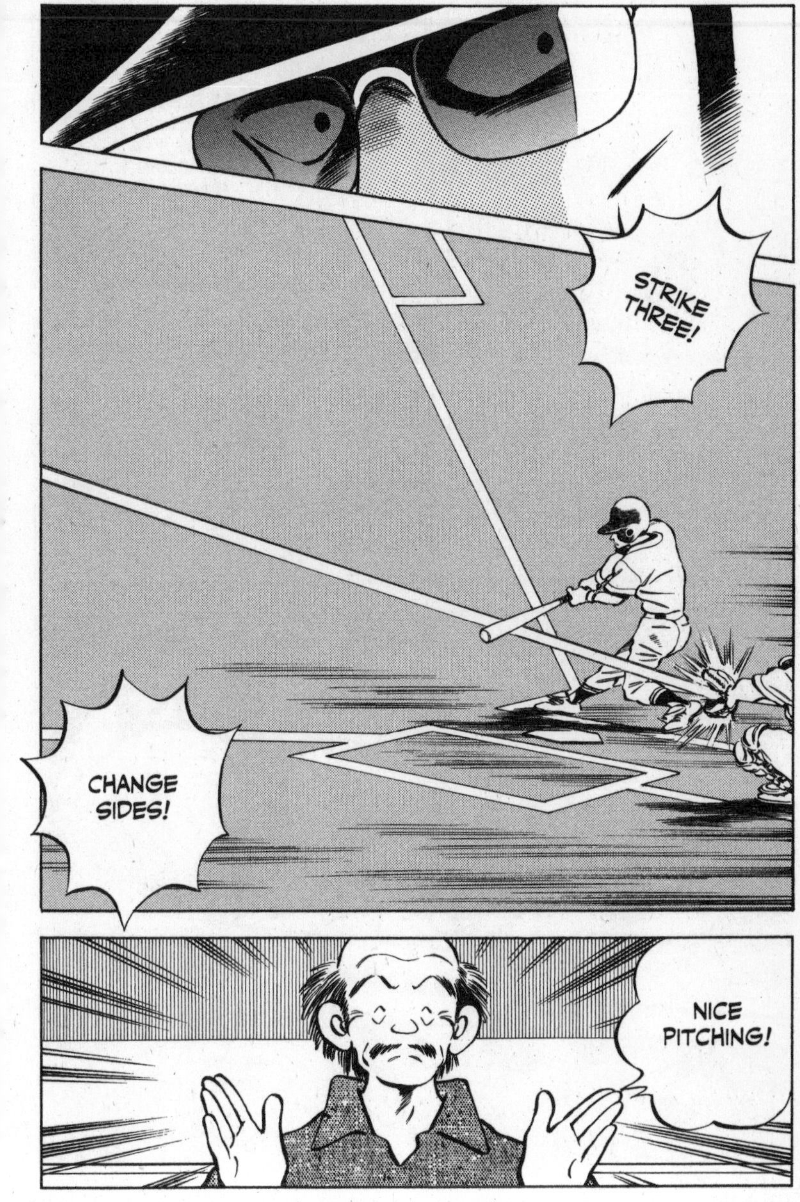
STRIKE THREE!
CHANGE SIDES!
NICE PITCHING!

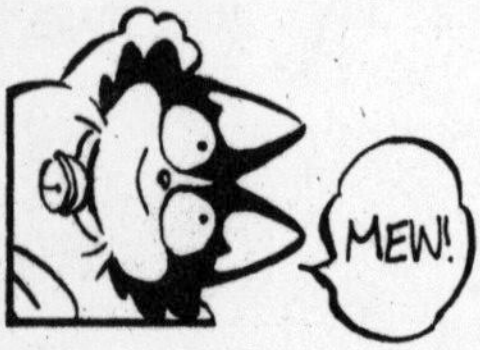
MEW!

Cross Game

7

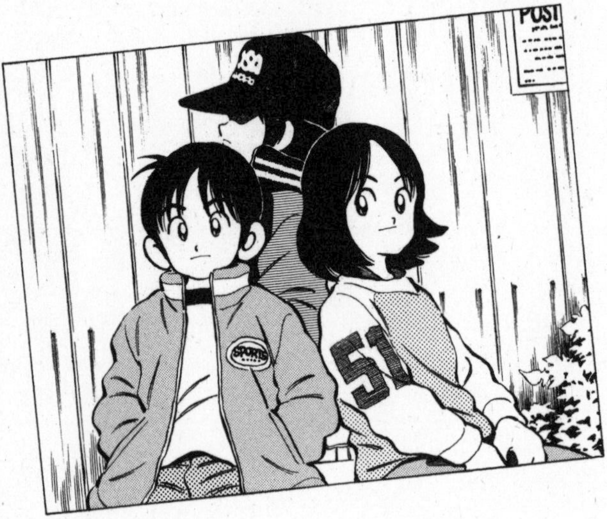
POST
SPORTS
51

Story & Art by

Mitsuru Adachi

CHAPTER 51
BETRAYED ME AGAIN

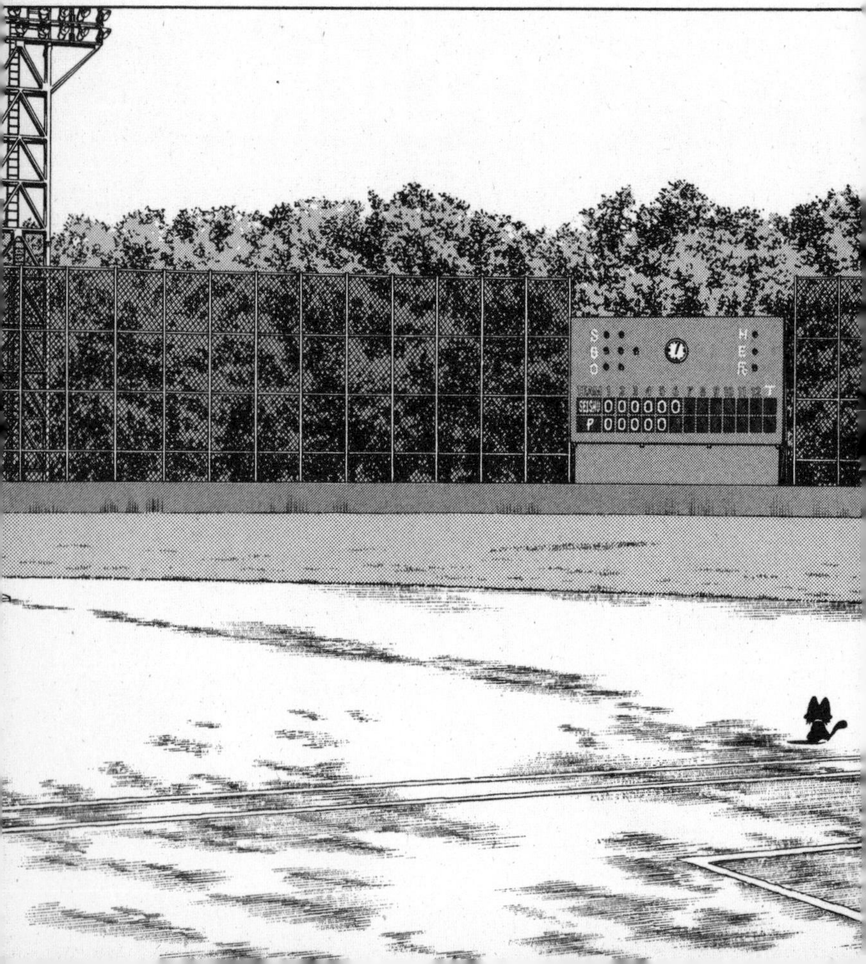
SEISHU 000000
P 00000

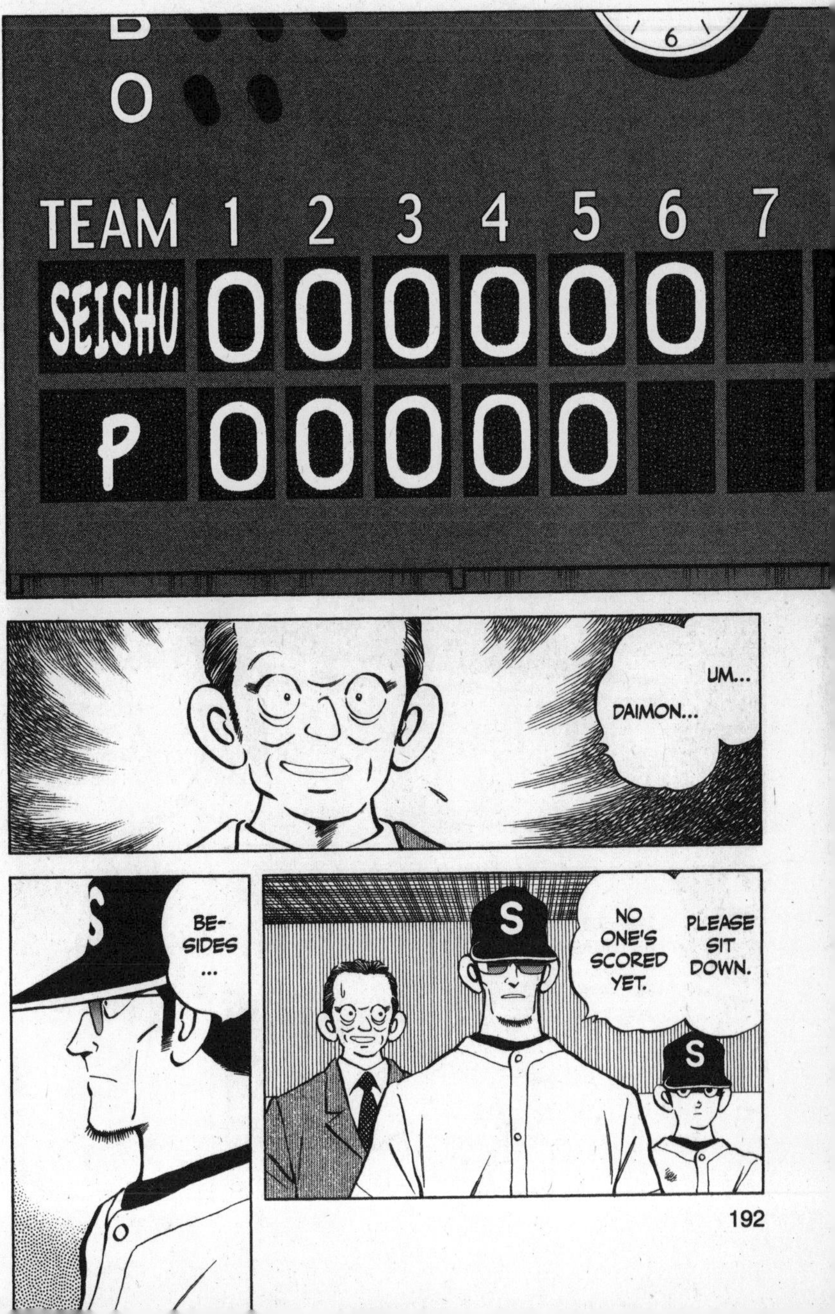
B
O
TEAM 1 2 3 4 5 6 7
SEISHU 0 0 0 0 0 0
P 0 0 0 0 0
UM...
DAIMON...
PLEASE SIT DOWN.
NO ONE'S SCORED YET.
BE-SIDES...

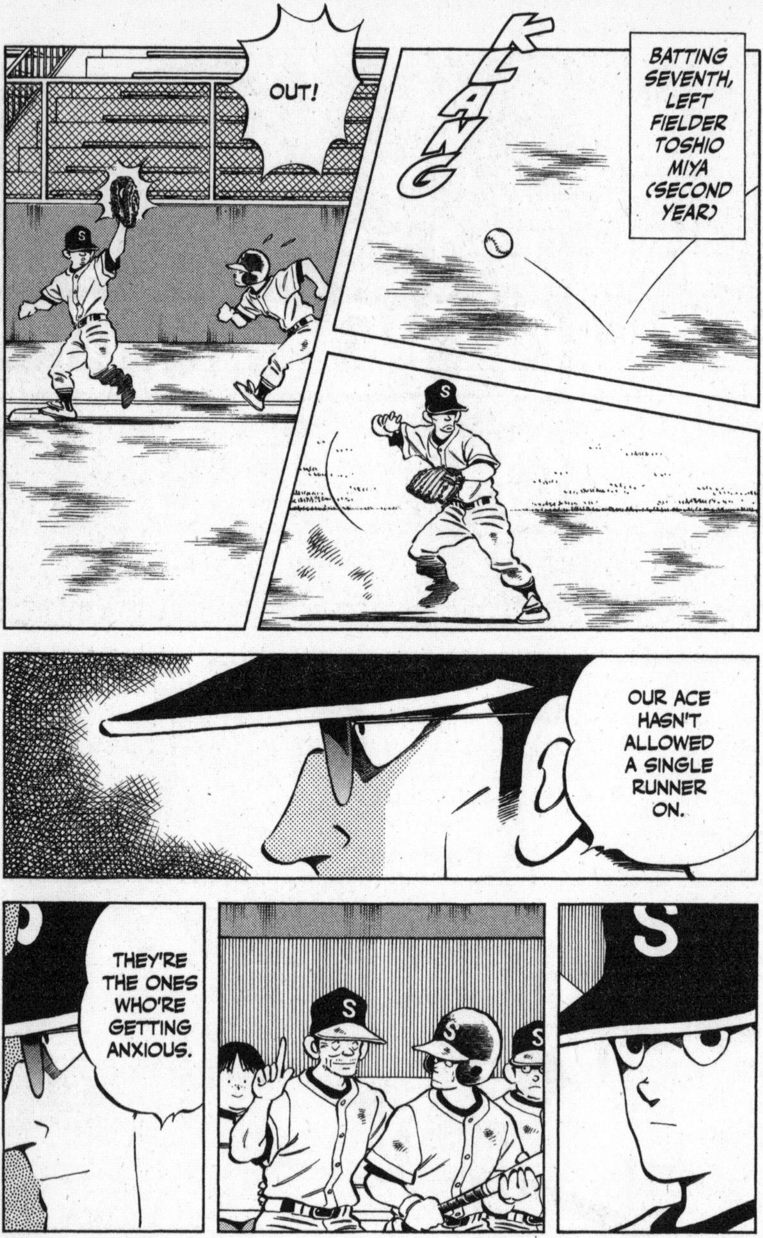
BATTING SEVENTH, LEFT FIELDER TOSHIO MIYA (SECOND YEAR)
KLANG
OUT!
OUR ACE HASN'T ALLOWED A SINGLE RUNNER ON.
THEY'RE THE ONES WHO'RE GETTING ANXIOUS.

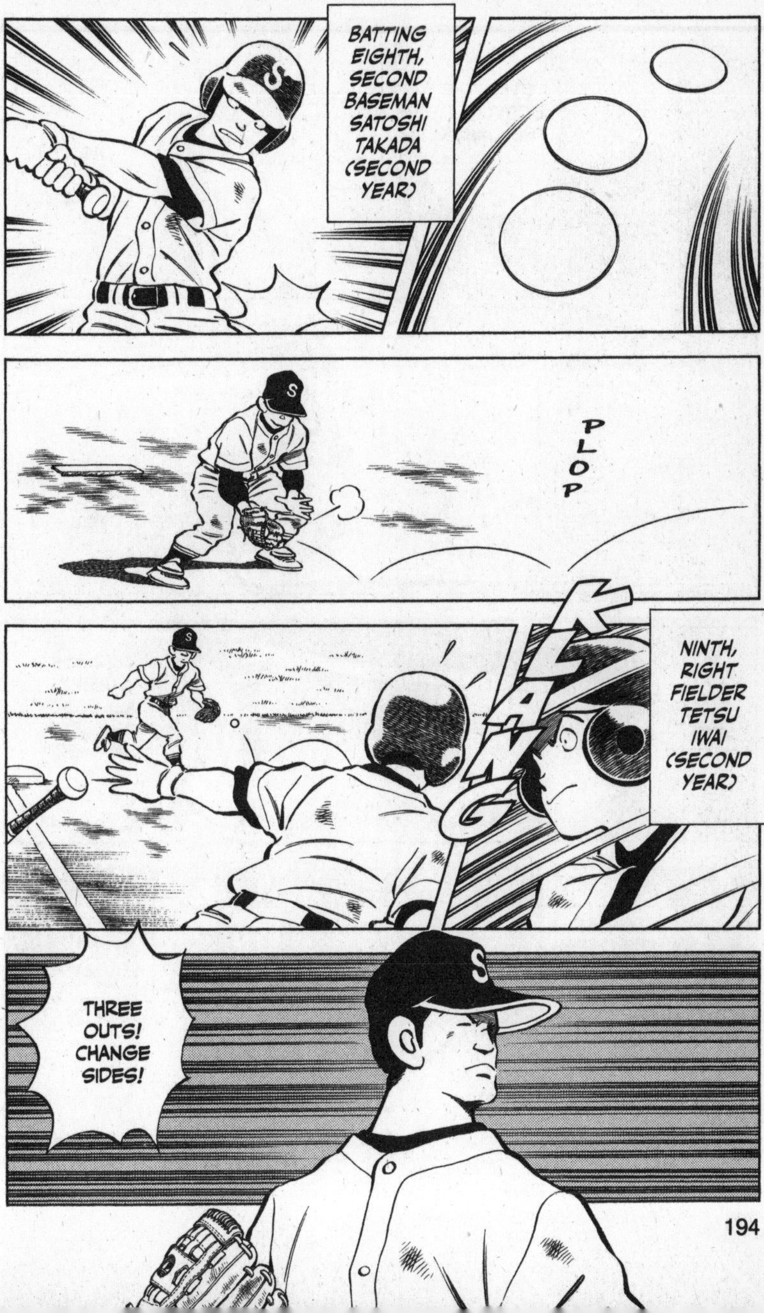
BATTING EIGHTH, SECOND BASEMAN SATOSHI TAKADA (SECOND YEAR)
PLOP
NINTH, RIGHT FIELDER TETSU IWAI (SECOND YEAR)
KLANG
THREE OUTS! CHANGE SIDES!

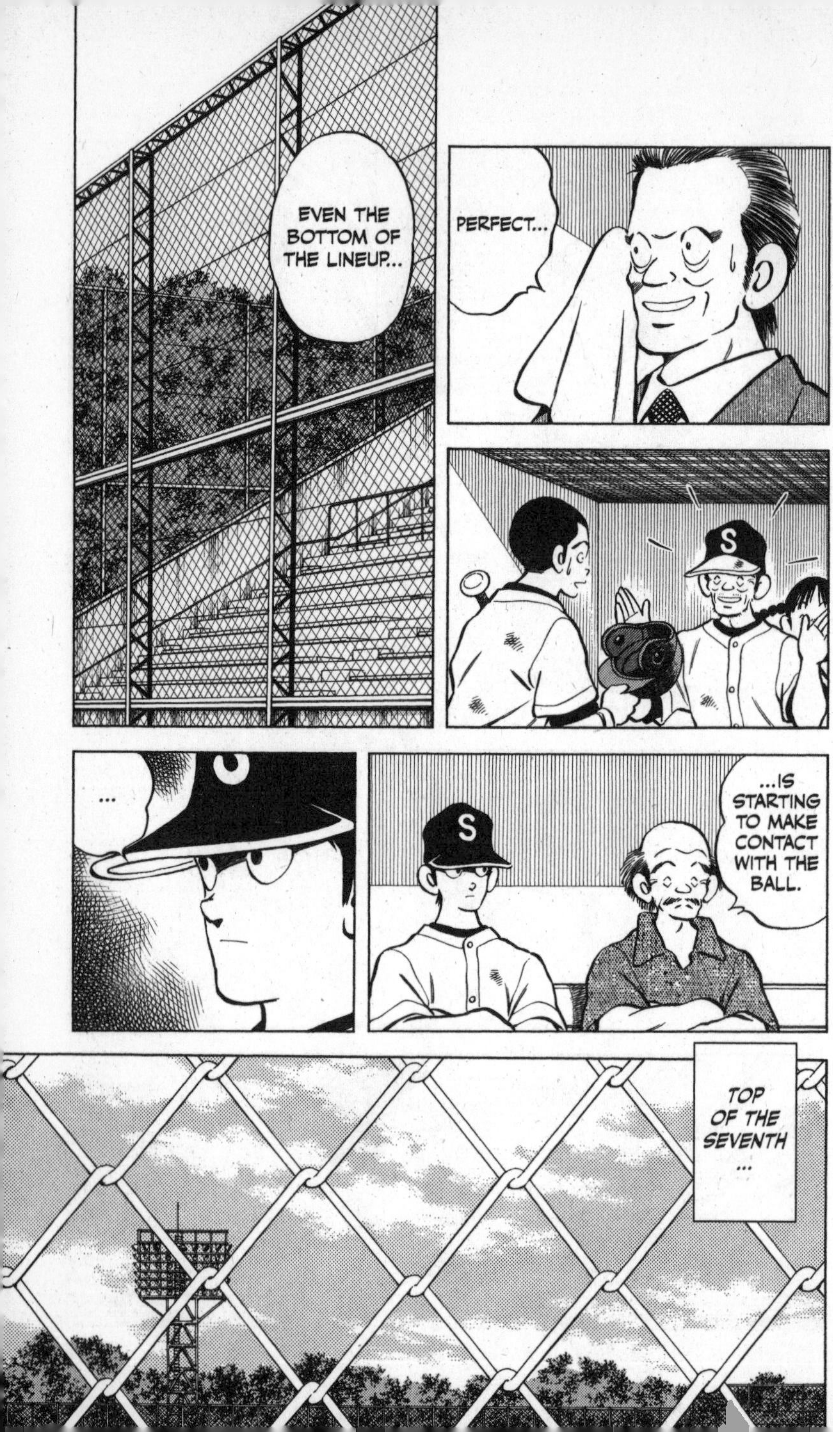
PERFECT...
EVEN THE BOTTOM OF THE LINEUP...
...IS STARTING TO MAKE CONTACT WITH THE BALL.
...
TOP OF THE SEVENTH ...

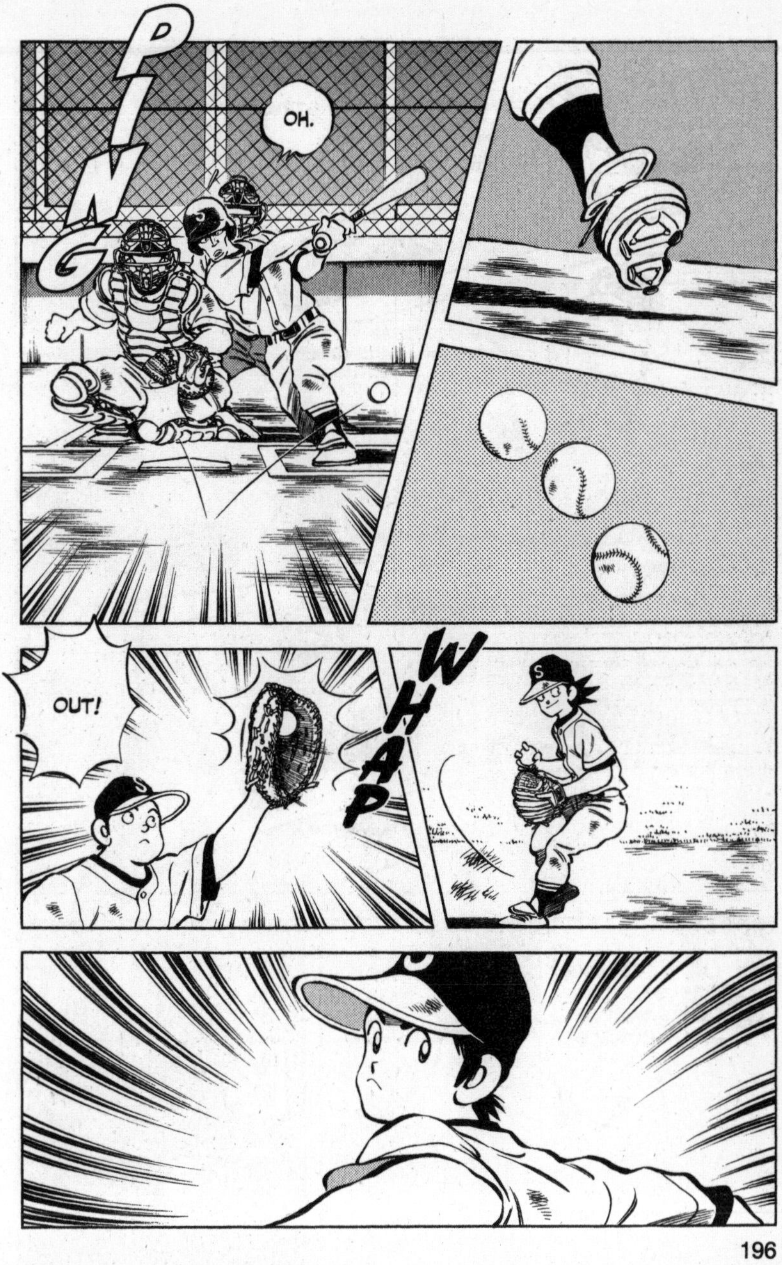
PING
OH.
WHAP
OUT!

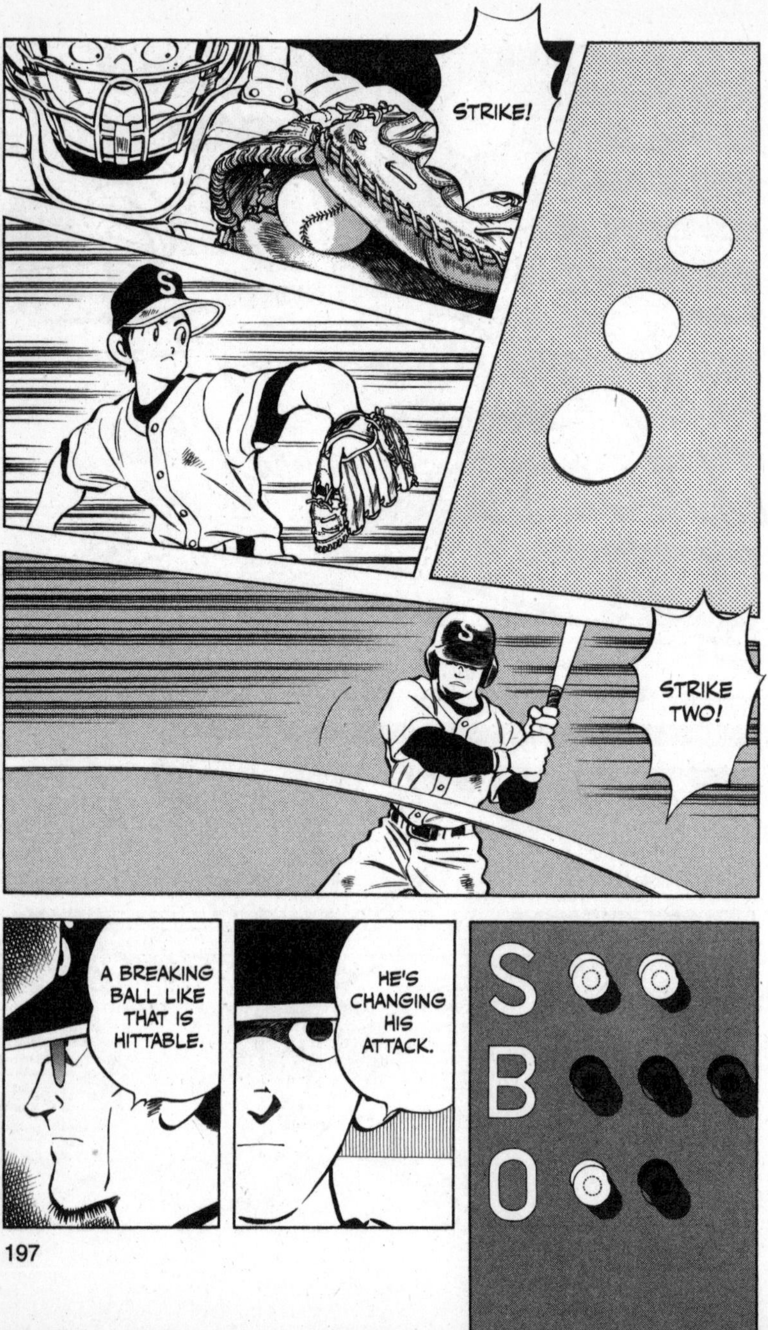
STRIKE!
STRIKE TWO!
S
B
O
HE'S CHANGING HIS ATTACK.
A BREAKING BALL LIKE THAT IS HITTABLE.

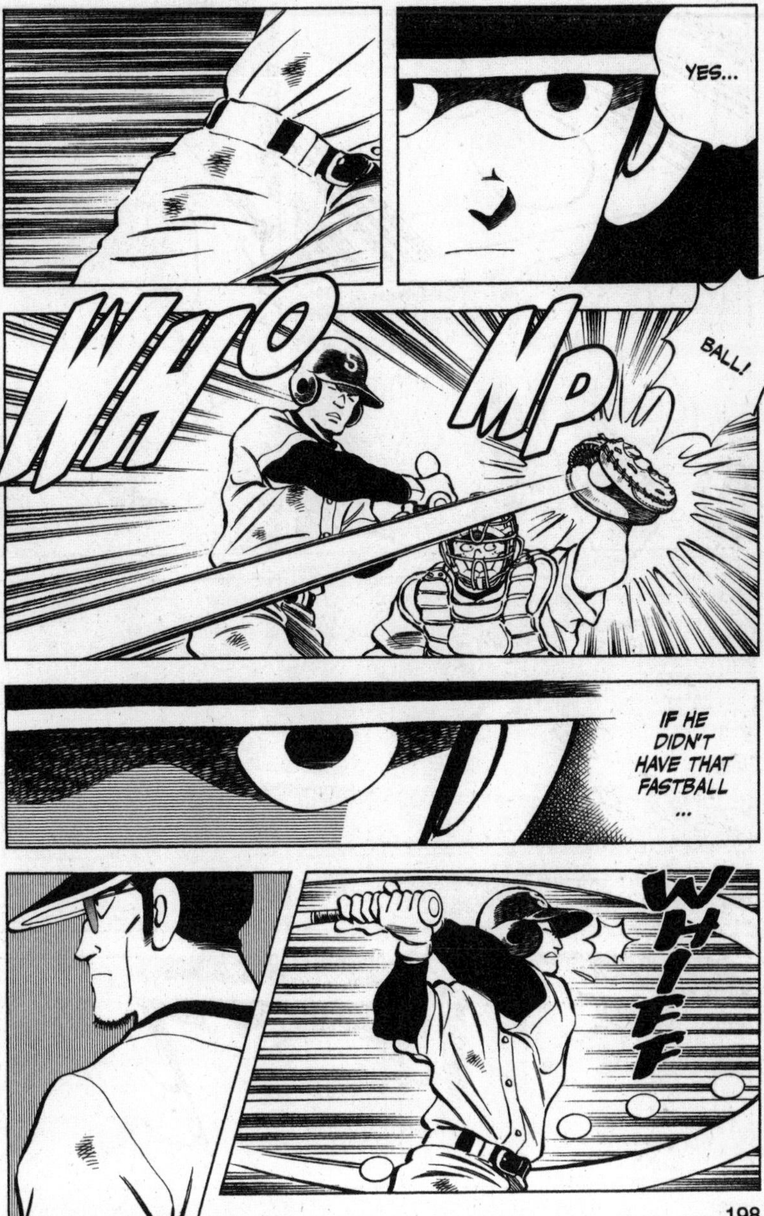
YES...
WHOMP
BALL!
IF HE DIDN'T HAVE THAT FASTBALL ...
WHIFF

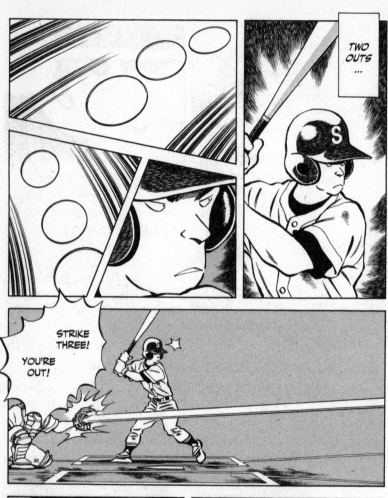

TWO OUTS ...

STRIKE THREE!

YOU'RE OUT!

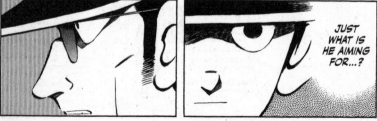

JUST WHAT IS HE AIMING FOR...?

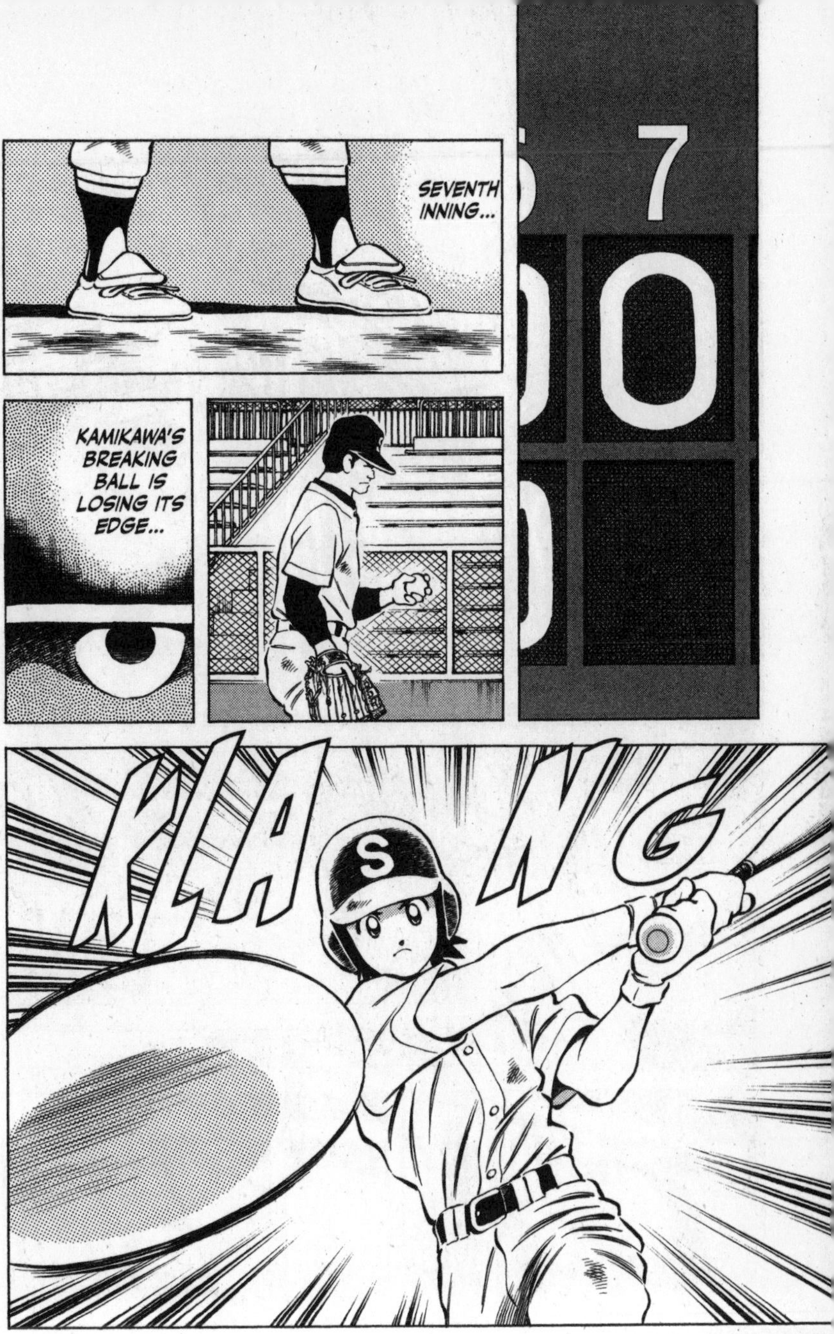
SEVENTH INNING...
KAMIKAWA'S BREAKING BALL IS LOSING ITS EDGE...
KLANG

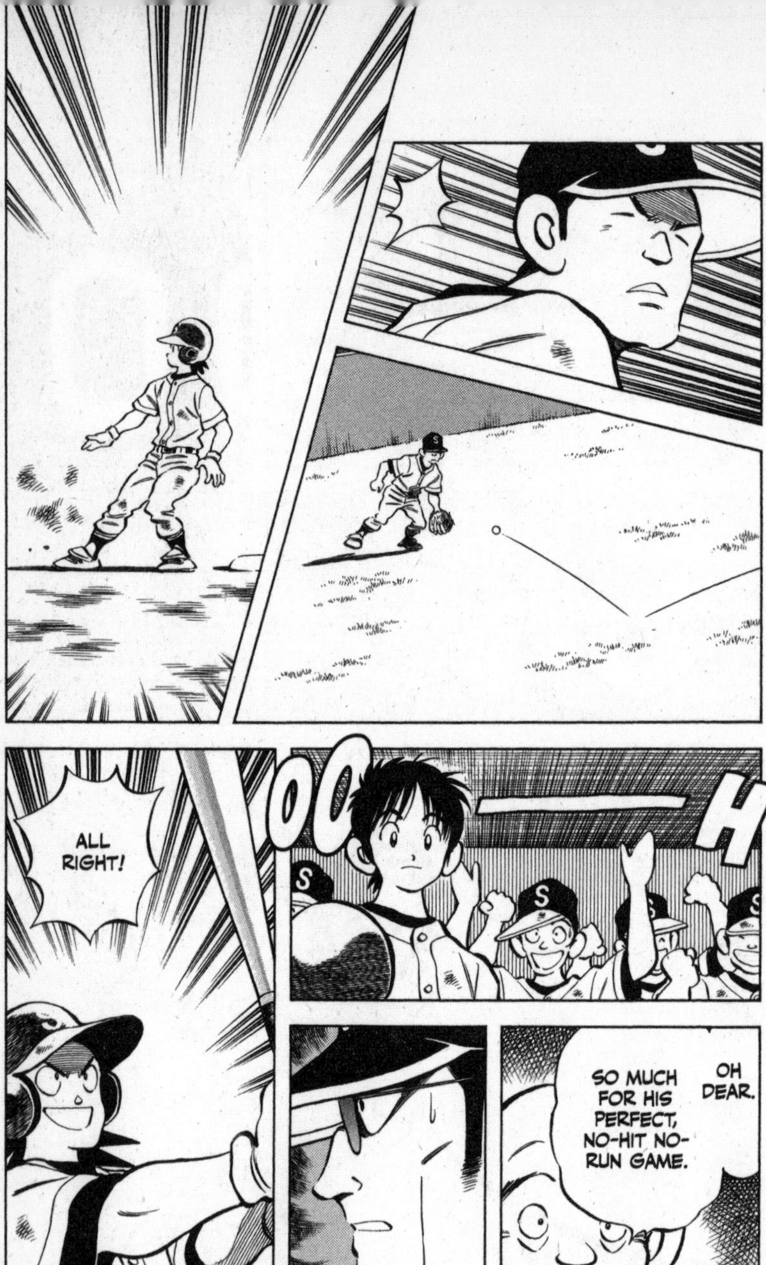

OO—H
OH DEAR.
SO MUCH FOR HIS PERFECT, NO-HIT NO-RUN GAME.
ALL RIGHT!

A SACRIFICE BUNT?
NOPE...
GOING!
WHAP
KLANG!
SAFE!

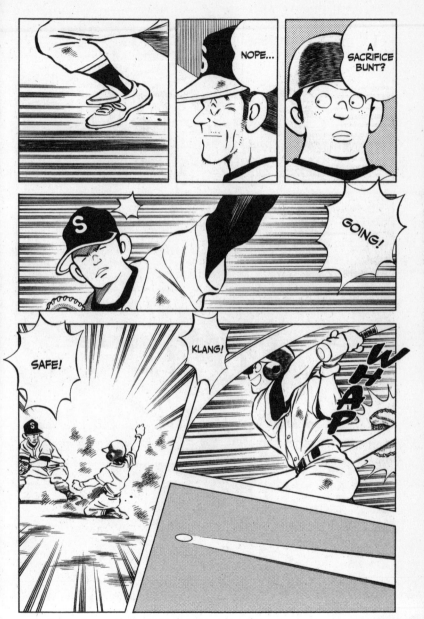

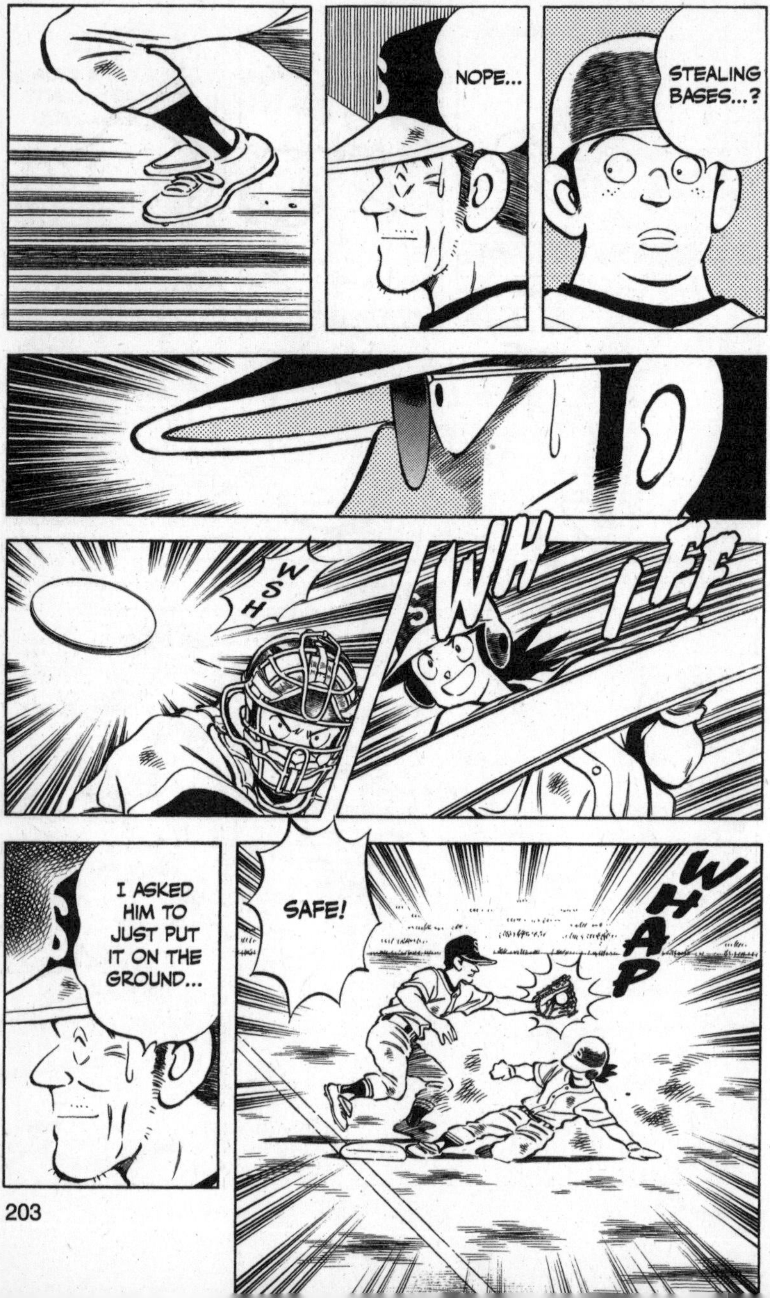
STEALING BASES...?
NOPE...
WHIFF
WSH
SAFE!
WHAP
I ASKED HIM TO JUST PUT IT ON THE GROUND...

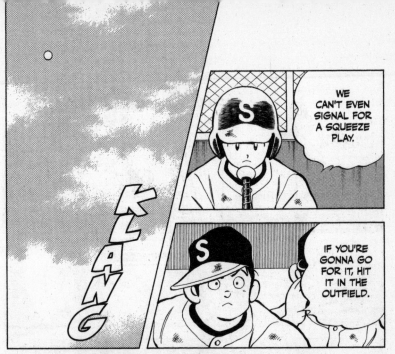

WE CAN'T EVEN SIGNAL FOR A SQUEEZE PLAY.

KLANG

IF YOU'RE GONNA GO FOR IT, HIT IT IN THE OUTFIELD.

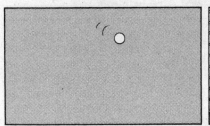

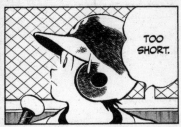

TOO SHORT.

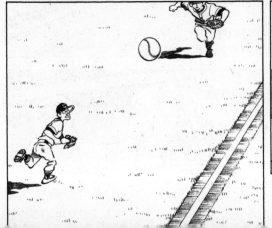

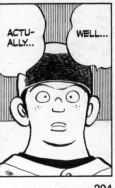

ACTUALLY...

WELL...

204

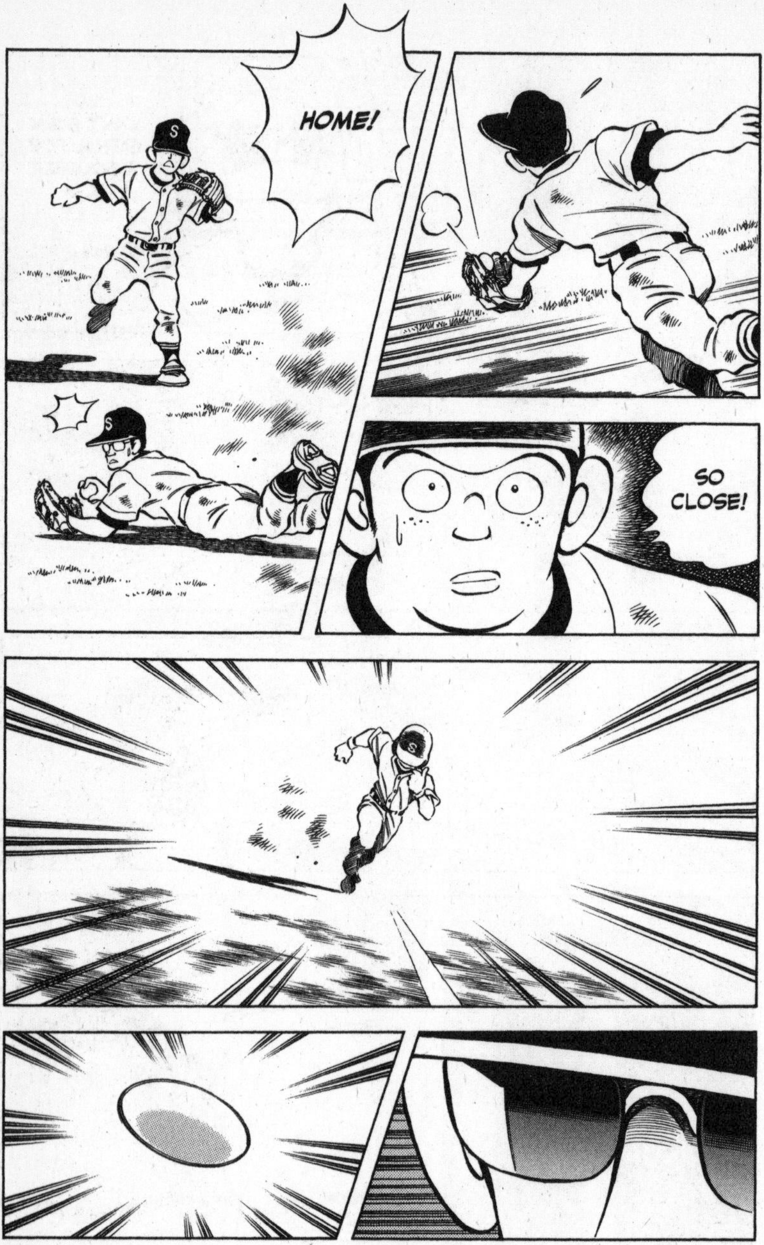
HOME!
SO CLOSE!

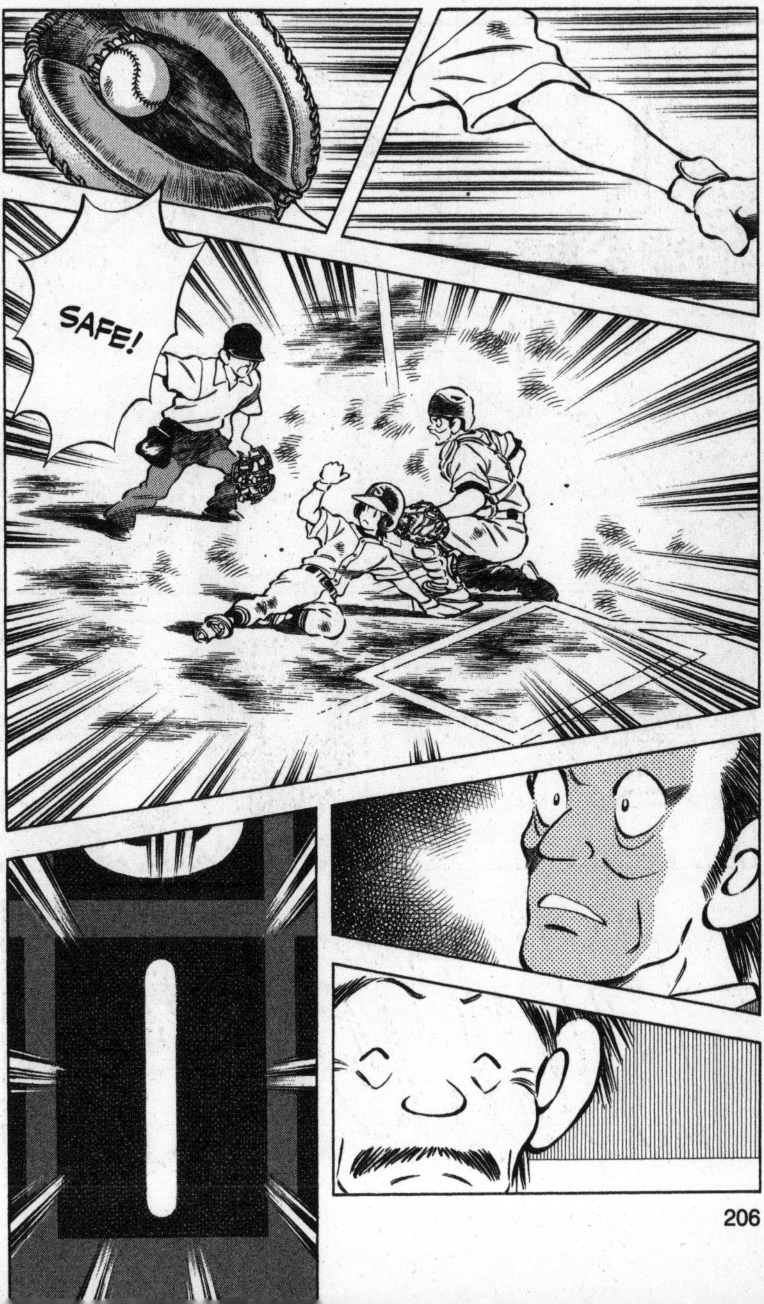
SAFE!

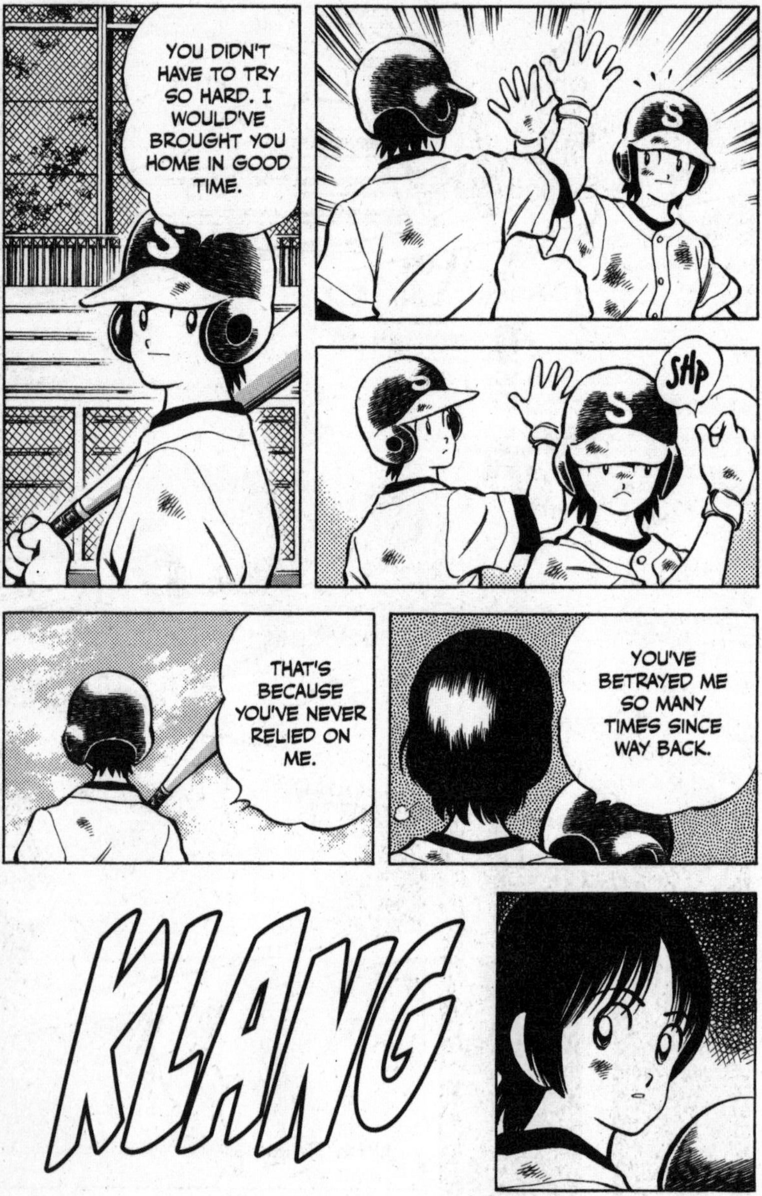
SHP
YOU DIDN'T HAVE TO TRY SO HARD. I WOULD'VE BROUGHT YOU HOME IN GOOD TIME.
YOU'VE BETRAYED ME SO MANY TIMES SINCE WAY BACK.
THAT'S BECAUSE YOU'VE NEVER RELIED ON ME.
KLANG

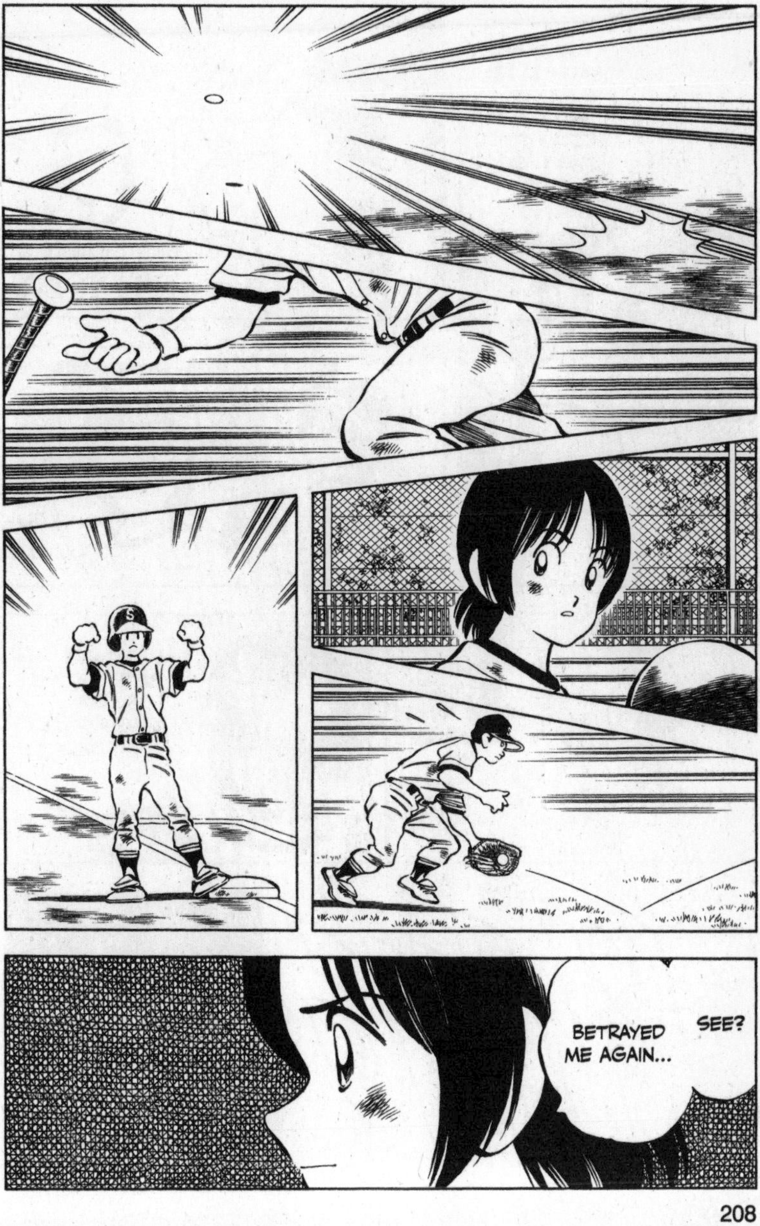
SEE?
BETRAYED ME AGAIN...

CHAPTER 52
WOULDN'T YOU KNOW IT

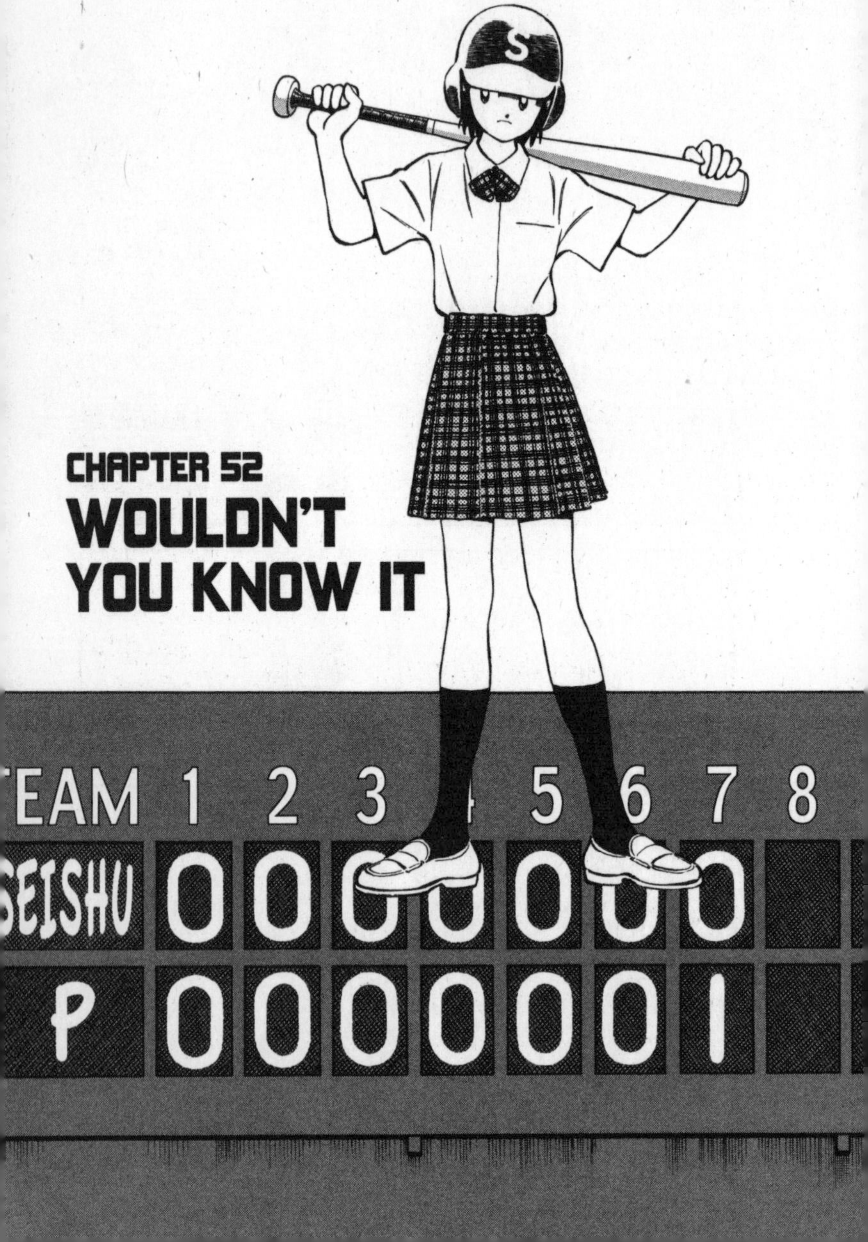
TEAM 1 2 3 4 5 6 7 8
SEISHU 0 0 0 0 0 0 0
P 0 0 0 0 0 0 1

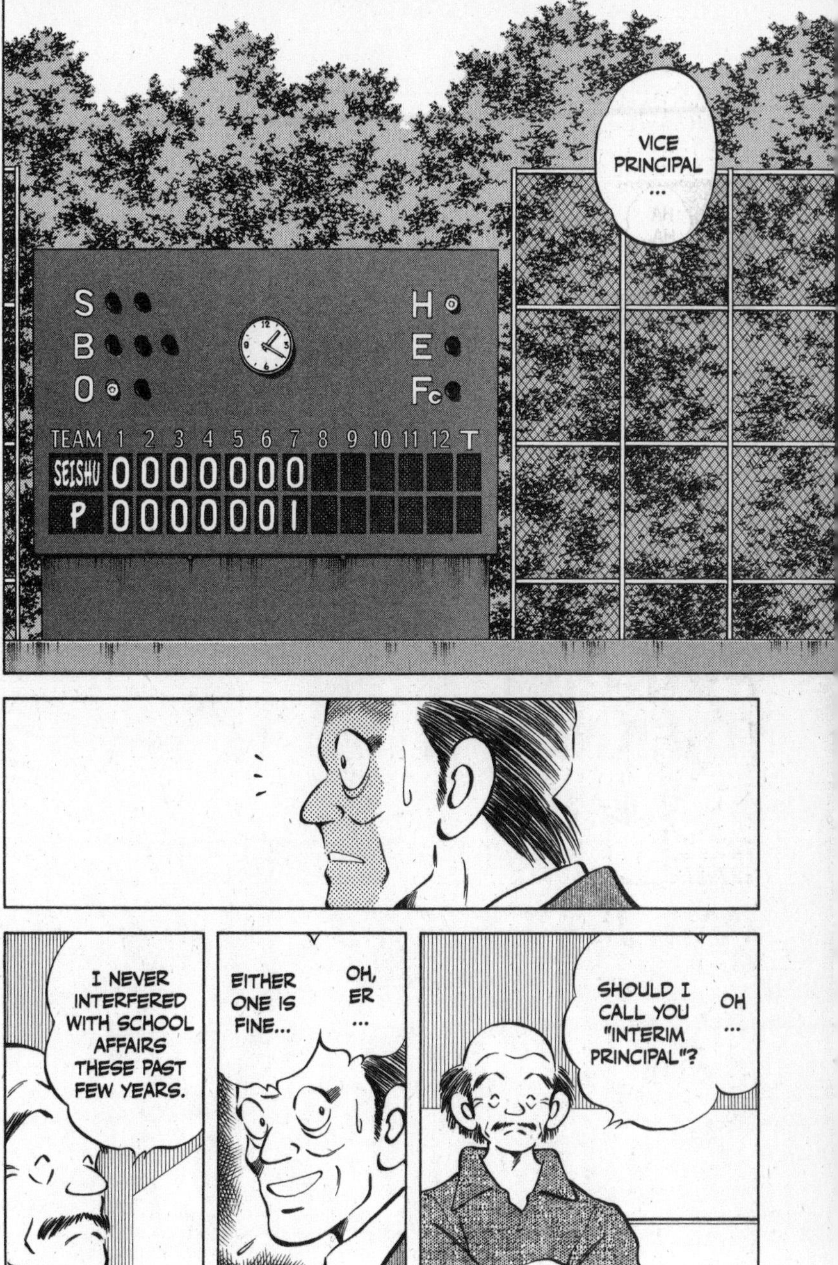
VICE PRINCIPAL ...
S
B
O
H
E
Fc
TEAM 1 2 3 4 5 6 7 8 9 10 11 12 T
SEISHU 0 0 0 0 0 0 0
P 0 0 0 0 0 0 1
OH ...
SHOULD I CALL YOU "INTERIM PRINCIPAL"?
OH, ER ...
EITHER ONE IS FINE...
I NEVER INTERFERED WITH SCHOOL AFFAIRS THESE PAST FEW YEARS.

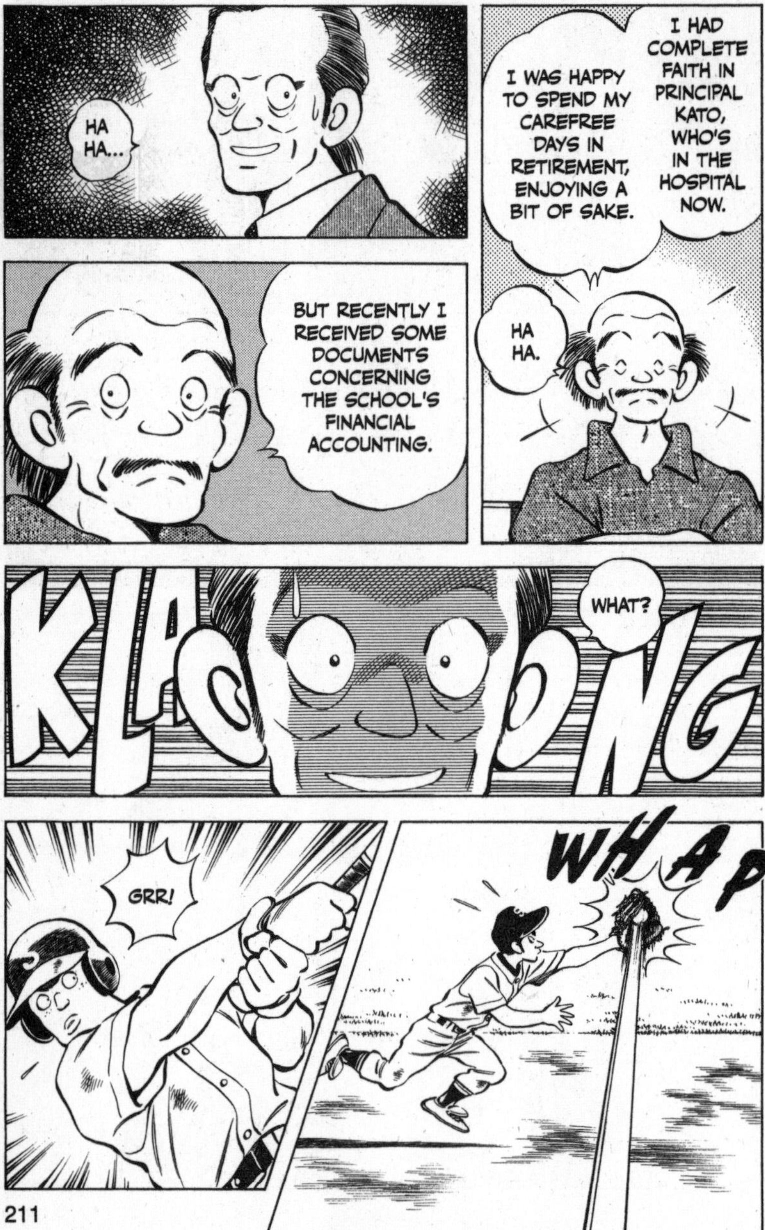
I HAD COMPLETE FAITH IN PRINCIPAL KATO, WHO'S IN THE HOSPITAL NOW.
I WAS HAPPY TO SPEND MY CAREFREE DAYS IN RETIREMENT, ENJOYING A BIT OF SAKE.
HA HA.
HA HA...
BUT RECENTLY I RECEIVED SOME DOCUMENTS CONCERNING THE SCHOOL'S FINANCIAL ACCOUNTING.
WHAT?
KLAOONG
WHAP
GRR!

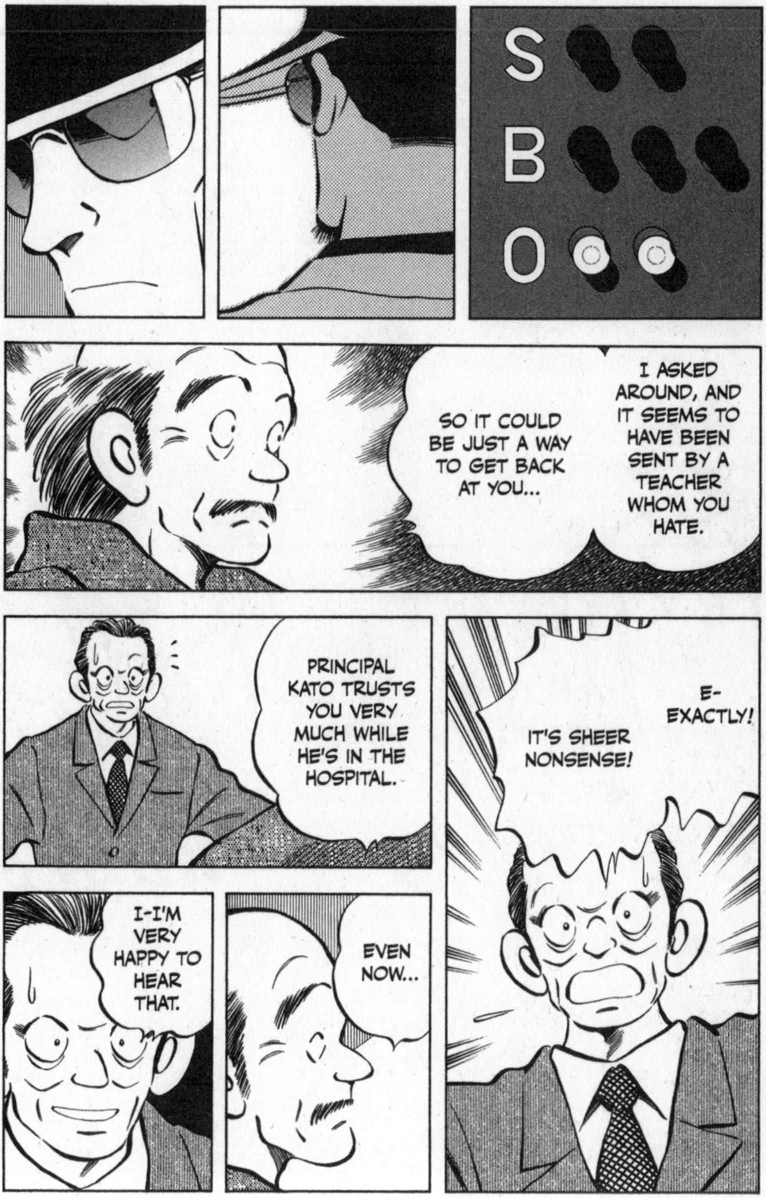
S
B
O
I ASKED AROUND, AND IT SEEMS TO HAVE BEEN SENT BY A TEACHER WHOM YOU HATE.
SO IT COULD BE JUST A WAY TO GET BACK AT YOU...
E- EXACTLY!
IT'S SHEER NONSENSE!
PRINCIPAL KATO TRUSTS YOU VERY MUCH WHILE HE'S IN THE HOSPITAL.
EVEN NOW...
I-I'M VERY HAPPY TO HEAR THAT.

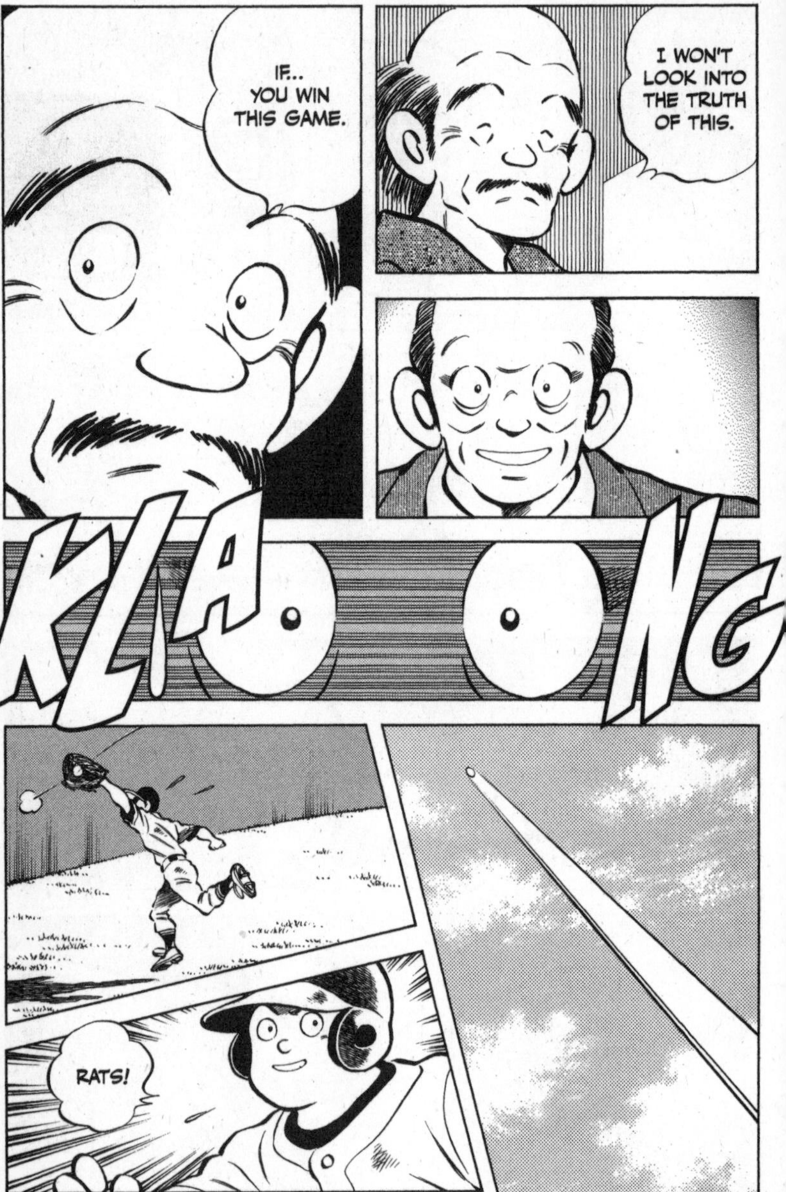

I WON'T LOOK INTO THE TRUTH OF THIS.
IF... YOU WIN THIS GAME.
KLAOONG
RATS!

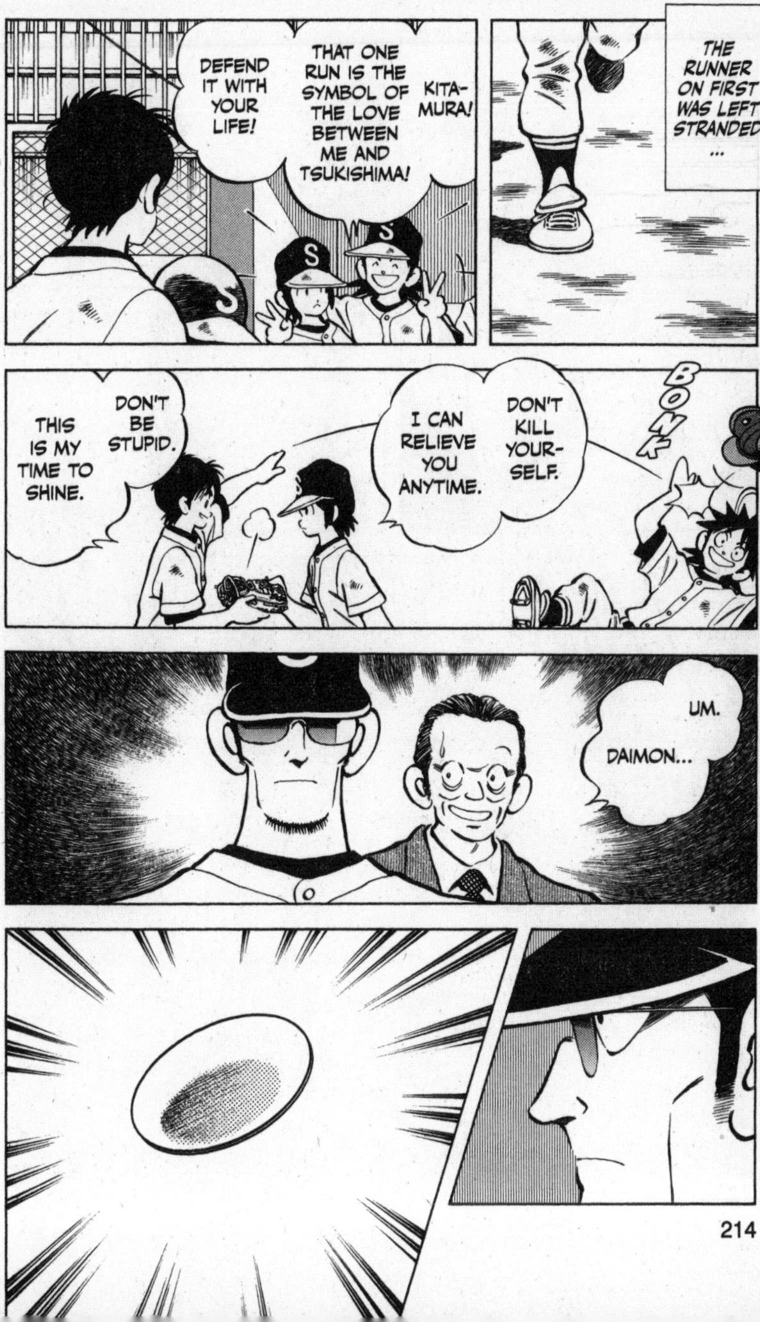
THE RUNNER ON FIRST WAS LEFT STRANDED...
KITA-MURA!
THAT ONE RUN IS THE SYMBOL OF THE LOVE BETWEEN ME AND TSUKISHIMA!
DEFEND IT WITH YOUR LIFE!
BONK
DON'T KILL YOURSELF.
I CAN RELIEVE YOU ANYTIME.
DON'T BE STUPID.
THIS IS MY TIME TO SHINE.
UM.
DAIMON...

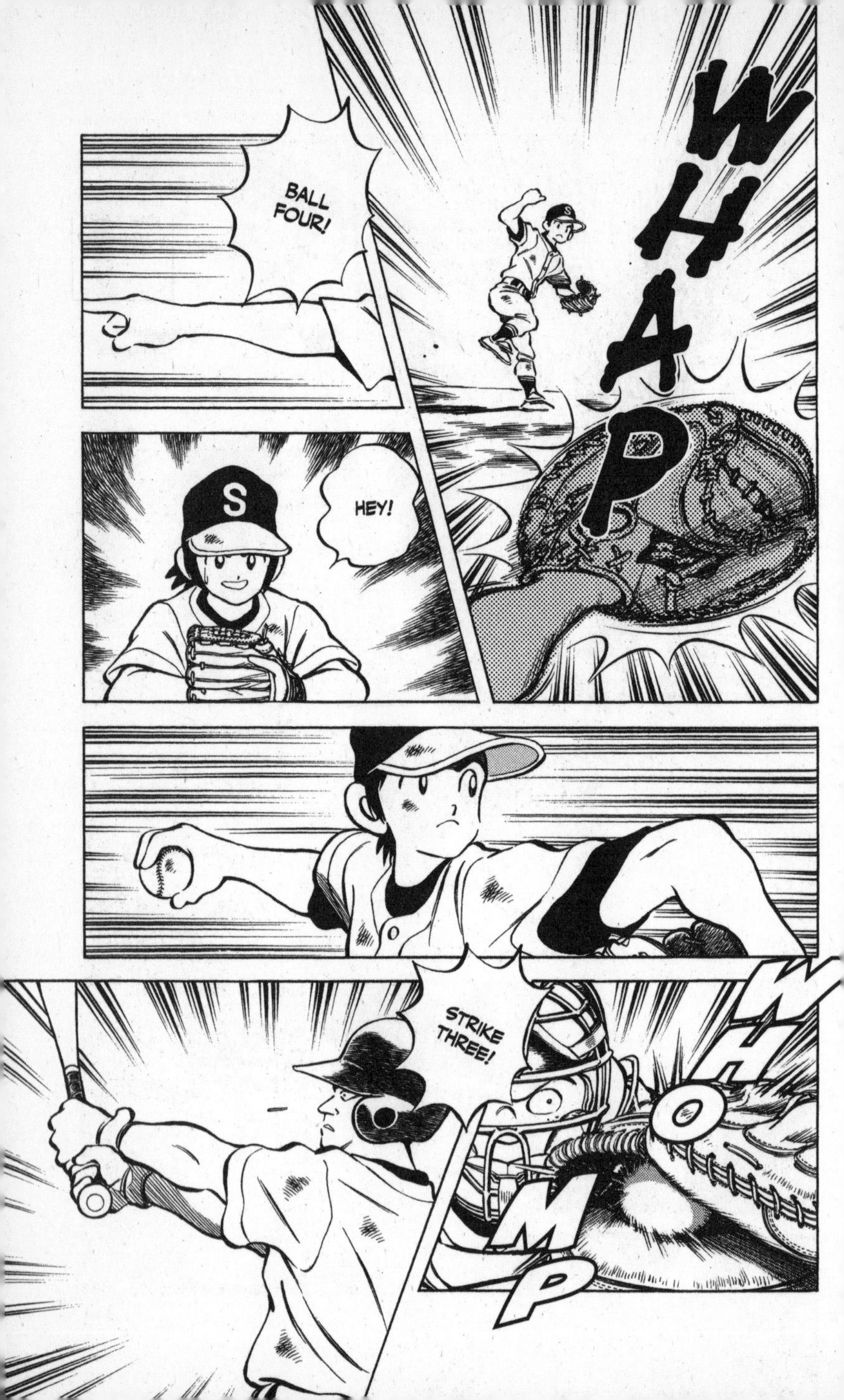
WHAP
BALL FOUR!
HEY!
WHOMP
STRIKE THREE!

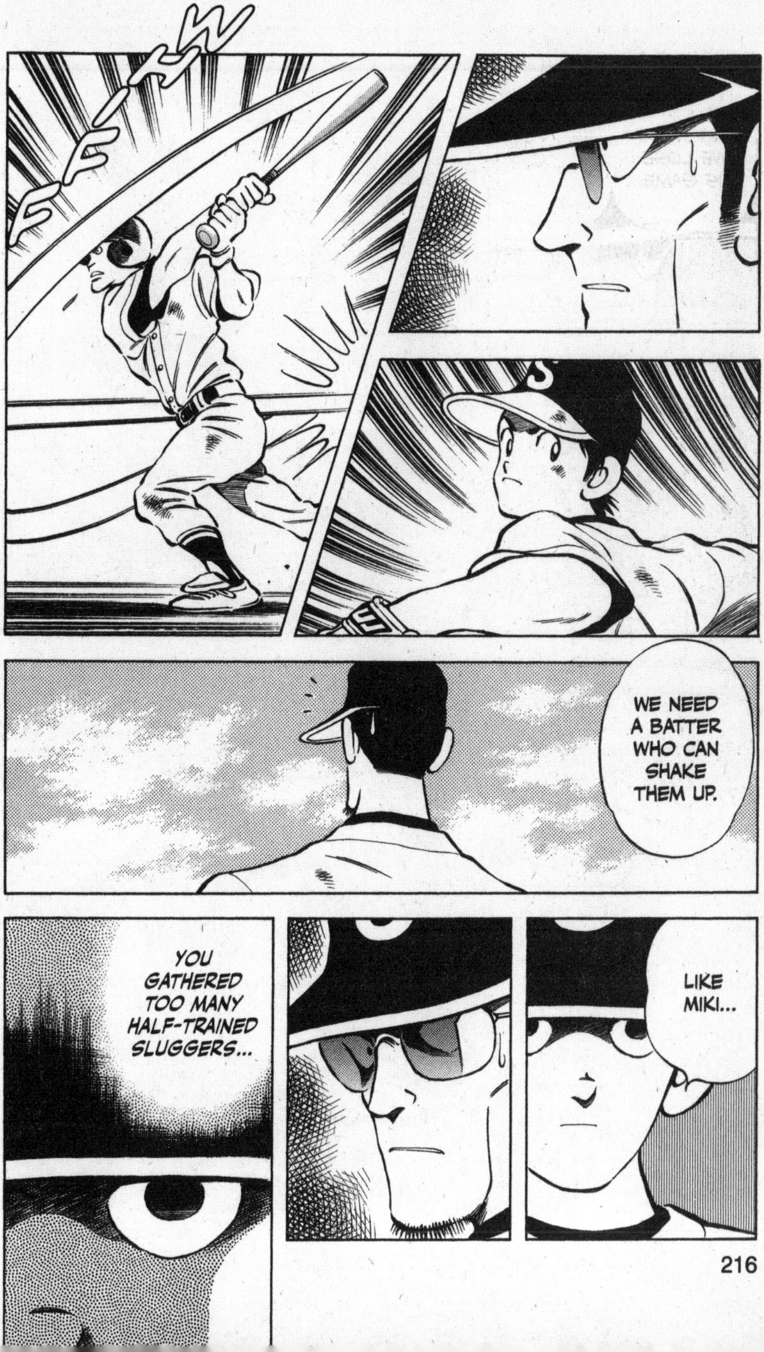
FF-KW
WE NEED A BATTER WHO CAN SHAKE THEM UP.
LIKE MIKI...
YOU GATHERED TOO MANY HALF-TRAINED SLUGGERS...

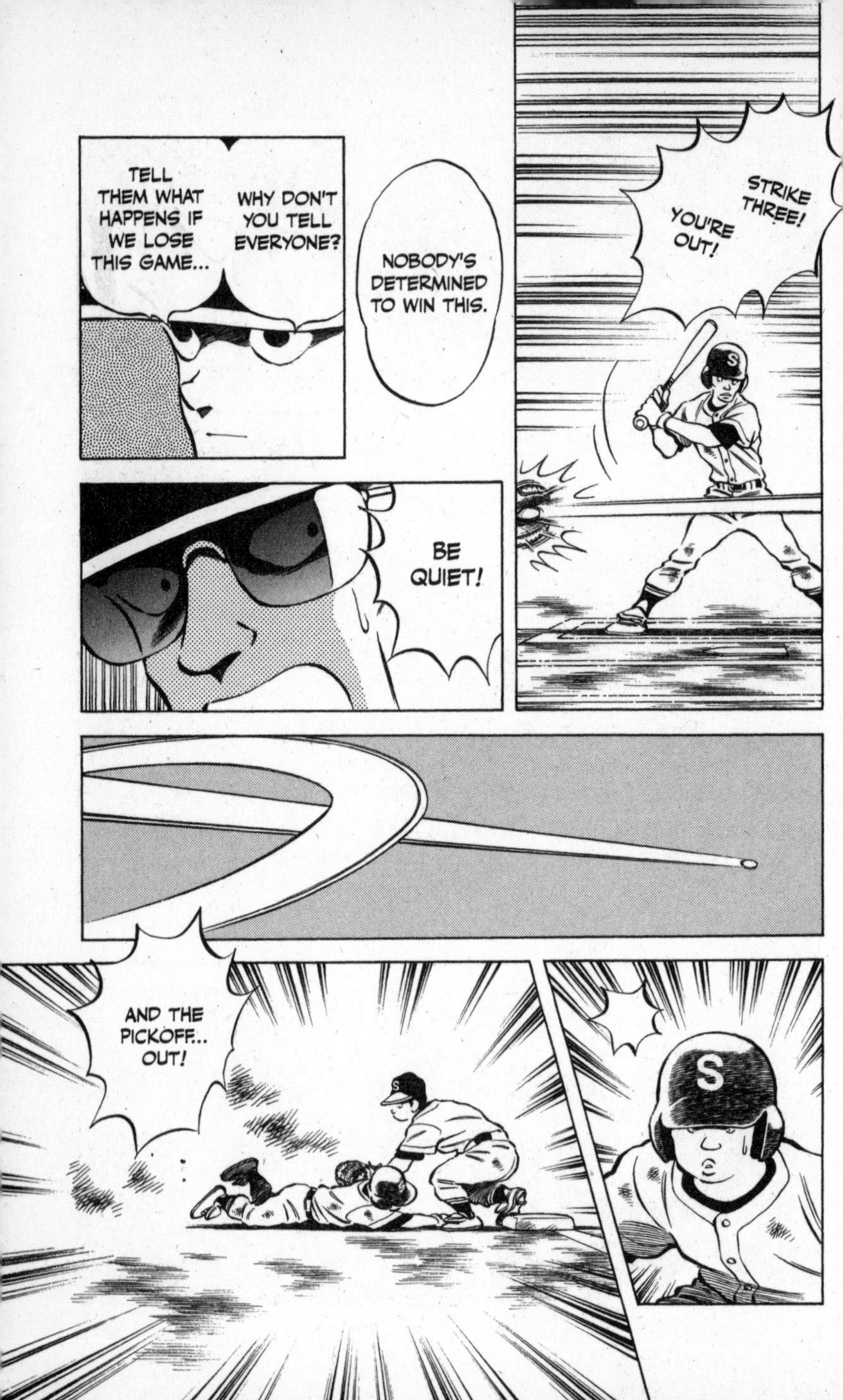
STRIKE THREE! YOU'RE OUT!
NOBODY'S DETERMINED TO WIN THIS.
WHY DON'T YOU TELL EVERYONE?
TELL THEM WHAT HAPPENS IF WE LOSE THIS GAME...
BE QUIET!
AND THE PICKOFF... OUT!

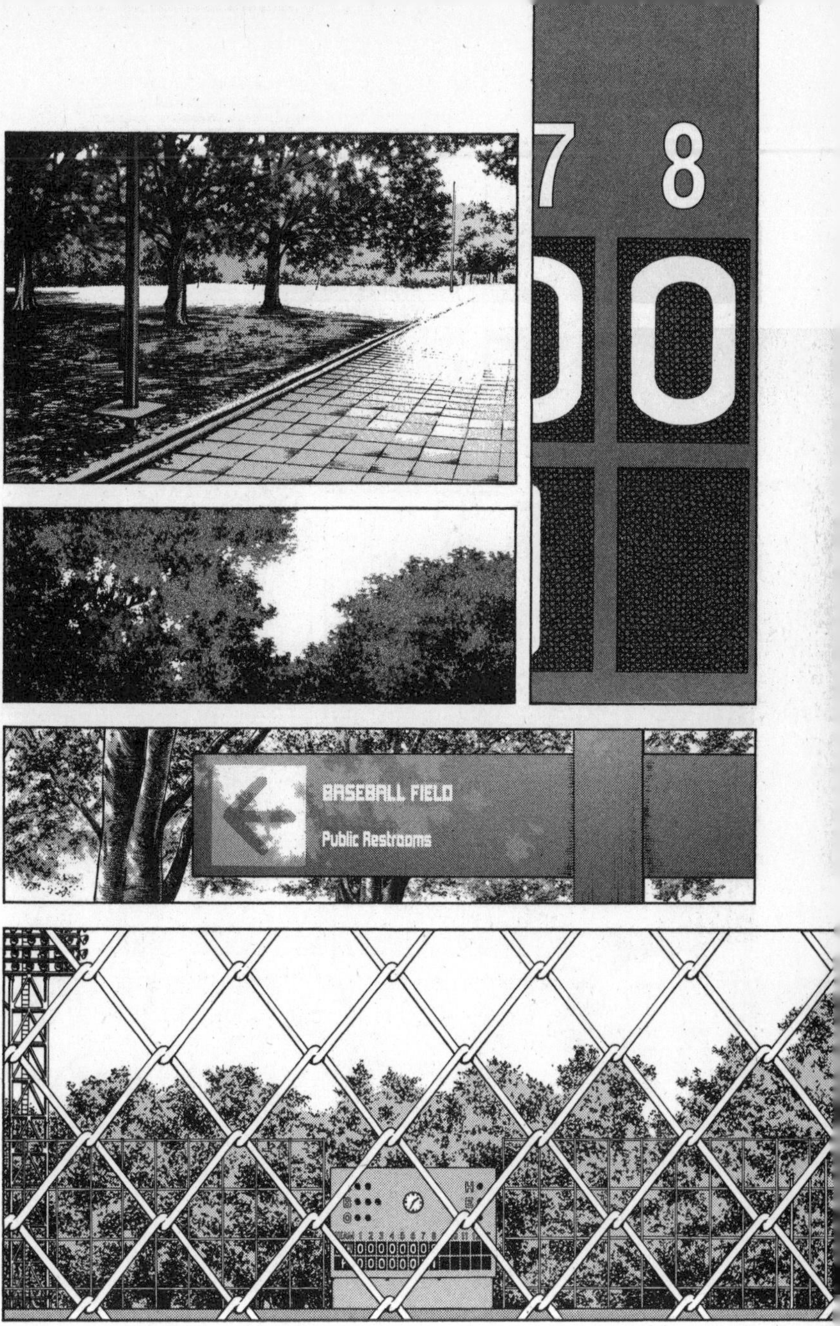
BASEBALL FIELD
Public Restrooms

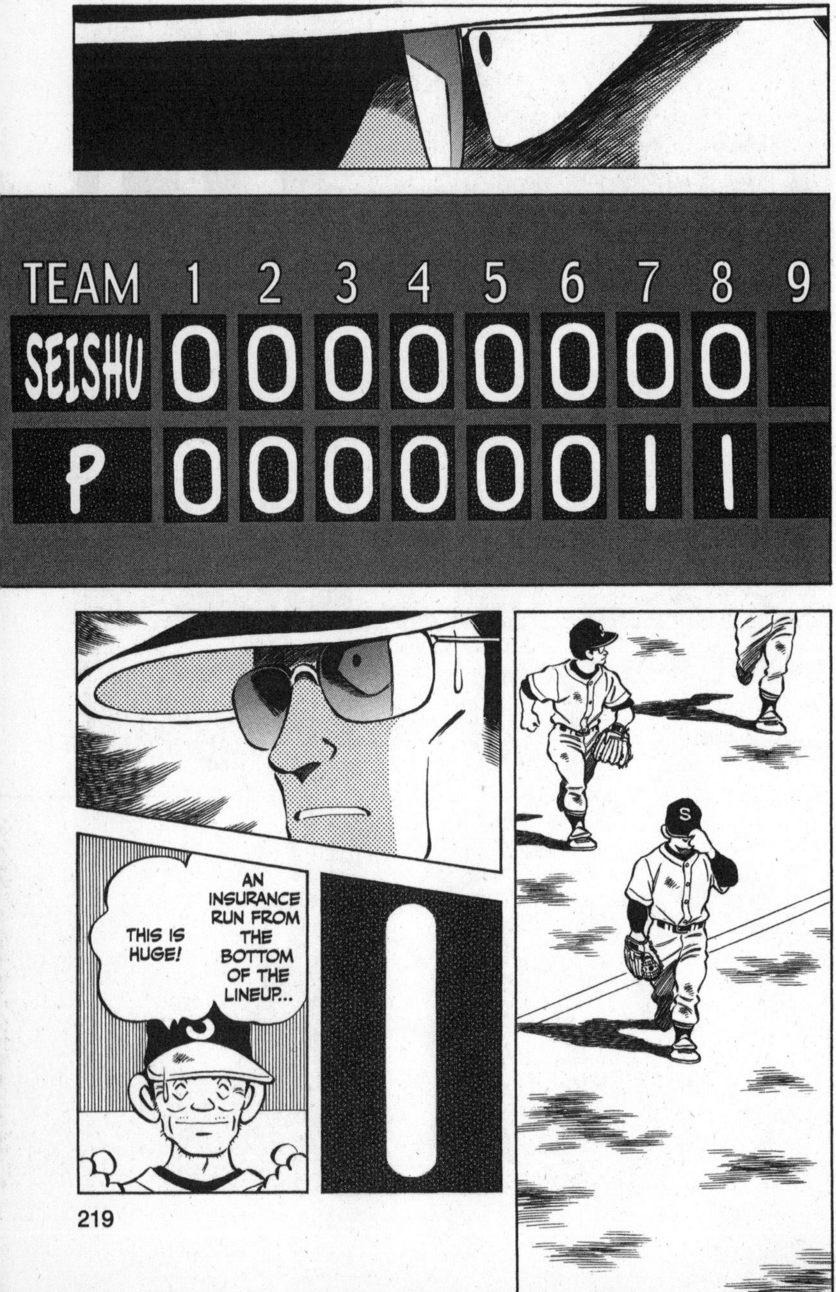
TEAM 1 2 3 4 5 6 7 8 9
SEISHU 0 0 0 0 0 0 0 0
P 0 0 0 0 0 0 1 1
0
AN INSURANCE RUN FROM THE BOTTOM OF THE LINEUP...
THIS IS HUGE!

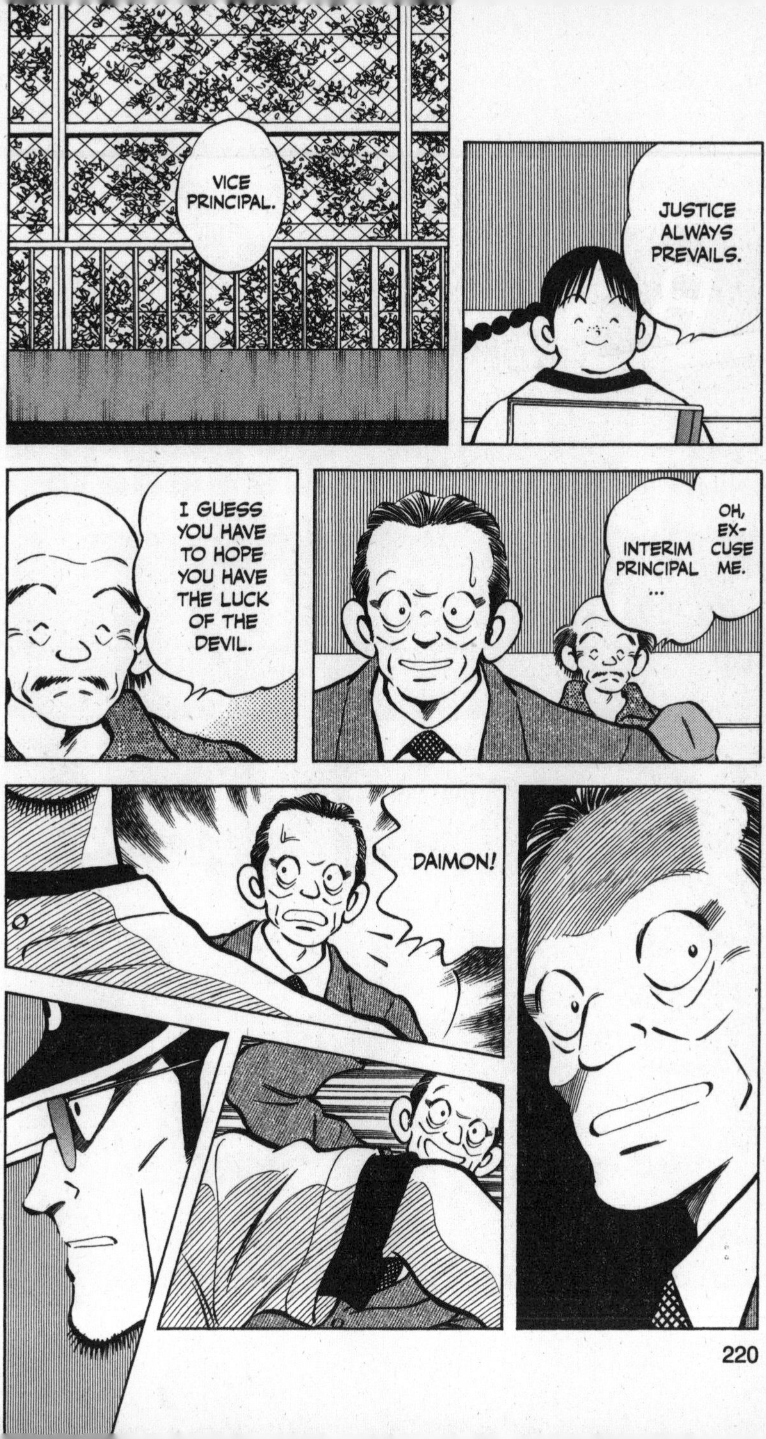
JUSTICE ALWAYS PREVAILS.
VICE PRINCIPAL.
OH, EXCUSE ME.
INTERIM PRINCIPAL ...
I GUESS YOU HAVE TO HOPE YOU HAVE THE LUCK OF THE DEVIL.
DAIMON!

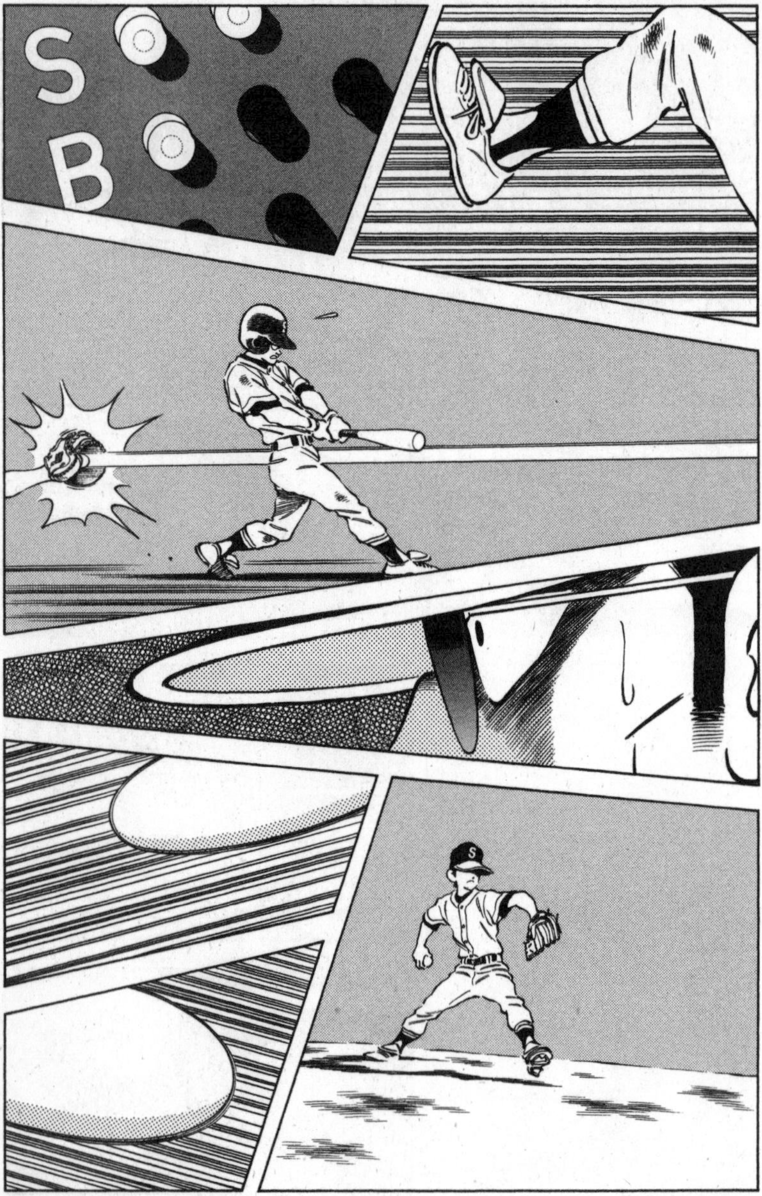
S
B

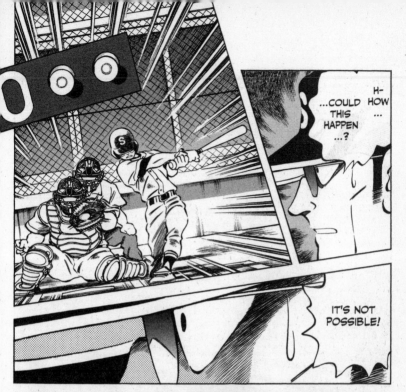

H- HOW ...COULD THIS HAPPEN ...?

IT'S NOT POSSIBLE!

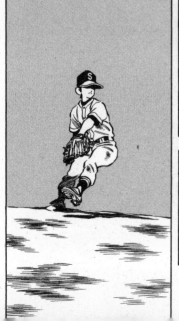

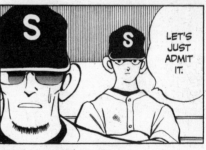

LET'S JUST ADMIT IT.

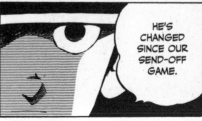

HE'S CHANGED SINCE OUR SEND-OFF GAME.

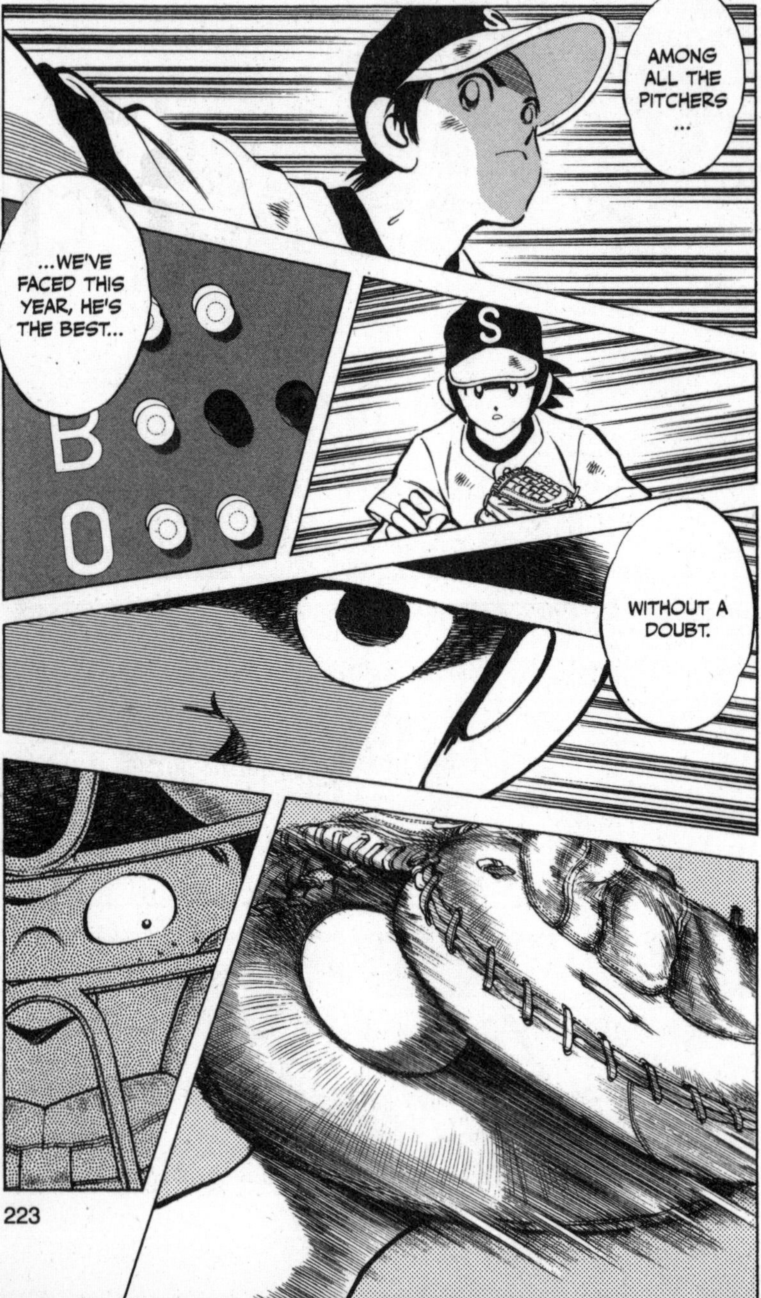
AMONG ALL THE PITCHERS ...
...WE'VE FACED THIS YEAR, HE'S THE BEST...
B
O
WITHOUT A DOUBT.

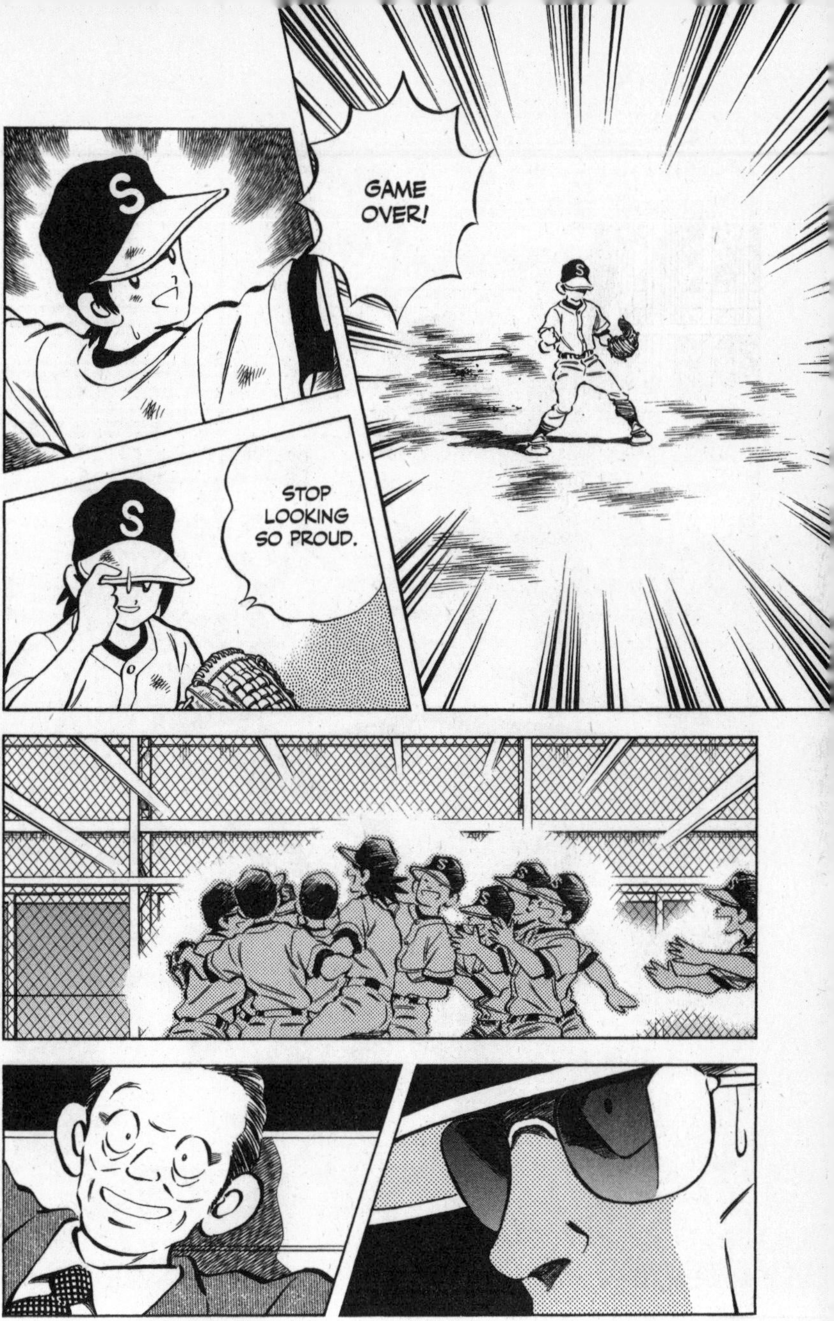
GAME OVER!
STOP LOOKING SO PROUD.

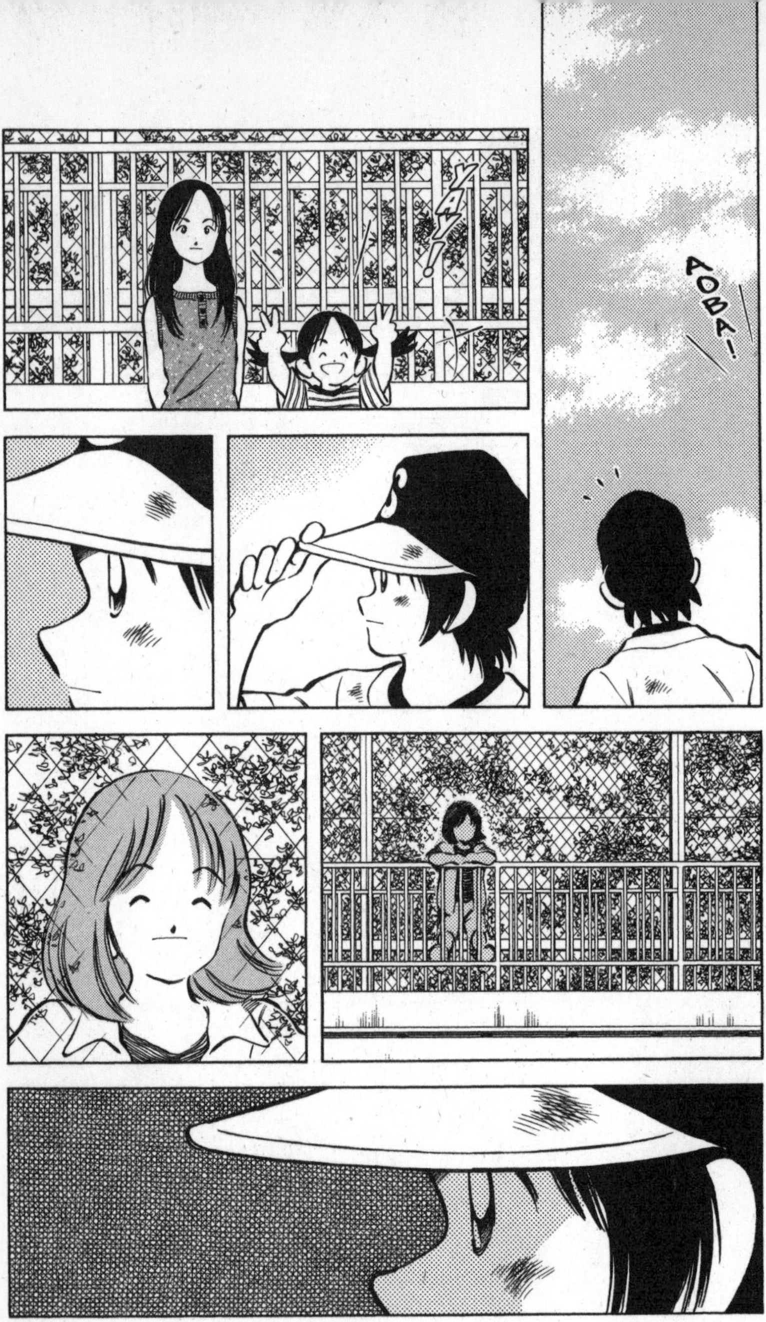
AOBA!
YAY!

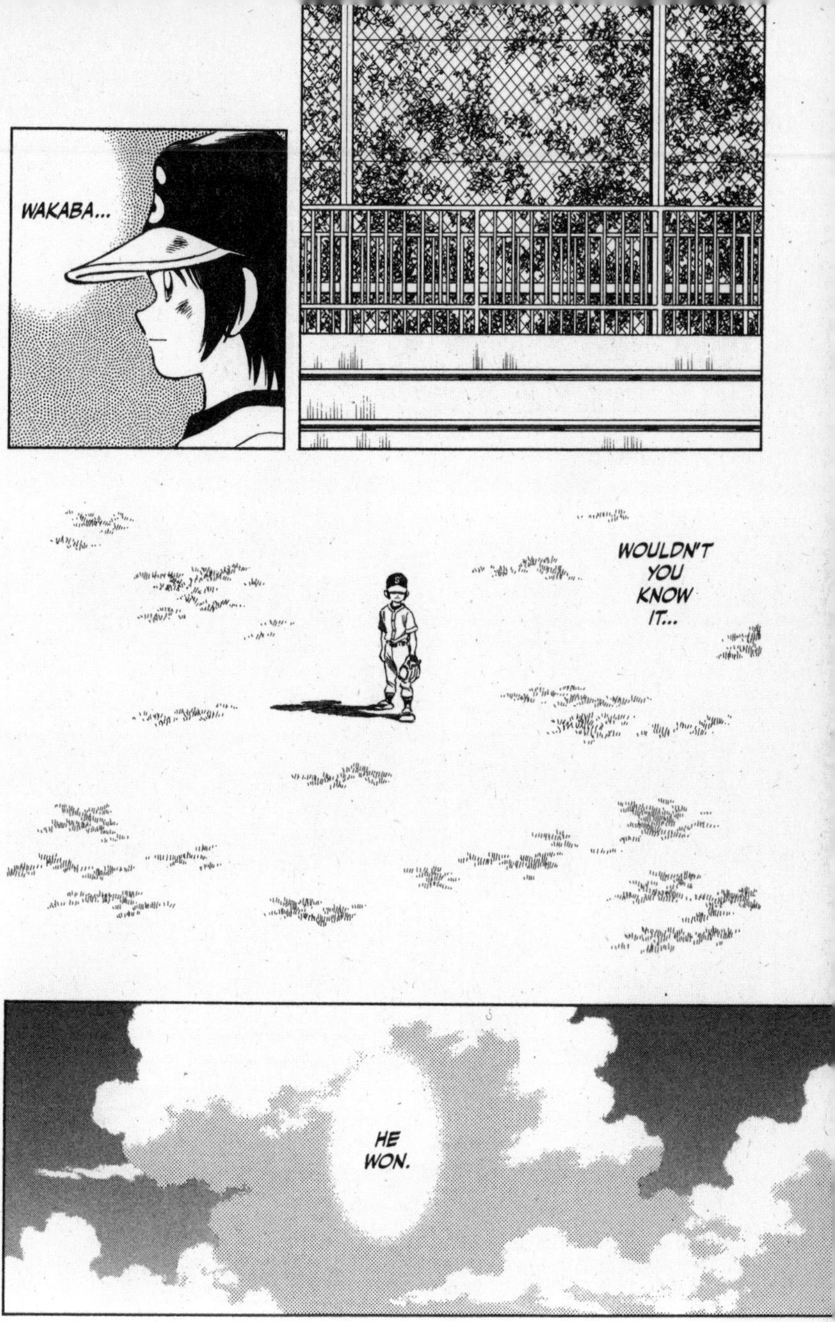
WAKABA...
WOULDN'T YOU KNOW IT...
HE WON.

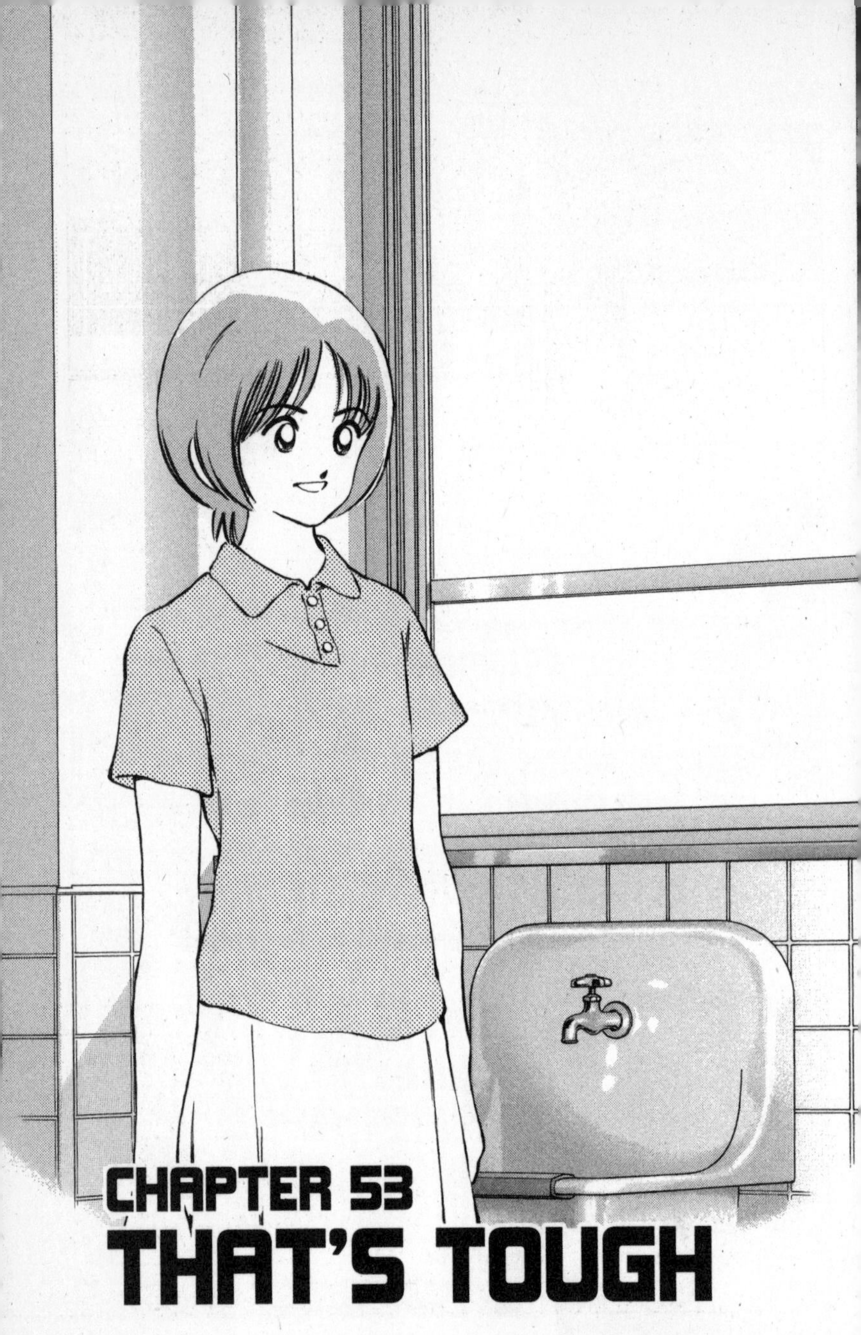

CHAPTER 53
THAT'S TOUGH

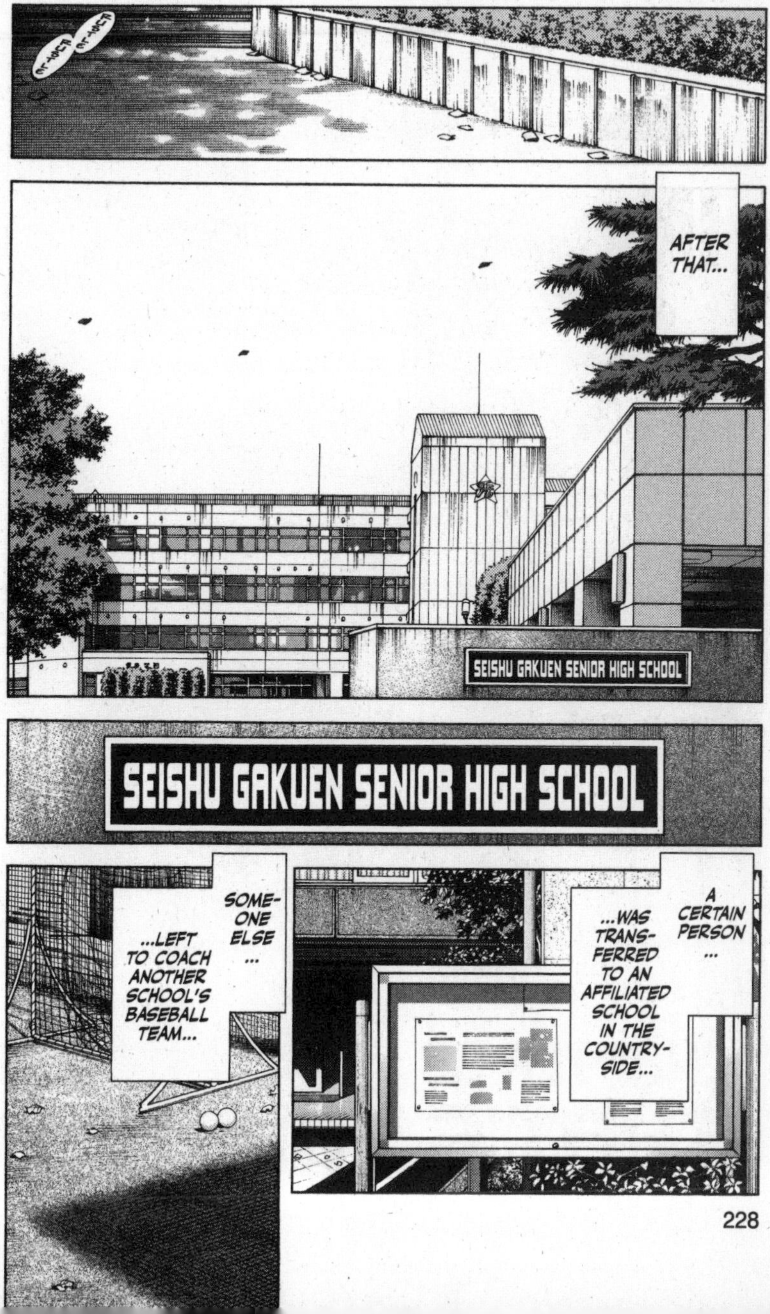
AFTER THAT...
SEISHU GAKUEN SENIOR HIGH SCHOOL
SEISHU GAKUEN SENIOR HIGH SCHOOL
A CERTAIN PERSON...
...WAS TRANSFERRED TO AN AFFILIATED SCHOOL IN THE COUNTRYSIDE...
SOMEONE ELSE...
...LEFT TO COACH ANOTHER SCHOOL'S BASEBALL TEAM...

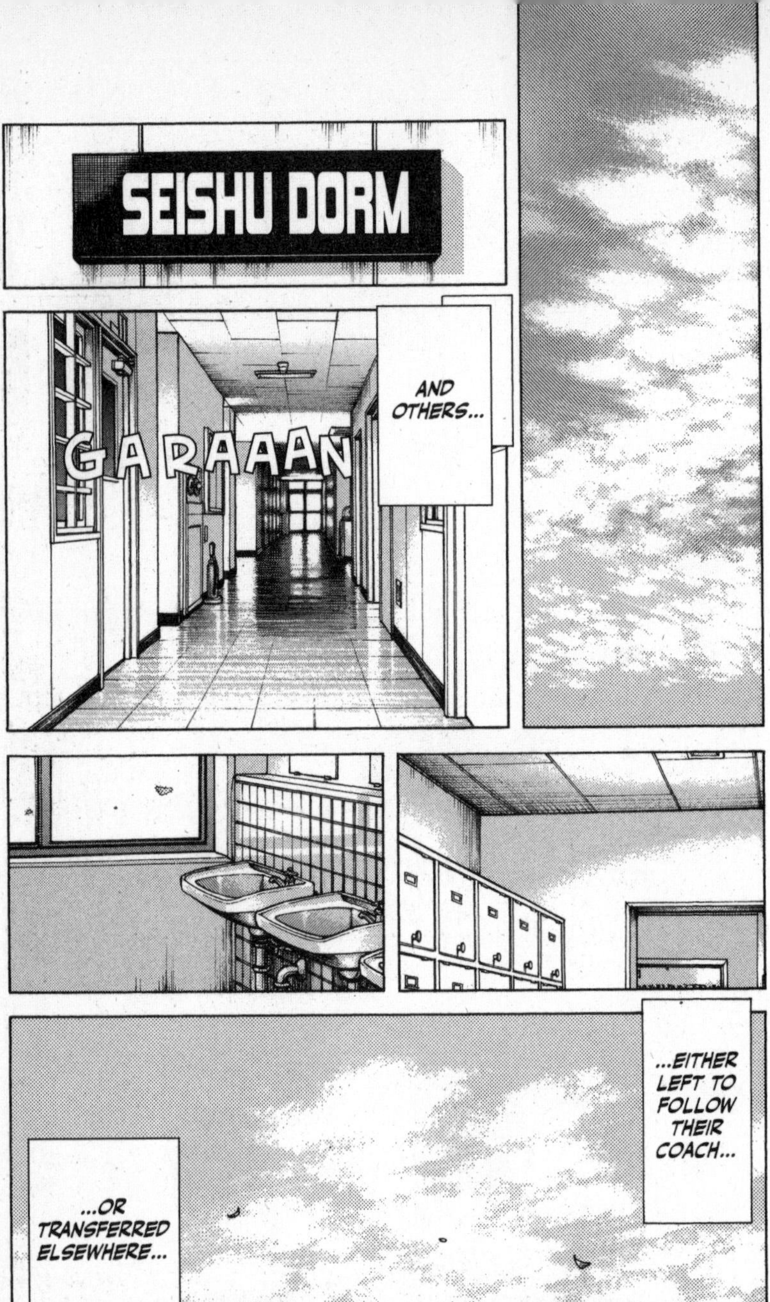
SEISHU DORM
AND OTHERS...
GARAAAN
...EITHER LEFT TO FOLLOW THEIR COACH...
...OR TRANSFERRED ELSEWHERE...

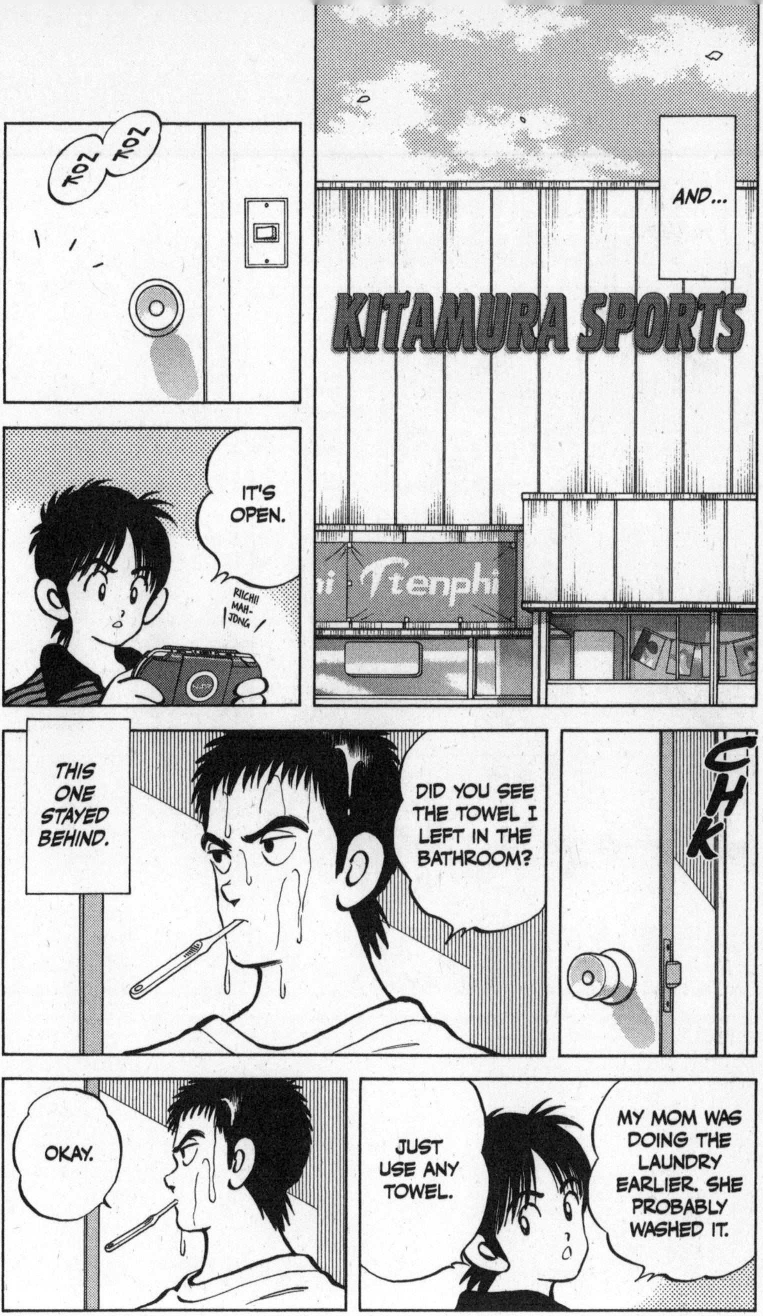
AND...
KITAMURA SPORTS
tenphi
KNOK KNOK
IT'S OPEN.
RIICHI! MAH-JONG
CHK
DID YOU SEE THE TOWEL I LEFT IN THE BATHROOM?
THIS ONE STAYED BEHIND.
MY MOM WAS DOING THE LAUNDRY EARLIER. SHE PROBABLY WASHED IT.
JUST USE ANY TOWEL.
OKAY.

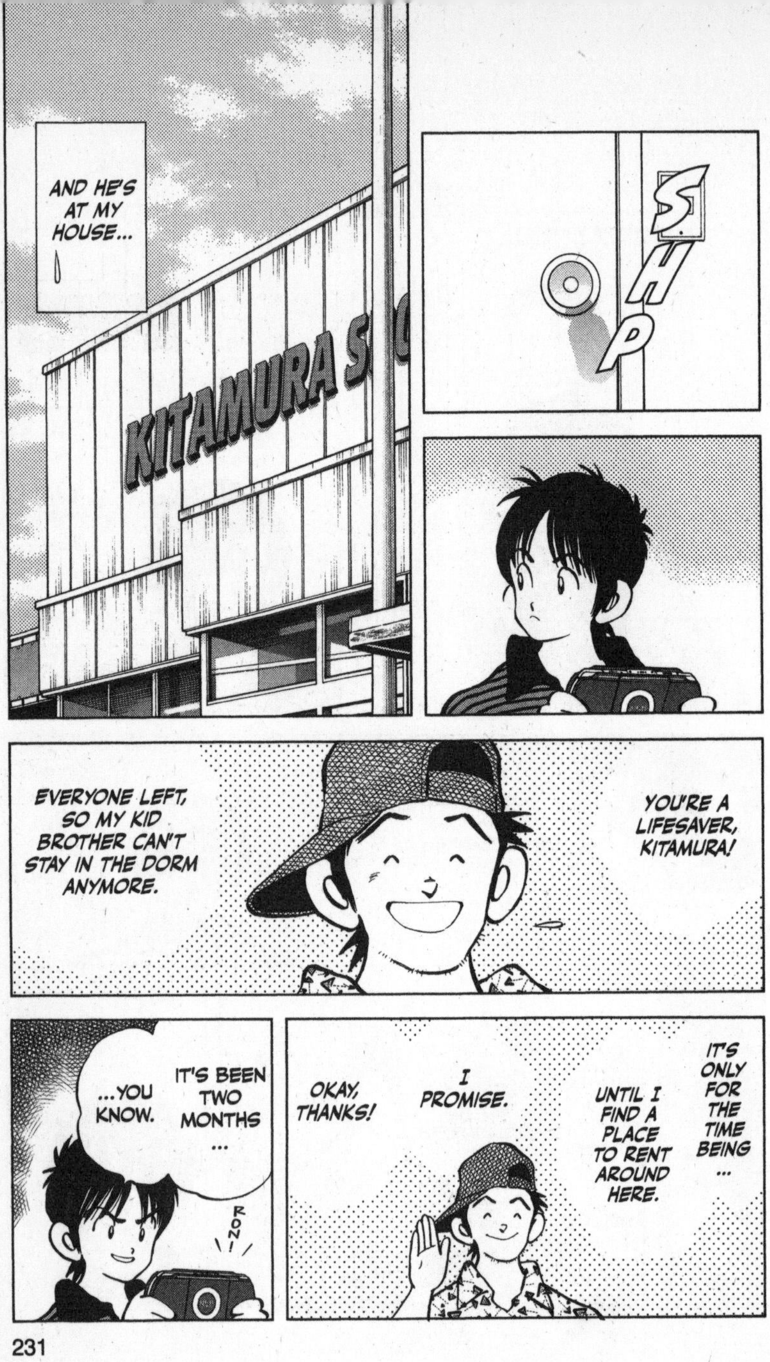
S
H
P
AND HE'S AT MY HOUSE...
KITAMURA S
YOU'RE A LIFESAVER, KITAMURA!
EVERYONE LEFT, SO MY KID BROTHER CAN'T STAY IN THE DORM ANYMORE.
IT'S ONLY FOR THE TIME BEING...
UNTIL I FIND A PLACE TO RENT AROUND HERE.
I PROMISE.
OKAY, THANKS!
IT'S BEEN TWO MONTHS...
...YOU KNOW.
RON!

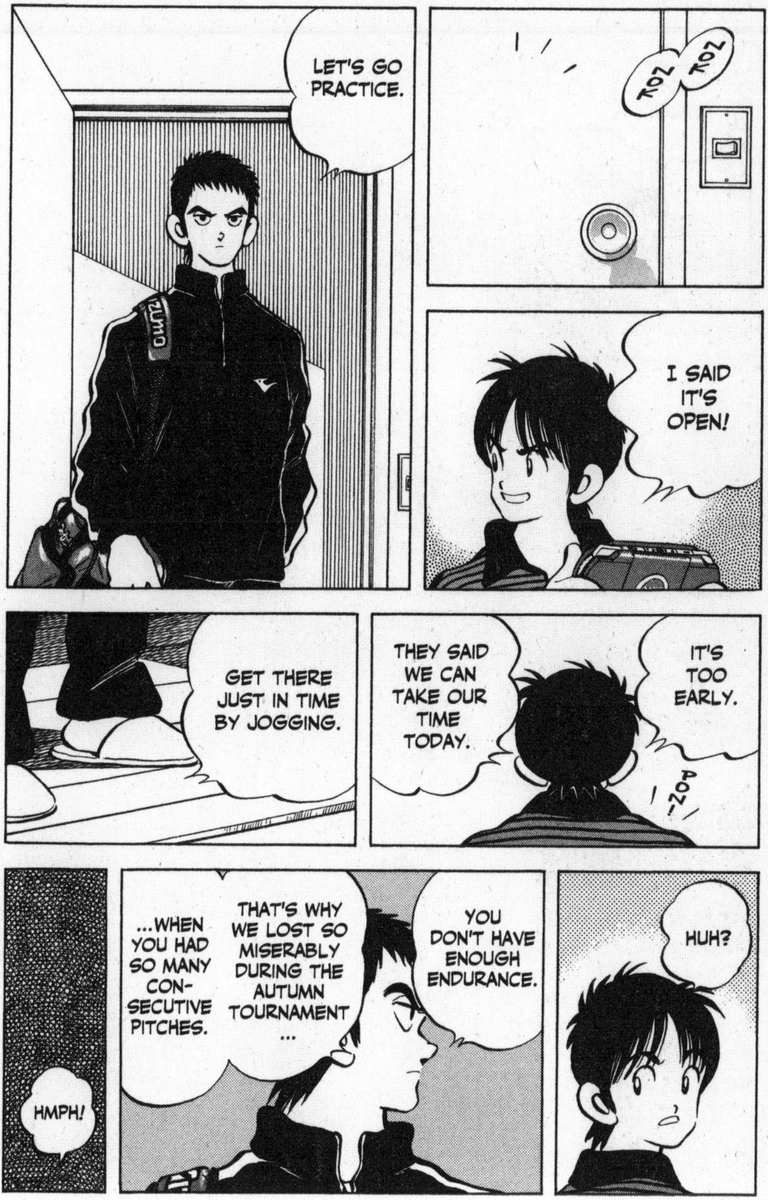
TOK TOK
I SAID IT'S OPEN!
LET'S GO PRACTICE.
IT'S TOO EARLY.
THEY SAID WE CAN TAKE OUR TIME TODAY.
PON!
GET THERE JUST IN TIME BY JOGGING.
HUH?
YOU DON'T HAVE ENOUGH ENDURANCE.
THAT'S WHY WE LOST SO MISERABLY DURING THE AUTUMN TOURNAMENT...
...WHEN YOU HAD SO MANY CON-SECUTIVE PITCHES.
HMPH!

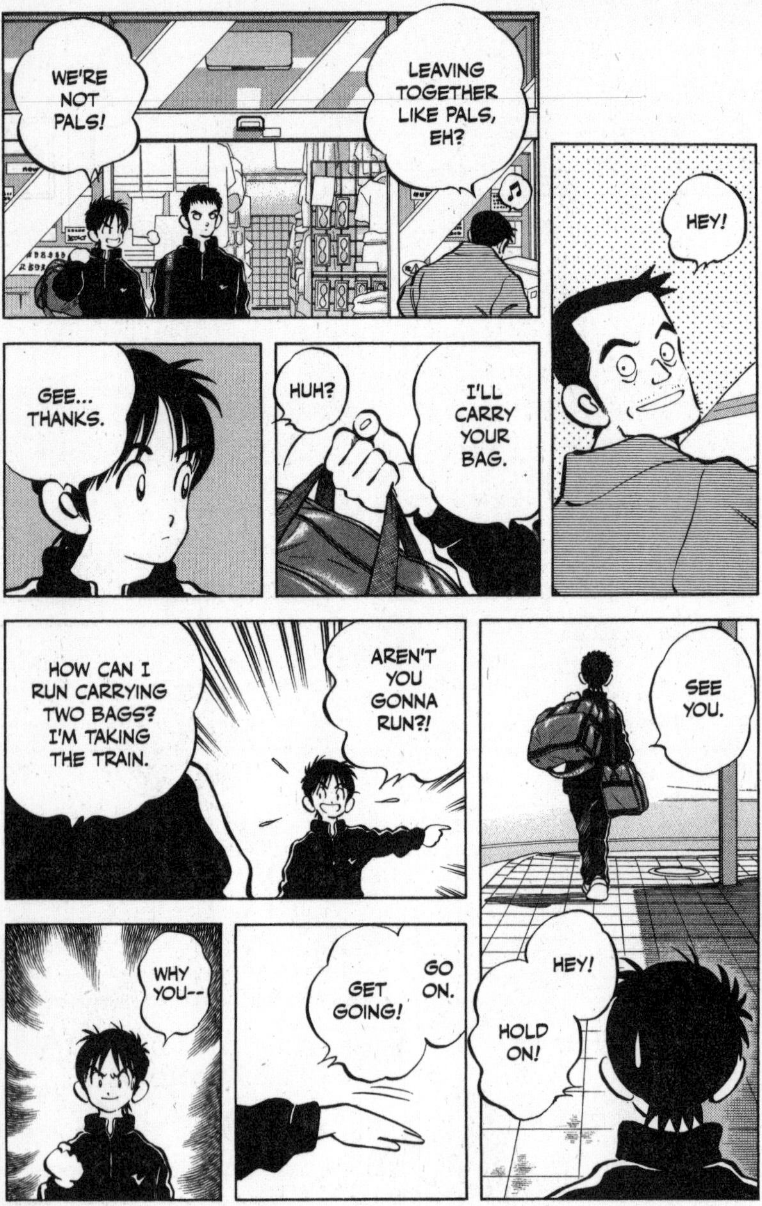
LEAVING TOGETHER LIKE PALS, EH?
WE'RE NOT PALS!
HEY!
I'LL CARRY YOUR BAG.
HUH?
GEE... THANKS.
AREN'T YOU GONNA RUN?!
HOW CAN I RUN CARRYING TWO BAGS? I'M TAKING THE TRAIN.
SEE YOU.
HEY!
HOLD ON!
GO ON.
GET GOING!
WHY YOU--

COFFEE
CLOVER
野菜・果物
東
azuma
produce

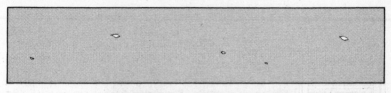

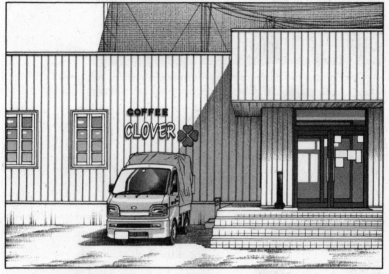

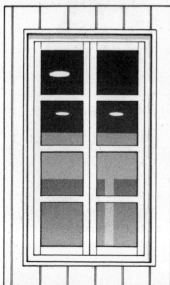

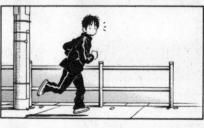

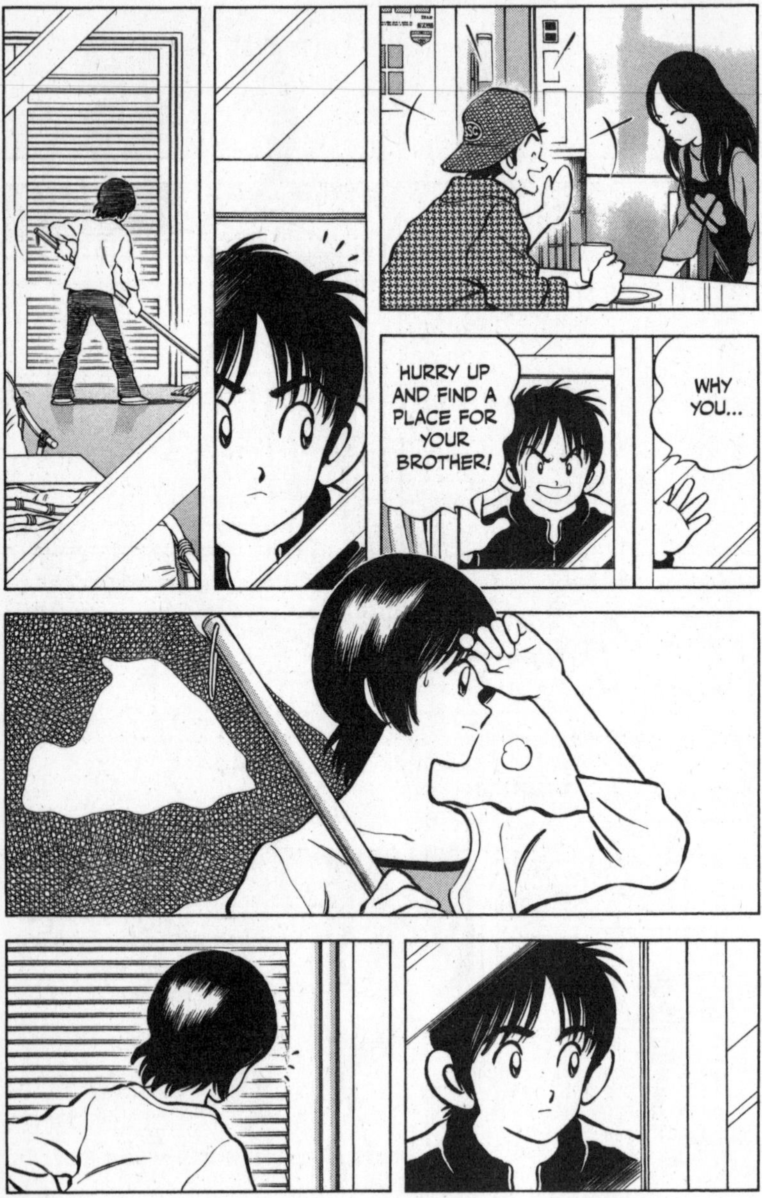
HURRY UP AND FIND A PLACE FOR YOUR BROTHER!
WHY YOU...

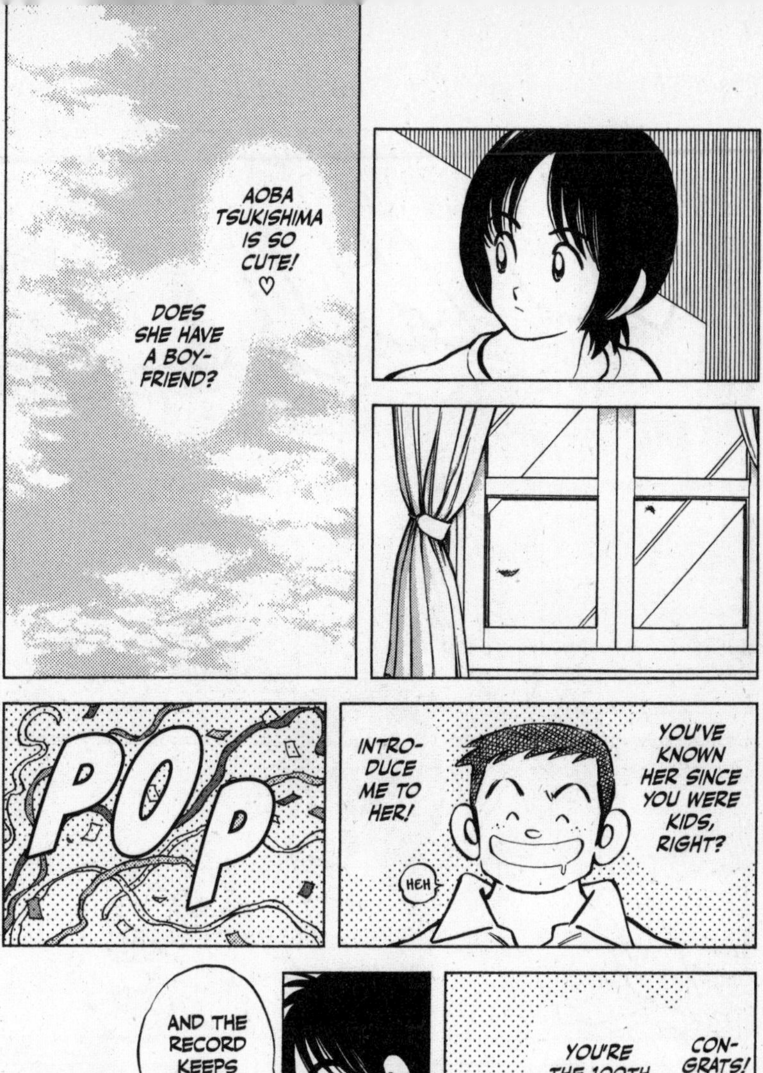
AOBA TSUKISHIMA IS SO CUTE! ♡
DOES SHE HAVE A BOY-FRIEND?
YOU'VE KNOWN HER SINCE YOU WERE KIDS, RIGHT?
INTRO-DUCE ME TO HER!
HEH
POP
CON-GRATS!
YOU'RE THE 100TH PERSON TO ASK ME THAT!
AND THE RECORD KEEPS GROWING ...

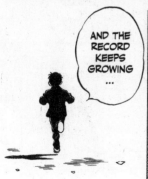

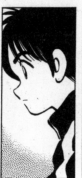

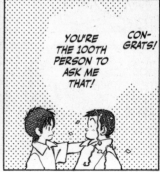

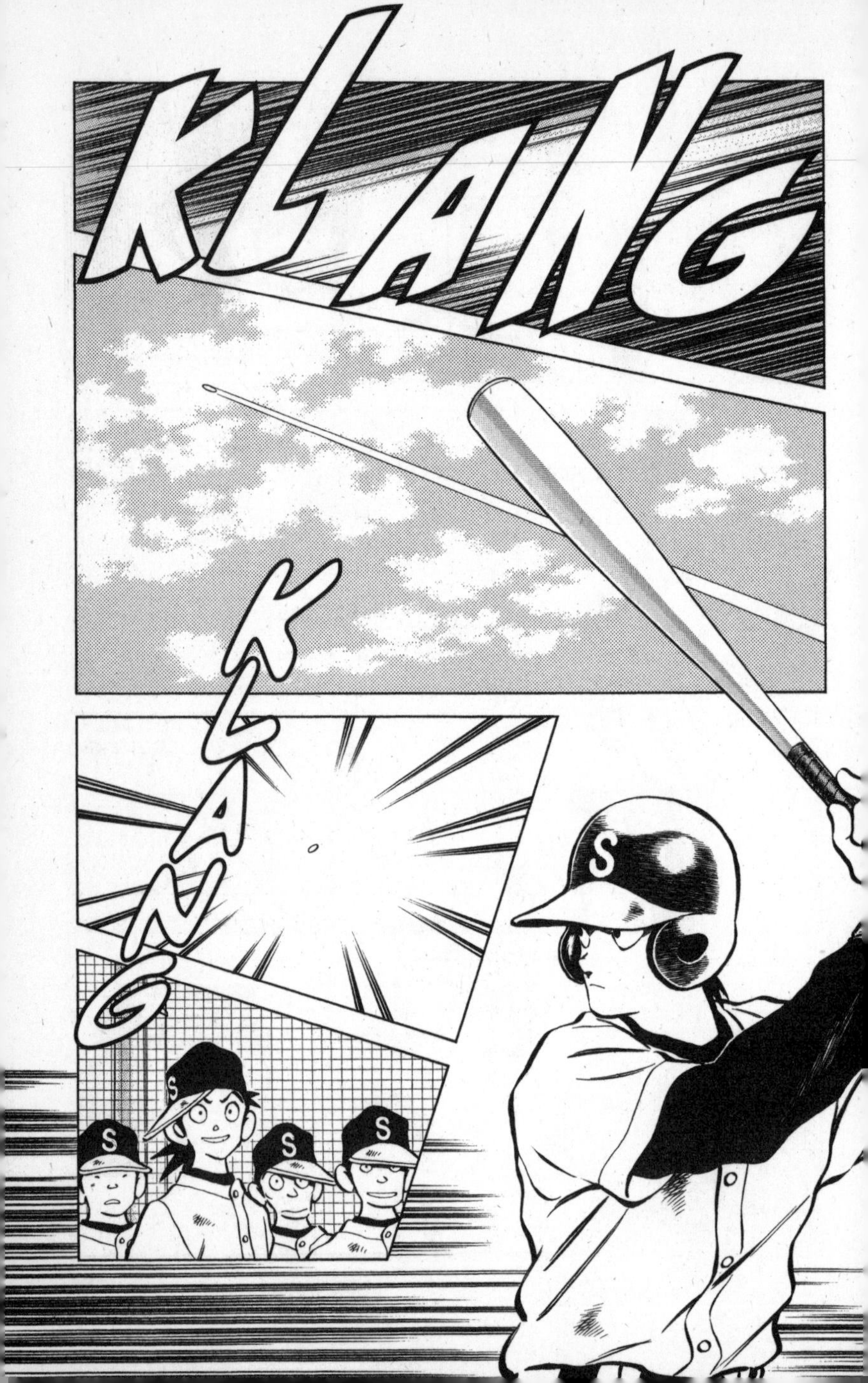
KLANG
KLANNG

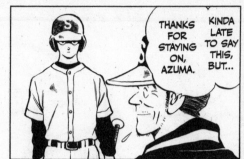

KINDA LATE TO SAY THIS, BUT...
THANKS FOR STAYING ON, AZUMA.
YEAH, RIGHT.
THANKS TO YOU, NOW I'M ON THIRD.
I'M SOOO HAPPY.
YOU NEED TO MOVE A LITTLE...
...THEN MAYBE YOU'D LOSE SOME WEIGHT.
OINK!
READY, AKAISHI?
YEAH!

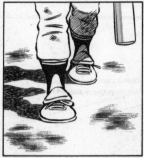

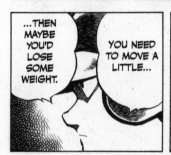

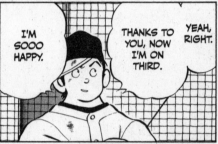

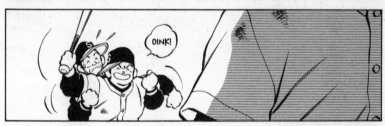

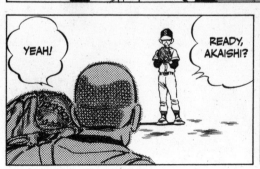

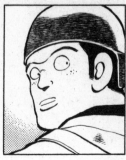

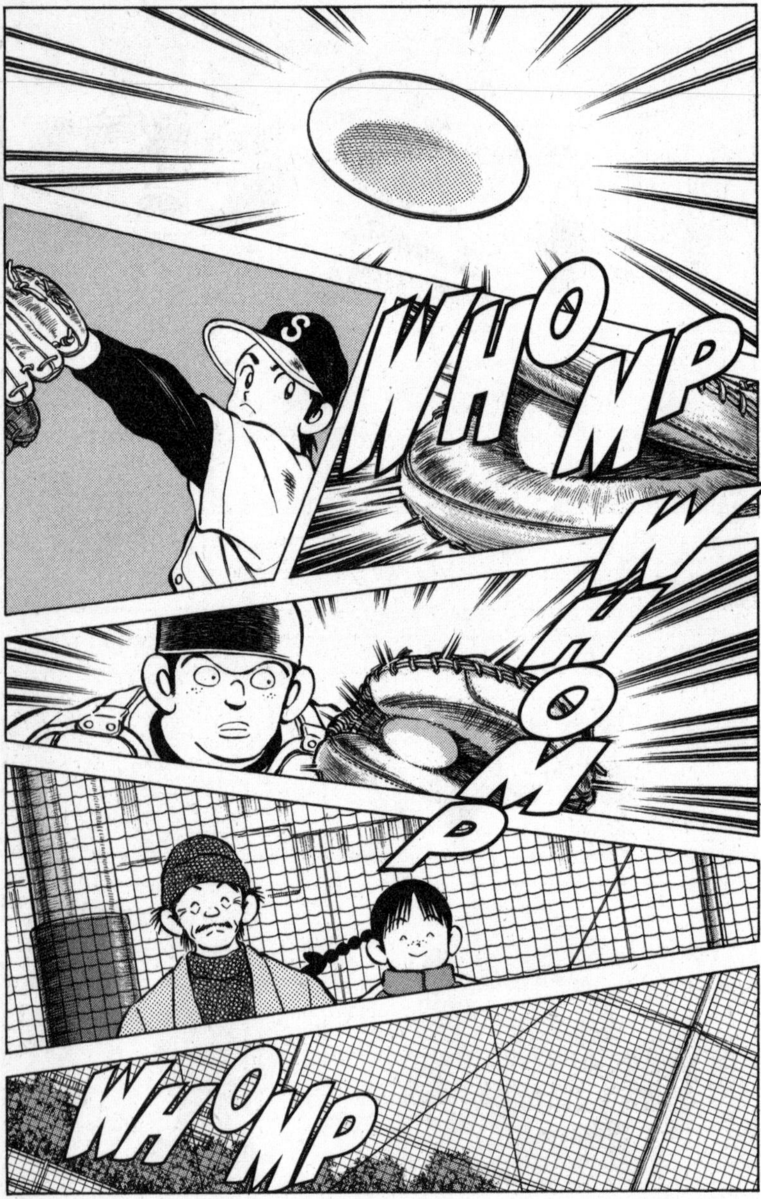
WHOMP
WHOMP
WHOMP

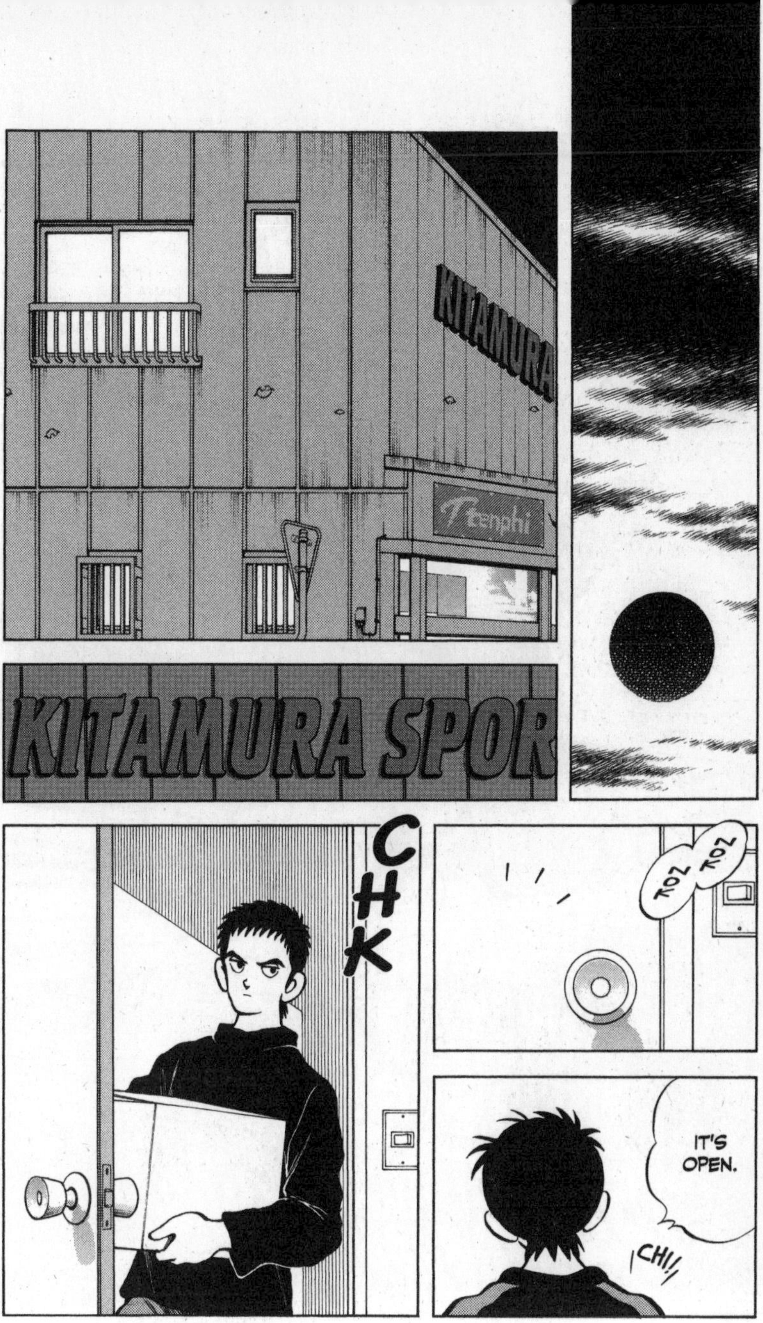
KITAMURA
tenphi
KITAMURA SPOR
KON KON
IT'S OPEN.
CHI!
CHK

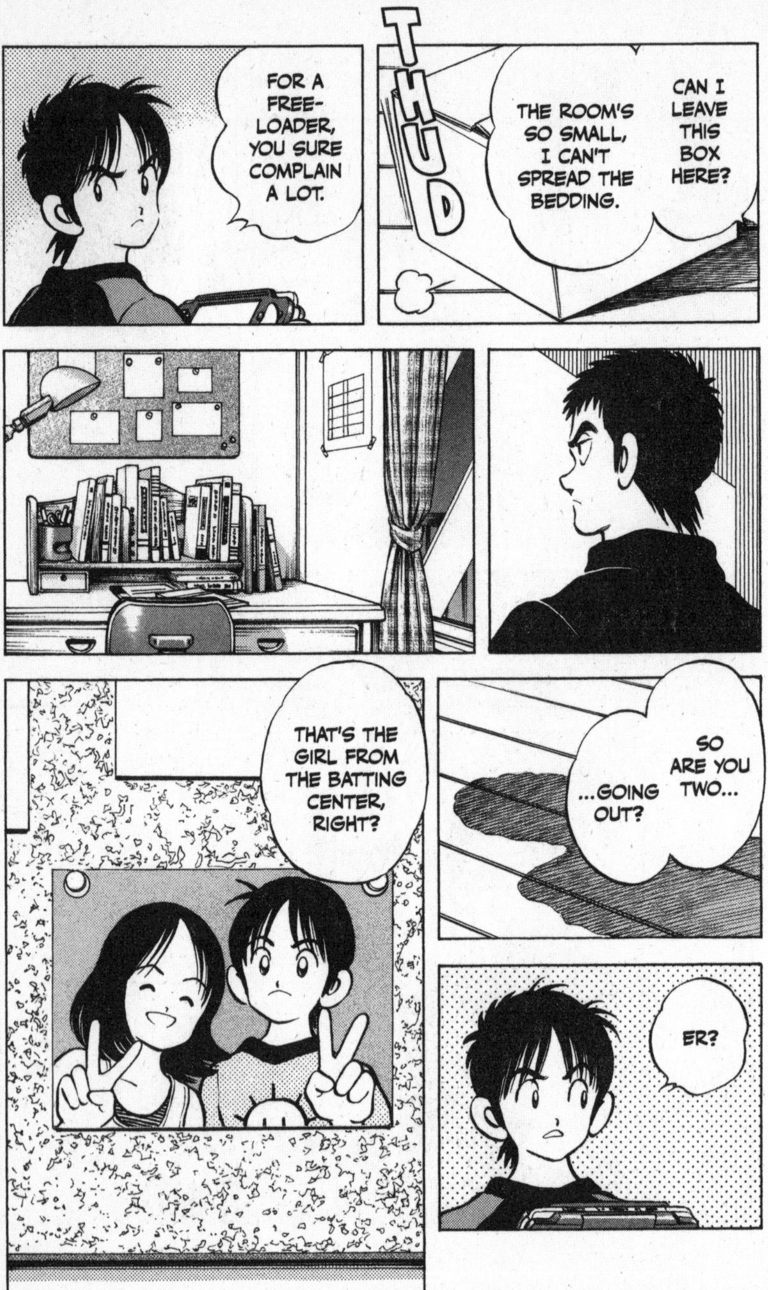
THUD
CAN I LEAVE THIS BOX HERE?
THE ROOM'S SO SMALL, I CAN'T SPREAD THE BEDDING.
FOR A FREE-LOADER, YOU SURE COMPLAIN A LOT.
SO ARE YOU TWO...
...GOING OUT?
ER?
THAT'S THE GIRL FROM THE BATTING CENTER, RIGHT?

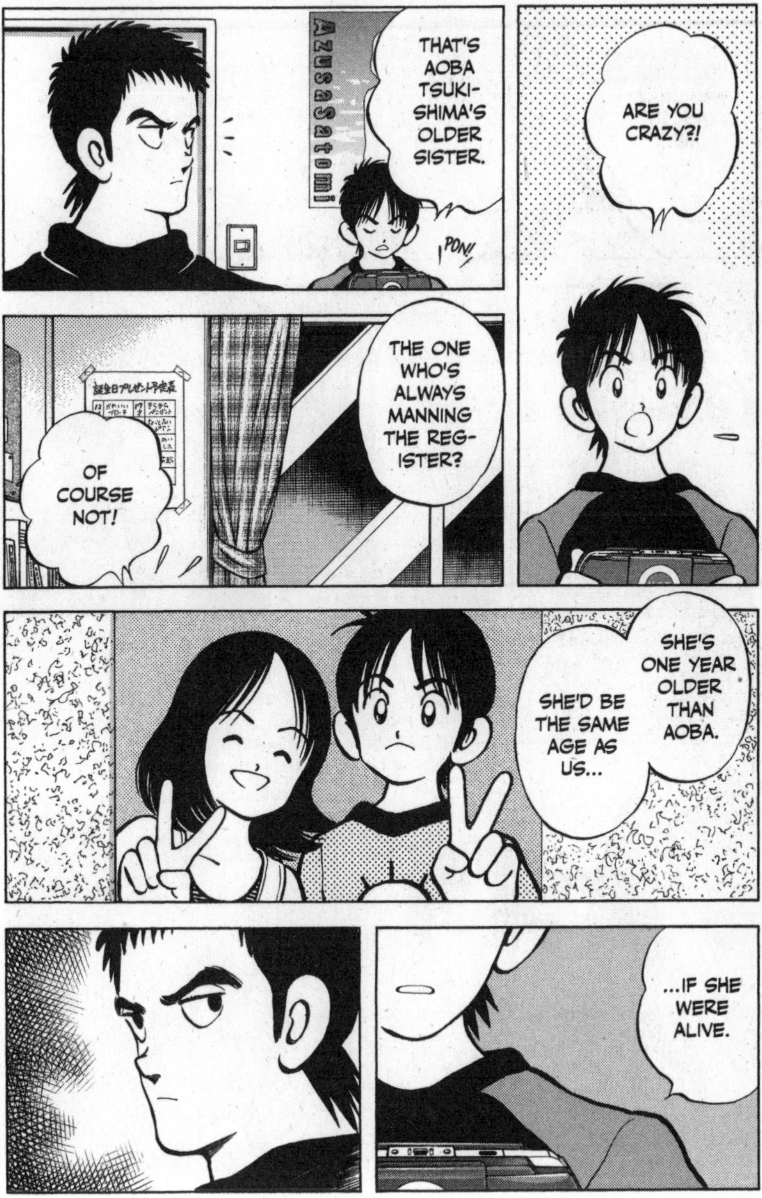
ARE YOU CRAZY?!
THAT'S AOBA TSUKISHIMA'S OLDER SISTER.
Azusa Satomi
PON!
THE ONE WHO'S ALWAYS MANNING THE REGISTER?
誕生日プレゼント予定表
OF COURSE NOT!
SHE'S ONE YEAR OLDER THAN AOBA.
SHE'D BE THE SAME AGE AS US...
...IF SHE WERE ALIVE.

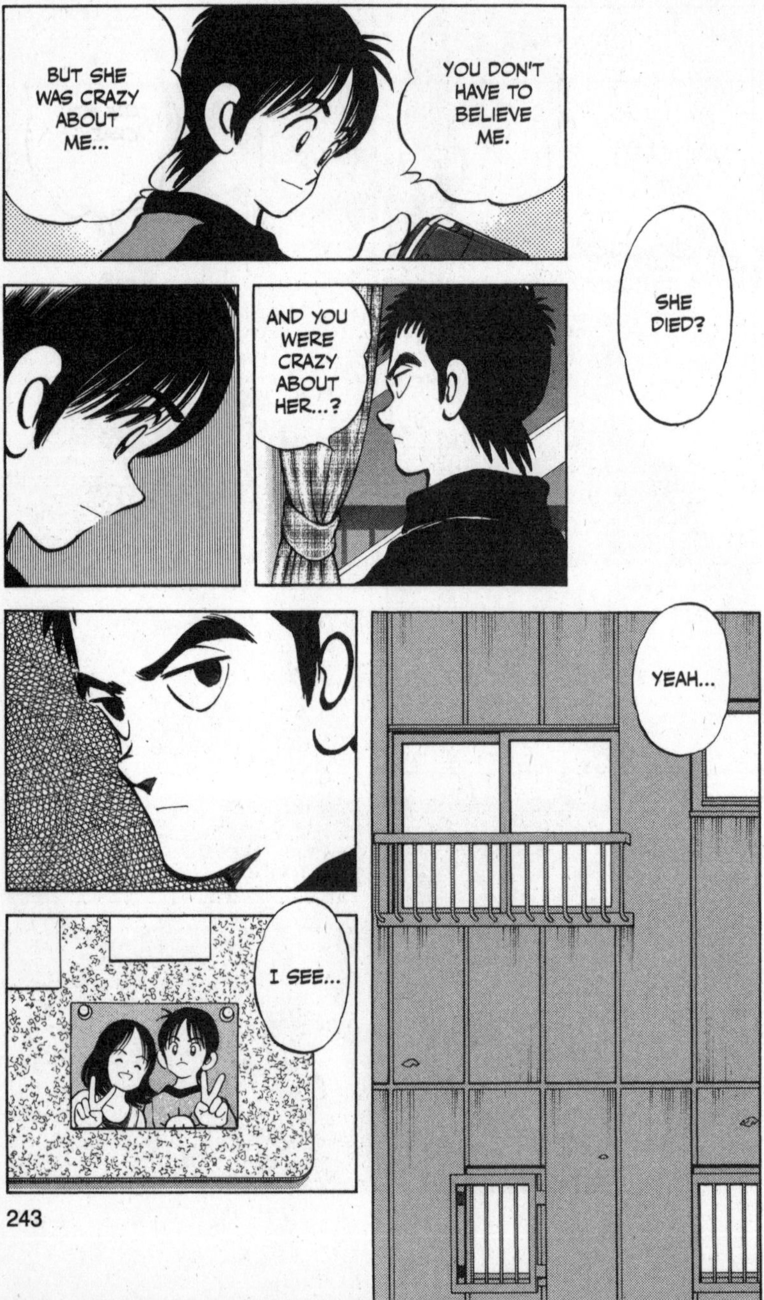
YOU DON'T HAVE TO BELIEVE ME.
BUT SHE WAS CRAZY ABOUT ME...
SHE DIED?
AND YOU WERE CRAZY ABOUT HER...?
YEAH...
I SEE...

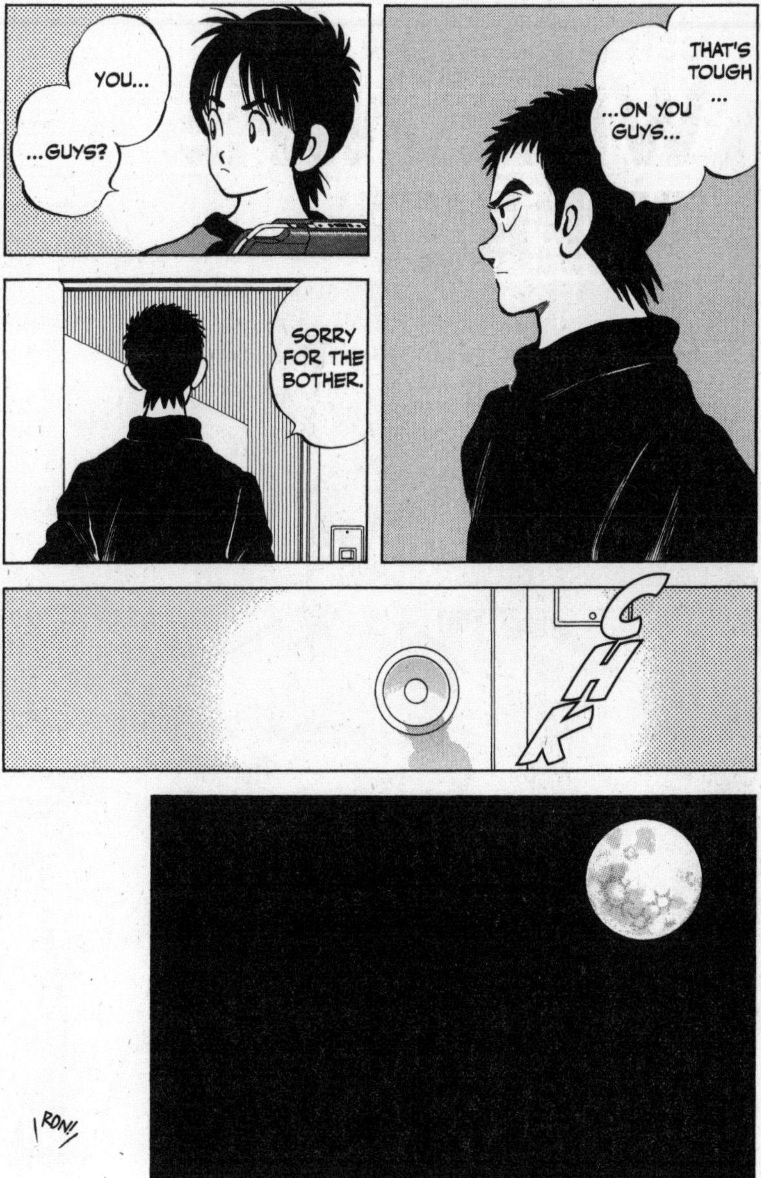
THAT'S TOUGH ...
...ON YOU GUYS...
YOU...
...GUYS?
SORRY FOR THE BOTHER.
CHK
RON!

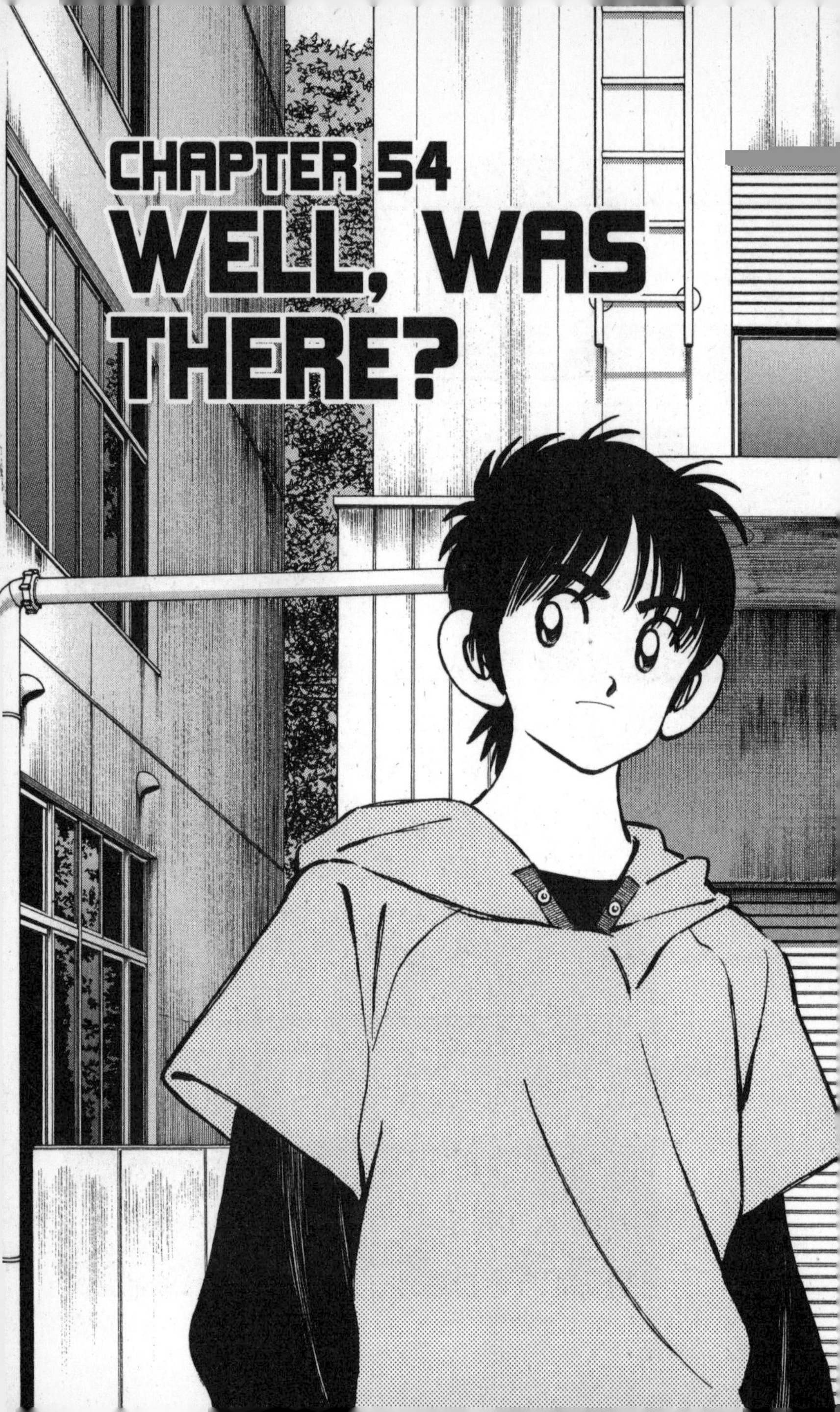
CHAPTER 54
WELL, WAS THERE?

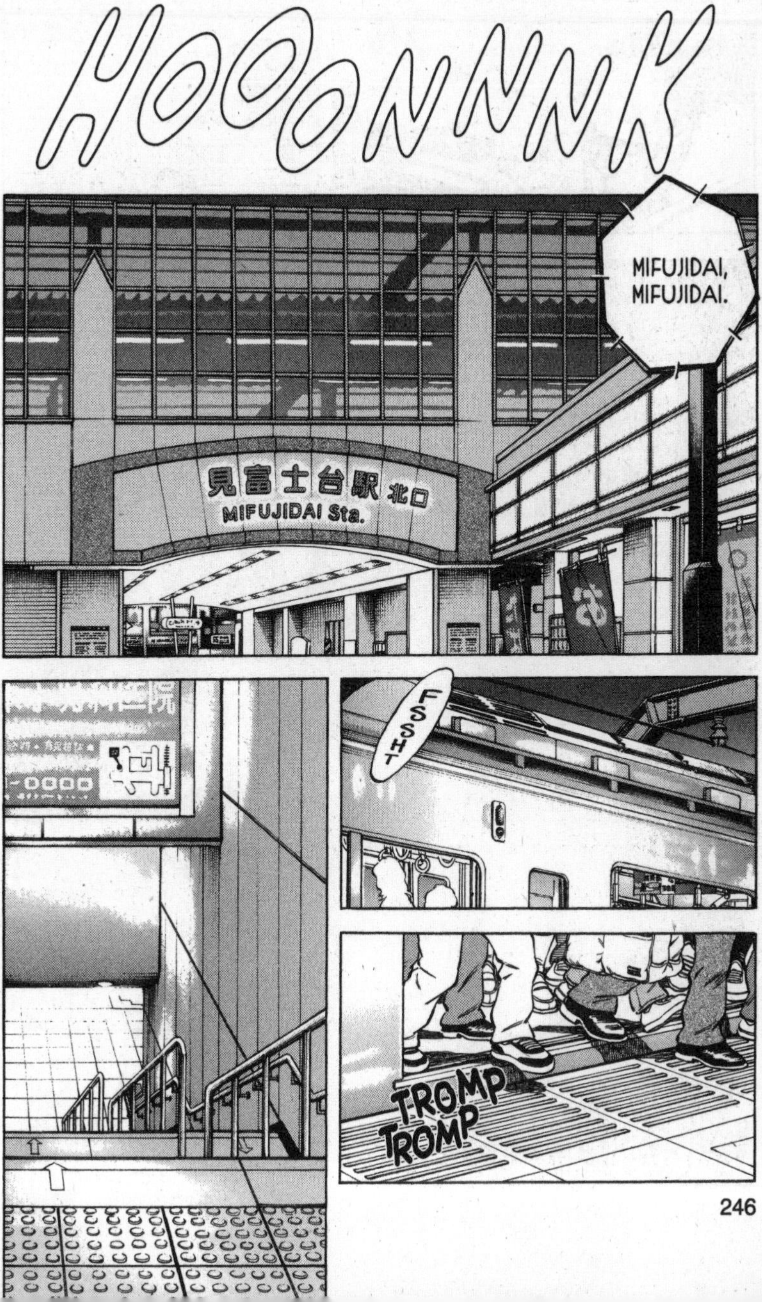
HOOONNNK
見富士台駅 北口
MIFUJIDAI Sta.
MIFUJIDAI, MIFUJIDAI.
FSSHT
TROMP TROMP

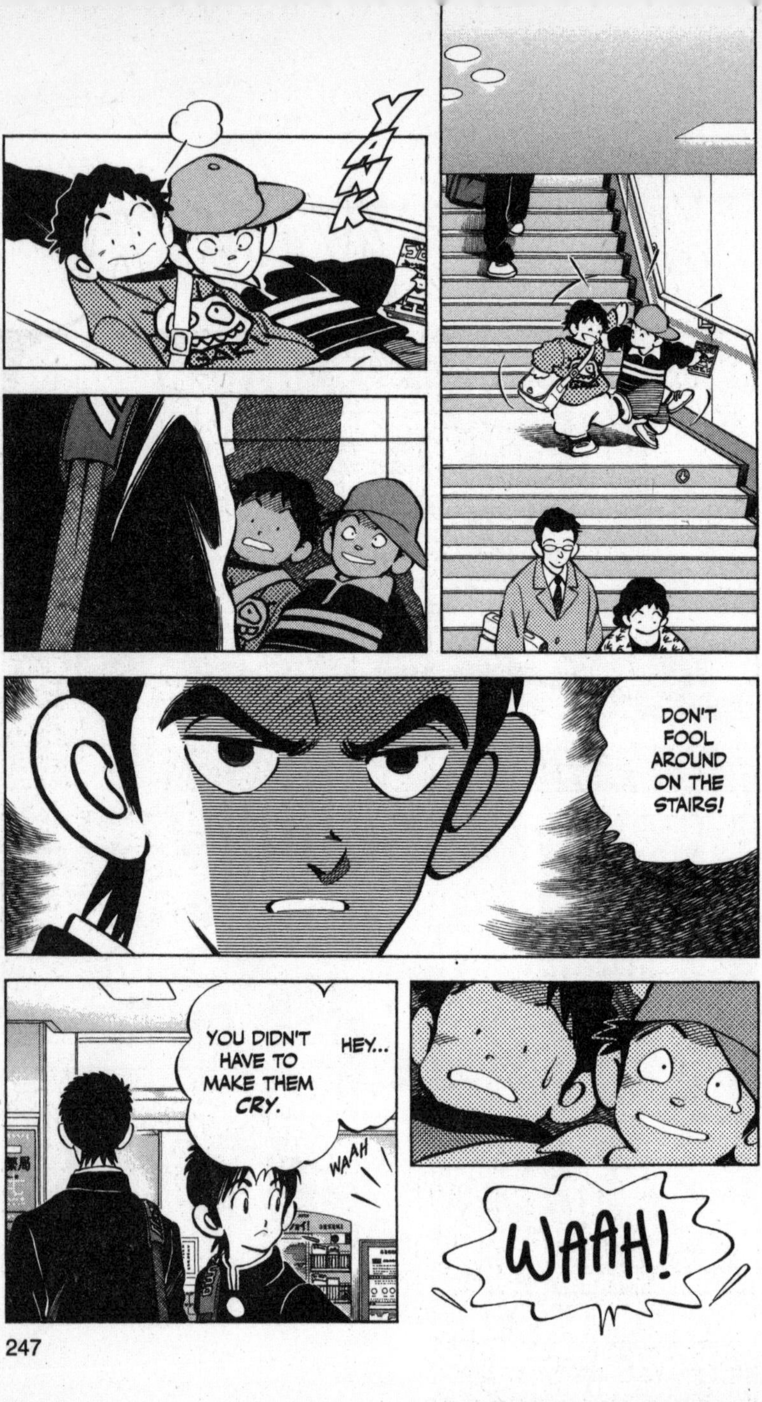
YANK
DON'T FOOL AROUND ON THE STAIRS!
WAAH!
HEY...
YOU DIDN'T HAVE TO MAKE THEM CRY.
WAAH

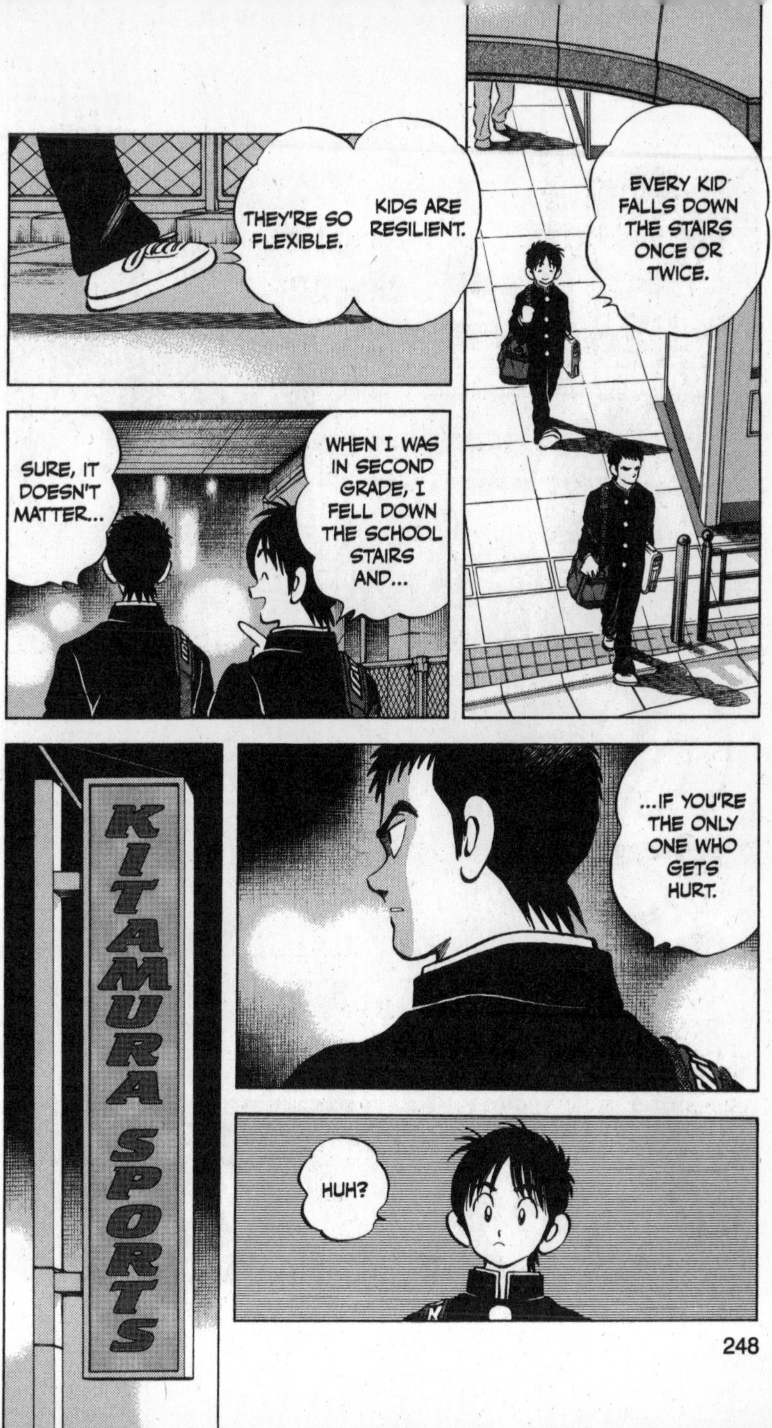
EVERY KID FALLS DOWN THE STAIRS ONCE OR TWICE.
KIDS ARE RESILIENT.
THEY'RE SO FLEXIBLE.
WHEN I WAS IN SECOND GRADE, I FELL DOWN THE SCHOOL STAIRS AND...
SURE, IT DOESN'T MATTER...
...IF YOU'RE THE ONLY ONE WHO GETS HURT.
HUH?
KITAMURA SPORTS

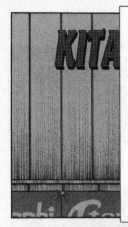

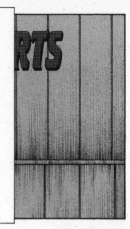

TODAY IS OUR WEDDING ANNIVERSARY, SO WE'RE GOING OUT ON A DATE.

YOU'RE ON YOUR OWN FOR DINNER.

(^^)/~ ♡

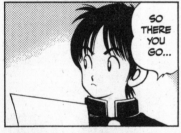

SO THERE YOU GO...

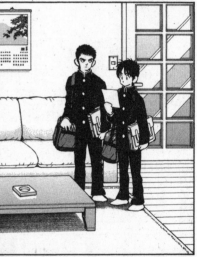

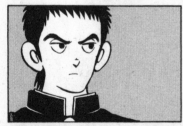

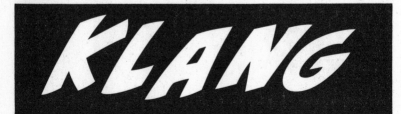

KLANG

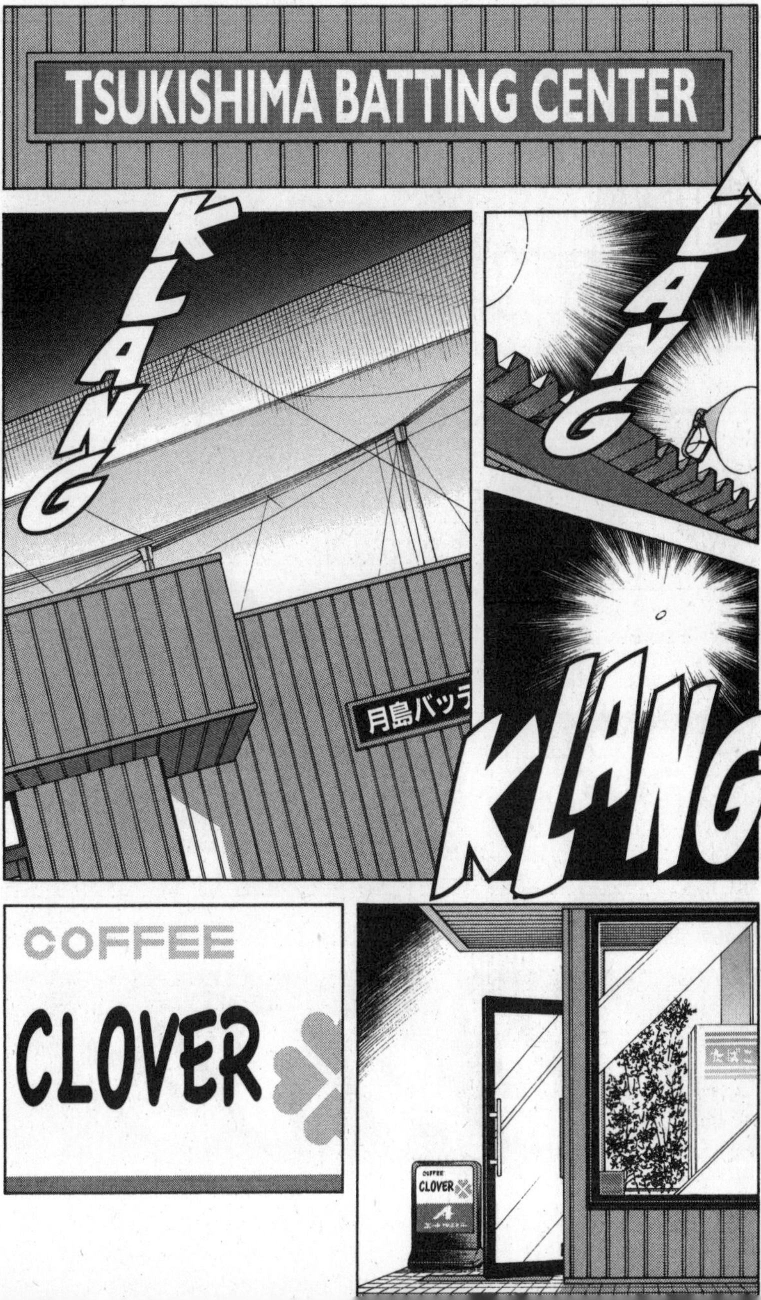
TSUKISHIMA BATTING CENTER
KLANG
KLANG
KLANG
COFFEE
CLOVER
たばこ
COFFEE
CLOVER

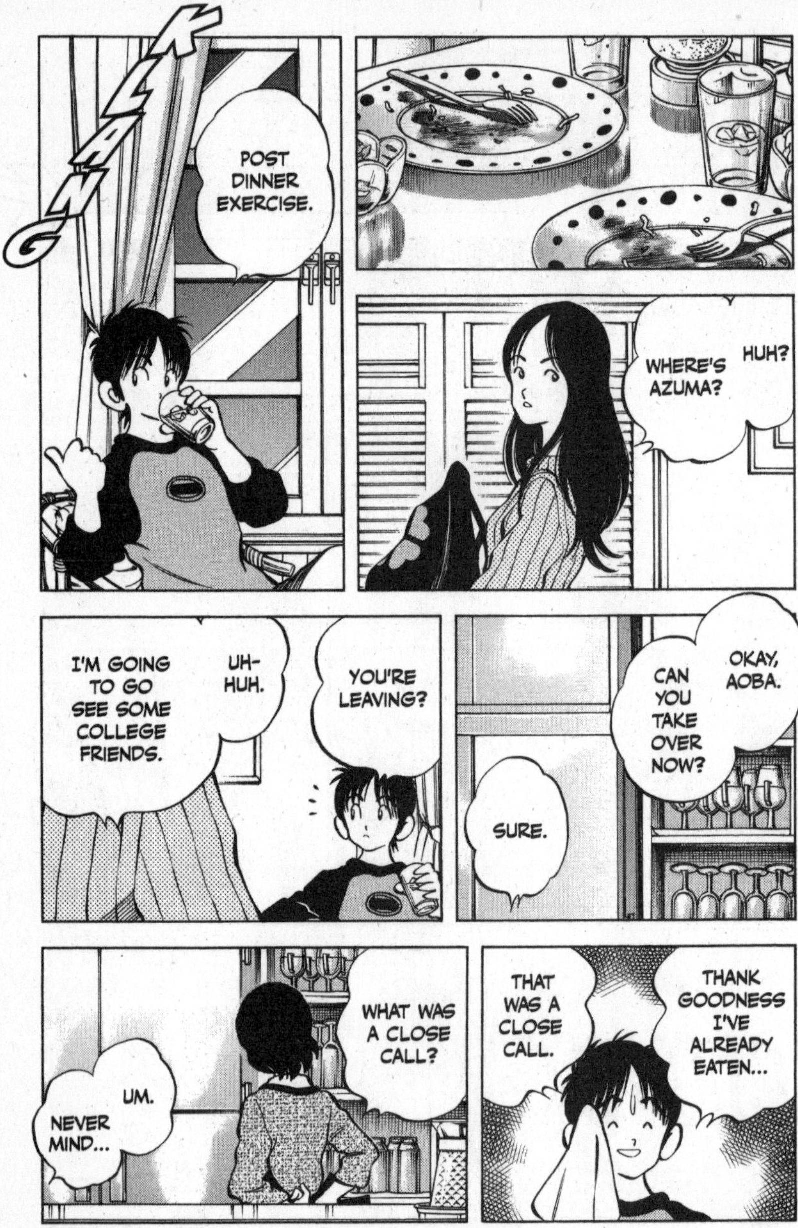

HUH?
WHERE'S AZUMA?
KLANG
POST DINNER EXERCISE.
OKAY, AOBA.
CAN YOU TAKE OVER NOW?
SURE.
YOU'RE LEAVING?
UH-HUH.
I'M GOING TO GO SEE SOME COLLEGE FRIENDS.
THANK GOODNESS I'VE ALREADY EATEN...
THAT WAS A CLOSE CALL.
WHAT WAS A CLOSE CALL?
UM.
NEVER MIND...

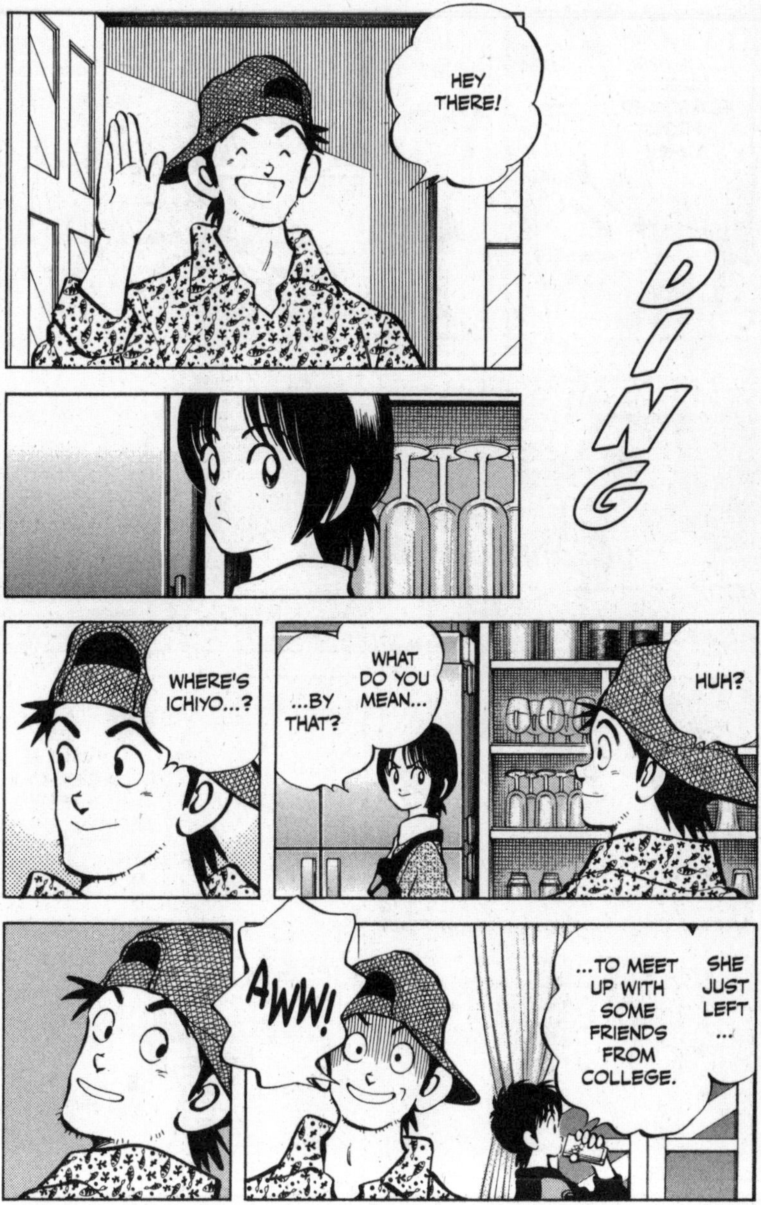
DING
HEY THERE!
HUH?
WHAT DO YOU MEAN...
...BY THAT?
WHERE'S ICHIYO...?
SHE JUST LEFT...
...TO MEET UP WITH SOME FRIENDS FROM COLLEGE.
AWW!

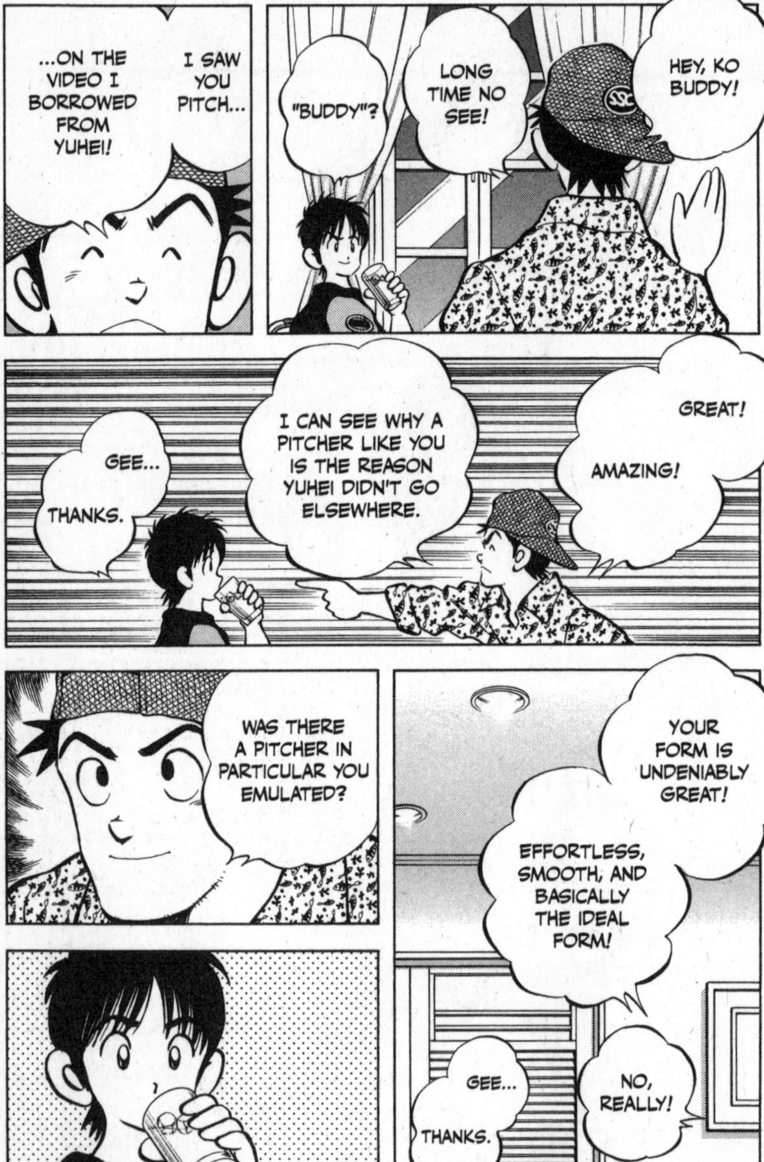
HEY, KO BUDDY!
LONG TIME NO SEE!
"BUDDY"?
I SAW YOU PITCH...
...ON THE VIDEO I BORROWED FROM YUHEI!
GREAT!
AMAZING!
I CAN SEE WHY A PITCHER LIKE YOU IS THE REASON YUHEI DIDN'T GO ELSEWHERE.
GEE...
THANKS.
YOUR FORM IS UNDENIABLY GREAT!
EFFORTLESS, SMOOTH, AND BASICALLY THE IDEAL FORM!
NO, REALLY!
GEE...
THANKS.
WAS THERE A PITCHER IN PARTICULAR YOU EMULATED?

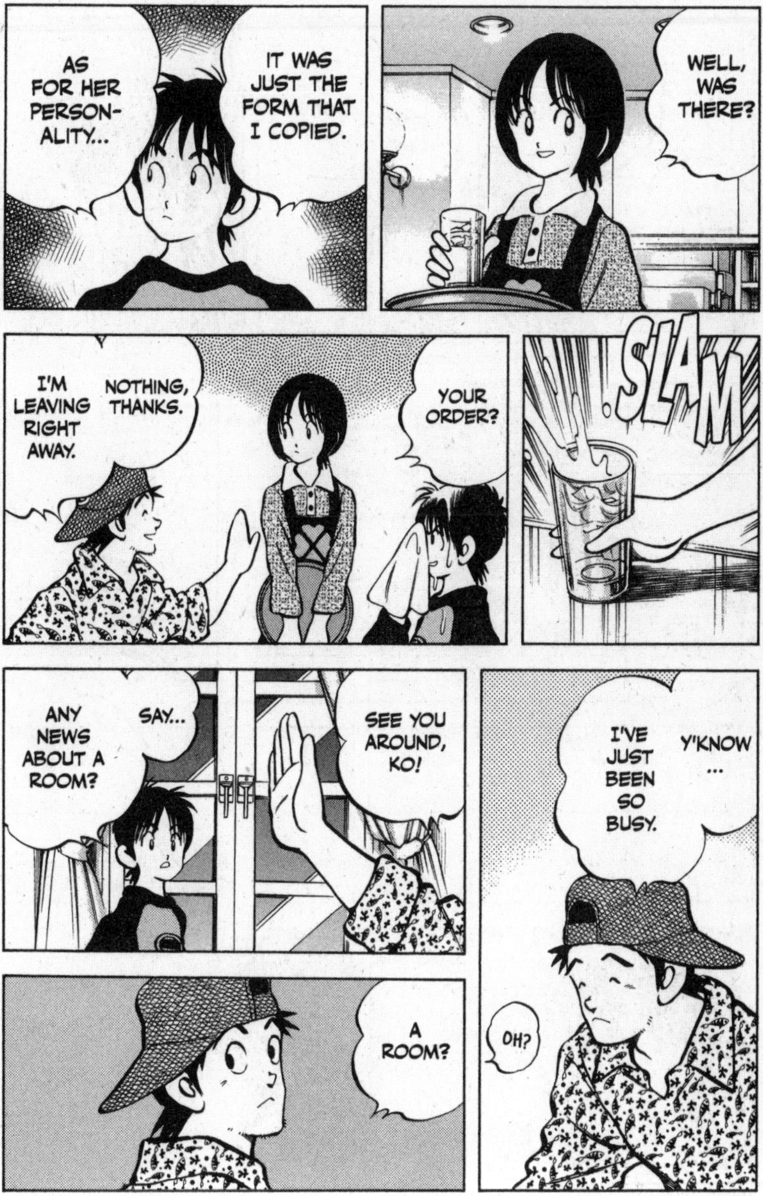
WELL, WAS THERE?
IT WAS JUST THE FORM THAT I COPIED.
AS FOR HER PERSON-ALITY...
SLAM
YOUR ORDER?
NOTHING, THANKS.
I'M LEAVING RIGHT AWAY.
Y'KNOW...
I'VE JUST BEEN SO BUSY.
OH?
SEE YOU AROUND, KO!
SAY...
ANY NEWS ABOUT A ROOM?
A ROOM?

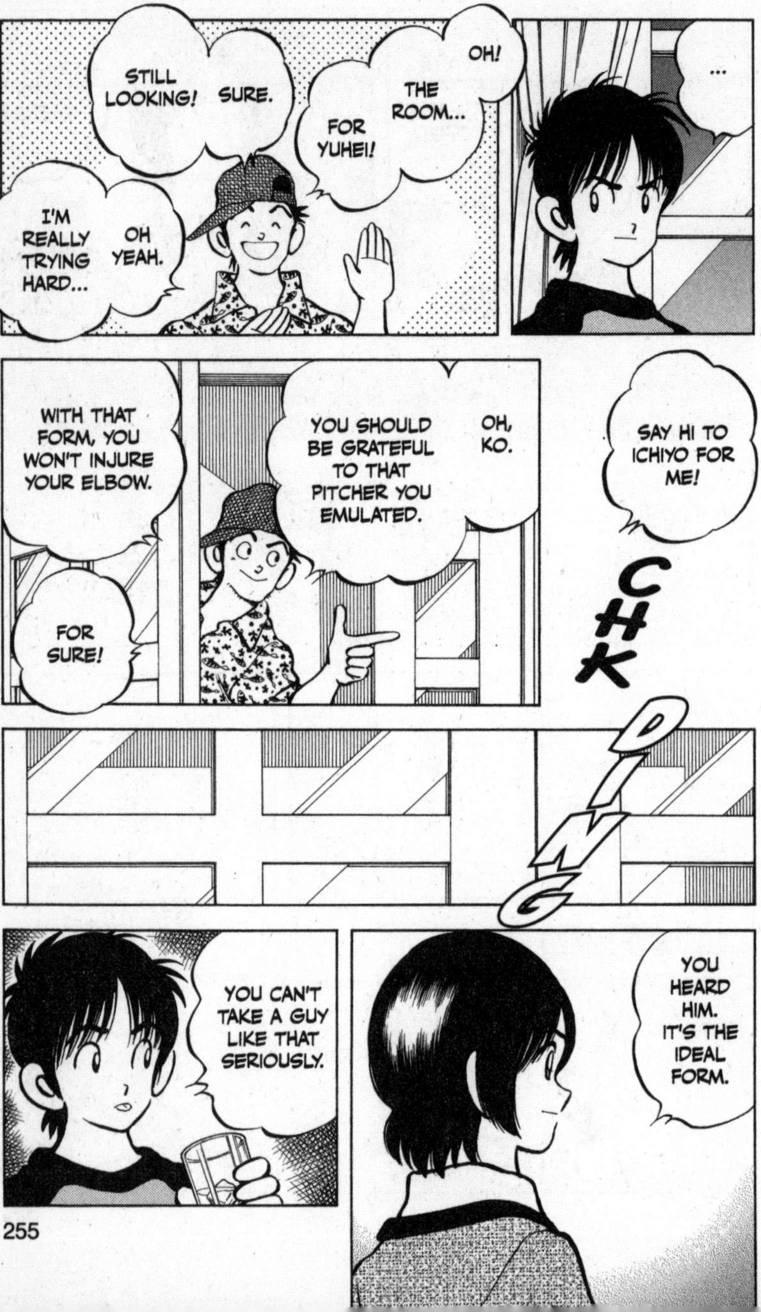
...
OH!
THE ROOM...
FOR YUHEI!
SURE.
STILL LOOKING!
OH YEAH.
I'M REALLY TRYING HARD...
SAY HI TO ICHIYO FOR ME!
OH, KO.
YOU SHOULD BE GRATEFUL TO THAT PITCHER YOU EMULATED.
WITH THAT FORM, YOU WON'T INJURE YOUR ELBOW.
FOR SURE!
CHK
DING
YOU HEARD HIM. IT'S THE IDEAL FORM.
YOU CAN'T TAKE A GUY LIKE THAT SERIOUSLY.

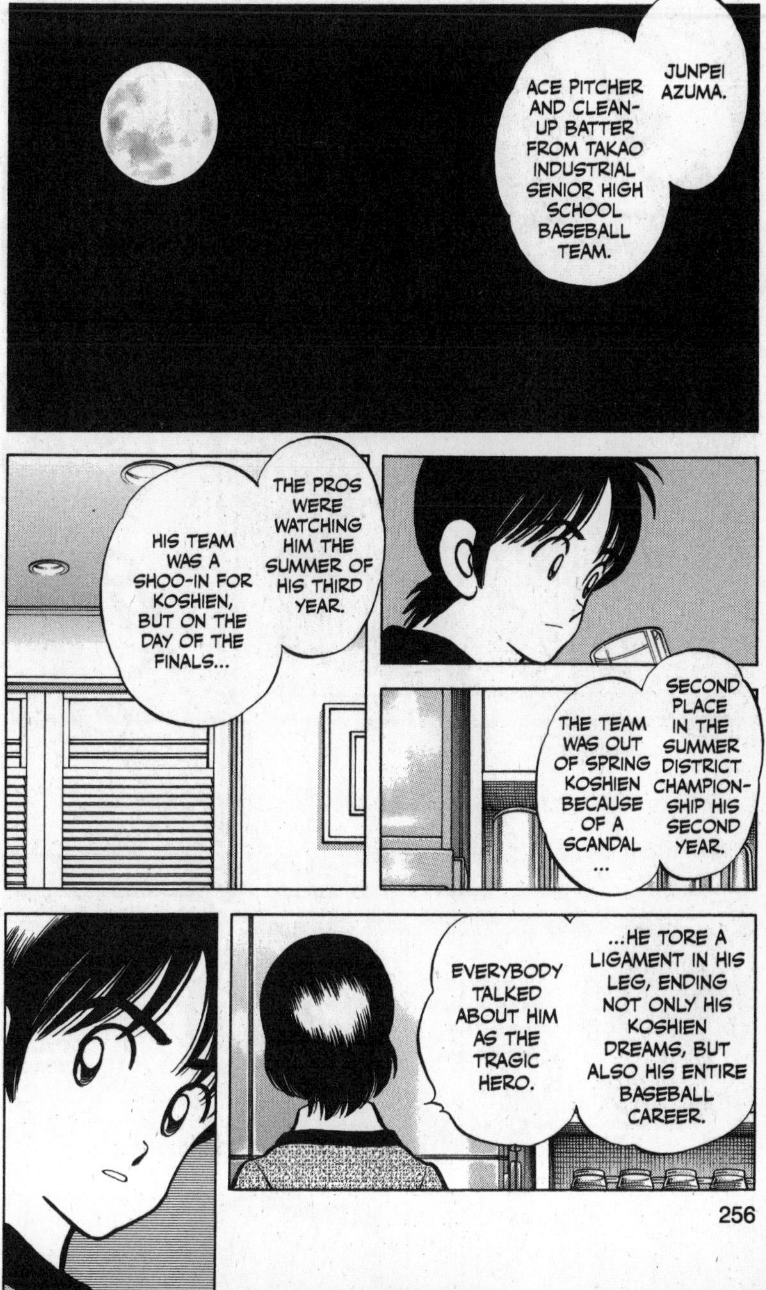
JUNPEI AZUMA.
ACE PITCHER AND CLEAN-UP BATTER FROM TAKAO INDUSTRIAL SENIOR HIGH SCHOOL BASEBALL TEAM.
SECOND PLACE IN THE SUMMER DISTRICT CHAMPIONSHIP HIS SECOND YEAR.
THE TEAM WAS OUT OF SPRING KOSHIEN BECAUSE OF A SCANDAL ...
THE PROS WERE WATCHING HIM THE SUMMER OF HIS THIRD YEAR.
HIS TEAM WAS A SHOO-IN FOR KOSHIEN, BUT ON THE DAY OF THE FINALS...
...HE TORE A LIGAMENT IN HIS LEG, ENDING NOT ONLY HIS KOSHIEN DREAMS, BUT ALSO HIS ENTIRE BASEBALL CAREER.
EVERYBODY TALKED ABOUT HIM AS THE TRAGIC HERO.

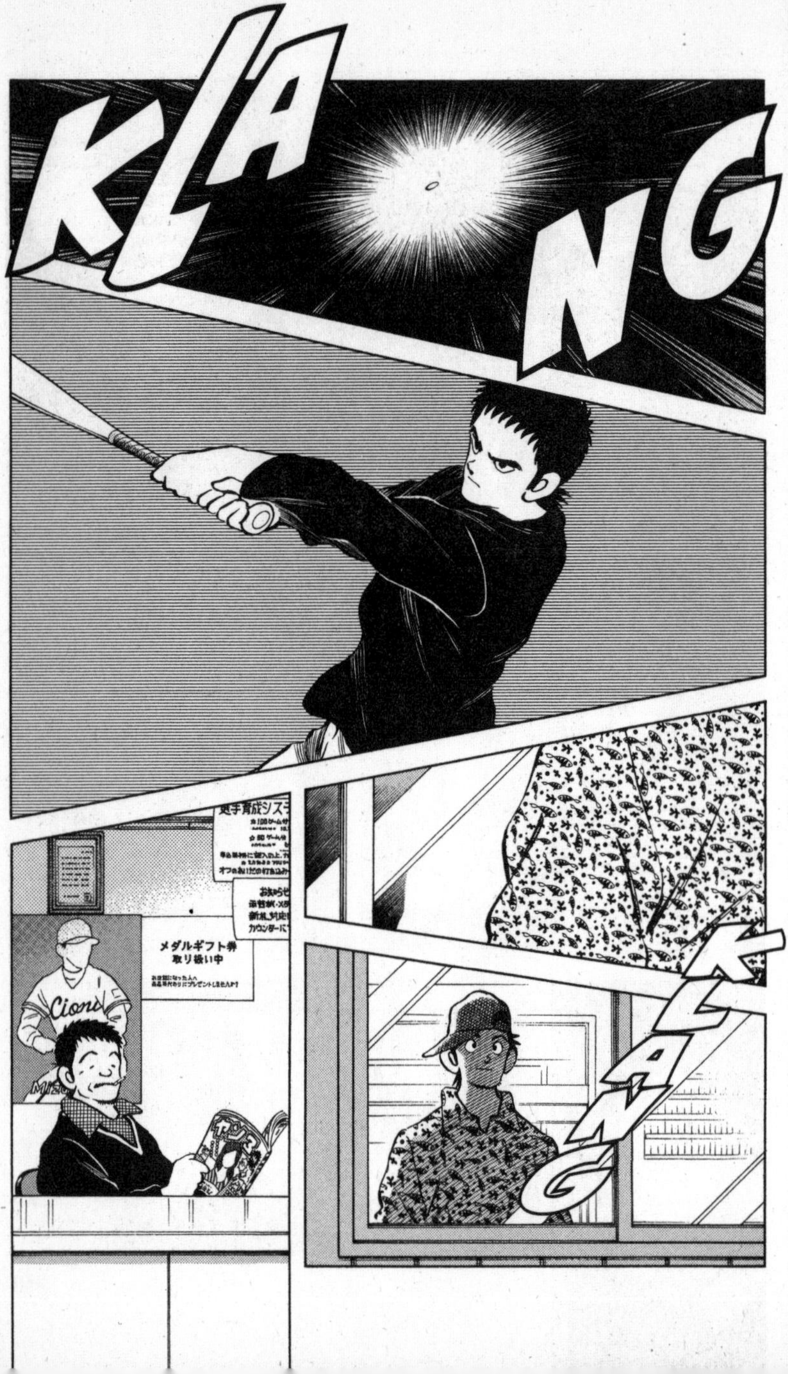
KLANG
KLANG
メダルギフト券
取り扱い中

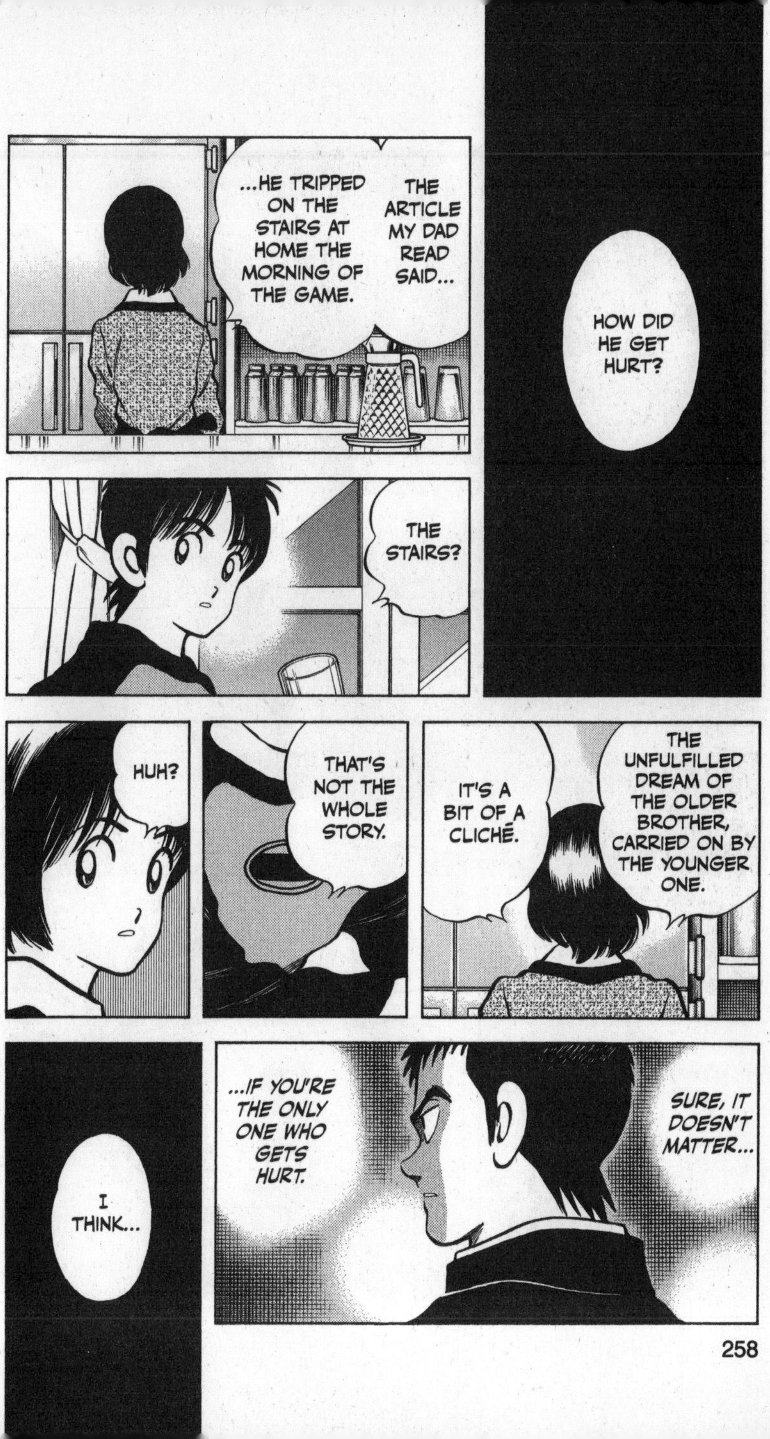
HOW DID HE GET HURT?
THE ARTICLE MY DAD READ SAID...
...HE TRIPPED ON THE STAIRS AT HOME THE MORNING OF THE GAME.
THE STAIRS?
THE UNFULFILLED DREAM OF THE OLDER BROTHER, CARRIED ON BY THE YOUNGER ONE.
IT'S A BIT OF A CLICHÉ.
THAT'S NOT THE WHOLE STORY.
HUH?
SURE, IT DOESN'T MATTER...
...IF YOU'RE THE ONLY ONE WHO GETS HURT.
I THINK...

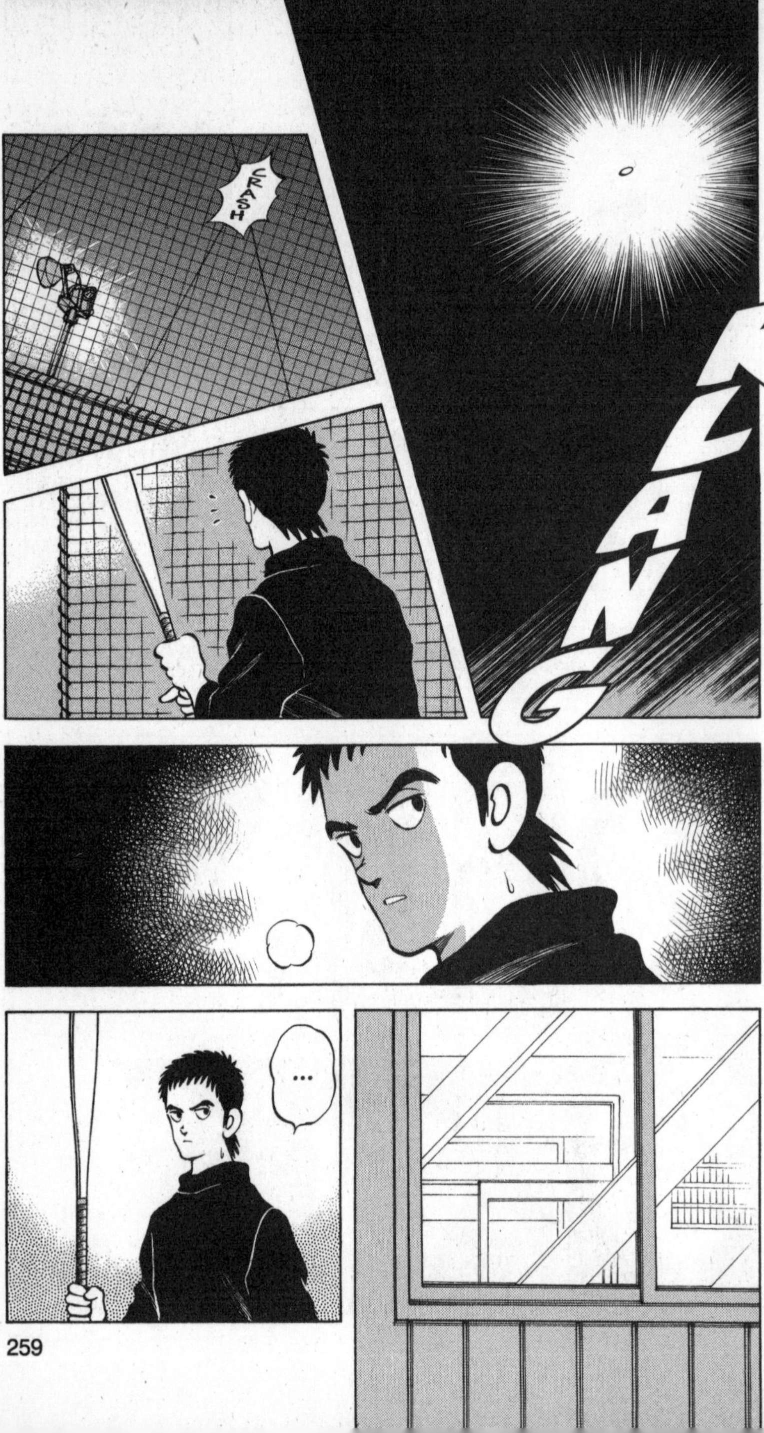
KLANG
CRASH
...

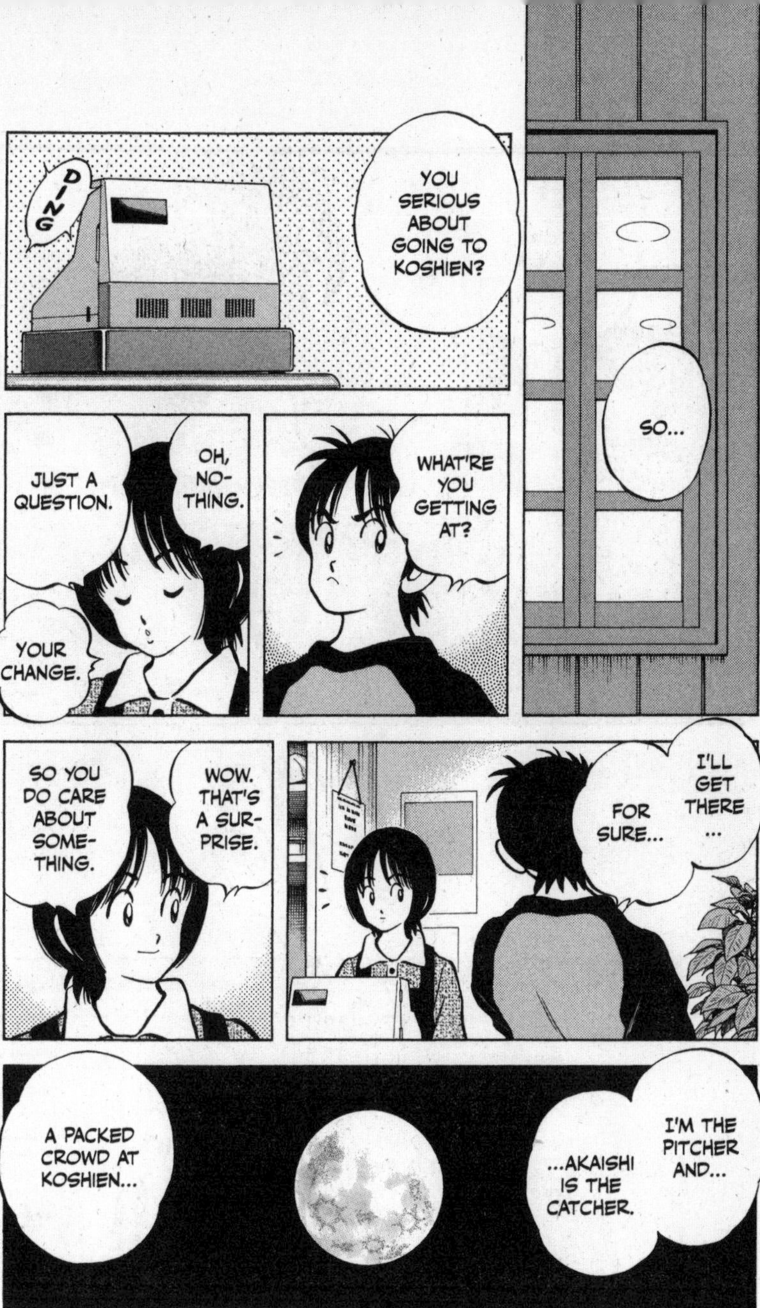
SO...
YOU SERIOUS ABOUT GOING TO KOSHIEN?
DING
WHAT'RE YOU GETTING AT?
OH, NO-THING.
JUST A QUESTION.
YOUR CHANGE.
I'LL GET THERE ...
FOR SURE...
WOW. THAT'S A SUR-PRISE.
SO YOU DO CARE ABOUT SOME-THING.
I'M THE PITCHER AND...
...AKAISHI IS THE CATCHER.
A PACKED CROWD AT KOSHIEN...

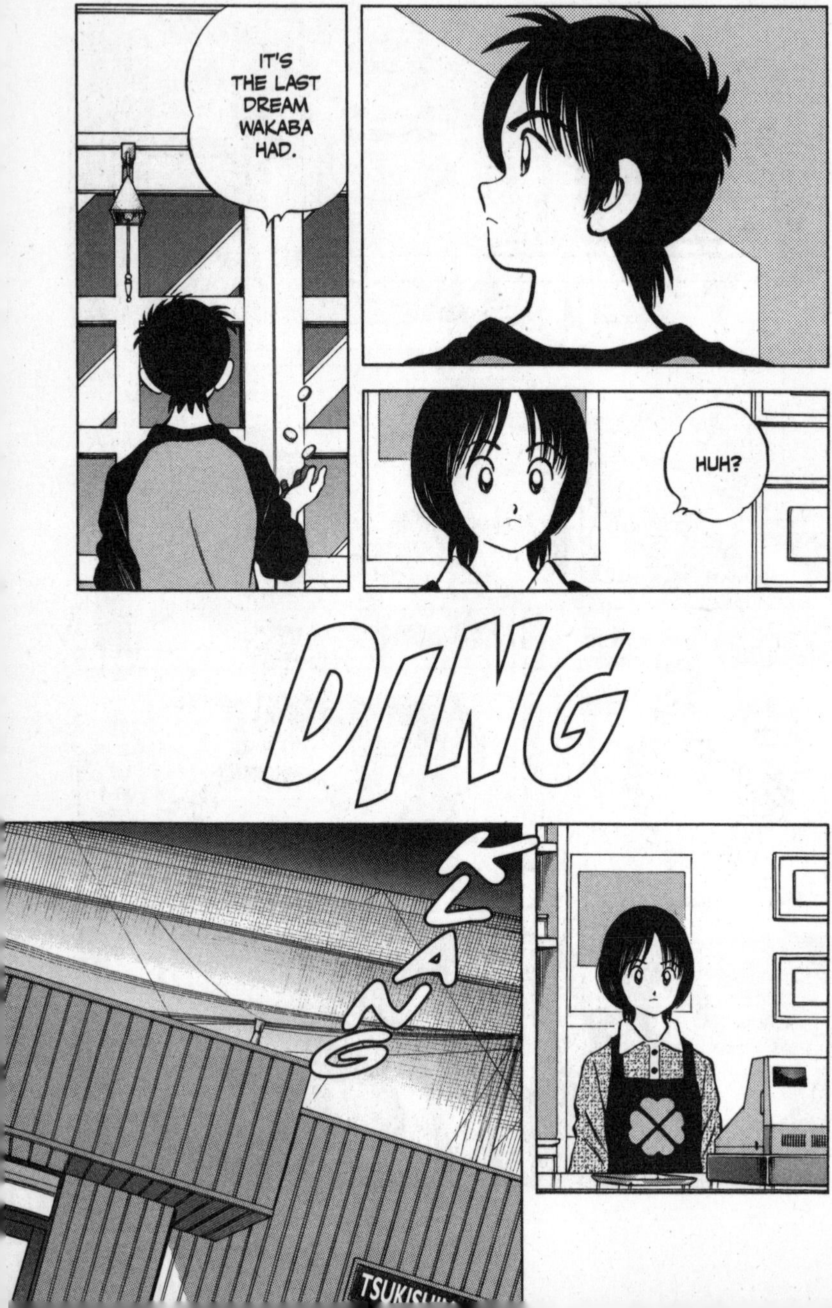
HUH?
IT'S THE LAST DREAM WAKABA HAD.
DING
KLANG

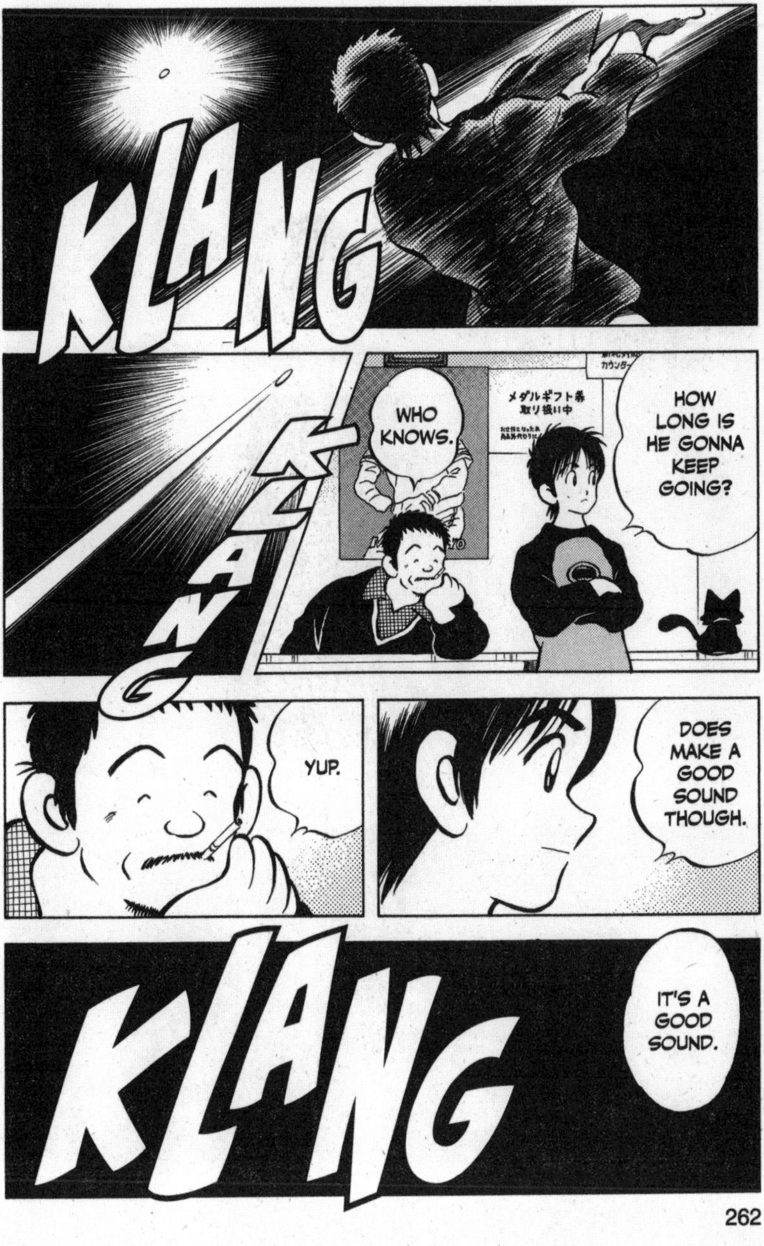
KLANG
HOW LONG IS HE GONNA KEEP GOING?
メダルギフト券
取り扱い中
WHO KNOWS.
KLANG
DOES MAKE A GOOD SOUND THOUGH.
YUP.
IT'S A GOOD SOUND.
KLANG

CHAPTER 55
GOING ON A DATE

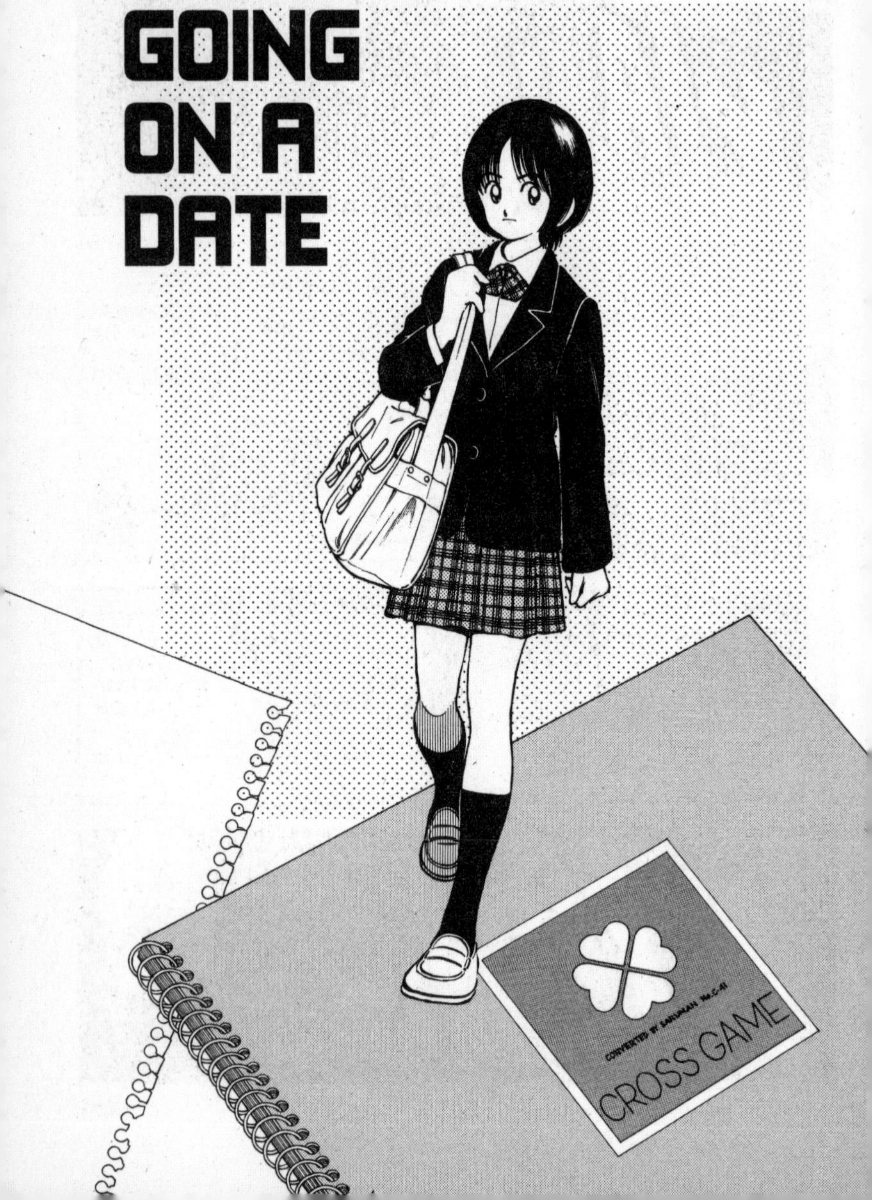

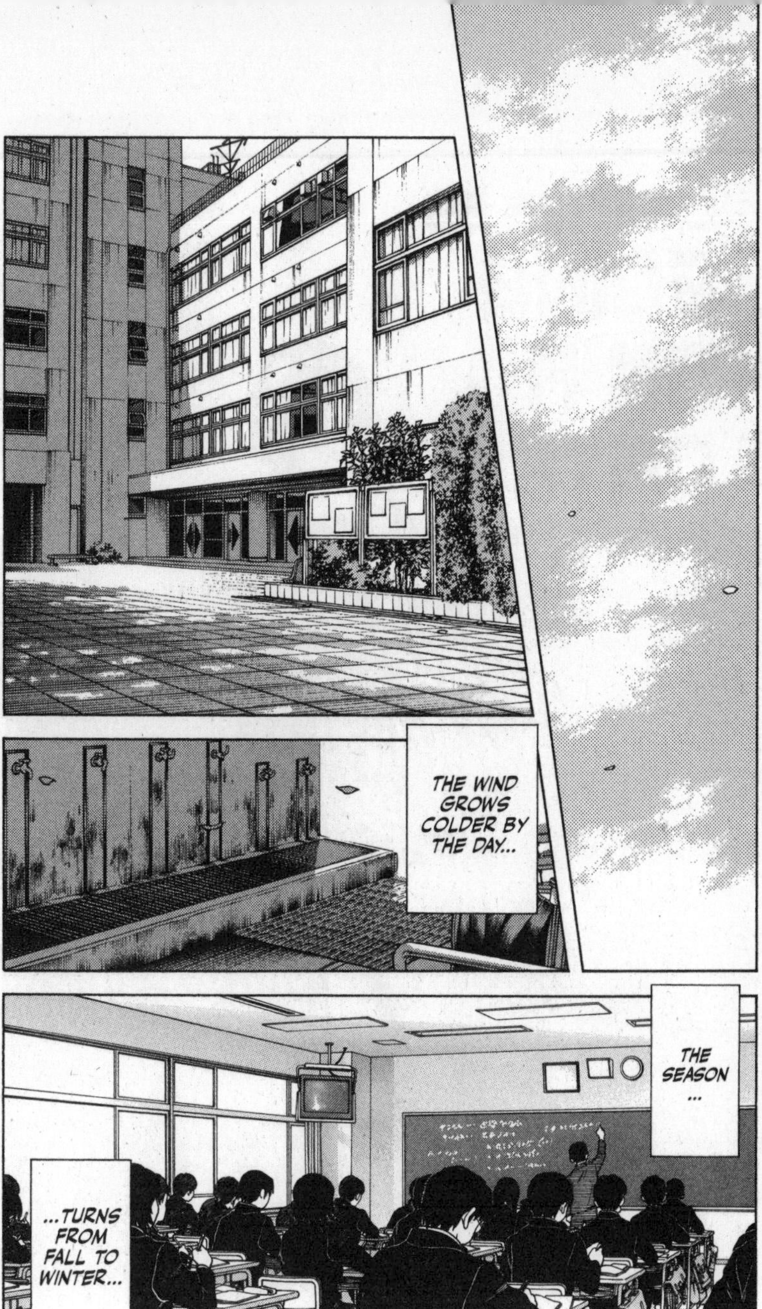
THE WIND GROWS COLDER BY THE DAY...
THE SEASON ...
...TURNS FROM FALL TO WINTER...

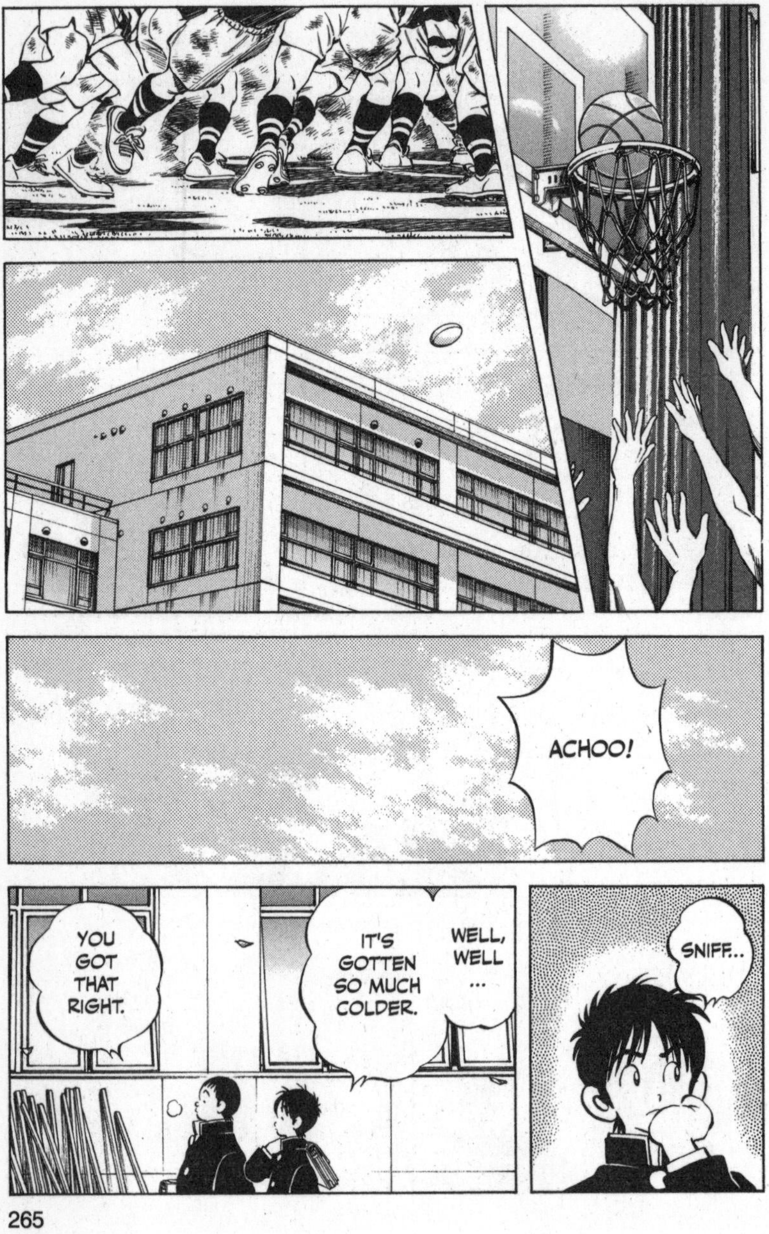
ACHOO!
SNIFF...
WELL, WELL ...
IT'S GOTTEN SO MUCH COLDER.
YOU GOT THAT RIGHT.

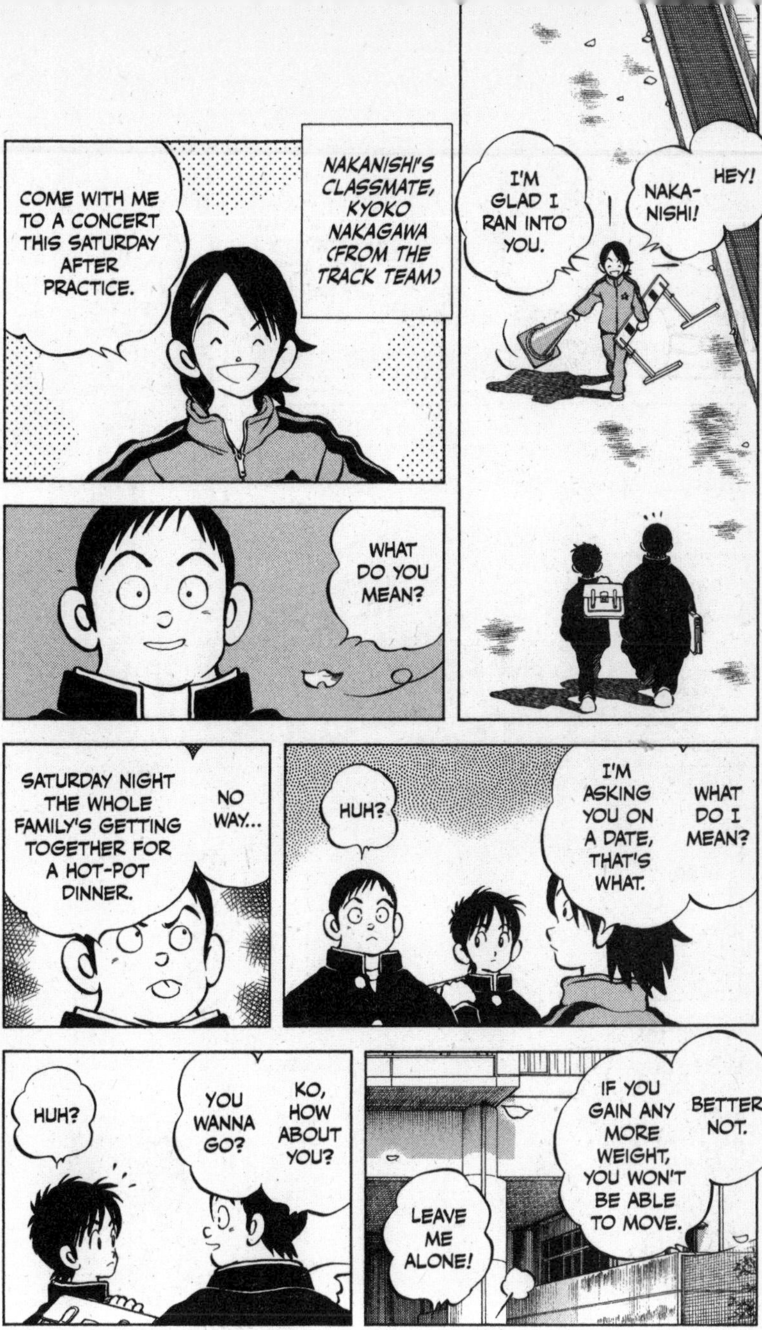
HEY! NAKA-NISHI!
I'M GLAD I RAN INTO YOU.
NAKANISHI'S CLASSMATE, KYOKO NAKAGAWA (FROM THE TRACK TEAM)
COME WITH ME TO A CONCERT THIS SATURDAY AFTER PRACTICE.
WHAT DO YOU MEAN?
WHAT DO I MEAN?
I'M ASKING YOU ON A DATE, THAT'S WHAT.
HUH?
NO WAY...
SATURDAY NIGHT THE WHOLE FAMILY'S GETTING TOGETHER FOR A HOT-POT DINNER.
BETTER NOT.
IF YOU GAIN ANY MORE WEIGHT, YOU WON'T BE ABLE TO MOVE.
LEAVE ME ALONE!
KO, HOW ABOUT YOU?
YOU WANNA GO?
HUH?

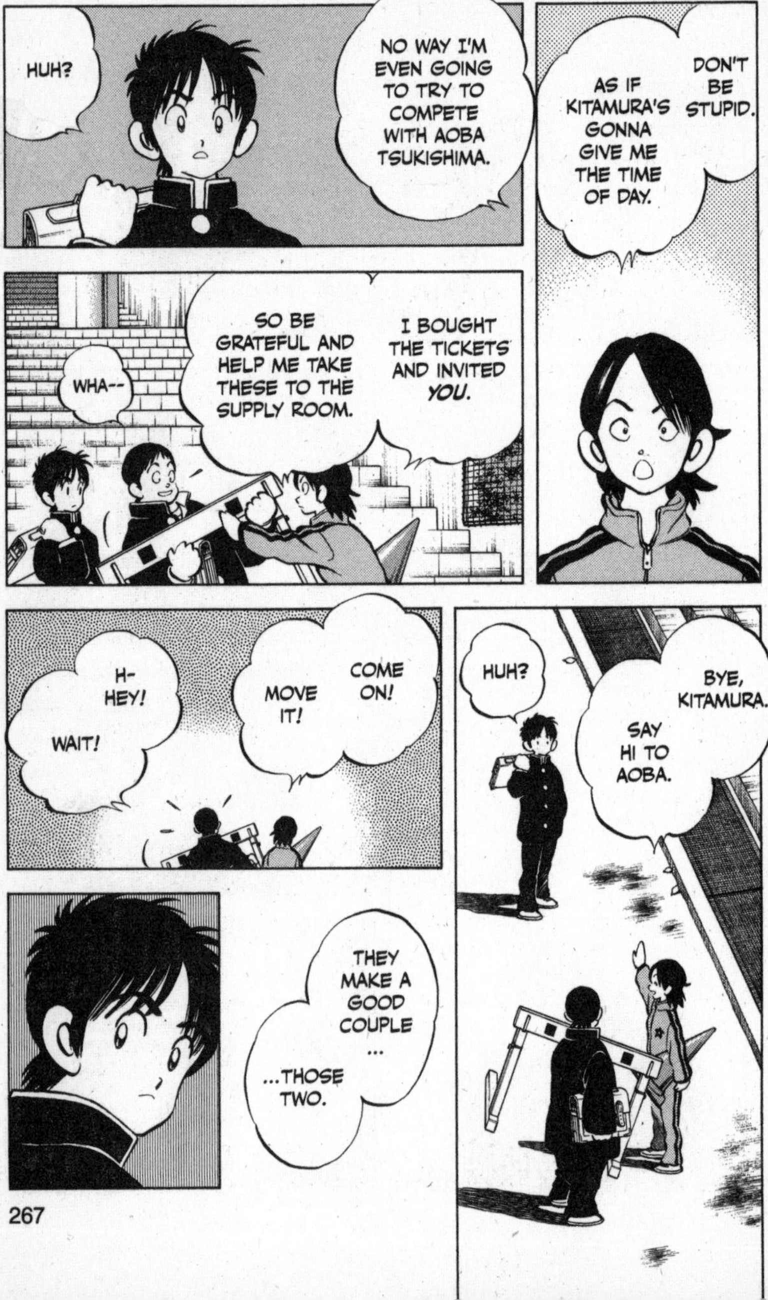
DON'T BE STUPID.
AS IF KITAMURA'S GONNA GIVE ME THE TIME OF DAY.
NO WAY I'M EVEN GOING TO TRY TO COMPETE WITH AOBA TSUKISHIMA.
HUH?
I BOUGHT THE TICKETS AND INVITED *YOU*.
SO BE GRATEFUL AND HELP ME TAKE THESE TO THE SUPPLY ROOM.
WHA--
BYE, KITAMURA.
SAY HI TO AOBA.
HUH?
COME ON!
MOVE IT!
H- HEY!
WAIT!
THEY MAKE A GOOD COUPLE ...
...THOSE TWO.

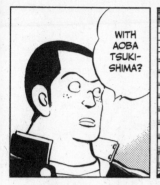

ARE YOU GOING OUT?
HUH?
WITH AOBA TSUKI-SHIMA?
OF COURSE NOT!
WHO'S SPREADING THESE RUMORS ANYWAY?!
I MEAN REALLY!
GUILTY AS CHARGED.
THERE ARE QUITE A FEW GIRLS IN CLASS WHO ASK ME TO INTRODUCE YOU TO THEM.
SO I'VE JUST BEEN TELLING THEM YOU AND TSUKI-SHIMA ARE AN ITEM.
THEN EVERYONE SIMPLY BACKS OFF.

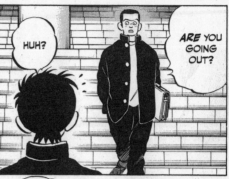

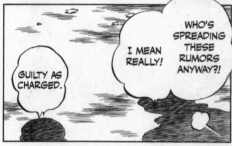

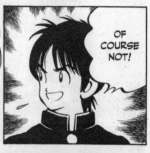

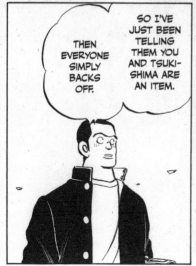

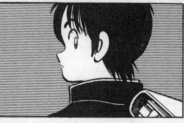

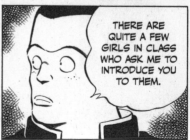

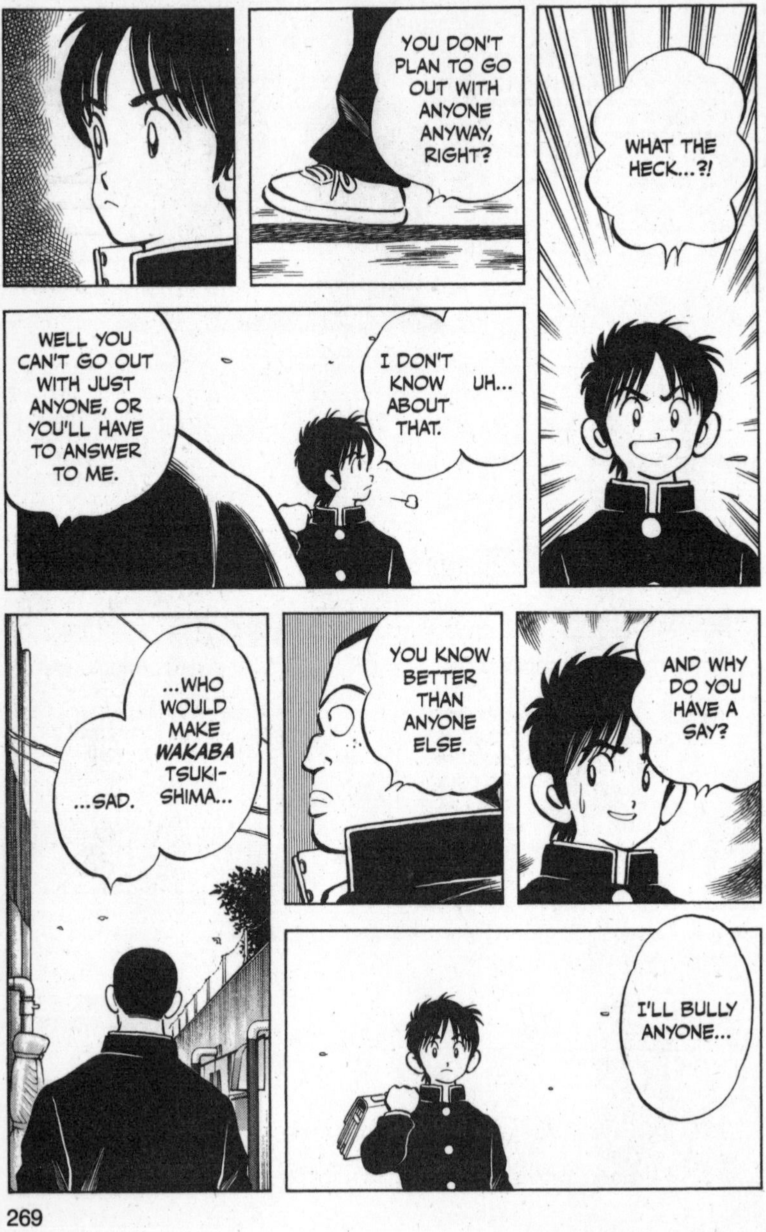
WHAT THE HECK...?!
YOU DON'T PLAN TO GO OUT WITH ANYONE ANYWAY, RIGHT?
UH...
I DON'T KNOW ABOUT THAT.
WELL YOU CAN'T GO OUT WITH JUST ANYONE, OR YOU'LL HAVE TO ANSWER TO ME.
AND WHY DO YOU HAVE A SAY?
YOU KNOW BETTER THAN ANYONE ELSE.
I'LL BULLY ANYONE...
...WHO WOULD MAKE *WAKABA* TSUKI-SHIMA...
...SAD.

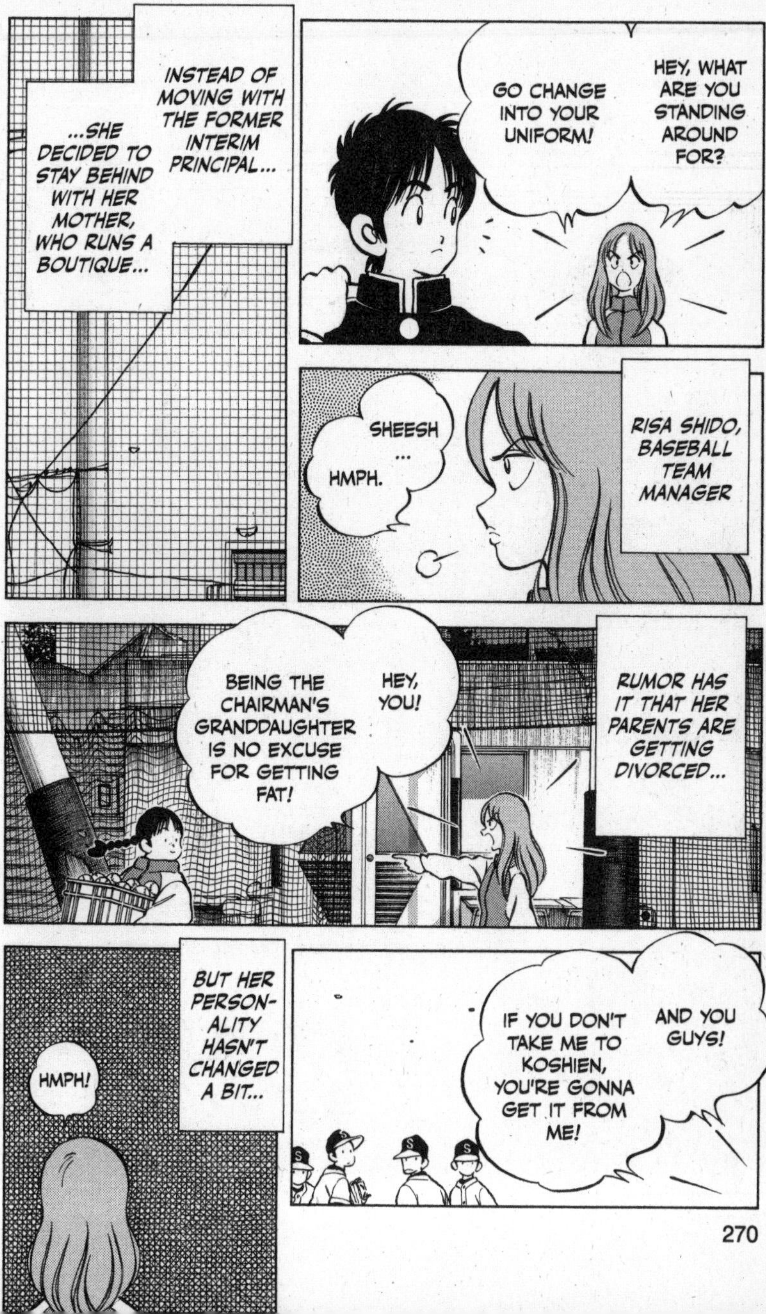
HEY, WHAT ARE YOU STANDING AROUND FOR?
GO CHANGE INTO YOUR UNIFORM!
RISA SHIDO, BASEBALL TEAM MANAGER
SHEESH ... HMPH.
INSTEAD OF MOVING WITH THE FORMER INTERIM PRINCIPAL...
...SHE DECIDED TO STAY BEHIND WITH HER MOTHER, WHO RUNS A BOUTIQUE...
RUMOR HAS IT THAT HER PARENTS ARE GETTING DIVORCED...
HEY, YOU!
BEING THE CHAIRMAN'S GRANDDAUGHTER IS NO EXCUSE FOR GETTING FAT!
AND YOU GUYS!
IF YOU DON'T TAKE ME TO KOSHIEN, YOU'RE GONNA GET IT FROM ME!
BUT HER PERSON-ALITY HASN'T CHANGED A BIT...
HMPH!

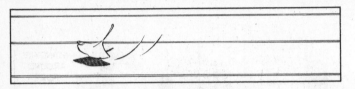

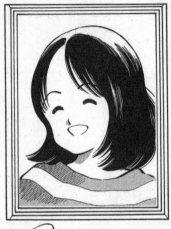

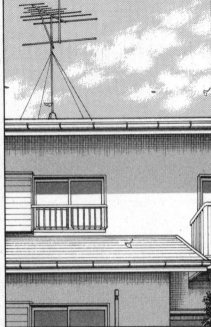

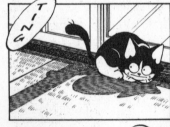

TING

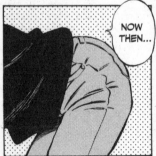

NOW
THEN...

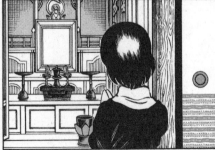

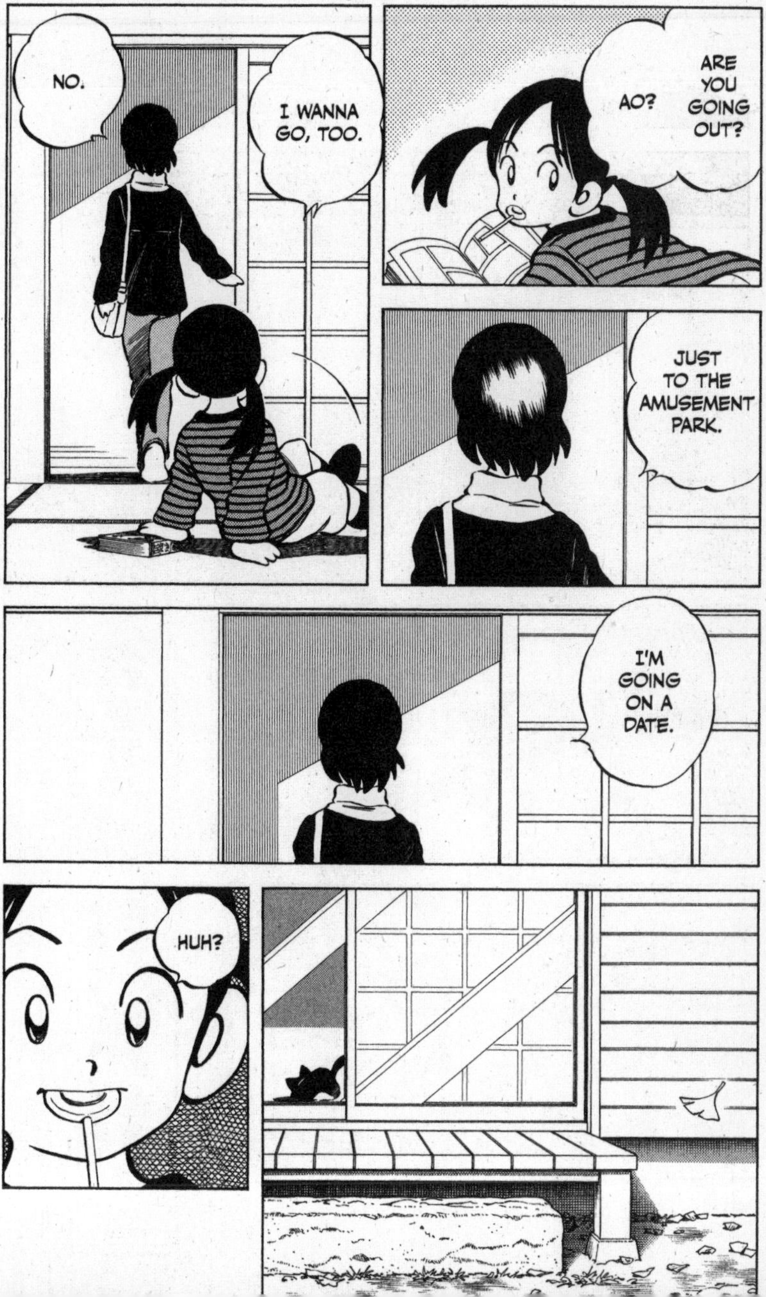
AO? ARE YOU GOING OUT?
JUST TO THE AMUSEMENT PARK.
I WANNA GO, TOO.
NO.
I'M GOING ON A DATE.
HUH?

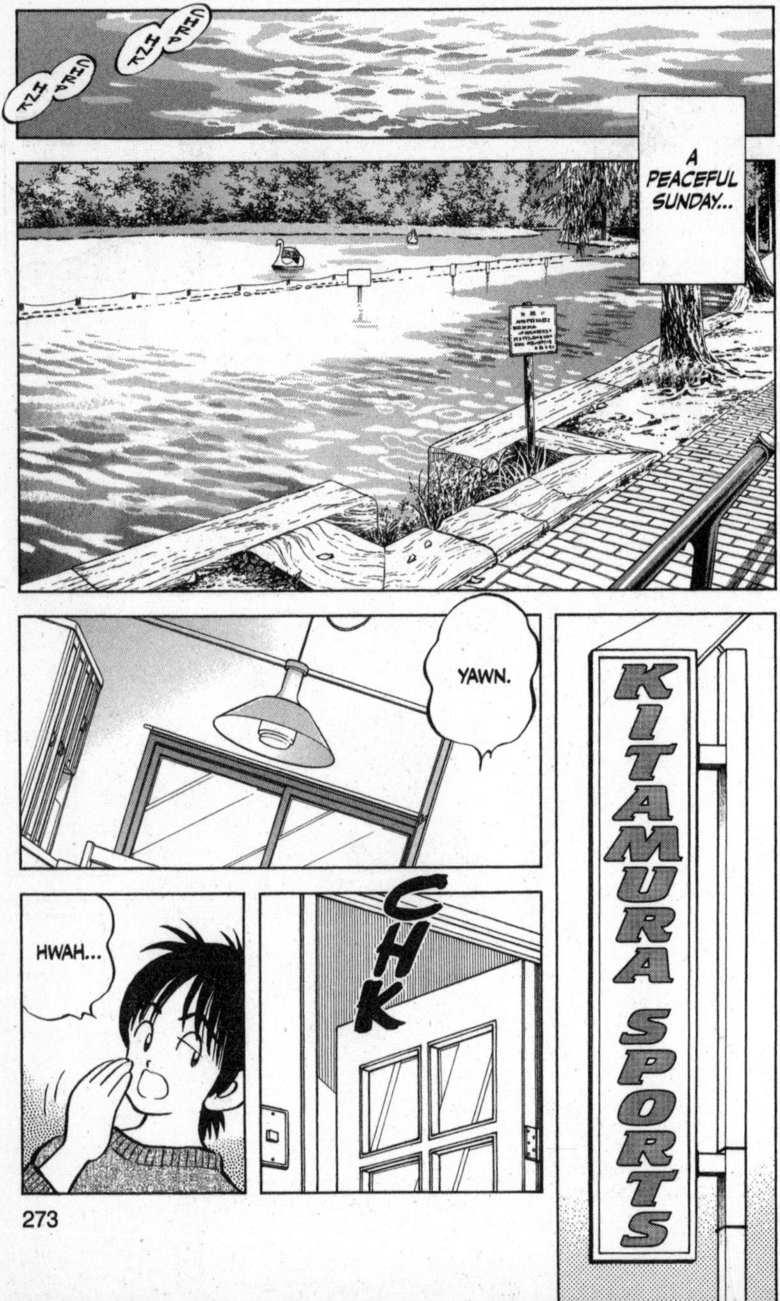
CHRP
HNK
CHRP
HNK
A PEACEFUL SUNDAY...
KITAMURA SPORTS
YAWN.
CHK
HWAH...

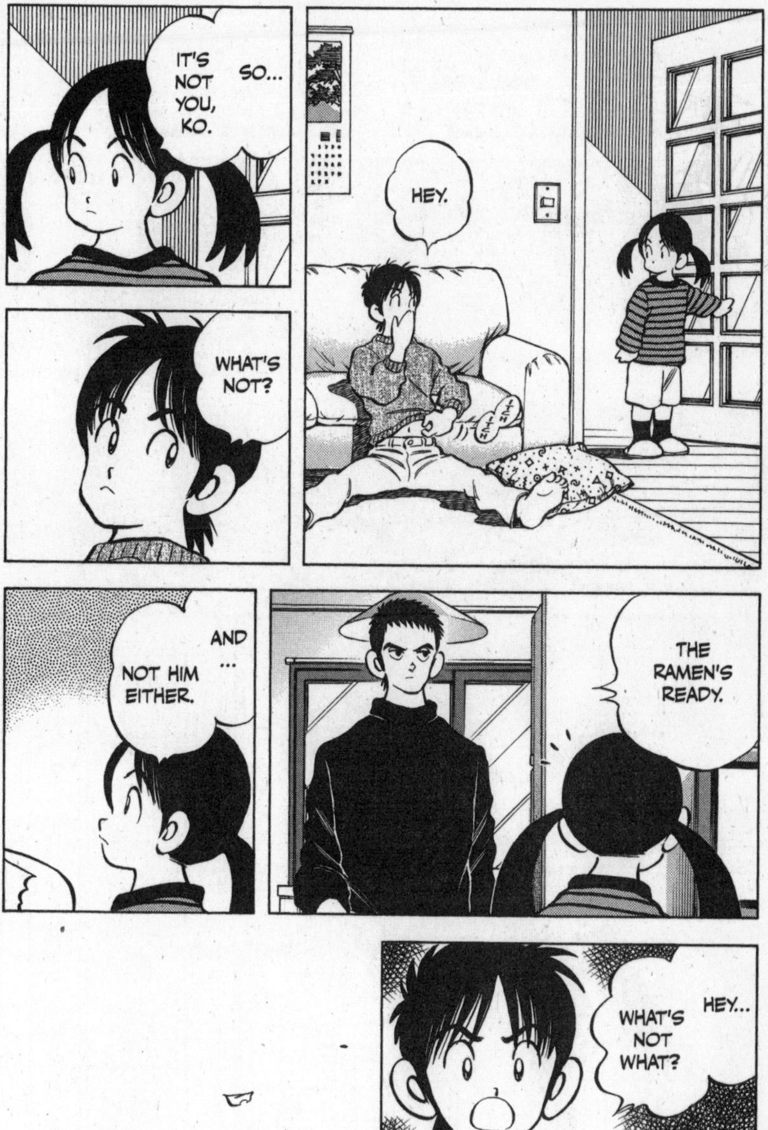
HEY.
SO... IT'S NOT YOU, KO.
WHAT'S NOT?
THE RAMEN'S READY.
AND... NOT HIM EITHER.
HEY... WHAT'S NOT WHAT?

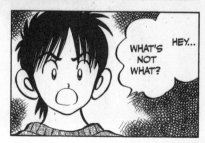

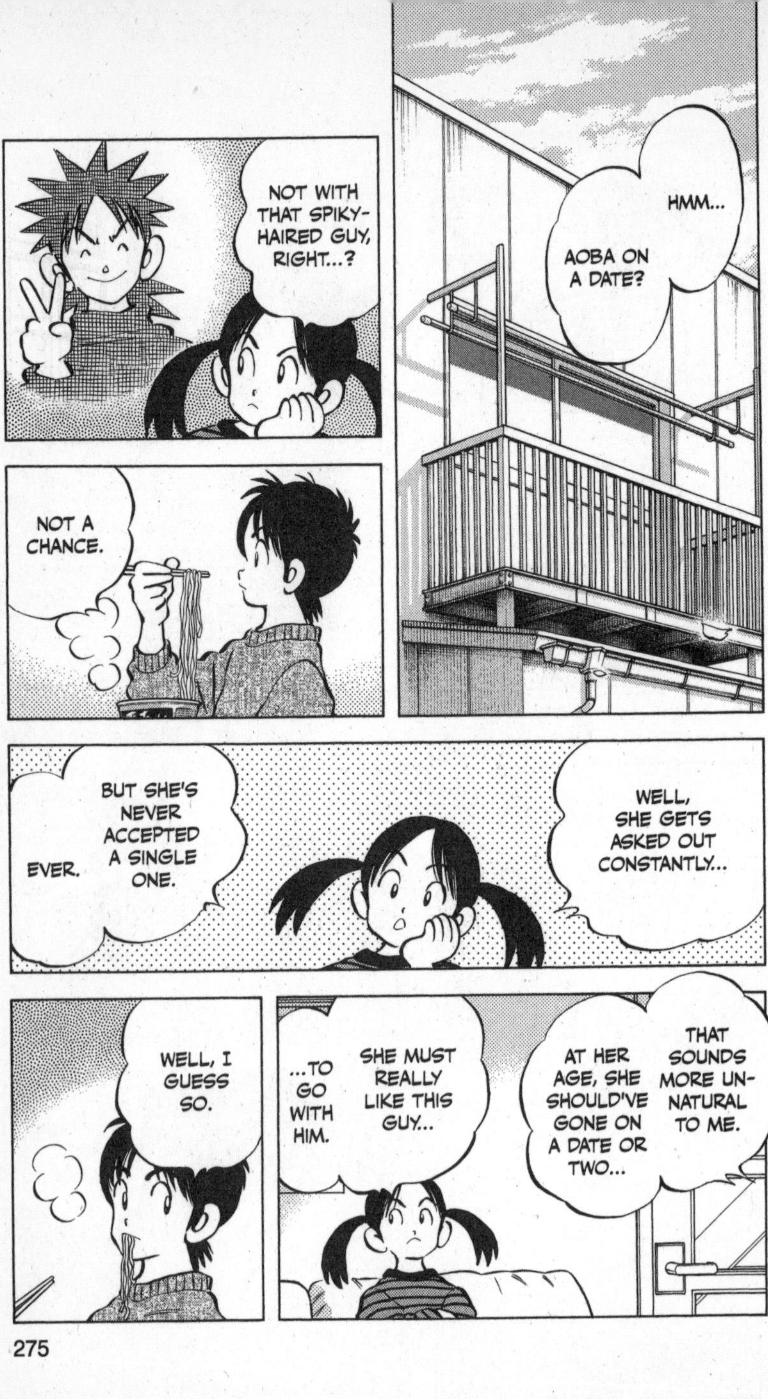
HMM...
AOBA ON A DATE?
NOT WITH THAT SPIKY-HAIRED GUY, RIGHT...?
NOT A CHANCE.
WELL, SHE GETS ASKED OUT CONSTANTLY...
BUT SHE'S NEVER ACCEPTED A SINGLE ONE.
EVER.
THAT SOUNDS MORE UN-NATURAL TO ME.
AT HER AGE, SHE SHOULD'VE GONE ON A DATE OR TWO...
SHE MUST REALLY LIKE THIS GUY...
...TO GO WITH HIM.
WELL, I GUESS SO.

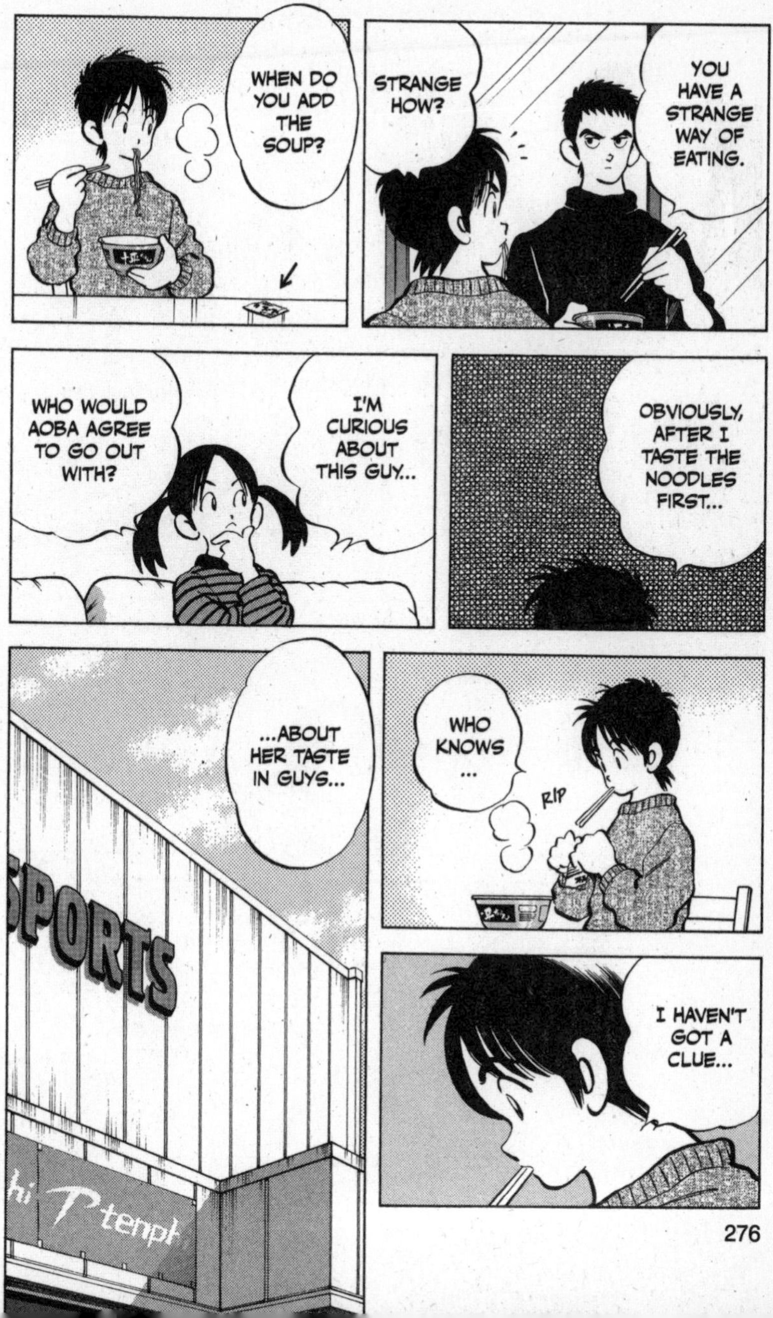
YOU HAVE A STRANGE WAY OF EATING.
STRANGE HOW?
WHEN DO YOU ADD THE SOUP?
OBVIOUSLY, AFTER I TASTE THE NOODLES FIRST...
I'M CURIOUS ABOUT THIS GUY...
WHO WOULD AOBA AGREE TO GO OUT WITH?
WHO KNOWS ...
RIP
I HAVEN'T GOT A CLUE...
...ABOUT HER TASTE IN GUYS...
SPORTS

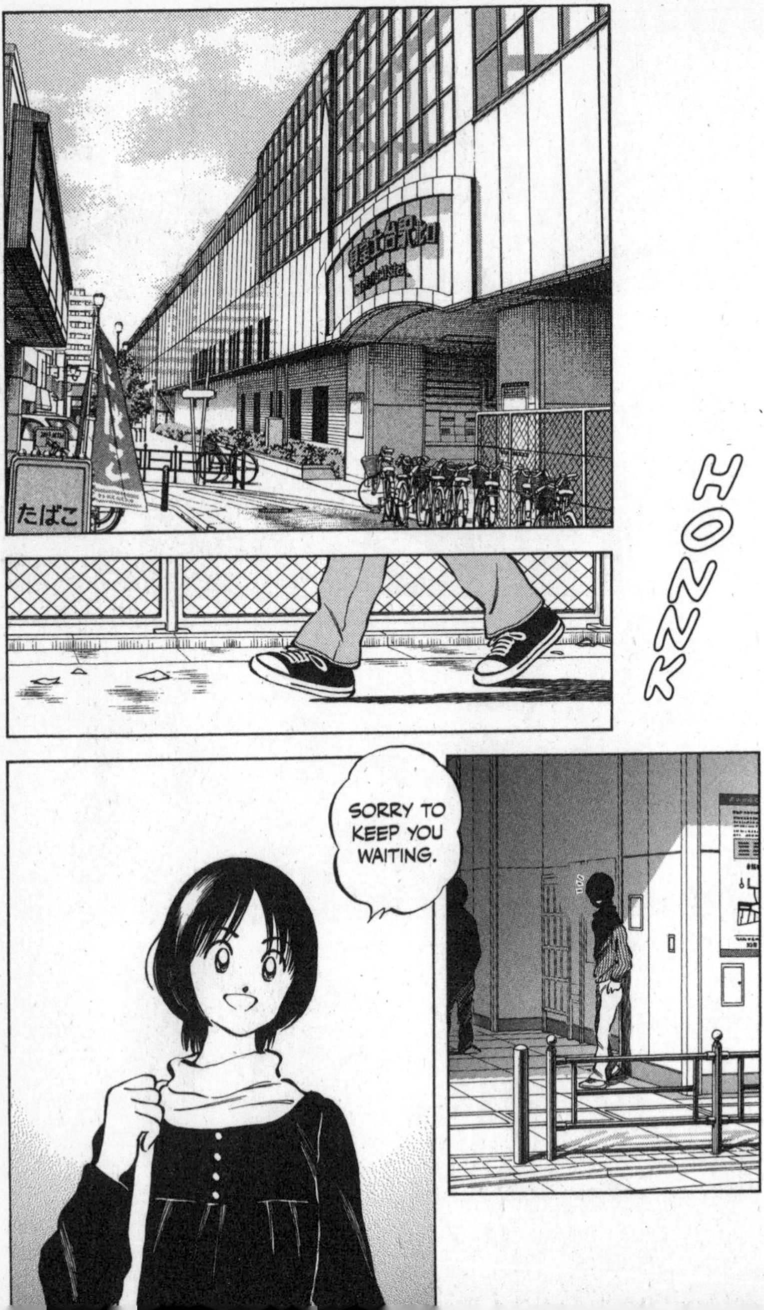
たばこ
HONNK
SORRY TO KEEP YOU WAITING.

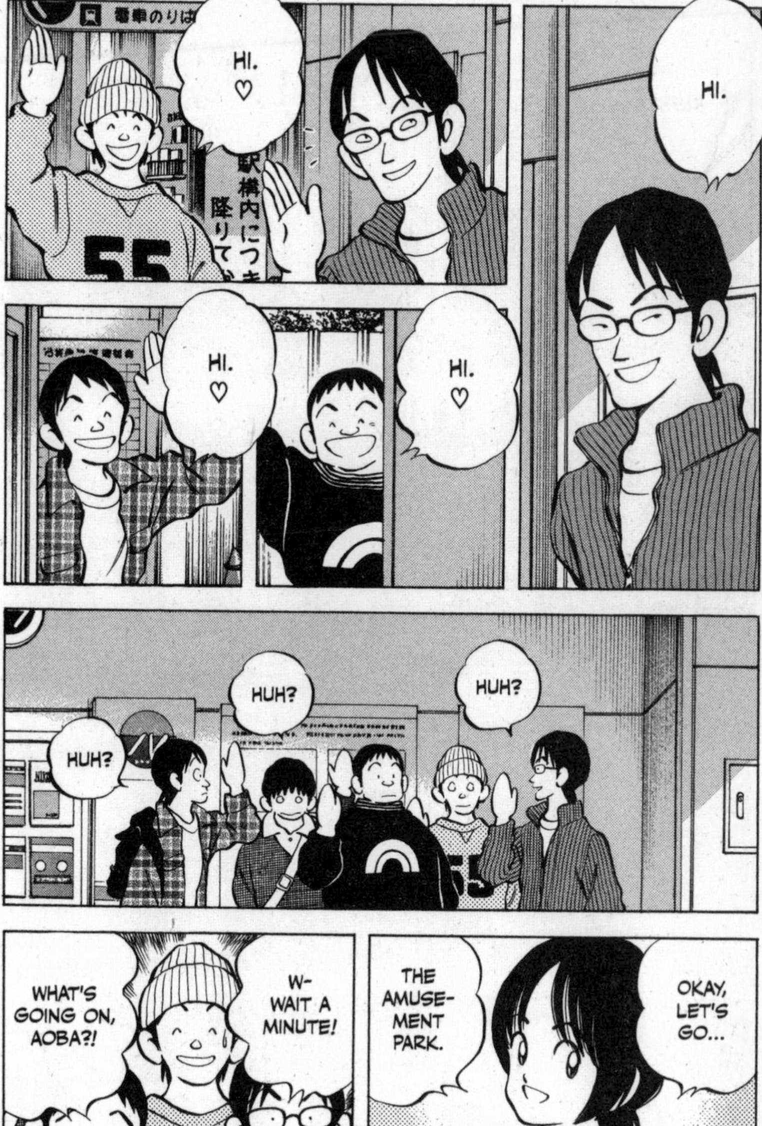
HI.
電車のりは
HI. ♡
駅構内につき
降りて
HI. ♡
HI. ♡
HUH?
HUH?
HUH?
OKAY, LET'S GO...
THE AMUSE-MENT PARK.
W- WAIT A MINUTE!
WHAT'S GOING ON, AOBA?!

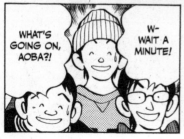

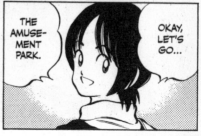

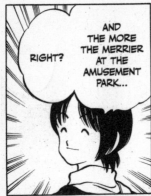

I KEEP TURNING YOU DOWN, BUT YOU'RE ALL SO PER-SISTENT.
IF I GO OUT WITH YOU ONCE, YOU'LL BE SATISFIED, RIGHT?
AND THE MORE THE MERRIER AT THE AMUSEMENT PARK...
RIGHT?
THE MORE ...
THE MERRIER ...?
COME ON!
WE'RE ON A DATE!
ROA——RR

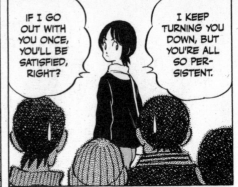

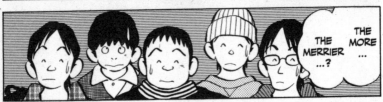

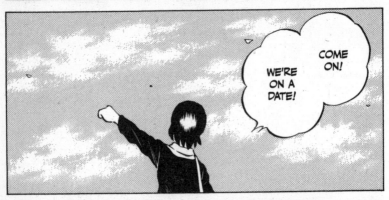

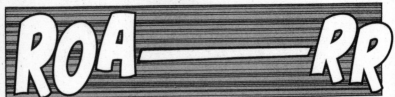

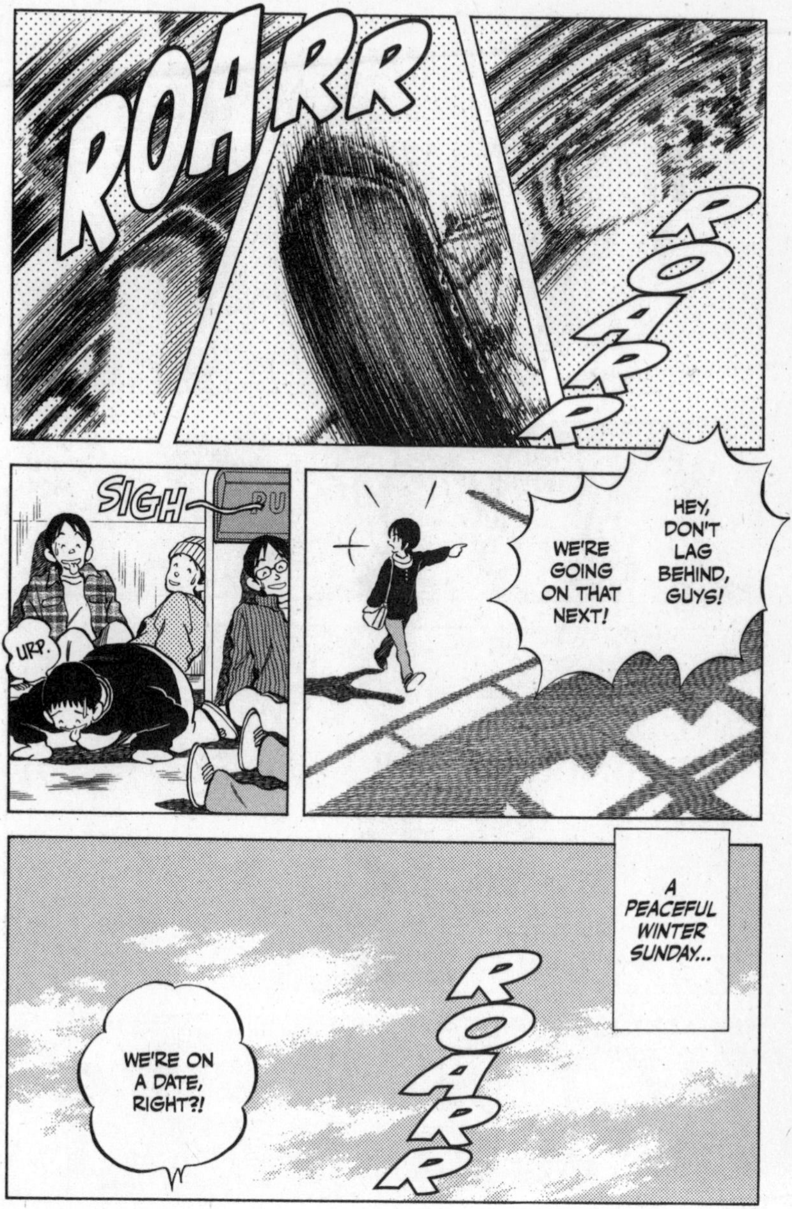
ROARR
ROARR
HEY, DON'T LAG BEHIND, GUYS!
WE'RE GOING ON THAT NEXT!
SIGH
URP.
A PEACEFUL WINTER SUNDAY...
ROARR
WE'RE ON A DATE, RIGHT?!

CHAPTER 56

FIRST DREAM OF THE NEW YEAR

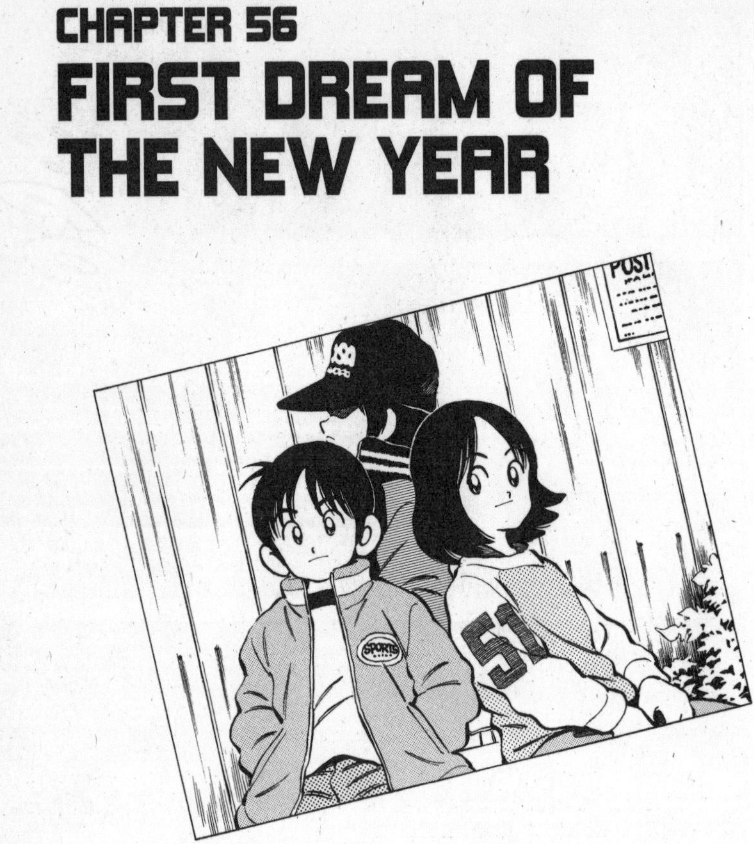
POST
SPORTS

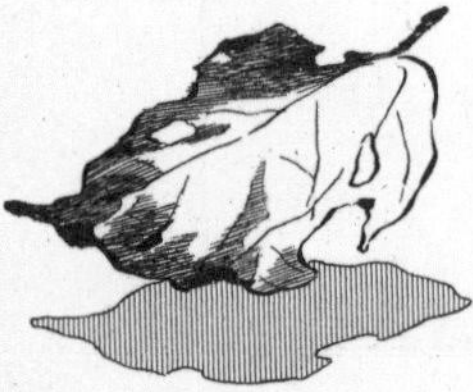

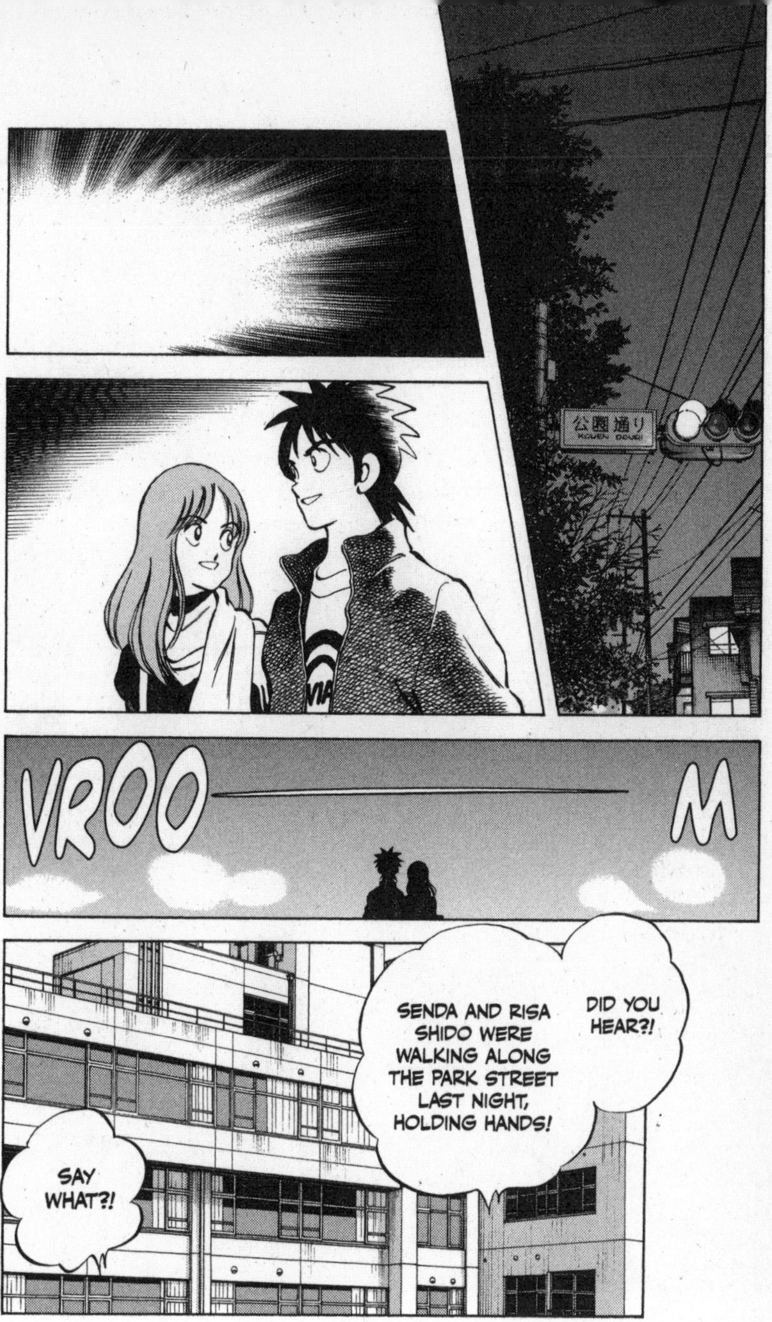
公園通り
VROOM
DID YOU HEAR?!
SENDA AND RISA SHIDO WERE WALKING ALONG THE PARK STREET LAST NIGHT, HOLDING HANDS!
SAY WHAT?!

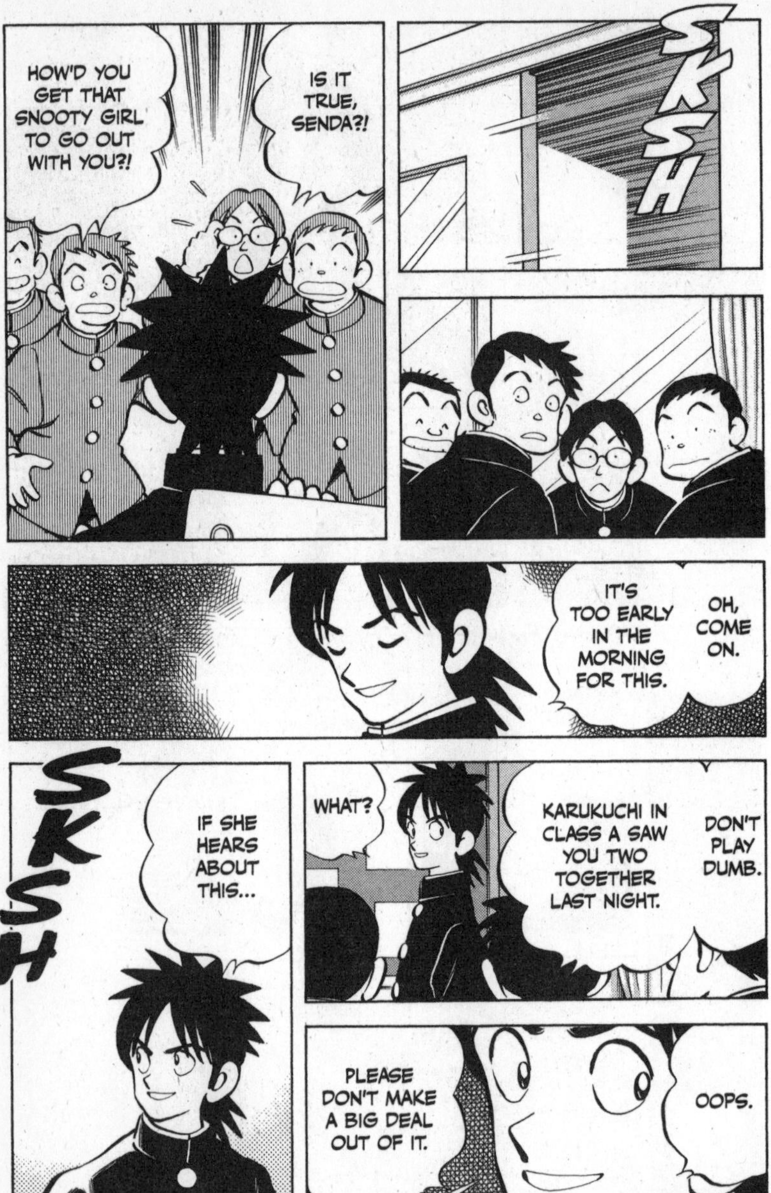
SKSH
IS IT TRUE, SENDA?!
HOW'D YOU GET THAT SNOOTY GIRL TO GO OUT WITH YOU?!
OH, COME ON.
IT'S TOO EARLY IN THE MORNING FOR THIS.
DON'T PLAY DUMB.
KARUKUCHI IN CLASS A SAW YOU TWO TOGETHER LAST NIGHT.
WHAT?
OOPS.
PLEASE DON'T MAKE A BIG DEAL OUT OF IT.
SKSH
IF SHE HEARS ABOUT THIS...

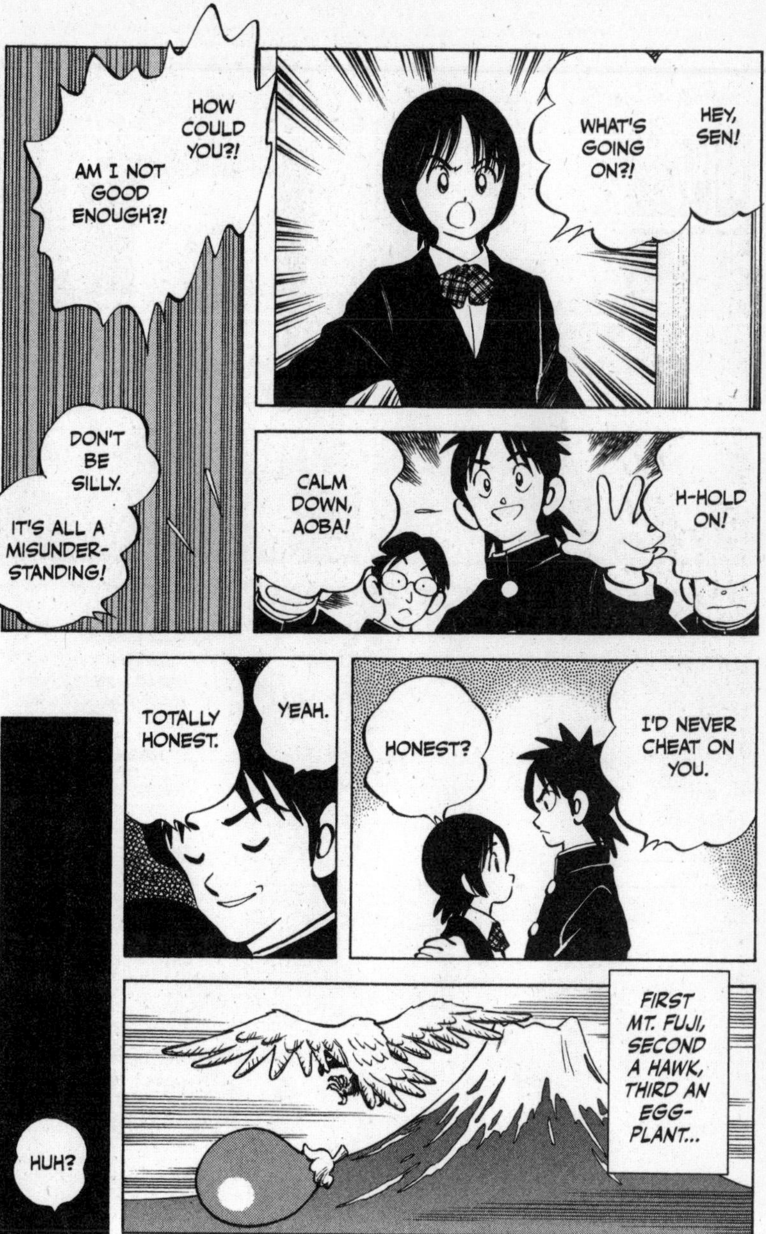
HEY, SEN!
WHAT'S GOING ON?!
H-HOLD ON!
CALM DOWN, AOBA!
HOW COULD YOU?!
AM I NOT GOOD ENOUGH?!
DON'T BE SILLY.
IT'S ALL A MISUNDERSTANDING!
I'D NEVER CHEAT ON YOU.
HONEST?
YEAH.
TOTALLY HONEST.
FIRST MT. FUJI, SECOND A HAWK, THIRD AN EGGPLANT...
HUH?

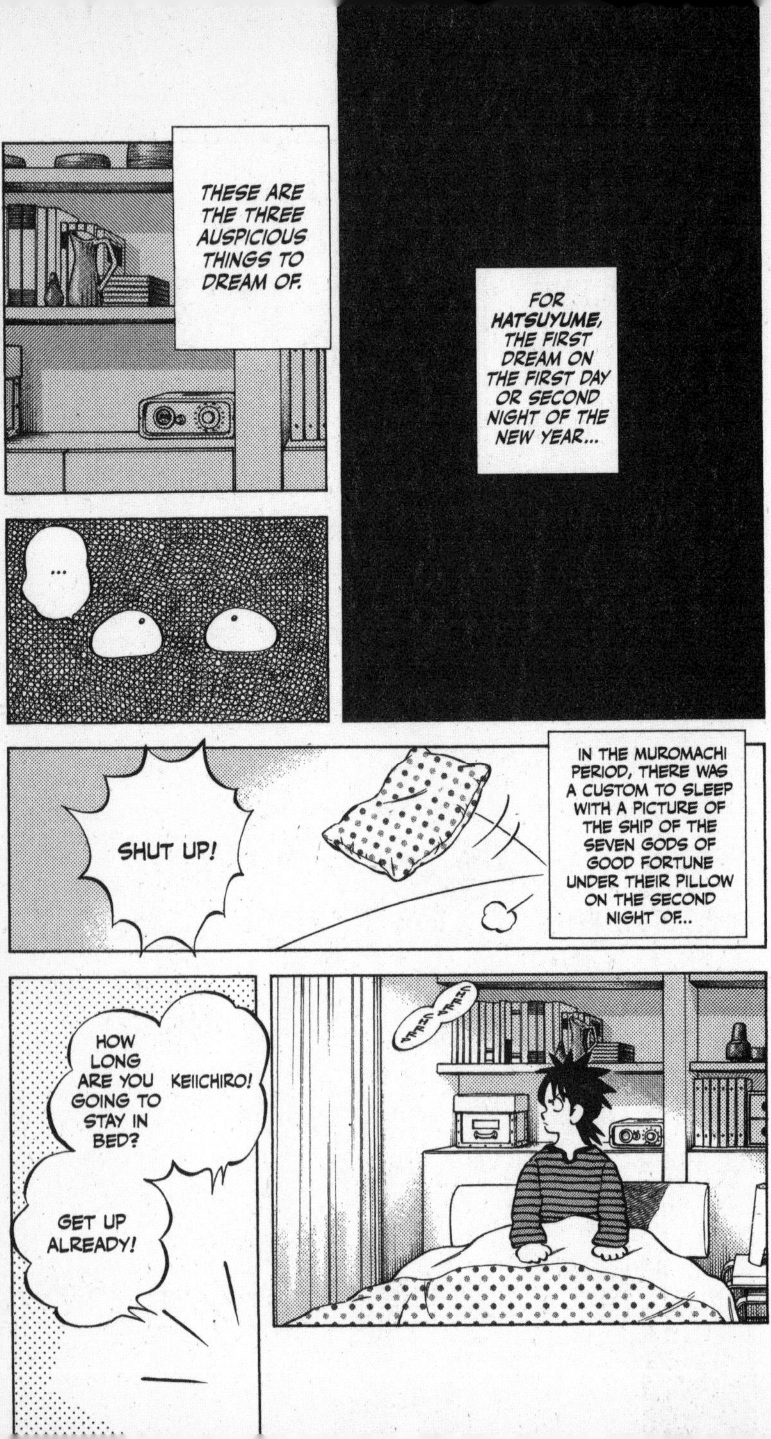
FOR HATSUYUME, THE FIRST DREAM ON THE FIRST DAY OR SECOND NIGHT OF THE NEW YEAR...
THESE ARE THE THREE AUSPICIOUS THINGS TO DREAM OF.
...
IN THE MUROMACHI PERIOD, THERE WAS A CUSTOM TO SLEEP WITH A PICTURE OF THE SHIP OF THE SEVEN GODS OF GOOD FORTUNE UNDER THEIR PILLOW ON THE SECOND NIGHT OF...
SHUT UP!
KEIICHIRO!
HOW LONG ARE YOU GOING TO STAY IN BED?
GET UP ALREADY!

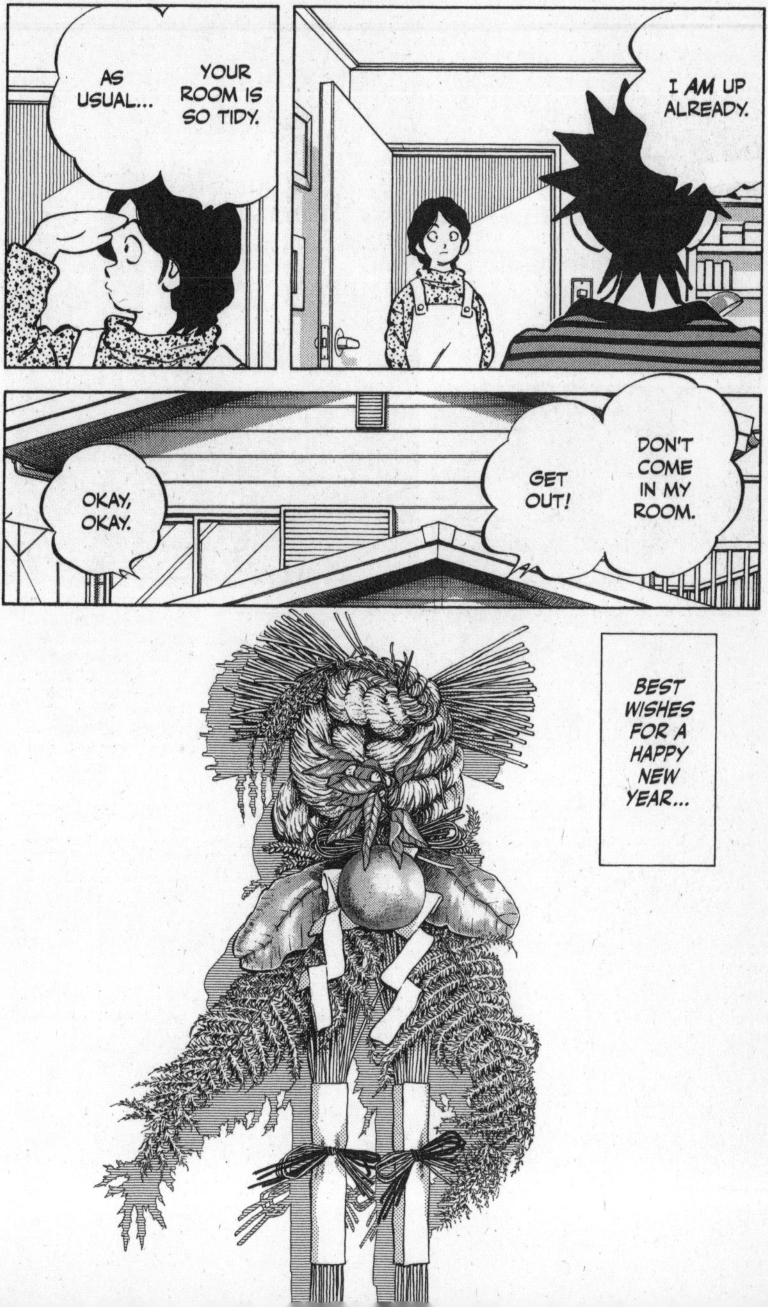
I AM UP ALREADY.
AS USUAL... YOUR ROOM IS SO TIDY.
DON'T COME IN MY ROOM.
GET OUT!
OKAY, OKAY.
BEST WISHES FOR A HAPPY NEW YEAR...

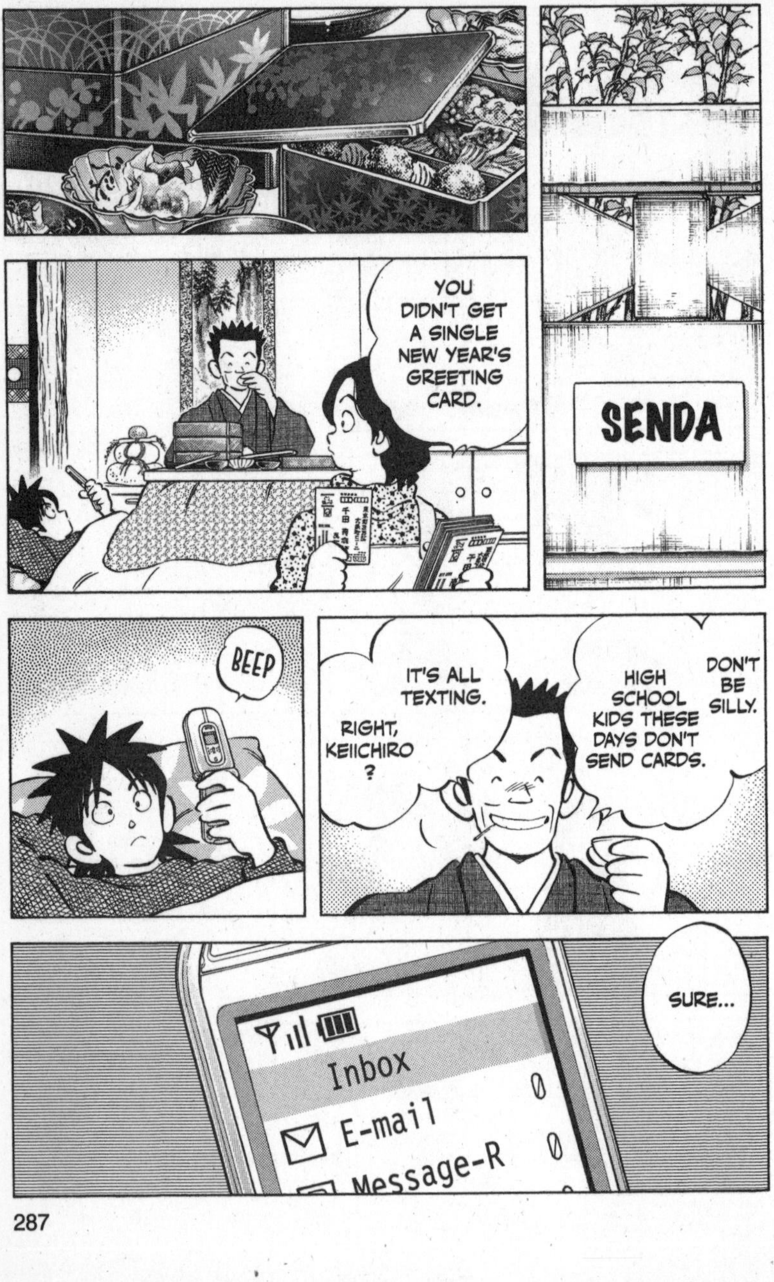
SENDA
YOU DIDN'T GET A SINGLE NEW YEAR'S GREETING CARD.
DON'T BE SILLY.
HIGH SCHOOL KIDS THESE DAYS DON'T SEND CARDS.
IT'S ALL TEXTING.
RIGHT, KEIICHIRO?
BEEP
SURE...
Inbox
E-mail 0
Message-R 0

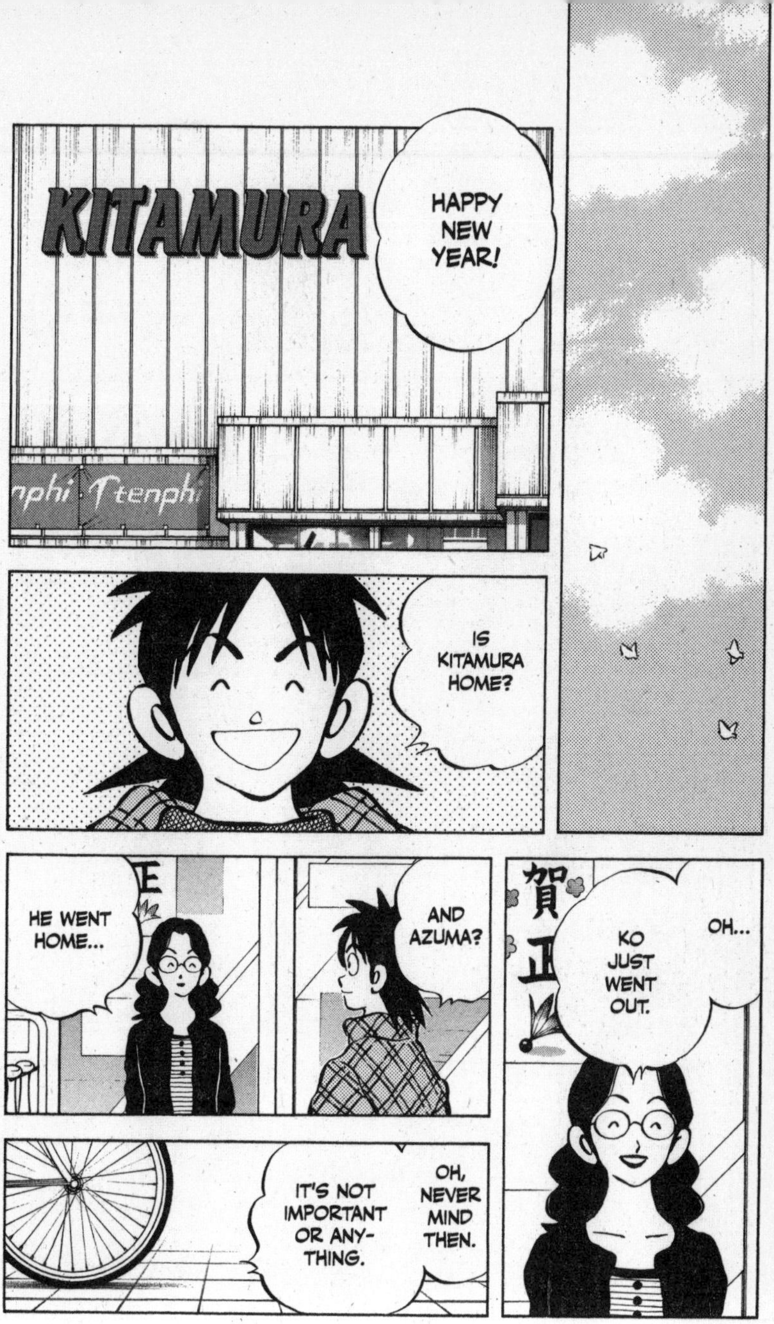
KITAMURA
HAPPY NEW YEAR!
IS KITAMURA HOME?
OH...
KO JUST WENT OUT.
AND AZUMA?
HE WENT HOME...
OH, NEVER MIND THEN.
IT'S NOT IMPORTANT OR ANY-THING.

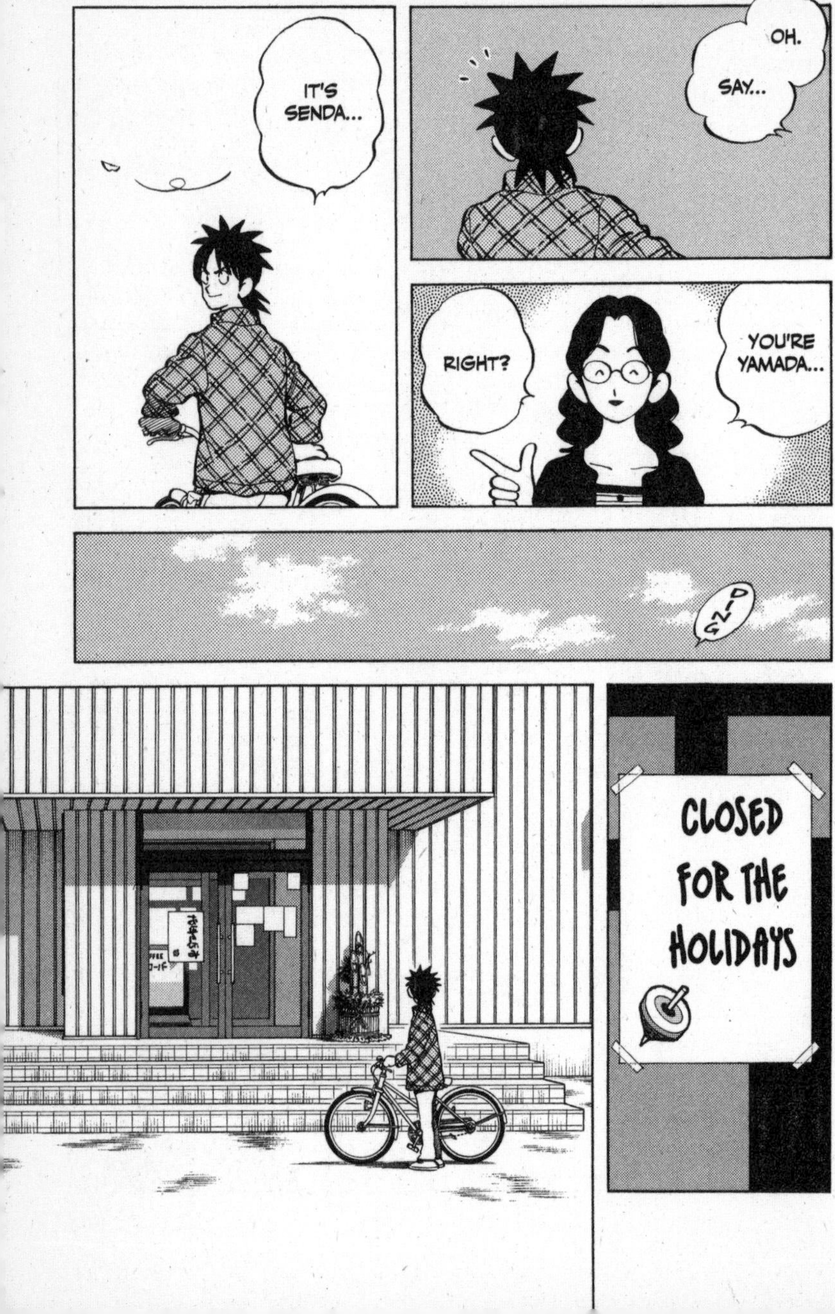
OH.
SAY...
YOU'RE YAMADA...
RIGHT?
IT'S SENDA...
DING
CLOSED FOR THE HOLIDAYS

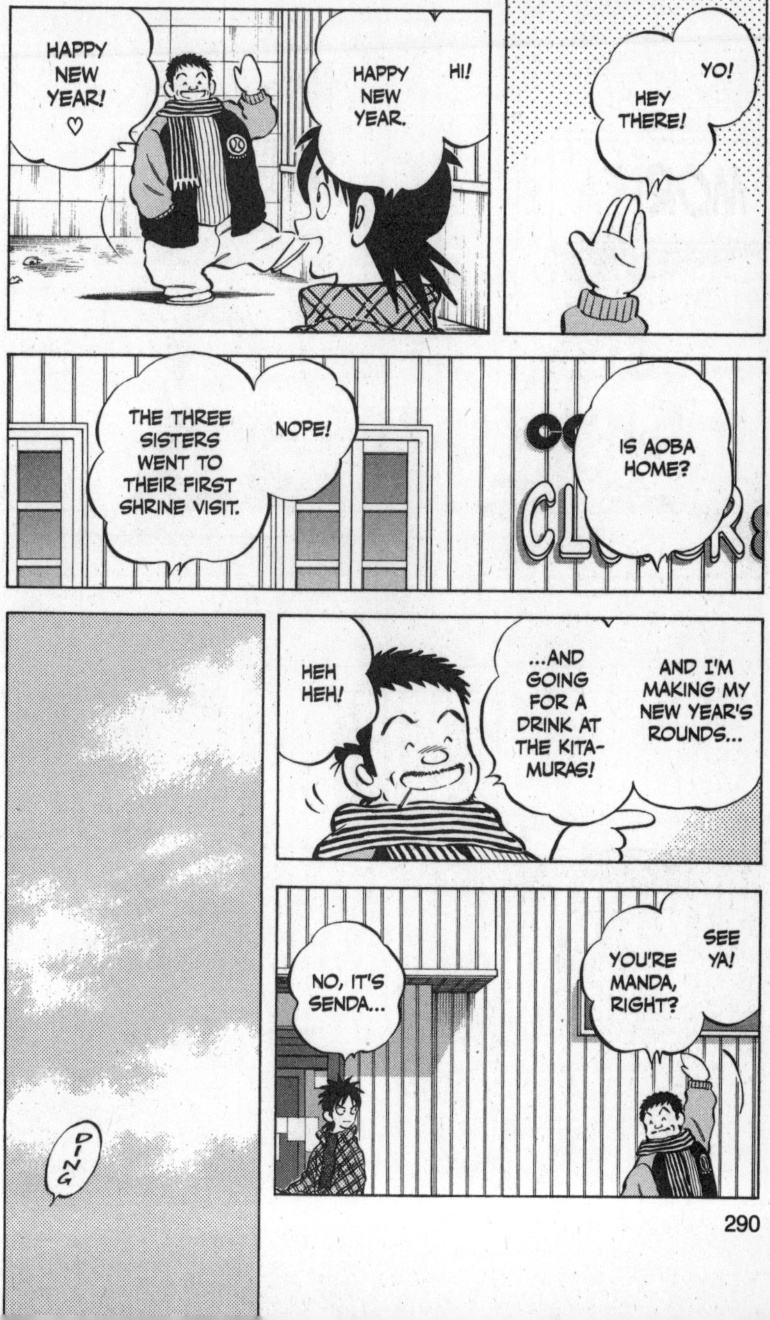
YO! HEY THERE!
HI! HAPPY NEW YEAR.
HAPPY NEW YEAR! ♡
IS AOBA HOME?
NOPE! THE THREE SISTERS WENT TO THEIR FIRST SHRINE VISIT.
AND I'M MAKING MY NEW YEAR'S ROUNDS...
...AND GOING FOR A DRINK AT THE KITA-MURAS!
HEH HEH!
SEE YA! YOU'RE MANDA, RIGHT?
NO, IT'S SENDA...
DING

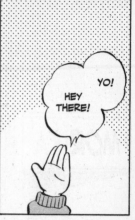

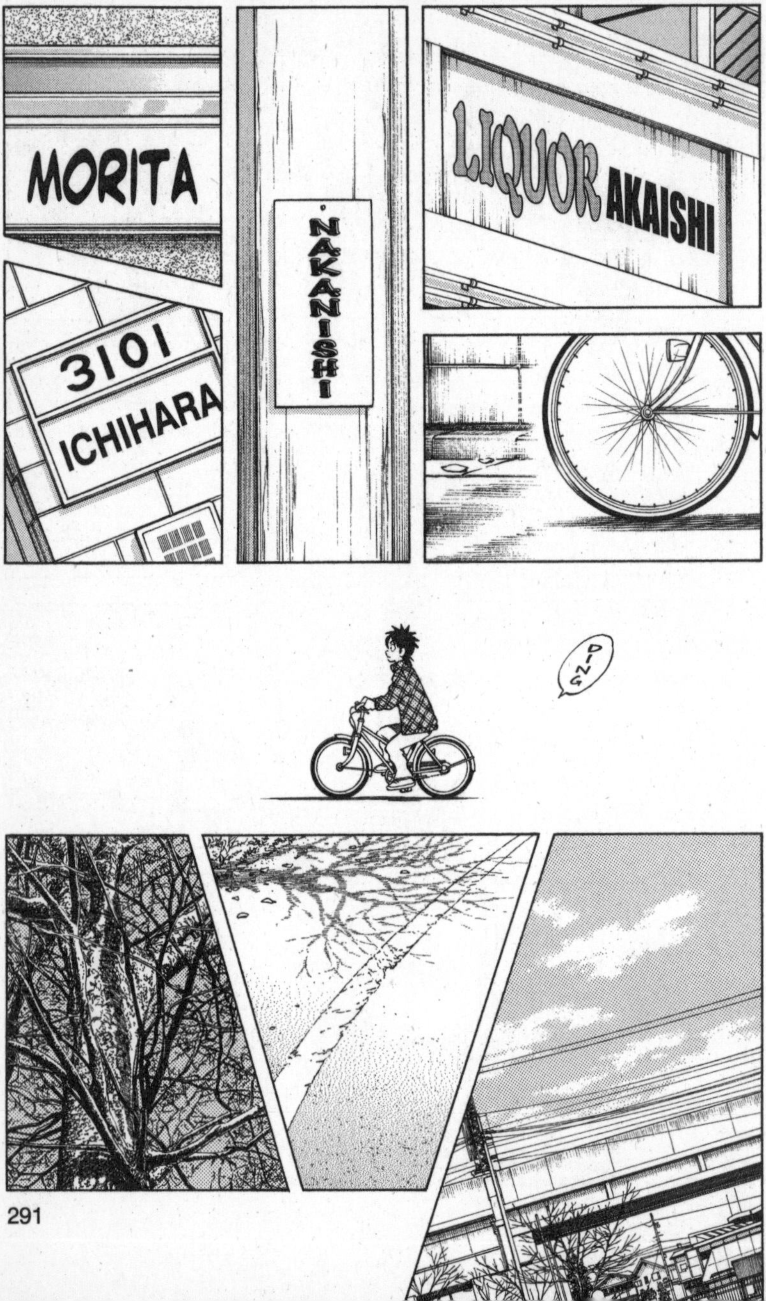
LIQUOR AKAISHI
NAKANISHI
MORITA
3101
ICHIHARA
DING

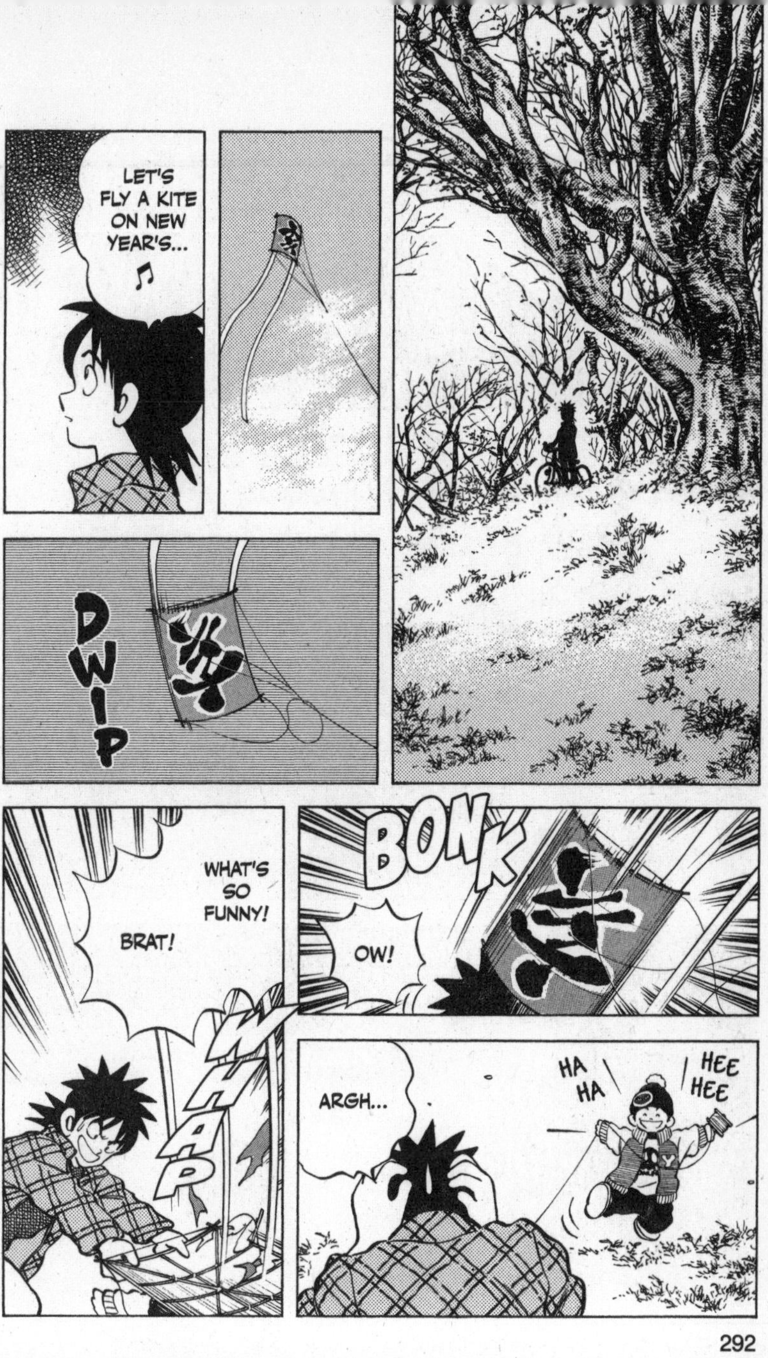
LET'S FLY A KITE ON NEW YEAR'S... ♪
DWIP
BONK
OW!
HA HA
HEE HEE
ARGH...
WHAT'S SO FUNNY!
BRAT!
WHAP

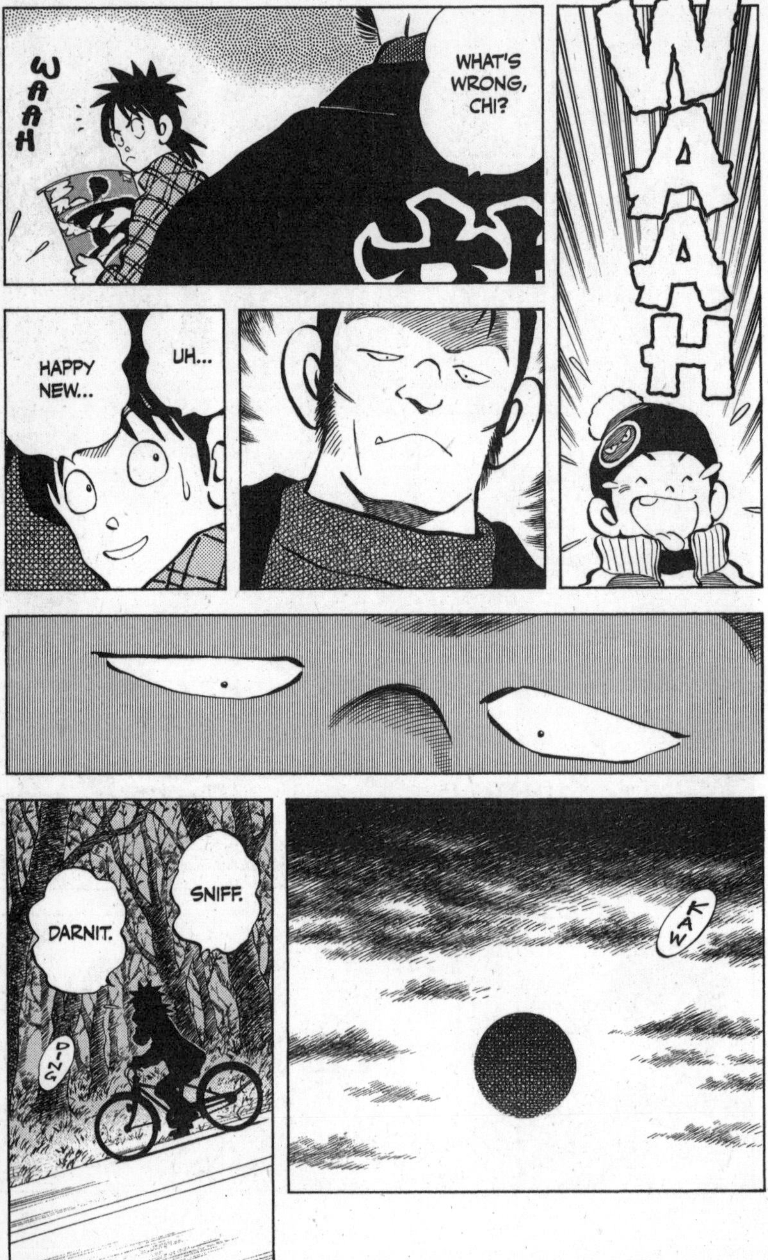
WAAH
WHAT'S WRONG, CHI?
WAAH
UH...
HAPPY NEW...
KAW
SNIFF.
DARNIT.
DING

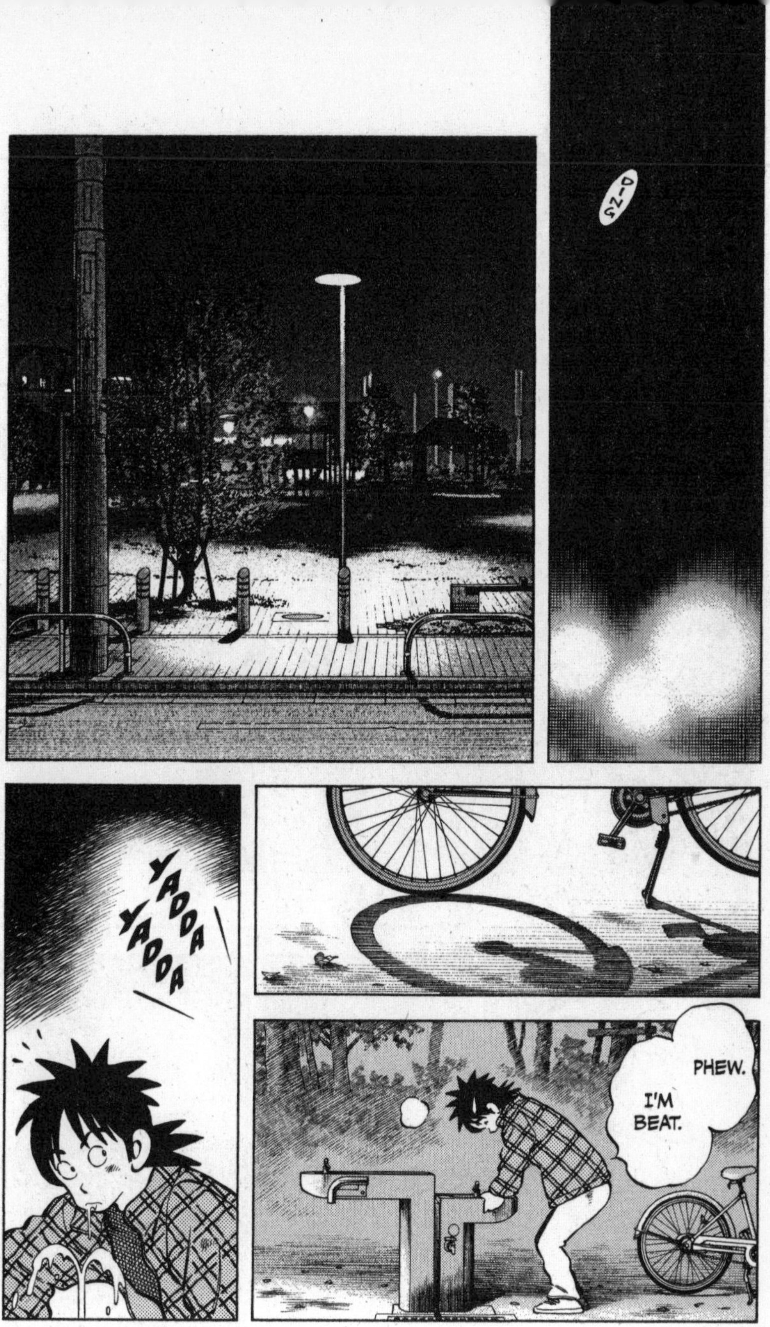
DING
PHEW.
I'M BEAT.
YADDA YADDA

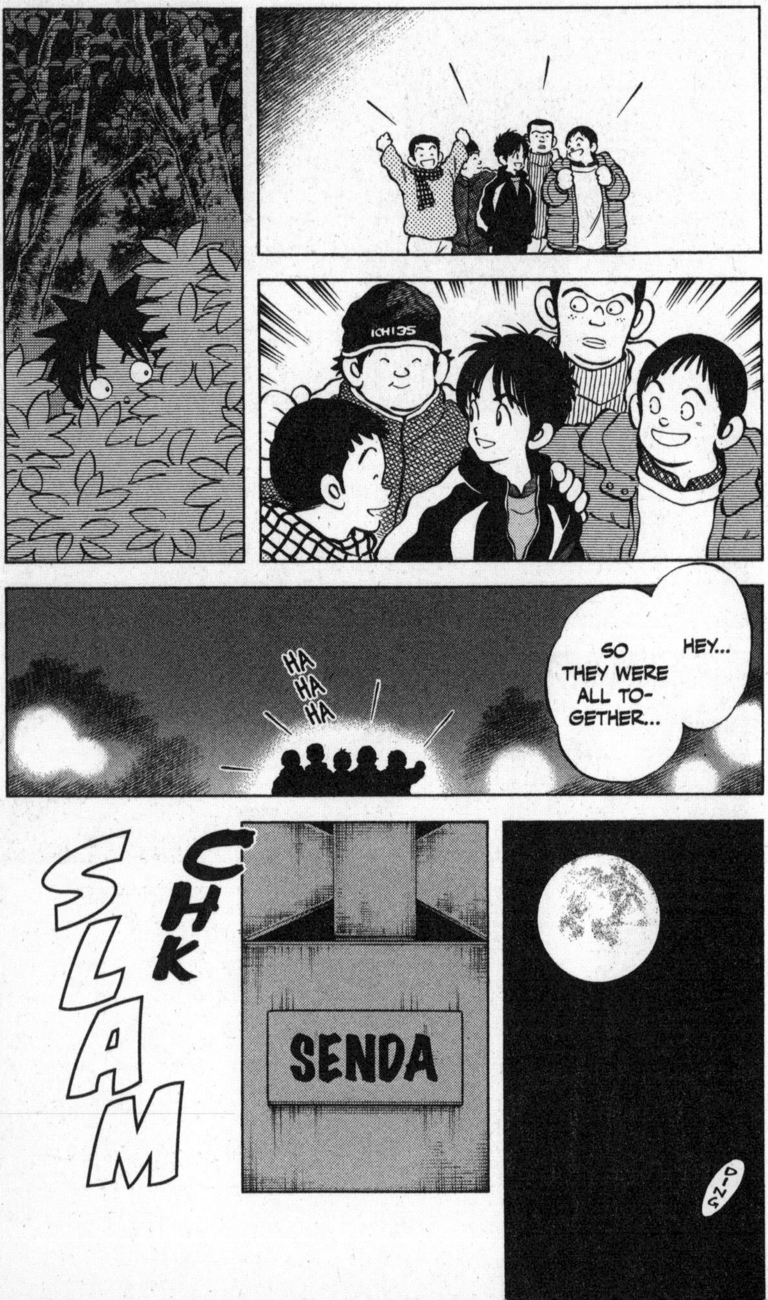
ICHI35
HEY...
SO THEY WERE ALL TO-GETHER...
HA HA HA
DING
CHK
SENDA
SLAM

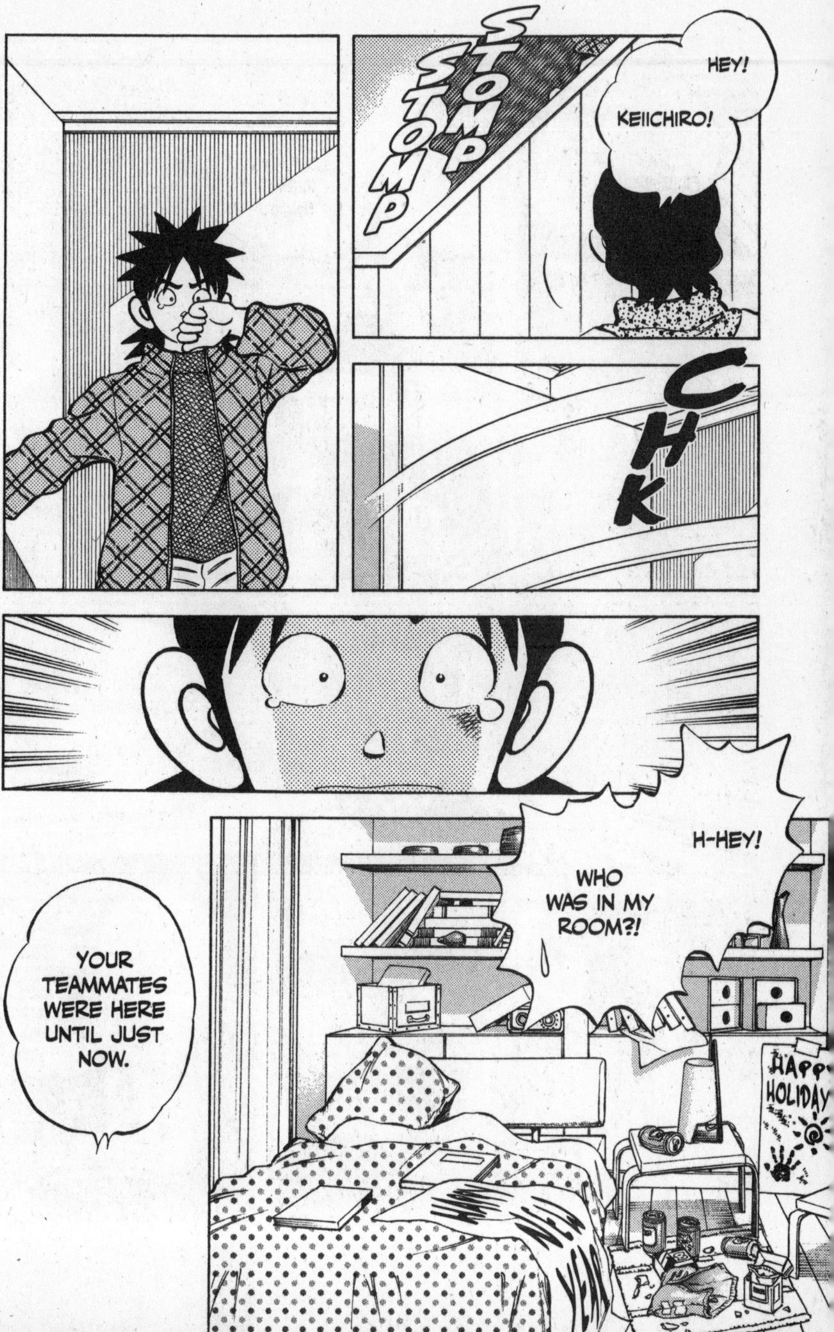
STOMP STOMP
HEY!
KEIICHIRO!
CHK
H-HEY!
WHO WAS IN MY ROOM?!
YOUR TEAMMATES WERE HERE UNTIL JUST NOW.

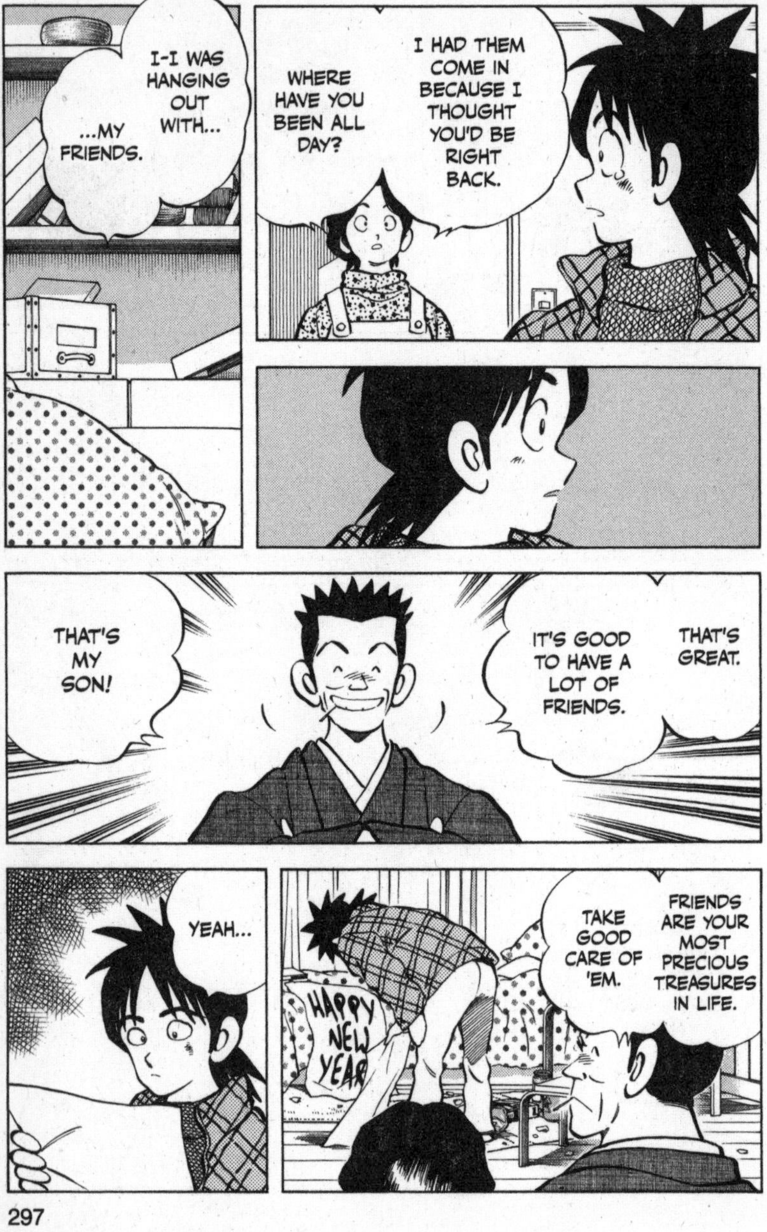
I HAD THEM COME IN BECAUSE I THOUGHT YOU'D BE RIGHT BACK.
WHERE HAVE YOU BEEN ALL DAY?
I-I WAS HANGING OUT WITH...
...MY FRIENDS.
THAT'S GREAT.
IT'S GOOD TO HAVE A LOT OF FRIENDS.
THAT'S MY SON!
FRIENDS ARE YOUR MOST PRECIOUS TREASURES IN LIFE.
TAKE GOOD CARE OF 'EM.
HAPPY NEW YEAR
YEAH...

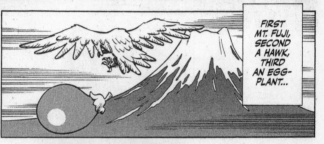

AIM FOR KOSHIEN! SEISHU GAKUEN BASEBALL TEAM

I KNOW.

KOFF

FIRST MT. FUJI, SECOND A HAWK, THIRD AN EGG-PLANT...

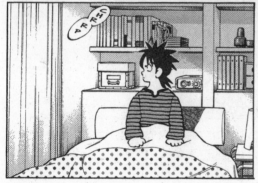

AAAH

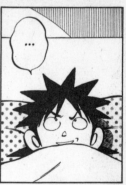

...

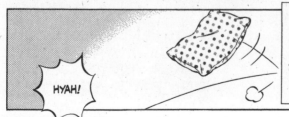

HYAH!

IN THE MUROMACHI PERIOD, THERE WAS A CUSTOM TO SLEEP WITH THE PICTURE OF THE SHIP OF THE SEVEN GODS OF GOOD FORTUNE...

CHAPTER 57

WHAT A BUNCH OF HOGWASH

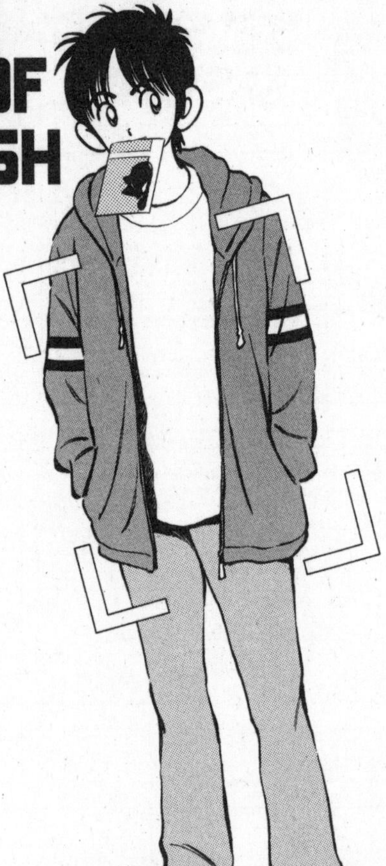

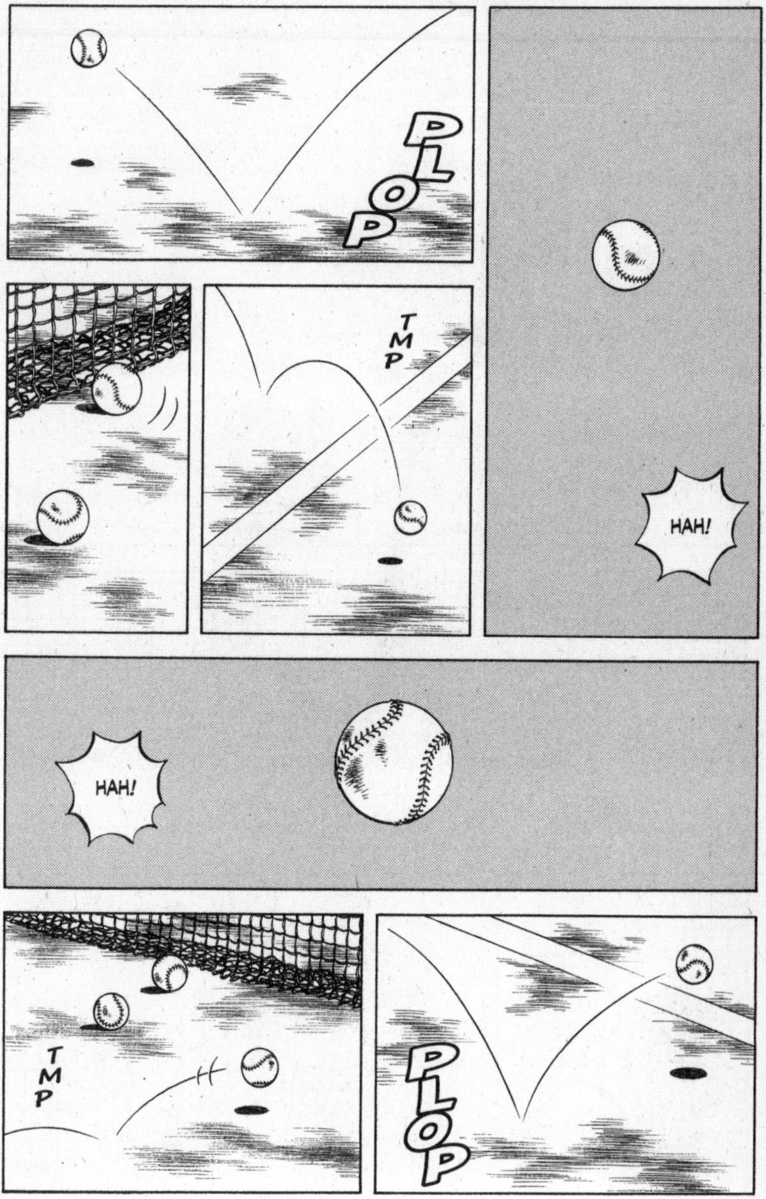
HAH!
PLOP
TMP
HAH!
PLOP
TMP

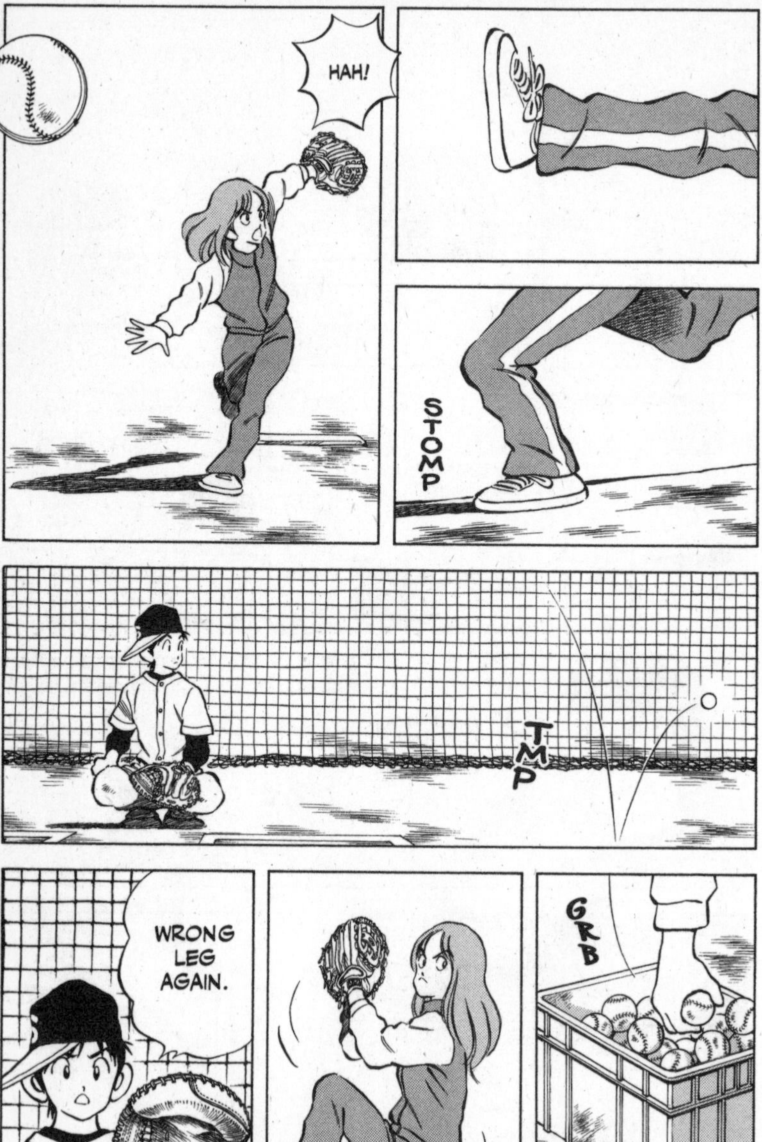
STOMP
HAH!
TMP
GRB
WRONG LEG AGAIN.

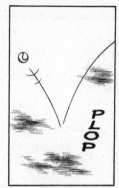

PLOP

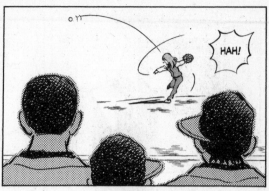

HAH!

PITCHING PRACTICE. AS YOU CAN SEE ...

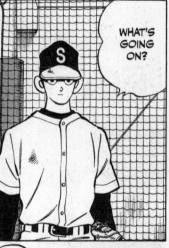

WHAT'S GOING ON?

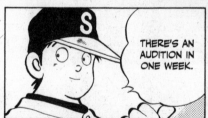

THERE'S AN AUDITION IN ONE WEEK.

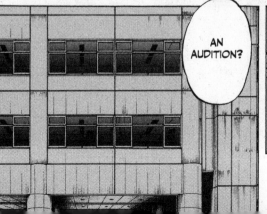

AN AUDITION?

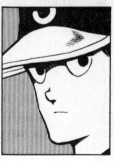

302

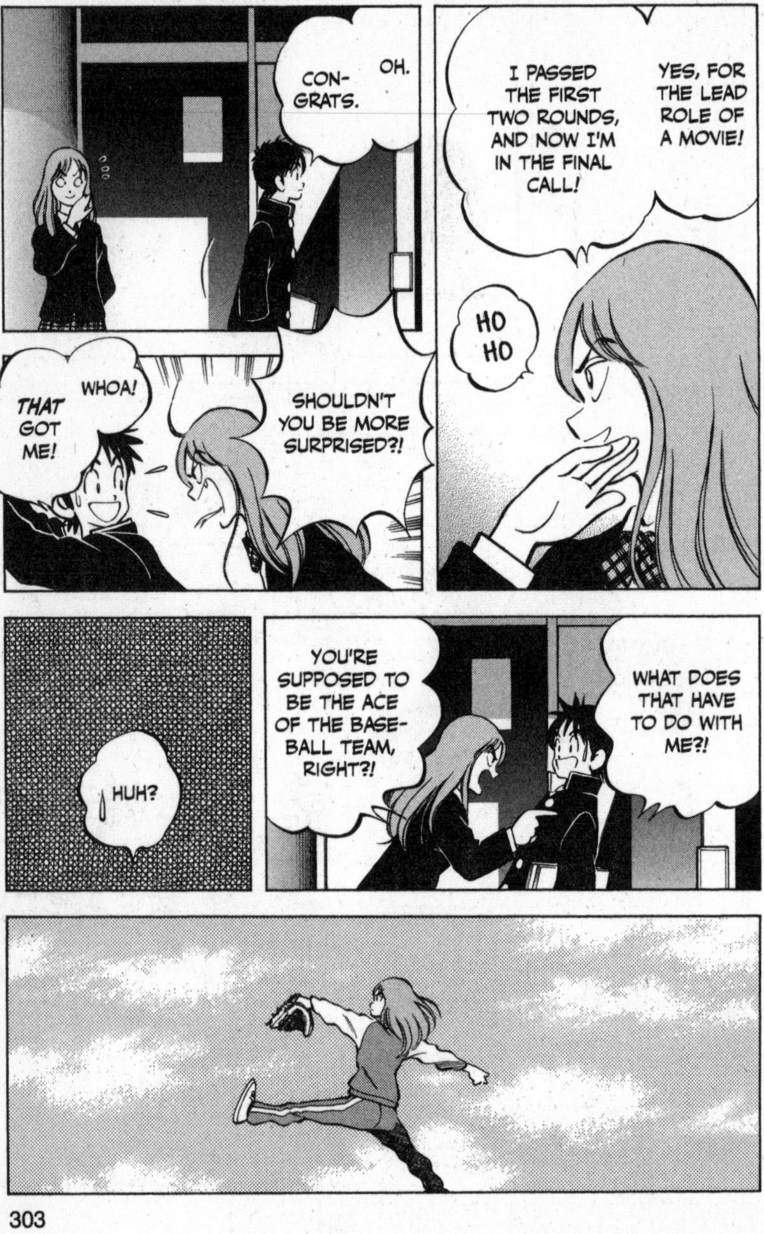
YES, FOR THE LEAD ROLE OF A MOVIE!
I PASSED THE FIRST TWO ROUNDS, AND NOW I'M IN THE FINAL CALL!
HO HO
OH.
CON-GRATS.
SHOULDN'T YOU BE MORE SURPRISED?!
WHOA!
THAT GOT ME!
WHAT DOES THAT HAVE TO DO WITH ME?!
YOU'RE SUPPOSED TO BE THE ACE OF THE BASE-BALL TEAM, RIGHT?!
HUH?

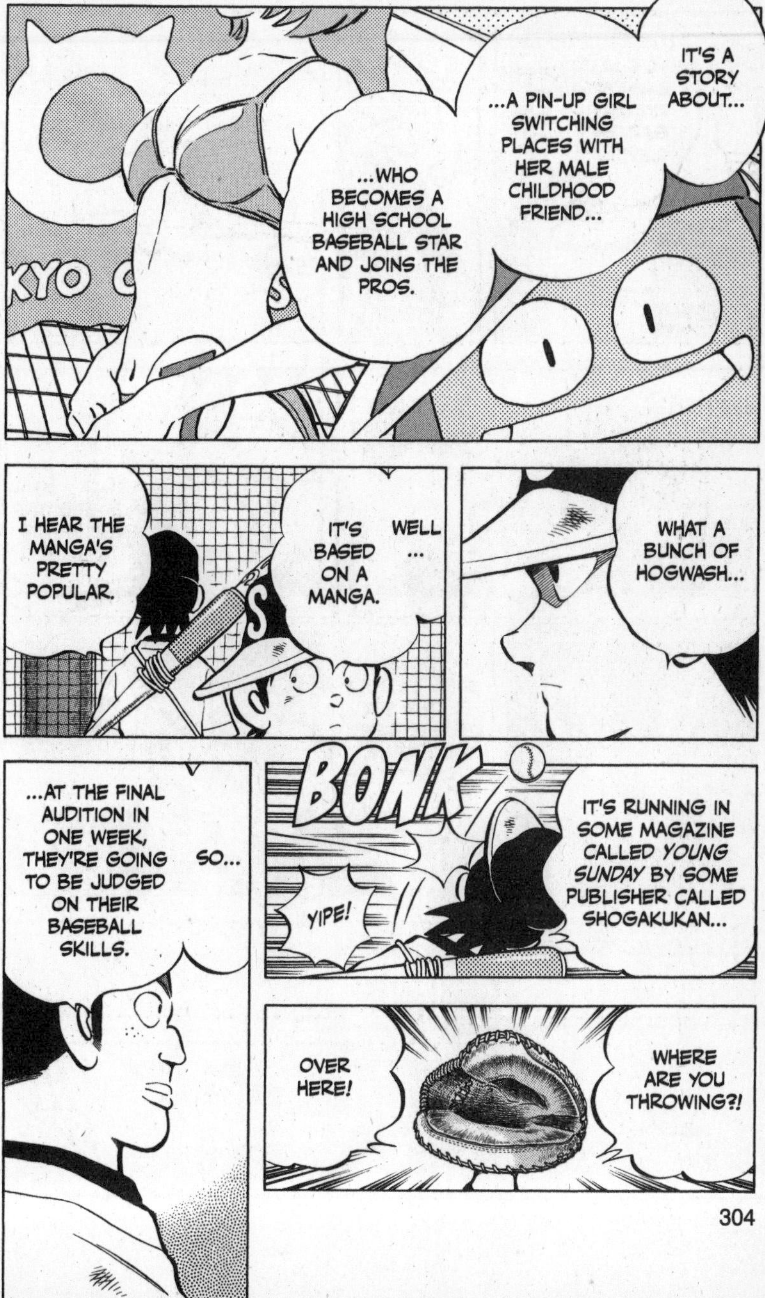
IT'S A STORY ABOUT...
...A PIN-UP GIRL SWITCHING PLACES WITH HER MALE CHILDHOOD FRIEND...
...WHO BECOMES A HIGH SCHOOL BASEBALL STAR AND JOINS THE PROS.
WHAT A BUNCH OF HOGWASH...
WELL ...
IT'S BASED ON A MANGA.
I HEAR THE MANGA'S PRETTY POPULAR.
IT'S RUNNING IN SOME MAGAZINE CALLED *YOUNG SUNDAY* BY SOME PUBLISHER CALLED SHOGAKUKAN...
BONK
YIPE!
WHERE ARE YOU THROWING?!
OVER HERE!
SO...
...AT THE FINAL AUDITION IN ONE WEEK, THEY'RE GOING TO BE JUDGED ON THEIR BASEBALL SKILLS.

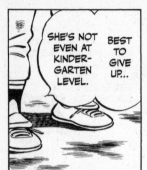

PLOP
HAH!
BEST TO GIVE UP...
SHE'S NOT EVEN AT KINDER-GARTEN LEVEL.
SEEMS SHE WROTE IN HER RESUME THAT SHE'S BEEN HOLDING A BALL SINCE SHE WAS THREE YEARS OLD.
SHE'S NOT LYING IF...
...ALL SHE DID WAS HOLD THE BALL.
THAT'S TRUE...
PLOP

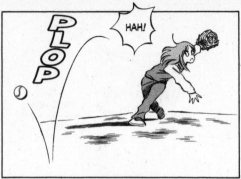

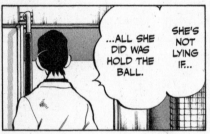

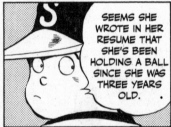

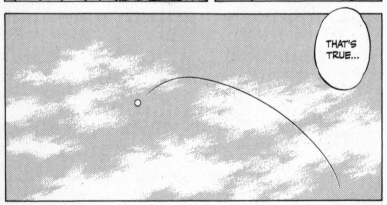

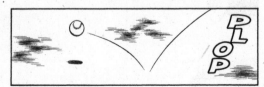

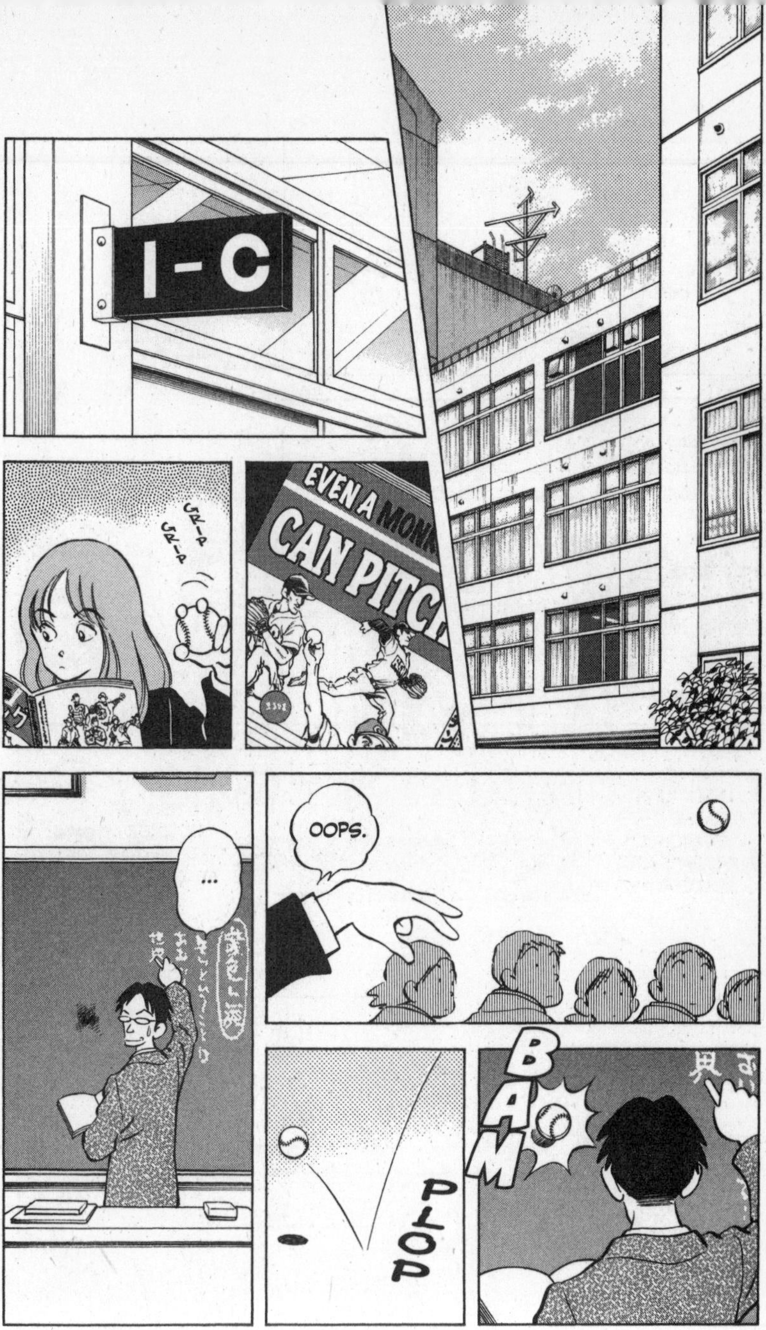
I-C
CAN PITC
GRIP
GRIP
OOPS.
BAM
PLOP
...

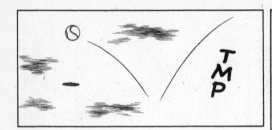

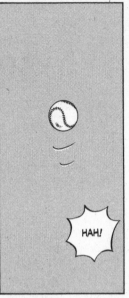

HAH!
TMP
TMP
SHE WON'T NEED A CATCHER FOR A WHILE...
YOU'RE IN EVERY-ONE'S WAY.
GO TO THAT CORNER AND THROW AT THE NET.
JUST KEEP IN MIND THE BASICS I TAUGHT YOU YESTERDAY.
HEY!
I'LL COME LATER AND WATCH YOU THROW.
MUMBLE GRUMBLE

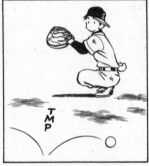

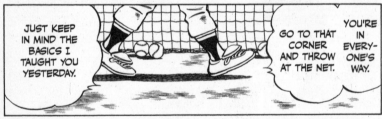

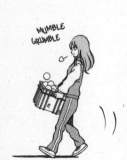

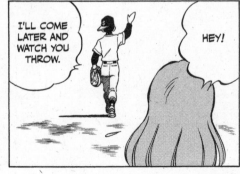

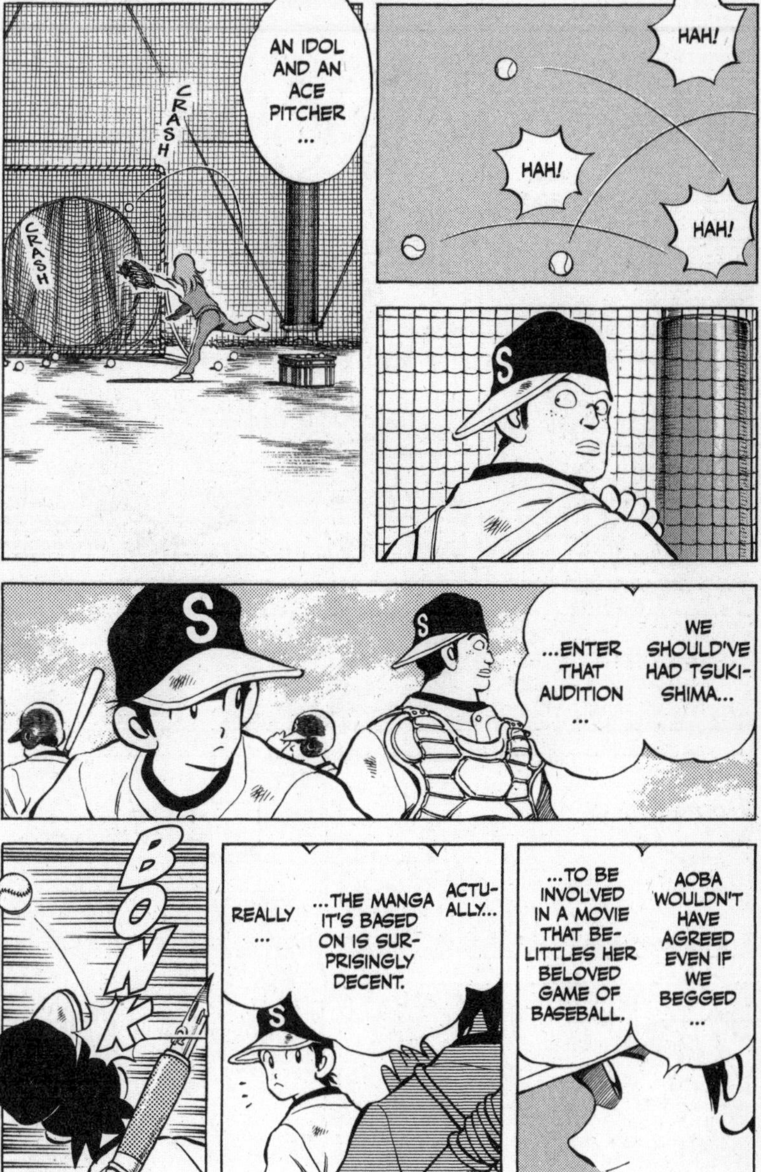
HAH!
HAH!
HAH!
CRASH
CRASH
AN IDOL AND AN ACE PITCHER ...
WE SHOULD'VE HAD TSUKI-SHIMA...
...ENTER THAT AUDITION ...
AOBA WOULDN'T HAVE AGREED EVEN IF WE BEGGED ...
...TO BE INVOLVED IN A MOVIE THAT BE-LITTLES HER BELOVED GAME OF BASEBALL.
ACTU-ALLY...
...THE MANGA IT'S BASED ON IS SUR-PRISINGLY DECENT.
REALLY ...
BONK

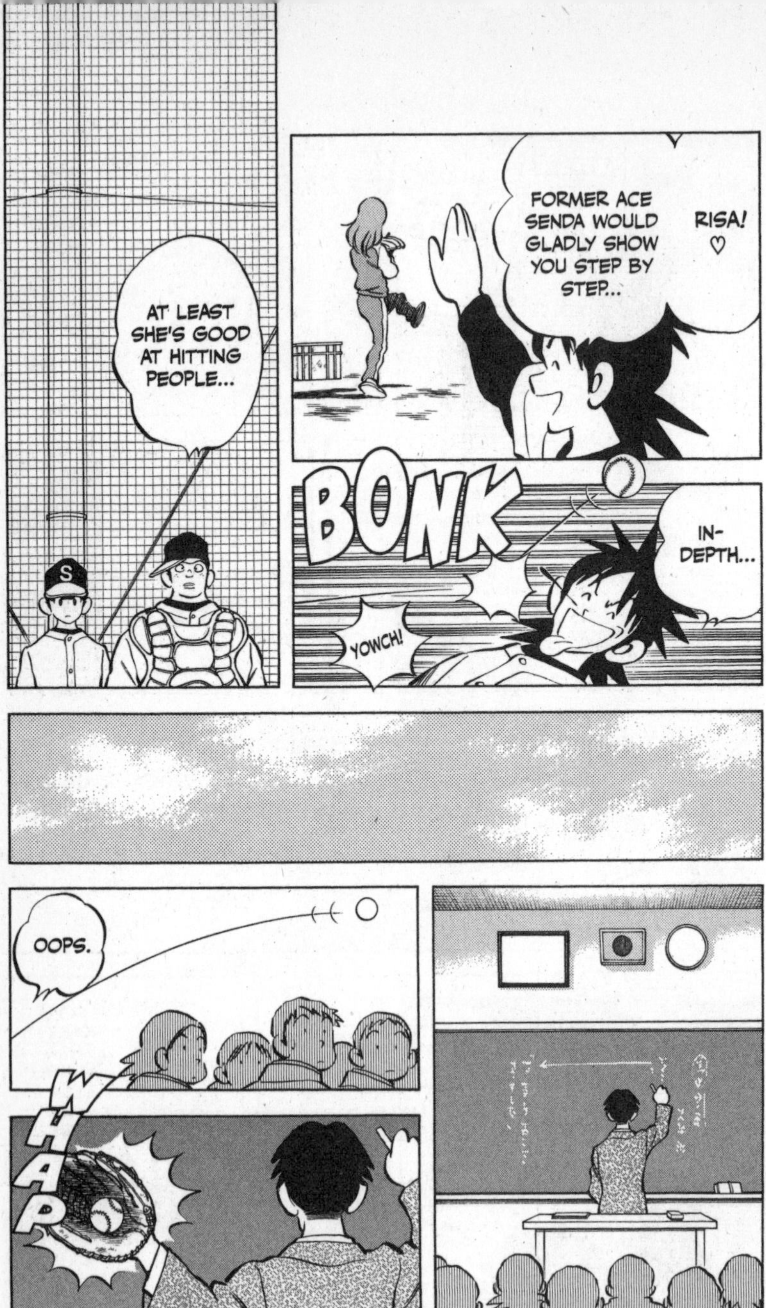
RISA! ♡
FORMER ACE SENDA WOULD GLADLY SHOW YOU STEP BY STEP...
IN-DEPTH...
BONK
YOWCH!
AT LEAST SHE'S GOOD AT HITTING PEOPLE...
OOPS.
WHAP

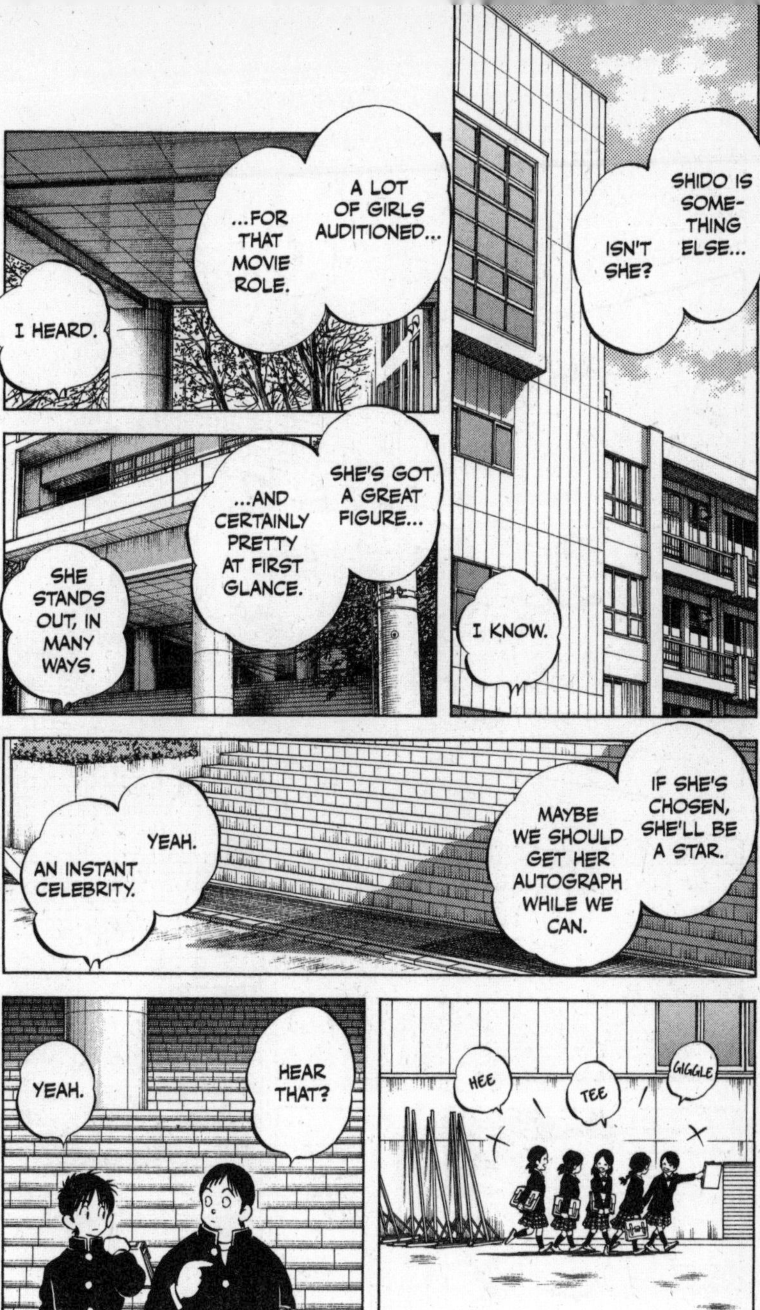
SHIDO IS SOMETHING ELSE...
ISN'T SHE?
I KNOW.
A LOT OF GIRLS AUDITIONED...
...FOR THAT MOVIE ROLE.
I HEARD.
SHE'S GOT A GREAT FIGURE...
...AND CERTAINLY PRETTY AT FIRST GLANCE.
SHE STANDS OUT, IN MANY WAYS.
IF SHE'S CHOSEN, SHE'LL BE A STAR.
MAYBE WE SHOULD GET HER AUTOGRAPH WHILE WE CAN.
YEAH.
AN INSTANT CELEBRITY.
GIGGLE
TEE
HEE
HEAR THAT?
YEAH.

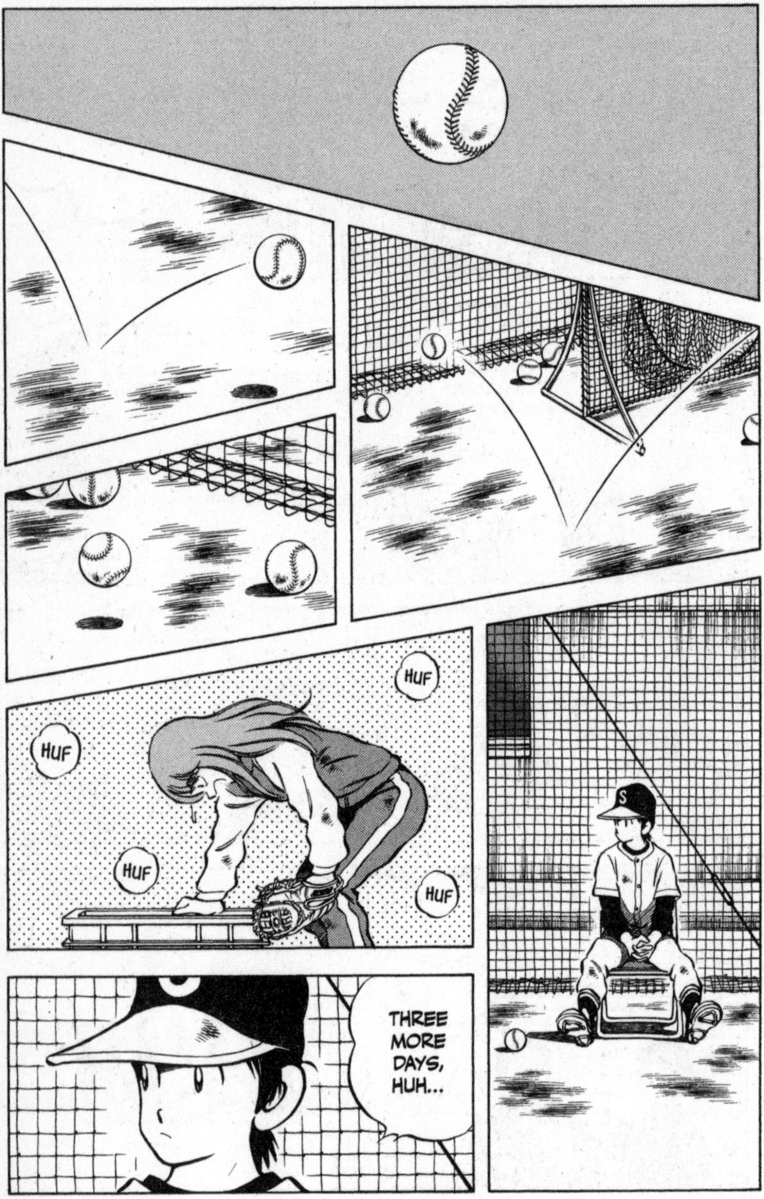
HUF
HUF
HUF
HUF
THREE MORE DAYS, HUH...

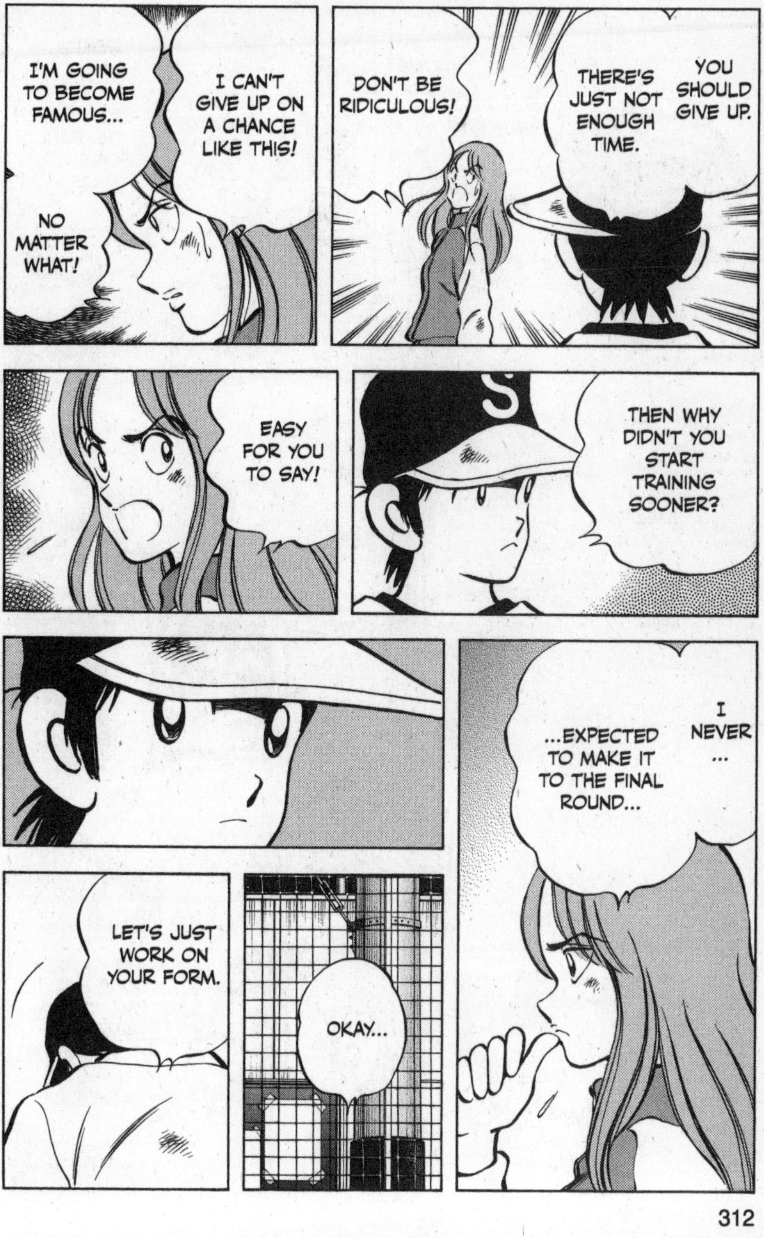
YOU SHOULD GIVE UP.
THERE'S JUST NOT ENOUGH TIME.
DON'T BE RIDICULOUS!
I CAN'T GIVE UP ON A CHANCE LIKE THIS!
I'M GOING TO BECOME FAMOUS...
NO MATTER WHAT!
THEN WHY DIDN'T YOU START TRAINING SOONER?
EASY FOR YOU TO SAY!
I NEVER...
...EXPECTED TO MAKE IT TO THE FINAL ROUND...
OKAY...
LET'S JUST WORK ON YOUR FORM.

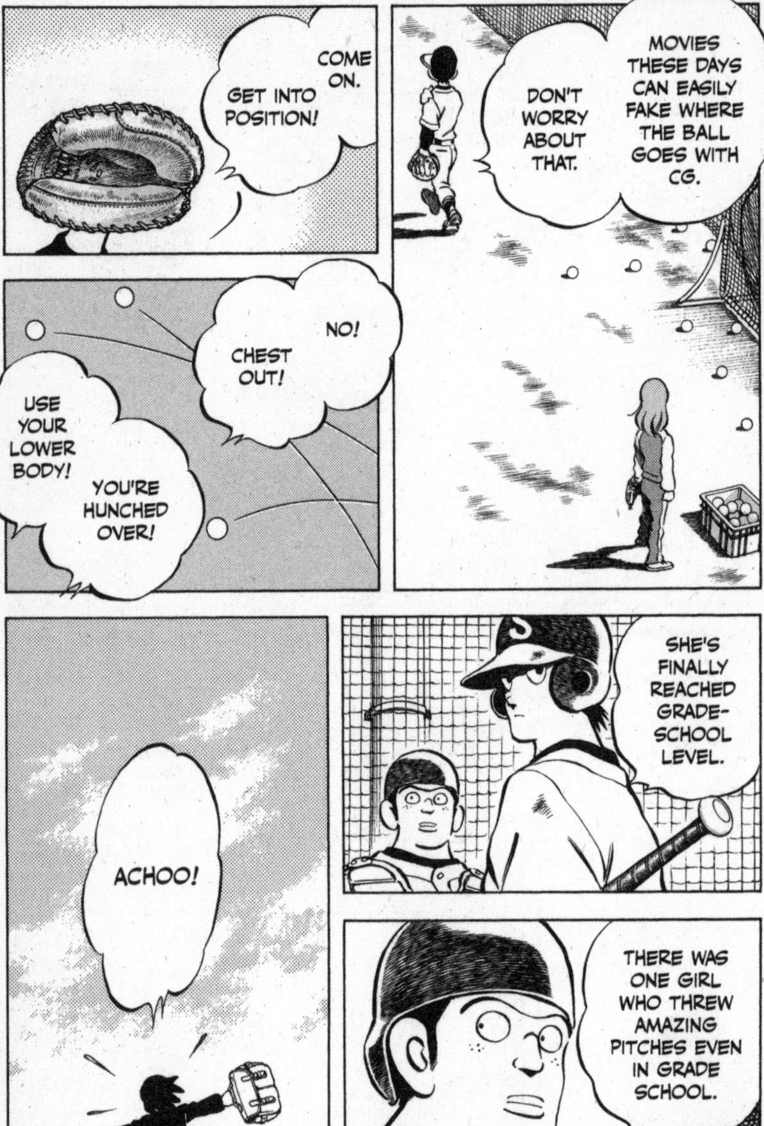

DON'T WORRY ABOUT THAT.
MOVIES THESE DAYS CAN EASILY FAKE WHERE THE BALL GOES WITH CG.
COME ON.
GET INTO POSITION!
NO!
CHEST OUT!
USE YOUR LOWER BODY!
YOU'RE HUNCHED OVER!
SHE'S FINALLY REACHED GRADE-SCHOOL LEVEL.
THERE WAS ONE GIRL WHO THREW AMAZING PITCHES EVEN IN GRADE SCHOOL.
ACHOO!

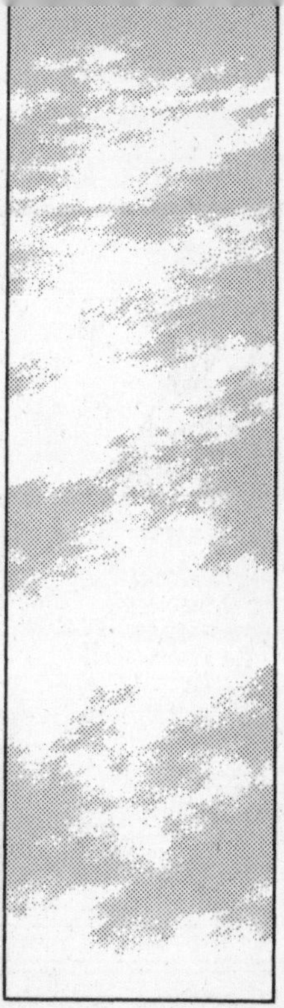

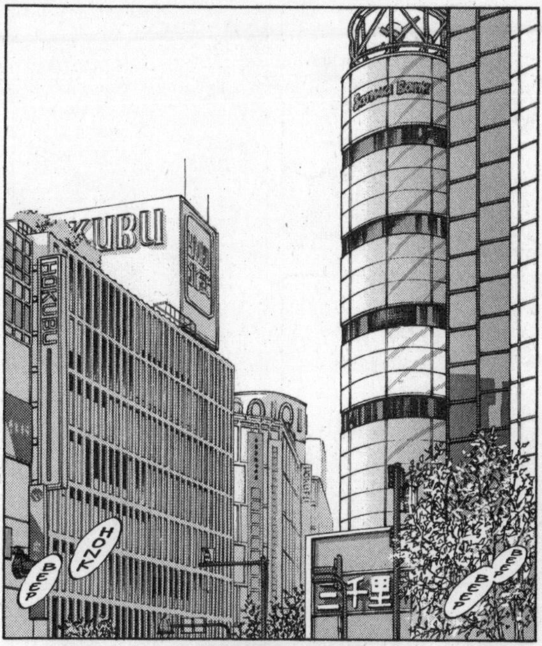
BEEP BEEP
KUBU
HOKUBU
二千里
HONK
BEEP

Movie: IDOL ACE

Auditions for leading role

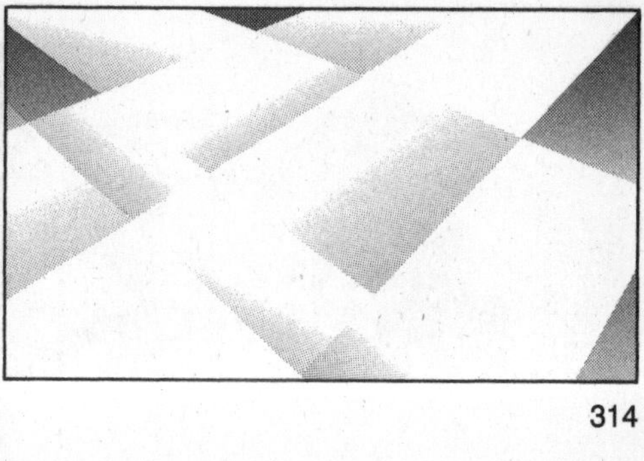

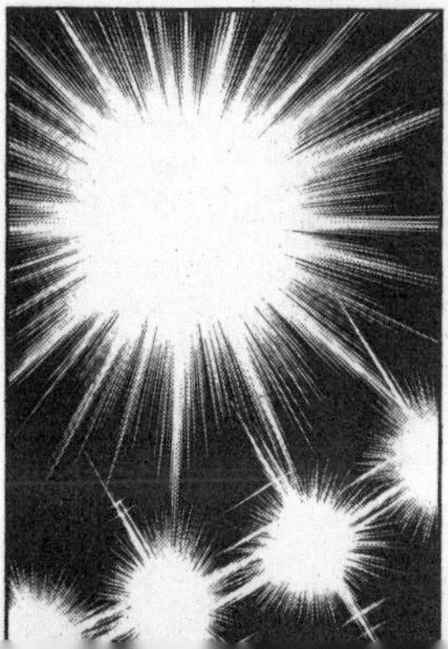

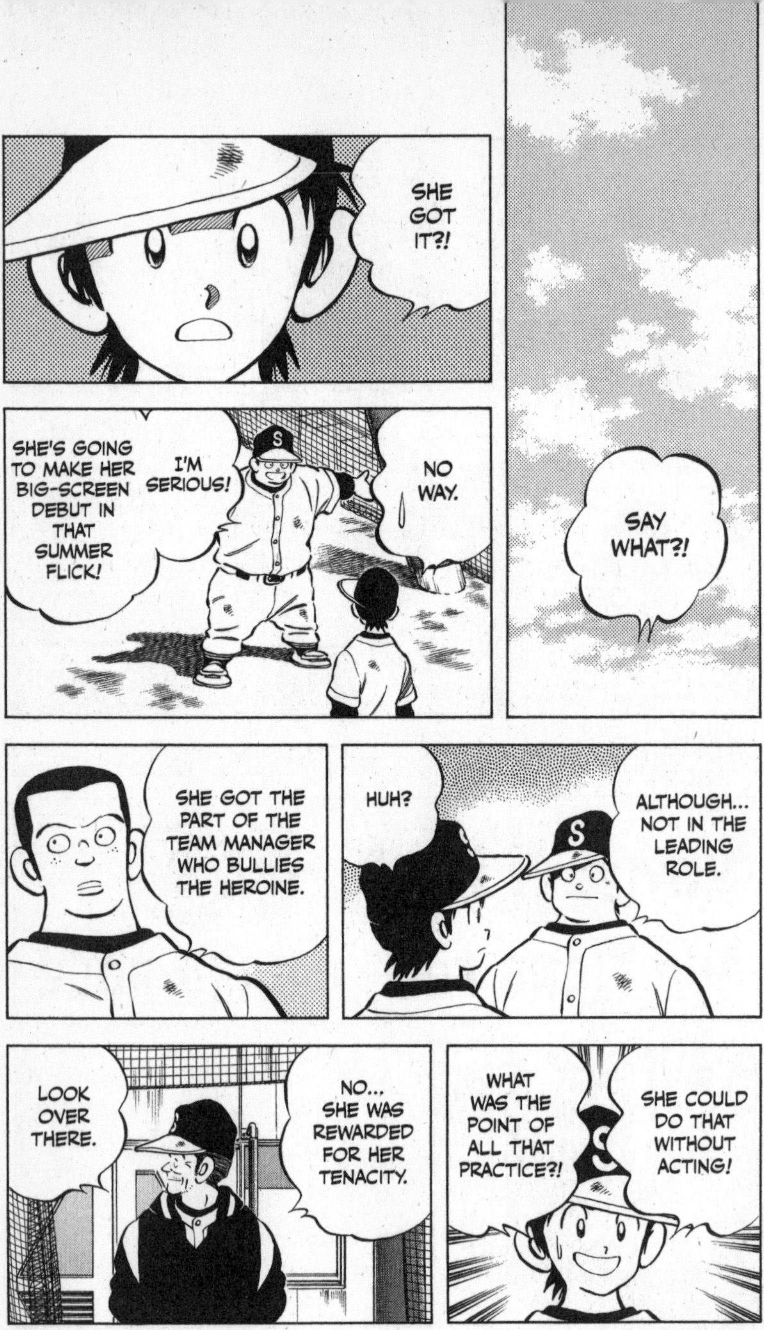
SAY WHAT?!
SHE GOT IT?!
NO WAY.
I'M SERIOUS!
SHE'S GOING TO MAKE HER BIG-SCREEN DEBUT IN THAT SUMMER FLICK!
ALTHOUGH... NOT IN THE LEADING ROLE.
HUH?
SHE GOT THE PART OF THE TEAM MANAGER WHO BULLIES THE HEROINE.
SHE COULD DO THAT WITHOUT ACTING!
WHAT WAS THE POINT OF ALL THAT PRACTICE?!
NO... SHE WAS REWARDED FOR HER TENACITY.
LOOK OVER THERE.

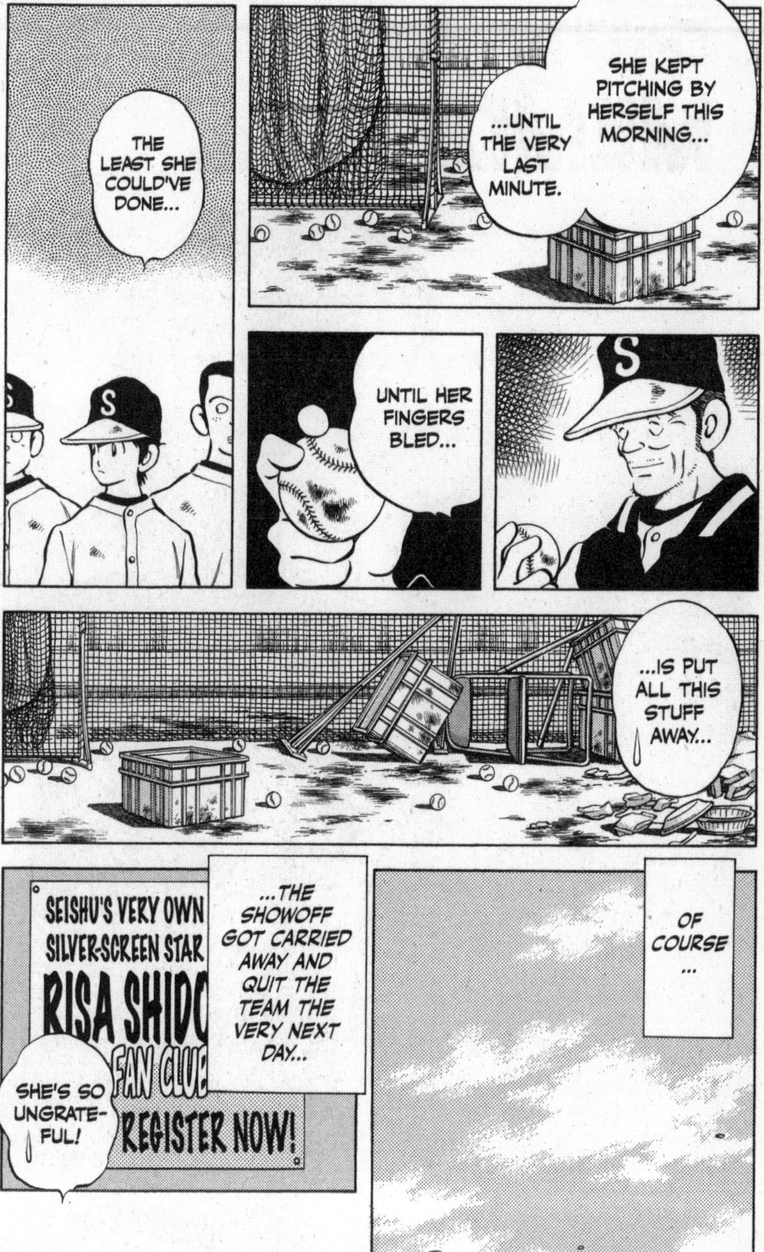
SHE KEPT PITCHING BY HERSELF THIS MORNING...
...UNTIL THE VERY LAST MINUTE.
UNTIL HER FINGERS BLED...
THE LEAST SHE COULD'VE DONE...
...IS PUT ALL THIS STUFF AWAY...
OF COURSE...
...THE SHOWOFF GOT CARRIED AWAY AND QUIT THE TEAM THE VERY NEXT DAY...
SEISHU'S VERY OWN SILVER-SCREEN STAR
RISA SHIDO
FAN CLUB
REGISTER NOW!
SHE'S SO UNGRATE-FUL!

CHAPTER 58
MEMORIES...

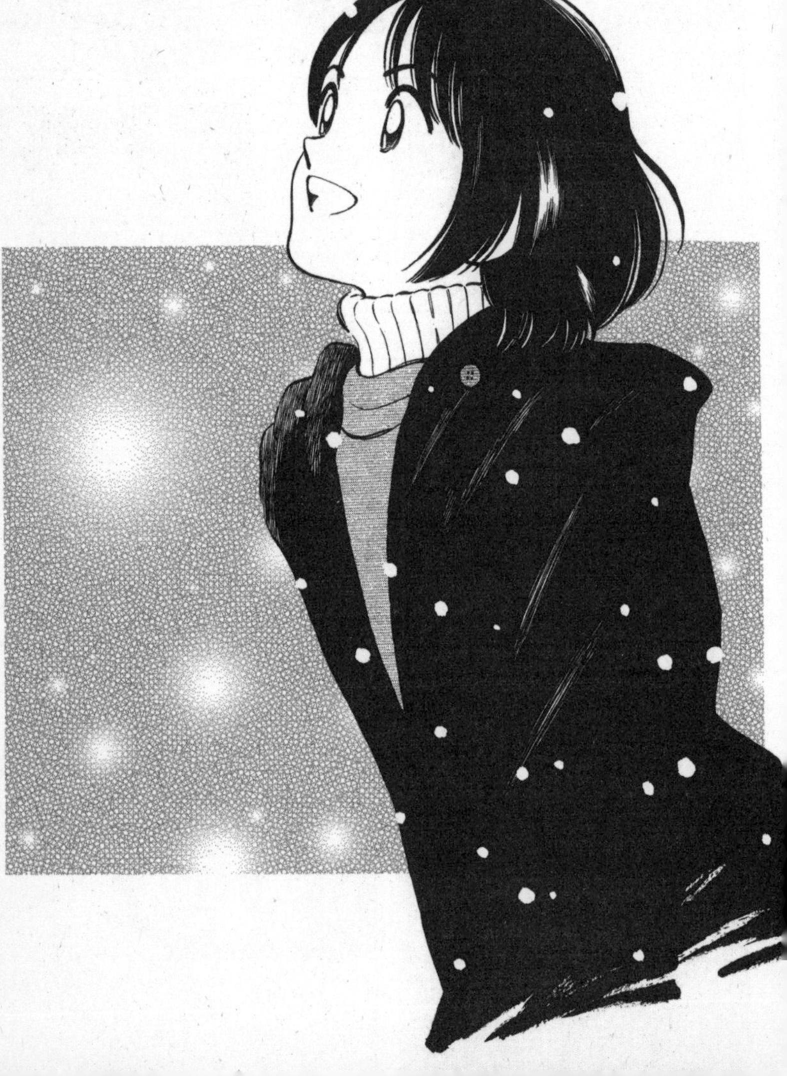

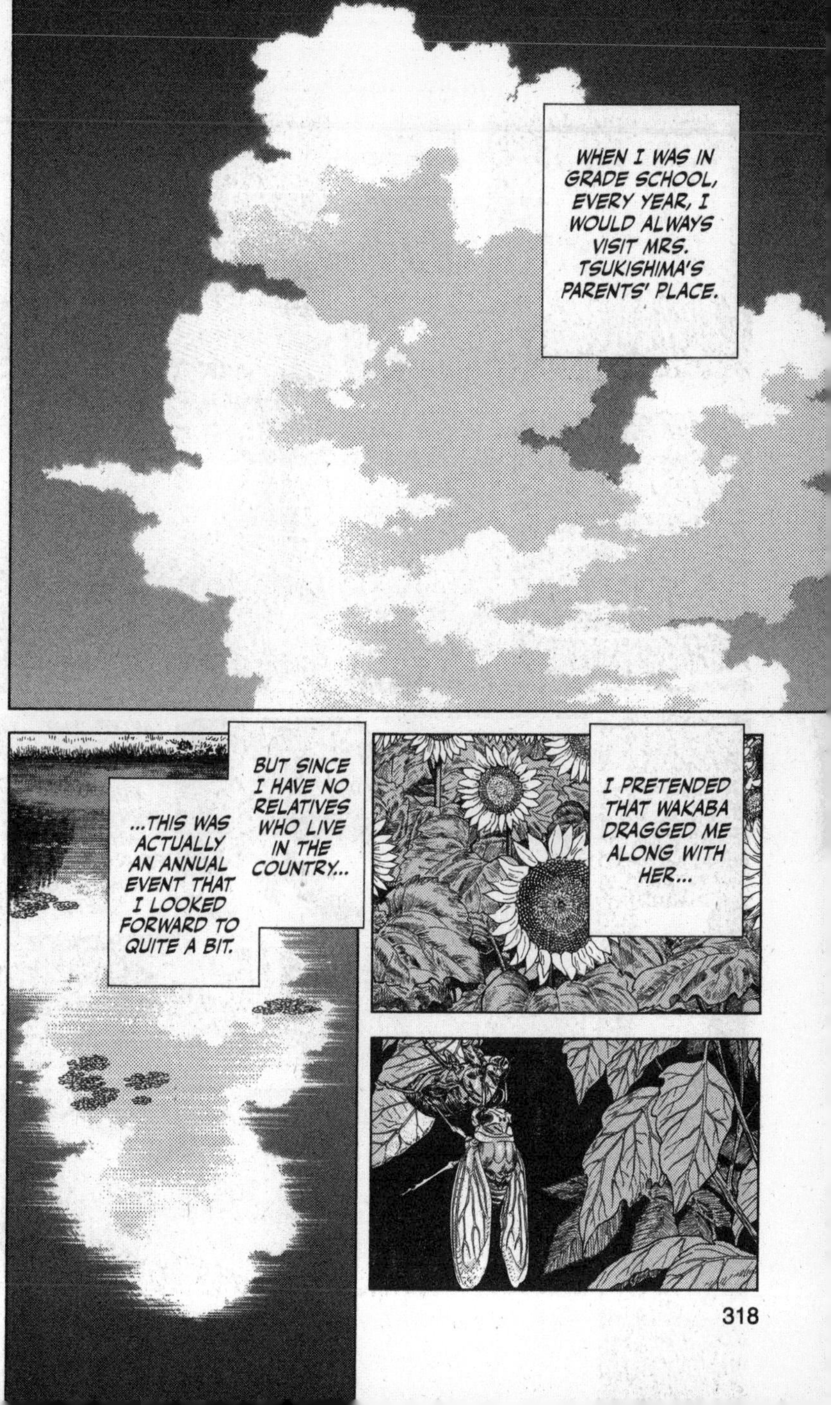
WHEN I WAS IN GRADE SCHOOL, EVERY YEAR, I WOULD ALWAYS VISIT MRS. TSUKISHIMA'S PARENTS' PLACE.
I PRETENDED THAT WAKABA DRAGGED ME ALONG WITH HER...
BUT SINCE I HAVE NO RELATIVES WHO LIVE IN THE COUNTRY...
...THIS WAS ACTUALLY AN ANNUAL EVENT THAT I LOOKED FORWARD TO QUITE A BIT.

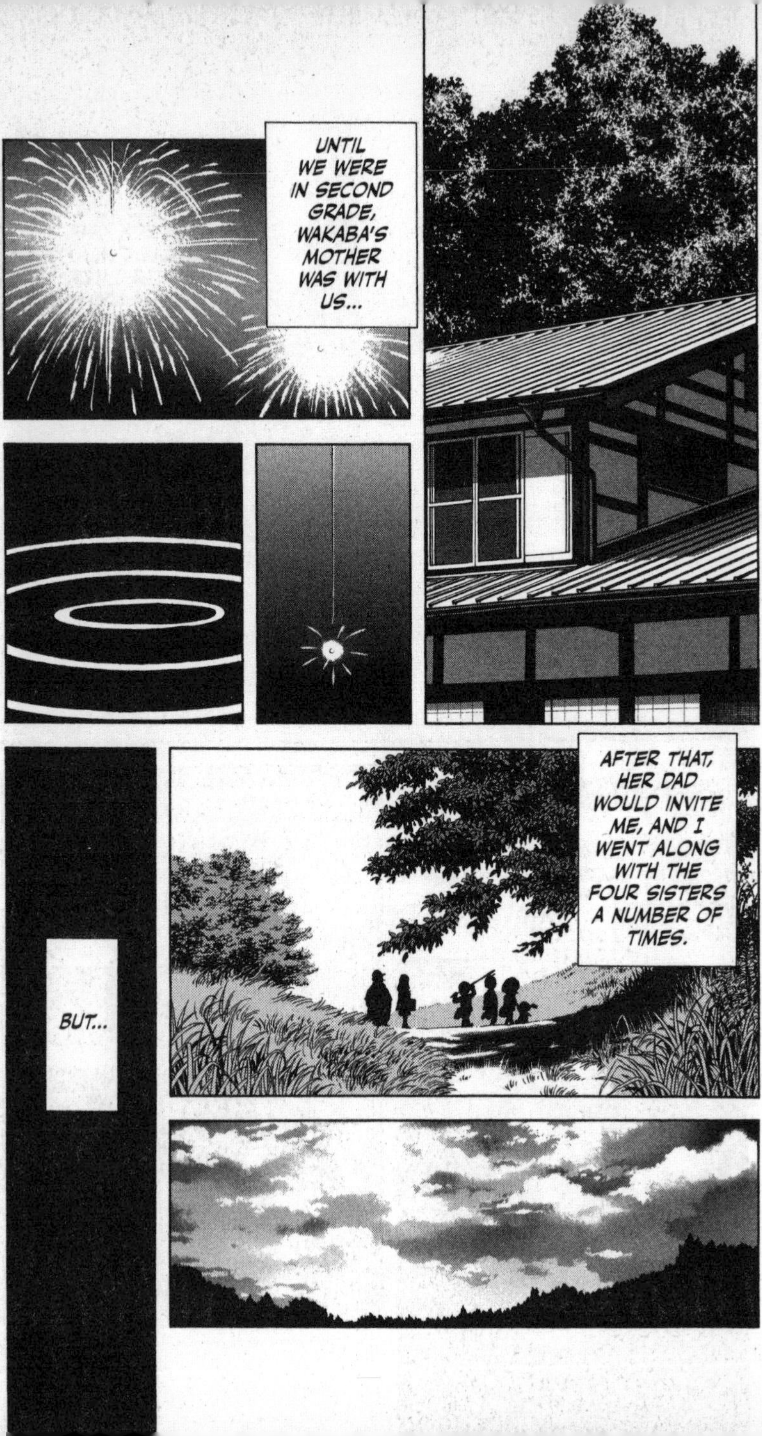
UNTIL WE WERE IN SECOND GRADE, WAKABA'S MOTHER WAS WITH US...
AFTER THAT, HER DAD WOULD INVITE ME, AND I WENT ALONG WITH THE FOUR SISTERS A NUMBER OF TIMES.
BUT...

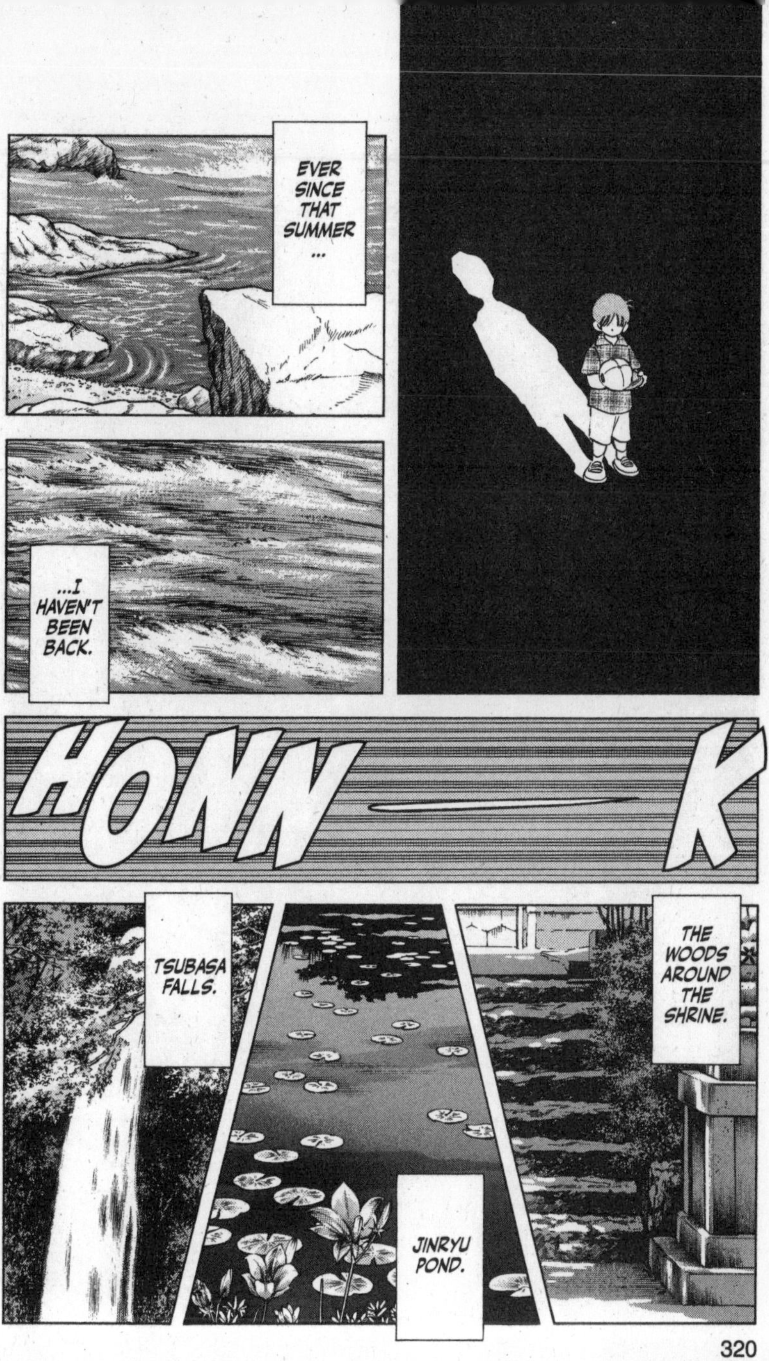
EVER SINCE THAT SUMMER ...
...I HAVEN'T BEEN BACK.
HONN K
THE WOODS AROUND THE SHRINE.
JINRYU POND.
TSUBASA FALLS.

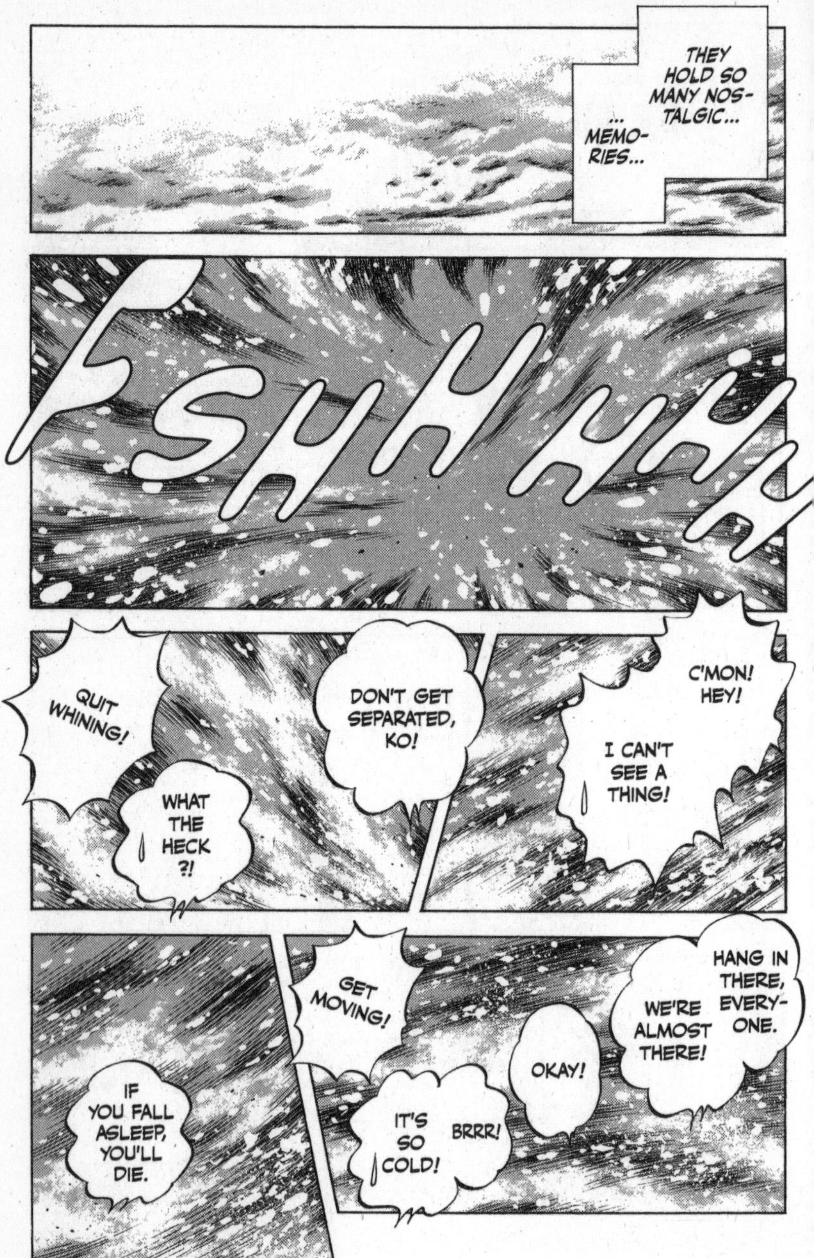
THEY HOLD SO MANY NOSTALGIC...
...MEMORIES...
SHHHHH
C'MON! HEY!
I CAN'T SEE A THING!
DON'T GET SEPARATED, KO!
QUIT WHINING!
WHAT THE HECK?!
HANG IN THERE, EVERYONE.
WE'RE ALMOST THERE!
OKAY!
GET MOVING!
BRRR!
IT'S SO COLD!
IF YOU FALL ASLEEP, YOU'LL DIE.

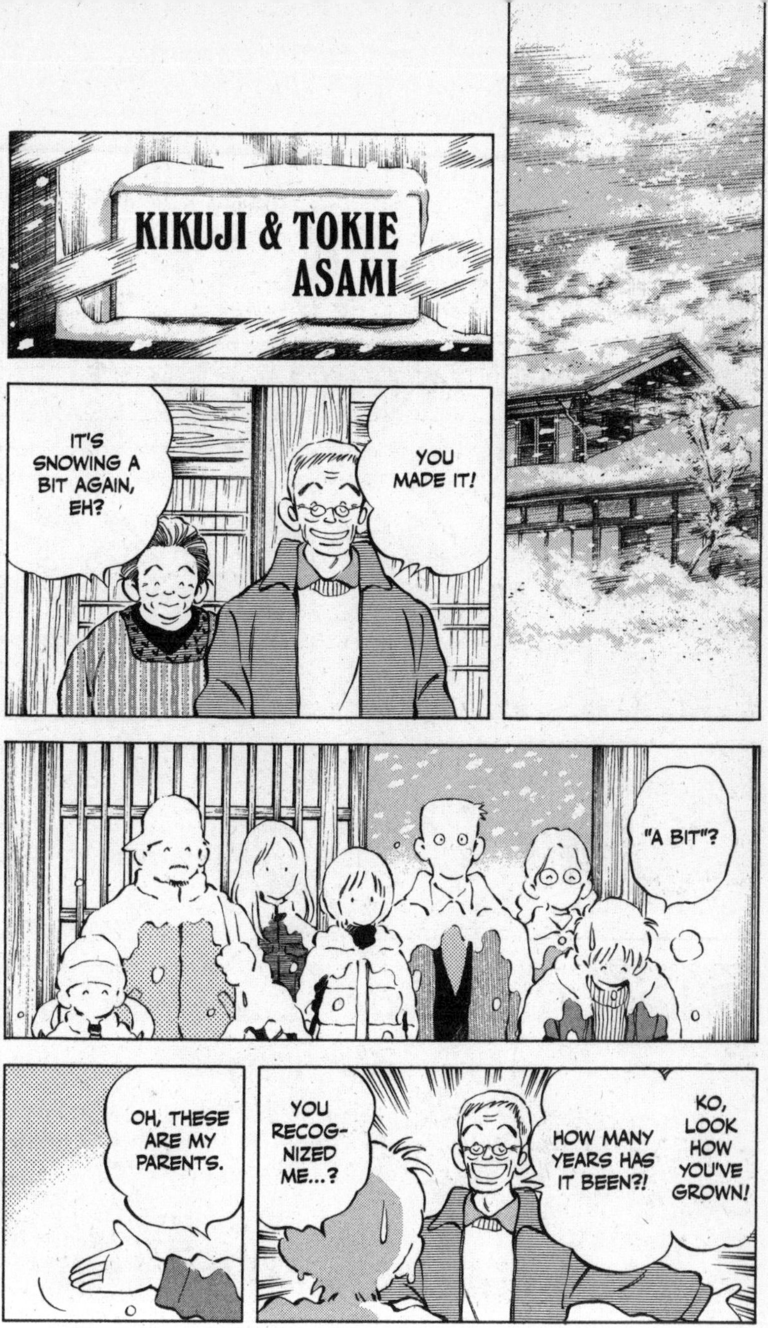
KIKUJI & TOKIE ASAMI
YOU MADE IT!
IT'S SNOWING A BIT AGAIN, EH?
"A BIT"?
KO, LOOK HOW YOU'VE GROWN!
HOW MANY YEARS HAS IT BEEN?!
YOU RECOG-NIZED ME...?
OH, THESE ARE MY PARENTS.

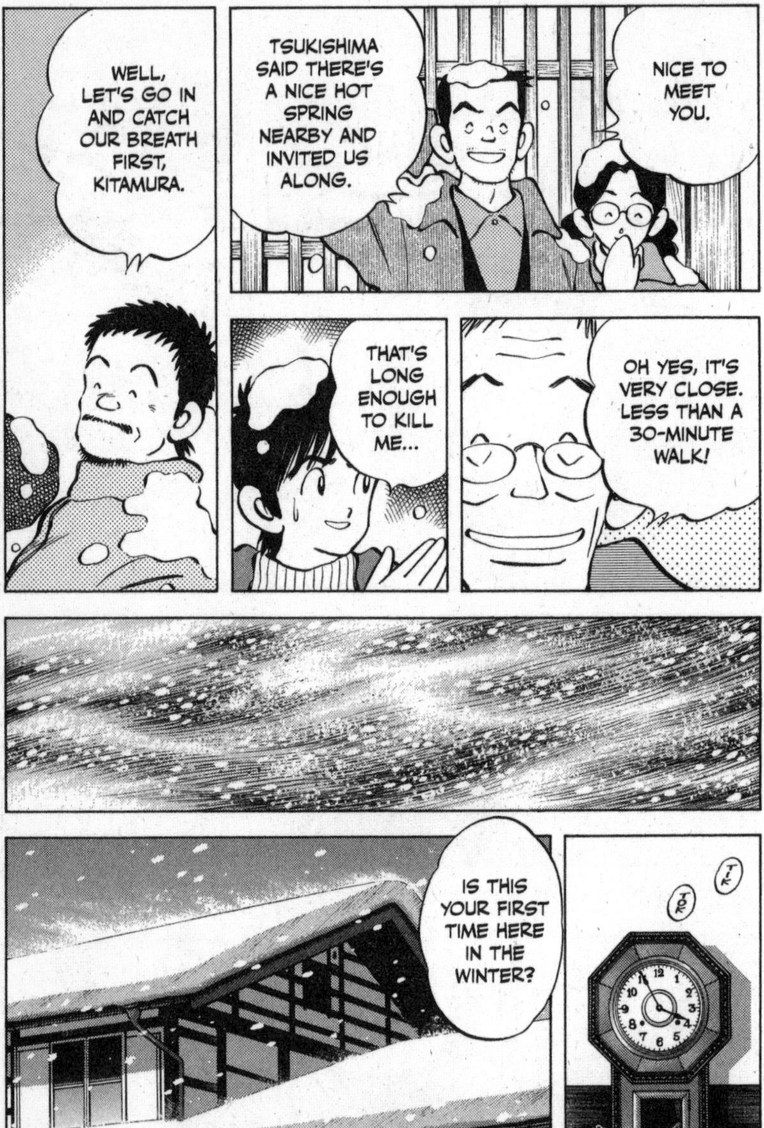
NICE TO MEET YOU.
TSUKISHIMA SAID THERE'S A NICE HOT SPRING NEARBY AND INVITED US ALONG.
OH YES, IT'S VERY CLOSE. LESS THAN A 30-MINUTE WALK!
THAT'S LONG ENOUGH TO KILL ME...
WELL, LET'S GO IN AND CATCH OUR BREATH FIRST, KITAMURA.
TIK
TOK
IS THIS YOUR FIRST TIME HERE IN THE WINTER?

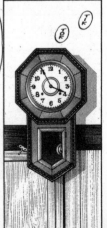

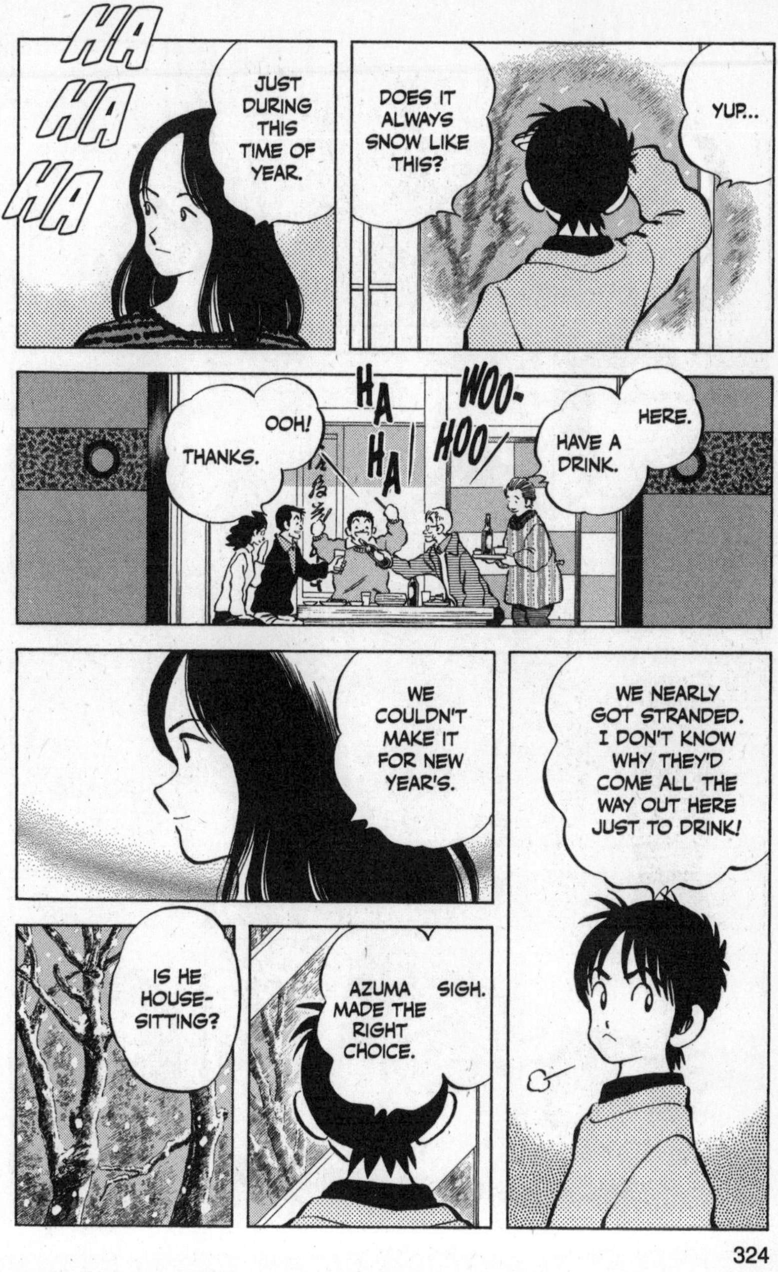
YUP...
DOES IT ALWAYS SNOW LIKE THIS?
JUST DURING THIS TIME OF YEAR.
HA HA HA
HERE. HAVE A DRINK.
WOO-HOO
HA HA
OOH! THANKS.
WE NEARLY GOT STRANDED. I DON'T KNOW WHY THEY'D COME ALL THE WAY OUT HERE JUST TO DRINK!
WE COULDN'T MAKE IT FOR NEW YEAR'S.
SIGH.
AZUMA MADE THE RIGHT CHOICE.
IS HE HOUSE-SITTING?

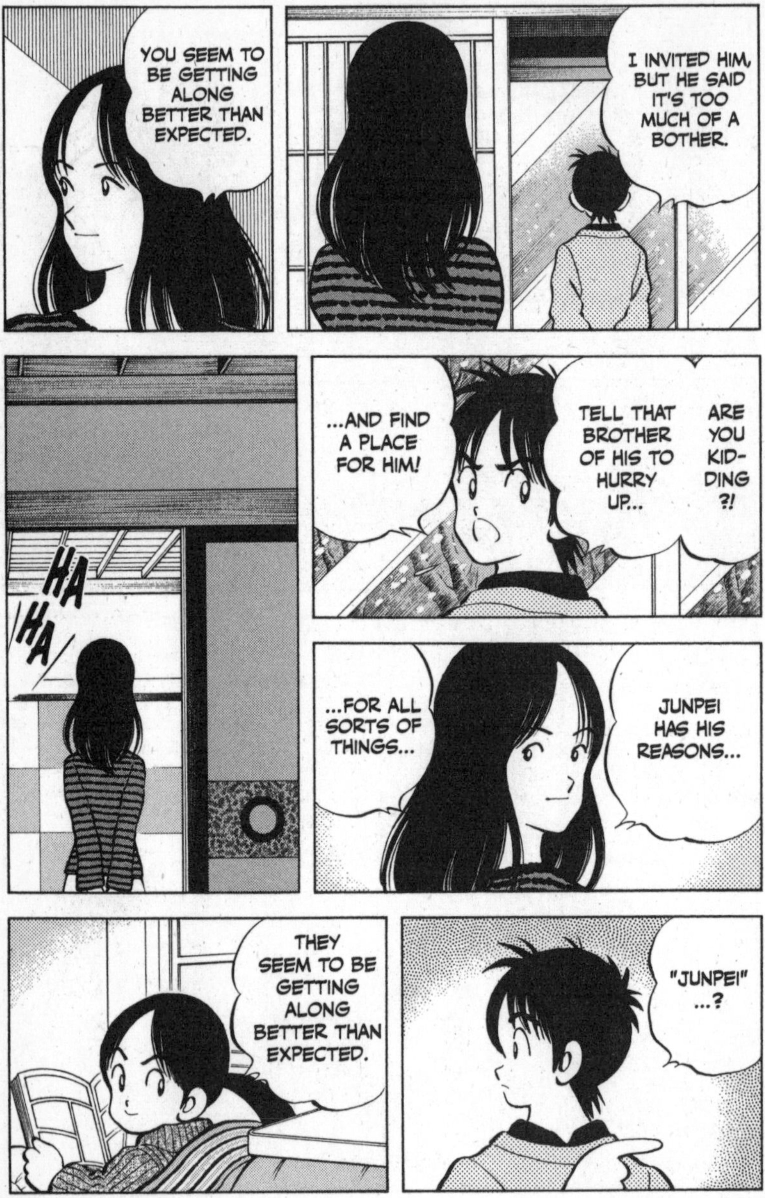
I INVITED HIM, BUT HE SAID IT'S TOO MUCH OF A BOTHER.
YOU SEEM TO BE GETTING ALONG BETTER THAN EXPECTED.
ARE YOU KIDDING?!
TELL THAT BROTHER OF HIS TO HURRY UP...
...AND FIND A PLACE FOR HIM!
JUNPEI HAS HIS REASONS...
...FOR ALL SORTS OF THINGS...
HA HA
"JUNPEI" ...?
THEY SEEM TO BE GETTING ALONG BETTER THAN EXPECTED.

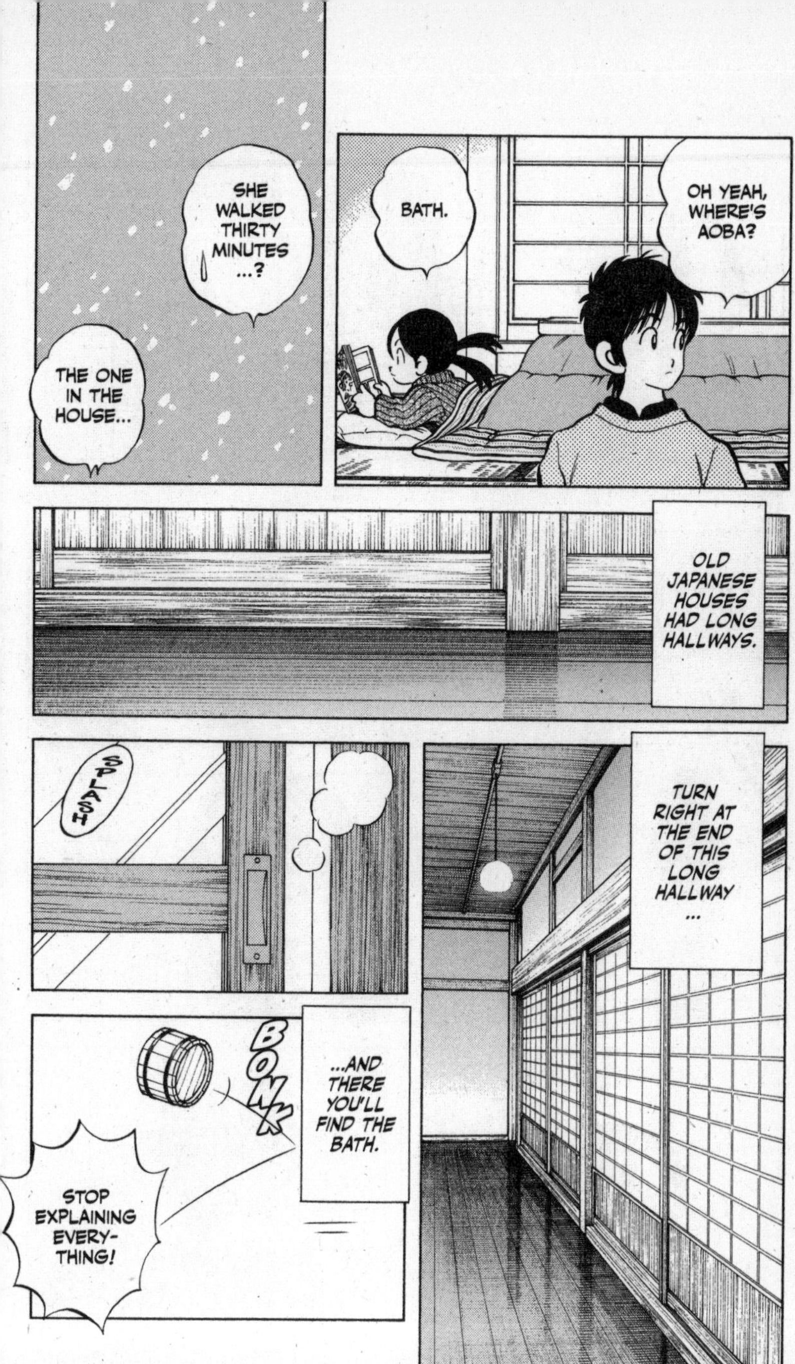
OH YEAH, WHERE'S AOBA?
BATH.
SHE WALKED THIRTY MINUTES ...?
THE ONE IN THE HOUSE...
OLD JAPANESE HOUSES HAD LONG HALLWAYS.
TURN RIGHT AT THE END OF THIS LONG HALLWAY ...
SPLASH
...AND THERE YOU'LL FIND THE BATH.
BONK
STOP EXPLAINING EVERY-THING!

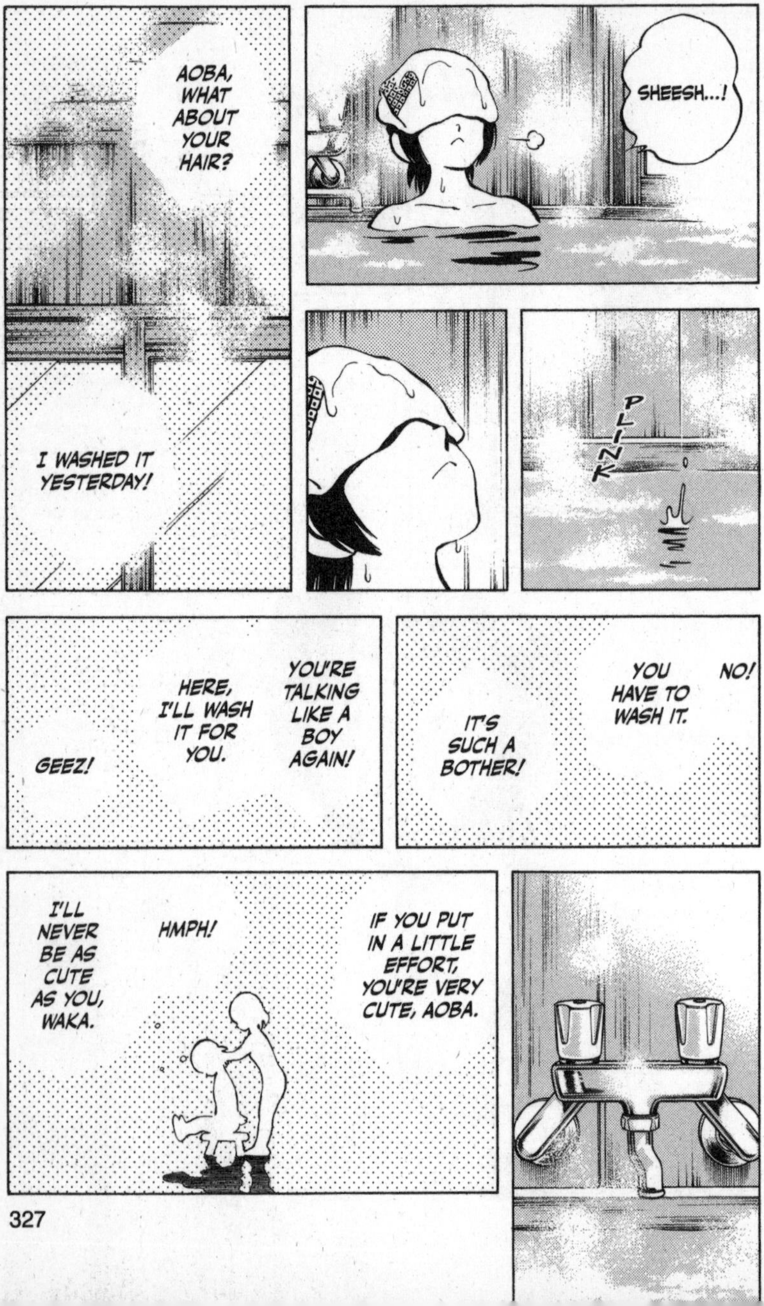
SHEESH...!
PLINK
AOBA, WHAT ABOUT YOUR HAIR?
I WASHED IT YESTERDAY!
NO!
YOU HAVE TO WASH IT.
IT'S SUCH A BOTHER!
YOU'RE TALKING LIKE A BOY AGAIN!
HERE, I'LL WASH IT FOR YOU.
GEEZ!
IF YOU PUT IN A LITTLE EFFORT, YOU'RE VERY CUTE, AOBA.
HMPH!
I'LL NEVER BE AS CUTE AS YOU, WAKA.

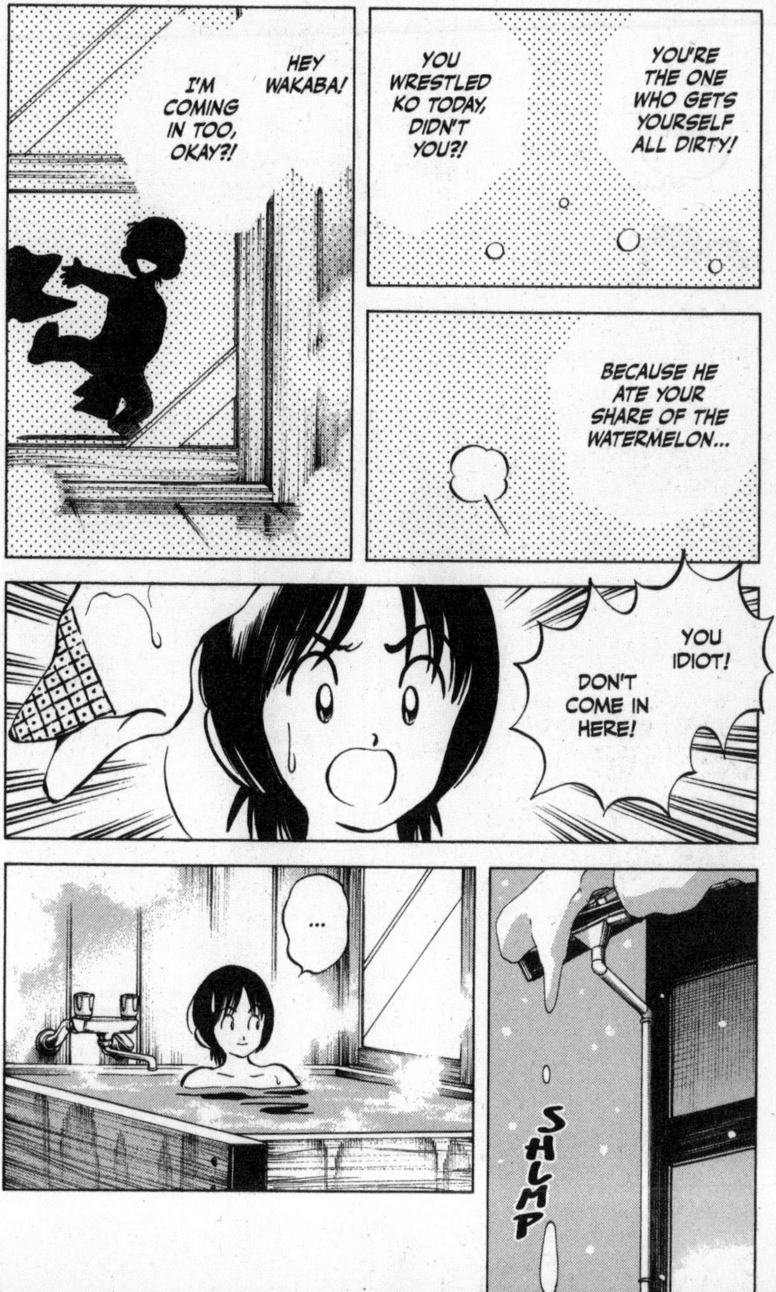

YOU'RE THE ONE WHO GETS YOURSELF ALL DIRTY!
YOU WRESTLED KO TODAY, DIDN'T YOU?!
BECAUSE HE ATE YOUR SHARE OF THE WATERMELON...
HEY WAKABA!
I'M COMING IN TOO, OKAY?!
YOU IDIOT!
DON'T COME IN HERE!
SHLMP
...

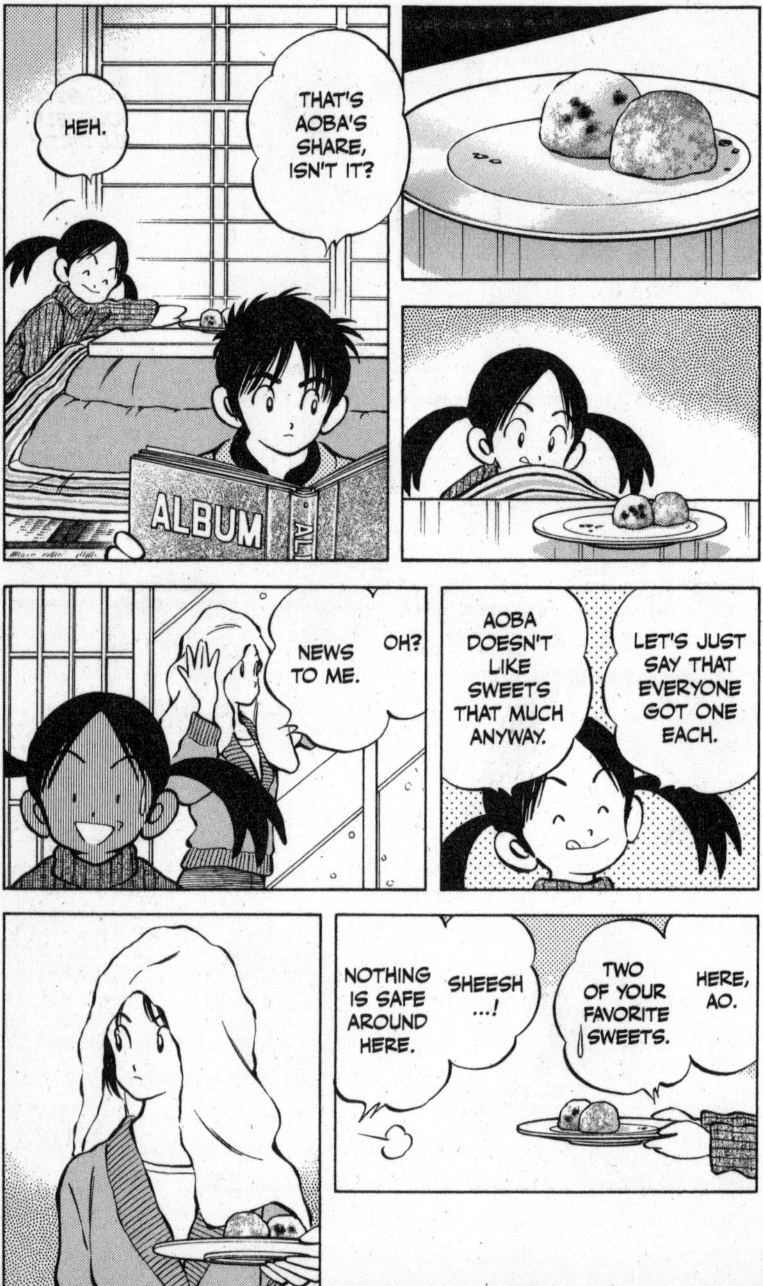
THAT'S AOBA'S SHARE, ISN'T IT?
HEH.
LET'S JUST SAY THAT EVERYONE GOT ONE EACH.
AOBA DOESN'T LIKE SWEETS THAT MUCH ANYWAY.
OH?
NEWS TO ME.
HERE, AO.
TWO OF YOUR FAVORITE SWEETS.
SHEESH ...!
NOTHING IS SAFE AROUND HERE.

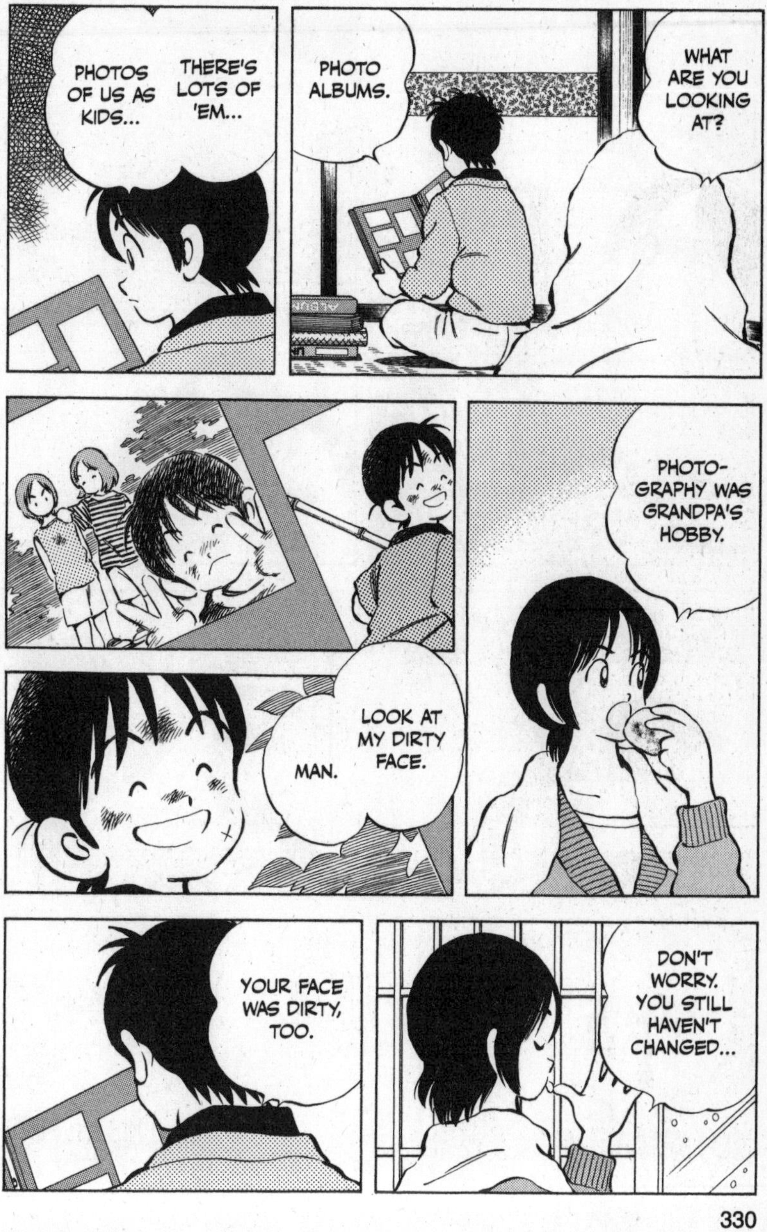
WHAT ARE YOU LOOKING AT?
PHOTO ALBUMS.
THERE'S LOTS OF 'EM...
PHOTOS OF US AS KIDS...
PHOTOGRAPHY WAS GRANDPA'S HOBBY.
LOOK AT MY DIRTY FACE.
MAN.
DON'T WORRY. YOU STILL HAVEN'T CHANGED...
YOUR FACE WAS DIRTY, TOO.

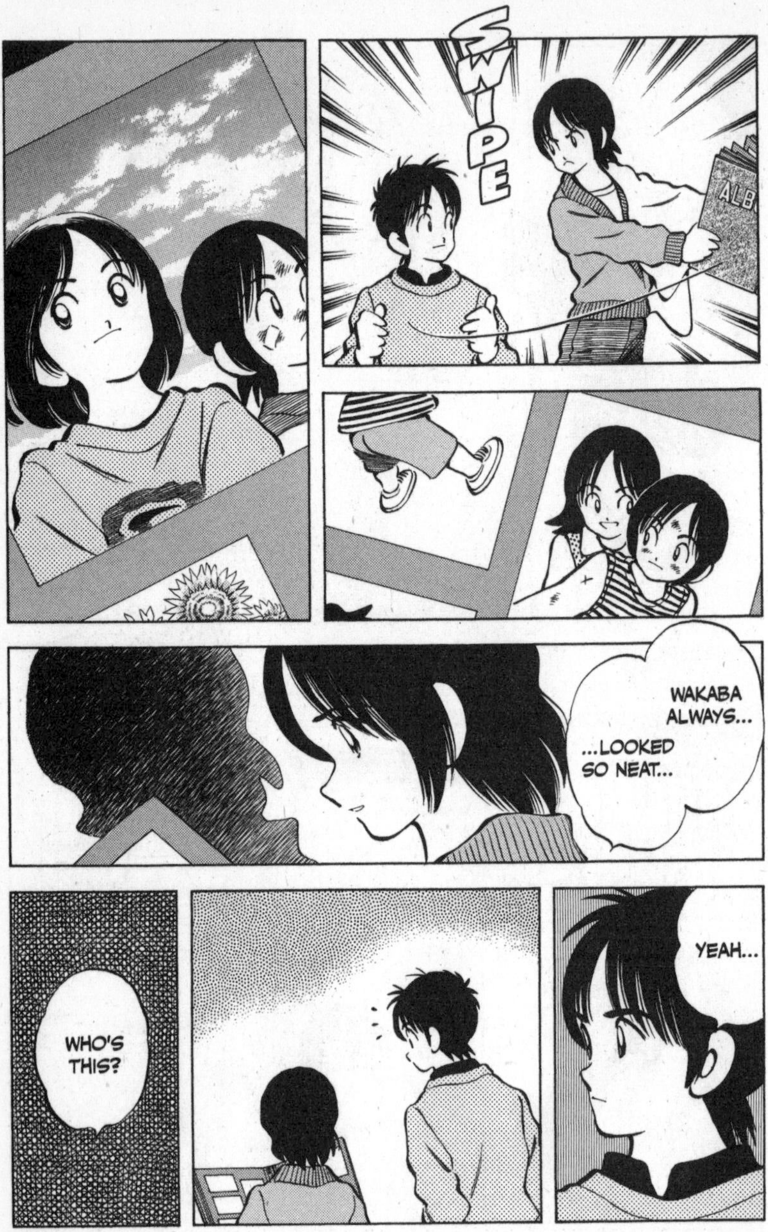
SWIPE
WAKABA ALWAYS...
...LOOKED SO NEAT...
YEAH...
WHO'S THIS?

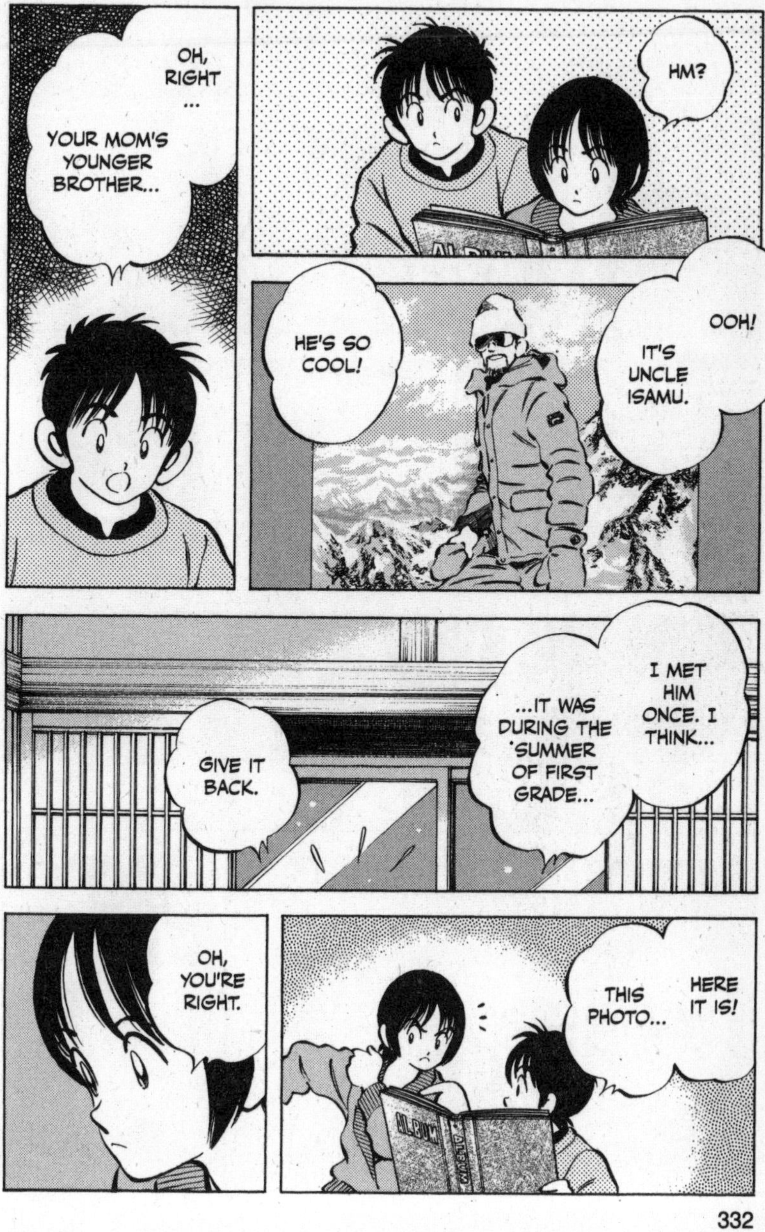
HM?
OOH! IT'S UNCLE ISAMU.
HE'S SO COOL!
OH, RIGHT ...
YOUR MOM'S YOUNGER BROTHER...
I MET HIM ONCE. I THINK...
...IT WAS DURING THE SUMMER OF FIRST GRADE...
GIVE IT BACK.
HERE IT IS!
THIS PHOTO...
OH, YOU'RE RIGHT.

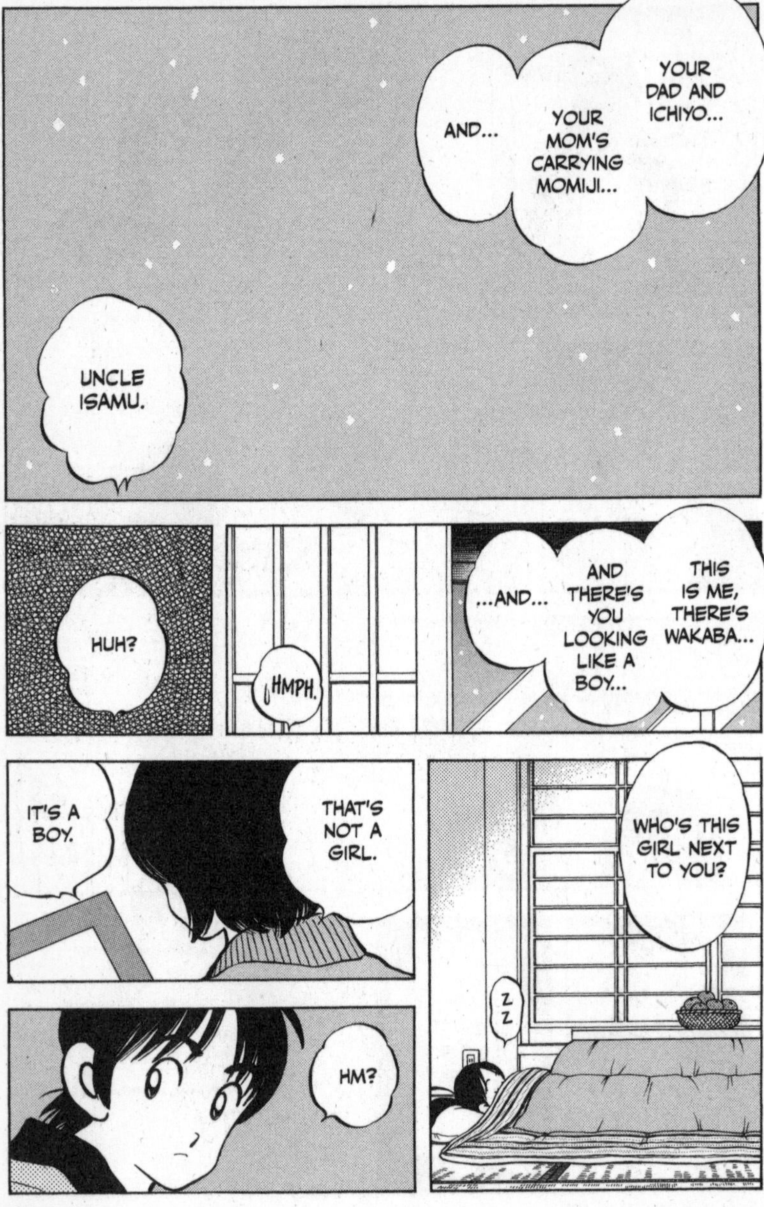
YOUR DAD AND ICHIYO...
YOUR MOM'S CARRYING MOMIJI...
AND...
UNCLE ISAMU.
THIS IS ME, THERE'S WAKABA...
AND THERE'S YOU LOOKING LIKE A BOY...
...AND...
HMPH.
HUH?
WHO'S THIS GIRL NEXT TO YOU?
Z Z
THAT'S NOT A GIRL.
IT'S A BOY.
HM?

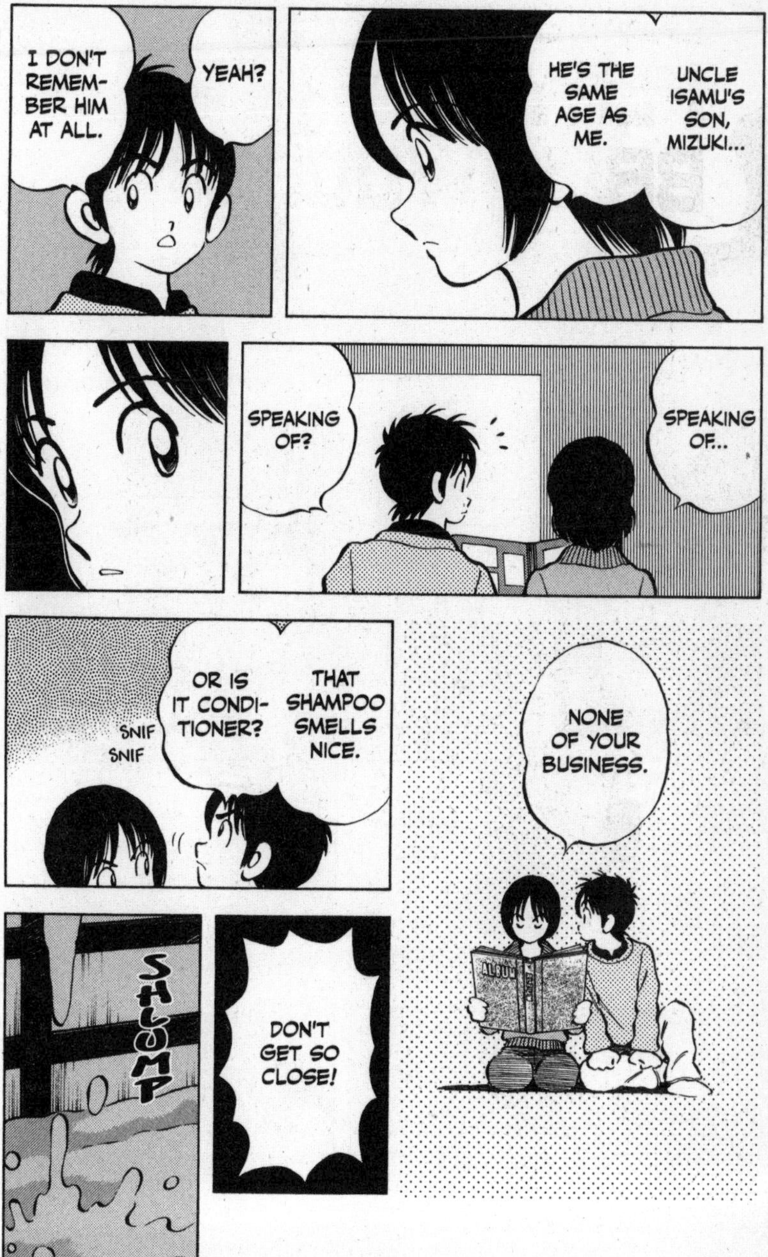
UNCLE ISAMU'S SON, MIZUKI...
HE'S THE SAME AGE AS ME.
YEAH?
I DON'T REMEMBER HIM AT ALL.
SPEAKING OF...
SPEAKING OF?
NONE OF YOUR BUSINESS.
ALBUM
THAT SHAMPOO SMELLS NICE.
OR IS IT CONDITIONER?
SNIF SNIF
DON'T GET SO CLOSE!
SHLUMP

CHAPTER 59
PLAYING IN THE BACK WOODS

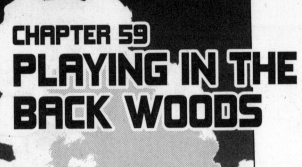

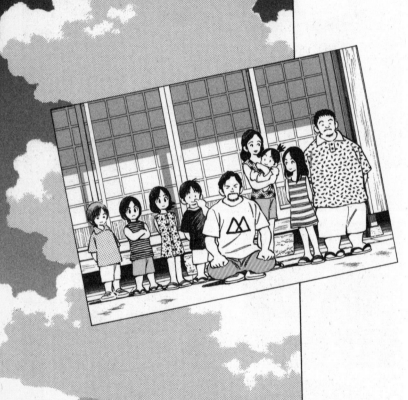

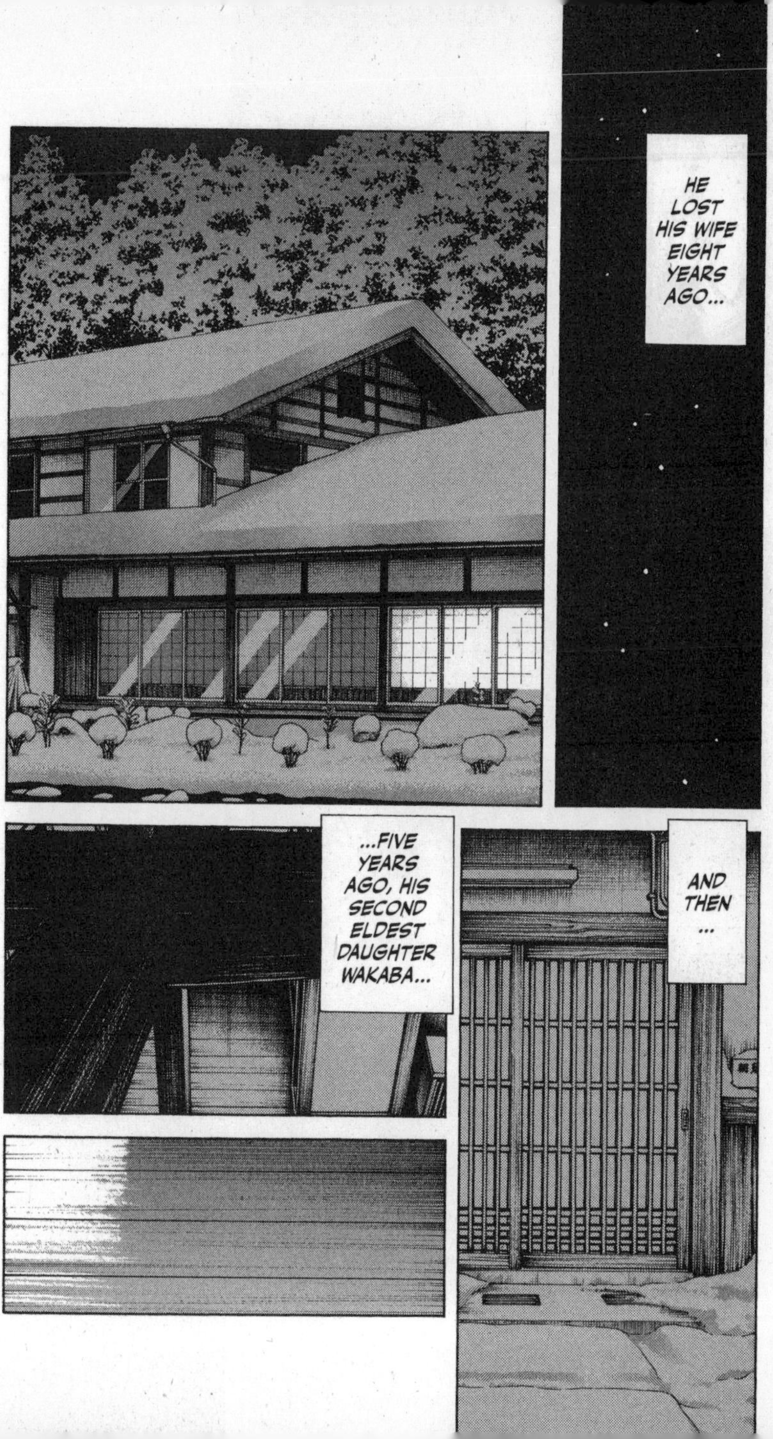
HE LOST HIS WIFE EIGHT YEARS AGO...
...FIVE YEARS AGO, HIS SECOND ELDEST DAUGHTER WAKABA...
AND THEN...

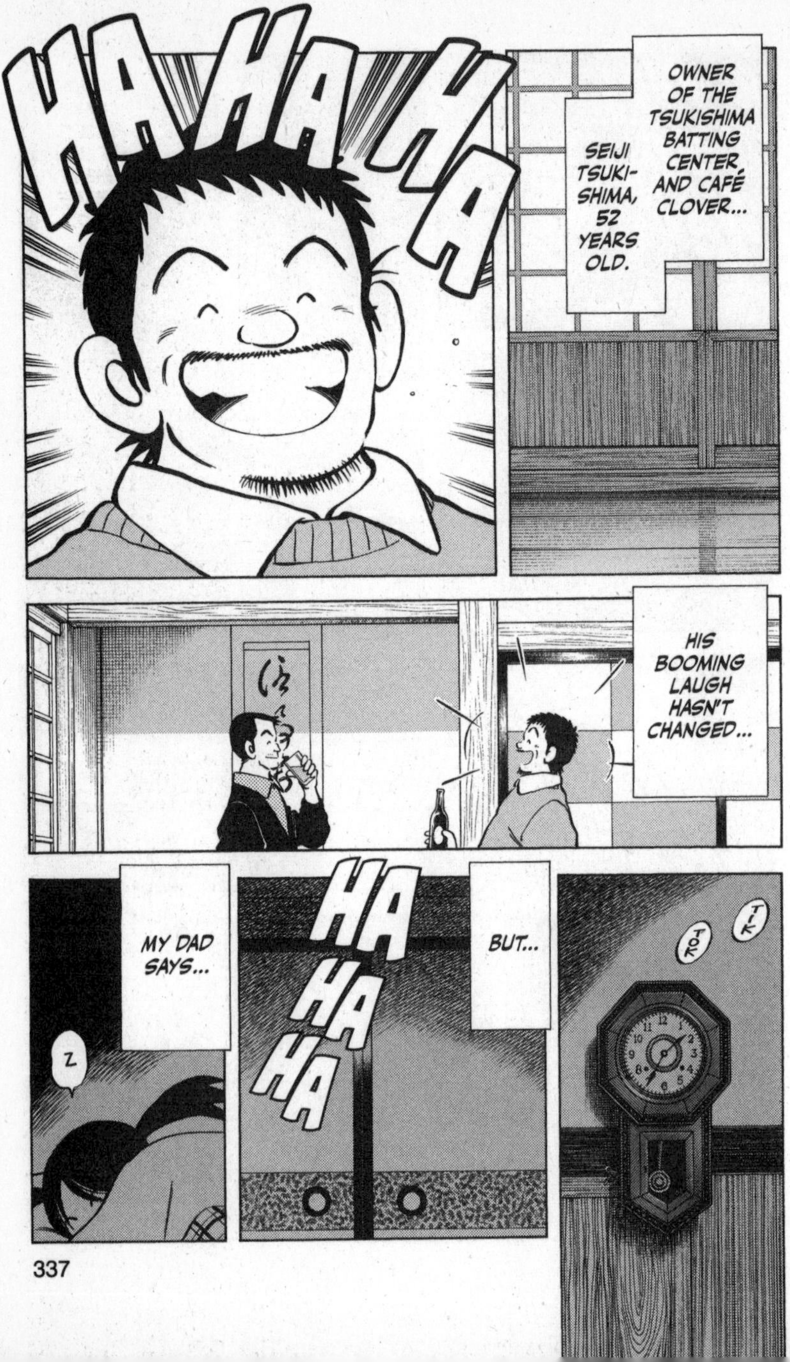

OWNER OF THE TSUKISHIMA BATTING CENTER AND CAFÉ CLOVER...
SEIJI TSUKISHIMA, 52 YEARS OLD.
HAHAHAHA
HIS BOOMING LAUGH HASN'T CHANGED...
TIK
TOK
BUT...
HA HA HA HA
MY DAD SAYS...
Z

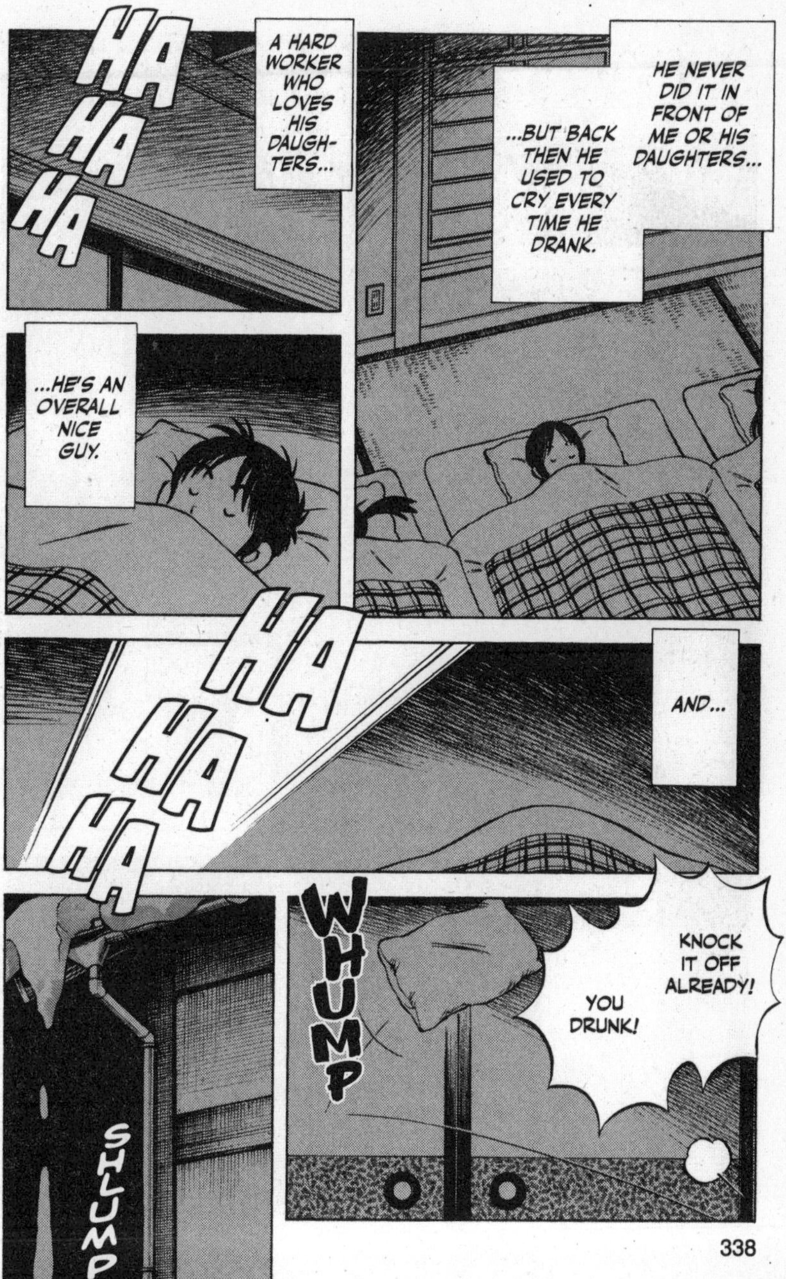
HE NEVER DID IT IN FRONT OF ME OR HIS DAUGHTERS...
...BUT BACK THEN HE USED TO CRY EVERY TIME HE DRANK.
A HARD WORKER WHO LOVES HIS DAUGH-TERS...
HA HA HA HA
...HE'S AN OVERALL NICE GUY.
AND...
HA HA HA HA
KNOCK IT OFF ALREADY!
YOU DRUNK!
WHUMP
SHLUMP

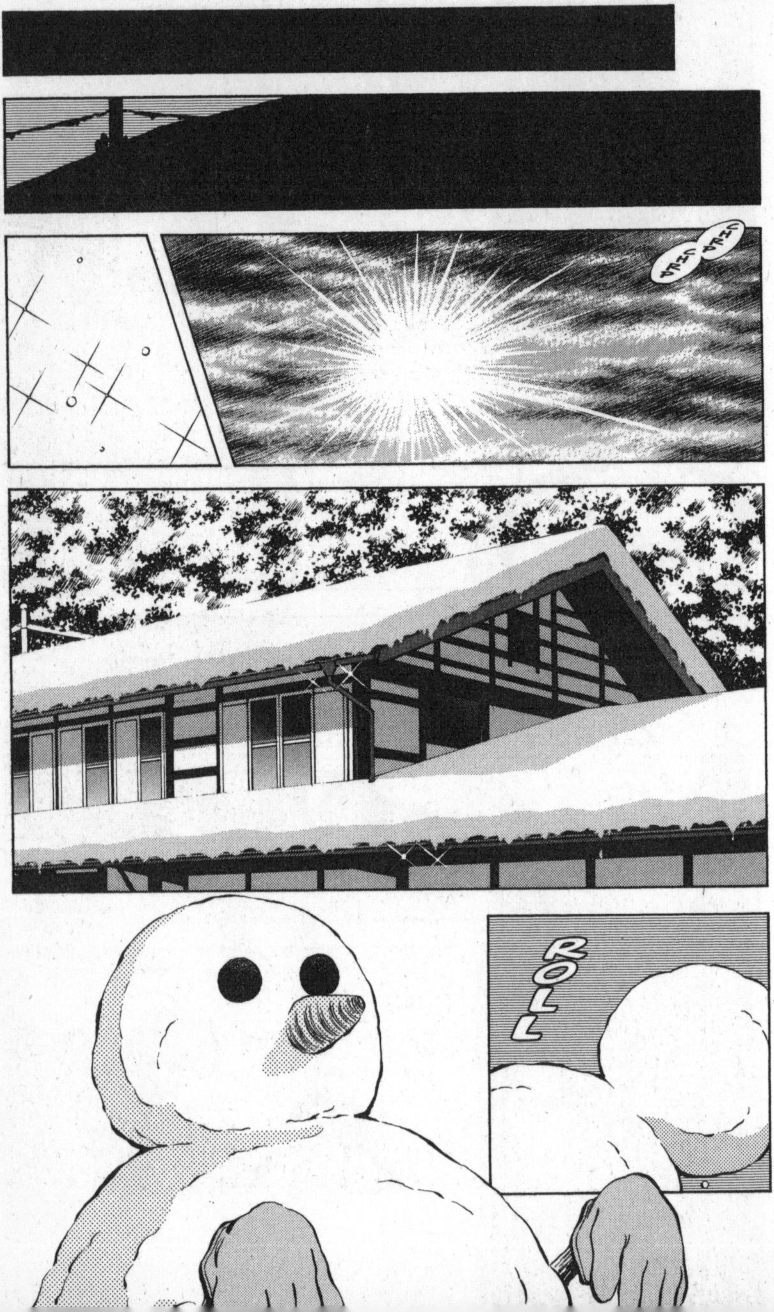
CHRP CHRP
ROLL

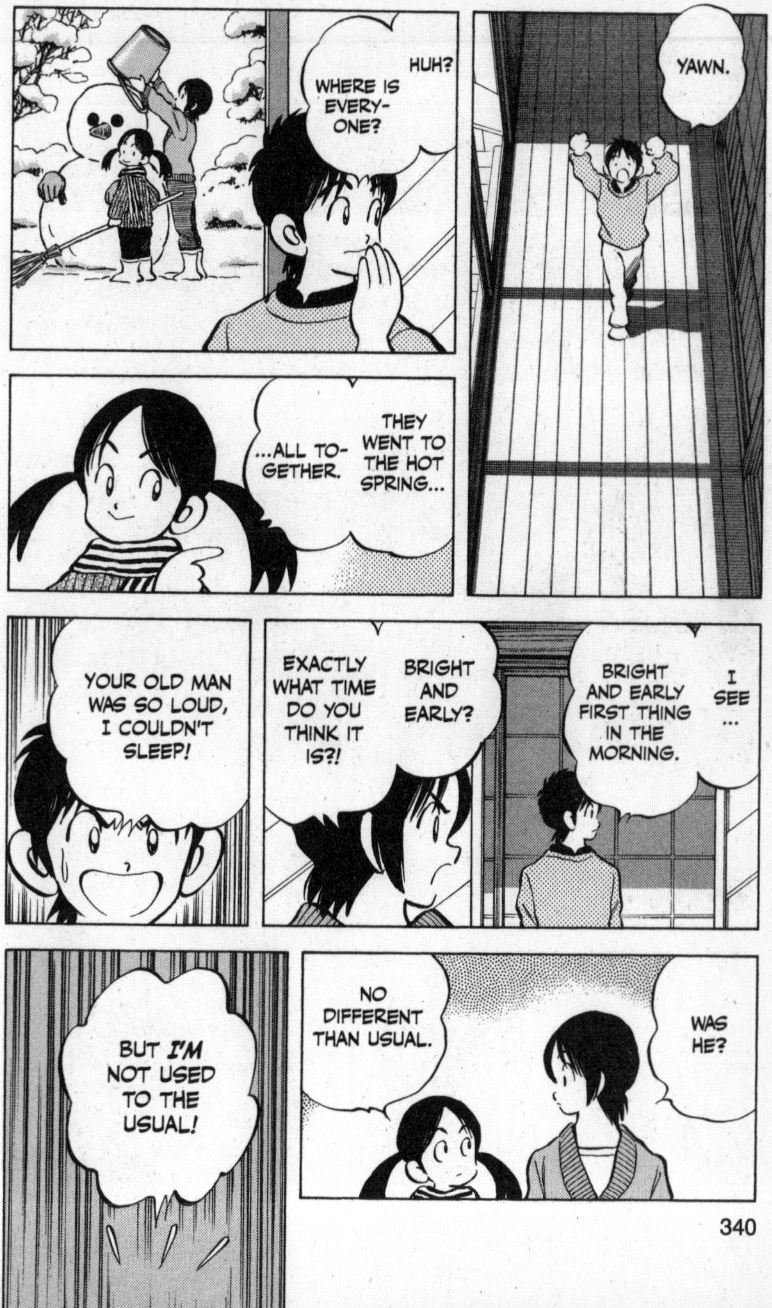
YAWN.
HUH?
WHERE IS EVERY-ONE?
THEY WENT TO THE HOT SPRING...
...ALL TO-GETHER.
I SEE ...
BRIGHT AND EARLY FIRST THING IN THE MORNING.
BRIGHT AND EARLY?
EXACTLY WHAT TIME DO YOU THINK IT IS?!
YOUR OLD MAN WAS SO LOUD, I COULDN'T SLEEP!
WAS HE?
NO DIFFERENT THAN USUAL.
BUT *I'M* NOT USED TO THE USUAL!

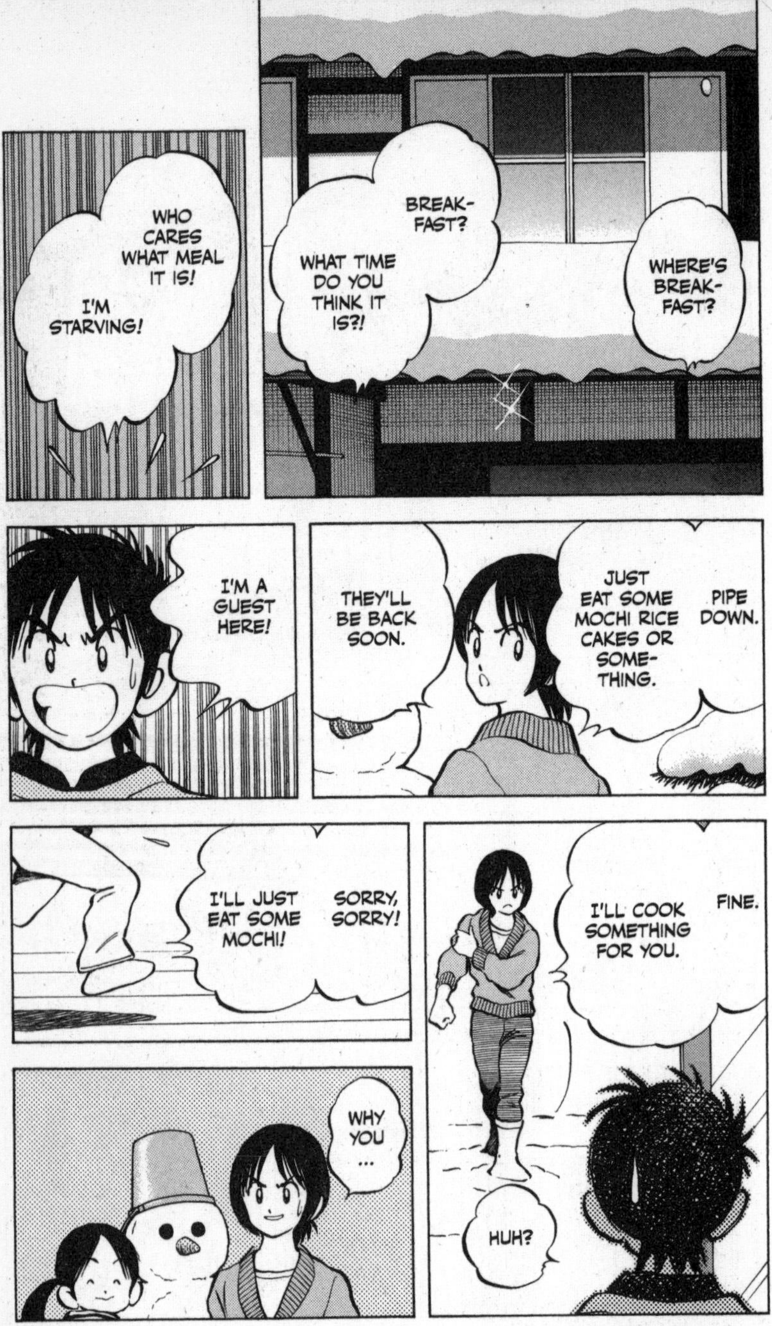
WHERE'S BREAK-FAST?
BREAK-FAST?
WHAT TIME DO YOU THINK IT IS?!
WHO CARES WHAT MEAL IT IS!
I'M STARVING!
PIPE DOWN.
JUST EAT SOME MOCHI RICE CAKES OR SOME-THING.
THEY'LL BE BACK SOON.
I'M A GUEST HERE!
FINE.
I'LL COOK SOMETHING FOR YOU.
HUH?
SORRY, SORRY!
I'LL JUST EAT SOME MOCHI!
WHY YOU ...

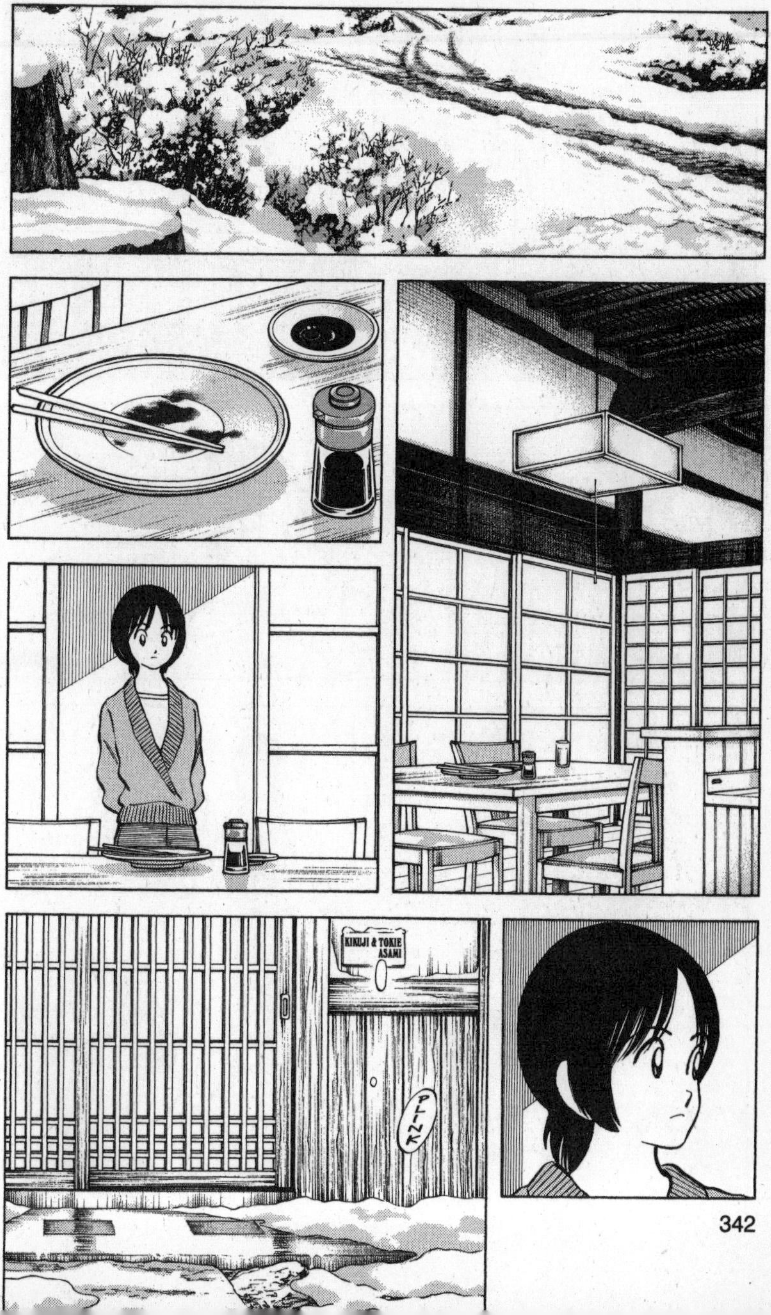
KIKUJI & TOKIE ASAMI
PLINK

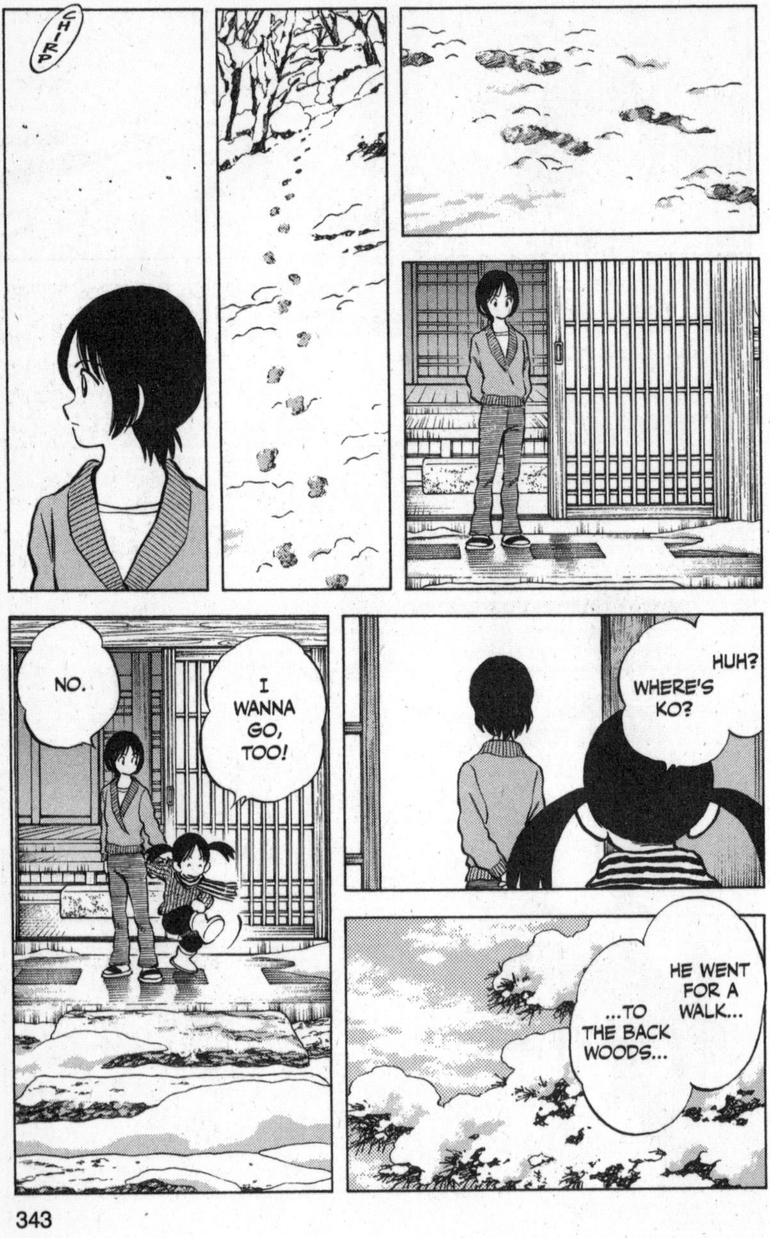
CHIRP
HUH? WHERE'S KO?
HE WENT FOR A WALK...
...TO THE BACK WOODS...
I WANNA GO, TOO!
NO.

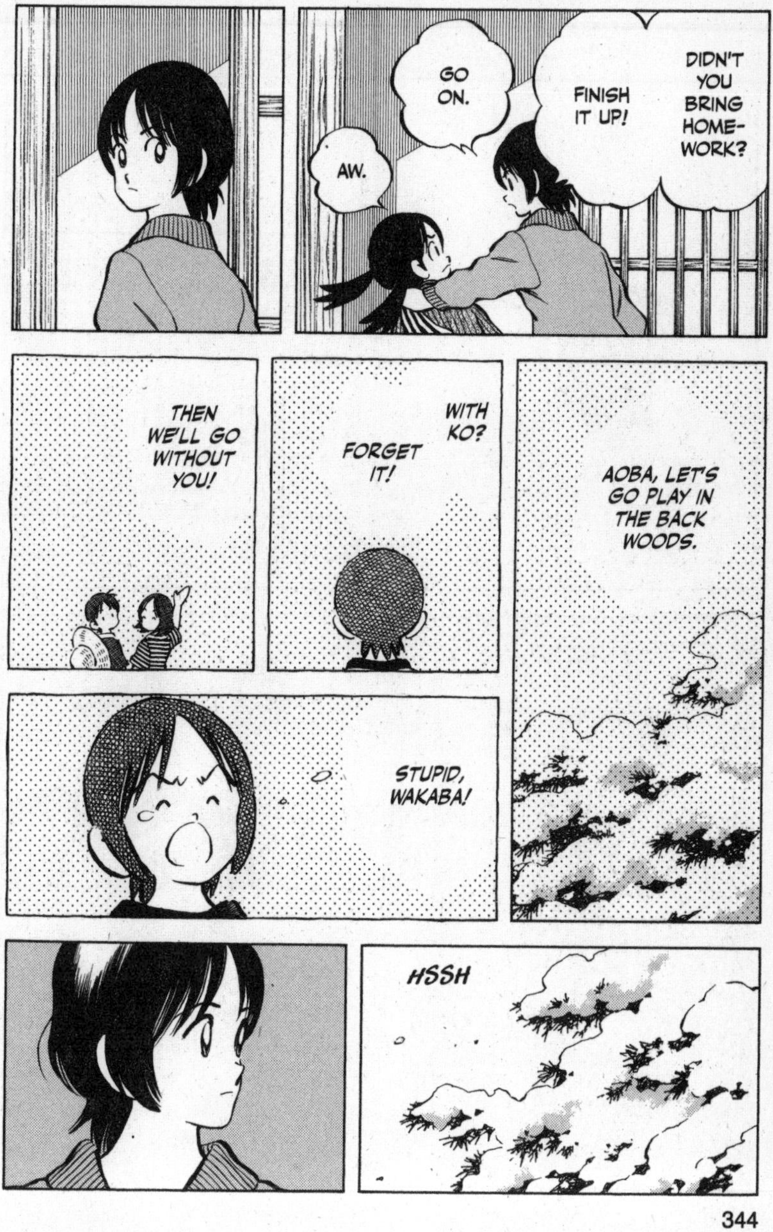
DIDN'T YOU BRING HOME-WORK?
FINISH IT UP!
GO ON.
AW.
AOBA, LET'S GO PLAY IN THE BACK WOODS.
WITH KO?
FORGET IT!
THEN WE'LL GO WITHOUT YOU!
STUPID, WAKABA!
HSSH

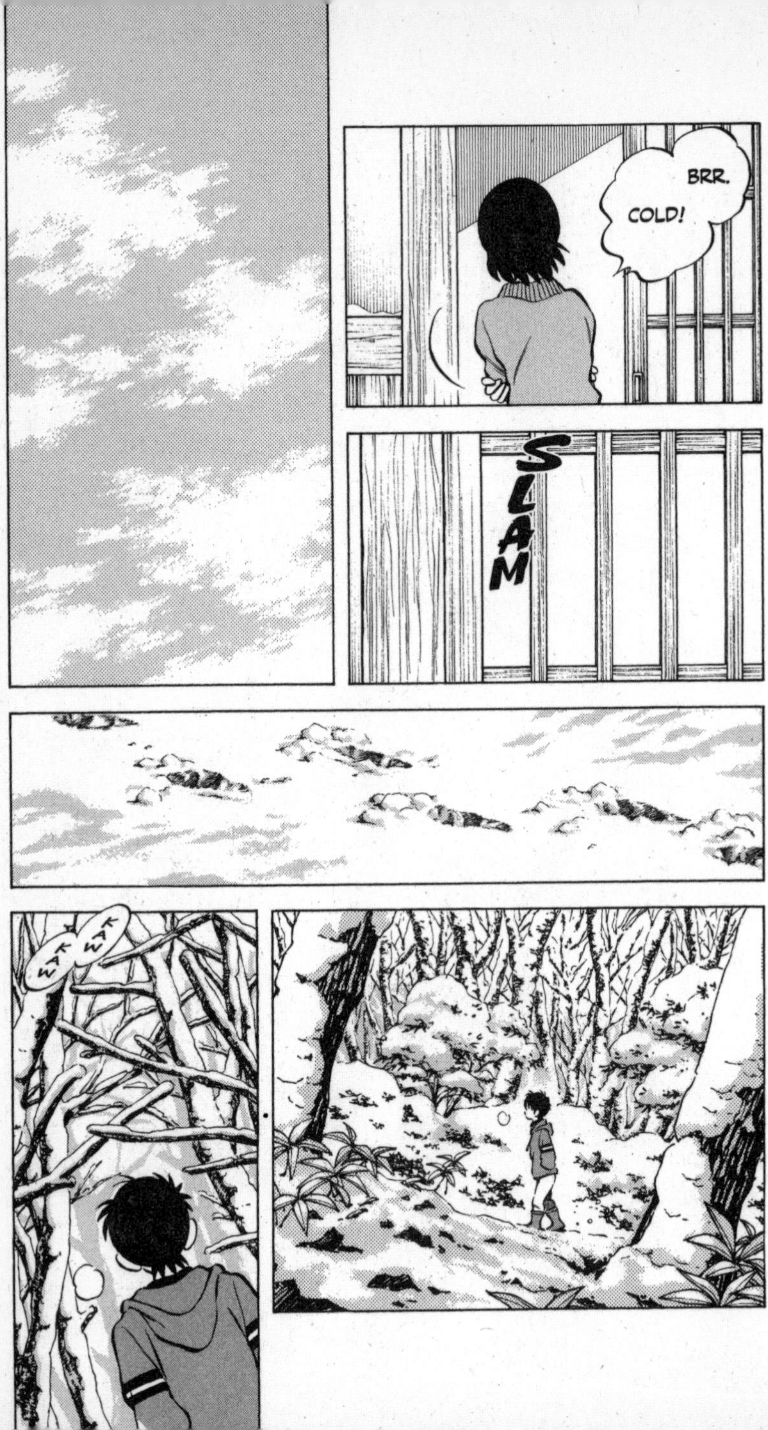
BRR.
COLD!
SLAM
KAW
KAW

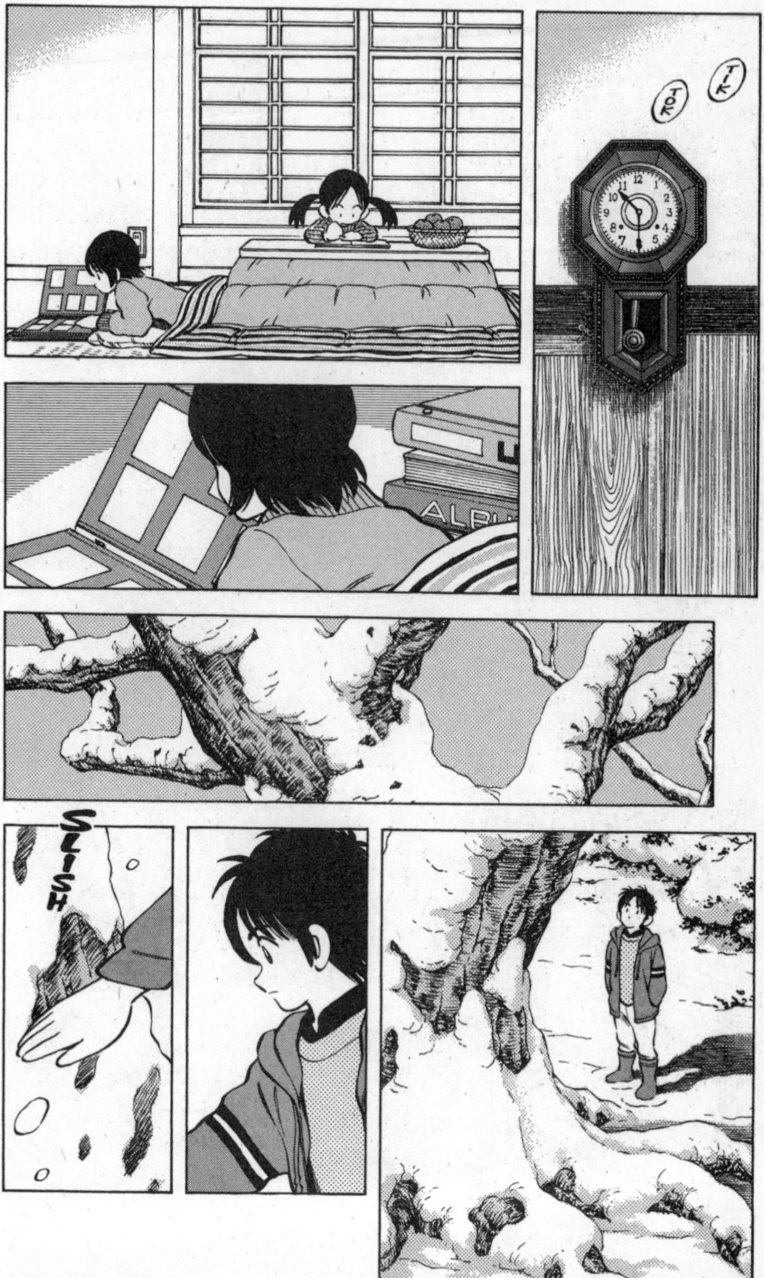
TIK
TOK
ALBU
SLISH

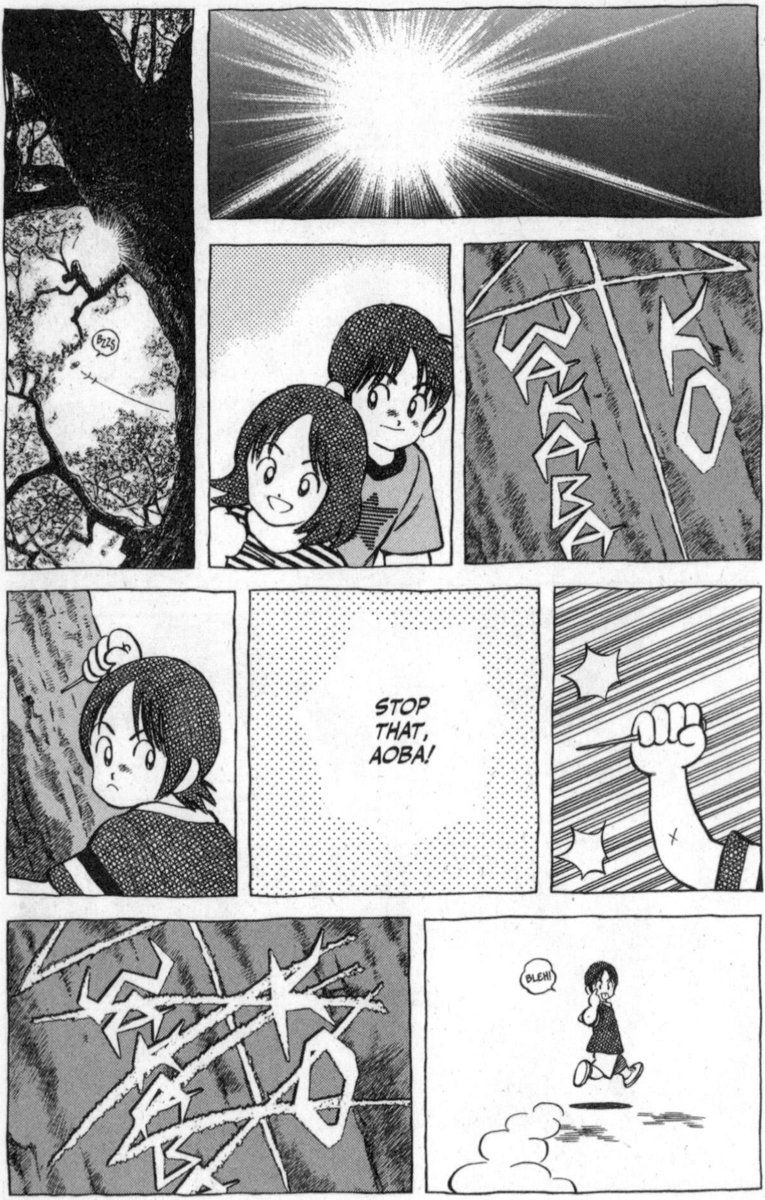
KO
WAKABA
BZZS
STOP THAT, AOBA!
BLEH!

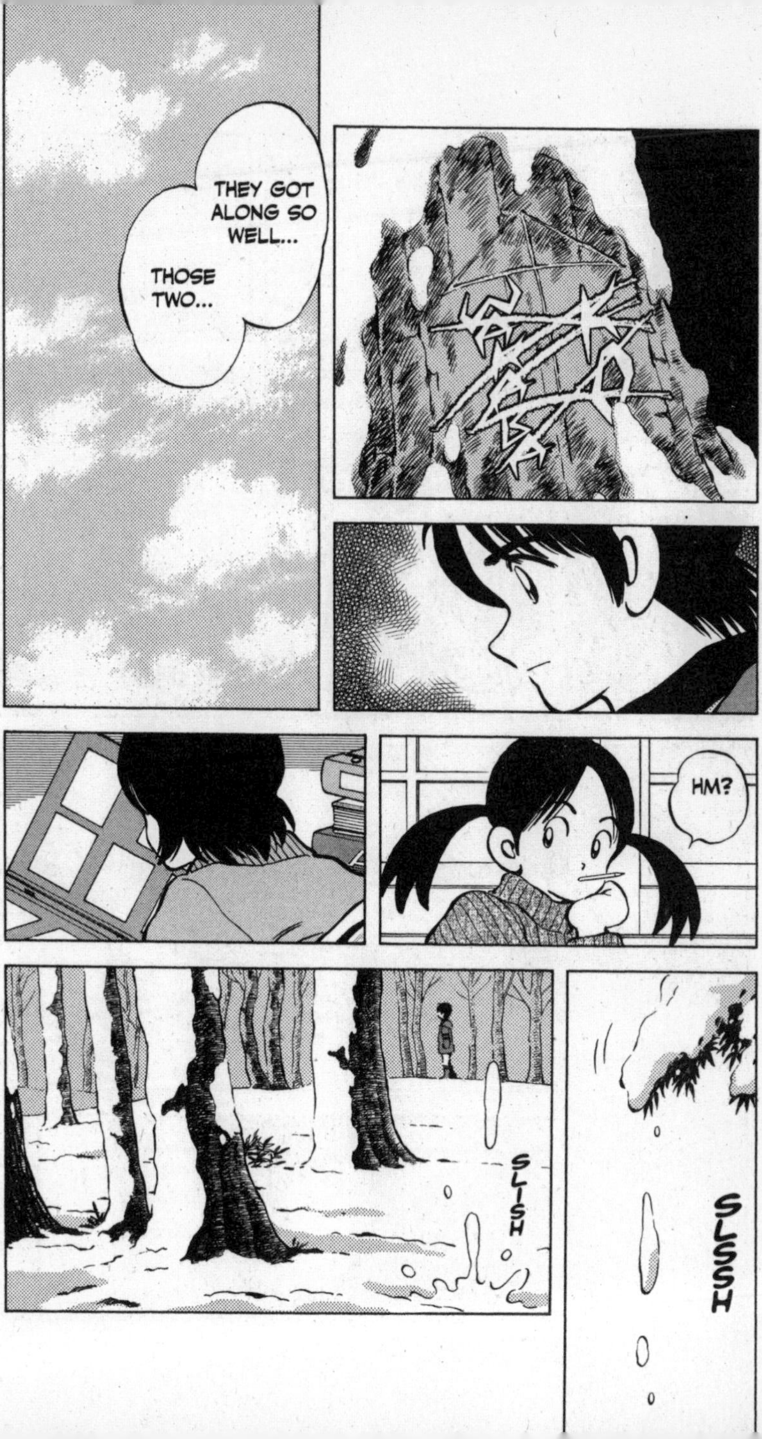
THEY GOT ALONG SO WELL...
THOSE TWO...
HM?
SLSSH
SLISH

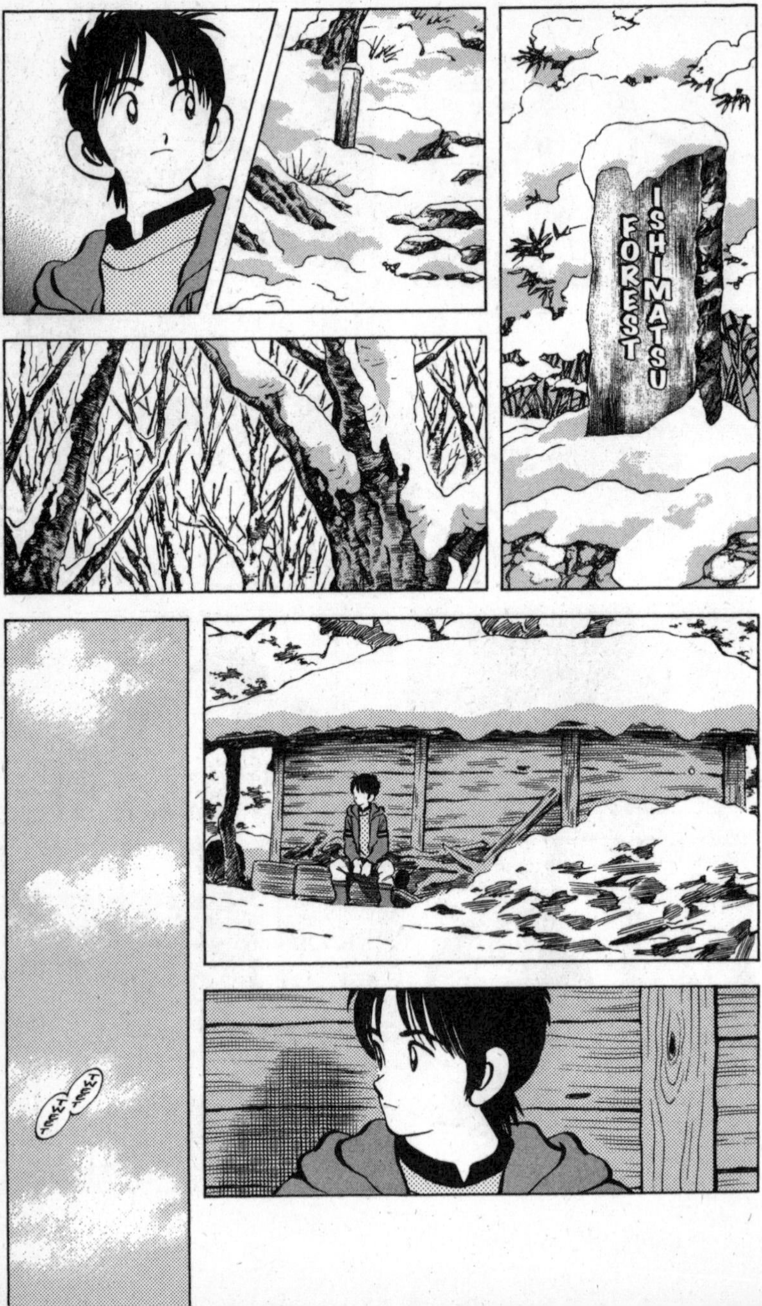
ISHIMATSU FOREST
TWEET TWEET

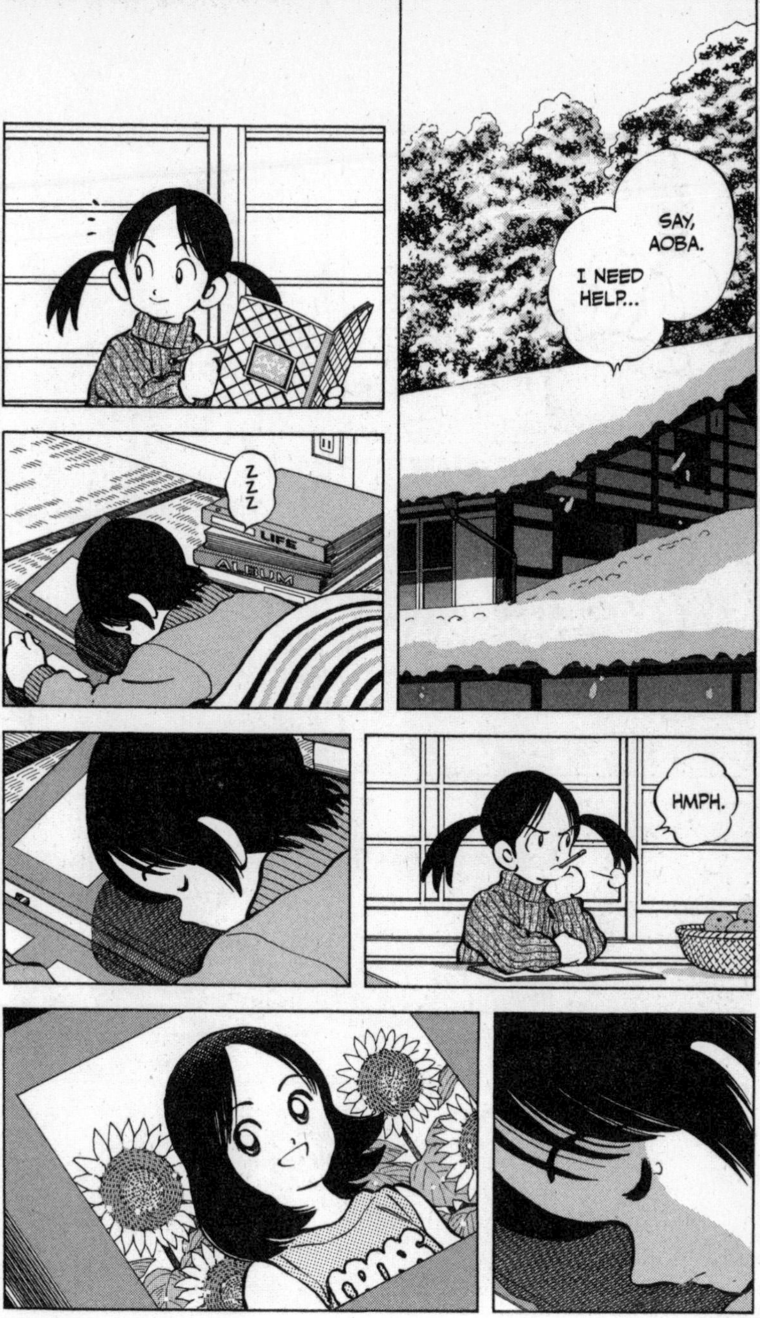
SAY, AOBA.
I NEED HELP...
ZZZ
LIFE
ALBUM
HMPH.

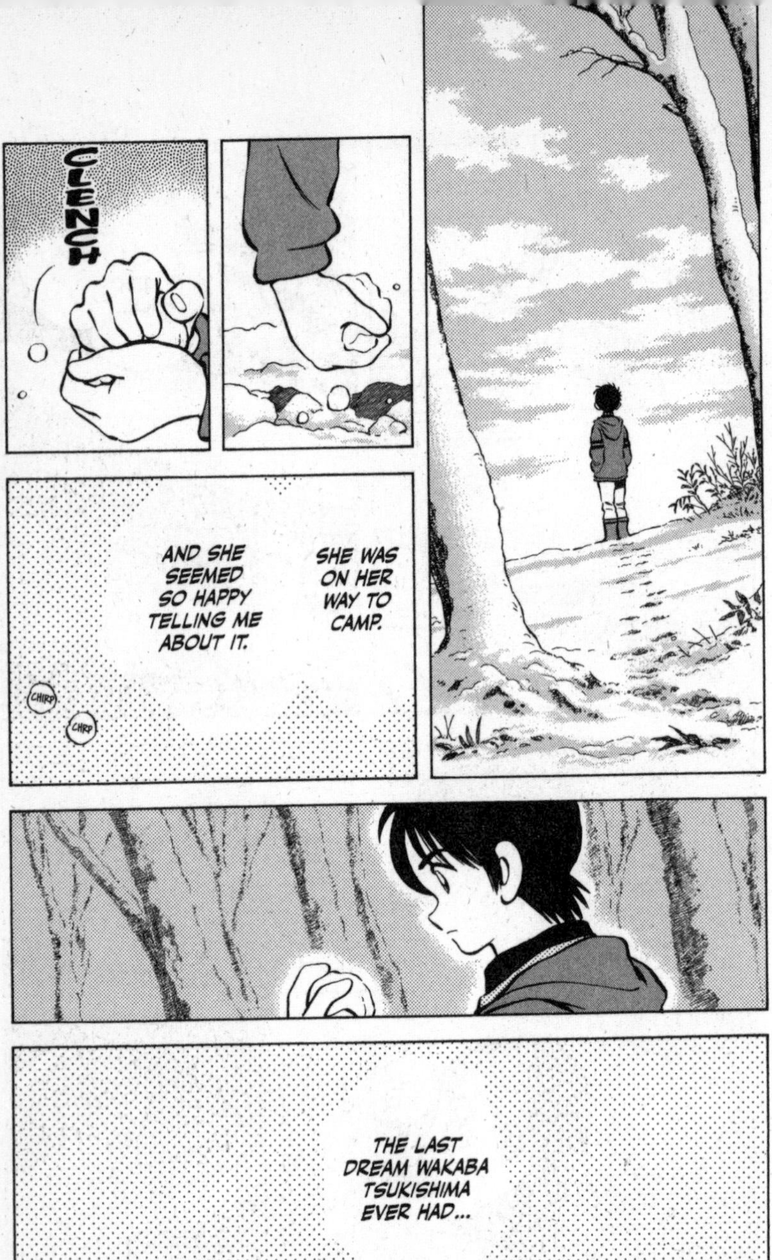

CLENCH
SHE WAS ON HER WAY TO CAMP.
AND SHE SEEMED SO HAPPY TELLING ME ABOUT IT.
CHIRP
CHIRP
THE LAST DREAM WAKABA TSUKISHIMA EVER HAD...

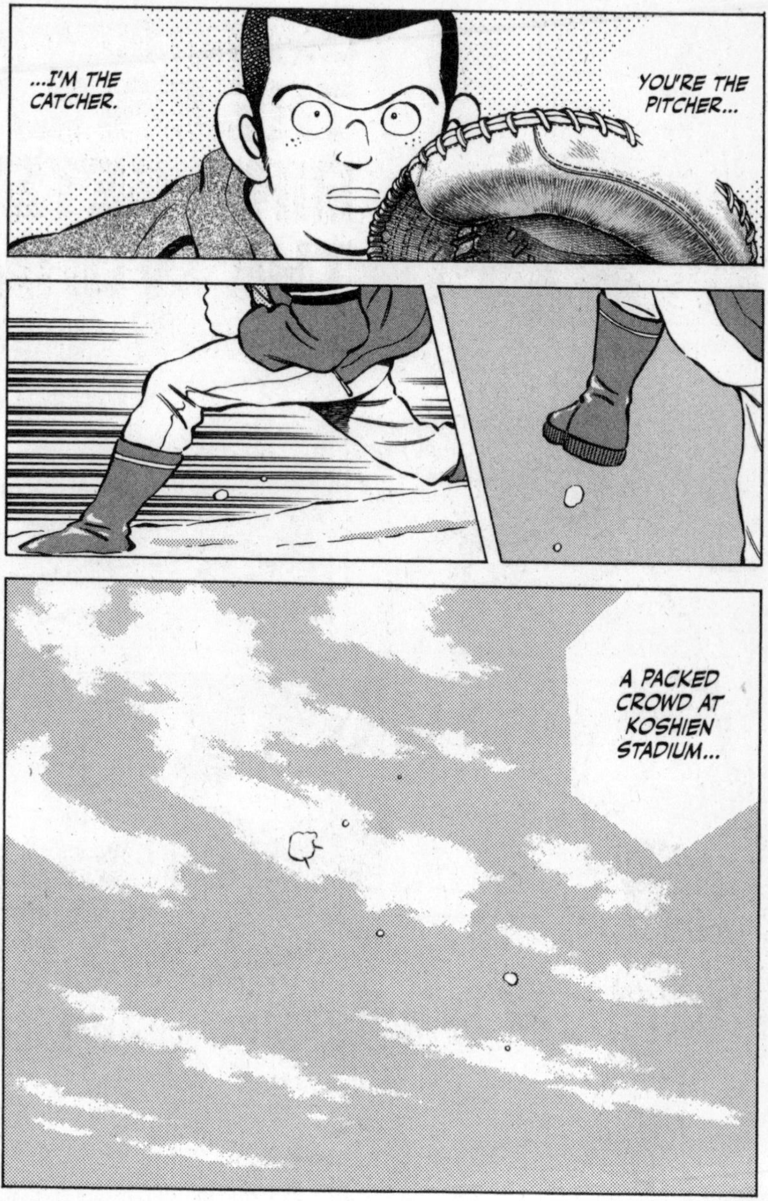
YOU'RE THE PITCHER...
...I'M THE CATCHER.
A PACKED CROWD AT KOSHIEN STADIUM...

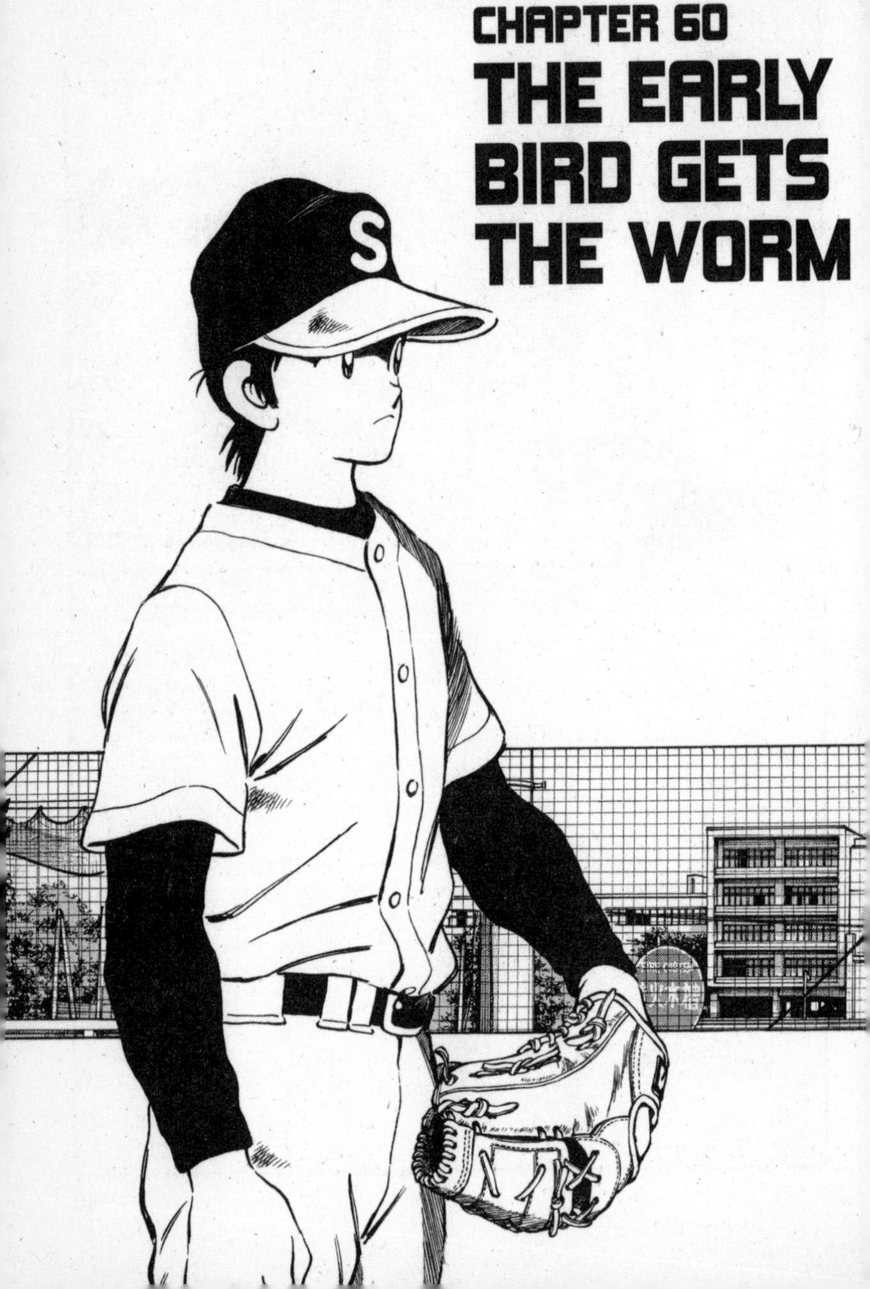
CHAPTER 60
THE EARLY BIRD GETS THE WORM

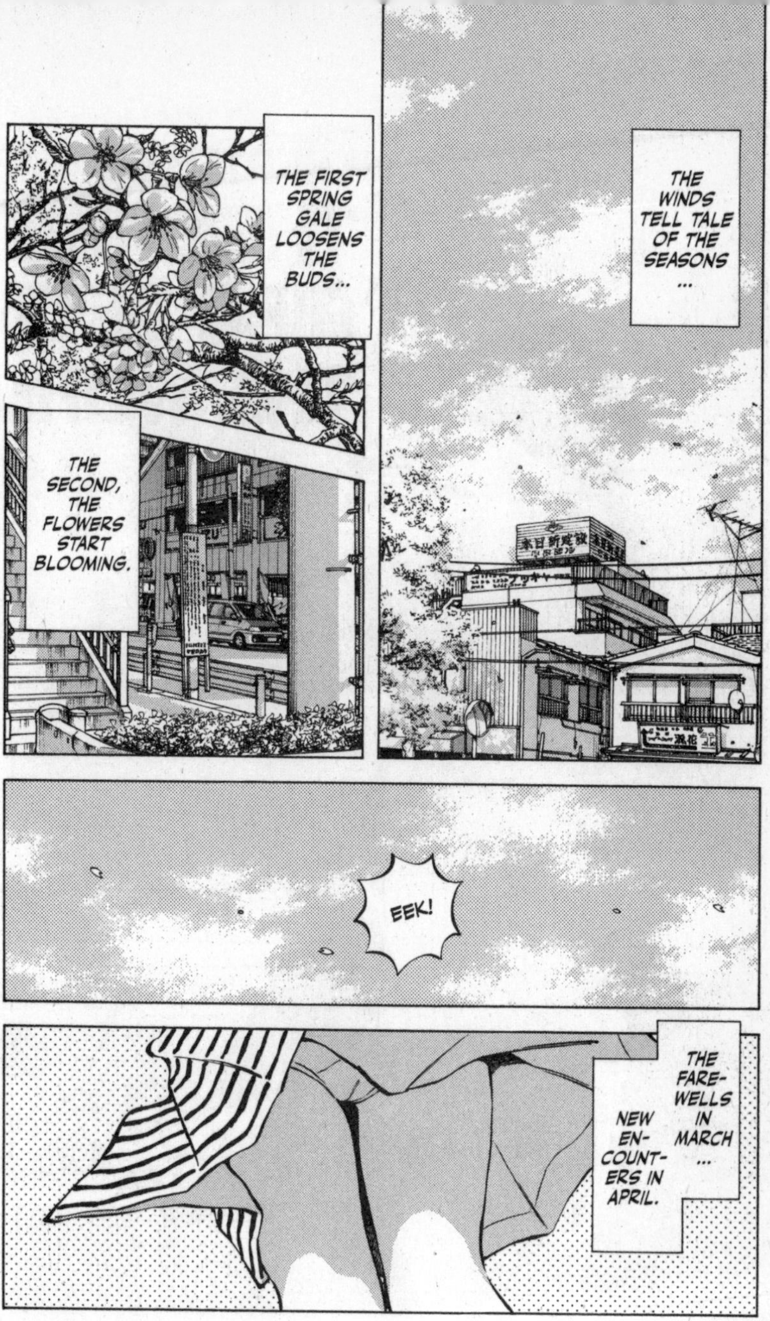
THE WINDS TELL TALE OF THE SEASONS ...
THE FIRST SPRING GALE LOOSENS THE BUDS...
THE SECOND, THE FLOWERS START BLOOMING.
EEK!
THE FAREWELLS IN MARCH ...
NEW ENCOUNTERS IN APRIL.

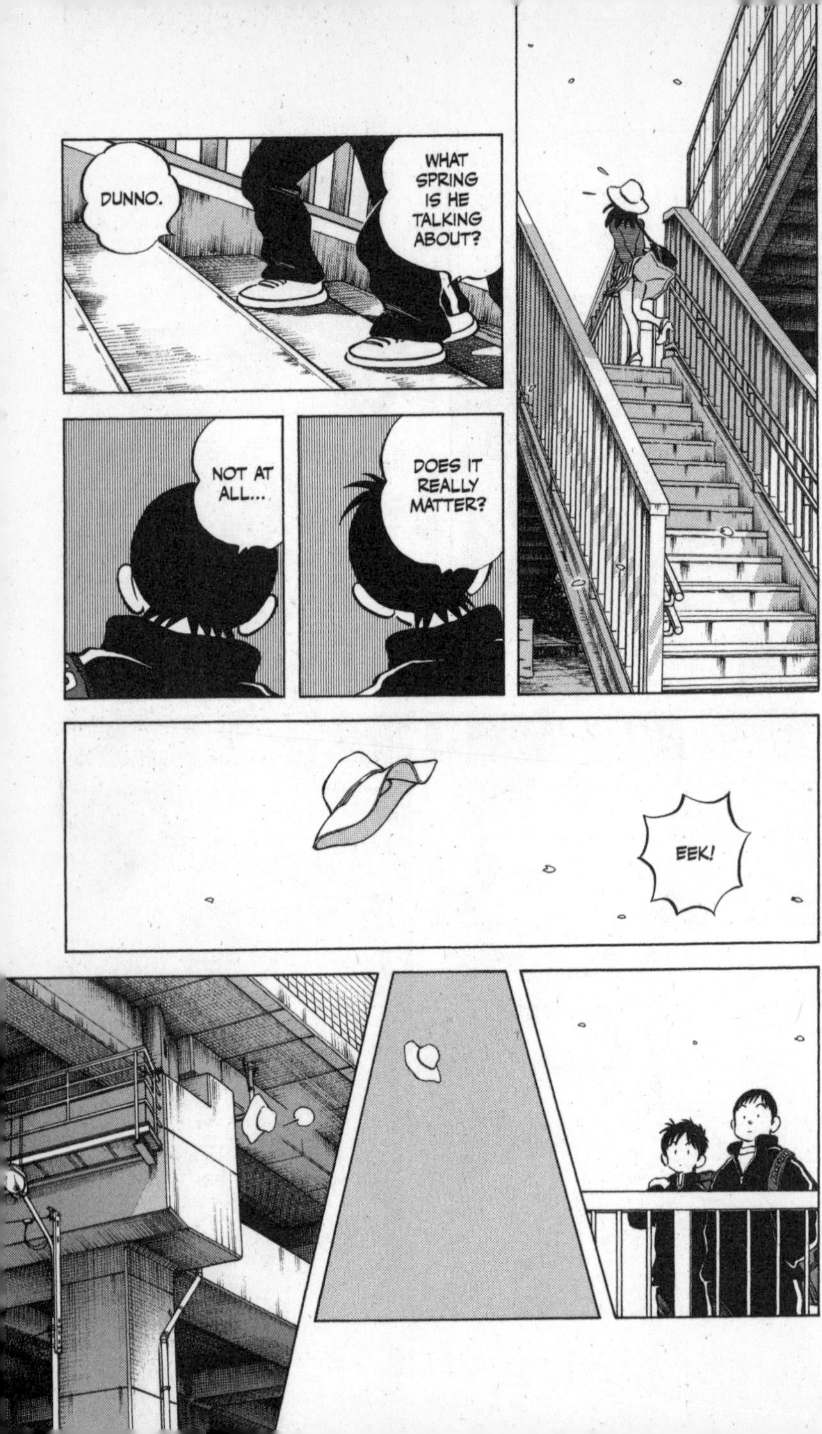
WHAT SPRING IS HE TALKING ABOUT?
DUNNO.
DOES IT REALLY MATTER?
NOT AT ALL...
EEK!

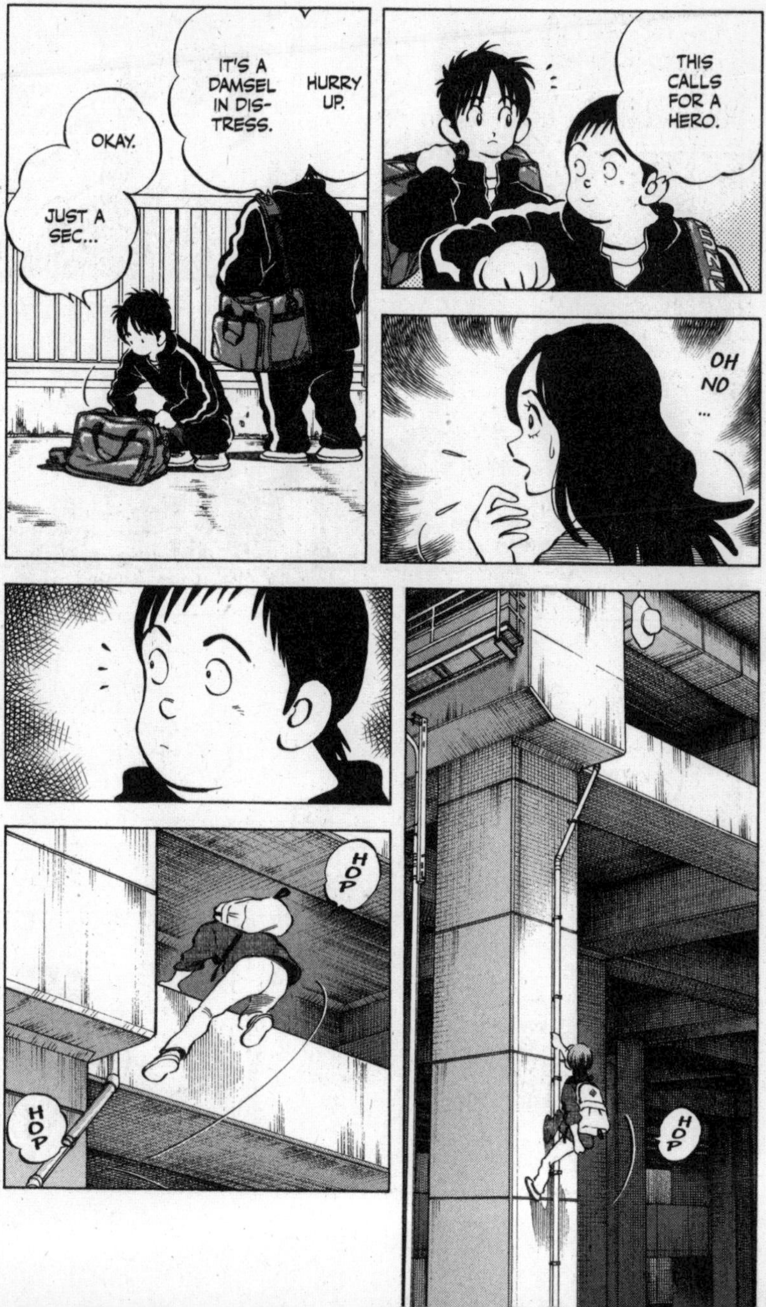
THIS CALLS FOR A HERO.
OH NO ...
HURRY UP.
IT'S A DAMSEL IN DIS-TRESS.
OKAY.
JUST A SEC...
HOP
HOP
HOP

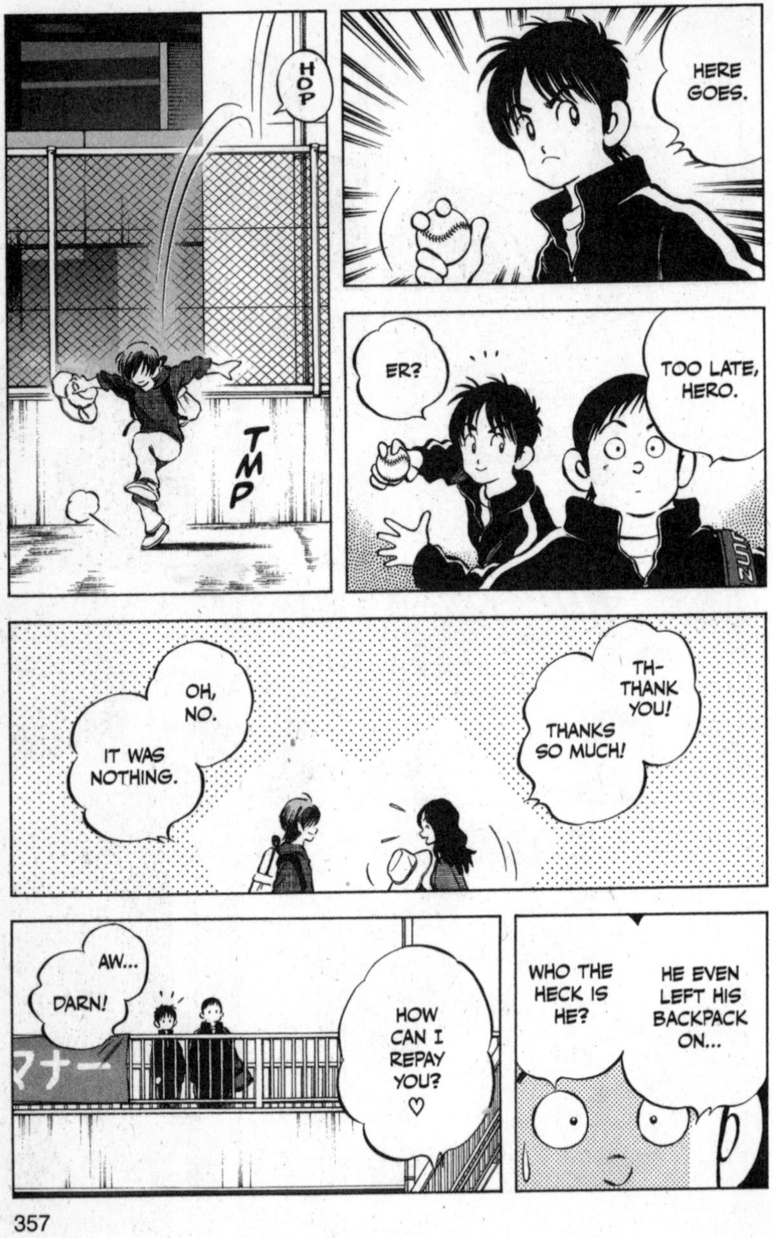
HERE GOES.
TOO LATE, HERO.
ER?
HOP
TMP
TH- THANK YOU!
THANKS SO MUCH!
OH, NO.
IT WAS NOTHING.
HE EVEN LEFT HIS BACKPACK ON...
WHO THE HECK IS HE?
HOW CAN I REPAY YOU? ♡
AW...
DARN!
マナー

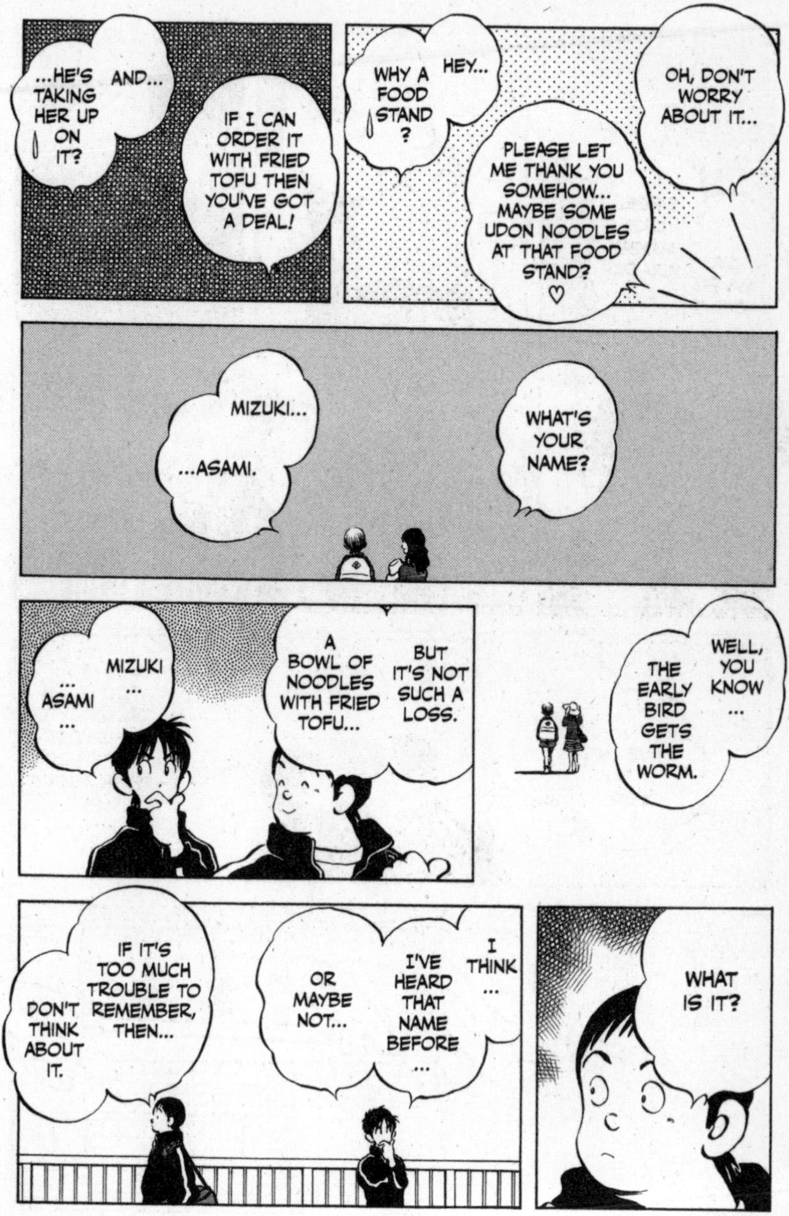
OH, DON'T WORRY ABOUT IT...
PLEASE LET ME THANK YOU SOMEHOW... MAYBE SOME UDON NOODLES AT THAT FOOD STAND? ♡
HEY...
WHY A FOOD STAND?
IF I CAN ORDER IT WITH FRIED TOFU THEN YOU'VE GOT A DEAL!
AND...
...HE'S TAKING HER UP ON IT?
WHAT'S YOUR NAME?
MIZUKI...
...ASAMI.
WELL, YOU KNOW...
THE EARLY BIRD GETS THE WORM.
BUT IT'S NOT SUCH A LOSS.
A BOWL OF NOODLES WITH FRIED TOFU...
MIZUKI...
...ASAMI...
WHAT IS IT?
I THINK...
I'VE HEARD THAT NAME BEFORE...
OR MAYBE NOT...
IF IT'S TOO MUCH TROUBLE TO REMEMBER, THEN...
DON'T THINK ABOUT IT.

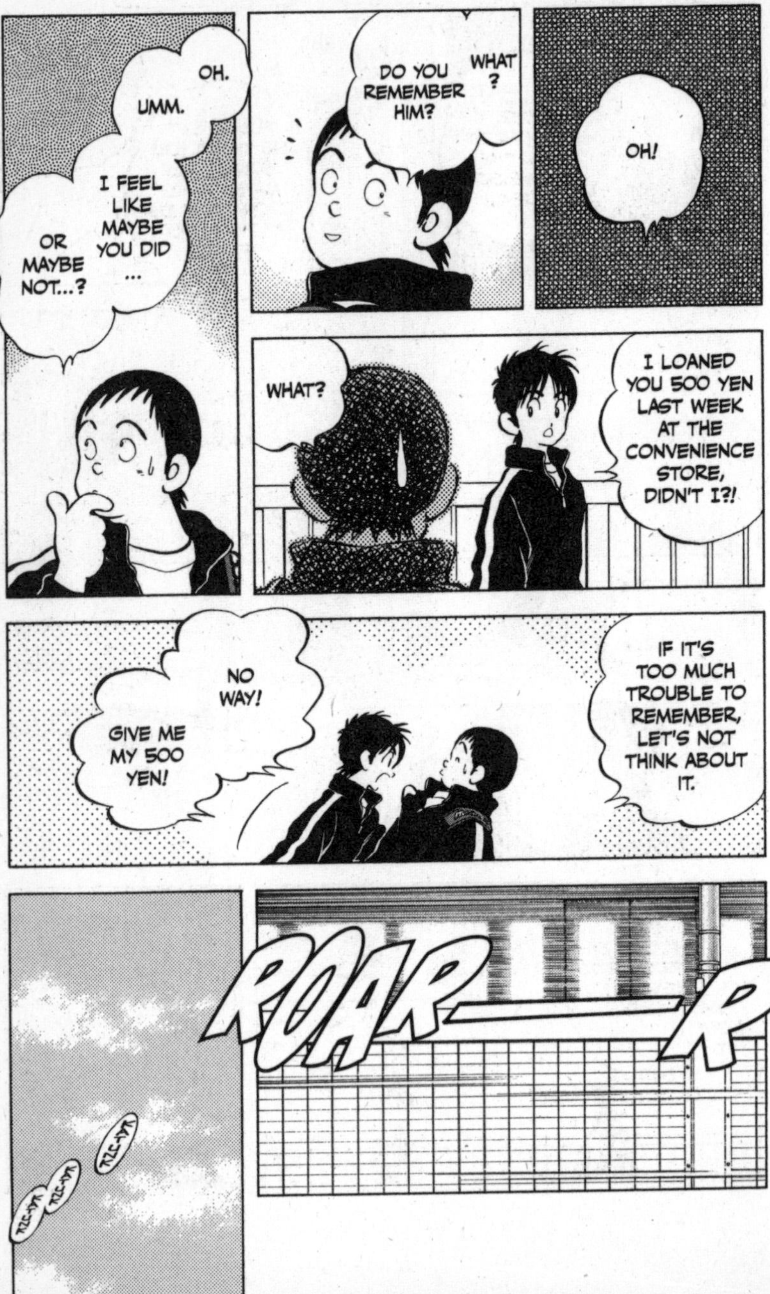
OH!
WHAT?
DO YOU REMEMBER HIM?
I LOANED YOU 500 YEN LAST WEEK AT THE CONVENIENCE STORE, DIDN'T I?!
WHAT?
OH.
UMM.
I FEEL LIKE MAYBE YOU DID...
OR MAYBE NOT...?
IF IT'S TOO MUCH TROUBLE TO REMEMBER, LET'S NOT THINK ABOUT IT.
NO WAY!
GIVE ME MY 500 YEN!
ROAR—R

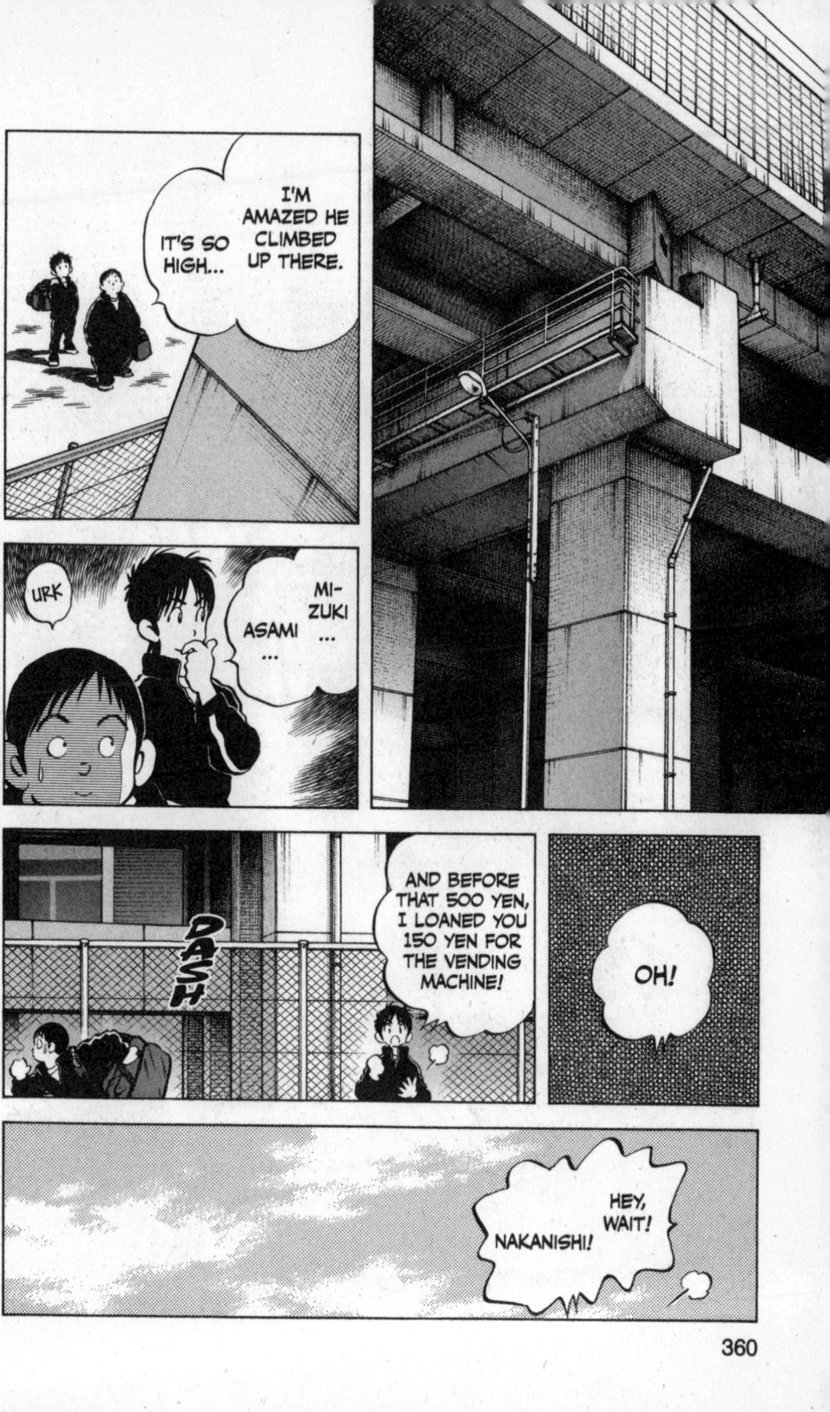
I'M AMAZED HE CLIMBED UP THERE.
IT'S SO HIGH...
MI-ZUKI ...
ASAMI ...
URK
OH!
AND BEFORE THAT 500 YEN, I LOANED YOU 150 YEN FOR THE VENDING MACHINE!
DASH
HEY, WAIT!
NAKANISHI!

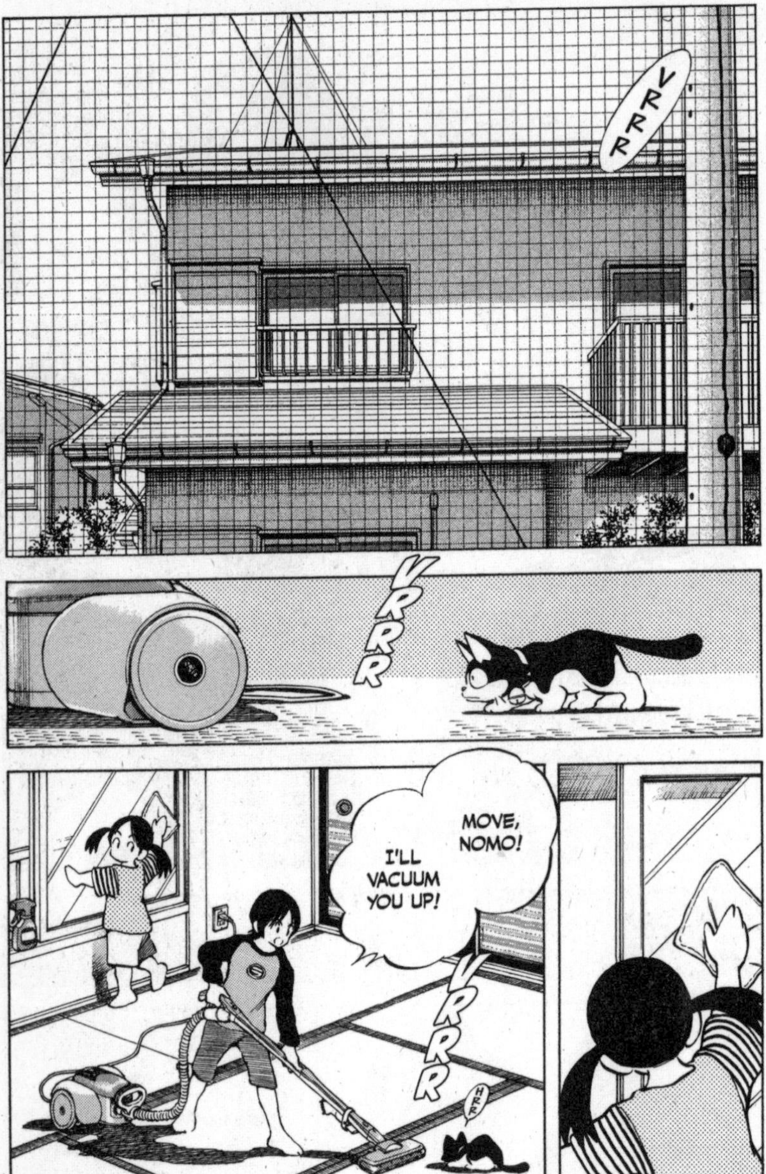
VRRR
VRRR
MOVE, NOMO!
I'LL VACUUM YOU UP!
VRRR
HRR

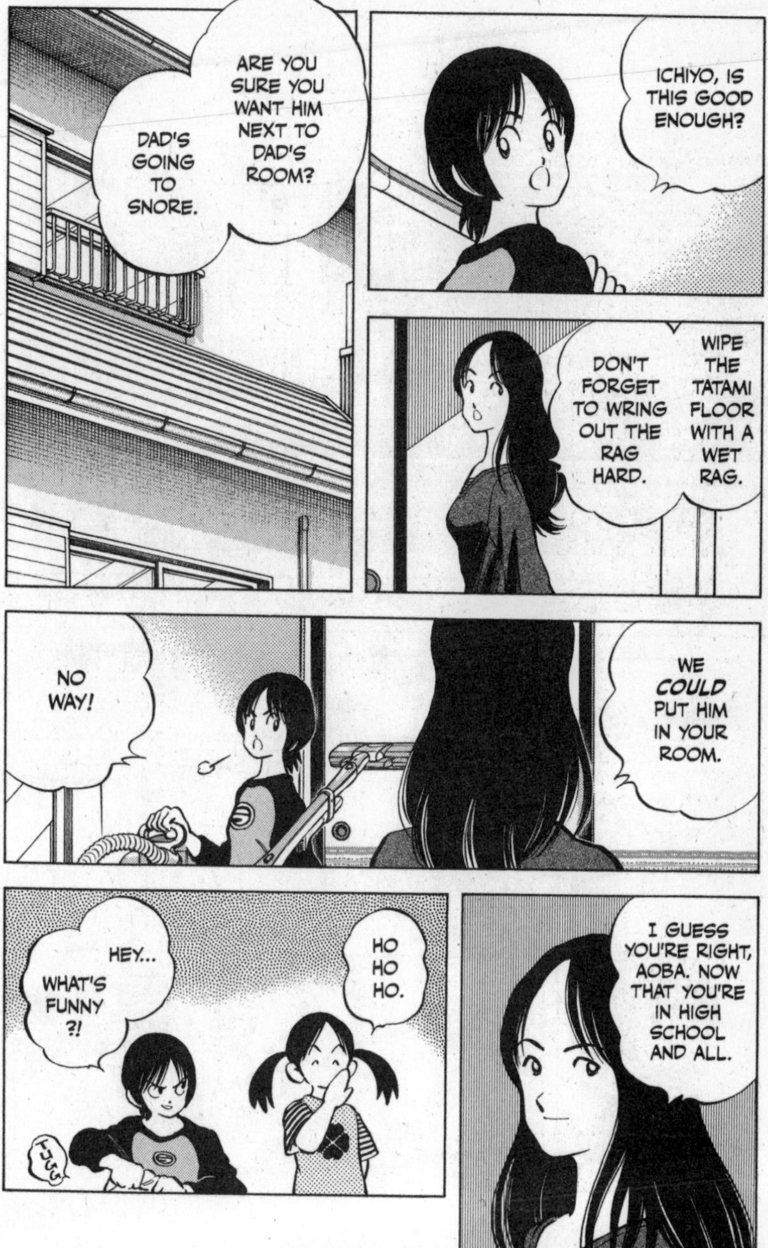
ICHIYO, IS THIS GOOD ENOUGH?
WIPE THE TATAMI FLOOR WITH A WET RAG.
DON'T FORGET TO WRING OUT THE RAG HARD.
ARE YOU SURE YOU WANT HIM NEXT TO DAD'S ROOM?
DAD'S GOING TO SNORE.
WE *COULD* PUT HIM IN YOUR ROOM.
NO WAY!
I GUESS YOU'RE RIGHT, AOBA. NOW THAT YOU'RE IN HIGH SCHOOL AND ALL.
HO HO HO.
HEY...
WHAT'S FUNNY ?!
TUGG

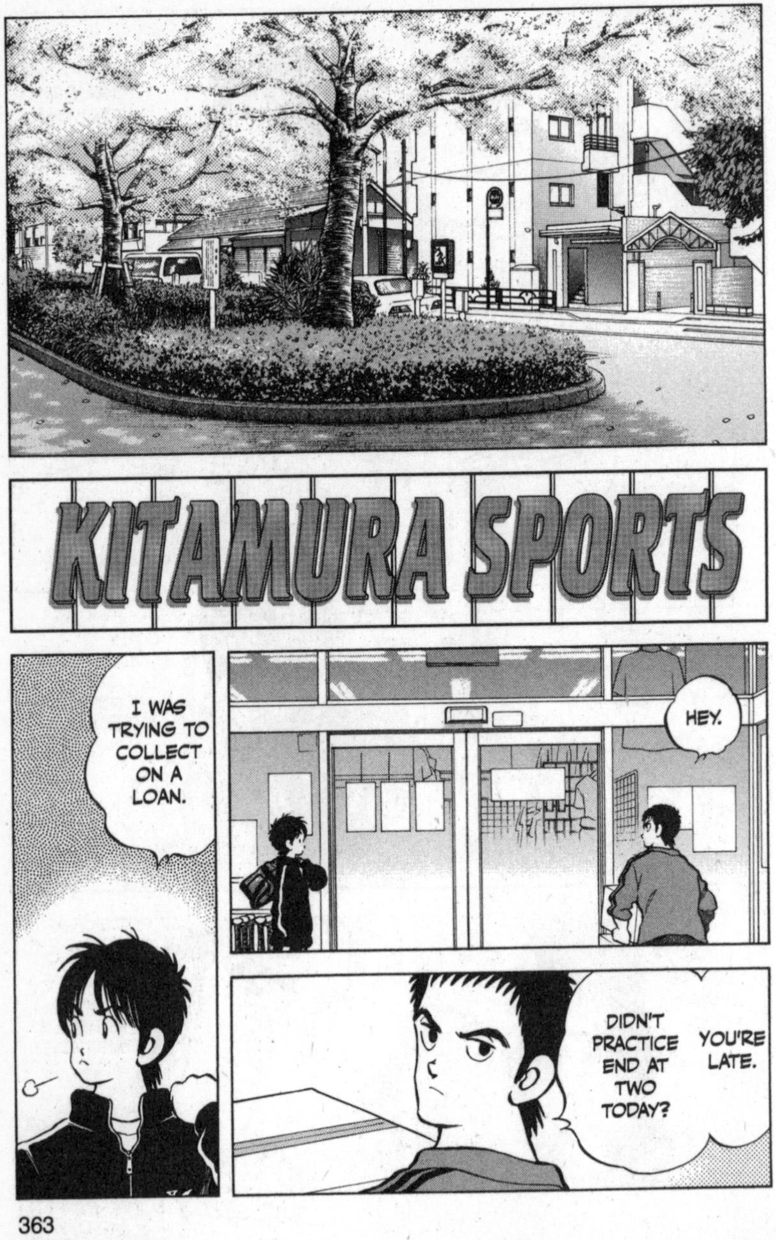
KITAMURA SPORTS
HEY.
YOU'RE LATE.
DIDN'T PRACTICE END AT TWO TODAY?
I WAS TRYING TO COLLECT ON A LOAN.

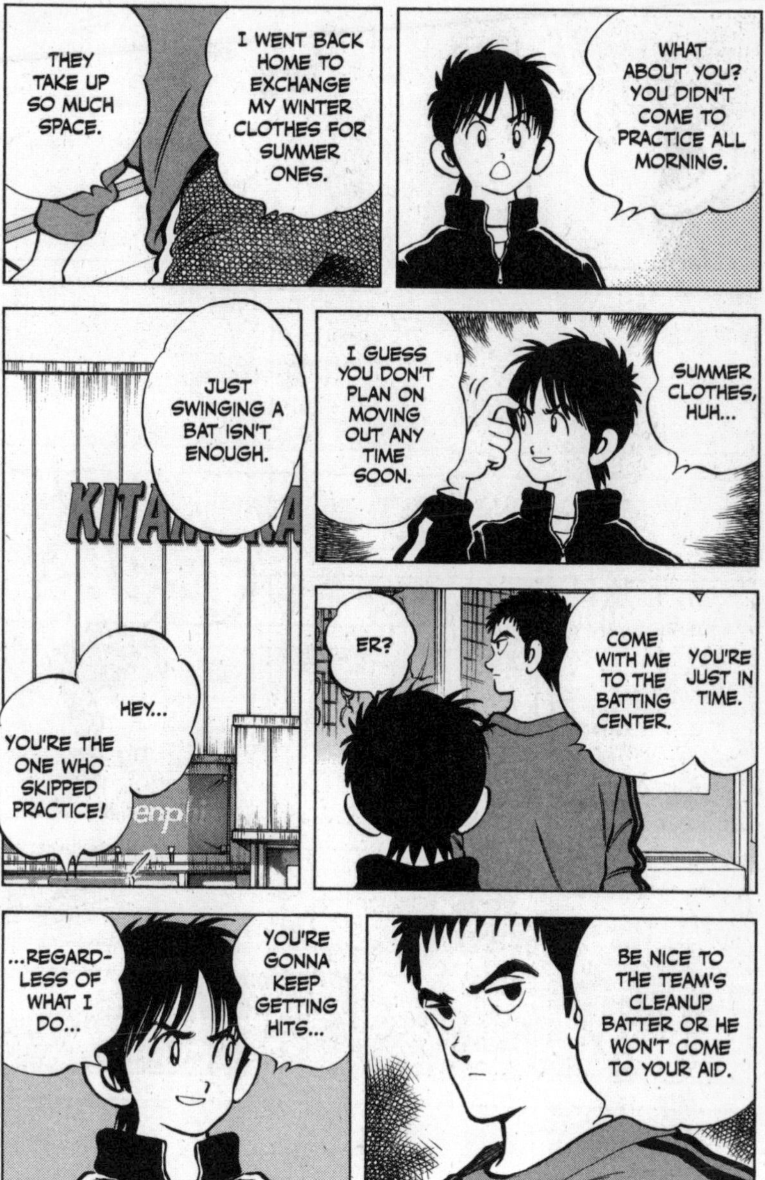
WHAT ABOUT YOU? YOU DIDN'T COME TO PRACTICE ALL MORNING.
I WENT BACK HOME TO EXCHANGE MY WINTER CLOTHES FOR SUMMER ONES.
THEY TAKE UP SO MUCH SPACE.
SUMMER CLOTHES, HUH...
I GUESS YOU DON'T PLAN ON MOVING OUT ANY TIME SOON.
YOU'RE JUST IN TIME.
COME WITH ME TO THE BATTING CENTER.
ER?
JUST SWINGING A BAT ISN'T ENOUGH.
HEY...
YOU'RE THE ONE WHO SKIPPED PRACTICE!
BE NICE TO THE TEAM'S CLEANUP BATTER OR HE WON'T COME TO YOUR AID.
YOU'RE GONNA KEEP GETTING HITS...
...REGARD-LESS OF WHAT I DO...

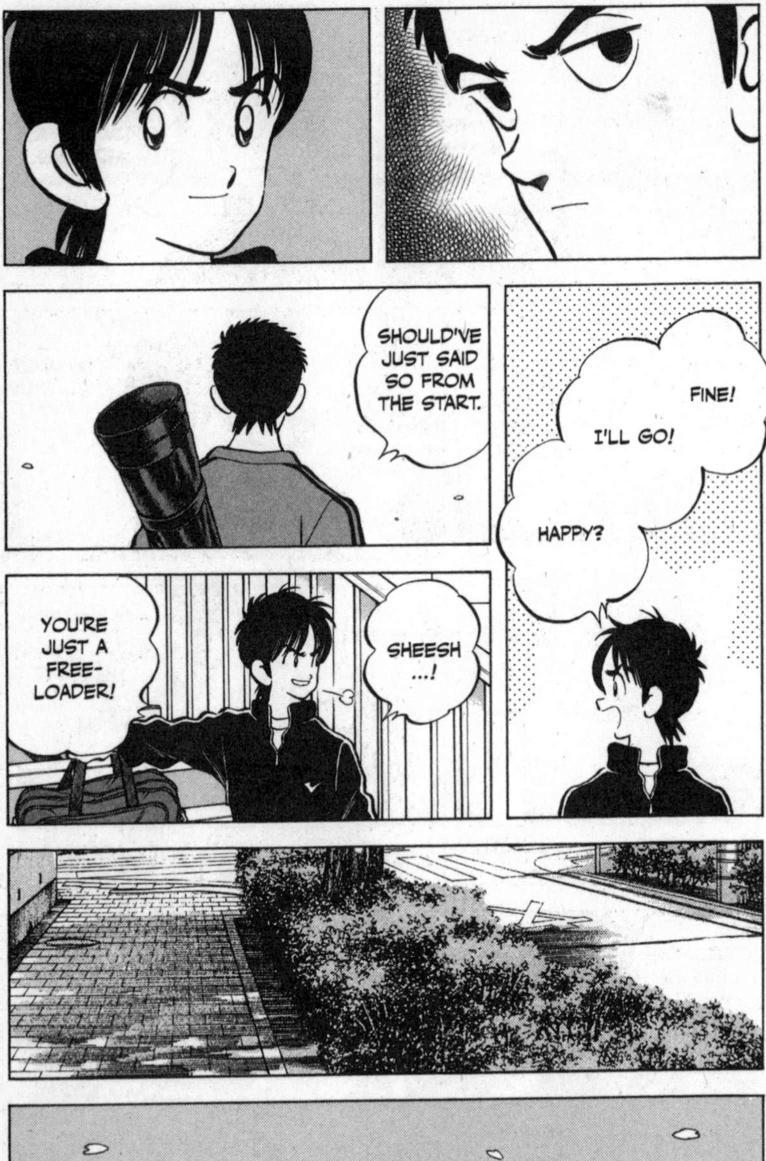
FINE! I'LL GO! HAPPY?
SHOULD'VE JUST SAID SO FROM THE START.
SHEESH ...!
YOU'RE JUST A FREE-LOADER!

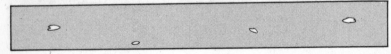

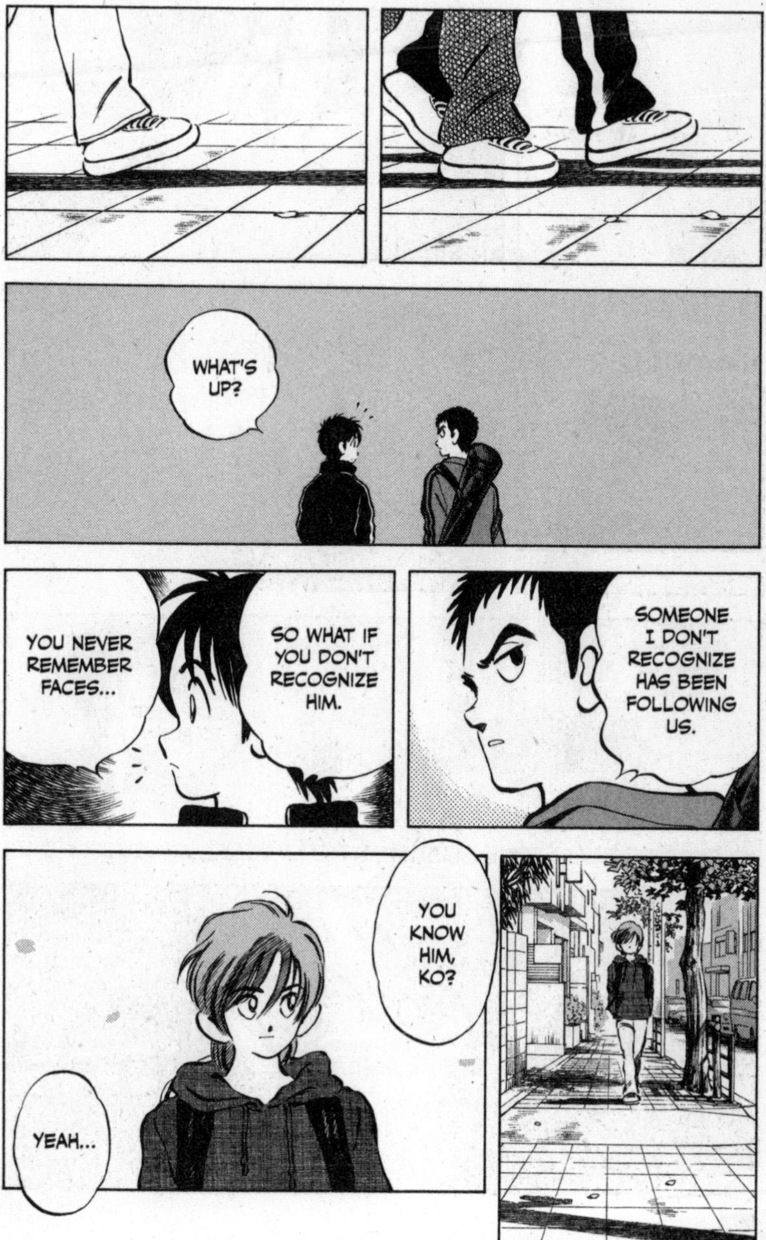
WHAT'S UP?
SOMEONE I DON'T RECOGNIZE HAS BEEN FOLLOWING US.
SO WHAT IF YOU DON'T RECOGNIZE HIM.
YOU NEVER REMEMBER FACES...
YOU KNOW HIM, KO?
YEAH...

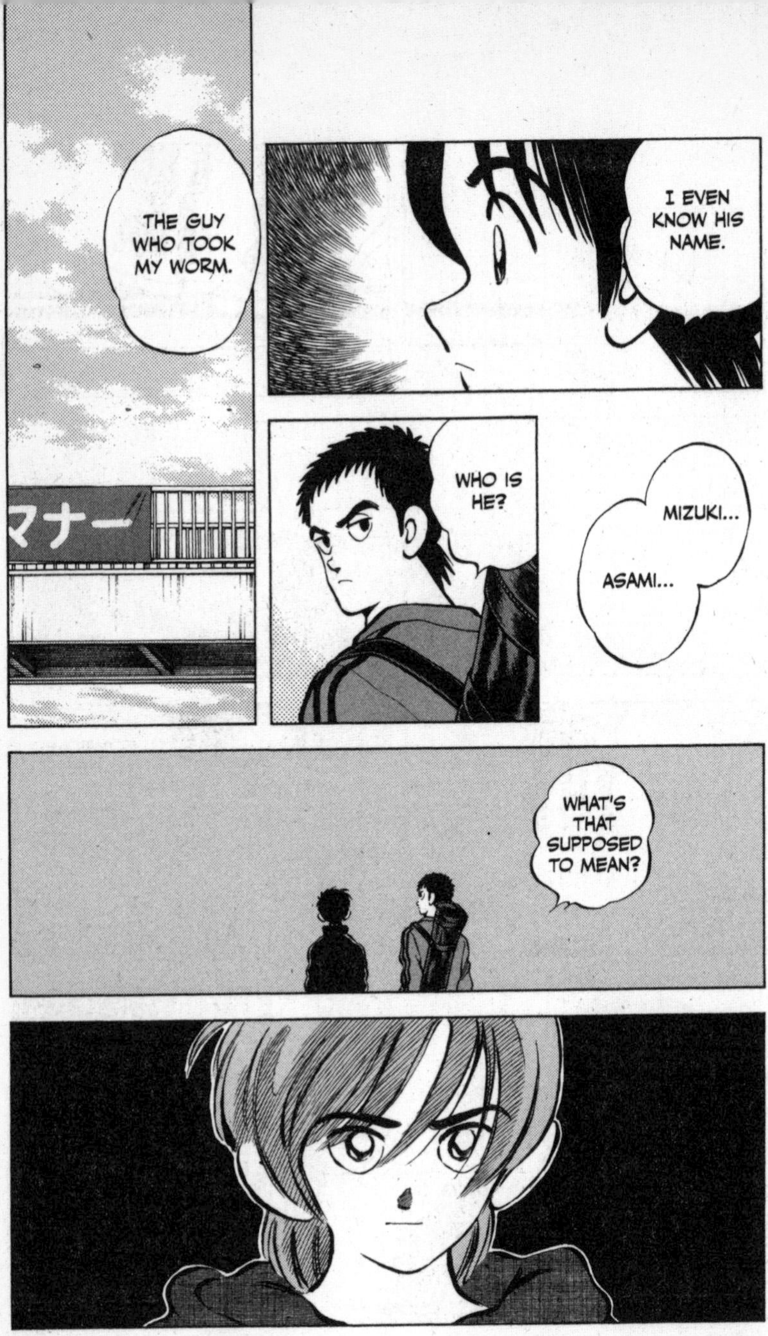
I EVEN KNOW HIS NAME.
MIZUKI...
ASAMI...
WHO IS HE?
THE GUY WHO TOOK MY WORM.
WHAT'S THAT SUPPOSED TO MEAN?

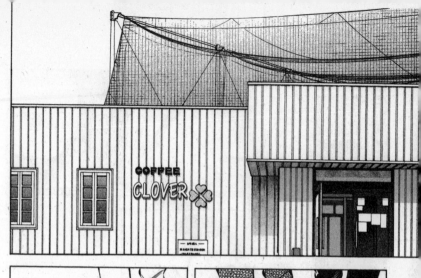

COFFEE
CLOVER

TSUKISHIMA BATTING CENTER

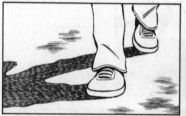

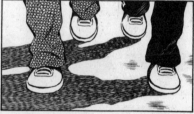

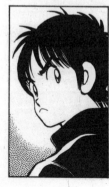

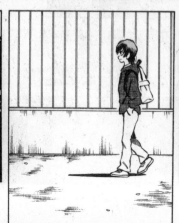

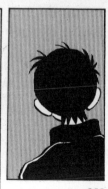

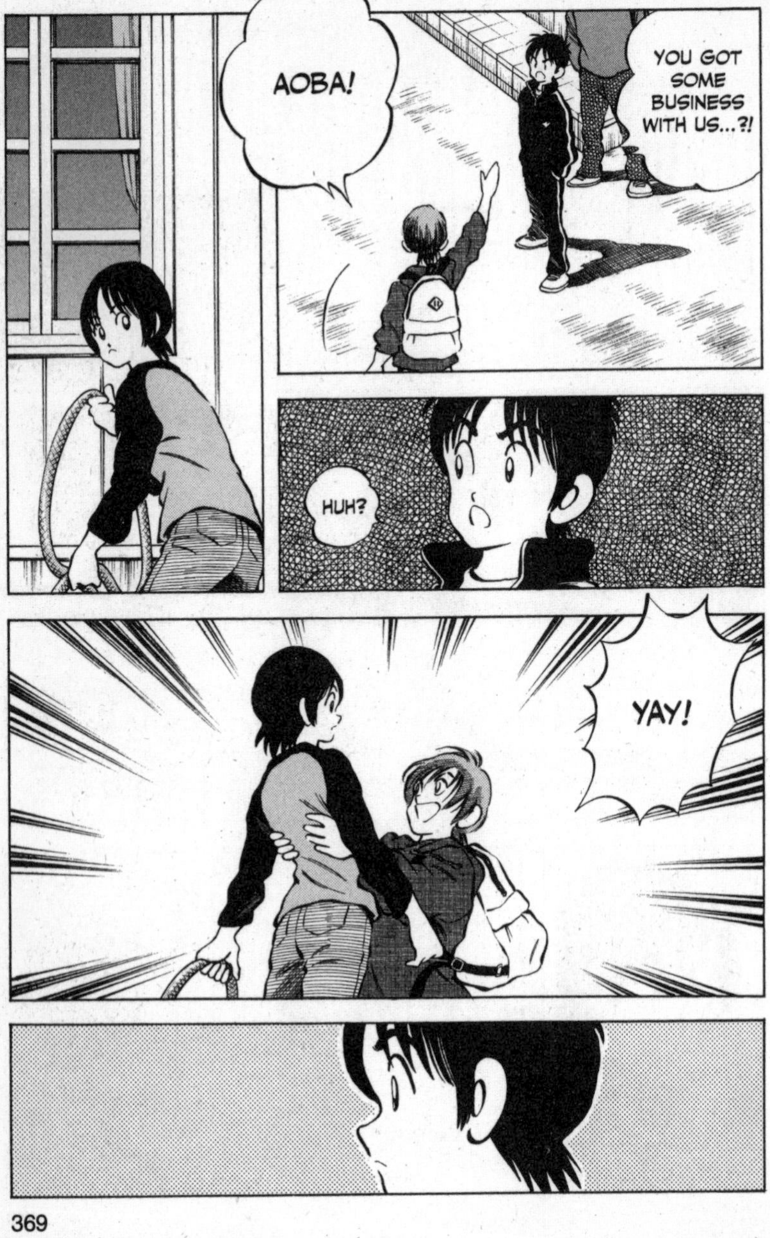
YOU GOT SOME BUSINESS WITH US...?!
AOBA!
HUH?
YAY!

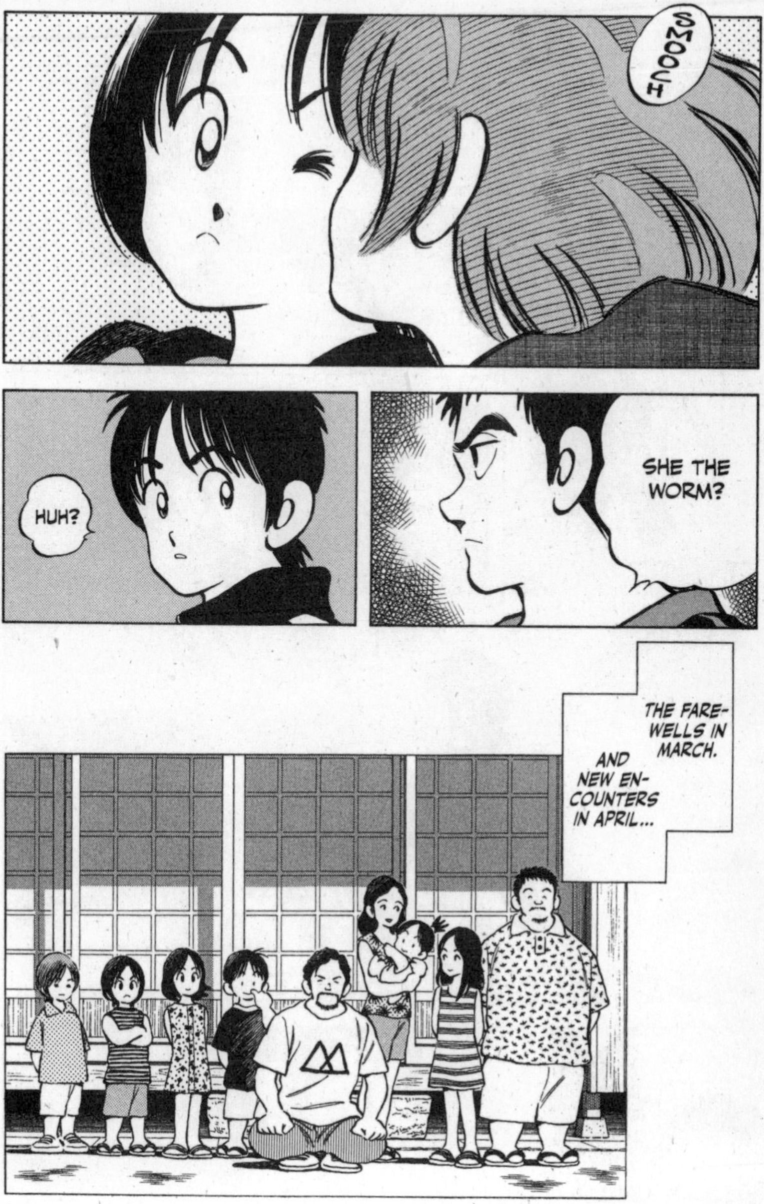
SMOOCH
SHE THE WORM?
HUH?
THE FAREWELLS IN MARCH.
AND NEW ENCOUNTERS IN APRIL...

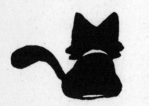

One of the biggest names in the manga industry today, Mitsuru Adachi made his debut in 1970 with *Kieta Bakuon* in the pages of *Deluxe Shonen Sunday*. The creator of numerous mega-hits such as *Touch*, *Miyuki*, and *Cross Game*, Adachi Sensei received the Shogakukan Manga Award for all three of the aforementioned series. Truly in the top echelon of the manga industry, his cumulative works have seen over 200 million copies sold, and many of his series have been adapted into anime, live-action TV series and film. A master of his medium, Adachi has come to be known for his genious handling of dramatic elements skillfully combined with romance, comedy and sports. He, along with Rumiko Takahashi, has become synonymous with the phenomenal success of *Shonen Sunday* in Japan.

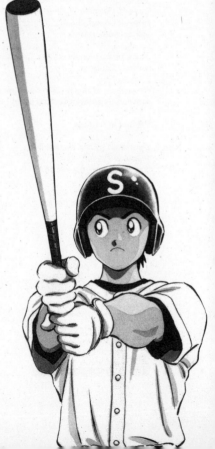

CROSS GAME
VOLUME 3
Shonen Sunday Edition

STORY AND ART BY
MITSURU ADACHI

© 2005 Mitsuru ADACHI/Shogakukan
All rights reserved.
Original Japanese edition "CROSS GAME" published by SHOGAKUKAN Inc.

Translation/Lillian Olsen
Touch-up Art & Lettering/Mark McMurray
Cover Design/John Kim, Yukiko Whitley
Interior Design/Yukiko Whitley
Editor/Andy Nakatani

Printed in Canada

Published by VIZ Media, LLC
P.O. Box 77010
San Francisco, CA 94107

10 9 8 7 6 5 4 3 2 1
First printing, April 2011

www.viz.com   WWW.SHONENSUNDAY.COM

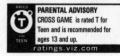

	DATE DUE		
AUG 2 3 2011		APR 0 2 2013	
OCT 1 6 2011			
NOV 2 2 2011			
JAN 0 8 2012